Physiological Bases
of Phytoplankton Ecology

The *Canadian Bulletins of Fisheries and Aquatic Sciences* are designed to interpret current knowledge in scientific fields pertinent to Canadian fisheries and aquatic environments.

The *Canadian Journal of Fisheries and Aquatic Sciences* is published in annual volumes of monthly issues. *Canadian Special Publications of Fisheries and Aquatic Sciences* are issued periodically. These series are available from authorized bookstore agents and other bookstores, or you may send your prepaid order to the Canadian Government Publishing Centre, Supply and Services Canada, Hull, Que. K1A 0S9. Make cheques or money orders payable in Canadian funds to the Receiver General for Canada.

Director and Editor-in-chief
of Scientific Information   J. WATSON, PH.D.

Deputy Director and Editor   JOHANNA M. REINHART, M.SC.

Assistant Editors   D. G. COOK, PH.D.
LORRAINE C. SMITH, PH.D.

Production-Documentation   J. CAMP
G. J. NEVILLE
B. I. PATTERSON

Department of Fisheries and Oceans
Scientific Information and Publications Branch
Ottawa, Canada
K1A 0E6

Participants in the picture are W.G. Harrison, T. Malone, D. Smith, P. Syrett, B. Thake, J. Raven, J. Feuillade, D. Cushing, P. Holligan, J. McCarthy, V. Ittekkot, S. Weiler, J. Smith, I. Morris, L. Legendre, F. Morel, P. Franco, R. Dugdale, P. Harrison, G. Magazzu, T. Platt, L. Guglielmo, G. Carrada, G. Honsell, G. Socal, T. Thordardottir, D. Marino, C. Descolas-Gros, M. Marzocchi, S. Puiseux-Dao, A. Zingone, M. Modigh, J. Horner, B. Heimdal, T. Smayda, L. Lazzara, C. Tomas, J. Myers, D. Bonin, D. Blasco, J. Gostan, R. Barber, B. Irwin, A. Sournia, E. Sakshaug, M. Estrada, S. Maestrini, R. Jackson, G. Fogg, T. Sertorio, B. Prézelin, P. Falkowski, C. Videau, P. Wheeler, R. Eppley, N. Morel, S. Chisholm, M. Karydis, and L. Mazzella. Other participants, not in the picture, include G. Jacques, W. Gieskes, M. Brogueira, S. Panella, C. Andreoli, M. Moita, W. Admiral, H. Glover, J.-C. Therriault, J. Lenz, N. Carr, and E. Toselli.

BULLETIN 210

Physiological Bases
of Phytoplankton Ecology

TREVOR PLATT [ed.]

Department of Fisheries and Oceans
Marine Ecology Laboratory
Bedford Institute of Oceanography
Dartmouth, Nova Scotia   B2Y 4A2

Based on an Advanced Study Institute
sponsored by NATO Scientific Affairs
Division

DEPARTMENT OF FISHERIES AND OCEANS
Ottawa 1981

Canada : $17.95   Catalog No. Fs94-210E
Other countries : $21.55   ISBN 0-660-11089-X
                                    ISSN 0706-6503

Price subject to change without notice
Ottawa

Printed in Canada
by
K.G. Campbell Corporation

Correct citation for this publication:

PLATT, T. [ED.] 1981. Physiological bases of
    phytoplankton ecology. Can. Bull. Fish.
    Aquat. Sci. 210: 346 p.

Contents

Foreword

This Bulletin is a compilation of the major contributions to an Advanced Study Institute, sponsored by NATO with important assistance from the University of Messina, held on the island of Lipari, Sicily, in October 1980. The aim of the Workshop was an exchange of ideas and results between field ecologists and laboratory physiologists working on phytoplankton. It was motivated by the belief that conventional phytoplankton ecology, as practised by biological oceanographers, has been slow to assimilate and exploit the progress made by laboratory physiologists and biochemists working on phytoplankton. If the science of the physiological ecology of phytoplankton is to develop rapidly and efficiently, it could profit from a meeting of the two sides. Those who participated, on both sides, found it a stimulating and memorable experience.

The idea for the Workshop was first conceived in conversation with Richard Dugdale, and developed by an Organizing Committee including Giuseppe Magazzú, Ian Morris, and Alain Sournia. The magnificent local organization was made possible through the help of Letterio Guglielmo.

We also received help, at key points, from Prof. Battaglia of Padova, Prof. Genovese of Messina, Drs N. J. Campbell and J. Watson of Ottawa, and the Mayor and Municipality of Lipari. To all those people, and particularly to the authors of the chapters, I am grateful for their contributions. Finally, it is a pleasure to thank my secretary, Mrs M. Landry, for her valued help at every stage of the organization.

TREVOR PLATT
Editor and Director of the
Advanced Study Institute

Abstract

PLATT, T. [ED.] 1981. Physiological bases of phytoplankton ecology. Can. Bull. Fish. Aquat. Sci. 210: 346 p.

   This book is a collection of 18 essays aimed at the elucidation and exposition of the physiological first principles that underlie phytoplankton ecology. It is based on a successful Advanced Study Institute of which the object was to expose field phytoplankton ecologists to the most recent advances made by laboratory-based physiologists in their understanding of algal photosynthesis, metabolism, and growth, and also to review the physiological principles on which these advances are founded. A second theme is the attempt to incorporate this new knowledge into the interpretation of measurements made on natural assemblages of phytoplankton in the field. The subject matter treated includes the light reactions of photosynthesis; the dark reactions of photosynthesis; respiration and photorespiration; numerical analysis of photosynthesis experiments; application of radioactive tracer techniques to metabolic studies; dynamics of the cell cycle and synchrony; nitrogen metabolism; nutrient uptake kinetics; the relationship between assimilation and growth; adaptation of the metabolic parameters to environmental change; and the physiological and morphological bases of competition and succession.

Key words: phytoplankton, ecology, photosynthesis, cell cycle, unicellular algae, growth rate, nutrient assimilation

Résumé

PLATT, T. [ED.] 1981. Physiological bases of phytoplankton ecology. Can. Bull. Fish. Aquat. Sci. 210: 346 p.

   Le présent ouvrage groupe 18 essais visant à la clarification et à l'exposition des premiers principes physiologiques soustendant l'écologie du phytoplancton. Il est le résultat d'un programme d'études avancées dont l'objectif était d'exposer les écologistes spécialistes du phytoplancton sur le terrain aux plus récents progrès accomplis par les physiologistes en laboratoire sur la photosynthèse, le métabolisme et la croissance des algues, et aussi de passer en revue les principes physiologiques sur lesquels reposent ces progrès. Comme deuxième thème, on traite des efforts entrepris en vue d'incorporer ces nouvelles connaissances dans l'interprétation des données recueillies sur des groupements naturels de phytoplancton sur le terrain. Parmi les sujets traités, on note : réactions de photosynthèse à la lumière; réactions de photosynthèse à l'obscurité; respiration et photorespiration; analyse numérique d'essais sur la photosynthèse; application des techniques de marquage par isotopes aux études de métabolisme; dynamique du cycle et du synchronisme cellulaire; métabolisme de l'azote; cinétique de l'assimilation des éléments nutritifs; relation entre assimilation et croissance; adaptation des paramètres métaboliques au changement du milieu; et fondements physiologiques et morphologiques de la concurrence et de la succession.

Light Reactions in Photosynthesis

BARBARA B. PRÉZELIN

Marine Science Institute and
Department of Biological Sciences
University of California
Santa Barbara, CA 93106, USA

Introduction

As approaches to the study of primary productivity in algae advance, to include new knowledge about the photosynthetic processes regulating plant growth, biological oceanographers must be impressed and perhaps feel deluged with the amount of photosynthetic information now available. Here, an attempt is made to sort the molecular photosynthetic literature and provide a summary that details present understanding of the light reactions in photosynthesis and emphasizes their relevance to studies of algal growth. Because of the wealth of information available, many areas covered had to be simplified. First, emphasis was placed on how the light reactions proceed at the molecular level, i.e. the processes of light absorption, excitation energy transduction to the photochemical reaction centers, and the generation of electrochemical energy and electron flow between two distinct phototraps. The associated reactions of water splitting, NADP reduction, and transmembrane proton flux which lead eventually to the generation of ATP, are also discussed. Once the functional architecture of the light reactions has been outlined, some regulatory aspects of the cellular processes of photosynthesis on primary productivity are considered. Examples are taken from algal literature whenever possible, and special attention is given to topics related to present-day lab/field techniques which are routinely used or recently introduced to biological oceanography, i.e. pigmentation, fluorescence probes, photosynthetic unit concepts, and parameters of the photosynthesis–irradiance curve. In all, it is hoped that a useful framework of information is provided to researchers involved in studies of algal physiology and efforts to estimate rates of in situ primary productivity.

Algal Chloroplasts

Plants take their characteristic color from pigmented membranes termed thylakoids and are found within distinct cellular organelles called chloroplasts (Fig. 1). It is in this highly colored organelle that photosynthesis occurs, i.e. where absorbed light

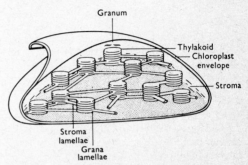

FIG. 1. Cut-away representation of a chloroplast to show three-dimensional structure. (By permission, Hall and Rao 1977.)

energy is channeled into photochemical reactions that lead eventually to the formation of ATP and reduced NADP, and which in turn are utilized in the biochemical reactions incorporating CO_2 into sugars and proteins. The light and dark reactions of photosynthesis are separated physically within the chloroplast. All structural components of the light reactions are localized within the pigmented membranes, while the soluble enzymatic components of the dark reactions are found in the aqueous matrix (stroma) surrounding the exterior surface of the thylakoid. Thylakoids have distinct sidedness, being made of two double membranes joined at the edges to form an internal aqueous phase (the intrathylakoid space) separated off from the stroma. Structural components of the light reactions are arranged in an organized manner across the thylakoid, so that certain steps in the photochemistry occur on the inside of the membranes (i.e. the water-splitting reactions) while others are directed toward the exterior (i.e. ATP and reduced NADP formation) (Hall and Rao 1978; Kirk and Tilney-Bassett 1978).

Nonphotosynthetic structures also are found in the chloroplast and are localized in the stroma. Plastid DNA, RNA, and ribosomes are present, giving the chloroplast some autonomy in protein, lipid, and pigment synthesis. There are also pyrenoid bodies, i.e. spherical regions of high density containing one or more enzymes of CO_2 fixation in or closely associated with the chloroplasts of some algae. Unlike most algal groups, in higher plants/green algae the photosynthetic storage products (fixed

1

carbon) accumulate inside the chloroplast as starch grains in the stroma or as a shell around pyrenoid bodies if present. In addition there can be eyespots in the chloroplasts of some flagellated algae and, depending on the algal class, may be found in association with the flagellum. Algae also contain other osmiophilic globules besides eyespots although they are not generally very predominate. Although they have no direct function in photosynthesis, these globules do appear to be storage pools for such photosynthetic components as plastoquinone, vitamin K, and thylakoid membrane lipid precursors.

The chloroplast envelope, a semipermeable limiting double membrane in green algae and higher plants, keeps the contents of the chloroplast intact and separate from other components of the cytoplasm. The outermost membrane is believed to function primarily in maintaining the structural integrity of the chloroplast. A number of functions have been assigned to the inner membrane of the chloroplast envelope, including the control of solute passage and synthesis of structural components required for the differentiation of the thylakoids (Bisalputra 1974; Kirk and Tilney-Bassett 1978).

By comparison, the photosynthetic machinery of blue-green algae and photosynthetic bacteria is not compartmentalized into chloroplasts. (The blue-green algae are described more accurately as cyanobacteria, being true procaryotes. However, as their photosynthetic machinery is similar to eucaryotic algae and quite distinct from photosynthetic bacteria, the former term is used here). Their photosynthetic membranes are formed from invaginations of the cell envelope and extend as single lamellar membranes throughout the cytoplasm. As a result, although the intrathylakoid space is preserved, the stroma does not exist in these organisms. Thus the components that would be segregated in the stroma of eucaryotic plants are part of the cytosol of blue-green algae and photosynthetic bacteria.

The number of chloroplasts per cell varies widely in different cell types and between different plant groups, but generally they increase with cell size. Chloroplasts are most often found around the periphery of the cytoplasm, close to the cytoplasmic membranes. The particular characteristics of chloroplast shape and internal structure also varies widely, but two observations can be described that often distinguish the chloroplasts of several algal groups from those of higher plants or green algae. First, unlike higher plants or red and green algae, the cryptomonads, chrysophytes, diatoms, dinofla-

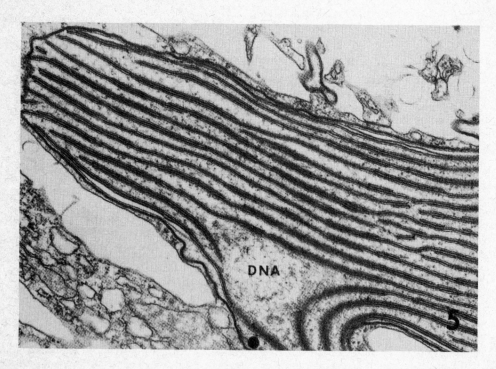

FIG 2. Chloroplast in the contracted form from *Gonyaulax* cells fixed at 1800 ct., from a culture held in continuous light. Also shown are an area of the chloroplast containing DNA fibrils and chloroplast ribosomes in the interlamellar spaces. × 38 000. (By permission, Herman and Sweeney 1975.)

gellates, Euglenoids, Chloromonads, and brown algae all have a third membrane surrounding the existing double membranes of the chloroplast envelope. In some cases, this third membrane that lies outside the chloroplast envelope is referred to as the "chloroplast endoplasmic reticulum," as connections between it and the endoplasmic reticulum of the cytoplasm have been observed in some groups. In addition, ribosomes have been noted on its outer surface in some species and connections with the nuclear envelope have been seen (Kirk and Tilney-Bassett 1978; Bisalputra 1974).

Second, all algal chloroplasts usually contain thylakoids that extend the full length of the organelle. However, algal classes differ in their arrangement of thylakoids within the chloroplast. The red and blue-green algae have the simplest thylakoid arrangement, with single thylakoids that lie separate and parallel to one another throughout the length of the stroma. Cryptomonad algae have paired thylakoids, whereas most other algal groups have sets of threes. Such stacks of thylakoids, referred to as compound lamellae, can be seen as bands in cross sections of chloroplasts (Fig. 2). An elaborate arrangement of thylakoids is found in green algae, similar in arrangement to the thylakoids of higher plants. The compound lamellae of green algae may have as many as seven thylakoids. In some species of greens there are clearly recognized regions of stacked thylakoids (grana) interdispersed by regions of unstacked thylakoids traversing the stroma and connecting separate grana stacks to one another (Kirk and Tileny-Bassett 1978; Hall and Rao 1978).

Photosynthetic Pigments

Photosynthetic energy conversion is initiated when the pigments of the thylakoid membranes absorb light energy. There are three classes of photosynthetic pigments: chlorophylls (chl), phycobilins, and carotenoids. Of these, only chl a must be present for photosynthesis to proceed. The other pigments serve a light-harvesting function for chl a, and expand the spectral range of visible light energy that can be absorbed in the chloroplast and transferred to chl a to drive the photochemical reactions of photosynthesis. The differential distribution of the various photosynthetic pigments into specific plant groups (Table 1) gives them characteristic whole cell absorption properties, some of which are represented in Fig. 3.

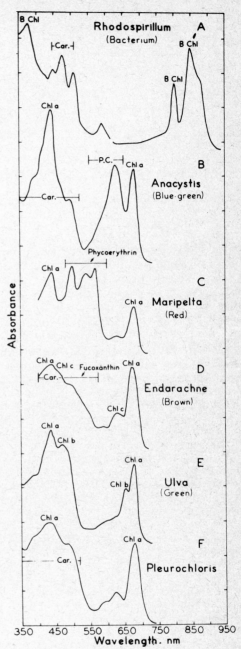

FIG. 3. Absorption spectra made in vivo for the major kinds of photosynthetic organisms. Spectrum A was measured by chromatophores of the nonsulfur purple bacterium, *Rhodospirillum spheroides*. Other spectra were obtained with intact organisms. The deep-water red alga, *Maripelta rotata*, grows in submarine canyons off California at depths to 60 m. The approximate absorption maxima and, in some cases, the range of absorption of photosynthetic pigments are shown. (Car., carotenoid; P.C., phycocyanin.) (By permission, Fork 1977.)

TABLE 1. Distribution of photosynthetically active pigments in major plant groups.

	Chl a	Chl b	Chl c_1	Chl c_2	Phyco-erythrin	Phyco-cyanin	Allophy-cocyanin	b-caro-tene	Major xanthophylls
Blue-green algae	+				+	+	+	+	Myxoxanthin
Red algae	+				+	+	+	+	Lutein
Cryptomonad algae	+			+	+	+		trace	Alloxanthin
Dinoflagellates	+			+				+	Peridinin
Brown algae, diatoms	+		+	+				+	Fucoxanthin
Chrysophytes	+		+	+				+	Fucoxanthin
Green algae, higher plants	+	+						+	Lutein

CHLOROPHYLLS AND CHLOROPHYLL–PROTEIN COMPLEXES

The chlorophylls include chl a, chl b, chl c_1, and chl c_2 and give most plants their typical green color. They are characterized by their porphyrin ring structure, where magnesium is chelated in the center and liganded at four sites to pyrole nitrogen atoms (Fig. 4). These porphyrin rings are essentially planar complexes surrounded by dense clouds of pi-electrons. Polypeptides are believed to attach through linkages with side groups of the planar ring. Through substitutions of different side groups on the ring, electronic states of the molecule are altered and give rise to the characteristic absorption properties of the different chlorophylls (Fig. 4 and 5).

When chl a is freed from the chloroplast and membrane proteins by extraction with acetone, its typical absorption spectrum shows two peaks of approximately equal intensity in the red and blue region of the visible spectrum at 660 and 430 nm, respectively (Fig. 5). Chl b under the same conditions has a blue Soret band near 453 nm, which is about 2.85 times more intense than its red absorption peak at 643 nm (Seely 1966). Similarly, the two forms of chl c found in most phytoplankton species are primarily blue light absorption pigments, with the Soret band of chl c_2 at almost 10 times as intense as the weak red absorption band around 630 nm (Jeffrey 1969). Thus, the accessory chlorophylls partially fill in the absorption window left by chl a, especially in the blue region of the visible spectrum.

While the porphyrin ring gives chlorophylls their absorption properties, the long phytol chain of chl a and chl b molecules presumably provides

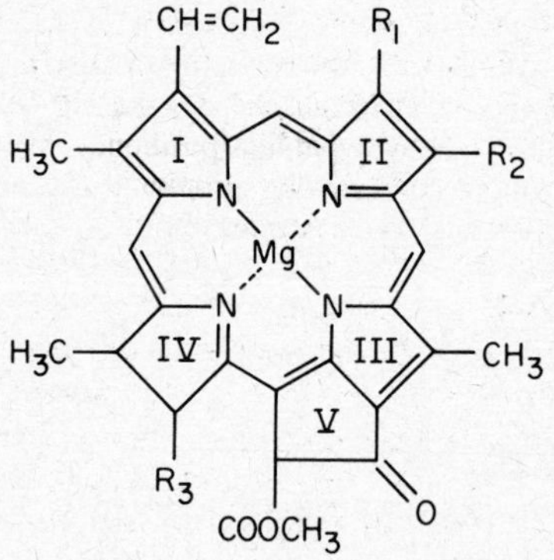

	R_1	R_2	R_3
Chl $\underline{a}$	CH_3	CH_2CH_3	$(H_2C)_2 -$ PHYTOL
Chl $\underline{b}$	CHO	CH_2CH_3	$(H_2C)_2 -$ PHYTOL
Chl $\underline{c_1}$	CH_3	CH_2CH_3	$HC=CH_2-$ COOH
Chl $\underline{c_2}$	CH_3	$CH=CH_2$	$HC=CH_2-$ COOH

FIG. 4. Structures of chlorophylls. (Redrawn from Seely 1966; Dougherty et al. 1966.)

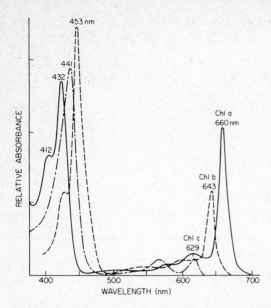

FIG. 5. Absorption spectra of chlorophylls extracted in acetone. (Redrawn and adapted from Hall and Rao 1977.)

a lipophilic side group important in the insertion of the pigments into the thylakoid membrane. Phytol is a hydrophobic terpenoid ($COOC_{20}H_{39}$) attached via an ester linkage to a propionic acid side group on ring IV. By comparison, neither type of chl c has a phytol group attached at this position, but the acrylic side group is replaced by propionic acid. With no phytol chain, chl c molecules are only $2/3$ the size of chl a or chl b (610 versus about 900 daltons) and presumably should be more hydrophilic than either chl a or b. But chl c appears to be closely associated with detergent-solublized thylakoid components.

The absorption properties of free chlorophylls can be modified significantly when bound to membrane proteins and inserted into the thylakoid. In vivo chlorophylls generally display spectral shifts of their long wavelength absorption peaks further into the red region of the visible spectrum by anywhere from 5 to more than 40 nm (Stoke's shift). Furthermore, the absorption band of chl a in vivo is comprised of several types of chl a–protein complexes, each absorbing light energies at slightly different wavelengths. Deconvolution of chl a absorption spectra (Fig. 6) and fluorescence spectral analyses led to the hypothesis that there are at least four universal forms of chl a in vivo, with low temperature (77K) absorption maxima at 662, 670, 677, and 684 nm. The existence of more than one spectral form of chl b and c has not been documented.

It now appears that virtually all functional chlorophylls in vivo are conjugated with proteins (Thorn-

ber and Barber 1979; Markwell et al. 1979). Specific chlorophyll–proteins are difficult to isolate intact or functionally unaltered because chlorophylls are not linked covalently to proteins and the complexes are located in the water-insoluble membranes of the chloroplast. However, recent efforts with detergent extraction techniques have been successful in isolating a variety of chl a–protein complexes from higher plants and now several groups of algae. The procedures are discussed in some detail in several review articles characterizing plant chlorophyll proteins (Anderson 1975; Thornber and Alberte 1977; Thornber et al. 1977, 1979; Boardman et al. 1978; Thornber and Barber 1979).

One of the best characterized chlorophyll–proteins is the P700–chl a–protein complex, representing photosystem I reaction center and some of its immediate antenna chlorophyll. This complex must be present for the photochemical events of photosynthesis to proceed and, therefore, is found in all oxygen-evolving photosynthetic plants (Brown et al. 1974). The P700–chl a–protein shows a characteristic chl absorption peak centered around 675–677 nm (Fig. 7), which is due to the presence of light-harvesting (LH) chl a molecules specifically associated with each Ps I reaction center. The light energy absorbed by these chl a_1 molecules is preferentially directed to the photochemical reaction center of Ps I. The amount of light-harvesting chl a_1 and b-carotene (the latter giving rise to the absorption shoulder around 500 nm in Fig. 7) isolated with the P700–chl a–protein complex varies with the isolation procedure, but usually the complexes have a chl a/P700 ratio between 20:1 and 40:1 and a b-carotene/P700 ratio of 1:1 (Thornber et al. 1977). It has been suggested that b-carotenes function in the complex to protect P700 from photochemical damage and that quinones, generally present, may function in early photochemical events (Thornber and Alberte 1977).

At the heart of the complex is P700, a chlorophyll dimer that provides the reaction center of photosystem I with physical, absorption, and fluorescence properties different from antenna chlorophyll (Katz et al. 1979). The long wavelength absorption properties of P700 result presumably from the chl–chl interactions in the dimer, secondarily influenced by the protein binding of the complex in a specific chl–membrane environment. Both the reaction center of Ps I in vivo and the isolated P700 complex are characterized by a photobleaching signal resolved around 700 nm (Fig. 8). This light or chemically induced oxidized-minus-reduced negative signal at 700 nm arises from a charge separation reaction in the P700 dimer excited by absorbed light energy and can be used to quantify the number of Ps I reaction centers present in a sample.

5

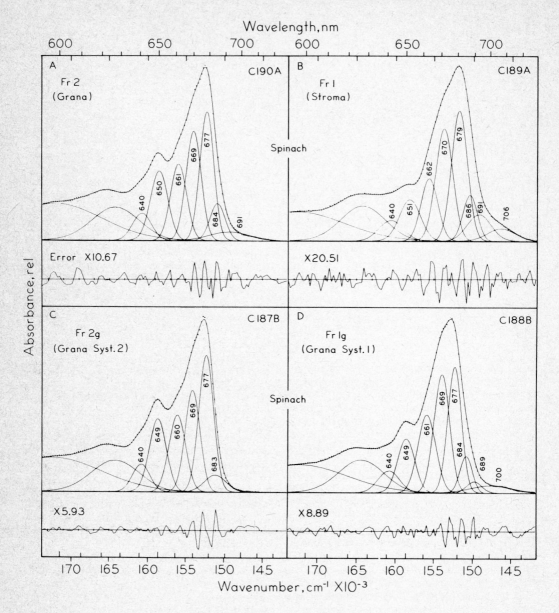

Fɪɢ. 6. Curve analyses of the absorption spectra of fragments from spinach stroma and grana membranes at −196°C. The error of fit at each point is shown on a scale below each curve with the designated magnification; the higher the magnification, the better the fit. (By permission, Brown et al. 1972.)

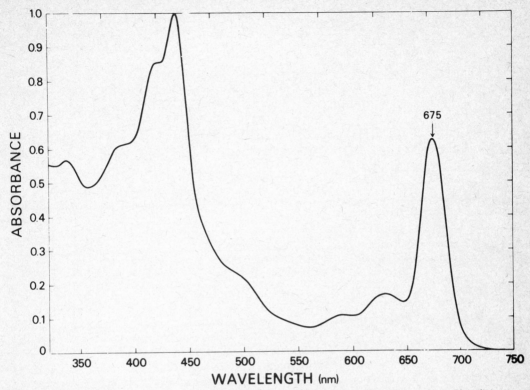

FIG. 7. Room temperature (300K) absorption spectrum of the P_{700}–chl a–protein isolated from *Glenodinium* sp. (By permission, Prézelin and Alberte 1978.)

Attempts to isolate a single chlorophyll–protein complex representing the functional reaction center of photosystem II (Ps II) have been more difficult, presumably because of susceptibility of the complex to degradation by ionic detergents. Whole cell absorption studies have suggested that the reaction center of Ps II contains a special chl a form, which undergoes an absorption decrease at 680 nm when oxidized and, thus, the phototrap of Ps II was termed P680. However, this signal is not used to quantify Ps II reaction centers, as it is not resolved simply and occurs in a part of the visible spectrum where secondary optical signals from P700 and antenna chl a molecules would interfere (Fig. 8).

It is not clear if P680 represents a chl a dimer structure similar to that described for P700 (Katz et al. 1979) or a ligated chl a monomer whose function as a Ps II phototrap is determined by its membrane environment (Fajer et al. 1979). Closely associated with P680, and perhaps reflecting a primary or secondary electron acceptor for Ps II, is an unidentified spectral component that undergoes a characteristic light-induced absorbance change in the 550-nm region of the visible spectrum. Termed C550, this optical signal is best resolved at low temperature (77K) and has proven a strong diagnostic

indicator of Ps II activity in higher plants and green algae (cf. Butler 1977). Unfortunately, little or no work is available on the use of this signal in the phycobilin–chl and carotenoid–chl c–chl a pigment systems found in most aquatic plant groups. In studies of whole cell fluorescence excitation spectra and fluorescence induction curves (Murata et al. 1966; Krey and Govindjee 1966; Govindjee and Yang 1966; Murata 1969), it has been suggested that the in vivo fluorescence maximum of Ps II is at 685 nm (room temperature) and 685–695 nm (77K). The association of these particular chl a forms with the antenna pigments of Ps II have been confirmed in recent studies on isolated Ps II particles (Satoh and Butler 1978; Satoh 1980).

The major light-harvesting component from higher plants and green algae has been isolated and the characterization of the chl a–chl b protein complexes from all chl b-containing plants are becoming quite detailed. Functioning as antenna pigments for the two photosystems, these chl–proteins have been shown to contain approximately equal concentrations of both chl a and chl b (Fig. 9). In addition some of higher plant/green algae carotenoids are found associated with these complexes, in particular b-carotene and lutein, as well

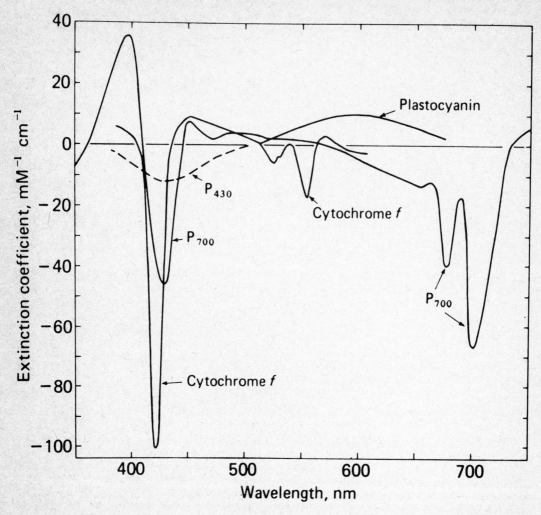

FIG. 8. Oxidized-minus-reduced difference spectra for the electron transfer components P700, P430, cytochrome *f*, and plastocyanin. The difference spectra for P700, cytochrome *f*, and plastocyanin are produced on conversion by light from the reduced to the oxidized form. The negative P430 band results from the reduction of an unidentified compound. (By permission, Fork 1977.)

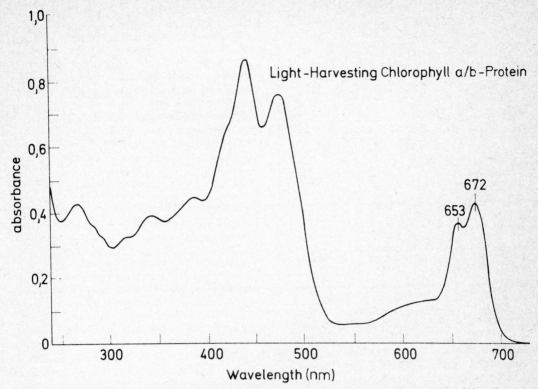

FIG. 9. Room temperature absorption spectrum of light-harvesting chl *a*/*b*–protein of green alga, *Chlamydomonas reinhardii*. (By permission, Thornber and Alberte 1977.)

as trace amounts of galactolipids and phospholipids. The most recent structural model for this complex would suggest a chl *a*/chl *b*–protein monomer of molecular weight 29 500, comprised of a single polypeptide apoprotein of molecular weight 24 000 associated through noncovalent linkages to three molecules each of chl *a* and chl *b* (cf. Thornber and Barber 1979). Apparent oligomers of the chl *a*– chl *b*–protein complex have also been isolated, although the characterization of their supposed aggregate structure is incomplete (Thornber et al. 1979; Markwell et al. 1979).

In most marine phytoplankton, the major light-harvesting chlorophyll is chl *c*, not chl *b*. Little work had been done until recently to elucidate the organization of chl *c* in vivo. Problems arose when detergent-solubilization techniques designed for the chl *a*– chl *b* pigments system of higher plants/green algae were applied directly to phytoplankton pigment systems. The general result was the rapid dissociation of chl *c* and carotenoids from the thylakoid membranes (Prézelin 1976; Prézelin and Alberte 1978; Boczar et al. 1979, 1980; Prézelin and Boczar 1980a, b). However, three chlorophyll aggregate structures containing chl *a* and chl *c* have been isolated from brown algae, one of which was also enriched in

fucoxanthin (Barrett and Anderson 1977; Anderson and Barrett 1979). From dinoflagellates, where chl *c* always predominates over chl *a* in whole cells (i.e. 1.4:1.0 molar chl *c*:chl *a* in low light cells), a single small molecular weight (38 000–50 000) chl *a*–chl c_2–protein complex has been isolated from *Glenodinium* sp. This complex contains nearly all the chl *c* in the cell, about 20% of the total chl *a*, no peridinin, but some yellow xanthophylls (diadino-xanthin and dinoxanthin). Its spectral characteristics are shown in Fig. 10, and illustrate how the predominance of chl *c* contributes to the blue light-absorbing capabilities of these phytoplankters. The chl *c*/chl *a* chromophore molar ratio approaches 5:1. The chl *a*–chl c_2–protein complex of *Glenodinium* sp. appears to be a functional analog of the monomer form of the chl *a*–chl *b*–protein of higher plants/ green algae, functioning as major light-harvesting components for the photosynthetic apparatus (Boczar et al. 1979; Prézelin and Boczar 1980a, b; Boczar et al. 1980).

PHYCOBILINS AND BILIPROTEINS

Red and blue-green algae have derived their names from the color of the photosynthetic pigments

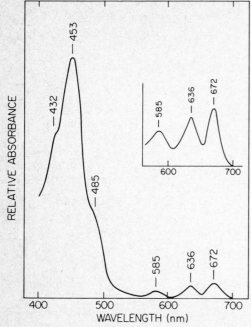

FIG. 10. Room temperature absorption spectrum of the chl a–chl c–protein complex of *Glenodinium* sp. (By permission, Boczar et al. 1980.)

that make up the light-harvesting components of their photosynthetic apparatus. (However, some red algae are not red and some blue-green algae are red.) The accessory pigments of these algae are easily isolated as water-soluble, pigment–protein complexes, termed biliproteins, and are distinguished by their color. The red, blue, and purple biliproteins are phycoerythrin (PE), phycocyanin (PC), and allophycocyanin (APC), respectively. Phycoerythrin absorbs light energy over a broad range of the visible spectrum between 500 and 570 nm. Phycocyanin absorbs light at slightly longer wavelengths, between 550 nm and 650 nm. Allophycocyanin is the longest wavelength absorbing phycobilin, with absorption maximum centered at 650 nm.

All three biliprotein types are found in most species of red and blue-green algae, with PE predominant in the reds and PC predominant in the blue-green algae. Cryptomonad algae also contain PE and PC but not APC, the most central component in the light-harvesting apparatus of most phycobilin-containing organisms (Stanier 1974) (Table 2). In cryptomonads, it has been suggested that the functional role of APC may have been replaced by a long wavelength PC (PC645) or perhaps even mediated by chl c_2, which is also present in these unusual algae (MacColl and Berns 1978).

TABLE 2. Properties of algal biliproteins.[a] (Adapted from Glazer 1977.)

Biliprotein	Phycobilin[b]	Absorption maxima (nm)	Fluorescence maxima (nm)	Molecular weight	Probable subunit structure
C-phycoerythrin	PE	565	575	226 000	$(\alpha\beta)_6$
C-phycocyanin	PC	615	635	224 000	$[(\alpha\beta)_3]_2$
Allophycocyanin (APC II & III)	PC	(620), 650	660	105 000	$(\alpha\beta)_3$
Allophycocyanin (APC I & B)	PC	654	673–680	145 000	$(\alpha\beta)_3$
R-phycoerythrin	PE + PU	498, 540, 565	578	290 000	$(\alpha\beta)_3$
B-phycoerythrin	PE + PU	545, 563	575	290 000	$(\alpha\beta)_3$
R-phycocyanin	PC + PE	553, 615	635	273 000	$[(\alpha\beta)_3]_2$
Cryptomonad phycoerythrins					
PE 544	PE	544	–	30 800	–
PE 555	PE	555	580	27 800	$\alpha\beta$
PE 568	PE	568	–	30 800–35 000	–
Cryptomonad phycocyanins					
PC 615	PC + PV	558,615	637	–	–
PC 630	PC + PV	558,630	–	37 300	–
PC 645	PC + PV	583,645	660	24 000–34 000	–

[a] Values are based on data derived mainly from Brooks and Gantt (1973), Glazer and Bryant (1975), O'Carra and O'hEocha (1976), Bennett and Siegelman (1977), Ley et al. (1977), Glazer (1977), Zilinskas et al. (1978).
[b] PE, phycoerythrobilin; PC, phycocyanobilin; PU, phycourobilin; PV, phycoviolin.

As different groups of algae were analyzed, it became apparent that the spectral characteristics of PE and PCs varied widely (Fig. 11–13). At first, believing that the different spectral types of biliproteins followed a taxonomic pattern, prefixes were added to designate various taxonomic groups (C, Cyanophyceae; R, Rhodophyceae; B, Bangiophyceae, a subclass of lower red algae). Generally, PEs isolated from the red algae have three major absorption maxima, whereas those isolated from blue-green and cryptomonads have only one. Similarly, PCs from red and cryptomonad algae have two absorption maxima between about 550 and 650 nm, whereas C–PC has a single broad absorption maximum which varies between 615 and 620 nm depending on ionic strength. APCs can have one or two absorption maxima, with the major peak centered around 650 nm. Initially, it was suggested that the large spectral differences observed in each of the individual biliprotein classes was the result of conformational stresses imposed on the same chromophore by the specific protein environments in each of the different algal groups.

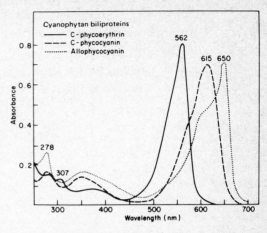

FIG. 11. Biliproteins from blue-green algae: C-phycoerythrin from *Phormidium persicinum* (solid line), C-phycocyanin from *Nostoc muscorum* (broken line), allophycocyanin from *Nostoc muscorum* (dotted line). (By permission, O'Carra and O'hEocha 1976.)

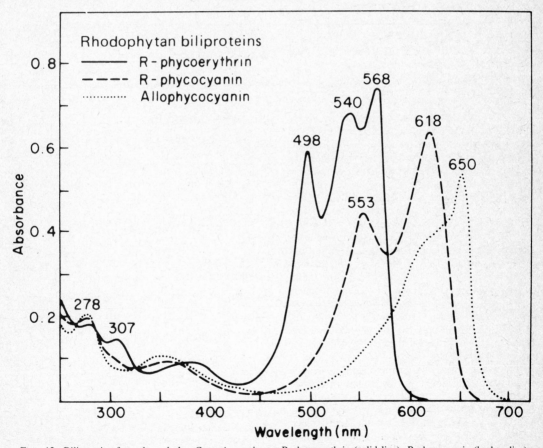

FIG. 12. Biliproteins from the red alga *Ceramium rubrum*: R-phycoerythrin (solid line), R-phycocyanin (broken line), allophycocyanin (dotted line). (By permission, O'Carra and O'hEocha 1976.)

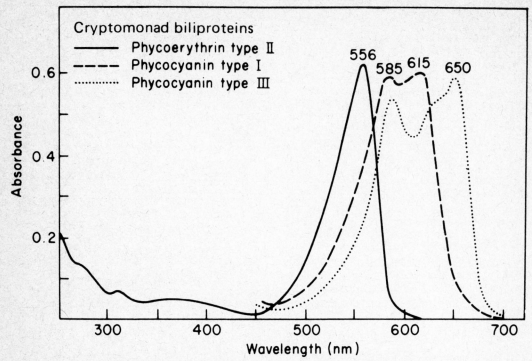

FIG. 13. Some cryptomonad biliproteins: phycoerythrin from *Hemiselmis fugescens* (solid line), phycocyanin from *Hemiselmis virescens* (broken line), phycocyanin from *Croomonas* sp. (dotted line). (By permission, O'Carra and O'hEocha 1976.)

Later, as the biliprotein chromophores were chemically characterized, it became apparent that spectral differences were related to the fact that the composition of the chromophores was not always the same in similarly colored biliproteins isolated from different algal taxonomic groups (cf. reviews of Glazer 1977; Bennett and Siegelman 1978; Gantt 1980). When the chromophore composition of four spectrally distinct PEs was analyzed, one representing the PE of blue-greens and three isolated from cryptomonads, the chromophore was the same in all cases and contained a single phycobilin pigment, phycoerythrobilin (Fig. 14). By contrast, two distinct phycobilin pigments were found in the chromophore of R–PE. In addition to phycoerythobilin, phycourobilin was also isolated and shown to account for the short wavelength absorption maximum seen in R–PE of red algae, but not seen in the PEs isolated from the two other algal groups (Glazer 1977).

Similarly, the C–PC chromophore contains a single type of phycobilin (phycocyanobilin), whereas both phycocyanobilin and phycoerythrobilin are found in the R–PC chromophore. The cryptomonad PCs are also unique in their chromophore composition, containing phycocyanobilin in combination with phycoviolin (Table 2). By contrast, the chromophore of allophycocyanins isolated from red and

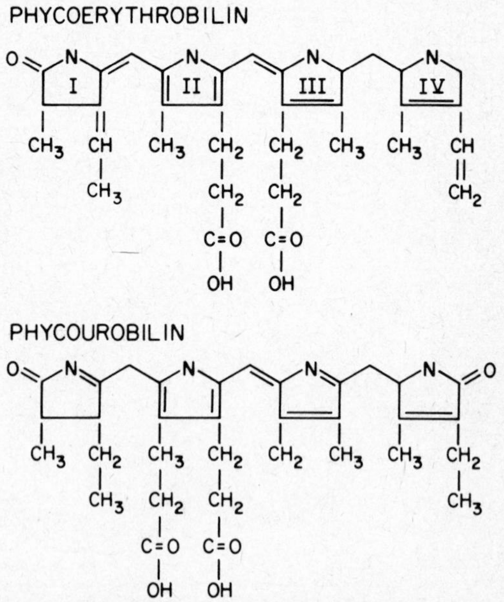

FIG. 14. (A) Structure of phycoerythrobilin. Phycocyanobilin is similar in structure, with the C_2H_3 group of the IV ring saturated to become C_2H_5. (B) Proposed structure of phycourobilin. (Redrawn from O'Carra and O'hEocha 1976.)

12

blue-green algae are all the same, containing only phycocyanobilin. Thus, the composition of the purple APCs and the blue C–PCs chromophores are identical, and the difference in color presumably arises from differences in the protein environment in which the phycobilin pigment resides.

Two different polypeptides, alpha and beta, make up the subunits of the apoprotein of biliproteins. These subunits usually occur in a 1:1 stoichiometry, with at least one chromophore attached to each polypeptide. The primary structure of the apoproteins from different biliproteins has been examined and it appears that the amino acid composition is highly conserved, regardless of the algal source (Chapman 1973; O'Carra and O'hEocha 1976; Glazer 1978; Gantt 1980). The heterodimer structure of biliproteins is the alpha–beta configuration, weighing approximately 30 000 and exemplified in the cryptomonad pigment system (Table 2).

As the individual biliprotein polypeptides aggregate to form the higher molecular biliprotein complexes (i.e. dimers and trimers in Table 2), the extinction coefficents of the phycobilins increase and the absorption and fluorescence emission spectra of the aggregate alters significantly. These aggregation states of heterodimer biliproteins can be affected by several factors, including ionic strength, pH, and the concentration of the biliproteins (Chapman 1973; Gantt and Conti 1976; Glazer 1977; Trench and Ronzio 1978).

The biliproteins not only aggregate with like kinds of biliproteins, but these aggregates further can combine with different kinds of biliproteins to form large organized aggregate structures on the stromal surface of the thylakoid membranes. Aggregates of PE, PC, and APC are termed phycobilisomes in red and blue-green algae. They can be seen as granules with diameters to 300 Å on the exterior surface of the thylakoid membrane (Gantt et al. 1976; Glazer 1977) (Fig. 15). Light energy transduction occurs from most externally placed PE (fluorescing orange-yellow at 580 nm) to PC (fluorescing its absorbed light energy

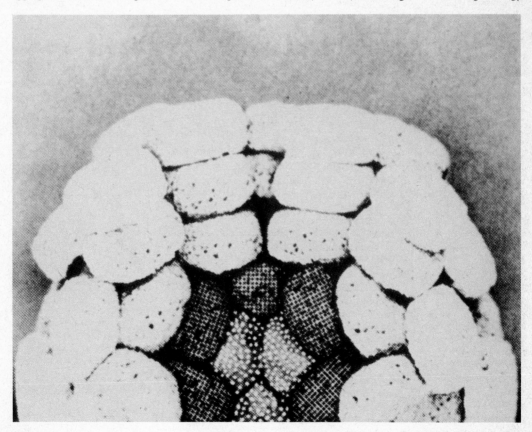

FIG. 15. Model of a phycobilisome as envisioned to exist in the red alga, *Porphyridium cruentum*. Allophycocyanin as a core (white stipples) is in the center and near the photosynthetic membrane. R-phycocyanin (black stipples) surrounds the allophycocyanin, and phycoerythrin (light gray) constitutes the outer layer (stroma surface). (By permission, Gantt et al. 1976.)

between 635 and 660 nm) to APC (fluorescing a deep red with a emission maximum between 660 nm and 680 nm) located on the thylakoid surface in contact with chl *a*. It is from APC that light energy is transferred from the phycobilin antenna pigments to the chl *a* molecules making up the antenna and phototraps of the two photosystems. By contrast, the biliproteins of cryptomonads are not aggregated into supermolecular structures but are packed evenly on the internal surfaces of thylakoid membranes, between the pairs of photosynthetic membranes.

It can be concluded that the absorption properties of different biliproteins are influenced both by the chromophore composition and by membrane pigment–protein interactions at higher order organizational levels. As the hydrophobic tetrapyroles become protein-bound, they are shielded from the external environment and are subject to influences of the internal apoprotein environment. The resulting protein-induced conformational changes account for much of the spectral changes observed in bound phycobilins where different apoproteins modify the absorption spectrum in different ways. Interestingly, these tetrapyroles only become fluorescent when they become protein bound, suggesting that the apoprotein also plays an important functional role in providing the optimal environment for effective energy transfer to occur. These spectral characteristics are further modified as the different biliproteins assemble together to form supermolecular phycobilisomes (Chapman 1973; Gantt et al. 1977; Glazer 1977; Gartt 1980).

CAROTENOIDS AND CAROTENOID–CHLOROPHYLL–PROTEIN COMPLEXES

The chemistry of carotenoids has been extensively reviewed (cf. Isler 1971; Goodwin 1976; Moss and Weedon 1976). The structure of carotenoids can be generally described as tetraterpenes made of eight isoprenoid (branched five carbon chains) units. Carotenoids can be divided into two groups, depending on whether they are hydrocarbons (carotenes) or contain some oxygen molecules (xanthophylls) (Fig. 16). These pigments can be synthesized de novo only by plants and photosynthetic bacteria. Animals derive their carotenoid pigmentation by grazing on these food sources and altering the chemical structure of ingested carotenoids, usually through the oxidizing effects of their digestive enzymes.

The carotenoids found in the photosynthetic tissues of plants can play several functional roles. Very small amounts of β-carotene are found in all photosynthetic membranes, presumably with both a photoprotective role and a stabilizing influence for the highly reactive P700 complex of Ps I. Yellow carotenoids (about 20% total carotenoid content of most phytoplankton algae) have been shown to

increase their proportions under bright light conditions and function as photoprotective screens or effective chemical quenchers in photooxidative reactions (Isler 1971; Krinsky 1979). These yellow carotenoids may also serve as biosynthetic precursors for the major light-harvesting carotenoids present in photosynthetic algae. The role of carotenoids as photosynthetic light-harvesting components has been examined extensively only in a few of these pigment systems. The efficient transfer of light energy from lutein to chl *a* within a chl *a*–chl *b* protein complex has been suggested (Satoh and Butler 1978). However, lutein and similar carotenoids have not been considered significant contributors to total light absorption in higher plants/green algae where chlorophylls dominate the pigment system or in the red algae where the biliproteins predominate.

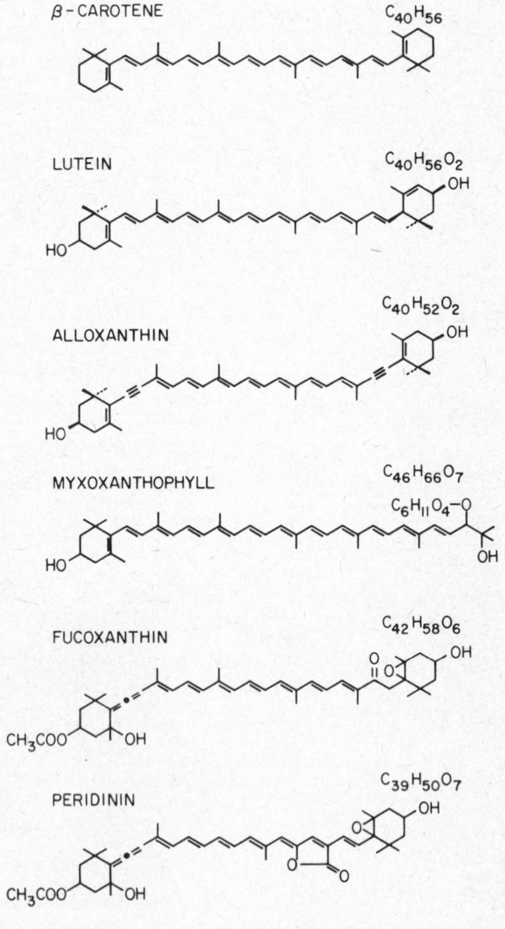

FIG. 16. Structures of representative plant carotenoids. (From Isler 1971.)

14

The major carotenoids of most phytoplankton are fucoxanthin and peridinin, present in the carotenoid–chl *a*–chl *c* pigment system of dinoflagellates, diatoms, brown algae, and chrysophytes in amounts that exceed that of either chl *a* or chl *c*. These two carotenoids are similar in structure (Fig. 16), differ from most other carotenoids in their high oxygen content, and have absorption properties that make them excellent photoreceptors for the blue-green light that penetrates to depth in the ocean. Photosynthetic action spectra of oxygen evolution in phytoplankton have long indicated the effective role peridinin and fucoxanthin play in gathering light energy for photosynthesis (Tanada 1951; Haxo 1960; Prézelin et al. 1976).

The protein binding of fucoxanthin was established by Margulies (1970), but attempts to isolate a fucoxanthin-protein by higher plant extraction techniques have been generally unsuccessful (Mann and Myers 1968). Barrett and Anderson (1977, 1980) and Berkaloff et al. (1980) recently isolated a chl *a*–chl *c* fraction enriched in fucoxanthin, but the detailed structural information on the organization of fucoxanthin and its binding to protein in these complexes is not yet available.

There has been major success in isolating peridinin–chl *a*–protein (PCP) complexes from a variety of free-living and symbiotic dinoflagellates (Haidak et al. 1966; Haxo et al. 1976; Prézelin and Haxo 1976; Siegelman et al. 1977; Chang and Trench 1981; Meeson and Sweeney 1981). Characterized in detail in *Glenodinium* sp. and *Gonyaulax polyedra*, the PCPs of these organisms appear to contain all the peridinin of the cell in a 4:1 molar ratio with chl *a* and are noncovalently attached to either one or two apoproteins with a total complex molecular weight around 35 000. The four peridinins of the chromophore occur as two dimers around a monomer of chl *a* (Fig. 17). Presumably it is this combination of dimerization and protein-binding environment that accounts for the absorption properties of peridinin within the pigment–protein complex (Fig. 18). Like the biliproteins, PCP is a water-soluble complex with its chromophore buried inside a hydrophobic pocket of the apoprotein (Song et al. 1976). Unlike the biliproteins, PCP contains a single chl *a* molecule in its chromophore which receives light energy from peridinin within the chromophore with 100% efficiency (Prézelin and Haxo 1976; Song et al. 1976). It is tempting to suggest that fucoxanthin, so structurally and functionally similar to peridinin, also might be localized in a pigment–protein complex similar to PCP.

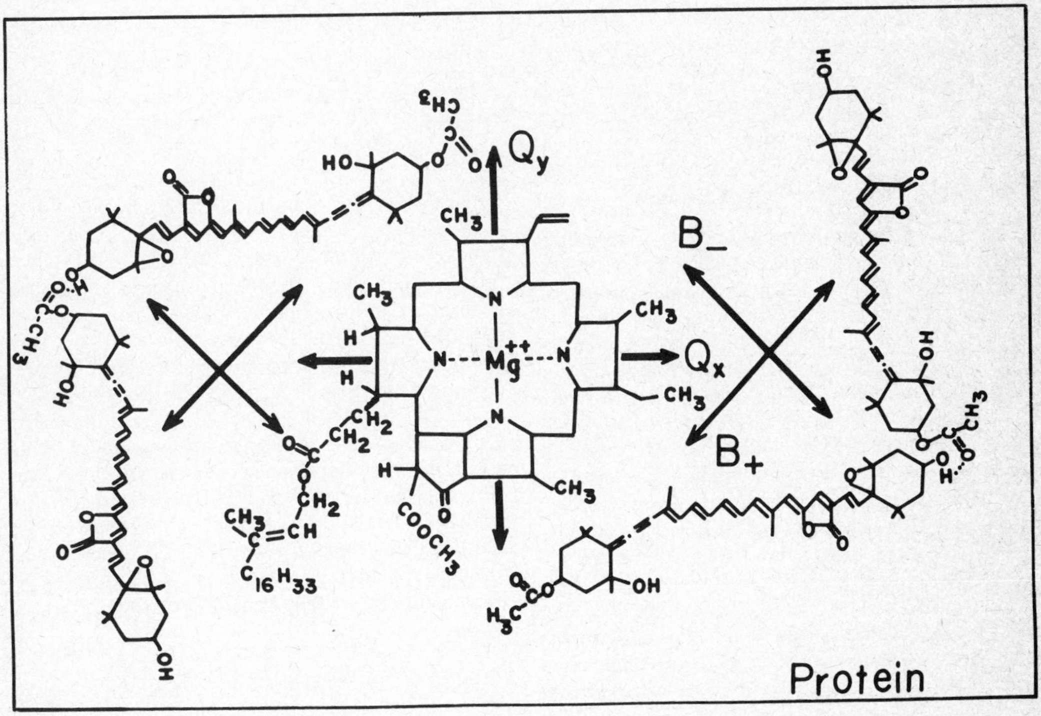

FIG. 17. A probable molecular arrangement of chlorophyll *a* and peridinins based on relative orientations of transition moments (double arrows of Qy fluorescence and B$^+$ exciton transitions. (By permission, Song et al. 1976.)

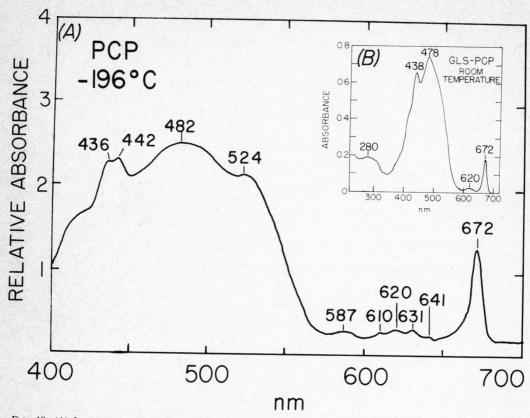

FIG. 18. (A) Low temperature (77K) absorption spectrum of purified pI 7.3 PCP from *Glenodinium* sp. in 5 m*M* Tris pH 8.4 buffer. (B) Room temperature absorption spectrum of purified pI 7.3 PCP from *Glenodinium* sp. in 5 m*M* Tris pH 8.4 buffer. (By permission, Prézelin et al. 1976.)

THE PHOTOSYNTHETIC UNIT CONCEPT

The chemical fractionation of chloroplasts has revealed different structural subunits for antenna pigments. In addition, each phototrap is bound in apparent protein complexes with discrete groups of chl *a* molecules that absorb light energy for that reaction center. Within Ps I there are an estimated 40–120 chl a_I molecules bound in a protein complex with P700, as compared with an estimated 20–60 chl a_{II} molecules associated with P680 in Ps II. A third chl *a*–protein complex, containing only chl *a*, also has been hypothesized to link the reaction centers of Ps I and II, serving no photochemical function but regulating light energy distribution between the two photosystems in the spillover process (Thornber et al. 1977; Hayden and Hopkins 1977; Anderson et al. 1978; Miles et al. 1979; Anderson 1980). This chl *a* core is thought to be conservative in pigment composition under most conditions and has been suggested to be the same in all organisms that contain chl *a* (Oquist 1974; Thornber et al. 1977; Vierling and Alberte 1980) (Fig. 19). If so, differences in pigment composition of dif-

ferent algal groups would then reflect differences only in the pigment–protein complexes that make up their light-harvesting components, i.e. the chl *a*–chl *b* protein complex in higher plants and green algae, the composite of biliproteins in red, blue-green, and cryptomonad algae, and the carotenoid–chl *a*–protein complexes in association with chl *a*– chl *c* protein complexes in diatoms, dinoflagellates, and brown algae (Fig. 19). The minimal and simplest functional composite structure, comprised of two photosystems and their light-harvesting components, has been termed a photosynthetic unit (PSU). This organization implies a 1:1 relationship between closely spaced Ps I and II reaction centers, although recent experimentation suggests this may not be the case (Haehnel 1976; Kawamura et al. 1979; Anderson 1980).

FUNCTIONS OF THE PHOTOSYNTHETIC APPARATUS

In the first steps of photosynthesis, light is absorbed by antenna pigments and transferred to the

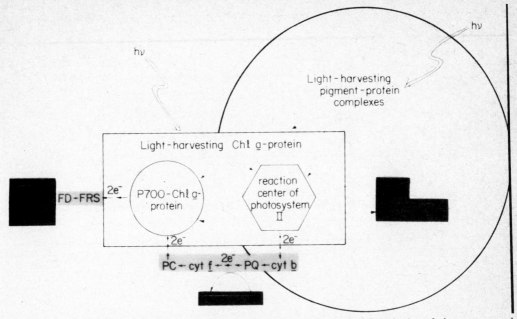

FIG. 19. Schematic model of the photosynthetic unit of chl *a*-containing plants. Organization of photosystems and light-harvesting components based on model proposed by Thornber et al. (1977).

phototraps of the photochemical reaction centers. There, absorbed light energy drives electron flow from water molecules to NADP and is tightly coupled to the formation of ATP. The reducing power of NADPH and the chemical potential of ATP are then used in the carbon dioxide fixation reactions in the stroma. Although the photosynthetic events of the light-driven reactions are described most easily as a sequence of events, it should be kept in mind that these are interdependent processes. For instance, there are possible exchanges of electromagnetic energy between antenna serving different PSUs, as well as electron flow between similar electron carriers of different electron transport chains linking Ps II and Ps I reaction centers. Moreover, it is the combined photochemical events of all functional reaction centers that establishes the electrochemical gradients within the thylakoid membrane and are crucial to the regulation of overall photosynthetic events (Junge 1977; Witt 1979).

Light absorption and energy transduction — When light energy is absorbed into the molecular structure of a pigment, electrons become redistributed into a set of excited singlet states (Fig. 20). The absorption spectrum of a pigment molecule or a pigment–protein complex reflects the light energy levels most effectively absorbed into the electronic states characteristic of the chromophore structure and conformation (cf. Clayton 1970; Sauer 1975; Malkin 1977; Knox 1977). The increased energy of the excited singlet state can be dissipated in several ways

(Fig. 20; Table 3). In a well-coupled photosynthetic

TABLE 3. Excited-states reaction scheme (by permission, Malkin 1977).

				Typical values* of the rate constants (s^{-1})
$M + h\nu$	$\rightarrow$	$^1M_n^*$	(absorption of the nth excited singlet state)	—
$^1M_n^*$	$\rightarrow$	$^1M^*$	(cascading to the lowest excited singlet by radiationless transitions)	10^{12}
$^1M_1^*$	$\xrightarrow{kF}$	$M + h\nu'$	(fluorescence)	10^9
$^1M_1^*$	$\xrightarrow{kH}$	M	(radiation transitions)	10^7–10^{11}
$^1M_1^*$	$\xrightarrow{kT}$	$^3M_1^*$	(transition to the lowest excited triplet state by radiationless transition — intersystem crossing)	10^7–10^{11}
$^1M_1^*$	$\xrightarrow{kp}$	P	(formation of photochemical products from the excited singlet state)	—
$^3M_1^*$	$\xrightarrow{k'F}$	$M + h\nu''$	(phosphorescence)	1
$^3M_1^*$	$\xrightarrow{k'H}$	M	(radiationless transition to the ground state [singlet] — intersystem crossing)	10^2–10^5 $(10^{-1}$–10^{-2} at 77K)
$^3M_1^*$	$\xrightarrow{k'p}$	P'	(photochemistry)	—

17

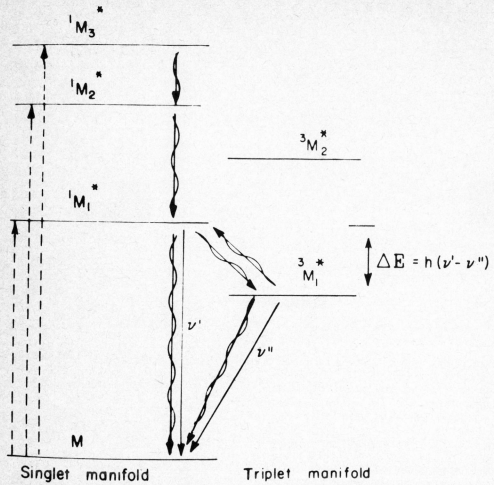

Singlet manifold   Triplet manifold

FIG. 20. Diagram of electronic state transitions for a typical polytomic milecule. M represents the ground-state (singlet). $^1M_n^*$ represents the n-excited singlet state. $^3M_n^*$ represents the n-excited triplet state. Light absorption is mainly restricted to either singlet or triplet manifolds. Broken arrows indicate absorption; wavy arrows indicate nonradiative transitions; solid arrows indicate radiative transitions: fluorescence (frequency ν'–photon energy $h\nu'$) and phosphorescence (frequency ν''–photon energy $h\nu''$). (By permission, Malkin 1977.)

apparatus, most energy of the excited singlet state of antenna pigments is transduced between neighboring pigment molecules until it reaches the phototraps of the reaction center. The energy transfer process usually is complete within a nanosecond, thereby competing successfully with dissipating processes (Table 3).

A second excited state also can be produced from the excited singlet state by nonradiative transition processes. Termed the triplet state, it is characterized by decreased energy and a longer lifetime (10 ms) than the excited singlet state. The transition from the singlet to triplet state involves the unpairing of an electron spin in an outer orbital of the pigment molecule. The probability of a singlet to triplet conversion and vice versa is considered small among

most antenna pigments (Malkin 1977). However, it has been suggested that the long-lived triplet state may be important in the reaction center phototraps, where excitation energy is quenched by primary electron acceptors (cf. Sauer 1975) (Fig. 20, Table 3).

Triplet–triplet state conversions among excited state molecules also can occur and serve a photoprotective function. In the presence of bright light, more energy is absorbed into excited singlet states than can be used in the photochemical reactions. This situation seems relevant when algae with large amounts of light-harvesting pigments (i.e. low light cells) experience a large and sudden increase in light intensities in their environment. Under these conditions, even though some excess light energy is dissipated through light emission and nonradiative decay, triplet states of antenna chl *a* can be formed and combined with oxygen molecules to become chemically altered. A loss of chl molecules can result and seriously affect photosynthetic potential of the algae at high light levels. One way to avoid the photooxidation of chl *a* molecules is to transfer quickly the energy of the chl *a* triplet state to neighboring carotenoids, where the excitation energy is released as heat (Fig. 20, 21). This process of carotenoid quenching of chl *a* triplet states has been described in some detail for those yellow xanthophylls found in most algal groups, whose concentrations increase at high light intensities but not noted for their photosynthetic light-harvesting capabilities (cf. Krinsky 1979). There is also evidence that the light-harvesting peridinin molecules also effectively protect the chl *a* monomer within the PCP chromophore from photodestruction (Song et al. 1980).

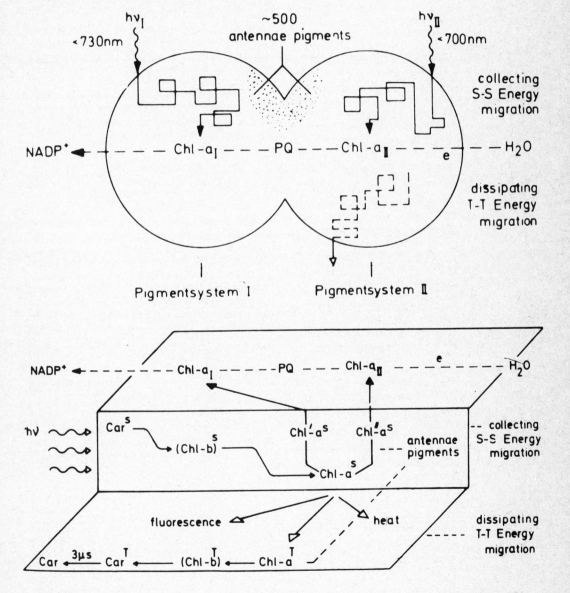

FIG. 21. Collection and dissipating energy migrations in the antennae pigments of photosynthesis. (By permission, Witt 1979.)

However, the dominant means of dissipating excess light energy from the excited states of photosynthetic pigments is through luminescence. Light emission is most easily observed in solutions of free chlorophylls, where coupled energy transfer, photochemistry, and membrane-mediated thermal transitions are eliminated. However, whereas chlorophylls fluoresce, extracted carotenoids and phycobilins removed from biliproteins do not fluoresce. Fluorescence is the light-emitting process by which pigments in the excited singlet state can return to ground state if their excess energy is not funneled through other processes within the fluorescence lifetime of the molecule (Fig. 20, Table 3). The transfer time between closely neighboring chl a molecules is estimated at less than a picosecond, while the fluorescence lifetime of chl a is on the order of 5 ns. Fluorescence occurs only from the lowest excited singlet state and, because of thermal relaxation prior to light emission, the fluorescence maximum is a few nanometres longer than the longest absorption maximum of the chromophore. In vivo, the majority ($>$ 90%) of fluorescence at room temperature arises from Ps II, as Ps I is much more likely to dissipate excess light energy through nonradiative thermal conversion processes (Fig. 21).

Light emission as the triplet state returns to ground state is also possible and is termed phosphorescence. It occurs much later (about 1 s) and with much less energy release than fluorescence (Table 3). A related process is delayed light emission, which can only occur in vivo and is closely related to the photochemical properties of Ps II and the energized state of the thylakoid membrane (cf. Malkin 1977). It is a complex phenomenon, occurring over a time scale from 1 μs to 1 min, and involves a triplet-to-singlet reconversion with the subsequent fluorescence of light coming from the excited singlet state.

Generally, the light energy absorbed by antenna pigments reaches the phototraps with high efficiency, suggesting the mechanism(s) of energy transduction to the reaction center must be very rapid and compete successfully against the wasteful processes mentioned above. The speed of electromagnetic transfer between pigment molecules depends on the strength of their resonant transition dipoles, which in turn depends on the distance between the pigments and their relative orientation to one another (Junge 1977). For sufficient resonance to keep energy transfer times less than the fluorescence lifetime, chl a molecules need to be closer than 100 Å. It appears that the proteins in the membrane and pigment complexes serve to optimally space chl molecules in vivo. Any membrane changes that alter the distances and orientation of pigment molecules so as to interfere with the strength and speed of their interaction will subsequently disrupt, weaken,

or alter energy transduction between the pigment molecules and can enhance the dissipation processes.

Charge separation and electron transport — Several excellent reviews have been written that thoroughly detail present knowledge of the primary photochemical events (Sauer 1975; Malkin and Ke 1978) and electron transport reactions of photosystems I and II (Trebst 1974; Bearden and Malkin 1975; Avron 1975; Golbeck et al. 1977; Junge 1977; Bolton 1977; Amesz 1977; Ke 1978; Knaff and Malkin 1978; Crofts and Wood 1978; CIBA Foundation Symposium 1979; Muhlethaler 1980; Velthuys 1980). Presented here is a summary of the latest views on charge separation and electron transport reactions. An attempt is made to highlight differences between algae and higher plants and indicate where concurrent information on algal groups is lacking.

The primary photochemical events in photosynthesis occur when reaction centers of Ps I and II are excited by absorbed light energy (Fig. 21, 22). The charge separation reaction can be visualized as the following:

$$DPA \xrightarrow{H\nu} D^1(P^*A_1) \xrightarrow{\text{5 ps}} D^1(P^+A_1^-)$$
$$\longrightarrow D^3(P^+A_1^-) \xrightarrow{\text{200 ps}} D^+PA_1A_2^-$$

where P is the photoactive P680 and P700 chl a pairs, and D and A represent electron donor and acceptors, respectively. In the excited singlet state, both P680 and P700 eject an electron which is rapidly transferred (5 ps) to a closely associated primary electron acceptor (A). A conversion from the singlet to a triplet state of the radical ion pair results and, from the triplet state, electron transfer to secondary

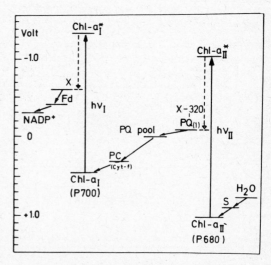

FIG. 22. Energy diagram of the electron transfer and midpoint potentials. (By permission, Witt 1979b.)

acceptors occurs in about 200 ps. At this point, back reactions are less likely. Where recombinations do occur, delayed fluorescence from Ps II may be observed. Secondary electron donors and acceptors complete the charge separation and the reaction center returns to its original condition through the oxidation of electron donors. In both photosystems, the primary electron donors lie near the inner surface of the thylakoid, the reaction centers are buried in the thylakoid membrane, and the electron acceptors are found near the outer stoma surface of the thylakoids. Thus, the photochemical events transfer one electron from each phototrap across the thylakoid membrane. In this manner, light energy is stabilized as stored chemical potential to be used in the formation of oxidizing and reducing compounds, transmembrane electric fields, ion gradients, and membrane conformational changes. The universality of the charge separation reaction in diverse pigment systems of different plant groups has yet to be demonstrated, as most studies to date have been done with higher plants and green algae. However, it is believed that differences may pertain more to details of molecular architecture and arrangement than to the fundamental nature of the charge separation process (Sauer 1981).

In Ps II, the primary electron donor is water and the acceptor is most probably a specialized plastoquinone molecule, historically termed Q for quencher or X–320 for the spectral changes associated with the charge separation phenomenon (Amesz 1977; Junge 1977; Knaff and Malkin 1978). Q is closely associated with the C550 signal previously described as indicative of Ps II photochemical events.

In Ps I of higher plants and some algae species, the primary electron donor is plastocyanin and the primary electron acceptor is possibly either a bound iron–sulfur protein or flavoprotein (Ke 1978; Croft and Wood 1978). The acceptor was first identified on the basis of spectral absorbance changes observed at 430 nm during the photochemical oxidation/reduction of P700 and was accordingly termed P430. Following electron transfer from plastocyanin to P700, the plastocyanin is rereduced by electron flow directed at photosystem I through a series of transmembrane electron carriers from the acceptor side of Ps II (Fig. 22, 23). From the acceptor side of Ps I, subsequent oxidation/reduction reactions transport electrons to the final electron acceptor NADP.

The electron transport chain can be discussed in three sections: the donor side of Ps II, the electron carriers between Ps I and II, and the acceptor side of Ps I (Fig. 22). The donor side of Ps II is least characterized and it is here that oxygen evolution and proton release from water occurs. Kok et al. (1970) observed oscillations in oxygen yield from cells illuminated with a series of flashes. Four successive flashes, and thus four electron transfers to P680, were required to produce a single oxygen molecule from two water molecules. The chemically uncharacterized water-splitting enzyme, known as S, Z, E, M, or Y by different workers, very efficiently donates electrons to P680 within 30 ns. To

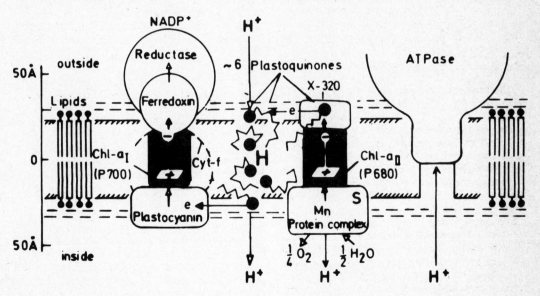

FIG. 23. Preliminary topography of the molecular machinery of photosynthesis based on functional experiments. The two black "trunks" symbolize the two photoactive centers, consisting of chl a_I and chl a_{II}, which probably are complexed with proteins. The porphyrin rings are located toward the inner surface. (By permission, Witt 1979a.)

21

form oxygen from water, the four electrons are extracted and stored in successive stages on the S complex, with the release of four protons to the intrathylakoid space. The work begun by Kok et al. (1970) has shown the S complex to include a charge storage enzyme with four oxidation states (S states) where one electron is removed from one of two associated water molecules within 0.2 ms of each flash (cf. Harriman and Barber 1979). All attempts to isolate the S complex have been unsuccessful although Spector and Winget (1980) have isolated a maganese-containing protein (molecular weight 65 000) which appears to be involved in oxygen evolution. It has been suggested that manganese is the charge accumulator in the S complex, although calcium and chloride also are known to be involved in oxygen evolution.

Localized between Ps I and Ps II are a series of chemical electron carriers. There has been controversy over the order and composition of electron acceptors in the chain, but the most favored simplified pathway is shown in Fig. 22. Following the primary acceptor, Q or X-320, electron transport moves out of Ps II via a second acceptor, R (or $PQ_{(1)}$). R is believed to be a pastoquionone ($PQ_{(1)}$), a lipophilic quinone with an isoprenoid side chain, bound to a special protein. It is between Q and R that the photosynthetic inhibitor 3-(3, 4-dichlorophenyl)-1, 1 dimethylurea (DCMU or diuron) acts to block electron flow. When R accepts electrons from Q it also takes up one proton from the stroma. However, since the addition or removal of two hydrogen atoms is needed to reduce or oxidize plastoquionones, R passes two pairs of electrons and protons on when subsequently oxidized by the neighboring plastoquinone (PQ) pool.

Perhaps the most important set of electron carriers is the PQ pool. Where the other electron carriers appear present in ratios of 1 or less per PSU, there are 5–10 PQ/electron chain. As such, the PQ pool innerconnects more than one electron transport chain, presumably providing alternate paths for electron flow when electron acceptors in one chain already are reduced. In this manner, PQ can provide an electron buffer in the transport systems and can regulate electron flow direction among different electron chains. In addition, as PQ is oxidized and passes its electrons along to plastocyanin (PC) or cyt c-552, two protons are released per molecules of PQ to the intrathylakoid space. The proton release from both PQ oxidation and water-splitting events to the interior phase of the thylakoid establishes the proton gradient across the thylakoid membrane, the driving force for photophosphorylation (cf. Junge 1977; Witt 1979).

The oxidation of reduced PQ by plastocyanin (a blue copper protein) is the slowest and, therefore,

the rate-limiting step in electron transport, setting the maximum quantum supply rate needed to drive electron flow (turnover time). As discussed by Crofts and Wood (1978), PC has been found in so many higher plants it is considered ubiquitous in all plant groups. However, the presence of PC has not been demonstrated in several algal species and the universal distribution of this electron carrier in photosynthetic algae has been questioned. Connected with these observations, an interesting suggestion has been made. One of the biggest differences known to occur between higher plants/green algae and other algal groups is the nature of another electron carrier, cyt f. Found in higher plants, cyt f is not always part of the electron transport chain. The cyt f of algae is very abundant and known not to have the same spectral or molecular weight characteristics as that isolated from higher plants (Wood 1977). This algal cyt f is also called cyt c-552 and is known to replace the function of PC in *Euglena* and to be present with PC in other algal species. It has been suggested that cyt c-552 serves a dual role for PC, especially under conditions of copper limitation when the PC content of plants declines.

An analogous situation also appears to occur on the acceptor side of Ps I. In some algae, the primary electron acceptor, the iron–sulfur protein ferredoxin, is partially replaced by flavodoxin. As it is able to substitute for almost all reactions involving ferredoxin, flavodoxin synthesis often is promoted by iron deficiency. It is suggested that ferredoxin is preferred in rich medium because it has better reaction properties than flavodoxin. But, because ferredoxin requires significant amounts of the cell's iron supply, flavodoxin is a useful alternative for growth when iron is limiting (cf. Croft and Wood 1979).

Ferredoxin reduces NADP with the aid of ferredoxin-NADP reductase, a FAD-containing flavoprotein (Fig. 23). Cyclic electron flow around Ps I in vivo also originates from ferredoxin, which passes electrons via cytochrome b-563 to PQ and back down the noncyclic portion of the chain to P700. Thus, during cyclic electron flow, additional protons are pumped to the intrathylakoid space. Cyclic electron flow, leading to cyclic photophosphorylation, is stimulated when carbon dioxide is limiting. Reduced NADPH cannot be reoxidized when the Cavin-Benson cycle activity is diminished and alternate electron acceptors from the acceptor side of Ps I must be utilized. In addition to cyclic flow, oxygen can also serve as a terminal electron acceptor in a process described as pseudocyclic photophosphorylation (cf. Gimmler 1977) (see Raven and Beardall 1981). Cyclic electron flow also appears to increase when Ps II activity is enhanced over Ps I, which can occur either when light energy distribution is not balanced between the two photosystems or when the number of Ps II centers predominates over the number of Ps I centers.

Photophosphorylation — The most accepted view of the coupling of electron transport, proton translocation, and ATP formation is based on Mitchell's (1974) chemiosmotic hypothesis and can be summarized as follows. Photophosphorylation can occur only within intact membrane vesicles impermeable to protons and with sufficient ADP and Pi available. Membrane potentials build up as a result of the primary photoact followed by the vectorial transport of protons (within 10 ms) to the interior of the vesicle (Fig. 23). Once a higher membrane potential is created by the proton flux, other ions can diffuse passively. Generally, chloride ions move in with protons and magnesium divalent ions move out. It is possible for most counterions present to pass through the thylakoid membrane to balance proton uptake. However, anion flow (i.e. Cl^-) inward results in membrane swelling and volume changes that can lead to membrane conformational changes uncoupling ATP synthesis and photosynthetic light reactions. Such alterations of membrane activity do not occur when cations (i.e. Mg^{2+}) are pumped out (Avron 1981).

A combination of the higher proton concentrations and net positive charge on the inside of the thylakoid tends to provide a "proton motive force" across the membrane to drive the protons out. The magnitude of proton movement depends on the light intensity (the driving force), the pH gradient in steady state, and the internal buffer capacity of the membrane. It appears that the internal proton concentration can reach magnitudes 10^4 times as great as the external proton concentration, with the pH of the intrathylakoid space being as low as 4.0. It is estimated that between 2.5 and 3.0 protons are pumped for each ADP phosphorylated. It is the proton motive force that drives ATP synthesis via a membrane-localized reversible ATPase, which is similar in both chloroplasts and bacterial chromatophores (cf. Jagendorf 1977; Avron 1981).

The actual mechanism by which ATP is formed from the dehydration of ADP and binding of Pi is not known. One scheme is Fig. 24. Here, hydroxyl and protons are released in ADP dehydration reactions, with the hydroxyl ions drawn toward the proton-rich interior to combine with the protons to form water. As a result the protons from the dehydration reaction are released in a stoichiometric 1:1 ratio with each proton hydrated on the interior, and thus a net proton release across the thylakoid membrane results (cf. Gimmler 1977). The reverse process is hypothesized to occur when ATP reserves are mobilized in the stroma, to allow the hydrolysis of ATP to ADP and Pi.

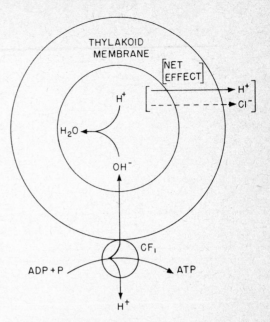

FIG. 24. Thermodynamic relations in ATP synthesis by membrane-bound, reversible, vectorial ATPase according to the chemiosmotic hypothesis. (By permission, Jagendorf 1977.)

Membrane Localization of Photosystems

In recent years, using techniques of freeze-fracture and freeze-etching, surfaces of the thylakoid membranes have been exposed to reveal the presence of particles embedded in or located on this membrane (Fig. 25). Presumably proteinaceous in nature, the particles are of different size and distribution and are increasingly regarded to represent discrete components of the photosynthetic apparatus. Detailed discussion of the freeze-fracture technique, descriptions of the substructure of the thylakoid membrane of green plants, and the molecular interpretations of observations are available in the review articles of Arntzen et al. (1977), Staehelin et al. (1977), Kirk and Tilney-Bassett (1978), Staehelin and Arntzen (1979), Staehelin et al. (1980). The substructure of the thylakoid membranes of phycobilin-containing organisms has been discussed in articles by Gantt and Conti (1966), Lefort-Tran et al. (1973), Gantt et al. (1977), and Gantt (1980). Until recently, no clear freeze-fracture micrographs of chl *c*-containing algal groups (browns, diatoms, dinoflagellates) have been obtained. A single study on the red tide dinoflagellate, *Gonyaulax polyedra*, is now available (Sweeney 1981).

Freeze-fracture techniques (Fig. 25a, b) reveal both the inner fracture face (PF) and the outer fracture face (EF) of the thylakoids. In green plants and algae

23

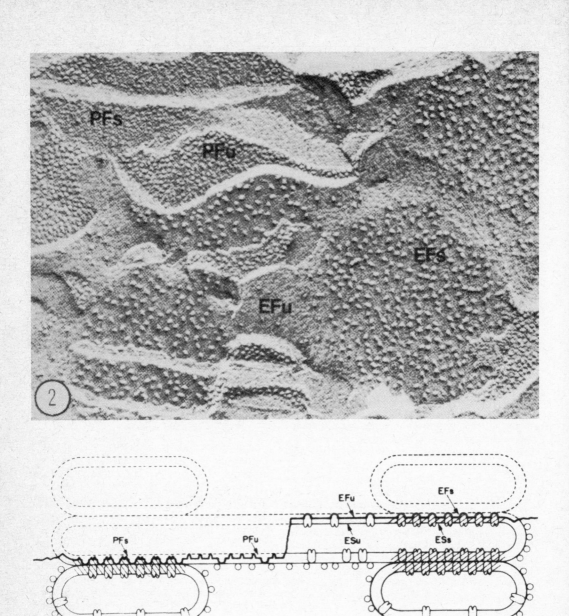

FIG. 25. (*Top*) Freeze-fractured isolated thylakoids of spinach illustrate the four types of fracture faces typical for such specimens. The faces EFs and PFs belong to stacked membrane regions, faces EFu and PFu to unstacked ones. × 85 000. (*Bottom*) Illustration of how the membrane faces EFs, EFu, PFs, and PFu in top arise during the fracturing of thylakoid membranes. (By permission, Staehelin et al. 1980.)

with recognized granum, a distinction is made between thylakoid surfaces of the grana and stoma lamellae. Granum membranes are considered stacked (s) and stroma membranes are considered unstacked (u). Thus, in higher plants, where grana stacks are most evident, four fracture faces (EFs, EFu, PFs, PFu) are recognized (Fig. 25).

The best characterized thylakoids are those of higher plants and green algae. On the inner fracture face of the granum thylakoid (EFs), there are characteristic large particles up to 164 Å in diameter. The largest of these particles are not found on similar fracture faces (EFu) of the stroma lamellae. Armond et al. (1977) observed the large particles to increase from a core diameter of 80 Å in etiolated pea leaves to three large size-classes of particles (105, 132, and 164 Å) in fully greened leaves. The only new polypeptide incorporated during this time was the chl a/b–protein of the light-harvesting component. Armond et al. (1977) suggested the inner fracture face particles represent a Ps II reaction center core (80 Å) in association with either 1, 2, or 4 aggregates of the chl a/b–protein complex. These observations are in accord with earlier studies of Sane et al. (1970) suggesting Ps II activity was absent from the stroma of higher plants.

The outer fracture face (PF) is similar in both the granum and stroma region, characterized by a high concentration of smaller sized particles ranging in size from 60 to 110 Å. These particles extend through the outer membrane surface slightly (Kirk and Tilney-Bassett 1978). It is believed that a sig-

nificant number of these particles may represent Ps I reaction centers (Staehelin et al. 1980), although the exact structural relationship is debated strongly. In addition, Staehelin (1976) found the EFs particles in one membrane to line up with rows of PFs particles in the other fracture face, suggesting the structurally close association of Ps I and II reaction centers. Along with other findings, Staehelin et al. (1977) and Arntzen et al. (1977) used these observations to design a model for intramembrane particle association in thylakoid stacked regions of chloroplast membranes (Fig. 26).

In electron micrographs of negatively stained thylakoids, 100 Å particles can be observed in large number over the outer surface (cf. Kirk and Tilney-Bassett 1978). These particles have been identified as the coupling factor for photophosphorylation. Likewise, both biochemical and immunological evidence is available to indicate the presence of the RUBP carboxylase as a 100–120 Å particle on this same surface. These particles are only found on external surfaces exposed to the stroma (Fig. 26). This is in contrast with outer surfaces of thylakoids closely aligned to other thylakoid membrane surfaces, i.e. stacked regions of higher plant chloroplasts or

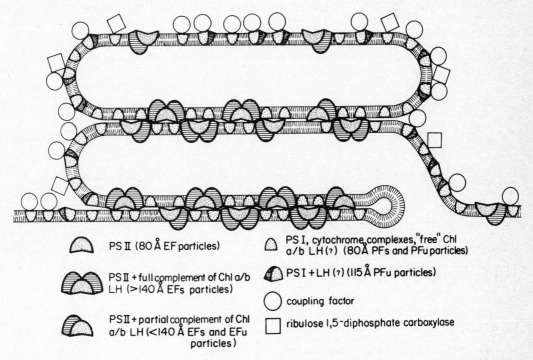

PS II (80 Å EF particles)

PS II + full complement of Chl a/b LH (>140 Å EFs particles)

PS II + partial complement of Chl a/b LH (<140 Å EFs and EFu particles)

PS I, cytochrome complexes, "free" Chl a/b LH(?) (80 Å PFs and PFu particles)

PS I + LH (?) (115 Å PFu particles)

coupling factor

ribulose 1,5-diphosphate carboxylase

FIG. 26. Schematic illustration of the supramolecular organization of thylakoid membranes of higher plants and green algae. Note the different composition of the stacked (grana) and unstacked (stroma) membrane regions. This differentiation appears to result from the adhesion between LHC–PS II complexes in adjacent membranes, and the concomitant physical exclusion of components not directly associated with the electron–transport chain. (By permission, Staehelin and Arntzen 1979.)

compound lamellae of overall algal classes. Only in the reds and blue-green algae, where thylakoids occur singularly, would a homogenous distribution of photosynthetic particles be expected along the external thylakoid surfaces.

In red and blue-green algae, where thylakoids occur singly so no distinction is made between contact and noncontact regions, a regular array of large particles (120–170 Å) can be observed on the exterior surfaces. They represent the phycobilisomes, whose arrangement may be ordered with underlying Ps II reaction centers (Fig. 27). As no light-harvesting chl *a/b*–protein complex is present in these organisms, large particles on the inner fraction face are not present. The overall distribution and sizes of particles within the thylakoid membranes are otherwise similar to that of agranual chloroplasts of higher plants (Lefort-Tran et al. 1973).

Very little detailed information on the molecular substructure of thylakoids in the major marine phytoplankton groups is available. However, the freeze-fracture study of *G. polyedra* does suggest some consistency of organization between the different algal groups (Fig. 28). Like other plant groups, the PF faces show many more particles than the EF faces (Sweeney 1981). Whereas the 160 Å particle correlated with the chl *a/b*–protein complexes is absence from the EFs face, the physical location of the peripheral light-harvesting peridinin–chl *a*–protein complex could not yet be identified (Sweeney).

Photosynthetic Unit Size and Density Determinations

As the discrete components of the two photosystems were identified and the concept of an organized arrangement of photosynthetic particles in the thylakoid membrane developed, attempts were made to estimate the pigment cross section (size) and density of photosystem reaction centers or combined PSUs in green plants. Such information is useful in studies which characterize photosynthetic particles and submolecular arrangements of thylakoid membranes, assess the regulatory responses of the photosynthetic apparatus to environmental change (ie. light, nutrients, temperature, etc.), and even attempt predictions of photosynthetic capacity. The measurement of size or number of PSUs is not a direct measure of photosynthetic activity. However, because the PSU represents a probable minimal unit of photosynthesis, it has been reasoned and debated that the number of PSUs should be directly correlated with photosynthetic capacity (Alberte et al. 1976a, b, 1977; Prézelin 1976; Terri et al. 1977; Armond and Mooney 1977; Malkin et al. 1977; Prézelin and Sweeney 1978; Prézelin and Alberte 1978; Perry et al. 1980). One instance where this correlation has not held is with the many phytoplankton species exhibiting a daily periodicity of photosynthesis in P_{max} and in situ photosynthesis, P_i, which is independent of both pigmentation and the shape of the photosynthesis-irradiance curves (Prézelin and Sweeney 1977; Prézelin and Ley 1980; Harding et al. 1981). Under such circumstances,

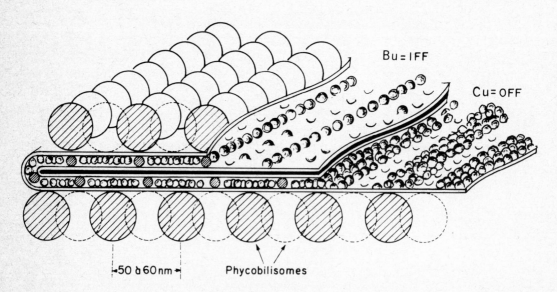

Fig. 27. Schematic representation of phycobilisome arrangement on thylakoids of red and blue-green algae, and the relationship to particle organization within the thylakoid membrane. (By permission, Lefort-Tran et al. 1973.)

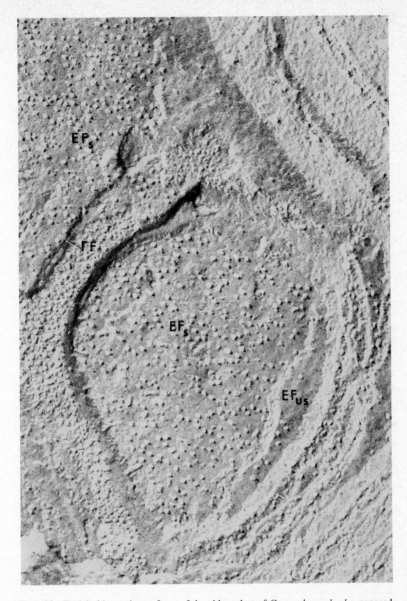

FIG. 28. Thylakoid membrane faces of the chloroplast of *Gonyaulax polyedra* exposed by freeze-fracture. All 4 faces of the thylakoid are × 120 000. (Courtsey of Sweeney 1981.)

the apparent PSU size and number stay relatively constant while the photosynthetic rate varies significantly over the day. In these cases, knowing the density of photosystems alone would add little and even be misleading in attempts to estimate daily rates of primary productivity.

Most work to date has been based on the assumption that an equal number of both Ps I and II reaction centers occur in most chloroplast membranes, and that measuring either the number of Ps I or Ps II reaction centers should reflect accurately the total number of functional PSU present. In higher plants the numbers of Ps I and II reaction centers does appear to be almost equal (Haehnel 1976). However, recent studies on blue-green algae indicate the Ps II:I ratio is not always unity, ranging from 1.2 to 3.9 depending on the species and light intensity used in culturing (Kawamura et al. 1979). Because only a few studies have been completed and error associated with the different measuring techniques is undefined, it is not possible at this time to assess what impact such results will have on the concepts of photosynthetic unit determinations and their usefulness in productivity estimates.

Also subject to some debate is which technique of measuring individual photosystem size and number is most accurate in reflecting total PSU size (absorptive cross section) and number. In the past, the most commonly used methods have been estimates of P700 content for Ps I and oxygen flash yields for Ps II. These two procedures are outlined below, as they are techniques of choice for most biologists. They require less investment of time and/or instrumentation than more intricate procedures, which include fluorescence-induction measurements (Malkin et al. 1977) and plastoquinone and chl a_1 flash absorbance measurements (Haehnel 1976).

P700 ASSAY

P700 can be detected in plant samples either by photochemical or chemical assays. Both approaches are based on measuring the oxidized-minus-reduced difference spectrum of P700 (Fig. 8) and applying a differential molar extinction coefficient to quantify the signal change induced at 700 nm. Coefficients varying from 64 to 70 mequiv. cm^{-1} have been reported for P700 (Hiyama and Ke 1972; Shiozawa et al. 1974; Ke 1978). PSU density is then expressed at P700/cell or area, and PSU size expressed as chl a/P700 ratios.

Light-induced oxidation/reduction changes can be measured in whole cell suspensions of many algal species. However, P700 signals apparently cannot be detected in whole cells of all phytoplankton (notably dinoflagellates, see Prézelin 1976; Govindjee et al. 1979). It is not clear why this is the case, as P700–chl a–protein complexes are known to be present (Prézelin and Alberte 1978). It is possible that recombination of light-induced charges separation in Ps I occurs so quickly it is not detected in the assay procedure. The instrumentation required for the photochemical assay is not readily available to most biologists and so the chemical assay of P700 more commonly is employed.

In the chemical assay, oxidants (i.e. potassium ferricyanide) and reductants (i.e. sodium ascorbate) are used to generate an oxidized-minus-reduced absorption spectrum of P700. However, several precautions must be taken to insure an accurate determination of P700 content (Markwell et al. 1980). First, cell fractionation and detergent solubilization of thylakoid membranes are required to insure exposure of all P700 complexes to redox reagents. Extracts of whole plants not clarified by initial centrifugation give poor results, presumably due to the redox-

buffering capacity of the extract (Markwell et al. 1980). In addition, if no detergent is used to solubilize large chloroplast fragments, scattering in the sample increases by an unknown amount, and increases sample absorption and the apparent P700 signal (Markwell, personal communication). Also, samples have to be temperature-equilibrated or large spectral shifts in the absorption spectrum result and interfere with the P700 signal.

Another major problem with the chemical assay is that the chemical oxidants often cause irreversible oxidations of antenna chlorophyll close to P700 and enhance the apparent P700 signal significantly. However, a procedural method outlined by Markwell et al. (1980) and involving a spectrophotometer coupled to a microprocessor has been successful in reducing the spectral interference of antenna chlorophyll around P700. Similarly, the type of solubilizing detergent can enhance or diminish the P700 signal, presumably altering redox interactions · of antenna chlorophylls (Markwell et al. 1980).

The maintainance of uniform measuring conditions insures that the estimates of the relative change in P700 content is possible in the same algal species under differing environmental conditions. However, it appears that great care must be taken to achieve a close estimate of the absolute number of Ps I reaction centers present. Also, few independent measurements have been made to assure that total exposure of P700 centers is achieved when the same extraction procedures are applied to plant groups with different membrane solubilization properties. Thus, while comparison of relative changes in PSU size and density within a single plant species is easily possible, it is not yet clear how much error may be involved when comparisons of absolute PS I number or PSU size and density are attempted within and between different plant groups (see Markwell et al. 1980; Perry et al. 1980).

OXYGEN FLASH YIELDS

The number of Ps II reaction centers has been estimated in whole cell algal suspensions by illuminating them with consecutive brief flashes of saturating light and determining the oxygen yield/flash/chlorophyll. These measurements were first made by Emerson and Arnold (1932) and are based on the concept that all reaction centers of a plant exposed to a brief intense light flash will react only once (turnover) during the flash. In the work on *Chlorella*, optimal oxygen yield was observed when the flash duration was about 1 μs and the time between flashes greater than 40 ms. Thus, the average light intensity is low and the dark period relatively long. The dark time is required to pass on the products from one flash and return all the reaction centers to a state that can fully utilize the energy of the next light flash. This reasoning appeared confirmed when it was determined by Emerson and co-workers that maximum flash yield was temperature independent and the dark time needed to complete the cycle of necessary enzyme reactions was temperature dependent. In *Chlorella* there are about 3000 chl *a* molecules present for each oxygen molecule evolved (Emerson and Arnold 1932) and this PSU size does not appear to vary with environmental conditions (Myers and Graham 1971).

The process can be time consuming, as flash yield as a function of both flash speed and intensity needs to be determined before the maximum flash yield can be obtained. These parameters are not the same for different species of phytoplankton (Kawamura et al. 1979). Also, significant respiration is possible during the relatively long dark period and may be accentuated over time by the relatively low average light level the algae can absorb during the measurement time. Interference with oxygen yield measurements is accentuated in those marine phytoplankton for which respiratory demands are proportionally much higher than those of green algae and higher plants (i.e. diatoms, and especially dinoflagellates). Respiration changes presumably can be corrected for by knowing the dark oxygen consumption rates and assuming they are unchanged during the brief intense light flash.

Regulation of Photosynthetic Cellular Processes which Alter Photosynthesis–Irradiance Relationships

The preceding sections attempted to present the current views on the structural and functional organization of the photosynthetic light reactions, but the emphasis now is shifted to highlight some regulatory aspects of the cellular processes of photosynthesis and their effect in altering rates of primary productivity at the whole plant level. While certainly not exhaustive, the following brief discussion is aimed at establishing that (i) discrete changes in the organization and/or activity of the photosynthetic apparatus are induced by changes in environmental and endogenous factors, (ii) the biochemical and structural nature of the cellular changes can now be identified in a fairly precise way by combining techniques which measure the amounts of various photosynthetic components (i.e., pigmentation, P700, and RUBP carboxylase) with the abundant information inherent in the photosynthesis–irradiance (P–I) relationships (cf. Bourdu and Prioui 1974), and (iii) knowing the cellular response mechanism(s) to environmental/endogenous variables considerably advances the knowledge and ability to predict the physiological consequences of the cellular changes on the photosynthetic characteristics at the whole plant level.

There are several ways the photosynthetic machinery may respond to external or endogenous environmental changes. The most obvious responses include alterations in (1) PSU size or the average amount of light-harvesting pigments per PS I/PS II pair; (2) PSU or individual photosystem density, (3) thylakoid membrane state leading to complete coupling/uncoupling of energy transduction and electron flow in discrete PSUs, and (4) reduction of dark enzyme activity and/or rates of electron flow from one electron carrier to another in Ps I and/or Ps II. A change in any one of the above processes should have a predictable effect on measureable photosynthetic components and their activity, with possible consequences for the magnitude (i.e. photosynthetic potential or capacity, P_{max}) and shape (i.e. α, the light-limited slope; $I = \frac{1}{2} P_{max}$, the light level at which photosynthesis is half saturated) of the P–I relationships. Each possibility is discussed briefly, with cited examples of the environmental/endogenous changes that bring about these cellular modifications in different plant groups. There always exists the possibility that more than one of the photosynthetic responses mentioned might result as a single external variable change, or that more subtle alterations in the photosynthetic apparatus might occur (i.e. changes in the Ps II/Ps I ratio). Their detection would require much more detailed measurements than those outlined below. However, it is still evident that development and usage of photosynthetic techniques designed to characterize the photosynthetic apparatus can be incorporated into biological oceanographic techniques to improve significantly the capabilities to both understand the mechanisms behind environmentally induced physiological changes in phytoplankton and to use that knowledge to improve the ability to predict the direction and even time course of photosynthetic change during environmental fluctuations.

A) PSU size (the average number of light-harvesting pigments per photosystem) changes can be estimated by looking for changes in either chl a/P700 or chl a/O_2 ratios.

Should such analytical procedures not be available, a change in PSU size (photosystem cross section) can be inferred from disproportionate changes in cellular pigmentation. Since the chl a core of the photosynthetic reaction centers and their spillover component are assumed fairly uniform in composition (Oquist 1974; Thornber et al. 1977; Vierling and Alberte 1980), changes in PSU size are evidenced through changes in the amount of light-harvesting component (LHC) associated with each PSU. Since the LHC of most marine plants (with the exception of green algae) is dominated by pigments other than chl a, a change in PSU size

29

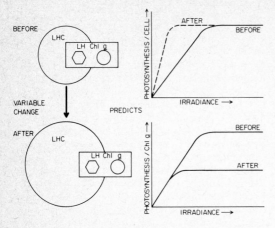

FIG. 29. Schematic representation of relationship between altered photosynthetic unit size and changes in the P–I curves, expressed either on a cellular basis (upper curves) or a chl a basis (lower curves). (See text for discussion.)

should lead to a change in whole cell pigment molar ratios.

The predicted effect of altered PSU size is illustrated in Fig. 29. When the P–I relationship is expressed on a chl a basis, P_{max} would be expected to change in direct proportion to the change in associated LHC chl a. In phycobilin systems, where no chl a is in the LHC, changes in the P–I relationship would only be seen if one or more of the phycobilins were used to standarized photosynthetic rates. On a cellular or area basis, P_{max} would not be expected to change as the density of PSU remained constant. However, since the size of the LHC was altered, the light intensity required to saturate photosynthesis should change in some inverse proportion to the size of the PSU and be reflected in both slope and half-saturation constant changes.

Unfortunately, not all these measurements have been made simultaneously in most studies of environmentally induced changes in photosynthesis. Increases in chl a/P700 ratios, with no alterations in P700/cell or area ratios, have been observed when higher plants are grown under lowered light conditions (Brown et al. 1974; Alberte et al. 1976a), when corn is subjected to decreased water stress (Alberte et al. 1977), when the halophytic green algae Dunaliella is released from hypotonic salt stress (Brown et al. 1974), and when diatoms generally are exposed to lowered light levels or increased nutrient supply (Perry et al. 1981). Decreased PSU size is commonly associated with aging and senescence in higher plants (Alberte 1981). In the majority of these examples the effects on photosynthetic characteristics is not available. However, in dinoflagellates, changes in photosynthesis-irradiance

curves similar to those in Fig. 29 are seen when bright-light cultures are low-light adapted. The changes occur within a generation time and are associated with major increases in pigmentation and specifically in association with increased amounts of LHC, i.e. PCP and the chl a/chl c–protein complexes (Prézelin 1976; Prézelin and Sweeney 1978, 1979; Prézelin and Matlick 1980). Although all the necessary data are not available, pigmentation and P–I data suggest similar low light responses may also occur in the blue-green alga, Synechoccocus elogatus (Jorgensen 1969), the diatom, Skeletonema costatum (Brooks 1964), the green algae, D. tertiolecta, and to a lesser extent in Chlorella vannielli (Reger and Krauss 1970) and in some seaweed (Ramus et al. 1967a, b).

B) PSU (or photosystem) density changes should be seen in changes in both P700/cell and total O_2 flash yields, while chl a/P700 and chl a/O_2 remain unaltered. Amounts of pigmentation would change, although pigment molar ratios do not, as the composition of PSU is the same. PSU density changes should not affect PSU/chl a values (Fig. 30), therefore, no significant changes in the P–I chl a curves should be evident. But, since P_{max}/cell should change in direct proportions to P700, the magnitude of the P–I/cell curves should change in direct proportion to pigmentation.

Although not often documented, this strategy has been seen in photoadaptive responses of a few dinoflagellates, notably Peridinium cinctum (Prézelin and Sweeney 1979) and Ceratium furca (Meeson and Sweeney 1981), and suggested by the photosynthetic data available for the green alga, Chlamydomas moewussi, and the xanthophyte, Monodus subterraneus (Jorgensen 1969, 1970). Changes in P700/cell have been seen in light-induced responses in diatoms (Perry et al. 1980) and cotton (Patterson

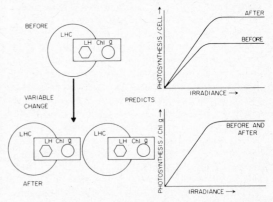

FIG. 30. Schematic representation of relationship between altered photosynthetic unit density and changes in the P–I curves, expressed either on a cellular basis (upper curves) or a chl a basis (lower curves). (See text for discussion.)

et al. 1977), as well as in mutants of three hybrids of corn (Terri et al. 1977). In all cases there was good correlation between P700/cell or area and P_{max}/cell or area. An exception is a recent study in blue-greens, where P700/cell doubled at low light, phycocyanin concentration tripled, P_{max}/cell stayed the same, and P_{max}/chl a declined (Vierling and Alberte 1980). It appears to be an example of simultaneous increase in Ps I density and LHC size of Ps II at low light levels.

C) Changing photosynthetic efficiency refers here to the coupling/uncoupling of energy transduction or electron flow between a discrete number of total photosystems. In other words, the energy flow through existing PSUs can be reversibly interrupted without disturbing the size and density of Ps I and Ps II per cell. In this case, no pigmentation changes are observed, but both light-limited and light-saturated rates of photosynthesis are dramatically altered (Fig. 31). This phenomenon appears basic to thermal liability in higher plants and algae (Bjorkman 1972), daily photosynthetic periodicity (often controlled by a biological clock) in dinoflagellates (Prézelin et al. 1977; Prézelin and Sweeney 1977, diatoms (Prézelin and Ley 1980; Harding et al. 1981), *Euglena* (Lonegran and Sargent 1978), and *Acetabularia* (Terbourgh and Mcleod 1967), and life cycle changes in the photosynthetic activity of blue-green algae (Senger 1970a, b).

D) Changing enzymatic rates (rates of electron transport and carbon dioxide fixation) are detected in changes in specific enzyme activities and not in pigmentation, PSU size or density, or light-limited rates of photosynthesis (Fig. 32). The major effect is on light-saturated rates of photosynthesis, which

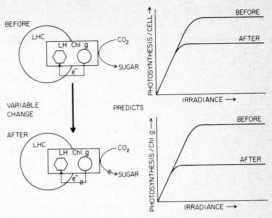

FIG. 32. Schematic representation of relationship between altered photosynthetic enzymatic reactions and changes in the P–I curves, expressed either on a cellular basis (upper curves) or a chl a basis (lower curves). (See text for discussion.)

decline in proportion to decreased enzyme activity. Such responses generally have been linked to low light responses in higher plants and green algae (Bjorkman 1972), carbon dioxide availability studies for several groups of plants (Kelley et al. 1976), and aging in plants (Thimann 1980; Prézelin unpublished results).

In Vivo Fluorescence as a Photosynthetic Probe

Here, an effort is made to introduce a few general types of fluorescence parameters routinely used in photosynthesis studies today. Some discussion of regulating parameters is included to indicate complexities in interpreting fluorescence signals which are rich in photosynthetic information. The following is far from a complete review, as fluorescence studies in photosynthesis have expanded considerably during the past 15 yr. Those wishing more detailed information are referred to the review articles of Papageorgiou (1975), Lavorel and Etienne (1977), Butler (1977), the CIBA Foundation Symposium (1979), and the many articles on fluorescence in the Proceedings of the 5th International Congress on Photosynthesis (1981).

FLUORESCENCE INTENSITY $+/-$ DCMU INDICES

Since the early 1960s, the fluorescence intensity of extracted chl a has been used as a routine field measurement reliably indicating the quantity of chlorophylls and their breakdown products in dilute field

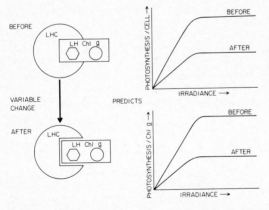

FIG. 31. Schematic representation of relationship between altered photosynthetic energy transduction and changes in the P–I curves, expressed either on a cellular basis (upper curves) or a chl a basis (lower curves). (See text for discussion.)

samples. With the advent of flow-through fluorimeters, in vivo chl a fluorescence profiles could be measured easily. Assuming a reasonable correlation between in vivo and extracted chl a fluorescence intensity, in vivo fluorescence profiles are now commonly used to indicate the spatial distribution of plant biomass in aquatic habitats. This approach not only assumed that the in vivo fluorescence intensity (F) was a consistent and accurate index of chl a content, but that the chl a content of the sample also was an accurate and consistent index of plant standing crop. The latter assumption was discredited early on, as widely varying chl a/biomass ratios were observed under a variety of changing environmental conditions. And recently, the constancy of chl a fluorescence yield (F/chl a, referred to as R in some literature) also has been challenged. As a result, it has been suggested now that the addition of the photosynthetic inhibitor, DCMU, would release in vivo F/chl a from all modifying effects of the cell and thereby be a more true index of chl a concentrations (Slovceck and Hannon 1977). This is challenged also. While blocking electron flow and thus increasing fluorescence, DCMU does nothing to control the natural dynamics of the thylakoid membrane which determine the changing physical/chemical environment in which chl a molecules reside. The modifying effects of a variety of parameters, including redox potential, ion flow, membrane stacking, protein phosphorylation, and other aspects of membrane state changes, on fluorescence yield have been documented in recent years (Wraight and Crofts 1970; Telfer et al. 1976; Mills et al. 1976; Murata 1969; Barber 1979; Homann 1979; cf. Proceedings of the 5th International Congress on Photosynthesis 1981).

So, while fluorescence intensity indices may not be reliable measures of chl a concentrations, changes in these indices often reflect physiological state changes within the plant and, in some instances, correlate well with changes in photosynthetic activity. For instance, changes in F/chl a have been associated with light and nutrient stress (Kiefer 1973a; Loftus and Seliger 1975; Cullen and Renger 1979; Prézelin and Ley 1980) as well as with diurnal periodicity in photosynthesis (Prézelin and Sweeney 1977; Prézelin and Ley 1980; Vincent 1980). In some but not all cases, good correlations also have been recorded between various fluorescence indices and photosynthetic rates (Samuelsson and Oquist 1977; Samuelsson et al. 1978; Prézelin and Ley 1980; Kulandaivelu and Daniell 1980). To analyze critically the usefulness of these indices in future phytoplankton studies, it is first necessary to review the parameters which comprise and regulate the measurement of in vivo fluorescence intensity and, second, to then review the studies where such indices have or have not been successfully employed.

Fluorescence intensity (F) instantly monitors all the competing processes in primary photosynthetic events. At room temperature, 90% or more of the fluorescence intensity arises from back reactions of primary photochemical events occurring in the reaction centers and antenna chlorophyll of photosystem II. Membrane state changes, which reflect physiological state changes and which alter F, are removed when fluorescence measurements are made at low temperature (i.e. in the presence of liquid nitrogen, at 77 K). For instance, the daily changes observed in F/chl a and F_{DCMU}/chl a associated with circadian rhythmicity in photosynthesis of phytoplankton are abolished when measurements are done at low temperature, suggesting the regulation of diurnal periodicity of photosynthesis of many phytoplankton species is closely related to endogenous regulatory changes in the membrane state of the thylakoids (Prézelin and Sweeney 1977; Govingjee et al. 1979; Sweeney et al. 1979; Prézelin and Ley 1980). Also, low temperature usually but not always increases F as fluorescence contributions from Ps I become more significant. For biological oceanographers working with in vivo fluorescence measurements of natural phytoplankton populations, F may be considered a probe of Ps II activity, which can be strongly influenced by several variables. Summarized from the review of Lavorel and Etienne (1977), fluorescence intensity can be described generally by:

$$(2) \qquad F = I \cdot \varphi_f \,(It, t, \lambda_e, \lambda_f, \text{state})$$

where I = absorbed light energy, and

$$(3) \quad \varphi_f - \text{fluorescence yield} =$$
$$k_f/(k_f + k_p + k_d + k_t)$$

where k_f = fluorescence rate constant, and k_p = photochemical rate constant, and k_d = nonradiative de-excitation rate constant, and k_t = excitation transfer rate constant, and φ_f depends on several factors affecting photosynthetic rate, including t = time of illumination, It = density of illumination, λ_e = excitation wavelength, λ_f = fluorescence emission wavelength, and state physiological conditions of the sample due to pretreatment or growth status (i.e. temperature, dark adaptatime, addition of oxidants/reductants/inhibitors, light, and nutrient status, etc.).

If the light source (I) is kept constant, then changes in detected F should reflect changes in φ_f. This is generally the case in fluorescence intensity studies where the light source is the actinic beam of a fluorimeter, and is not the case where fluorescence is detected off the surface of the ocean by remote sensing. When cells of a single type with identical pretreatment are placed in a fluorimeter and a constant

I used to detect fluorescence, it is then possible to study changes in F that accurately reflect changes in φ_f. Such conditions have been used widely in molecular studies to analyze the effects of various chemicals and environmental conditions (i.e. reduced temperature, ion changes, nutrient stress, etc.) on the photochemical events in photosynthesis. It should be cautioned that while the uniform state of the same cells placed in such conditions can be assured, the same state can not be assured in the same cells from different conditions or from different cells under the same conditions (Papageorgiou 1975; Lavorel and Etienne 1977).

The light source (I) also photochemically alters the F signal with time, giving the well-known fluorescence induction curve. Generally, standard fluorimeters are not equipped to keep I small enough ($< 1 \ \mu W \ cm^{-2}$) or illumination time short enough to keep φ_f independent of It, and, therefore, the time at which measurements are made after the onset of illumination become important in determining the intensity of the F signal. Equally important in determining the intensity of F are the emission wavelengths monitored and the excitation wavelengths used to promote fluorescence.

When the photosynthetic inhibitor DCMU is added to algal suspensions, an eventual block to electron flow between Ps II and I occurs and usually can be monitored as an increase in fluorescence intensity (F_{DCMU}) to a new higher steady-state level. (The time for the F_{DCMU} signal to maximize appears to vary in different algal preparations, from less than 30 s (Cullen and Renger 1979) to 30 min, and may well reflect differences in membrane permeability or sensitivity to the DCMU block (Prézelin and Ley 1980)). With k_p now presumably equal to zero, the F_{DCMU} signal then should reflect the total light energy absorbed by the photosynthetic apparatus of Ps II when both k_d and k_t are considered small and unchanged. Under such conditions, if the fluorescence yield of chl (φ_f/chl) has not been altered by the addition of membrane-bound DCMU and the photosynthetic activity of Ps I and II are generally equivalent, then the fluorescence ratios F/F_{DCMU} and $I-F/F_{DCMU}$ should reflect that proportion of absorbed light energy which is reemitted as fluoresced light or used in the photochemical events of Ps II, respectively. If all assumptions hold true, then F/F_{DCMU} and $1-F/F_{DCMU}$, respectively, vary inversely and directly with the photosynthetic activity of untreated algal suspensions. There are several cases where one or more of the above assumptions do not hold true and the reliability of the fluorescence indices is questioned (cf. Lavorel and Etienne 1977; Proc. 5th Int. Cong. Photosynth. 1981). However, examples do exist where good correlation between

fluorescence indices and photosynthetic activity are found. A few examples follow.

Studies of diurnal periodicity in photosynthetic capacity (P_{max}) in laboratory cultures of dinoflagellates and field samples of mixed diatom populations have shown that correlated changes in fluorescence indices F/chl a, F_{DCMU}/chl a, and F/F_{DCMU} occur over the day (Prézelin and Sweeney 1977; Sweeney et al. 1979; Prézelin and Ley 1980). The mechanism of regulation of the photosynthesis and fluorescence periodicity appear closely linked, unrelated to pigmentation, and subject to regulation of the thylakoid membrane activity of a fixed number and fixed-size PSUs by a biological clock (Prézelin and Sweeney 1977; Sweeney and Prézelin 1978; Sweeney et al. 1979). The apparent inverse correlation between F/F_{DCMU} and P_{max} resulted from the larger changes in F_{DCMU}/chl a than in F/chl a occurring over the day (Sweeney et al. 1979; Prézelin and Ley 1980). Thus, in the case of diurnal periodicity of photosynthesis, the F/F_{DCMU} ratio does monitor accurately diurnal changes in photosynthetic activity in these populations, but does not reflect increased k_f in the presence of decreased k_p as was earlier predicted (Prézelin and Sweeney 1977). Instead, when k_p decreases at night apparently so does k_f, suggesting added de-excitation energy is dissipated more through membrane processes at night than during the day (Govindjee et al. 1979; Sweeney et al. 1979). These membrane-associated changes should be reflected in the rate constants k_d and k_t, which unfortunately are not easily quantified (cf. Papageorgiou 1975; Lavorel and Etienne 1977; Butler 1977).

These studies reinforce the growing awareness that F/chl a is not a constant that can be used reliably in mixed phytoplankton biomass estimates based on in vivo chl a fluorescence profiles (Kiefer 1973a, b; Loftus and Seliger 1975; Heany 1978). Likewise, in situations where strong photosynthesis rhythms are present, the addition of DCMU to uncouple chl fluorescence from photosynthesis may in fact enhance the fluorescence rhythm. Lastly, it should be mentioned that the correlation between photosynthesis and fluorescence over the day decreased with light limitation and sometimes with the age of the cultures. Thus, although good correlation may exist within any one set of measurements, the nature of the correlation or the degree of the correlation do not appear to occur reproducibly between different populations or the same population under different conditions. Handling, nutritional and light state of the culture, detection procedure, and time of day all combine to affect the fluorescence measurement.

Good correlation between fluorescence and photosynthesis also has been observed in aging cultures of green and blue-green algae (Samuelsson and Oquist 1977; Samuelsson et al. 1978) and higher

33

plants (Kulandaivelu and Daniell 1980). In the first case, the integrated signal of F/chl a and F_{DCMU}/chl a within the first 5 s of illumination is determined and the calculated $1-F/F_{DCMU}$ value is shown to be strongly correlated with P_{max} when compared in cells of different culture age. However, the components of this ratio are F/chl a and F_{DCMU}/chl a and they appear to follow the photosynthetic rate during exponential growth and only become inversely related as the cells enter the stationary phase. Again, as with the daily periodicity studies, the fluorescence ratios in the presence and absence of DCMU do appear to reflect accurately but not predict changes in photosynthetic activity. Furthermore, the studies on laboratory cultures of green and blue-green algae indicated that the largest increases in DCMU-induced fluorescence ($F_{DCMU}-F$) occurred in cell suspensions where photosynthetic activity was the highest. Similar observations were made by Rey (1978) and showed a remarkable degree of correlation in studies of freshwater and marine mixed phytoplankton populations. Together, these workers have suggested the possibility of using "variable" fluorescence (here defined as $F_{DCMU}-F$) as an indirect field measure of primary production and photosynthetic capacity.

The observation that DCMU does not always increase fluorescence intensity (F) to the same degree has been studied in some detail in the blue-green alga *Oscillatoria chalybea* by Bader and Schmid (1981). They recently reported that ammonium sulfate-grown cells of *O. chalybea* exhibited DCMU-enhanced fluorescence in the presence of DCMU. They argue that, unlike higher plants, the site of the DCMU block shifts in nitrate-grown algae from the acceptor side to the donor side of Ps II. That nutrient

state can alter the sensitivity of fluorescence yield to DCMU adds one more consideration to the interpretation of fluorescence indices.

In conclusion, it appears that fluorescence indices provide a wealth of photosynthetic information, only some of which can now be applied clearly to field studies. The fact that F/chl a and F_{DCMU}/chl a vary widely under different conditions makes them poor indices for chl a or photosynthetic activity calculations. However, changes in these indices and their ratios, which are susceptible to environmental regulation, make them possibly good indices of physical/chemical gradient changes between different water masses or physiological state changes between different populations within the same water mass (Kiefer 1973a; Loftus and Seliger 1975; Heany 1978; Cullen and Renger 1979; Vincent 1980). But, before fluorescence indices of photosynthetic rate can be used reliably, it appears necessary to improve our present very limited understanding of in vivo fluorescence prperties, as well as to standardize the varied sampling and measuring techniques being used presently.

FLUORESCENCE INDUCTION CURVES

Fluorescence induction curves measure the time-varying fluorescence signal following the onset of constant illumination and provide information on the activity of Ps II and its interaction with Ps I (Fig. 33, 34). Letters (O, I, D, P, S, M, T) designate the main features of fluorescence kinetic changes described by the curves and often are used with the assumption that each phase corresponds to specific aspects of the basic photochemistry associated with Ps II (cf. Papageorgiou 1975; Lavorel and Etienne 1977).

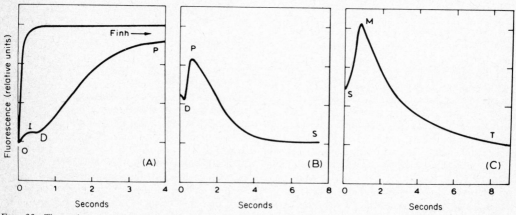

FIG. 33. The various stages of the fluorescence time course of chl a invivo: (A) fast rise in isolated broken (class II) spinach chloroplasts in the absence (lower curve) and presence (upper curve) of the electron transport inhibitor DCMU; (B) fast rise, and ensuing fast decay of chl a fluorescence in the red alga *Porphyridium cruentum* (redrawn from Mohanty et al. 1971b); (C) slow fluorescence change in the green alga *Chlorella pyrenoidosa*. (By permission, Papageorgiou 1975.)

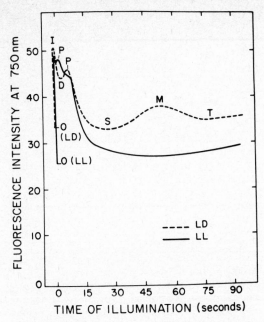

FIG. 34. Chl *a* fluorescence transients of *G. polyedra* cultured on a light–dark cycle (LD, broken line) and transferred to continuous dim illumination (LL, solid line); temperature, 22°C; dark adaptation, 10 min. (By permission, Govindjee et al. 1979.)

Usually, upon illumination with bright light (cf. Munday and Govindjee 1969; Mohanty and Govindjee 1974; Papageorgiou 1975; Lavorel and Etienne 1977), chl *a* fluorescence intensity (1) rises from an initial level labeled "O" (for origin) to an intermediary peak labeled "I" (due to the reduction of the primary electron acceptor of Ps II, Q, to Q⁻), (2) declines to a dip, "D" (due to interaction with Ps I which reoxidizes Q⁻ back to Q), (3) rises to the peak "P" (due to filling up of the plastoquinone pool, thus preventing the oxidation of Q⁻ to Q), (4) declines to a quasi steady state "S" (due to the conversion of Q⁻ to a quenching but non-active form of Q, labeled Q', and possibly changes in the thylakoid membrane following changes in pH and/or spillover of energy from the strongly fluorescent Ps II to the weakly fluorescent Ps I), and (5) the "SMT" transient, where M refers to a maximum and T to a terminal steady state (due to changes in the thylakoid membrane caused by changes in photophosphorylation, redox potential, etc.). The time courses for the fluorescence phases can vary considerably with algal species and preconditions (Fig. 33, 34), but have been described to fall in the following ranges: IDP ($\sim$ 1 s), PS (5–10 s), SM ($\sim$ 0.5 min), MT ($\sim$ 1.5 min) (Lavorel and Etienne 1977).

Following suitable dark adaptation, the time course of light-induced O_2 burst and evolution rates were found to be antiparallel to the IDP and PS

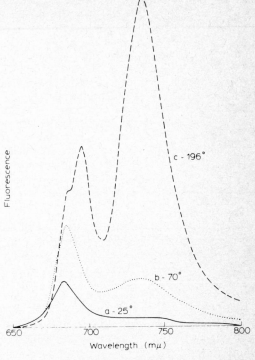

FIG. 35. Fluorescence emission spectra of spinach chloroplasts. Excitation light, 475 nm. (A) 25°C; (b) −70°C; (c) −196°C. Emission measured with a 5-nm half band width. (By permission, Murata et al. 1966b.)

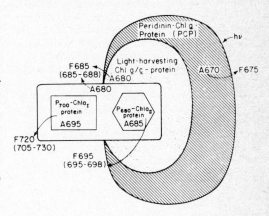

FIG. 36. A working model for the possible assignment of absorption (A) and emission (F) maxima, in nm, to the various chl *a* complexes in dinoflagellates. (By permission, Govindjee et al. 1979.)

phases of the fluorescence induction curve (the SMT stages run parallel), and argues strongly that the early stages of fluorescence induction accurately reflected the photochemical activity of Ps II (cf. Joliot 1981). It should be made clear that this observation (the

Kautsky effect) is distinct from the recent lab/field measurements of in vivo fluorescence intensity and its subsequent correlation to integrated steady-state photosynthetic rates determined by standard ^{14}C or O_2 procedures. Thus, the Kautsky effect may offer little insight into why supposedly similar fluorescence intensity measurements of phytoplankton are often completely out of phase with each other. For instance, instantaneous measurements by Kiefer (1973b) of diatom populations fluorescence ran antiparallel to photosynthesis, while 30-s and 2-min measurements of F in similar mixed diatom populations were parallel and antiparallel, respectively, to photosynthesis (Prézelin and Ley 1980). Lab studies on the dinoflagellate G. polyedra indicated all phases in the first 90 s of the fluorescence induction curve were parallel to integrated 15-min measurements of photosynthetic rates (Sweeney et al. 1979). It appears that before fluorescence induction data can be used reliably in the prediction of photosynthetic activity, it will be necessary to (1) characterize fluorescence induction characteristics and their variability in a wider range of phytoplankton species (to date, G. polyedra is the only major marine phytoplankton species to be partially characterized), and (2) to improve techniques to resolve and integrate fluorescence and photosynthesis changes over a short period of time (however, see Samuelsson et al. 1978).

The addition of DCMU abolishes the IDP phase of the fluorescence induction curve and often increases the overall F signal. Changes in the position and shape of this phase have been shown to depend on the relative Ps II/Ps I rates of excitation (Munday and Govindjee 1969) and on the presence of HCO_3^- in chloroplasts (Stemler and Govindjee 1974). For instance, cells of G. polyedra grown on a light–dark (LD) cycle had the same pigmentation but a distinct fluorescence induction curve from similar cells grown under continuous light (LL) (Fig. 36). Among the changes was a shorter time needed to reach "P" in LL cells (3 s compared with 10 s), which suggested a higher ratio of Ps II/Ps I activity than LD cells, due to either a more efficient use of absorbed quanta in the initial transformations of Ps II or to a slower interaction with Ps I (Govindjee et al. 1979).

The slow fluorescence phase "SMT" appears to be a "thermal" stage not linked directly to the photochemistry of photosynthesis. However, it is quite sensitive to conformational state changes of the thylakoid membrane and can provide some useful insights into photosynthetic regulation phenomena. For instance, cations like Mg^{2+} induce conformational changes in the membrane, which decrease the rate of excitation spillover from Ps II to Ps I, visualized in the fluorescence induction curve as an increase in the S level. Likewise, the S level increases with preillumination with Ps I light but decreases with Ps II light (Lavorel and Etienne 1977). Many similar kinds of fluorescence spectroscopy studies of fluorescence kinetics have been useful in examining how excitation energy distribution among the two photosystems are affected by changes in endogenous/ environmental variables.

FLUORESCENCE EMISSION/EXCITATION SPECTRA

Fluorescence emission and excitation spectra, respectively, provide information on the presence of different fluorescence species of chl–proteins and biliproteins (carotenoid fluorescence is not detectable in vivo or in vitro) and on the direction and efficiency of excitation energy transfer among these pigment–protein complexes (cf. Goedheer 1972; Govindjee et al. 1979). In fluorescence emission measurements, fluorescence intensity (F) is shown to vary as a function of excitation wavelength (λ_e). The resulting fluorescence emission maxima (λ_f) are characteristic of discrete fluorescing pigment complexes present in the sample (Fig. 35). By monitoring individual fluorescence emission maximum (λ_f) as a function of excitation wavelength (λ_e), spectral components can be identified that best transfer their absorbed light energy to the fluorescing pigment component. In this manner, the direction of excitation energy flow between various pigment components can be mapped. When the absorption intensities of the spectral components also are known, then transfer efficiencies also can be calculated. In this way, the uses of fluorescence excitation spectra are similar to those of oxygen action spectra, with the exception that fluorescence measurements can examine the activity of a single or a mix of pigment components while oxygen measurements are restricted to measuring the composite activity of all the components affecting Ps II. Finally, studying the same fluorescent system under different conditions can provide information on how changes in various stimuli alter the relative concentration, activity, and direction of energy transfer flow between different fluorescence species and supposedly influence associated photosynthetic activities.

In higher plants and green algae, the room-temperature emission spectrum is essentially a red-shifted chl a fluorescence spectrum where accessory pigments (chl b and carotenoids) contribute to chl a emission but their own fluorescence cannot be detected. The same appears to be true for the chl a– chl c–carotenoid system of brown algae, diatoms, and dinoflagellates (Goedheer 1972). However, the phycobilins present in red and blue-green algae fluoresce in vivo, even though their transfer efficiencies to chl a approached 100%. This difference can be used to detect even small amounts of phyco-bilin-containing organisms in field samples (i.e.

Prézelin and Ley 1980). The fluorescence intensities of emitting pigments are usually strongly increased as temperatures are lowered to liquid nitrogen temperatures (77 K), especially at the longer wavelengths associated with Ps I. The resultant band sharpening and band shifts of emission bands at low temperature make fluorescence excitation studies easier and are believed to result from reduced interactions between different excited states and/or altered rates of energy transfer between the various chl–protein complexes.

Three- or four-peaked low-temperature emission curves have been described for higher plants and red, green, and blue-green algae (cf. Papageorgiou 1975; Lavorel and Etienne 1977) and interpreted as follows (Fig. 35). Since chl a fluorescence at 685 and 695 nm in the emission curve is sensitized mainly by wavelengths absorbed by chl b in higher plants and phycobilins in red and blue-green algae (determined from excitation spectrum analysis), these fluorescence maxima are assigned to two different chl a–proteins closely associated with Ps II. Likewise, a broad emission band extending from 710 to 735 nm becomes highly fluorescent at low temperature with peak emissions centered around 730 nm (F730). It is more sensitized by chl a than by accessory pigments and, therefore, is assigned to a chl a–protein complex closely associated with Ps I. It also has been possible through fluorescence emission/excitation studies to document changes in the excitation energy distribution within the two photosystems induced by changes in external stimuli of light color, temperature, redox state, salinity, etc. (Papageorgiou 1975; Lavorel and Etienne 1977; Ley 1981).

The situation is not the same in the chl a–chl c–carotenoid system of diatoms, dinoflagellates, and brown algae (Goedheer 1972; Govindjee et al. 1979). Only two of the low temperature emission bands (F690-695 and F705-715) are evident in diatoms and browns (Goedheer 1972), while dinoflagellates exhibit only a single major emission peak at 685–688 nm with a secondary band at 670 nm (Govindjee et al. 1979). Additional analysis of derived difference and ratio fluorescence spectra at low temperature does suggest that long wavelength components of Ps I analogous to those of higher plants are present in dinoflagellates. However, they are not susceptible to low temperature uncoupling in the same manner as those of higher plants (Govindjee et al. 1979).

In spite of the simplicity of the emission spectra presented for *G. polyedra*, a careful examination of the absorption spectra, emission spectra, difference emission spectra, excitation spectra of chl a fluorescence, and difference and ratio excitation spectra together revealed that the dinoflagellate contained at least four chl a complexes (in addition to those in the two reaction centers which were so weakly fluorescent they could not be observed) (Govindjee

et al. 1979). This information was used to construct a working model for the possible assignment of absorption (A) and emission (F) maxima to various chl a–protein complexes known to be present in dinoflagellages (cf. Prézelin and Alberte 1978; Boczar et al. 1980; Prézelin and Boczar 1981) (Fig. 36). It is not known, but tempting to suggest, that a similar approach might be useful to interpret the organization and activity of photosynthetic pigment in most chl a–chl c–carotenoid containing plants. Based on approximate Stoke's shifts of 5–15 nm, with possible absorption peaks used as subscripts and their possible emission peakes as superscripts, the following chl a spectral forms must be present in *G. polyedra*: Chl a_{670}^{675} (antenna chl a in peridinin–chl a–protein complexes); Chl $a_{678-681}^{686-687}$ (antenna chl a, possibly in chl a–chl c protein complexes; chl c is nonfluorescent because it transfers energy with 100% efficiency to this chl a invivo); Chl $a_{\parallel 685}^{690-695}$ (associated with Chl a 685 close to reaction center II); and Chl $a_{690-705}^{705-720}$ (associated with chl a 695, close to reaction center I). Working with this model, it has been possible to follow a change in light energy distribution between the two photosystems when the light period is lengthened from 12 to 24 h (Govindjee et al. 1979) and to show little or no change in light energy distribution between the two photosystems over the day when cells were cultured on a 12:12 light–dark cycle of moderate light intensity (Sweeney et al. 1979).

Conclusion

Information on the molecular processes of photosynthesis and the architecture of the photosynthetic apparatus is accumulating at a rapid rate. The majority of research effort to date has been directed toward understanding green plant photosynthesis. Where major algal groups have been studies, the fundamental photosynthetic light-process appears the same, but with sufficient variation in details to prompt and encourage further detailed analyses of their photochemical and fluorescence characteristics. From this newer understanding of photosynthetic light processes have come suggestions for new probes of physiological state and/or photosynthetic rate (i.e. PSU number or fluorescence intensity indices) which have been applied with varying success to phytoplankton productivity studies. Future studies into the molecular basis of photosynthetic processes in phytoplankton promise new insights into how the photosynthetic apparatus is organized and functions, as well as perceives external stimuli, and then uses these cues to effect a change in photosynthesis and perhaps other cellular processes regulating growth phenomena at the whole plant level.

Acknowledgments

Dr R. Trench, Dr J. P. Thornber, and Dr B. M. Sweeney, as well as B. Boczar, are gratefully acknowledged for their editorial assistance in reviewing the manuscript content. Special appreciation is given to Deborah Rupp for her excellent secretarial assistance. Financial Support was provided by funds from USDA research grant PL95-224 (BBP) and NSF research grant OCE 78-13919 (BBP).

Abbreviations

APC	allophycocyanin
chl	chlorophyll
PC	phycocyanin
PCP	peridinin–chl a–protein
PE	phycoerythrin
P–I	photosynthesis–irradiance
PS	photosystem
PSU	photosynthetic unit
PQ	plastoquinone
LHC	light-harvesting component
α	light-limited slope
I =	$^1/_2$ P_{max} half-saturation constant for photosynthesis or the light level at which photosynthesis is half saturated
P_i	photosynthetic preformance or in situ rate of photosynthesis
F	fluorescence intensity
λ	wavelength

References

ALBERTE, R. S. 1981. Dynamics of the photosynthetic apparatus: prospects for genetic engineering and crop improvement. Can. J. Genet. Cytol. (In press)

ALBERTE, R. S., E. L. FISCUS, AND J. P. THORNBER. 1971. Water stress effects on the content and organization of chlorophyll in mesophyll and bundle sheath chloroplasts of maize. Plant Physiol. 59: 351–353.

ALBERTE, R. S., ET AL. 1974. Comparison and activity of the photosynthetic apparatus in temperature-sensitive mutants of higher plants. Proc. Natl. Acad. Sci. USA 71: 2414–2418.

ALBERTE, R. S., J. D. HESKETH, AND J. A. KIRBY. 1976a. Comparisons of photosynthetic activity and lamellar characteristics of virescent and normal grean peanut leaves. Z. Pflanzenphysiol. 77: 152–159.

ALBERTE, R. S., P. R. McLURE, AND J. P. THORNBER. 1976b. Photosynthesis in trees. Plant Physiol. 58: 341–344.

AMESZ, J., AND L.N.M. DUYSENS. 1977. Primary and Associated Reactions of System II, p. 149–186. In Scientific Publication J. Barber [ed.] Primary processes of photosynthesis. Elsevier Co., Amsterdam.

ANDERSON, J. M. 1975. The molecular organization of chloroplast thylakoids. Biochim. Biophys. Acta 416: 191–235.

——— 1980. Chlorophyll–protein complexes of higher plant thylakoids: distribution, stoichiometry and organization in the photosynthetic unit. FEBS Lett. 117: 327–331.

ANDERSON, J. M., AND J. BARRETT. 1979. Chlorophyll–protein complexes of brown algae: P700 reaction centre and light-harvesting complexes, p. 81–96. In Chlorophyll organization and energy transfer in photosynthesis. CIBA Found. Symp. 61, Excerpta Medica.

ANDERSON, J. M., J. C. WALDRON, AND S. W. THORNE. 1978. Chlorophyll–protein complexes of spinach and barley thylakoids. Spectral characteristics of six complexes resolved by an improved electrophoretic procedure. FEBS Lett. 92: 227–233.

ARMOND, P. A., AND H. A. MOONEY. 1977. Correlation of photosynthetic unit size and density with photosynthetic capacity. Carnegie Inst. Washington Yearb. 77: 234–237.

ARNTZEN, C. J., P. A. ARMOND, J. M. BRIANTAIS, J. J. BURKE, AND W. P. NOVITZKY. 1977. Dynamic interactions among structural components of the chloroplast membrane, p. 316–337. In Chlorophyll–proteins, reaction centers, and photosynthetic membranes. Brookhaven Natl. Symp. 28.

AVRON, M. 1975. The electron transport chain in chloroplasts, p. 374–388. In Govindjee [ed.] Bionergetics of photosynthesis. Academic Press, New York.

——— 1981. Proton movement and transmembrane electrochemical potential. 5th Int. Cong. Photosyn.

BADER, K. P., AND G.H. SCHMID. 1980. Dependence of fluorescence behavior and other photosystem II characterists on the nature of the nitrogen source for the filamentous cyanobacterium. Abst. 5th Int. Cong. Photosynthesis. Haliki, Greece. p. 33.

BARBER, J. 1979. Energy transfer and its dependence on membrane properties, p. 283–304. In Chlorophyll organization and energy transfer in photosynthesis. CIBA Found. Symp. 61, Excerpta Medica.

BARRETT, J., AND J. M. ANDERSON. 1977. Thylakoid membrane fragments with different chlorophyll a, chl c, and fucoxanthin compositions isolated from the brown seaweed, Ecklonia radiata. Plant Sci. Lett. 9: 275–283.

——— 1980. The P-700 chlorophyll a–protein complex and two major light-harvesting complexes of Acrocarpia paniculata and other brown seaweeds. Biochim. Biophys. Acta 49(3): 309–323.

BEARDEN, A. J., AND R. MALKIN. 1975. Primary photochemical reactions in chloroplast photosynthesis. Rev. Biophys. 7: 131–177.

BENNETT, A., AND H. W. SIEGELMAN. 1978. Bile pigments of plants. In D. Dolphin [ed.] The porphyrins. Academic Press, New York.

BERKALOFF, C., J. C. DUVAL, H. JUPIN, F. CHRISSOVERGIS, AND L. CARON. 1980. Spectroscopic studies of isolated pigment protein complexes of some brown algae thylakoids. Abst. 5th Int. Cong. Photosynthesis. Haliki, Greece. p. 60.

BISALPUTRA, T. 1974. Plastids, p. 124–160. In W. D. P. Stewart [ed.] Algal physiology and biochemistry. Univ. California Press, Los Angeles.

BJORKMAN, O. 1972. Photosynthetic adaptation to contrasting light climates. Carnegie Inst. Plant Biol. p. 82.
_____ 1974. Thermal stability of the photosynthetic apparatus in intact leaves. Carnegie Inst. Plant. Biol. p. 748–751.

BOARDMAN, N. K., J. M. ANDERSON, AND D. J. GOODCHILD. 1978. Chlorophyll-protein complexes and structure of nature and developing chloroplasts, p. 35–109. *In* D. Rao Sanadi and L. P. Vernon [ed.] Current topics in bioenergetics. Academic Press, New York, NY.

BOCZAR, B. B. PRÉZELIN, J. MARKWELL, AND J. P. THORNBER. 1979. Evidence for the isolation of a chlorophyll *a*–chlorophyll *c*–protein complex from a dinoflagellate. Abst. Photochem. Photobiol. Asilomar, CA. p. 80.
_____ 1980. A chlorophyll *c*-containing pigment-protein complex from the marine dinoflagellate, *Glenodinium* sp. FEBS Lett. 120: 243–247.

BOLTON, J. R. 1977. Photosystem I photoreactions, p. 187–202. *In* J. Barber [ed.] Primary processes of photosynthesis. Elsevier Scientific Publications Co., Amsterdam.

BOURDU, R., AND J. L. PRIOUL. 1974. Réponses photosynthétiques de type adaptatif aux climats lumineux de croissance: étude théorétique, applications et diagnostic précoce. Physiol. Veg. 12: 35–51.

BROOKS, J. E. 1964. Acclimation to light intensity in two species of marine phytoplankton, *Dunaliella tertiolecta* Butcher and *Skeletonema* (Greve) Cleve. M.S. Thesis. Univ. Southern California. 30 p.

BROOKS, C., AND E. GANTT. 1973. Comparison of phycoerythrins (542, 566 nm) from cryptophycean algae. Arch. Mikrobiol. 88: 193–204.

BROWN, J. S., R. S. ALBERTE, AND J.P. THORNBER. 1974. Comparative studies on the occurrence and spectral composition of chlorophyll–protein complexes in a wide variety of plant material, p. 1951–1962. *In* 3rd Int. Congr. Photosyn. Res.

BROWN, J.S., R. A. GASANOV, AND C. S. FRENCH. 1972. A comparative study of the forms of chlorophyll and photochemical activity of system 1 and system 2 fractions form spinach and *Dunaliela*. Carnegie Inst. Yearb. 72: 351–359.

BUTLER, W. L. 1977. Chlorophyll fluorescence: a probe for electron transfer and energy transfer, p. 149–167. *In* A. Trebst and M. Avron [ed.] Photosynthetic electron transport and photophosphorylation. Springer-Verlag, Berlin.

CHANG, S., AND R. TRENCH. 1981. Variation of *Symbiodinium* (= *Gymnodinium*) *microadriaticum* (Freudenthal): analysis of peridinin–chlorophyll *a*–protein complexes. Proc. R. Soc. London (Submitted)

CHAPMAN, D. J. 1973. Biliproteins and bile pigments, p. 162–185. *In* N. G. Carr and B. A. Whitton [ed.] The biology of blue-green algae. Univ. California Press, Berkeley.

CIBA Foundation Symposium 61. 1979. Chlorophyll organization and energy transfer in photosynthesis. Excerpta Medica: 374 p.

CLAYTON, R. K. 1970. Light and living matter, Vol. 1. The physical part. McGraw-Hill, New York, 148 p.

CROFTS, A. R., AND P. M. WOOD. 1978. Photosynthetic electron-transport chains of plants and bacteria and their role as proton pumps, p. 175–245. *In* D. P. Sanadi and L. P. Vernon [ed.] Current topics in bioenergetics, Vol. 7. Photosynthesis: Part A. Academic Press, New York.

CULLEN, J. J., AND E. H. RENGER. 1979. Continuous measurement of the physiological state of natural phytoplankton populations as inferred from in vivo fluorescence response. Mar. Biol. 53: 13–20.

DOUGHERTY, R. C., H. H. STRAIN, W. A. SVEC, R. A. UPHAUS, AND J. J. KATZ. 1966. Structure of chlorophyll *c*. J. Am. Chem. Soc. 88: 5037–5038.

EMERSON, R., AND W. ARNOLD. 1932. The photochemical reaction in photosynthesis. J. Gen. Physiol. 16: 191–205.

FAJER, J., C. K. CHANG, M. S. DAVIS, I. FUJITA , AND T. L. NETZEL. 1979. Primary donors and acceptors of plant photosynthesis: in vitro studies. Abst. 7th Annu. Meet. Am. Soc. Photobiol. p. 83.

FORK, D.C. 1977. Photosynthesis, p. 329–370. *In* K. C. Smith [ed.] The science of photobiology. Plenum/Rosette, New York, NY.

GANTT, E. 1980. Structure and function of phycolilisomes: light harvesting pigment complexes in red and blue-green algae. Int. Rev. Cytol. 66: 45–80.

GANTT, E., AND S. F. CONTI. 1966. Phycobiliprotein location in algae. J. Cell Biol. 29: 423–434.

GANTT, E., C. A. LIPSCHULTZ, AND B. A. ZILINSKAS. 1976. Further evidence for a phycobilisome model from selective dissociation, fluorescence emission, immunoprecipitation and electron microscopy. Biochim. Biophys. Acta 430: 375–381.
_____ 1977. Phycobilisomes in relation to the thylakoid membranes, p. 347–357. *In* Chlorophyll–proteins, reaction centers, and photosynthetic membranes. Brookhaven Symp. 28.

GIMMLER, H. 1977. Photophosphorylation in vivo, p. 448–472. *In* A. Trebst and M. Avron [ed.] Photosynthesis I: photosynthetic electron transport and photophosphorylation. Springer-Verlag, Berlin.

GLAZER, A. N. 1977. Structure and molecular organization of the photosynthetic accessory pigments of cyanobacteria and red algae. Mol. Cell. Biochem. 18: 125–140.

GLAZER, A. N., AND D. A. BRYANT. 1975. Allophycocyanin B (λ_{max}) 671, 618 nm, a new cyanobacterial phycobiliprotein. Arch. Microbiol. 104: 15–22.

GOEDHEER, J. C. 1972. Fluorescence in relation to photosynthesis. Annu. Rev. Plant Physiol. 23: 87–112.

GOLDBECK, J. H., S. LIEN, AND A. SAN PIETRO. 1977. Electron transport in chloroplasts, p. 94–116. *In* A. Trebst and M. Avron [ed.] Photosynthetic electron transport and photophosphorylation. Springer-Verlag, Berlin.

GOODWIN, T. W. [ed.] 1976. Distribution of carotenoids, p. 225–262. *In* Chemistry and biochemistry of plant pigments. Academic Press, London.

GOVINDJEE, D. WONG, B. B. PRÉZELIN, AND B. M. SWEENEY. 1979. Chlorophyll *a* fluorescence of *Gonyaulax polyedra* grown on a light–dark cycle after transfer to constant light. Photochem. Photobiol. 30: 405–411.

GOVINDJEE, AND L. YANG. 1966. Structure of the red fluorescence band in chloroplasts. J. Gen. Physiol. 49: 763–780.

HAEHNEL, W. 1976. The ratio of the two light reactions and their coupling in chloroplasts. Biochim. Biophys. Acta 423: 499–509.

HAIDAK, D., C. MATTHEWS, AND B. M. SWEENEY. 1966. Pigment protein complex from *Gonyaulax*. Science (Washington, D.C.) 152: 212–213.

HALL, D. O., AND K. K. RAO. 1977. Photosynthesis. Edward Arnold Publications, London. 71 p.

HARDING, L. W., B. W. MEESON, B. B. PRÉZELIN, AND B. M. SWEENEY. 1981. Diel periodicity of photosynthesis in marine phytoplankton. Mar. Biol. 61: 95–105.

HARRIMAN, A., AND J. BARBER. 1979. Photosynthetic water-spilling process and artificial chemical systems, p. 243–280. *In* J. Barber [ed.] Photosynthesis in regulation to model systems. Elsevier Scientific Publications Co., Amsterdam.

HAXO, F. T. 1960. The wavelength dependence of photo synthesis and the role of accessory pigments, p. 339–360. *In* M. B. Allen [ed.] Comparative biochemistry of photoreactive systems. Academic Press, New York.

HAXO, F. T., J. H. KYCIA, G. F. SOMERS, A. BENNETT, AND H. W. SIEGELMAN. 1976. Peridinin-chlorophyll *a* proteins of the dinoflagellate *Amphidinium carterae* (Plymouth 450). Plant Physiol. 57: 297–303.

HAYDEN, D. B., AND W. G. HOPKINS. 1977. A second distinct chlorophyll *a*–protein complex in maize mesophyll chloroplasts. Can. J. Bot. 55: 2525–2539.

HEANY, S. I. 1978. Some observations on the use of the in vivo fluorescence technique to determine chlorophyll *a* in natural populations and cultures of freshwater phytoplankton. Freshwater Biol. 8: 115–126.

HERMAN, E. M., AND B. M. SWEENEY. 1975. Circadian rhythm of chloroplast ultrastructure in *Gonyaulax polyedra*, concentric organization around a central cluster of ribosomes. J. Ultrastruc. Res. 50: 347–354.

HIYAMA, T., AND B. KE. 1972. Difference spectra and extinction coefficients of P700. Biochim. Biophys. Acta 267: 160–171.

HOMANN, P. H. 1979. The light dependence quenching of chloroplast fluorescence by cofactors of cyclic electron flow in photosystem I. Photochem. Photobiol. 29: 815–822.

ISLER, O. [ed.] 1971. Carotenoids. Halsted Press, New York. 932 p.

JAGENDORF, A. T. 1977. Photophosphorylation, p. 307–337. *In* A. Trebst and M. Avron [ed.] Photosynthesis I: Photosynthetic electron transport and photophosphorylation. Springer-Verlag, Berlin.

JEFFREY, S. W. 1969. Properties of two spectrally different components in chlorophyll *c* preparations. Biochem. Biophys. Acta 177: 456–467.

JOLIOT, P. 1981. Photosystem II and oxygen evolution. 5th Int. Cong. Photosyn. Halikidi, Greece. (In press)

JORGENSEN, E. G. 1969. The adaptation of plankton algae. IV. Light adaptation in different algal species. Physiol. Plant. 22: 1307–1315.

1970. The adaptation of plankton algae. V. Variation in the photosynthetic characteristics of *Skeletonema costatum* cells grown at low light intensity. Physiol. Plant. 23: 11–17.

JUNGE, W. 1977. Physical aspects of light harvesting, electron transport and electrochemical potential generation in photosynthesis of green plants, p. 59–93. *In* A. Trebst and M. Avron [ed.] Photosynthesis I. Photosynthetic electron transport and photophosphorylation. Springer-Verlag, Berlin.

KATZ, J. J., L. L. SHIPMAN, AND J. R. NORRIS. 1979. Structure and function in photoreaction-centre chlorophyll I, p. 1–40. *In* Chlorophyll organization and energy transfer in photosynthesis. CIBA Found. Symp. 61. Excerpta Medica.

KAWAMURA, M., M. MIMURO, AND Y. FUJITA. 1979. Quantitative relationship between two reaction centers in the photosynthetic system of blue-green algae. Plant Cell Physiol. 20: 697–705.

KE, B. 1978. The primary electron acceptors in green plant photosystem I and photosynthetic bacteria, p. 75–138. *In* D. R. Sanadi and L. P. Vernon [ed.] Current topics in bioenergetics, Vol. 7. Photosynthesis: Part A. Academic Press, New York.

KELLEY, G. J., E. LATZKO, AND M. GIBBS. 1976. Regulatory aspects of photosynthetic carbon metabolism. Annu. Rev. Plant Physiol. 27: 181–205.

KIEFER, D. A. 1973a. Chlorophyll *a* fluorescence in marine centric diatoms: responses of chloroplasts to light and nutrient stress. Mar. Biol. 23: 39–46.

1973b. Fluorescence properties of natural phytoplankton populations. Mar. Biol. 22: 263–269.

KIRK, J. T. O., AND R. A. E. TILNEY-BASSETT. 1978. The plastids. Elsevier N. Holland, Amsterdam. 960 p.

KNAFF, D. B., AND R. MALKIN. 1978. The primary reaction of chloroplast photosystem II, p. 139–174. *In* D. R. Sanadi and L. P. Vernon [ed.] Current topics in bioenergetics, Vol. 7. Photosynthesis: Part A. Academic Press, New York.

KNOX, R. S. 1977. Photosynthetic efficiency and excitation transfer and trapping, p. 55–98. *In* J. Barber [ed.] Primary processes of photosynthesis. Elsevier Scientific Publications Co., Amsterdam.

KOB, B., B. FORBUSH, AND M. MCGLOIN. 1970. Cooperation of charges in photosynthetic O_2 evolution. I. A linear four step mechanism. Photochem. Photobiol. 11: 457–475.

KREY, A., AND GOVINDJEE. 1966. Fluorescence studies on a red alga, *Porphyridium cruentum*. Biochim. Biophys. Acta 120: 1–18.

KRINSKY, N. I. 1979. Carotenoid pigments: multiple mechanisms for coping with the stress of photosensitized oxidations, p. 163–187. *In* M. Shilo [ed.] Strategies of microbial life in extreme environment, Vol. 13. Gustav Fisher Inc. New York.

KULANDAIVELU, G., AND H. DANIELL. 1980. Dichlorophenyl dimethylurea (DCMU) induced increase in chlorophyll *a* fluorescence intensity. An index of photosynthetic oxygen evolution in leaves, chloroplasts, and algae. Physiol. Plant. Pathol. 48: 385–388.

LAVOREL, J. 1975. Luminescence, p. 223–317. *In* Govindjee [ed.] Bionergetics of photosynthesis. Academic Press, New York.

LAVOREL, J., AND A.-L. ETIENNE. 1977. In vivo chlorophyll fluorescence, p. 203–268. *In* J. Barber [ed.] Primary processes of photosynthesis. Elsevier Scientific Publications Co., Amsterdam.

LEFORT-TRAN, M., G. COHEN-BAZIRE, AND M. POUPHILE. 1973. Les membranes photosynthétiques des algues à biliprotéines observées après cryodécapage. J. Ultrastruct. Res. 44: 199–209.

LEY, A. C. 1980. The distribution of absolved light energy for algal photosynthesis, p. 59–82. In P. G. Falkowski [ed.] Primary productivity in the sea. Plenum Press, New York, NY.

LEY, A. C., W. L. BUTLER, D. A. BRYANT, AND A. N. GLAZER. 1977. Isolation and function of allophycocyanin B of Porphyridium cruentum. Plant Physiol. 59: 974–980.

LOFTUS, M. E., AND H. H. SELIGER. 1975. Some limitations of the in vivo fluorescence technique. Chesapeake Sci. 16: 79–92.

LONEGRAN, T. A., AND M. L. SARGENT. 1978. Regulation of the photosynthesis rhythm in Euglena gracilis. Plant Physiol. 61: 150–153.

MACOLL, R., AND D. S. BERNS. 1978. Energy transfer studies on Cryptomonad biliproteins. Photochem. Photobiol. 27: 343–350.

MALKIN, S. 1977. Delayed luminescence, p. 349–432. In J. Barber [ed.] Primary processes of photosynthesis, Vol. 2. Elsevier Scientific Publications Co., Amsterdam.

MALKIN, S., D. C. FORK, AND P. A. ARMOND. 1977. Probing photosynthetic unit sizes of leaves by fluorescence-induction measurements. Carnegie Inst. Washington Yearb. 77: 237–247.

MANN, J. E., AND J. MYERS. 1968. On pigments, growth, and photosynthesis of Phaeodactylum tricornutum. J. Phycol. 4: 349–355.

MARGULIES, M. M. 1970. Changes in absorbance spectrum of the diatom Phaeodactylum tricornutum upon modification of protein structure. J. Phycol. 6: 160–164.

MARKWELL, J. P., C. C. MILES, R. T. BOGGS, AND J. P. THORNBER. 1979. Solubilization of chloroplast membranes by zwitterionic detergents. FEBS Lett. 99: 11–14.

MARKWELL, J.P., J. P. THORNBER, AND R. T. BOGGS. 1979. Evidence that in higher plant chloroplasts all the chlorophyll exists as chlorophyll–protein complexes. Proc. Natl. Acad. Sci. USA 76: 1233–1235.

MARKWELL, J. P., J. P. THORNBER, AND M. P. SKRDLA. 1980. Effect of detergents on the reliability of a chemical assay for P700. Biochim. Biophys. Acta 591: 391–399.

MARSHO, T. V., AND B. KOB. 1971. Detection and isolation of P700, p. 515–522. In A. San Peitro [ed.] Methods in enzymology, Vol. XXIII, Photosynthesis: Part A. Academic Press, New York.

MEESON, B., S. CHANG, AND B. M. SWEENEY. 1981. Characterization of the peridinin–chlorophyll a–protein (PCP) in the marine dinoflagellate Ceratium furca. (In prep.)

MEESON, B. W., AND B. M. SWEENEY. 1981. Adaptation to irradiance: photoadaptive mechanisms and growth rates for Ceratium furca and Gonyaulax polyedra at two growth temperatures. (In prep.)

MILES, C. D., J. P. MARKWELL, AND J. P. THORNBER. 1979. Effect of nuclear mutation in maize on photosynthetic activity and content of chlorophyll–protein complexes. Plant Physiol. 64: 690–694.

MILLS, J. D., A. TELFER, AND J. BARBER. 1976. Cation control of chlorophyll a fluorescence yield in chloroplasts. Location of cation sensitive sites. Biochim. Biophys. Acta 440: 495–505.

MITCHELL, P. 1974. A chemiosmotic molecular mechanism for protontranslocating adenosine triphosphatases. FEBS Lett. 43: 189–194.

MOHANTY, P., AND GOVINDJEE. 1974. The slow decline and the subsequent rise of chlorophyll fluorescence transients in intact algal cells. Plant Biochem. J. 2: 78–106.

MOSS, G. P., AND B. C. L. WEEDON. 1976. Chemistry of the Carotenoids, p. 149–224. In T. W. Goodwin [ed.] Chemistry and biochemistry of plant pigments. Academic Press, London.

MUHLETHALER, K. 1980. Introduction to structure and function of the photosynthesis apparatus, p. 503–520. In A. Trebst and M. Avron [ed.] Photosynthetic electron transport and photophosphorylation. Springer-Verlag, Berlin.

MUNDAY, J. C. JR., AND GOVINDJEE. 1969. Light-induced changes in the fluorescence yield of chlorophyll a in vivo. III. The dip and the peak in the fluorescence. Biophys. J. 9: 1–21.

MURATA, N. 1969. Control of excitation transfer in photosynthesis. II. Magnesium ion-dependent distribution of excitation energy between two pigment systems in spinach chloroplasts. Biochim. Biophys. Acta 189: 171–181.

MURATA, N., M. NISHIMURA, AND A. TAKAMIYA. 1966. Fluorescence of chlorophyll in photosynthetic systems. II. Induction of fluorescence in isolated spinach chloroplasts. Biochim. Biophys. Acta 126: 234–243.

MYERS, J., AND J. GRAHAM. 1971. The photosynthetic unit in Chlorella measured by repetitive short flashes. Plant Physiol. 48: 282–286.

O'CARRA, P., AND C. O'HEOCHA. 1976. Algal biliproteins and phycobilins, p. 328–376. In T. W. Goodwin [ed.] Chemistry and biochemistry of plant pigments. Academic Press, London.

OQUIST, G. 1974. Light-induced changes in pigment composition of photosynthetic lamellae and cell-free extracts obtained from the blue-green alga Anacystis nidulans. Physiol. Plant. 30: 38–44.

PAPAGEORGIOU, G. 1975. Chlorophyll fluorescence: an intrinsic probe of photosynthesis, p. 319–371. In Govindjee [ed.] Bioenergetics of photosynthesis. Academic Press, New York.

PATTERSON, D. T., J. A. BUNCE, R. S. ALBERTE, AND E. VAN VOLKENBURGH. 1977. Photosynthesis in relation to leaf characteristics of cotton from controlled and field environment. Plant Physiol. 59: 384–387.

PERRY, M. J., M. C. LARSEN, AND R. S. ALBERTE. 1981. Photoadaptation in marine phytoplankton: Response of the photosynthetic unit. Mar. Biol. 62: 91–101.

PRÉZELIN, B. B. 1976. The role of peridinin–chlorophyll a–proteins in the photosynthetic light adaptation of the marine dinoflagellate, Glenodinium sp. Planta 130: 225–233.

1982. Growth dynamics in Gonyaulax polyedra. I. Light dependent patterns of aging in photosynthesis and cell metabolism. Mar. Biol. (Submitted)

PRÉZELIN, B. B., AND R. S. ALBERTE. 1978. Photosynthetic characteristics and organization of chlorophyll in marine dinoflagellates. Proc. Natl. Acad. Sci. USA 75: 1801–1804.

PRÉZELIN, B. B., AND B. BOCZAR. 1982. Light-harvesting chlorophyll–protein complexes of dinoflagellates. Symposium on pigment–protein complexes in photosynthesis. Abst. Photochem. Photobiol. Colorado Springs, Col. p. 96–97.

———— 1981. Chlorophyll–protein complexes from the photosynthetic apparatus of dinoflagellates. 5th Int. Cong. Photosyn. Halikidi, Greece. (In press)

PRÉZELIN, B. B., AND F. T. HAXO. 1976. Purification and characterization of peridinin–chlorophyll a–proteins from the marine dinoflagellates Glenodinium sp. and Gonyaulax polyedra. Planta 128: 133–141.

PRÉZELIN, B. B., AND A. C. LEY. 1980. Photosynthesis and chlorophyll a fluorescence rhythms of marine phytoplankton. Mar. Biol. 55: 295–307.

PRÉZELIN, B. B., A. C. LEY, AND F. T. HAXO. 1976. Effects of growth irradiance on the photosynthetic action spectra of the marine dinoflagellate, Glenodinium sp. Planta 130: 251–256.

PRÉZELIN, B. B., AND H. A. MATLICK. 1980. Timecourse of photoadaptation in the photosyntheses-irradiance relationship of a dinoflagellate exhibiting photosynthetic periodicity. Mar. Biol. 58: 85–96.

PRÉZELIN, B. B., B. W. MEESON, AND B. M. SWEENEY. 1977. Characterization of photosynthetic rhythms in marine dinoflagellates. I. Pigmentation, photosynthetic capacity and respiration. Plant Physiol. 60: 384–387.

PRÉZELIN, B. B., AND B. M. SWEENEY. 1977. Characterization of photosynthetic rhythms in marine dinoflagellates. II. Photosynthesis-irradiance curves and in vivo chlorophyll a fluorescence. Plant Physiol. 60: 388–392.

———— 1978. Photoadaptation of photosynthesis in Gonyaulax polyedra. Mar. Biol. 48: 27–35.

———— 1979. Photoadaptation of photosynthesis in two bloom-forming dinoflagellates, p. 101–106. In C. Ventsch [ed.] Proc. 2nd Int. Conf. Toxic Dinoflagellate Blooms.

RAMUS, J., S. I. BEALE, D. MAUZERALL, AND L. HOWARD. 1976a. Changes in photosynthetic pigment concentration in seaweeds as a function of water depth. Mar. Biol. 37: 223–230.

———— 1976b. Correlation of changes in pigment content with photosynthetic capacity of seaweeds as a function of water depth. Mar. Biol. 37: 231–238.

RAVEN, J. A., AND J. BEARDALL. 1981. Respiration and photorespiration. Can. Bull. Fish. Aquat. Sci. 210: 55–82.

REGER, B. J., AND R. W. KRAUSS. 1970. The photosynthetic response to a shift in the chlorophyll a to chlorophyll b ratio of Chlorella. Plant Physiol. 46: 568–575.

REY, F. 1978. Some results on the application of the in vivo chlorophyll fluorescence method to marine primary productivity studies, p. 36–47. In Symposium on fluorescence and luminescence. Dep. Plant Physiol., Univ. Umea, Sweden.

SAMUELSSON, G., AND G. OQUIST. 1977. A method for studying photosynthetic capacities of unicellular algae based on in vivo chlorophyll fluorescence. Physiol. Plant. 40: 315–319.

SAMUELSSON, G., G. OQUIST, AND P. HALLDAL. 1978. The variable chlorophyll a fluorescence as a measure of photosynthetic capacity in algae. Mitt. Int. Ver. Theor. Angew. Limnol. 21: 207–215.

SANE, P. V., D. J. GOODCHILD, AND R. B. PARK. 1970. Characterization of chloroplast photosystem 1 and 2 separated by a non-detergent method. Biochim. Biophys. Acta 216: 162–178.

SATOH, K. 1980. F-695 emission from the purified photosystem II chlorophyll a–protein complex. FEBS Lett. 110: 53–56.

SATOH, K., AND W. L. BUTLER. 1978. Low temperature spectral properties of subchloroplast fractions purified from spinach. Plant Physiol. 61: 373–379.

SAUER, K. 1975. Primary events and the trappings of energy, p. 115–181. In Govindjee [ed.] Bioenergetics of photosynthesis. Academic Press, New York.

———— 1981. Charge separation in the light reactions of photosynthesis 5th Int. Cong. Photosyn. Halikidi, Greece. (In press)

SEELEY, G. R. 1966. The structure and chemistry of functional groups, p. 67–110. In L. P. Vernon and G. R. Seeley [ed.] The chlorophylls, physical, chemical and biological properties. Academic Press, New York.

SENGER, H. 1970a. Characterization of a synchronous culture of Scenedesmus obliques: its potential photosynthetic capacity and its photosynthetic quotient during the life cycle. Planta 92: 243–266.

———— 1970b. Quantum yield and variable behavior of the two photosystems of the photosynthetic apparatus during the life cycle of Scenedesmus obliques in synchronous culture. Planta 92: 327–346.

SHIOZAWA, J. A., R. S. ALBERTE, AND J. P. THORNBER. 1974. The P700 chlorophyll a–protein. Isolation and some characteristics of the complex in higher plants. Arch. Biochem. Biophys. 165: 388–397.

SIEGELMAN, H. W., J. H. KYCIA, AND F. T. HAXO. 1977. Peridinin–chlorophyll a–proteins of dinoflagellate algae. Brookhaven Natl. Symp. 28: 162–169.

SLOVACECK, R. E., AND P. J. HANNAN. 1977. In vivo fluorescence determinations of 197 phytoplankton chlorophyll a. Limnol. Oceanogr. 22: 919–925.

SONG, P.-S., P. KOKA, B. B. PRÉZELIN, AND F. T. HAXO. 1976. Molecular topology of the photosynthetic light-harvesting pigment complex, peridinin–chlorophyll a–protein, from marine dinoflagellates. Biochemistry 15: 4422–4427.

SONG, P. S., E. B. WALKER, J. JUNG, R. A. AUERBACH. G. W. ROBINSON, AND B. B. PRÉZELIN. 1980. Primary processes of phytobiological receptors. In New horizons in biological chemistry. Acad. Publ. Cent. Tokyo, Japan.

SONNEVELD, A., H. RADEMAKER, AND L. N. M. DUYSENS. 1979. Chlorophyll a fluorescence as a monitor of nanosecond reduction of the photooxidized primary donor P-680+ of photosystem II. Biochim. Biophys. Acta 548: 536–551.

SPECTOR, M., AND G. D. WINGET. 1980. Purification of a manganese-containing protein involved in photosynthetic oxygen evolution and its use in reconstituting an active membrane. Proc. Natl. Acad. Sci. USA 77: 957–959.

STAEHELIN, L. A. 1976. Reversible particle movements associated with unstacking and restacking of chloroplast membranes in vitro. J. Cell Biol. 71: 136–158.

STAEHELIN, L. A., P. A. ARMOND, AND K. R. MILLER. 1977. Chloroplast membrane organization at the supramolecular level and its functional implications, p. 278–315. In Chlorophyll–proteins, reaction centers, and photosynthetic membranes. Brookhaven Symp. Biol. 28.

STAEHELIN, L. A., AND C. J. ARNTZEN. 1979. Effects of ions and gravity forces on the supramolecular organization and excitation energy distribution in chloroplast membranes, p. 147–175. In Chlorophyll organization and energy transfer in photosynthesis. CIBA Found. Symp. 61, Excerpta Medica.

STAEHELIN, L. A., D. P. CARTER, AND A. McDONNEL. 1980. Adhesion between chloroplast membranes: experimental manipulation and incorporation of the adhesion factor into artificial membranes, p. 1–179. In B. Gilula [ed.] Membrane–membrane interactions. Raven Press, New York.

SWEENEY, B. M. 1981. Chloroplast membranes of Gaunyaulax polyedra (Pyrrophyta), a photosynthetic dinoflagellate with peridinin–chlorophyll–protein, studied by the freeze–fracture technique. J. Phycol. (In press)

SWEENEY, B. M., B. B. PRÉZELIN, D. WONG, AND GOVINDJEE. 1979. Chlorophyll a fluorescence of Gonyaulax polyedra grown on a light–dark cycle and after transfer to constant light. Photochem. Photobiol. 30: 405–411.

TANADA, T. 1951. The photosynthetic efficiency of carotenoid pigments in Navicula minima. Am. J. Bot. 38: 276–290.

TELFER, A., J. NICHOLSON, AND J. Barber. 1976. Cation control of chloroplast structure and chlorophyll a fluorescence yield and its relevance to the intact chloroplast. FEBS Lett. 65: 77–83.

TERBORGH, J., AND G. C. McLEOD. 1967. The photosynthetic rhythm of Acetabulana crenulata. I. Continuous measurements of oxygen exchange in alternating light-dark regimes and in constant light at different intensities. Biol. Bull. 133: 659–669.

TERRI, J. A., D. T. PATTERSON, R. S. ALBERTE, AND R. M. CASTELBERRY. 1977. Changes in the photosynthetic apparatus of maize in response to simulated natural temperature fluctuations. Plant Physiol. 60: 370–373.

THIMANN, K. V. [ed.] 1980. Senescence in plants. CRC Press, Boca Raton, FL. 238 p.

THORNBER, J. P., AND R. S. ALBERTE. 1977. The organization of chlorophyll in vivo, p. 574–582. In A. Trebst and M. Avron [ed.] Photosynthesis I: photosynthetic electron transport and photophosphorylation. Springer-Verlag, Berlin.

THORNBER, J. P., R. S. ALBERTE, F. A. HUNTER, J. A. SHIOZAWA, AND K. S. KAN. 1977. The organization of chlorophyll in the plant photosynthetic unit, p. 132–148. J. M. Olson and G. Hind [ed.] Chlorophyll–proteins, reaction centers, and photosynthetic membranes. Brookhaven Symp. Biol. 28.

THORNBER, J. P., AND J. BARBER. 1979. Photosynthetic pigments and models for their organization in vivo, p. 27–70. In J. Barber [ed.] Photosynthesis in relation to model systems. Topics in photosynthesis. Vol. 3. Elsevier Scientific Publications Co.

THORNBER, J. P., J. P. MARKWELL, AND S. REINMAN. 1979. Plant chlorophyll–protein complexes: recent advances. Photochem. Photobiol. Yrly. Rev. 29: 1205–1216.

TREBST, A. 1974. Energy conservation in photosynthetic electron transport of chloroplasts. Annu. Rev. Plant Physiol. 25: 423–458.

TRENCH, R. K., AND G. S. RONZIO. 1978. Aspects of the relation between Cyanophora paradoxa (Korschikoff) and its endosymbiotic cyanelles Cyanocyta korschikoffiana (Hall & Claus). II. The photosynthetic pigments. Proc. R. Soc. London Ser. B 202: 445–462.

VELTHUYS, B. R. 1980. Mechanisms of energy frow in photosystem II and toward photosystem I. Annu. Rev. Plant Physiol. 31: 545–567.

VIERLING, E., AND R. S. ALBERTE. 1980. Functional organization and plasticity of the photosynthetic unit of the cyanobacterium Anacystis nidulans. Physiol. Plant. 50: 93–98.

VINCENT, W. F. 1980. Mechanisms of rapid photosynthetic adaptation in natural phytoplankton communities. II. Capacity for non-cyclic electron transport. J. Phycol. 16: 368–577.

WILLIAMS, W. P. 1977. The two photosystems and their interactions, p. 99–145. In J. Barber [ed.] Primary processes of photosynthesis. Vol. 2. Elsevier Scientific Publications, Amsterdam, Holland.

WITT, H. T. 1979. Energy conversion in the functional membrane of photosynthesis. Analysis by light pulse and electric pulse methods. The central role of the electric field. Biochim. Biophys. Acta 505: 355–427.

———— 1979. Charge separation in photosynthesis, p. 303–330. In H. Gerischer and J. J. Katz [ed.] Light-induced charge separation in biology and chemistry. H. Gerischer and Dahlem Konferenzen, Berlin.

WOOD, P. M. 1977. The roles of c-type cytochromes in algal photosynthesis. Extraction from algae of a cytochrome similar to higher plant cytochrome f. Eur. J. Biochem. 72: 605–612.

WRAIGHT, C. A., AND A. R. CROFTS. 1970. Energy dependent quenching of chlorophyll a fluorescence in isolated chloroplasts. Eur. J. Biochem. 17: 319–327.

ZILINSKAS, B. A., B. K. ZIMMERMAN, AND E. GANTT. 1978. Allophycocyanin forms isolated from Nostoc sp. phycobilisomes. Photochem. Photobiol. 27: 587–595.

Dark Reactions of Photosynthesis

BRUNO P. KREMER[1]

Universität zu Köln,
Seminar für Didaktik der Biologie
D-5000 Köln 41, West Germany

Introduction

All life on earth ultimately depends on assimilation of carbon dioxide as the main carbon source for production of organic material; the energy for this endergonic process is provided by light originating from nuclear fusions in the sun. Collectively, the reactions for this conversion of absorbed photons into stable chemical energy are termed photosynthesis. Usually, it is approached as a three-phase process comprising (i) the absorption of light quanta and retention of light energy, (ii) the conversion of light energy into chemical potential, and (iii) the interconversion, stabilization, and storage of the chemical potential. While the complex of light absorption, energy transduction, photochemical events, and finally the concomitant formation of products such as reducing (NADPH) and energy equivalents (ATP) represent the light reactions of photosynthesis (see Prézelin 1981), further steps involving the fixation and reduction of inorganic carbon at the expense of NADPH and ATP are the so-called dark reactions of photosynthesis.

Light is not directly required for the fixation and reduction of CO_2. During light–dark transients, however, the biochemical conversion steps involved rapidly decline due to steady exhaustion of the assimilatory power provided by the light reactions. On the other hand, the individual conversions can be studied in vitro with isolated systems, when NADPH and ATP are added to the test system instead of being derived directly from irradiated thylakoids. In addition, there are some further, presumably regulatory, effects of the light reactions on individual reaction steps in the biochemical reactions of photosynthesis other than those requiring ATP and NADPH. They will not be considered further in this context.

Photosynthesis is the basic process that provides living organisms with the organic material needed for growth and maintenance, but, in turn, plant cells or their products also yield the foodstuff for all other components of the biosphere. All organisms have to consume energy by means of degradation

[1] Correspondence to: Dr B. P. Kremer, Andreasstrasse 51, D-5300 Bonn 2 (FRG).

involving oxidative metabolic processes that demand an oxidizing environment, allowing for final conversion of all carbon compounds to the most oxidized form ($= CO_2$). Photosynthesis restores the balance by generating oxygen and by fixation of CO_2, resulting in more reduced carbon being made available to catabolism. Thus, photosynthesis supports all forms of life on earth by a rather unique complex of reactions that can utilize and conserve radiant energy from outside.

Photosynthetic organisms capable of these reactions include all plants equipped with chlorophyll *a* together with at least one major accessory pigment. Among them are vascular plants and mosses, the wide variety of blue-green, red, green, and brown pigmented algae, the lichens, as well as a number of photosynthesizing bacteria belonging to the Thiorhodaceae (purple sulfur bacteria), Athiorhodaceae (purple nonsulfur bacteria), and Chlorobacteriaceae (green sulfur bacteria). Photosynthesizing organisms sensu lato are also aquatic invertebrate animals that contain unicellular algae or even algal organelles as functional endosymbiotic units (cf. Trench 1979).

Basis of Autotrophy: Reductive Pentose Phosphate Cycle

CARBON SOURCE

The initial steps among the dark reactions of photosynthesis involve uptake, incorporation, and fixation of inorganic carbon by carboxylation of a preformed substrate, ribulose-1, 5-bisphosphate. Inorganic carbon is available to terrestrial plants as atmospheric carbon dioxide. Under normal conditions (20°C, 1 bar (1 bar = 100 kPa)), the atmosphere contains at least 0.03% CO_2 (already in 1980 about 360 ppm), which is equivalent to $\sim 15~\mu mol \cdot L^{-1}$. Marine plants live in an environment that contains inorganic carbon either as dissolved CO_2 or as H_2CO_3 as well as HCO_3^- and CO_3^{2-}. The total carbon content in seawater is a function of pH, temperature, and salinity (see Skirrow 1975). In the normal pH range (between 7.8 and 8.2) HCO_3^- is by far the predominant form, comprising more than 90% of the total inorganic carbon present. The average content amounts to about 2.2–2.5 mmol $\cdot$ L^{-1}. Some aquatic plants take up unhydrated CO_2, while others utilize the bicarbonate (HCO_3^-) (Jolliffe and Tregunna 1970). Those operating with CO_2 rely on only about 10 μL $\cdot$ L^{-1} as a carbon source, whereas those incorporating HCO_3^- usually have more than 2 mmol $\cdot$ L^{-1} available.

The bicarbonate concentration of seawater is not likely to limit the rate of photosynthesis in plankton or seaweeds; it is usually far more than saturating (cf. Harris 1978). It must be considered, however, that the diffusion constant of CO_2 in the atmosphere is about 0.16 cm^2 $\cdot$ s^{-1}, whereas it is 2×10^{-5} cm^2 $\cdot$ s^{-1} in seawater. This ratio of about 10^4 in the diffusion velocities compensates for any possible advantage that a bicarbonate-utilizing marine plant might have over a terrestrial species, with regard to concentrations of inorganic carbon in the respective environments (cf. Raven 1970).

The carboxylating enzyme initiating photosynthetic carbon incorporation, ribulose-1,5-bisphosphate carboxylase, has been found to use unhydrated CO_2 rather than HCO_3^- (cf. Raven 1970). Those aquatic species relying on bicarbonate must, therefore, be able to convert HCO_3^- to unhydrated CO_2. The appropriate enzyme system, carbonic anhydrase (= carbonate dehydratase), catalyzes this conversion effectively. It is present in various representatives of algae (Graham and Smillie 1976), and it appears reasonable to ascribe to it a significant role in photosynthesis. Nonetheless, various aspects of the function and importance of this peculiar enzyme remain elusive (cf. Lamb 1977).

The CO_2 of the atmosphere is a mixture of the stable isotopes $^{12}C^{16}O^{16}O$, $^{13}C^{16}O^{16}O$, and $^{12}C^{18}O^{18}O$, but the isotope ^{12}C in total contributes 98.89% to atmospheric CO_2. Most photosynthesizing plants have been found to prefer this lightest of the carbon isotopes. Usually, the ratio $^{12}C/^{13}C$ as determined by mass spectroscopy is expressed as the $\delta^{13}C$ (‰) value. Most plant $\delta^{13}C$ values are negative, indicating that the proportions of the isotopes in organic compounds arising from photosynthesis do not exactly reflect the relative amounts present in the abiotic atmosphere, but that living organisms are somewhat depleted in ^{13}C.

In aquatic environments, the equilibrium reactions of CO_2 complicate the situation. As bicarbonate already has a $\delta^{13}C$ value which is somewhat lower than that of atmospheric CO_2, algae utilizing HCO_3^- are expected to show a comparable shift. In fact, such shifts have been found for a variety of marine algae in the range of the isotope fractionation between HCO_3^- and CO_2 (Smith and Epstein 1971; Black and Bender 1976).

Carbon isotope fractionation between ^{12}C and ^{13}C (and, moreover, between ^{12}C and ^{14}C) is also indicative of the nature of the primary carboxylation event of the photosynthetic pathway. The resulting ^{13}C values allow discrimination between C_3 and C_4 plants (see discussion below).

REACTIONS OF REDUCTIVE PENTOSE PHOSPHATE CYCLE

The basic biochemical pathway that provides fixation of inorganic carbon and converts it to highly reduced organic compounds is the reductive pentose phosphate cycle (RPP cycle below). The reaction sequence originally proposed (see Bassham and Calvin 1957) has required no essential additions or changes since its discovery, and is obviously a universally operating metabolic pathway, as may be determined from experimental findings by a wide variety of photosynthesizing organisms. This brief consideration of the reactions involved follows the more comprehensive treatment by Bassham (1979), which should be consulted for additional information.

Three operational phases in series can be distinguished, comprising the carboxylation, the reduction, and the cyclic regeneration of the starting material.

Carboxylation — The enzyme ribulose-1,5-bisphosphate carboxylase (= RuBPCase, EC 4.1.1.39) catalyzes the condensation of CO_2 supplied by inter-/intracellular diffusion with the C_2 atom of ribulose-1,5-bisphosphate (RuBP). There is convincing experimental evidence that the transition C_6 intermediate, resulting from the initial carboxylation step, is an enzyme-bound, 2-carboxy-3-ketoribitol-1,5-bisphosphate (Sjödin and Vestermark 1973). This short-lived intermediate is then hydrolytically split to give two molecules of 3-phosphoglycerate (PGA). PGA is a C_3 acid and the first stable, analytically traceable product of the photosynthetic carboxylation step. It was one of the earliest photosynthetic intermediates identified by kinetic tracer studies using $^{14}CO_2$. Cells were allowed to reach steady-state photosynthesis in $^{14}CO_2$ so that all pools of the presumably cycling intermediates were saturated with radiocarbon. When the further incubation was interrupted by darkening the cells, the immediate products of the photosynthetic light reactions (ATP and NADPH) were cut off, while carboxylation could continue. This resulted in the simultaneous disappearance of the CO_2 acceptor molecules (RuBP) and the appearance of the compounds derived from the carboxylation (PGA) (Fig. 1).

The C atom from CO_2 fixed to the C_2 atom of RuBP furnishes the carboxyl group of one PGA. This was demonstrated by chemical degradation of PGA, which allowed the further fate of the labeled carbon atom to be traced through the subsequent reactions of the RPP cycle.

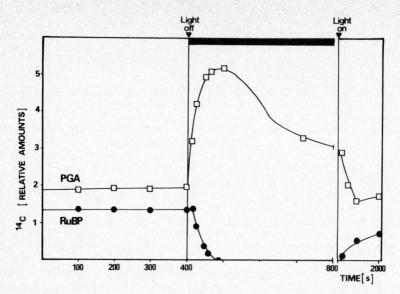

FIG. 1. Changes in concentrations of 3-phosphoglycerate (PGA) and ribulose-1,5-bisphosphate (RuBP) during light–dark transients (after Bassham and Calvin 1957).

Because the first product of the initiation phase of the cycle is a C_3 acid, this type of carbon fixation is usually termed C_3 photosynthesis.

Reduction of PGA — During the reduction phase of photosynthetic carbon assimilation, PGA is converted into glyceraldehyde 3-phosphate (GAP) representing a C_3 carbohydrate (triose phosphate). This conversion is strictly endergonic, requires coupling with an exergonic reaction, and occurs in two subsequent steps. First, PGA is phosphorylated to give the acylphosphate glycerate-1,3-bisphosphate (PPGA) at the expense of ATP as the donor of the phosphate group. The reaction is catalyzed by phosphoglycerate kinase.

The second conversion implies the reduction of PPGA to GAP by a NADPH-specific triose phosphate dehydrogenase. This is a typical and specific photosynthetic enzyme located exclusively in the photosynthesizing chloroplast. It differs considerably from the cytoplasmic NADH-linked enzyme participating in glycolysis. The overall reduction of PGA to GAP is energetically somewhat unfavorable.

Regeneration of the CO_2 acceptor — The third phase in the dark reactions of photosynthesis, following carboxylation and reduction of the first occurring photosynthate, includes a set of conversions designed to regenerate the specific acceptor molecule of CO_2, RuBP. For this purpose, the triose phosphate undergoes a series of isomerizations, condensations, and molecular rearrangements by which five molecules of GAP finally provide six molecules of a pentose phosphate (ribulose-5-phosphate, R5P).

These conversions include the following individual reactions, and are shown schematically in Fig. 2.

1) Two molecules of GAP are converted to dihydroxyacetone phosphate (DHAP) with triose phosphate isomerase.

2) The enzyme aldolase is able to condense two molecules of triose phosphate to give fructose-1,6-bisphosphate (FBP) in a reversible reaction.

3) FBP is subjected to dephosphorylation by fructose bisphosphatase yielding fructose-6-phosphate (F6P). GAP originating from the reduction phase of the cycle and F6P provided by conversions 1–3 form the substrates of the subsequent rearrangements which involve some changes in the chain length of the sugar phosphates participating in the sequence.

4) By action of the enzyme transketolase a C_2 unit is transferred from F6P to GAP leaving a C_4 sugar phosphate, erythrose-4-phosphate (E4P), and simultaneously yielding a C_5 sugar phosphate, xylulose-5-phosphate (Xu5P). This reaction is reversible. It provides one of the three pentose phosphates required for the regeneration of RuBP.

5) The aldose phosphate E4P then condenses with the triose phosphate DHAP in a reaction again mediated by aldolase (cf. step 2 of the regenerating phase) to form a C_7 compound, sedoheptulose-1,7-bisphosphate (SBP). Similar to RuBP, this compound is restricted to the photosynthetic pathway of carbon metabolism and does not occur in further metabolic sequences.

6) The ketose phosphate SBP is dephosphorylated to sedoheptulose-7-phosphate (S7P) with

46

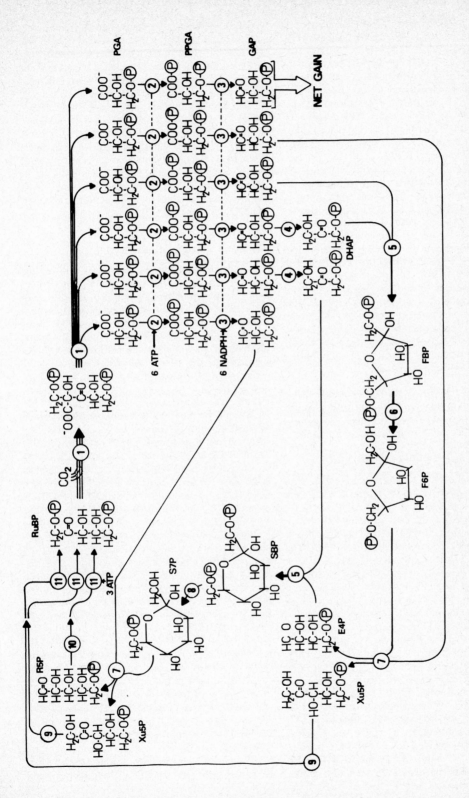

FIG. 2. Reactions of the reductive pentose phosphate cycle. Upon one turn of the cycle, three molecules of CO_2 are fixed and a net gain of one molecule of the C_3 compound glyceraldehyde phosphate is achieved. All further reactions are concerned with the cyclic regeneration of the CO_2 acceptor. For abbreviations see text. Enzymes involved in the conversions and molecular rearrangements: 1, ribulose-1,5-bisphosphate carboxylase; 2, phosphoglycerate kinase; 3, triosephosphate dehydrogenase; 4, triosephosphate isomerase; 5, aldolase; 6, fructose-1,6-bisphosphatase; 7, transketolase; 8, sedoheptulose-1,7-bisphosphatase; 9, phosphoketopentose epimerase; 10, phosphoketopentose isomerase; 11, ribulose-5-phosphate kinase.

catalysis by sedoheptulose-1,7-bisphosphatase, an enzyme that is obviously distinct from the phosphatase mediating step 3 of this cycle.

7) Finally, a further conversion catalyzed by transketolase occurs by which the C_1 and C_2 atoms of S7P are again transferred to GAP, resulting in the formation of two different pentose phosphates (Xu5P and ribose-5-phosphate; R5P). Both compounds are interconvertible by simple isomerization and represent the remaining C_5 compounds needed for the regeneration of RuBP.

As in Fig. 2, three molecules of RuBP are carboxylated by RuBPCase to form six molecules of PGA and, on reduction, six molecules of GAP. Five of these GAP molecules are consumed for the regeneration of three molecules of RuBP, thus completing the RPP cycle. The remaining sixth GAP represents the net gain of fixed organic carbon per turn of the cycle resulting from the initial input of three molecules of CO_2.

The further fate of the net gain GAP involves conversions similar to those formulated as the initial steps of the regenerating phase of the RPP cycle. They provide net photosynthate in the form of hexose phosphates (giving rise to accumulated free hexoses and related compounds) as well as the biosynthesis of polymeric storage carbohydrates. There are several branching points where intermediates of the RPP cycle can leave the photosynthetic pathway sensu stricto to be subsequently fed into other anabolic sequences for the biosynthesis of cellular constituents.

ENERGETICS AND STOICHIOMETRY

For each mole of CO_2 entering the carboxylation by RuBPCase, 1 mol of ATP is consumed for the formation of RuBP from Ru5P or Xu5P and R5P, respectively (see Fig. 2). Two further moles of ATP are required for the activation of 2 mol of PGA (arising from each mole of carboxylated RuBP) to PPGA. The subsequent reduction step strictly needs 2 mol of NADPH. As a complete turn of the RPP cycle involves uptake and fixation of three molecules of CO_2 to give a net gain of one GAP, a total of 9 mol of ATP and 6 mol of NADPH are the minimal investment required.

The 9 mol of ATP represent an energy equivalent of 68.8 kcal, the 6 mol of NADPH a total of 315.5 kcal. The energy input into one turn of the RPP cycle is thus, theoretically, in the range of 384.3 kcal. Energy recovered from the end product of the reduction phase, GAP, amounts to about 350.4 kcal/mol. Substracting the energy stored in GAP from that expended by consumption of ATP and NADPH, a difference of $\Delta G' = -33.9$ kcal is obtained, representing about 10% of the original input which is obviously wasted to drive the RPP cycle. The efficiency of carbon reduction during

the dark reactions of photosynthesis is thus very near 90%. However, if the actual, physiological in situ concentrations of the individual metabolic intermediates of the cycle are considered, a more realistic approach to the energetics and the overall efficiency can be achieved. From such calculations, which will not be detailed further here, the theoretical $\Delta G'$ values are corrected to physiological ΔG^s values. On this certainly more relistic and relevant background, the energy input of 6 mol of ATP and of 9 mol of ATP amounts to 427 kcal. The free energy finally converted to heat to keep the entire cycle running is $\Delta G^s = -73.4$ kcal. This would establish an efficiency in the range of 80% which, however, is still rather respectable (Bassham and Krause 1969).

MAPPING THE RPP CYCLE: METHODS AND DEVELOPMENTS

Several methodological advances initiated the research on photosynthetic carbon assimilation, which finally led to the formulation of the RPP cycle as given above. The most important progress was probably the introduction of the radioisotope tracer technique. Since then it became possible to follow the path of carbon from the carboxylation to the reduction of the triose phosphate and the cyclic regeneration of the acceptor molecule. In addition, this acquisition required further developments, including two-dimensional chromatography and autoradiography for the characterization and identification of small amounts of compounds involved. Only by such methods was it found that PGA, DHAP, FBP, and GAP were among the products formed during the first seconds of exposure to $^{14}CO_2$. Chemical degradation of such early photosynthates revealed that ^{14}C was located mostly in the carboxyl oe PGA or the C_3/C_4 atoms of the hexose phosphates, thus strongly suggesting that the C_3 acid once synthesized is rapidly converted to C_6 carbohydrates. Time-dependent changes in proporional ^{14}C labeling as obtained from kinetic studies of carbon flow confirmed this view. The methods originally applied have meanwhile been supplemented and improved in many respects. They are still an indispensable tool for the investigation of algal primary metabolism (see Kremer 1978).

Another fundamental approach to the dark reactions of photosynthesis was the characterization of the individual enzymes involved. Quayle et al. (1954) first demon trated the formation of PGA in vitro upon carboxylation, when radioactive CO_2 and RuBP were added to an enzyme preparation obtained from Chlorella cells. Comprehensive work has since been conducted on the properties of RuBPCase, which now appears to be one of the most important plant enzymes. During approximately the same period that the RPP cycle was formulated on the basis of radiotracer kinetic studies, an oxidative pentose phosphate cycle was discovered (see Horecker et al. 1953), and it soon became evident that some conversions formulated for this pathway were the exact reverse of the reactions of the RPP cycle, thus providing further biochemical evidence for the consolidation of the concept.

A third discovery should be mentioned. Arnon (1952) demonstrated the activity of an enzyme able to use NADPH as a coenzyme and to catalyze the reduction of PPGA to GAP. This enzyme, glyceraldehyde phosphate dehydrogenase, provides the fundamental reduction step from the activated C_3 acid to the level of a carbohydrate. This reaction utilizes the reducing power of NADPH and thus shows where and how an important product generated by the photosynthetic light reactions is consumed. The light and dark reactions of photosynthesis are intimately connected at this particular site of the RPP cycle, which, in addition, represents the site of an immediate on–off regulation of the entire cycling pathway.

Additional Mechanisms of Carbon Fixation

Experiments using the tracer technique to follow patterns and kinetics of ^{14}C labeling provide evidence that fixation of CO_2 by the RPP cycle is not the sole or an exclusive reaction by which carbon is fixed. There are further mechanisms for assimilation of inorganic carbon that should briefly be discussed in this connection. Such reactions are best associated with the term "C_4 metabolism," which is, as will be discussed below, not necessarily synonymous, or even identical with C_4 photosynthesis. Nonetheless, these reactions (often) show certain relationships to the RPP cycle and may, therefore, also be regarded as components of the photosynthetic dark reactions.

A common feature of the reactions to be considered here is the substrate to be carboxylated. It is a C_3 compound, usually phosphoenolpyruvate (PEP), which is condensed with CO_2 to form a C_4 dicarboxylic acid. In this particular connection, two enzymatic reactions have to be considered: phosphoenolpyruvate carboxylase and phosphoenolpyruvate carboxykinase. Both enzymes introduce a second carboxyl group ($= \beta$-carboxyl) into the C_3 acid PEP by a reaction generally termed β-carboxylation.

β-CARBOXYLATION VIA PHOSPHOENOLPYRUVATE CARBOXYLASE

A first indication of the existance of a further carboxylating mechanism involved in photosynthetic carbon fixation was obtained when Kortschak et al. (1957) found that in photosynthesizing sugarcane leaves the first occurring ^{14}C-labeled photosynthates were preponderingly C_4 dicarboxylic acids such as aspartate and malate rather than PGA, the traditional primary product of photosynthetic CO_2 fixation. Just one decade after the elucidation of the universally operating RPP cycle, Hatch and Slack (1966) presented a biochemical reaction scheme to account for the particular pattern of ^{14}C labeling among the early photosynthates observed in sugarcane. This was the onset of the C_4 wave.

C_4 photosynthesis has hitherto mostly been associated with green vascular plants exhibiting a specialized type of leaf anatomy. In contrast with the majority of angiosperms whose leaf tissue is usually organized into the two distinct cell types (the palisade layer and the spongy parenchyma), some other species have a so-called Kranz leaf anatomy. In such leaves the veins are much closer together, and each is surrounded by a particular layer of bundle sheath cells that contain large numbers of chloroplasts. The bundle sheath layer is embedded in mesophyll cells with only rather small air spaces between them.

The complex reactions of C_4 photosynthesis are compartmentated between bundle sheath cells (BSC) and mesophyll cells (MC). The entire context is schematically represented in Fig. 3. The basic reaction takes place in the MC and involves the β-carboxylation of PEP to oxaloacetate (OAA) by phosphoenolpyruvate carboxylase (PEPCase). Although it has originally, and then repeatedly, been proposed that this enzyme is associated with MC chloroplasts, it is now widely accepted that it is actually located in the cytoplasm (Coombs 1979). OAA is a rather unstable reaction product and will usually not be found after extraction and chromatographic isolation. It is immediately converted to either malate by malate dehydrogenase (NADPH-linked) and/or to aspartate by OAA–asparate aminotransferase. Whether prevailingly malate or aspartate is formed from OAA depends on the species investigated.

Accordingly, malate and/or aspartate is exported from MC and transferred to BSC. If malate is the C_4 dicarboxylic acid to be transferred, it is decarboxylated in the cytoplasm by malic enzyme, simultaneously regenerating the NADPH previously consumed for its synthesis. Transfer of malate from MC to BSC thus implies the transport of reduction equivalent. The C_3 compound resulting from decarboxylation of malate is pyruvate. It is returned to MC for restoring the pool of PEP.

If aspartate is transferred from MC to BSC, it is first reconverted to OAA and then decarboxylated by NAD-linked malic enzyme. In this case, pyruvate or alanine (formed from pyruvate on transamination to prevent increasing concentration of toxic NH_3

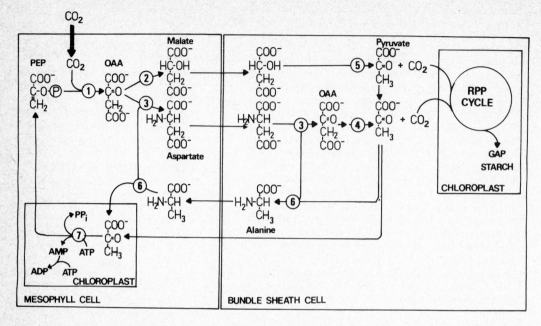

FIG. 3. Reactions and conversions in mesophyll and bundle sheath cells of C_4 plants. For abbreviations see text. Enzymes involved: 1, phosphoenolpyruvate carboxylase; 2, malate dehydrogenase; 3, oxaloacetate-aspartate aminotransferase; 4, NADH-linked malic enzyme (after reduction of OAA to malate by malate dehydrogenase); 5, NADPH-linked malic enzyme; 6, pyruvate-alanine aminotransferase; 7, pyruvate dikinase. In some plants reaction 4 involves decarboxylation of OAA by phosphoenolpyruvate carboxykinase to form PEP and CO_2. The scheme does not include any figure on the participation of mitochondria, although the NADH-linked malic enzyme is clearly of mitochondrial origin.

in BSC) is reimported into MC. In some C_4 plants, aspartate is decarboxylated by phosphoenolpyruvate carboxykinase in BSC and PEP is restored to MC.

Pyruvate contributed by BSC is regenerated to PEP in MC by an enzyme, pyruvate dikinase, which requires ATP and inorganic phosphate (P_i) to produce PEP, AMP, and pyrophosphate (PP_i). PP_i is hydro-lyzed into two P_i by a pyrophosphatase, and the AMP present reacts with another molecule of ATP to form two molecules of ADP. This powerfully exothermic reaction converting, in sum, two ATP into two ADP, runs strongly in the direction of PEP synthesis and, therefore, greatly facilitates the initial carboxylation step mediated by PEPCase.

The transfer of aspartate or malate, or in some species both, allows classification of the C_4 plants. The basic function of these transferred substrates is to serve as a CO_2 source in the BSC on decarboxy-lation. The so-formed CO_2 is immediately fixed in BSC chloroplasts via RPP cycle by the reactions as detailed above (C_3 photosynthesis).

The physiological and biochemical significance of C_4 photosynthesis is manifold. Plants possessing the C_4 machinery are capable of much higher rates of photosynthesis. As PEPCase exhibits a much higher affinity for CO_2 ($K_{m(CO_2)}$ about 20–70 μM)

than does RuBPCase ($K_{m(CO_2)}$ in the range of 400 μM), C_4 plants are able to absorb CO_2 from much lower concentrations than C_3 plants. Thus, the C_4 mech-anism concentrates effectively the intracellular CO_2 and keeps photosynthetic carbon fixation running, even if activity of RuBPCase would gradually de-crease due to unfavorable external conditions. C_4 photosynthesis, therefore, results in notably lower CO_2 compensation points (about 5 $\mu L \cdot L^{-1}$) than the 50 $\mu L \cdot L^{-1}$ determined for average C_3 plants.

Though C_4 plants usually show higher photo-synthetic rates and remarkable productivity, they are not necessarily more efficient than C_3 plants relying exclusively on the RPP cycle. In fact, C_4 plants consume more assimilatory power for the fixation of each molecule of CO_2. In addition to three ATP and two NADPH as the usual investment into the RPP cycle (C_3 photosynthesis in BSC), the C_4 mechanism preceding the C_3 pathway requires two further ATP for the biochemical operation of the MC, i.e. continuous supply of PEP. Therefore, C_4 plants can simply make better use of the excess light available in their environment to drive the C_4 machinery for the concentration of CO_2, and to maintain a higher level of inorganic carbon at the local environment of RuBPCase in the BSC, where it can be more rapidly fixed. The C_4 pathway is by no means an alternative to the RPP cycle, as it virtually results in no net reduction of the primarily fixed CO_2.

Crassulacean acid metabolism — Certain succulent plants possessing voluminous central vacuoles and a population of chloroplasts in the same cells increase their acid content in the night by accumulating malate in the vacuole(s), which, however, disappears during the subsequent day. Thus, the malate content of the vacuoles undergoes a distinct diurnal rhythm, usually accompanied by an inverse rhythm of polyglucan content. This type of metabolism is termed Crassulacean acid metabolism (CAM) because it has first been discovered in members of this angiosperm family. CAM involves the synthesis of malate by β-carboxylation mediated through PEPCase at night, and the degradation of this C_4 acid during daytime to liberate CO_2 for fixation via RPP cycle (Kluge and Ting 1978). CAM in many regards ressembles C_4 photosynthesis. The underlying reactions are basically the same. Again, PEPCase is concerned with harvesting CO_2 by carboxylation of PEP into OAA, which is subsequently reduced to malate by a NADH-linked malate dehydrogenase. Carboxylation and reduction take place in the cytoplasm. In the light, malate is released from the vacuoles into the cytoplasm and is there decarboxylated to yield free CO_2 and a C_3 residue. One group of CAM plants performs an oxidative decarboxylation by malic enzyme (NADP- or NAD- linked). Others show high activities of phosphoenol- pyruvate carboxykinase. In such species malate is first oxidized to OAA and then split into CO_2 and PEP. CO_2 is reintroduced into photosynthesis.

Although CAM enables certain plant species to cover their CO_2 demand by nocturnal CO_2 fixation, it does not provide an alternative to the RPP cycle either. In essence, the C_3 cycle, involving carboxylation via RuBPCase, is the central event and absolutely indispensible for net carbon assimilation. As in C_4 photosynthesis, the β-carboxylation represents some kind of a CO_2 supercharger. The implication of this preset reaction step solves the problem of how to effect maximum carbon gain with a minimum of water loss. Behind closed stomata, CO_2 is recycled from decarboxylation of malate and fed into the RPP cycle, while inversely the stored photosynthate provides the source for the generation of sufficient amounts of the primary CO_2 acceptor PEP.

In CAM plants, β-carboxylation of PEP and carboxylation of RuBP are not spatially (as in C_4 plants: MC vs. BSC), but temporally separated. CAM does not confer high rates of photosynthesis. In this regard, it is remarkably inefficient, but it permits the continuation of photosynthesis under extremely unfavorable environmental conditions.

β-CARBOXYLATION VIA PHOSPHOENOLPYRUVATE CARBOXYKINASE

There are several exclusive criteria such as specialized leaf anatomy, low CO_2 compensation points, low photorespiration, less extreme $^{12}C/^{13}C$ carbon isotope fractionation, primary CO_2 fixation into C_4 dicarboxylic acids, and a particular set of enzymes that must be fulfilled for unequivocal distinguishing of C_4 photosynthesis in any plant species. Unfortunately, in some cases only one of these basic features has been used to establish C_4 photosynthesis. This highly specialized pathway of carbon (pre-)fixation has been claimed for such diverse photosynthesizing plants as blue-green algae (Döhler 1974), seaweeds in general (Joshi and Karekar 1973), as well as a marine grass (Benedict and Scott 1976). These reports have caused considerable confusion in the (reviewing) literature and certainly require some further remarks.

The conclusion that the C_4 pathway of photosynthesis occurs in the blue-green alga *Anacystis nidulans* was based on the observation of considerable ^{14}C labeling of aspartate. Furthermore, this species was found to show activity of PEPCase. When ^{14}C-labeled exogenous aspartate was supplied, this compound was directly converted into other amino acids rather than into intermediates of the RPP cycle (Döhler 1974). There is no doubt that aquatic plants including algae incorporate appreciable amounts of photosynthetically fixed ^{14}C into C_4 compounds such as aspartate and malate. This labeling pattern simply requires β-carboxylation of a C_3 acid, but as such is far away from, and not necessarily identical with, C_4 photosynthesis.

In a variety of seaweeds, including *Ulva lactuca* and some further representatives of the major classes, the occurrence of C_4 photosynthesis was concluded on the basis of measurements of PEPCase activity (Joshi and Karekar 1973). However, in all marine algae so far investigated in detail, this enzyme is present in negligibly low amounts, insufficient to account for a CO_2-concentrating mechanism. Apart from that, PGA is the earliest ^{14}C-labeled photosynthate in seaweeds containing usually more than 80% of total ^{14}C assimilated during short-term photosynthesis (< 5–10 s) (Kremer and Willenbrink 1972; Kremer and Küppers 1977).

Undoubtedly, extreme caution is required when single characteristics are used to establish the presence of C_4 photosynthesis. In essence, if critically evaluated, so far there is no experimental evidence strongly suggesting the occurrence of C_4 photosynthesis in unicellular algae or in seaweeds. It has not (yet) been demonstrated that radiocarbon label in the C_4 position (β-carboxyl) of malate and/or aspartate is transferred quantitatively to the C_1 position of PGA through decarboxylation and subsequent

51

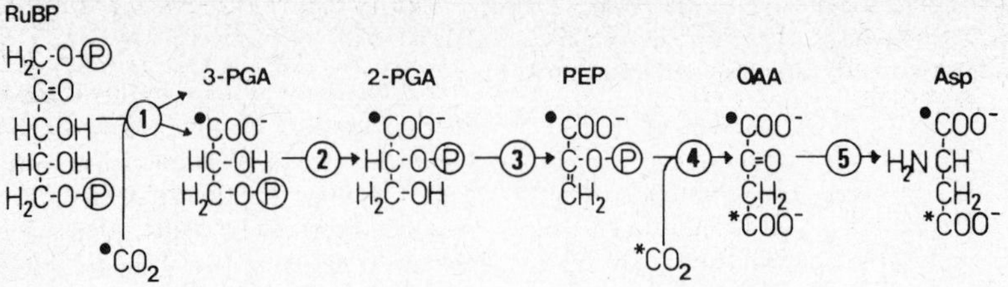

RuBP

H_2C-O-P
C=O
HC-OH — ①
HC-OH
H_2C-O-P

•CO_2

3-PGA
•COO$^-$
HC-OH — ② →
H_2C-O-P

2-PGA
•COO$^-$
HC-O-P — ③ →
H_2C-OH

PEP
•COO$^-$
C-O-P — ④
CH$_2$

*CO_2

OAA
•COO$^-$
C=O — ⑤ →
CH$_2$
*COO$^-$

Asp
•COO$^-$
H_2N CH
CH$_2$
*COO$^-$

FIG. 4. β-Carboxylation in the light. Reactions provide ^{14}C labeling in α- and β-carboxyl of aspartate. For abbreviations see text.

refixation, as it is in C_4 plants as well as CAM plants. Moreover, it is rather unlikely to expect that such a specialized metabolic apparatus, which certainly provides distinct advantages under peculiar ecological conditions as given in arid or xeric terrestrial environments, has been evolved independently in phytoplankton or seaweeds. In the environment of these plants there is no actual need to possess biochemical mechanisms for the concentration of intracellular CO_2.

As appreciable ^{14}C labeling in aspartate and malate is observed even after short-term photosynthesis in marine algae, β-carboxylation, to account for this labeling pattern, must be regarded as a carbon fixation mechanism supplementing carboxylation for initiation of the RPP cycle. However, the metabolic reactions and conversions involved should better be associated with the presumably less ambiguous term C_4 metabolism (Benedict 1978).

This phenomenon has attracted much attention during the last decade. Pioneering work was undertaken by Akagawa et al. (1972) who showed that the enzyme performing β-carboxylation in seaweeds is a phosphoenolpyruvate carboxykinase (PEPCKase). Originally, this enzyme was understood to be responsible for dark fixation (light-independent fixation) of CO_2. Carbon uptake and fixation into organic compounds during darkness is a special feature of macrophytic brown algae. In representatives of the Laminariales the rates of this nonphotosynthetic CO_2 incorporation may account for about 30% of the assimilation rates achieved under photosynthetic conditions at the same temperature and carbon supply. Particularly in young, differentiating frond areas β-carboxylation due to high activity of PEPCKase is significantly enhanced as compared with mature, differentiated frond tissue (Kremer and Küppers 1977; Küppers and Kremer 1978).

"Dark" carbon fixation yielding ^{14}C labeling of aspartate and malate upon β-carboxylation of PEP by PEPCKase is obviously not restricted to dark periods, but also occurs under photosynthetic conditions. From kinetic tracer studies using ^{14}C it became evident that maximum ^{14}C labeling of the C_4 dicarboxylic acids in the light is achieved distinctly later than in PGA. Furthermore, chemical degradation of [^{14}C]aspartate labeled in the light showed that ^{14}C is located in both C_1 and C_4 atoms. This suggests that the substrate of β-carboxylation already contained the ^{14}C labeling in the α-carboxyl (C_1 atom) when it was subjected to a further carboxylation step by PEPCKase. Hence, the C_3 acid PEP is derived from photosynthetically labeled PGA, and it must be concluded from the ^{14}C labeling pattern in the early photosynthates that radioactive carbon flows from an intermediate of the RPP cycle (PGA) to compounds usually associated with C_4 metabolism (aspartate and malate), but, at least in the representatives of brown macroalgae, under no circumstances in the opposite sense. In the dark, the substrate of PEPCKase, PEP, is provided by glycolytic catabolism of reserve carbohydrate. Thus, β-carboxylation can proceed in the light and in the dark with comparable efficiently (Kremer 1981a, b) (see Fig. 4).

Findings from marine phytoplankton, particularly diatoms, also strongly suggest that β-carboxylation must be regarded as a notable source of carbon in addition to CO_2 fixation provided by the RPP cycle. As has been shown in experiments with *Phaeodactylum cornutum* and *Skeletonema costatum*, designed to analyze different parameters of carbon input such as long- and short-term patterns of ^{14}C assimilation, as well as sensitivity of photosynthesis to environmental oxygen, a remarkable diversity in CO_2 fixation is found in marine algae (see Beardall and Morris 1975; Glover et al. 1975; Beardall et al. 1976; Mukerji et al. 1978). According to this work, the carboxylation of C_3 compounds to C_4 dicarboxylic acids is to be regarded as an important component of photosynthetic carbon metabolism supplementing the universally occurring reactions of the RPP cycle. Because diatoms and dinoflagellates exhibit considerable rates of carbon fixation in the dark due to continuation of β-carboxylation, their overall carbon strategy might be strictly comparable to that of the brown seaweeds.

Some discussion has arisen concerning the nature of the enzyme mediating β-carboxylation in phytoplankton species. Although Mukerji and Morris (1976) report the extraction of a PEPCase from *Phaeodactylum cornutum*, Holdsworth and Bruck (1977) and Kremer and Berks (1978) presented results strongly suggesting the participation of a PEPCKase. This qualification is now accepted (see Davies 1979). Whether the carbon flow from RPP cycle intermediates to C_1 compounds during β-carboxylation in the light is also similar to that evaluated for members of the Phaeophyceae awaits future investigation.

References

AKAGAWA, H., T. IKAWA, AND K. NISIZAWA. 1972. The enzyme system for the entrance of CO_2 in the dark fixation of brown algae. Plant Cell Physiol. 13: 999–1016.

ARNON, D. E. 1952. Glyceraldehyde phosphate dehydrogenase of green plants. Science (Washington, D.C.) 116: 635–637.

BASSHAM, J. A. 1979. The reductive pentose phosphate cycle and its regulation, p. 9–30. *In* M. Gibbs and E. Latzko [ed.] Encyclopedia of plant physiology. New Series. Vol. 6. Springer Verlag, Berlin, Heidelberg, New York.

BASSHAM, J. A., AND M. CALVIN. 1957. The path of carbon in photosynthesis. Prentice Hall Inc. p. 1–107.

BASSHAM, J. A., AND G. H. KRAUSE. 1969. Photosynthesis: energetics and related topics. Biochim. Biophys. Acta 189: 207–221.

BEARDALL, J., AND I. MORRIS. 1975. Effects of environmental factors on photosynthesis patterns in Phaeodactylum tricornutum (Bacillariophyceae). II. Effect of oxygen. J. Phycol. 11: 430–434.

BEARDALL, J., D. MUKERJI, H. E. GLOVER, AND I. MORRIS. 1976. The path of carbon in photosynthesis by marine phytoplankton. J. Phycol. 12: 409–417.

BENEDICT, C. R. 1978. Nature of obligate photoautotrophy. Annu. Rev. Plant Physiol. 29: 67–93.

BENEDICT, C. R., AND J. R. SCOTT. 1976. Photosynthetic carbon metabolism of a marine grass. Plant Physiol. 57: 876–880.

BLACK, C. C., AND M. M. BENDER. 1976. ^{13}C values in marine organisms from the Great Barrier Reef. Aust. J. Plant Physiol. 3: 25–32.

COOMBS, J. 1979. Enzymes of C_1 metabolism, p. 251–262. *In* M. Gibbs and E. Latzko [ed.] Encyclopedia of plant physiology. New Series. Vol. 6. Springer Verlag, Berlin, Heidelberg, New York.

DAVIES, D. D. 1979. The central role of phosphoenolpyruvate in plant metabolism. Annu. Rev. Plant Physiol. 30: 131–158.

DÖHLER, G. 1974. C_4–Weg der Photosynthese in der Blaualge Anacystis nidulans. Planta 118: 259–269.

GLOVER, H., J. BEARDALL, AND I. MORRIS. 1975. Effects of environmental factors on photosynthetis patterns in Phaeodactylum tricornutum (Baccillario-

phyceae). I. Effect of nitrogen deficiency and light intensity. J. Phycol. 11: 424–429.

GRAHAM, D., AND R. M. SMILLIE. 1976. Carbonate dehydratase in marine organisms of the Great Barrier Reef. Aust. J. Plant Physiol. 3: 113–119.

HARRIS, G. P. 1978. Photosynthesis, productivity and growth. The physiological ecology of phytoplankton. Arch. Hydrobiol. Suppl. 10: 1–171.

HATCH, M. D., AND C. R. SLACK. 1966. Photosynthesis by sugarcane leaves. Biochem. J. 101: 103–111.

HOLDSWORTH, E. S., AND K. BRUCK. 1977. Enzymes concerned with β-carboxylation in marine phytoplankter. Purification and properties of phosphoenolpyruvate carboxykinase. Arch. Biochem. Biophys. 182: 87–94.

HORECKER, B. L., P. Z. SMYRNIOTIS, AND H. KLENOW. 1953. Characterization of a transketolase from spinach leaves. J. Biol. Chem. 218: 769–783.

JOLLIFFE, E. A., AND E. B. TREGUNNA. 1970. Studies on HCO_3^- ion uptake during photosynthesis in benthic marine algae. Phycologia 9: 293–303.

JOSHI, G. V., AND M. D. KAREKAR. 1973. Pathway of $^{14}CO_2$ fixation in marine algae. Proc. Indiana Acad. Sci. B 39: 489–493.

KLUGE, M., AND I. P. TING. 1978. Crassulacean acid metabolism. Ecological studies. Vol. 30. Springer Verlag, Berlin, Heidelberg, New York. p. 1–180.

KORTSCHAK, H.P., C. E. HARTT, AND G. O. BURR. 1965. Carbon dioxide fixation in sugarcane leaves. Plant Physiol. 40: 209–213.

KREMER, B. P. 1978. Determination of photosynthetic rates and ^{14}C photoassimilatory products of brown seaweeds, p. 269–283. *In* J. A. Hellebust and J. S. Craigie [ed.] Handbook of phycological methods. Vol. II. Cambridge University Press.

1981a. Metabolic implications of non-photosynthetic carbon assimilation in brown seaweeds. Phycologia 20. (In press)

1981b. Aspects of carbon metabolism in marine macroalgae. Oceanogr. Mar. Biol. Annu. Rev. 19: 41–94.

KREMER, B. P., AND R. BERKS. 1978. Photosynthesis and carbon metabolism in marine and freshwater diatoms. Z. Pflanzenphysiol. 87: 149–167.

KREMER, B. P., AND U. KÜPPERS. 1977. Carboxylating enzymes and pathway of photosynthetic carbon assimilation in different marine algae — evidence for the C_4 pathway? Planta 133: 191–196.

KREMER, B. P., AND J. WILLENBRINK. 1972. CO_2-Fixierung und Stofftransport in benthischen marinen Algen. I. Zur Kinetik der $^{14}CO_2$-Assimilation bei Laminaria saccharina. Planta 103: 55–64.

KÜPPERS, U., AND B. P. KREMER. 1978. Longitudinal profiles of CO_2 fixation capacities in marine macroalgae. Plant Physiol. 62: 49–53.

LAMB, J. E. 1977. Plant carbonic anhydrase. Life Sci. 20: 393–406.

MUKERJI, D., H. E. GLOVER, AND I. MORRIS. 1978. Diversity in the mechanisms of carbon dioxide fixation in Dunaliella tertiolecta (Chlorophyceae). J. Phycol. 14: 137–142.

MUKERJI, D., AND I. MORRIS. 1976. Photosynthetic carboxylating enzymes in *Phaeodactylum tricornu-*

tum. Assay methods and properties. Mar. Biol. 36: 199–206.

PRÉZELIN, B. B. 1981. Light reactions in photosynthesis. Can. Bull. Fish. Aquat. Sci. 210: 1–43.

QUAYLE, J. R., R. C. FULLER, A. A. BENSON, AND M. CALVIN. 1954. Enzymatic carboxylation of ribulose diphosphate. J. Am. Chem. Soc. 76: 3610–3611.

RAVEN, J. A. 1970. Exogenous inorganic carbon sources in plant photosynthesis. Biol. Rev. 45: 167–221.

SJÖDIN, B., AND A. VESTERMARK. 1973. The enzymatic formation of a compound with the expected properties of carboxylated ribulose-1,5-diphosphate. Biochim. Biophys. Acta 297: 165–173.

SKIRROW, G. 1975. The dissolved gases — carbon dioxide, p. 1–192. *In* J. P. Hiley and G. Skirrow [ed.] Chemical oceanography. Academic Press: New York.

SMITH, B. N., AND S. EPSTEIN. 1971. Two categories of $^{13}C/^{12}C$ ratios for higher plants. Plant Physiol. 47: 380–384.

TRENCH, R. K. 1979. The cell biology of plant–animal symbiosis. Annu. Rev. Plant Physiol. 30: 485–531.

Respiration and Photorespiration

JOHN A. RAVEN AND JOHN BEARDALL

Department of Biological Sciences, University of Dundee,
Dundee DD1 4HN, Scotland, U.K.

Introduction

A number of processes in phytoplankters run counter to the main energy-dependent process of photosynthesis. Photosynthesis involves the generation of "high-energy intermediates" (reductant, proton gradient, ATP) with the evolution of O_2 and, ultimately, the consumption of the "high energy intermediates" in the generation of reduced organic compounds from CO_2. The processes which run counter to this reductive, energy-storing trend of photosynthesis are included under the headings of "photorespiration" and "dark respiration," and involve the uptake of O_2 in the oxidation of some reduced compound and (often) the evolution of CO_2.

A simplified scheme which relates these various "respiratory" processes to photosynthesis is given in Fig. 1. The respiratory process closest to the photochemistry of photosynthesis (and often considered as a part of photosynthesis) is the re-oxidation of redox intermediates of the "light reactions" of photosynthesis (Mehler reaction = pseudocyclic electron flow = O_2-linked noncyclic electron flow). Experimentally this process is difficult to distinguish from the O_2 uptake component of the RuBPc-o and PCOC reactions, as they are both strictly light dependent. The oxygenase function of the primary carboxylase of photosynthesis (RuBPc-o) is competitive with the carboxylase function, and is O_2 consuming. The phosphoglycolate produced in this reaction is converted to glycolate which can be excreted, or metabolized via the PCOC, with further uptake of O_2 and evolution of CO_2. The final respiratory process, and the one that is most remote from photosynthesis, is that complex of reactions subsumed under the heading of "dark respiration"; as its name implies this process can occur in the dark but may also be important in the light. The dark respiratory reactions have a more clearly understood function than do the photorespiratory reactions, in that they supply the NADPH, ATP, and C skeletons required for growth and maintenance processes in all aerobic organisms.

The approach which we shall adopt in analyzing the role of these respiratory processes in the life of phytoplankton organisms will be a quantitative one. We shall see that there are considerable difficulties in quantifying the various O_2 uptake and CO_2 evo-

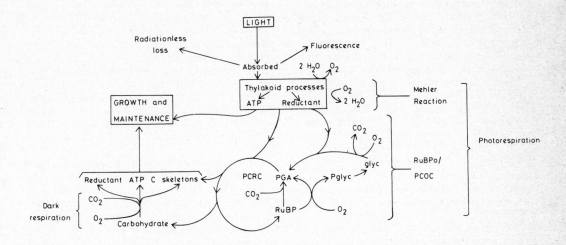

FIG. 1. Outline of the pathways of energy, carbon, and oxygen in photosynthesis, photorespiration, dark respiration, and growth of a phytoplankter. No attempt is made to represent stoichiometries. (Abbreviations: Glyc, glycolate; PCOC, photorespiratory carbon oxidation cycle; PCRC, photosynthetic carbon reduction cycle; PGA, 3-phosphoglycerate; Pglyc, phosphoglycolate; RuBP, ribulose bisphosphate; RuBPo, ribulose bisphosphate oxygenase.

lution processes, particularly under natural conditions and in the light when the opposing photosynthetic and respiratory fluxes must be distinguished. Having quantified the metabolic fluxes of O_2 and CO_2 on the basis of biomass or growth rate, we can then explore the relationship of the processes to growth and maintenance; for this analysis three criteria will be used. One is the impact of the process on the growth efficiency in terms of running costs; using the commonly limiting resource of light as an example, we can ask what influence the process has on the quantum requirement for growth. Pseudocyclic electron flow strictly coupled to ATP synthesis, and generation of NADPH and ATP in tightly coupled dark respiration, are examples of the generation of compounds essential for growth and maintenance involving a certain minimum quantum input per unit of growth; "uncoupled" operation of these pathways, and most manifestations of RuBPo and the PCOC represent a use of quanta which is not essential for growth under all circumstances. A second criterion in natural selection is the efficiency with which capital resources are deployed: we may ask what investment of potentially limiting resources (light, N, P, etc.) is involved in producing the metabolic machinery for the various pathways of respiration, and what would be the investment for such alternative pathways as may serve the same end (e.g. photophosphorylation rather than oxidative phosphorylation as a source of ATP in the light for processes other than the photosynthetic production of carbohydrates). A third consideration is that of safety and stability; do the respiratory processes act as stabilizing or as destabilizing processes with respect to (for example) the dissipation of light energy absorbed in excess of what can be used in growth under a certain set of conditions? The Mehler reaction could act to dissipate excess energy which would otherwise generate triplet chlorophyll, but it can also serve to generate toxic O_2 derivatives (O_2^-, H_2O_2).

Recent reviews of the topics covered in this article include Jackson and Volk (1970), Raven (1976a), and Foyer and Hall (1980) (Mehler reaction (Mehler and Brown 1952) and pseudocyclic photophosphorylation), Merrett and Lord (1973), Tolbert (1974), Andrews and Lorimer (1978), Lorimer et al. (1978a), Heber and Krause (1980), and Raven (1980a, b) (glycolate metabolism, RuBPo, PCOC, photoinhibition, inorganic C concentration mechanism), and ap Rees (1974), Lloyd (1974a, b), Lloyd and Turner (1980), and Raven (1971, 1972a, b, 1976a, b) (dark respiration). Where important comparative considerations are involved, or data on algae are lacking, the metabolism of other organisms will be discussed. Heterotrophy (Droop 1974; Nielson and Lewin 1974) and the role of respiratory incapacity in obligate autotrophy (Whittenbury and Kelly 1977) will not be discussed in detail.

Mehler Reaction
(Pseudocyclic Electron Flow)

Once the problems of extracellular diffusion barriers to O_2 exchange had been appreciated (see Jackson and Volk 1970), experiments on tracer O_2 exchange in microalgae consistently showed a light-stimulated O_2 uptake; this process occurred in all of the algal classes tested (Bacillariophyceae: Bunt 1965; Bunt et al. 1966; Chlorophyceae: Brown and Weis 1959; Hoch et al. 1963; Fock et al. 1980; Radmer and Ollinger 1980; Chrysophyceae: Weis and Brown 1959; Euglenophyceae: Gerster and Tournier 1977; Cyanophyceae (Cyanobacteria): Hoch et al. 1963; Owens and Hoch 1963; Lex et al. 1972; Radmer and Kok 1976). This light-stimulated O_2 uptake is underestimated by the tracer O_2 technique to the extent that O_2 is recycled between the O_2 evolution and O_2 uptake sites without becoming available to the sensor (mass spectrometer inlet) employed; this underestimate is the same in *absolute* terms for O_2 uptake and O_2 evolution, but the *fractional* underestimation is larger for the process of smaller magnitude, i.e. O_2 uptake.

This light-stimulated O_2 uptake in photosynthetically competent algae depends on the functioning of photosystem II: this is shown by studies of action spectra, photosynthetic mutants, and the effects of photosynthetic inhibitors (Govindjee et al. 1963; Hock et al. 1963; Owens and Hoch 1963; Radmer and Ollinger 1980). The involvement of photosystem one is likely, although studies of the "Emerson Enhancement Effect" (the classical method of demonstrating the involvement of two photosystems in plant photosynthesis) show negative rather than positive effects (Govindjee et al. 1963; Owens and Hoch 1963). These steady-state effects can be interpreted in terms of interactions of cyclic and pseudocyclic redox processes (see Glidewell and Raven 1975, 1976) and an involvement of photosystem one in the light-dependent O_2 uptake; this view is supported by net O_2 exchange phenomena under transient conditions (French and Fork 1960), and by analogy with studies on subcellular systems from higher plants (Elstner and Konze 1976; Foyer and Hall 1980).

In general the tracer O_2 uptake in the light exceeds that attributable to the sum of dark respiration and of RuBPo/PCOC activity. As will be seen later (see Table 1) the O_2 uptake capacity of dark respiration is relatively limited (especially in cyanobacteria and nonmotile eukaryotes), so even if this process were proceeding at its maximum rate in the light (cf. the blue light stimulation of algal respiration: Sargent and Taylor 1965) it could not account for the observed O_2 uptake rate in the light. The contribution of RuBPo/PCOC to this light-stimulated O_2 uptake is limited by the relatively high exogenous

TABLE 1. Comparison of some properties of the major O_2-consuming processes in phytoplankton organisms (data from Sargent and Taylor 1972; Radmer et al. 1978; Raven and Glidewell 1978; Palmer 1979; Badger 1980; Fock et al. 1981).

| | Oxygen-consuming reaction | | | |
Property	Mehler reaction (pseudocyclic electron flow)	RuBPo	Cytochrome oxidase	Alternate oxidase
V_{max} (catalytic capacity at substrate saturation)	$\leqslant V_{max}$ for gross oxygen evolution	≈ 0.15 of V_{max} for RuBPc or gross O_2 evolution	Typically 0.1 of V_{max} of gross O_2 evolution (range 0.02–0.3)	As for cytochrome oxidase, *but not additive with it*
$K_{\frac{1}{2}(O_2)}$, μM	100–150	500–1000	2	6
In vivo effect of full noncyclic chain[a]	Absolute requirement	Absolute requirement	Variable (inhibits or stimulates)	Variable (inhibits or stimulates)
Inhibition by HCN	No	Yes	Yes	No
Inhibition by substituted hydroxamic acids	(No)	(No)	No	Yes

[a] In organisms using H_2O as redox donor to photosynthesis rather than those adapted to H_2S or H_2.

CO_2 levels employed in many experiments (particularly the earlier ones), and by the occurrence of a "CO_2 concentrating mechanism" (see below) in algae grown at low CO_2 concentrations; these two factors together mean that RuBPo activity is considerably suppressed by the competitive inhibitor CO_2. Thus a substantial fraction of the observed light-stimulated O_2 uptake is most reasonably attributed to the Mehler reaction.

The extent of the Mehler reaction under natural conditions is probably substantially greater than that reported in many of the papers cited above as the half-saturation constant for O_2 is quite high and (for technical reasons) many of the earlier experiments used O_2 concentrations well below the $K_{\frac{1}{2}}$ for O_2 in the Mehler reaction. Recent estimates of the $K_{\frac{1}{2}}$ for O_2 uptake in algal cells (using tracer O_2) gave values of 8–11% and 12.5% O_2 in the gas phase for *Scenedesmus obliquus* and *Chlamydomonas reinhardtii*, respectively, corresponding to 100–150 μM in solution at 25°C (Radmer et al. 1978; Fock et al. 1981). These values were obtained under conditions in which RuBPo activity was only sufficient to account for a small fraction of the O_2 uptake, and the $K_{\frac{1}{2}}$ for O_2 in the light is much higher than that for dark respiration in algae via either the alternate oxidase (~ 6 μM) or cytochrome oxidase

(~ 2 μM) (Sargent and Taylor 1972; see Table 1). Thus we may attribute the great majority of the low-affinity O_2 uptake to a Mehler reaction in vivo. The low affinity found for these algae is consistent with the O_2 affinity in *Hydrodictyon africanum* for phosphate uptake energized ultimately by ATP from pseudocyclic photophosphorylation (Raven and Glidewell 1975a), but much higher affinities are found in isolated higher plant chloroplasts (e.g. Asada and Nakano 1978) for the Mehler reaction.

A major discrepancy exists between measurements conducted in different laboratories with respect to the magnitude of the Mehler reaction relative to gross photosynthetic O_2 evolution. Radmer and associates (Radmer and Kok 1976; Radmer et al. 1978; Radmer and Ollinger 1980) find that there is a constant gross O_2 evolution with varying CO_2 fixation rates, with any decrease in electron flow to CO_2 caused by limiting CO_2 concentration, or by inhibition of the PCRC, being compensated quantitatively by increased O_2 uptake. The O_2 uptake in the light varies from about 0.1 of gross O_2 evolution when the PCRC is operating at its maximum rate to 1.0 of gross O_2 evolution at the CO_2 compensation point or in the presence of PCRC inhibitors. By contrast, other recent work (Fock et al. 1981), in agreement with earlier results, shows that O_2 uptake in the light does not completely compensate for decreased PCRC activity as an electron sink, i.e. gross O_2 evolution falls as the rate of CO_2 fixation falls, and while O_2 uptake may increase at low CO_2 fixation rates it does not *quantitatively* compensate for the reduced availability of CO_2 as electron acceptor.

The reasons for these discrepancies are not clear; despite the large quantitative variation in the magnitude of the Mehler reaction estimated by different workers, it is possible to discuss the possible roles on this process under the headings proposed in the introduction.

Dealing first with running costs, there is evidence that the Mehler reaction is at least *facultatively* coupled to ATP synthesis in vivo (see Raven and Glidewell 1975a; Raven 1976a; Gimmler 1977). It is thus a possible contender (with cyclic photophosphorylation and oxidative phosphorylation) for the role of supplier of any "extra" ATP used in photosynthetic production of reduced carbon, and other ATP-requiring growth and maintenance processes in illuminated photosynthetic cells. By "extra" ATP is meant ATP in addition to that supplied by noncyclic photophosphorylation during the generation of the reductant for CO_2 fixation and for the reduction of NO_3^- and SO_4^{2-}. Current opinion (cf. Raven 1976a; Rosa 1979) seems to favor a P/e_2 ratio in noncyclic (and pseudocyclic) photophosphorylation of less than 1.5 (Kaplan et al. 1980b), so that "extra" ATP is needed even for carbohydrate production in "pure PCRC" photosynthesis when 3 ATP are needed per 4 electrons (2 NADPH) used in CO_2 reduction. If pseudocyclic ATP synthesis has a maximum quantum yield of 0.33 ATP/quantum (1.33 ATP/e_2, 2 quanta per electron), we can compare its efficiency with that of cyclic photophosphorylation and oxidative phosphorylation. If the H^+/e_2 in cyclic electron flow is 4, and 1 quantum absorbed by photosystem one moved 1 electron, an H^+/ATP of 3 in the ATP synthetase will give a maximum quantum yield of 0.67 ATP/quantum, in accord with in vivo data (Raven 1976a, 1980a, b; cf. Olsen et al. 1980). Oxidative phosphorylation yields (see below) 5.60 ATP per C (at the redox level of carbohydrate) oxidized, so with the minimum quantum requirement for CO_2 fixation of 8.5 quanta/CO_2 (3 ATP and 2 NADPH generated by a mixture of noncyclic and cyclic photophosphorylation), the maximum quantum yield is 0.66 ATP/quantum. Thus, granted optimal efficiency in coupling of ATP synthesis to redox reactions and in diverting excitation energy to the most needy photoreaction (Ried and Reinhardt 1980), it is clear that cyclic photophosphorylation and oxidative phosphorylation are each about twice as efficient as pseudocyclic photophosphorylation. The option of reoxidizing the reductant

generated in noncyclic photophosphorylation by the external pyridine nucleotide dehydrogenase of mitochondria (Fig. 5) with a P/e_2 of 2 in oxidative phosphorylation added to the P/e_2 of 1.33 in noncyclic photophosphorylation to give a quantum yield of 0.83 does not seem to have been realized in nature.

The inefficiency of pseudocyclic ATP generation may seem to militate against its occurrence during growth of algae under light-limiting conditions where it is often difficult to balance ATP and reductant requirements for growth with quantal input even with the most efficient mechanisms of energy conversion (Raven 1976a; cf. Pirt et al. 1980). However, there is considerable evidence that the Mehler reaction does occur under light-limiting conditions (e.g. Hoch et al. 1963; Fock et al. 1981) to an extent which could (granted complete coupling) supply much of the "extra" ATP needed for growth.

Turning to considerations of capital costs for the Mehler reaction, we may again compare its economics (as a means of generating "extra" ATP) with that of cyclic and oxidative phosphorylation. Because it has a quantum yield which may be only half of that of cyclic photophosphorylation, the generation of a certain quantity of ATP per unit time by cyclic photophosphorylation requires only half the investment in antenna chlorophyll, and in reaction centers, than does pseudocyclic photophosphorylation. Again, cyclic photophosphorylation appears to be superior under light-limiting conditions. The other alternative for the generation of "extra" ATP, i.e. oxidative phosphorylation following complete photosynthesis, seems even more inefficient with respect to capital investment than does pseudocyclic photophosphorylation, as all the mitochondrial machinery is needed as well as the thylakoid and stroma apparatus, thus doubling the cost of a given rate of ATP synthesis in terms of energy, C, or N invested (Raven 1976a, b, 1980a, b). However, as pointed out by Raven (1976a), if the ATP-using as well as the ATP-producing investments are considered, oxidative phosphorylation is less costly, as the ATP-using machinery can, in principle, be used over a full 24-h light–dark cycle when oxidative phosphorylation is the ATP source whereas the direct use of photophosphorylative ATP means that the ATP-consuming machinery is standing idle in the dark (cf. Foy et al. 1976; Foy and Smith 1980; van Liere et al. 1979).

The final point for consideration is that of safety; does the process under consideration produce toxic compounds which some other process is required to detoxify, or is the process itself a detoxifying procedure? For the Mehler reaction the answer seems to be "both"; it is involved with the potentially dangerous outcome of having more excitation energy supplied to the photochemical apparatus than can be used in the energy-requiring processes of growth and maintenance, and it can act as a sink for possibly dangerous accumulations of excited states of chlorophyll at the expense of generating toxic, partly H_2O_2). The "energy-sink" role of the Mehler reaction would, ideally, only come into play at irradiances in excess of those at which light is limiting the reduction of the essentials for growth and maintenance (when natural selection would favor strictly coupled electron flow in the Mehler reaction); at such supersaturating irradiances uncoupled pseudocyclic electron flow could act to dissipate excess excitation (in concert with enhanced excretion of organic products of photosynthesis related to an excess of photosynthetic rate over growth rate: Fogg 1975). The finding that the Mehler reaction increases in parallel with CO_2 fixation as the light intensity increases up to that required to saturate photosynthesis, and then continues to increase (in parallel with an increment of gross O_2 evolution) as irradiance is increased to values higher than those needed to saturate CO_2 fixation, is consistent with such an "energy-dissipating" role (Brown and Weis 1969; Weis and Brown 1959; Hoch et al. 1963; Fock et al. 1980). The findings of Radmer and co-workers concerning the quantitative replacement of CO_2 fixation by O_2 uptake in the Mehler reaction whenever the PCRC cannot operate at its maximal rate would constitute an effective energy sink under low-CO_2 conditions, and accordingly one would not expect photoinhibition to be manifested at irradiances similar to those required to saturate CO_2 fixation (under CO_2-saturating conditions), regardless of the CO_2 concentration. A similar argument applies to the "induction phase" of CO_2 fixation at a dark–light transition, when the high Mehler reaction rate could (if uncoupled) act as an energy sink in addition to supplying (if coupled) the "priming" ATP needed during induction (Radmer and Kok 1976). However, in cases in which this quantitative replacement of CO_2 uptake by O_2 uptake at low CO_2 concentrations does not occur, photoinhibition occurs at low CO_2 concentrations at an irradiance which does not photoinhibit at higher CO_2 concentrations (Fock et al. 1981), suggesting that the Mehler reaction is an imperfect energy sink under these conditions.

The other aspect of safety with respect to the Mehler reaction is its role in generating toxic O_2 radicals and H_2O_2; indeed, H_2O_2 production has been used as a (qualitative) indicator of Mehler reaction activity (Patterson and Myers 1973; cf. Radmer and Kok 1976). The generation of these toxic intermediates of the reduction of O_2 to H_2O is probably much more quantitatively significant in photosynthetic organisms than in other aerobic

organisms (on either a growth rate or a biomass basis), and their detoxification involves inter alia superoxide dismutase and catalase (Halliwell 1974; Elstner and Konze 1976; Foyer and Hall 1980).

A final aspect of the functioning of the Mehler reaction is the possibility that, in addition to catalyzing photophosphorylation, it can also have a regulatory role in "redox poising" and in permitting the optimal activity of the cyclic and noncyclic photophosphorylation pathways (see Ziem-Hanck and Heber 1980, for an up-to-date discussion of this hypothesis).

Glycolate Synthesis and Metabolism: Ribulose Bisphosphate Oxygenase and the Photorespiratory Carbon Oxidation Cycle

A major potential source of light-dependent O_2 uptake (and, to a lesser extent, CO_2 evolution) in illuminated photosynthetic cells is the synthesis and metabolism of glycolate (see Fig. 1). It is believed (see Lorimer and Andrews 1973; Andrews and Lorimer 1978; Somerville and Ogren 1979; Christen and Gasser 1980; Raven and Glidewell 1981) that the major pathway of glycolate synthesis in autotrophic organisms is via the oxygenase activity (RuBPo) of the major carboxylase, ribulose bisphosphate carboxylase-oxygenase (RuBPo, EC 4.1.1.39). This enzyme, in addition to catalyzing the carboxylase activity (RuBPc-o equation (1)):

(1) Ribulose-1,5-bisphosphate + CO_2 + H_2O
     $\rightarrow$ 2 (3-phosphoglyceric acid)

also catalyzes the oxygenase activity (RuBPo: equation (2)):

(2)   Ribulose-1,5-bisphosphate + O_2 $\rightarrow$
        3-phosphoglyceric acid +
        2-phosphoglycolic acid.

A report (Branden 1978) that the reactions shown in equations (1) and (2) are catalyzed by different enzymes has not been confirmed (McCurry et al. 1978).

The presence of RuBPo activity in phytoplankton organisms has been shown in two ways. One is the demonstration of the stoichiometry shown in equation (2) when extracted RuBPc-o from microalgae is incubated (after appropriate activation: Lorimer et al. 1977) with RuBP. This procedure has demonstrated RuBPo activity in RuBPc-o from members of the Bacillariophyceae (Beardall and Morris 1975), Chlorophyceae (Berry and Bowes 1973; Lord and Brown 1975; Berry et al. 1976; Nelson and Surzycki 1976a, b), Cyanophyceae (Okabe et al. 1979; Badger

1980), and Euglenophyceae (McFadden et al. 1979). In vivo demonstration of this activity can be investigated by the use of $^{18}O_2$: the reaction shown in equation (2) incorporates one O atom from O_2 into the carboxyl group of phosphoglycolate (and, after the action of phosphoglycolate phosphatase, of glycolate), the other O atom appearing in H_2O (Lorimer et al. 1973). Demonstration of a substantial enrichment of the carboxyl group of glycolate in ^{18}O during glycolate synthesis by illuminated algae in the presence of $^{18}O_2$ has been shown for members of the Chlorophyceae (Gerster and Tournier 1977; Lorimer et al. 1978b; Fock et al. personal communication) and Euglenophyceae (Dimon and Gerster 1976; Gerster and Tournier 1977). This in vivo demonstration of the role of RuBPo in glycolate synthesis fails to prove that RuBPo is the *unique* source of glycolate in microalgae for two reasons. One is that the enrichment of O in the carboxyl group of glycolate is never as high as it is in the $^{18}O_2$ supplied; this can be accounted for by dilution of the $^{18}O_2$ at the site of RuBPo activity by photosynthetic $^{16}O_2$ (Dimon and Gerster 1976; Lorimer et al. 1978b). The other problem is that it is implicitly assumed that RuBPo is the only mechanism of glycolate synthesis which leads to ^{18}O incorporation from $^{18}O_2$; while no other in vitro pathway shows substantial ^{18}O enrichment in glycolate (Lorimer et al. 1978b), Gerster and Tournier (1977) showed that ^{18}O from $^{18}O_2$ is still found in glycolate synthesized by *Chlorella* and *Euglena* in the presence of 1 mM KCN which might be expected to completely inhibit both the carboxylase and oxygenase activities of RuBPc-o (see Glidewell and Raven 1975, 1976; cf. Vennesland and Jetschmann 1976).

The data reviewed above are consistent with a large fraction of glycolate synthesis being a result of RuBPo activity in microalgae. Thus we may expect an (as yet unquantified) contribution of RuBPo to the total O_2 uptake in illuminated algae. Further O_2 uptake, and some CO_2 evolution, can result from the further metabolism of glycolate (Fig. 1, 2, and 3). Enzymic and in vivo labeling data support a role for the pathway (photosynthetic carbon oxidation cycle or PCOC) shown in Fig. 2 in glycolate metabolism in members of the Bacillariophyceae (Paul and Volcani 1976b; Burris 1977; Coughlan 1977), Chlorophyceae (Pritchard et al. 1961, 1963; Lord and Merrett 1970; Tolbert 1974; Burris 1977) and Euglenophyceae (Codd and Merrett 1971a, b). In some members of the Chlorophyceae (Badour and Waygood 1971a, b, 1972) there is enzymic and tracer evidence for the pathway shown in Fig. 3, involving glyoxylate carboligase and tartronic semialdehyde. The enzymes of this pathway are also present in members of the Bacillariophyceae (Paul and Volcani 1976b), although tracer

evidence for this pathway is not, as yet, available for these algae. In the Cyanophyceae the enzymes of the pathway shown in Fig. 2 are present, albeit at low activity (Codd and Stewart 1973); enzymic and inhibitor evidence, however, favors a major role for the pathway shown in Fig. 3 (Codd and Stewart 1973, 1974; Grodzinski and Colman 1975).

A number of comments about the pathways shown in Fig. 2 and 3 must be made briefly before the quantitative significance of glycolate synthesis and metabolism in relation to the running costs, capital costs, and safety of algal growth are considered.

1) The enzyme which catalyzes the oxidation of glycolate to glyoxylate is, in most algae, a glycolate dehydrogenase rather than the glycolate oxidase found in bryophytes and tracheophytes and their green algal (charophyte) ancestors. Glycolate dehydrogenase is the characteristic glycolate-oxidizing enzyme of the Bacillariophyceae (Paul and Volcani 1974, 1975; Paul et al. 1975), Chlorophyceae (Frederick et al. 1973; Gruber et al. 1974; Stewart and Mattox 1975; Floyd and Salisbury 1977; cf. Codd and Schmid 1972; Bullock et al. 1979), Cyanophyceae (Codd and Stewart 1973, 1974; Codd and Sellal 1978), and Euglenophyceae (Codd and Merrett 1971a, b). Glycolate dehydrogenase is a membrane-associated enzyme. In the prokaryotic cyanobacteria it is associated with the thylakoid membranes (Codd and Sellal 1978), while in the eukaryotes it is associated with the inner mitochondrial membrane (Stabenau 1974a, b; Paul et al. 1975; Paul and Volcani 1976a), although there is also glycolate dehydrogenase activity associated with microbodies in *Euglena* (Collins and Merrett 1975). The oxidation of glycolate via the dehydrogenase can lead to ATP synthesis via the "sites" between UQ and O_2 (Collins and Merrett 1975; Paul and Volcani 1975, 1976a; Paul et al. 1975). The magnitude of this ATP synthesis for the energetics of algae is indicated in Table 2. The Charophyceae sensu lato have glycolate oxidase in microbodies; this direct coupling to O_2 precludes coupled ATP synthesis (Stewart and Mattox 1975; Stabenau 1975, 1980).

2) It is likely that there is some "leakage" from the pathways shown in Fig. 2 and via additional CO_2 release as some glyoxylate is oxidized (by glycolate oxidase/dehydrogenase, or by H_2O_2) to CO_2 plus formate, or to CO_2 alone (Halliwell 1978; Grodzinski 1979).

3) The glycine to serine step (Fig. 2) occurs in the mitochondria of eukaryotes; the NADH generated in this step is shown in Fig. 2 as being oxidized by the mitochondrial electron transport pathway with ATP generation. The NADH generated in this way probably cannot be used to reassimilate the NH_3 also released in the glycine to serine step within

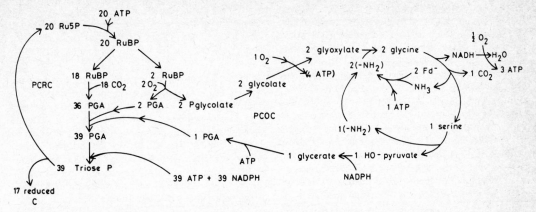

FIG. 2. Integrated PCRC/PCOC cycle for a RuBPc/RuBPo ratio of 9. With the in vitro RuBPc-o kinetics measured for *Anabaena variabilis* by Badger (1980), a RuBPc/ruBPo ratio of 9 could be achieved at 25°C (using equation (3)) if the "CO_2 concentrating mechanism" can maintain a steady-state intracellular CO_2 concentration of 67 μM; this is consistent with the data of Kaplan et al. (1980a). Per turn of the integrated cycle, there is a net fixation of 17 CO_2 (18 gross CO_2 fixed by RuBPc, 1 CO_2 produced in the PCOC), 17 O_2 are evolved (20.5 gross O_2 evolved in reductant generation for PCRC/PCOC, in 3.5 O_2 taken up in RuBPo/PCOC); 17 reduced C at the level of carbohydrate are produced. The energetics of this cycle, and of variants on it, are given in Table 2.

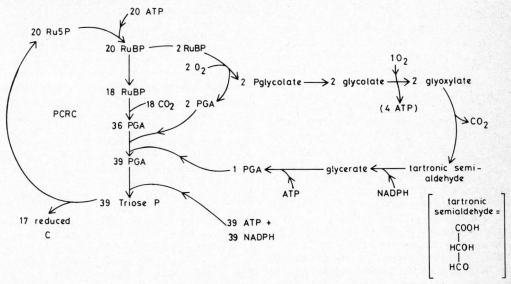

FIG. 3. Integrated PCRC/tartronic semialdehyde cycle for a RuBPc/RuBPo ratio of 9. The role of the "CO_2 concentrating mechanism" in bringing about a RuBPc/RuBPo of 9 is discussed in the caption of Fig. 2. Per turn of the integrated cycle, there is a net fixation of 17 CO_2 (18 gross CO_2 fixed by RuBPc, 1 CO_2 produced in the tartronic semi-aldehyde cycle); 17 O_2 are evolved (20 gross O_2 evolved in reductant generation for the PCRC/tartronic semialdehyde cycle, 3 O_2 taken up in RuBPo and glycolate oxidation); 17 reduced C at the level of carbohydrate are produced. The energetics of this cycle, and of variants on it, are given in Table 2.

the mitochondria as the glutamate dehydrogenase (at least in higher plants) in the mitochondria is very poor at glutamate synthesis (Hartmann and Ehmke 1980). It is more likely that ammonia assimilation occurs in the plastids, using the glutamine synthetase (GS) glutamate synthetase (GOGAT) pathway (Keys et al. 1978) and photoproduced ferredoxin as reductant for glutamate synthetase. The feasability of using the NADH generated in the glycine to serine step in the mitochondria in generating plastid reductant, via dicarboxylate shuttles at the mitochondrial inner membrane and the inner chloroplast envelope membrane, is questionable on thermodynamic grounds (cf. Krebs and Veech 1969; Woo and Osmond 1976; Moore et al. 1977; Wiskich 1977; Heber and Walker 1979). Few data are available for microalgae in this respect (cf. Syrett 1981).

4) The activity of the enzymes of the pathway of Fig. 2 are, in several members of the Chlorophyceae and *Euglena*, much higher when the algae are grown under "natural" concentrations of CO_2 (close to air equilibrium) rather than in air supplemented with 0.5–5% CO_2 (Pritchard et al. 1961, 1963; Nelson and Tolbert 1969; Lord and Merrett 1971; Stabenau 1977). The derepression of these enzymes is paralleled by increases in the activity of carbonic anhydrase and of catalase (Nelson et al. 1969; Graham and Reed 1971; Reed and Graham 1977; Stabenau 1977; cf. Kaplan et al. 1980a).

5) The operation of the pathway shown in Fig. 2 in eukaryotes involves the cooperation of a number of organelles. In bryophytes and tracheophytes the conversion of phosphoglycolate to glycolate, and the phosphorylation of glycerate, occurs in the chloroplasts; glycolate is converted to glycine, and serine is converted to glycerate, in the microbodies (peroxisomes); the glycine to serine conversion occurs in the mitochondria (Tolbert 1974). This distribution of the reactions is also found in those (charophyte) green algae which are the probable ancestors of the higher plants and which have glycolate oxidase rather than glycolate dehydrogenase (Stabenau 1975, 1980), although some of the microbody enzymes (e.g. hydroxypyruvate reductase and catalase, but not glycolate oxidase) are also found in an organelle distinct from the microbody. In the eukaryotic algae which possess glycolate dehydrogenase the entire sequence from glycolate to glycerate probably occurs in the mitochondria (Stabenau 1974a, b; Paul and Volcani 1975, 1976b; Paul et al. 1975), although some of the hydroxypuruvate reductase activity seems to be in the soluble fraction of cell extracts (Stabenau 1975, 1980).

In prokaryotes (Cyanophyceae) the pathway shown in Fig. 2 or, more significantly, that in Fig. 3, probably has glycolate dehydrogenase as the only membrane associated enzyme, the rest being free in the cytosol. In the eukaryotic microalgae the location of the glyoxylate to glycerate portion of the tartronic semialdehyde pathway (Fig. 3) is not clear.

6) The tartronic semialdehyde pathway (Fig. 3) seems to have considerable economy of capital investment compared with the glycine–serine pathway (Fig. 2); it is not clear what selective advantage the more cumbersome glycine–serine pathway might have which causes its dominance, at least in the higher plants. Tartronic semialdehyde has been characterized as an extracellular product in some algae (Badour and Waygood 1971b), and the occurrence of a "leaky" intermediate (in addition to glycolate and glyoxylate: Stewart and Codd 1980)

may be disadvantageous. However, there seems to be no good reason why tartronic semialdehyde should leak more than its isomer, hydroxypyruvate, which is an intermediate of the glycine–serine pathway (Fig. 2).

Having considered the biochemical potential of microalgae to synthesize and to metabolize glycolate by pathways which consume O_2 and generate CO_2, we now turn to a consideration of the extent to which these pathways function in these organisms. Starting with RuBPc-o, it is possible to predict the ratio of RuBPc to RuBPo activity at a given ratio of the concentrations of the mutually competitive substrates, O_2 and CO_2, using a relationship derived by Laing et al. (1974), equation (3):

$$(3) \qquad \frac{v_o}{v_c} = \frac{V_o}{V_c} \cdot \frac{K_c}{K_o} \cdot \frac{[O_2]}{[CO_2]}$$

where v_o and v_c are the achieved rates of RuBPo and RuBPc (measured in terms of specific reaction rates, s^{-1}, or other suitable units) at the O_2 and CO_2 concentrations prevailing at the site of RuBPc-o, respectively, V_o and V_c are the maximal rates of RuBPo (at saturating O_2) and RuBPc (at saturating CO_2), respectively, and K_c and K_o are the values of $K_{\frac{1}{2}}$ ($\approx K_i$) for the mutually competitive alternative substrates CO_2 and O_2, respectively.

Application of equation (3) to a number of C_3 higher plants for which the relevant data (net CO_2 exchange rates as a function of leaf intercellular space CO_2 and O_2 concentrations, and the in vitro kinetic characteristics of RuBPc-o) are available shows that much of the gas exchange characteristics can be explained in terms of the kinetics of RuBPc-o, assuming that the phosphoglycolate generated by RuBPo is metabolized as shown in Fig. 2 (Laing et al. 1974; Lorimer et al. 1978a; Farquhar et al. 1980; Raven and Glidewell 1981). Among the quantities predicted are the net CO_2 fixation rate in air, the stimulation of net CO_2 fixation at air levels of CO_2 by reducing O_2 to 1% or less (by increasing gross photosynthesis v_c when the competing O_2 is removed, and by decreasing CO_2 loss in the PCOC which is running at a much reduced rate corresponding to a much reduced v_o and hence much slower glycolate synthesis), and the magnitude of the CO_2 compensation concentration (the CO_2 concentration at which no net CO_2 exchange occurs and (ignoring dark respiration) $v_o = 2v_c$).

The only case in microalgae in which such a good fit between RuBPc-o kinetics in vitro and gas exchange and glycolate excretion data obtained in vivo has been obtained is that of *Chlamydomonas reinhardtii* grown at high CO_2 concentrations (Berry and Bowes 1973). Ogawara et al. (1980) found that the O_2 inhibition of growth in *Chlorella vulgaris* grown in the light with 1.0–2.4% CO_2 and 65% O_2 could be explained in terms of the competition between RuBPc and RuBPo (equation (3)) using the kinetic constants for higher plant RuBPc-o; however, as we shall see, the kinetics of the algal enzyme are not identical with those of the higher plant enzyme.

When we consider algae grown at "normal" CO_2 concentrations (i.e. a concentration in solution close to that in equilibrium with air, and thus relevant to the vast majority of limnological and oceanographic situations) a very different picture emerges. One striking observation is that, although the $K_{\frac{1}{2}CO_2}$ for the algal enzyme is *higher* than that for the higher plant enzyme, the $K_{\frac{1}{2}CO_2}$ in vivo is lower in air-grown algae than in higher plants; this difference between the $K_{\frac{1}{2}}$ values in vivo and in vitro in air-grown algae cannot be explained in terms of a large excess of the enzyme in the air-grown algae (Whittingham 1952; Bidwell 1977; Hogetsu and Miyachi 1977, 1979; Lloyd et al. 1977; Badger et al. 1978; Findenegg and Fischer 1978; Badger 1980; Coleman and Colman 1980a; Shelp and Canvin 1980a, b; Beardall and Raven 1981).

Another discrepancy between the in vivo and in vitro activities of the algal RuBPc-o in air-grown cells lies in the effect of changing O_2 concentrations from 21 to 1% or less; the stimulation of net photosynthesis is much smaller than is the case for C_3 terrestrial plants (Brown and Tregunna 1967; Bunt 1971; Beardall and Morris 1975; Beardall et al. 1976; Bidwell 1977; Lloyd et al. 1977; Coleman and Colman 1980a; Shelp and Canvin 1980a, b). Furthermore, the extent of CO_2 loss to CO_2-free air in the light is smaller than would be expected from equation (3) and the operation of the PCOC, provided techniques are used which do not lead to artifacts due to varying specific activities of the substrate for CO_2 production in tracer experiments (Bidwell 1977; Findenegg and Fischer 1978; Coleman and Colman 1980a). Finally, the CO_2 compensation concentration is much lower than equation (3) would predict, especially if the occurrence of dark respiration in the light is taken into account. Equation (3) applied to the in vitro kinetic data of Badger (1980) gives an estimated CO_2 compensation concentration ($v_c = 2v_o$, with PCOC) of some 4 μM for *Anabaena variabilis* in 21% O_2 at 25°C, while the measured CO_2 compensation concentrations in air-grown algae are generally 0.1–1.0 μM at pH 7 (Egle and Schenk 1952; Brown and Tregunna 1967; Bidwell 1977; Lloyd et al. 1977; Findenegg and Fischer 1978; Birmingham and Colman 1979; Shelp and Canvin 1980a, b).

These characteristics of air-grown algae resemble those of C_4 higher plants (see Raven and Glidewell 1978), where substantial suppression of RuBPo activity and enhancement of RuBPc activity is achieved by the operation of a "CO_2 pump" based on an auxilliary carboxylation of PEP and a C_4 acid cycle combined with specialized leaf anatomy. Although enhanced β-carboxylation has been suggested in some instances (Beardall et al. 1976; Appleby et al. 1980), the algae which show this "C_4-like" physiology generally have clear-cut C_3 biochemistry, i.e. RuBPc-o catalyzes the primary conversion of inorganic to organic C (Raven and Glidewell 1978; Coleman and Colman 1980b; Raven 1980a). We feel that the most plausible explanation of the "C_4 gas exchange but C_3 biochemistry" paradox lies in the occurrence of a "CO_2 concentrating mechanism" in many air-adapted algae. This is based on the active influx of some inorganic C species at some membrane between the bulk medium which supplies the inorganic C and the chloroplast stroma (eukaryotes) or the cytosol (cyanophytes) in which RuBPc-o fixes CO_2.

Direct evidence for such a "CO_2-concentrating mechanism" has been obtained for *Chlamydomonas reinhardtii* (Badger et al. 1977, 1978, 1980; Spalding and Ogren 1980), *Anabaena variabilis* (Badger et al. 1978; Kaplan et al. 1980a), *Dunaliella salina* (Zenvirt et al. 1980), and *Chlorella emersonii* (Beardall and Raven 1981). All of these experiments are based on estimations of the intracellular free inorganic C pool in photosynthesizing algal cells using a silicone oil centrifugation technique, and they all show that air-grown cells have a greater ratio of intracellular to extracellular inorganic C than can be accounted for by diffusive equilibration of CO_2 between medium and cells, taking the (measured) pH of the two compartments into account. The extent of accumulation in *Anabaena variabilis* is much higher than in the chlorophytes; this may reflect the absence of carbonic anhydrase in *A. variabilis* (Kaplan et al. 1980a) because if HCO_3^- is the transported inorganic carbon species, a high intracellular concentration is required to give a sufficiently high rate of (uncatalyzed) conversion to CO_2 to explain the observed rate of CO_2 fixation. In the chlorophytes with their relatively high carbonic anhydrase activity the HCO_3^-–CO_2 system is closer to equilibrium, and less intracellular HCO_3^- is needed in the steady state to maintain the CO_2 level. It thus appears that the actively maintained inorganic carbon pool is an essential intermediate in "C_4-like" photosynthesis in the air-grown algae and can account for the in vivo activities of RuBPc and RuBPo in terms of the in vivo CO_2 and O_2 concentrations, and the in vitro RuBPc-o kinetics (despite uncertainties as to the barrier behind which the accumulation occurs in eukaryote cells). The occurrence of this inorganic carbon pool to which "leaked" CO_2 is rapidly returned (see below) is likely to complicate the interpretation of "pulse-

TABLE 2. Energetics of photosynthesis: Required input of reductant and ATP from "light reactions" per C fixed into useful compounds under various conditions of operation of the "CO_2 concentration mechanism" and of pathways of glycolate metabolism. The operation of the "CO_2 concentrating mechanism" is assumed to require 3 ATP per net inorganic C transported; the kinetics of RuBP-co are assumed to be those described by Badger (1980) for *Anabaena variabilis*.

	Gas phase	Pathway of glycolate metabolism	Operation of "CO_2 concentrating mechanism"	(H)/C fixed	ATP/C fixed
(1)	CO_2/O_2 sufficient to suppress RuBPo	Not produced	No	4	3
(2)	Air	Not metabolized	Yes; $[CO_2]_i$ 67 μM[c]	5.4	7.1
(3)[a]	Air	PCOC/glyc dh, GS-GOGAT, NADH ox[b, d]	Yes; $[CO_2]_i$ 67 μM	4.8	6.1
(4)[a]	Air	PCOC/glyc ox, GS-GOGAT, NADH ox[b, d]	Yes; $[CO_2]_i$ 67 μM	4.8	6.4
(5)[a]	Air	PCOC/glyc dh, GS-GOGAT, NADH exp[b, d]	Yes; $[CO_2]_i$ 67 μM	4.7	6.3
(6)[a]	Air	Tartronic semi-aldehyde/glyc dh	Yes; $[CO_2]_i$ 67 μM	4.7	6.3
(7)	Air	Tartronic semi-aldehyde/glyc ox	Yes; $[CO_2]_i$ 67 μM	4.7	6.5
(8)[a]	Air	PCOC/glyc dh, GS-GOGAT, NADH ox[b, d]	No	12.5	4.5
(9)	Air	PCOC/glyc ox, GS-GOGAT, NADH exp[b, d]	No	11.3	8.5
(10)	Air	Not metabolized	No	No net CO_2 fixation	

[a]The rates of oxidative phosphorylation required for condition (8) are too high to be supported by the respiratory capacity of most phototrophic cells (see Table 1). The other rates of oxidative phosphorylation (conditions (3), (4), (5), (6)) are within the capacity of most phototrophic cells (Table 1).

[b]NADH ox means NADH produced in glycine to serine conversion oxidized with coupled ATP synthesis; NADH exp means this NADH is exported and used to support other reductive synthesis.

[c]The $[CO_2]$ to give a v_c/v_o ratio of 9.

[d]GS-GOGAT = glutamine synthetase–glutamine oxoglutarate aminotransferase.

chase" experiments designed to see if β-carboxylation, and decarboxylation of C_4 dicarboxylic acids, is an obligate reaction in net CO_2 fixation in photosynthesis by certain phytoplankters (see Raven 1980a).

Our inability to extract functional chloroplasts from the eukaryotic algae which exhibit the "CO_2 concentrating mechanism" means that the inorganic C species which is actively transported, as well as the membrane at which the transport occurs, is not clear. Even in the Cyanophyceae the situation is complicated by the occurrence of the typical gram-negative outer membrane which is not involved in active transport but which may influence experiments designed to determine whether CO_2 or HCO_3^- is the species transported across the plasmalemma (Beardall and Raven 1981). Data reviewed by Raven

(1980a) and Beardall and Raven (1981) suggest that the "CO_2 concentrating mechanism" can be manifested regardless of whether CO_2 or HCO_3^- is the species crossing the outer permeability barrier (outer membrane of Cyanophyceae, plasmalemma of eukaryotes). Further, experiments with the lipid-soluble cation tetraphenyl phosphonium (TPP^+) show that the inside-negative electrical potential difference across some membrane becomes more negative when cells in which the "CO_2 concentrating mechanism" is de-repressed are supplied with the inorganic C substrate for this transport mechanism; this has been shown for *Chlorella emersonii* (Beardall and Raven 1981) and for *Anabaena variabilis* (A. Kaplan personal communication). The most economical explanation of these findings involves a primary, electrogenic influx of HCO_3^- at the plasmalemma of the cyanophyte (A. Kaplan personal communication) and at the (?) inner membrane of the chloroplast envelope of the chlorophyte (Beardall and Raven 1981).

We may conclude that most of the apparent C_4-like photosynthetic characteristics which are exhibited to a greater or lesser extent by air-grown microalgae can be accounted for by the de-repression of the "CO_2 concentrating mechanism" with consequent suppression of RuBPo activity (see Table 2). This has been elegantly demonstrated by Fock et al. (1981) for *Chlamydomonas reinhardtii* using $^{18}O_2$: air-grown cells show very little incorporation of ^{18}O into glycolate, glycine, or serine, and the substantial light-stimulated $^{18}O_2$ uptake is very largely attributable to the Mehler reaction with a contribution from dark respiration (see above). Cells grown in high CO_2 show substantial ^{18}O labeling of glycolate when exposed to $^{18}O_2$-labeled air; these high CO_2 grown cells had not had time to de-repress their CO_2 concentrating mechanism (H. P. Fock personal communication).

To conclude our consideration of glycolate metabolism, the PCOC and RuBPc in relation to photorespiration in algae, we may consider the effect of these pathways on running costs, capital costs, and safety in microalgae.

Dealing first with running costs, it is clear that the energy input per unit reduced C produced is higher when RuPBo is operative than when it is not (Table 2); this is related to the energy costs of glycolate synthesis and of "scavenging" the glycolate back to some more useful compound via the PCOC (where present) and, a fortiori, to the costs of glycolate synthesis when glycolate is excreted rather than scavenged. These energy costs are fairly readily quantified (Table 2); what is less readily quantified is the energy cost of the "CO_2 concentrating mechanism" which (by favoring RuBPc over RuBPo) can spare much of the cost of glycolate synthesis and metabolism in air-grown algae. Raven (1980a) has computed an ATP requirement of 3/net CO_2 fixed for active transport of inorganic C in a microalgal cell, allowing for leakage through a barrier with $P_{CO_2} = 10^{-3}$ cm·s^{-1}; this is close to the P_{CO_2} determined by compartmental analysis in *Dunaliella salina* (D. Zenvirt and A. Kaplan personal communication). Experimental determinations of the quantum requirements for net CO_2 fixation in high — and low — CO_2-grown microalgae do not show very large differences (Shelp and Canvin 1980a; A. Kaplan personal communication). Further work is needed to quantify the running costs of the "CO_2 concentrating mechanism' vis a vis that of the RuBPo (with or without the PCOC) which would be incurred in the absence of the "CO_2 concentrating mechanism" under similar (air-equilibrium) CO_2 and O_2 concentrations.

Turning to capital costs, the CO_2-grown alga has minimal ancillary catalysts for carbon assimilation — the carbonic anhydrase, PCOC and "CO_2 concentrating mechanism" activities are minimal (see above, and Badger et al. 1977, 1978; Kaplan et al. 1980a; Beardall and Raven 1981). Under low CO_2 conditions these various accessory pathways are de-repressed (thus increasing the capital costs per unit C fixed) without any saving in terms of lowered levels of PCRC enzymes and, in particular, the very energy — and N — expensive RuBPc-o (Raven 1977, 1980a; Reed and Graham 1977; Badger et al. 1977, 1978; Hogetsu and Miyachi 1979; Kaplan et al. 1980a). This makes the hypothesis of Brown (1978) for terrestrial C_4 plants (i.e. that the energetic and, particularly, the N cost of producing the ancillary C_4 machinery is more than outweighed by the savings in the quantity of RuBPc and PCOC enzymes needed for unit C fixation) less readily applicable to microalgae with "C_4-like" physiology. How the capital costs of the "CO_2 accumulating mechanism" compare with those of the additional PCOC enzymes which would be required in the absence of this mechanism awaits further elucidation of the mechanism of "CO_2 accumulation."

Finally we turn to safety. RuBPo per se is not a good thing for a plant to possess in a high O_2 environment — witness the lethality of a *Chlamydomonas* mutation which has a higher than wild-type ratio of RuBPo to RuBPc when attempts are made to grow the organism at normal O_2 levels in the light (Nelson and Surzycki 1976a, b), and of the (higher plant) *Arabidopsis* mutants lacking phosphoglycolate phosphatase or serine-glyoxylate aminotransferase (Somerville and Ogren 1979, 1980) grown in 21% O_2 and with less than 1% CO_2. Justification for RuBPo activity in terms of the synthesis of glycine and serine in the PCRC is difficult in view of alternative pathways to these amino acids (Tolbert 1974). The major "use" for RuBPo, and the associated PCRC, seems to be as a means of energy dissipation when the rate of light absorption exceeds the rate at which energy can be used in C fixation by the PCRC, i.e. at low CO_2/O_2 ratios. Despite the relatively small fraction of light energy absorbed by a cell exposed to full sunlight which can be processed via the RuBPo–PCOC/RuBPc–PCRC pathways at the CO_2 compensation concentration, there is good empirical evidence of the efficacy of the pathway in C_3 land plants (Powles 1979; Heber and Krause 1980). The extent to which microalgae with a functional "CO_2 concentrating mechanism" can dissipate excess light energy at the CO_2 compensation concentration depends inter alia on the degree to which RuBPo is suppressed, and the "leakiness" of the inorganic C pump; Fock et al. (1981) find that photoinhibition rapidly sets in when air-grown

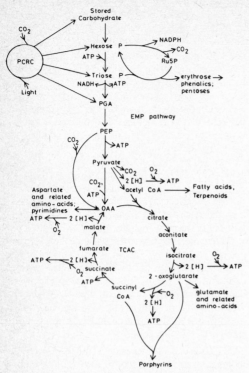

FIG. 4. The major "dark" respiratory processes in aerobic phototrophs, together with their major products.

NOTES: (1) The oxidative pentose phosphate pathway provides NADPH for reductive biosynthesis (and, in some obligate photolithotrophs with an incomplete TCAC, NADPH for oxidative phosphorylation); its role in generating C_4 and C_5 biosynthetic C skeletons can occur via the regenerative part of the cycle working alone (i.e. without the oxidative steps, or the reductive steps of the PCRC) (Raven 1972a, b; Raven 1976a). (2) The glycolytic pathway is probably the major pathway from sugar to pyruvate in phytoplankters other than the cyanobacteria, where a low activity of phosphofructokinase may mean an increased role for the oxidative PPP. (3) The TCAC, when complete (as is probably the case in most phytoplankters, including all facultative heterotrophs and some obligate photolithotrophs), has an important role in generating reductant for oxidative phosphorylation as well as in generation of C skeletons for biosynthesis. When the cycle is incomplete (as in some obligate photolithotrophs) the net generation of reductant is related stoichiometrically to the generation of biosynthetic C skeletons (reductant generated in right-hand limb *minus* reductant consumed in the left-hand limb). The relative operation of these limbs in producing a cell of a given composition depends on the pathway by which porphyrins are synthesized: the "classical" route involves the use of succinate and glycine to generate δ-aminolaevulinic acid, while the "C_5" route makes use of 2-oxoglutarate; the latter pathway predominates in most O_2-evolvers, particularly for chlorophyll synthesis (Beale 1978; Troxler and Offner 1979). (4) The biosynthetic use of the TCAC requires a net input of C_4 acids, achieved *either* by anaplerotic CO_2 fixation

Chlamydomonas is maintained under photosynthesis-saturating irradiances at the CO_2 compensation concentration. Sayre and Homann (1979) suggest that hydrogenase-mediated H_2 evolution may be a significant alternative route for the dissipation of excess excitation energy in microalgae with an efficient "CO_2 concentrating mechanism"; if such a mechanism is present in the strain of *Chlamydomonas* used by Fock et al. (1981) it is not very effective! In conclusion we concur with Andrews and Lorimer (1978) in regarding RuBPo as a necessary concomitant of CO_2 fixation by RuBPc-o in an air-equilibrated solution, and view the various mechanisms which have been described for suppressing RuBPo activity (C_4-like metabolism) or dealing with the glycolate produced (C_3-like metabolism) as representing the best selective compromise for a given organism between the various considerations of minimizing running costs and capital costs per unit growth or per unit maintenance which is consistent with the safe operation of the metabolic machinery.

Dark Respiration

INTRODUCTION

"Dark respiration" subsumes a heterogeneous collection of metabolic processes. The major components are shown in Fig. 1 and 4. The "core" of carbohydrate catabolism is the glycolytic (EMP) pathway; running partly in parallel with the glycolytic pathway is the oxidative pentose phosphate pathway, while the TCAC (Krebs cycle) is in series with glycolysis. These various processes make three major contributions to the economy of the cell, as follows (Davies et al. 1964; Beevers 1970; ap Rees 1974).

1) By providing ATP for biochemical and biophysical growth and maintenance processes. The ATP is generated in substrate-level phosphorylations in the glycolytic and TCAC pathways, and, in much larger quantities in the aerobic cell, by membrane-associated oxidative phosphorylation using reductant generated by dehydrogenases acting on organic substrates.

($C_1 + C_3$) as shown (Appleby et al. 1980) *or* by a glyoxylate cycle; this latter could overcome the restriction on reductant supply from organic acid metabolism imposed by an incomplete TCAC (Whittenbury and Kelly 1977) as well as permitting total cell synthesis from 2C compounds. (5) Recent work suggests that the "classical" oxidative PPP as portrayed in textbooks is wrong, and that a more complex variant involving octuloses is used (Mujaji 1980). (6) The CO_2 production related to C skeleton synthesis for growth is some 0.1–0.15 CO_2 per net C assimilated (Raven 1972a, b; 1976a, b).

2) By providing reductant, mainly as NADPH from the oxidative PPP, for reductive biosynthesis, e.g. the reduction of nitrate and nitrite.
3) As the "core" of metabolism, yielding essential C skeletons for biosynthesis.

Of these products, (1) and (2) are susceptible to being supplemented, or even replaced, by the direct use of the light (thylakoid) reactions of photosynthesis (ATP, NADPH/reduced ferredoxin: Raven 1971, 1972a, b, 1976a, b). This option is, of course, only open to photosynthetically competent cells in the light; nonphotosynthetic cells growing heterotrophically must obtain their ATP and reductant from the respiratory processes. Certain of the C skeletons mentioned under (3) are unique to "respiratory" processes, and cannot be generated in "photosynthetic" reactions. This applies particularly to the lower portion of glycolysis and to the TCAC (except for such (nonalgal) phototrophs as the Chlorobineae which may use a reversed, reductive TCAC in photosynthetic C fixation (Benedict 1978)).

LOCATION, STOICHIOMETRY, AND VARIABILITY OF THE PATHWAYS

The location within the photosynthetic eukaryotic cell of "dark" respiratory reactions has been discussed by Raven (1976a). Summarizing and bringing this information up to date, the entire EMP sequence is present in the cytosol; by comparison with higher plants the hexose phosphate-3PGA portion of the EMP pathway is probably also present in the plastids of green (chlorophyte and charophyte) algae (Stitt and ap Rees 1979). This is probably related to the storage of starch in these plastids; no other major taxon of algae, even the chlorophyll b containing Euglenophyceae, stores polysaccharide in the plastids, and such plastids may well lack those glycolytic enzymes not common to photosynthesis. The same may be true of the oxidative PPP; the enzymes (dehydrogenases) specific to this pathway are absent from the plastids of *Euglena*, but are probably present in the plastids of chlorophyte and charophyte algae as well as higher plants (Smillie 1963; Stitt and ap Rees 1979, 1980). The implications of the presence or absence of polysaccharide storage in the plastids for the location of enzymes of hexose metabolism should, perhaps, be reconsidered in relation to osmoregulation and the need for "compatible solutes" (often identical with the main soluble carbohydrate reserve) to occur within the plastids as well as in the cytosol if the relative volumes of these compartments are to be maintained at different internal osmolarities. The TCAC enzymes are located in the mitochondrial matrix, while the catalysts of oxidative phosphorylation are associated with the inner mitochondrial membrane (Lloyd 1974a, b; Lloyd and Turner 1980); see Fig. 5 and 6.

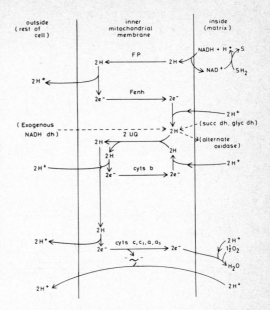

FIG. 5. The mitochondrial H$^+$-transporting redox chain. The chain represented here has a proton-translocating "loop" associated with the (endogenous) NADH to UQ step (Lawford and Garland 1972), a "proton-motive Q cycle" (Mitchell 1976), and a "conformational" (as opposed to a redox-loop) H$^+$ transport site associated with cytochrome oxidase (Wikstrom and Krab 1979; cf. Moyle and Mitchell 1978a). These mechanisms give a stoichiometry of 8 H$^+$ transported per 2e moving from NADH to O$_2$, as found by Brand et al. (1978) (cf. Moyle and Mitchell 1978b). Most of the evidence as to mechanisms and stoichiometry has been obtained with mammalian and fungal mitochondria; the specifically "plant" features have been best investigated on higher plant and fungal mitochondria (e.g. the NADHdh for exogenous NADH, and the alternate oxidase; Palmer 1979). The "alternate oxidase" represents a "physiological uncoupling" which has a very different mechanism from that found in vertebrates (Nicholls 1979), but which has a very similar end result and control mechanism (Sharpless and Buetow 1970; Nicholls 1979; Vanderleyden et al. 1980a, b). (dh = dehydrogenase)

The Cyanophyceae have the enzymes of the EMP pathway (often with low activity of phosphofructokinase), the oxidative PPP, and the TCAC (but without 2-oxoglutarate dehydrogenase) in the cytosol (Raven 1972a, b; Whittenbury and Kelly 1977). Oxidative phosphorylation is, of course, associated with membranes. Peschek (1980) has recently shown that the cell membrane of *Anacystis nidulans* cells which had lost, by photobleaching, their intracellular (thylakoid) membranes, still show respiratory activity, although with a lower specific activity (on a membrane protein basis) than did the pigmented membrane (cell membrane *plus* intracellular membrane) of control cells. It is likely that at least some

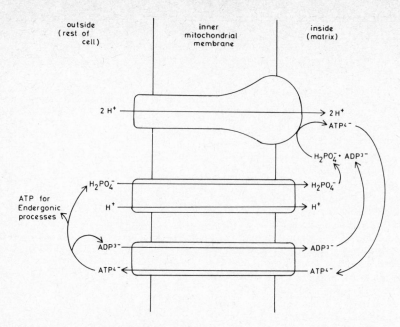

outside (rest of cell)	inner mitochondrial membrane	inside (matrix)

FIG. 6. The mitochondrial ATP synthetase and ADP, ATP, and P_i transport systems. The stoichiometry of the ATP synthetase is 2 H^+ per *internal* ADP + P_i converted to ATP, while the exchange of *internal* ATP for *external* ADP + P_i consumes another 1 H^+ per ATP generated. The overall stoichiometry of H^+ transported per exogenous (cytoplasmic) ADP + P_i converted to exogenous (cytoplasmic) ATP is thus 3:1 (Klingenberg 1979). With the H^+/e_2 of 8 in the oxidation of NADH by O_2 (Fig. 5), the P/e_2 ratio for NADH oxidation by O_2 would be 2.67 rather than the classical value of 3 (Brand et al. 1978; Brand 1979).

of the oxidative phosphorylation activity is normally in the thylakoid (Peschek and Schmetterer 1978; Peschek 1980).

The stoichiometry of generation of the products of respiration is quite well understood for the oxidative PPP; 2 NADPH are produced per CO_2 evolved. For use in reductive biosynthesis each NADPH generated by the oxidative PPP has a higher cost in absorbed quanta than does an NADPH generated directly by the photoacts; the generation of the carbohydrate substrate for the oxidative PPP involves the input of as many NADPH from photosynthesis as are later regenerated upon carbohydrate oxidation, together with the ATP required for the PCRC (plus the "CO_2 concentrating mechanism" and/or PCOC) and storing and mobilizing the carbohydrate product (see Raven 1976a). Thus the running costs for NADPH generation by the oxidative PPP exceed those for the direct use of photosynthetic NADPH. The stoichiometry of oxidative phosphorylation shown in Fig. 5 and 6 is still a matter of some debate; if it is accepted, then the ATP generated from the complete oxidation of one molecule of endogenous glucose is some 33.33 ATP (assuming 2 ATP are used in the hexokinase and phosphofructokinase reactions, and that the 2 NADH generated in glyco-

lysis are oxidized by the "external" NADH dehydrogenase of the inner mitochondrial membrane). The ATP production will be lower if site 1 of oxidative phosphorylation is bypassed in a trade-off of efficiency of conversion of sugar energy into ATP energy against the rate of ATP synthesis: bypassing site 1 can increase the rate of ATP synthesis per unit of mitochondrial machinery with internal NADH as substrate, although it is not clear if this bypass occurs in algae (Lloyd 1974a, b; Erecinska et al. 1978; Lloyd and Turner 1980; cf. Odum and Pinkerton 1955; Warncke and Slayman 1980). ATP production per unit carbohydrate oxidized will also be decreased if the "alternate oxidase" is operative; this pathway is widespread in phototrophs and fungi, and in trypanosomid protozoa, and bypasses all but site 1 of oxidative phosphorylation (Henry and Nyns 1975; Lloyd and Turner 1980; Kirst 1980). This pathway may be useful if operation of the TCAC is required for C skeleton biosynthesis but NADH oxidation in mitochondria is prevented by a suppression of oxidative phosphorylation by photophosphorylation (Marrè 1961). Thus the 33.33 ATP per glucose (corresponding to a P/e_2 of 2.8 overall) is an upper limit for the efficiency of oxidative phosphorylation in eukaryotic algae. The relative efficiency of oxidative phosphorylation and the various forms of photophosphorylation has already been mentioned in relation to the Mehler reaction. In Cyanophyceae (prokaryotes) one might expect a *higher* P/e_2 ratio from the H^+/e_2 and H^+/P ratios shown in Fig. 5 and 6, as the energy-requiring adenylate and phosphate transport across the inner mitochondrial membrane does not occur. However, the (chloroplast-type) coupling factor may have a higher H^+/ATP ratio than its mitochondrial equivalent, and the H^+/e_2 ratio may be lower due to a simpler cytochrome oxidase structure (Garland 1977; Fergusson et al. 1979; Yamanaka and Fujii 1980).

At all events in vivo estimates of the P/e_2 ratio in cyanobacteria give values of 2.63–3.08 (Pelroy and Bassham 1973).

CAPACITY OF DARK RESPIRATION

Any discussion of the role of dark respiratory processes in the life of microalgae requires an estimate of the capacity of the pathways, i.e. the maximum rates at which they can generate ATP, reductant, and C skeletons for comparison with rates of growth and the energy requirements of growth and maintenance. This is particularly important for phototrophs, as it is difficult to measure the *activity* of dark respiratory processes in the light in green cells, and an estimate of the *capacity* of the pathways of respiration at least puts an *upper* limit on the extent to which they contribute to metabolism in the light — the supply of the ATP, NADPH, and C skeletons which they carry out in the dark, together with any additional functions in the light (e.g. certain reactions of the PCOC which occur in the membranes catalyzing oxidative phosphorylation — see above, and Tables 1 and 3).

A number of approaches to the estimation of the capacity of dark respiratory processes in algae have been employed. In vitro methods involve the measurement of enzyme activities in extracts under optimal conditions; the *lowest* activity reflects the maximum capacity of the metabolic sequence in vivo (ap Rees 1974). In vivo methods include measurements of the rate of CO_2 and O_2 exchange in the dark under conditions designed to relieve as many constraints as possible on the rate of respiratory processes. These include the presence of an uncoupler of oxidative phosphorylation to maximize respiratory electron transport activity; the addition of some exogenous organic carbon source whose uptake and metabolism requires ATP (a method which can clearly only work for those algae with substantial capacities for transport and metabolism of exogenous substrates), or the addition of exogenous osmotica which stimulate ATP-requiring ion transport and compatible solute metabolism, also maximize electron transport

TABLE 3. Rates of membrane-associated O_2 uptake required to account for "photorespiratory" glycolate metabolism with a RuBPc/RuBPo of 9.

Pathway	O_2 uptake per 2 glycolate metabolized (i.e. 2 O_2 metabolized by RuBPo)	O_2 uptake per net C fixed
PCOC (glycolate oxidase, GS-GOGAT)	0.5	0.03
PCOC (glycolate dh, GS-GOGAT)	1.5	0.09
PCOC (glycolate oxidase, GDH)	0	0
PCOC (glycolate dh, GDH)[a]	1	0.06
Tartronic semi-aldehyde, glycolate oxidase	0	0
Tartronic semi-aldehyde, glycolate dh	1	0.06

[a]GDH = glutamic dehydrogenase.

rates (Ried et al. 1962; Soeder et al. 1962; Ried et al. 1963; Peschek and Broda 1973; Pelroy et al. 1976). The capacity of the oxidative PPP to generate reductant for biosynthesis can be tested by the addition of NO_3^- in the dark to N-deprived cells (Syrett 1955). Finally, the comparison of the ratio of inner mitochondrial membrane area to thylakoid area, or of ubiquinone (respiratory) to plastoquinone (photosynthetic) content of cells, can be used to estimate the ratio of oxidative phosphorylation to photosynthetic phosphorylation capacity of phototrophic cells, as the rate of ATP synthesis per unit membrane area or per unit quinone is similar in the two energy-coupling membranes (Shimikazi et al. 1978; Raven 1980a, b, and unpublished calculations).

Expressing the results of these calculations of respiratory capacity in the form (capacity for CO_2 production in dark respiration)/(maximum achieved growth rate), with both quantities expressed in $\log_e$ units h^{-1}, the results obtained show considerable variation between major taxa of algae. The data for respiratory capacities for the Bacillariophyceae, Chlorophyceae and Euglenophyceae compiled by Raven (1976a, b), and additional data on capacities derived from the references in Raven (1976a, b), Buetow (1968), and Werner (1977), together with those cited in the previous paragraph, suggest that the maximum CO_2 produced/unit of C assimilated during growth ($\mu_{r\,max}/\mu_g$, where $\mu_{r\,max}$ denotes dark respiratory capacity and μ_g denotes growth) in these

69

three classes can be as low as 0.3–0.5 for phototrophically grown cells, while for heterotrophically grown cells the ratio is 0.5–1.2. It is thus clear that the respiratory capacity associated with a given maximum specific growth rate is lower for phototrophs than for otherwise comparable heterotrophs. This difference in respiratory capacities is exemplified by comparisons of the fraction of the (non-vacuolar) volume of the cell which is occupied by mitochondria; this is significantly lower in phototrophic than in heterotrophic microalgae, even if the results are expressed in terms of the volume of cytoplasm excluding the plastids (whose volume can vary considerably between cells grown in the different trophic regimes) (Raven 1980a, b; Pellegrini 1980).

Data on $\mu_{r_{max}}/\mu_g$ for the Cyanophyceae suggest that the ratio can be substantially lower in these organisms that in the three eukaryote classes discussed above. For *Anacystis nidulans* the ratio is probably less than 0.05 (Kratz and Myers 1955; Peschek and Broda 1973; Doolittle and Singer 1974) in the wild type, and is even lower in revertants to mutant strain 704 which lack both of the dehydrogenases of the oxidative PPP (Doolittle and Singer 1974). Pelroy et al. (1976), in a study on the facultative heterotroph *Aphanocapsa* 6714 which dealt with the phosphorylation capacity under various light and dark conditions, showed that oxidative phosphorylation had only 0.05 of the capacity of (noncyclic plus cyclic) photophosphorylation.

By contrast, the Dinophyceae are a class of algae which seem to be characterized by high rates of dark respiration relative to the rate of growth or of net photosynthesis (Moshkind 1961; Dunstan 1973; Humphrey 1975; Prézelin and Sweeney 1978; Burris 1977; Falkowski and Owens 1978). The work of Prézelin and Sweeney (1978) gives a specific growth rate of 0.0086 h^{-1} at light saturation in a 12-h light:12-h dark cycle, while the *achieved* specific respiration rate is 0.0096 h^{-1}, in cultures of *Gonyaulax polyedra*. The *potential* respiratory rate is probably higher than the achieved rate (Hochachka and Teal 1964; cf. Thomas 1955). In phototrophic members of the Dinophyceae we may conclude that the capacity for dark respiration is as high as it is in heterotrophic cells of many other algae when expressed as a fraction of the growth rate.

The computations of respiratory capacity as a fraction of growth rate that have been performed here generally tend to underestimate the respiratory capacity, as other processes may be limiting the respiratory rate achieved in vivo; despite this, it is clear that there are variations of at least an order of magnitude in this ratio between different classes of algae.

ENERGY REQUIREMENTS FOR GROWTH AND MAINTENANCE IN RELATION TO THE ENERGY PROVIDED BY DARK RESPIRATION

The classic exposition of the relationship between growth rate and the rate of respiration for a heterotroph is (equation (4)):

$$(4) \qquad \mu_r = c \cdot \mu_g + \mu_o$$

where μ_r is the specific respiration rate (h^{-1}), μ_g is the specific growth rate (h^{-1}), μ_o is the specific maintenance rate (h^{-1}), and c is the ratio of C lost as CO_2 in growth-associated respiration to the C assimilated into cell material. The values of μ_r and μ_o are obtained from plots of μ_r vs. μ_g; the slope of the graph (ideally a straight line) gives c, while the intercept at $\mu_g = 0$ gives μ_0. The value of c should be related to the composition of the organism in that the CO_2 production should equal the net requirement for reductant in converting the organic and inorganic substrates into cell material (higher if nitrate rather than ammonium is the N source, and if acetate rather than glucose is the C source) *plus* the CO_2 production which equals the O_2 uptake involved in ATP generation in oxidative phosphorylation in order to produce sufficient ATP for growth (Raven 1971, 1972a, b, 1976a, b; Penning de Vries et al. 1974). Values of c which are higher than the values predicted from cell composition and the known mechanisms of transport and synthesis in the organism may be attributed to some kind of "slippage" or "uncoupling" (Beevers 1970; see below).

In the case of phototrophic growth we have the problem that, in the light, some of the ATP and NADPH required for processes other than the conversion of CO_2 into carbohydrate may be produced by the light reactions of photosynthesis rather than by the "dark" respiratory processes and that the extent to which the "dark" respiratory processes occur in the light is not easy to estimate (Ried 1970; Raven 1971, 1972a, b; 1976a, b). In this case the involvement of dark respiration in "growth" (conversion of photosynthate into cells) can be estimated by comparing the CO_2/C ratio which is required for the conversion of photosynthate into cells if all of the ATP and NADPH were supplied by respiration with likely values of the CO_2/C actually resulting from dark respiration. The energy requirements and the energy input must take maintenance into account (see below); two strategies may be followed in estimating the respiratory contribution. One is to take the measured dark respiration in the dark period (if any) of the daily cycle, and to add to it the respiration which would have occurred in the light period if the "dark" respiration rate during the light period was identical with the rates measured in the first steady-state CO_2 evolution found after cessation of long-term illumination (more than an hour). The other strategy is to take, as before, the respiration which was measured during the dark period of the delay cycle, and to add to it the respiration which would have occurred in the light period if dark respiration had been proceeding at its maximum rate (the *capacity* discussed above).

For *Chlorella* (see Raven 1976a, b) an appropriate value of c in equation (4) would be 0.46 for growth on ammonium as N source and 0.76 for growth on nitrate as N source. These figures both contain a CO_2/C of 0.36 for the generation of 2 ATP per C assimilated (P/e_2 of 2.8, respiratory quotient = 1; see above), and a term for the CO_2 produced in generating the reductant needed to bring (carbohydrate plus ammonium plus sulphate) or (carbohydrate plus nitrate plus sulphate) to the redox level of the final cell material. For ammonium as N source this CO_2/C increment is 0.1, and for nitrate as N source, 0.4 (Raven 1976a, b). From the discussion in Raven (1976a, b) it is clear that the *lower* estimate of dark respiration mentioned above (but which is still in accord with much experimental data) would give a "dark" respiratory input of ATP and NADPH considerably lower than that required according to a CO_2/C of 0.46 (ammonium) and 0.76 (nitrate). Even the *higher* estimate (assuming that "dark" respiration proceeded at its maximum rate throughout the light period) gives insufficient respiratory ATP and NADPH to supply growth requirements for either ammonium of nitrate as N source (bearing in mind that the capacity for the oxidative PPP in eukaryotes is not readily available to supply reductant to oxidative phosphorylation (ap Rees 1974). Thus for *Chlorella* and for other chlorophyceaeans, for members of the Bacillariophyceae and Chrysophyceae, and for some *Euglena* strains, it is likely that dark respiration cannot make all the ATP and NADPH required for growth processes during normal phototrophic growth (Laws and Caperon 1976; Raven 1976a, b; Laws and Wong 1978): some of the ATP and NADPH for growth, as well as that used in the conversion of CO_2 to carbohydrate, must come from noncyclic, pseudocyclic, and cyclic photophosphorylation.

This conclusion applies a fortiori to cyanophyceans even allowing for the (possible) greater flexibility in the use of reductant (NADPH) for *either* reductive biosynthesis *or* for ATP generation in oxidative phosphorylation; the respiratory capacity of cyanobacteria gives a CO_2/C for respiration of less than 0.1 in fast-growing cells while the required CO_2/C if respiration is to supply all of the ATP and NADPH for growth processes is similar to that for *Chlorella*, i.e. 0.4–0.8 depending on N source. For Dinophyceae, however, the CO_2/C from dark respiration is more than adequate to supply the requirement for ATP and NADPH for growth, and, if this respiration is not subject to great slippage or uncoupling, the direct use of photoproduced cofactors for growth need not be invoked.

The conclusion that (Dinophyceae aside) the direct use of photoproduced cofactors is important in supplying growth processes is reinforced if the temporal differences between respiratory supply and growth demand for energy is considered; this is particularly the case if very little growth processes occur in the dark period of the diurnal cycle although respiration exceeds the maintenance requirement (Raven 1976a, b).

The other energy-requiring process to which respiration may contribute is maintenance. Even when no growth occurs, the maintenance of viability and, more particularly, the ability to resume growth at a rapid rate as soon as the missing resource (e.g. light or some nutrient) is restored, requires a continued energy supply. This is used inter alia for resynthesizing unstable macromolecules, and for the active transport which recovers ions which have leaked through a membrane (Penning de Vries 1975). Maintenance respiration may be computed by the use of equation (4); this value for μ_o may be similar to the respiration rate measured after prolonged darkness. The alternative method of computing a maintenance requirement is to extrapolate the μ_g vs. incident irradiance relationship to zero irradiance, yielding a maintenance coefficient μ_e (van Liere and Mur 1979). In general, the measured rate of respiration in the dark period of a light–dark diurnal cycle is greater than the maintenance coefficients μ_o or μ_e computed by extrapolation (van Liere et al. 1979), particularly in the Cyanophyceae, where μ_e varies from 0.001 to 0.004 h^{-1} as compared with 0.007–0.015 h^{-1} in the Chlorophyceae. In this respect it is of interest that Doolittle and Singer (1974) found that revertant strains of *Anacystis nidulans* mutant 704 had specific respiration rates in the dark of below 0.005 h^{-1}, yet had as good an ability to remain viable in prolonged darkness as did the wild type whose specific respiration rate shortly after cessation of illumination was about 0.05 h^{-1}. The role of fermentation in maintenance in the revertant strains with negligible activity of the two dehydrogenases of the oxidative PPP remains to be explored (cf. Peschek and Broda 1973).

The remainder of this discussion of dark respiration is taken up with possible explanations for variations in specific respiration rates between organisms and between the same organism growing under different conditions.

VARIATIONS IN SPECIFIC RESPIRATION RATES: GENOTYPIC AND PHENOTYPIC EFFECTS AND POSSIBLE EXPLANATIONS

In the preceding section we saw that there were considerable differences in specific respiration rate between different phytoplankton organisms which could not be entirely explained by differences in μ_g according to equation (4) (cf. Laws 1975; Banse 1976). Three general classes of explanation may be investigated; one appeals to variability in the extent to which the direct use of photoproduced ATP and reductant "subsidizes" the respiratory provision of these cofactors; a second involves differences in cell composition which implies different energy requirements per unit cell growth as changes in the maintenance requirement; the third attributes differences in respiratory rate to different degrees of coupling between exergonic (respiratory) and endergonic (growth and maintenance) processes.

Dealing first with the notion of changes in the extent of the "energy subsidy" from photoproduced cofactors which "spares" the requirement to generate these cofactors by respiratory processes, the data discussed in the previous section showed that although there is an a priori case for such a subsidy in many classes of phytoplankters, the Dinophyceae yield no such evidence (assuming efficient coupling of respiratory and energy-requiring processes). This argues for considerable genotypic variation between algal classes with respect to this subsidy, with Cyanophyceae having the largest subsidy and Dinophyceae the smallest. The extent of phenotypic variation in the extent of the subsidy appears to be small, as equation (4) is obeyed with an essentially constant value of c when μ_g is altered by changes in light or (chemical) nutrient supply; this is exemplified by the measurements of Myers and Graham (1961) and Cook (1961) on light-limited cultures of *Chlorella* and *Euglena* respectively, and by the work of Laws and Caperon (1976) and Laws and Wong (1978) on nitrate-limited growth of *Thalassiosira*, *Monochrysis*, and *Dunaliella*. In all of these cases, specific respiration rate is a sufficiently low fraction of the specific growth rate that there is a requirement for an "energy subsidy" for growth and maintenance processes from photosynthetic partial reactions, and in each case this subsidy (as a fraction of the total energy required for processes other than carbohydrate generation in photosynthesis) is relatively invariant with growth rate. We may note that these conclusions only hold if there are not significant differences in the cell composition as a function of limitation of growth rate by lack of light or nutrients; as we shall see, there *are* changes in cell composition with growth rate.

Turning to the possibility that changes in c and μ_o (equation (4)) can be related to changes in cell composition, and hence changes in the ATP and NADPH required per unit C assimilated in growth, there are substantial differences in the energy costs of synthesizing, from "photosynthate" and inorganic nutrients, unit C in protein compared with unit C in polysaccharide; this is particularly the case if nitrate rather than ammonium or urea is the N source (Raven 1972a, b, 1976a, b; Penning de Vries et al. 1974; Raven and Glidewell 1975b). It has been suggested (Raven and Glidewell 1975b) that this may be significant in shade adaptation as a decreased fraction of the cell dry weight due to protein would reduce the "growth" energy requirement (from respiration or more directly from photosynthetic partial reactions) per unit C assimilated without decreasing gross photosynthesis at low irradiances, provided the protein economies were made in enzymes (not limiting at low irradiances) rather than in the light-harvesting pigment-protein complexes (see Prézelin 1981). This argument seems to be applicable to genotypically adapted "sun" and "shade" benthic macroalgae (compare Table 1 of Raven et al. 1979, with Table 7 of Raven 1981), but its validity for phytoplankton algae is less readily demonstrated. Here we are forced to rely on data from phenotypic adaptation of a given genotype to different irradiance regimes. The evidence on the activity of a major enzymic contributor to the cell protein level, RuBPc-o (see Raven 1980b), shows that its activity per unit cell protein decreases at low irradiances for growth in *Phaeodactylum tricornutum* (Beardall and Morris 1976) and *Scenedesmus obliquus* (Senger and Fleischhacker 1978) (cf. Molloy and Schmidt 1970), and that cell protein also declines at low irradiances (Beardall and Morris 1976; Parrot and Slater 1980). However, in other cases there is either no change in the fraction of cell weight contributed by protein or N as irradiance alters, or the N/C ratio *increases* at low irradiances (e.g. Yader 1979; Scott 1980; Tomas 1980).

We have already noted that the thorough investigations by Laws and Caperon (1976) and Laws and Wong (1978) showed that equation (4) held with a constant c value for cultures of *Thalassiosira*, *Monochrysis*, and *Dunaliella* in which growth rate was varied by nitrate supply although, as the cell analyses given in those papers show, the C:N ratio increases with decreasing (nitrate-limited) growth rates (cf. Goldman et al. 1979; Laws and Bannister 1980). Further investigation is needed to clarify the energy costs of synthesis under these culture conditions and its influence on the rate of respiration.

The effects of variation in photoperiod on specific respiration rate, specific growth rate, and cell composition are not identical with the effects of varied irradiance at constant photoperiod (Foy et al. 1976; Hobson et al. 1979; Humphrey 1979; Foy and Smith 1980). Ultimately these effects should be interpretable in terms of optimal temporal strategies of biosynthesis in varying photoperiods, as is discussed in this paper and by Cohen and Parnas (1976), van Liere et al. (1979), and Foy and Smith (1980).

Another compositional difference which might alter the energy cost of growth and maintenance is cell structure; this is an extension of the chemical composition differences discussed above. It is possible that the increased intracellular membrane content of eukaryotes compared with prokaryotes can, in part, explain the larger maintenance costs in the Chlorophyceae compared with the Cyanophyceae. The maintenance of the volume of the cytosol relative to that of "non-leaky" organelles (Raven 1980a) requires a constant input of energy to avoid "colloid-osmotic swelling" of the compartment with the higher content of macromolecules (Jakobssen 1980). However, van Gemerden (1980) points out that similar differences in maintenance requirement can occur *within* the prokaryotes (the Chlorobineae having values similar to the Cyanophyceae, and the Rhodospirillineae resembling the Chlorophytes), although this again may be related to differences in intracellular membrane arrangement (Raven and Beardall 1981).

Cell structure may be significant in accounting for the (usually) higher respiration rates of flagellate compared with nonflagellate microalgae (Moshkind 1961; Falkowski and Owens 1978). Raven (1976c, 1980a) has pointed out that flagellate cells are effectively wall-less with respect to osmoregulation even when (e.g. *Chlamydomonas*) they possess a wall, as the flagellar membrane is always wall-less. Volume regulation in wall-less cells requires a constant expenditure of energy, regardless of whether the cells are hypertonic in freshwater and osmoregulate by contractile vacuoles, or are isotonic in seawater but still have to deal with colloid-osmotic swelling (Raven 1976c; Jakobssen 1980). Walled cells, by contrast, have a volume regulation (the cell wall) built in during growth, and consequently may have a lower maintenance energy requirement for volume and osmotic regulation as far as the whole cell is concerned, although turgor maintenance probably involves energy input in a "pump and leak" system (Raven 1976c).

It is not easy to quantify these osmoregulatory energy requirements; it is easier (because the mechanism is better understood) to evaluate the suggestion (Moshkind 1961; cf. Falkowski and Owens 1978) that the high respiration rates of flagellates and, in particular, of dinoflagellates is related to their motility. A *Gonyaulax polyedra* cell 50 μm in diameter (Prézelin and Alberte 1978) has a specific respiration rate of up to 0.0096 h^{-1} (Prézelin and Sweeney 1978). Flagella have some 600 ATPase (dynein) molecules per micrometre length and a specific reaction rate of these ATPases of up to 100 s^{-1}

(Sleigh 1974); if *Gonyaulax* has a total flagella length of 250 μm, then the maximal ATP consumption per cell in flagella activity is 2.5. $\times$ 10^{-17} mol ATP·s^{-1}; with a P/e$_2$ of 2.8 and a C/cell volume of 0.125 g·cm^{-3}, the respiration associated with motility is only 0.000015 h^{-1}, which is only a small fraction of maintenance respiration (at least 0.001 h^{-1}). The total energy use by flagella (e.g. in nutrient uptake) is limited by ATP supply along the axoneme (see Raven 1980a). Thus flagellar motility is not a major contributor to the energy requirements of dinoflagellates.

A cell characteristic which has been frequently discussed with respect to rates of growth and of dark respiration in microalgae is cell size (e.g. Laws 1975; Banse 1976). The dependence of "pump and leak" maintenance energy requirements on cell size (via the ratio of plasmalemma area to cell volume) has been emphasized, although the area of intracellular membranes and the quantity of protein per unit volume is clearly also important in determining the maintenance requirement (see above, and Laws 1975). Empirically, the analysis by Laws (1975) suggests that there is a significant variation in the respiration/growth rate relationship with cell size, while Banse (1976) in a subsequent review of the data found no significant variation in this ratio with cell size. In view of the significance of cell size in the ecology of phytoplankton (Guillard and Kilham 1977), a mechanistic approach to the relationship between cell size, specific growth rate, and specific respiration rate would be desirable.

A further possible explanation of differences in the specific respiration rate (and the ratio specific respiration rate/specific growth rate) is related to stress. We have implicitly taken an "unstressed" organism as our paradigm; stress in general increases the rate of respiration relative to that of growth, if only because the decreased growth rate makes maintenance a greater fraction of the total respiration (as is the case for low irradiances or restricted nutrient availability which we have already considered). Aside from this, stress (e.g. temperatures or osmolarities which are nonoptimal) can increase c and μ_e as well as decrease μ_g. It is often difficult to decide if an increased c or μ_e results from a "respiratory control" response to an increased demand for energy as part of adaptation or is increased "slippage" as a result of damage to the respiratory or energy-consuming processes. The data are generally not easy to interpret (e.g. Guillard and Ryther 1962; Ryther and Guillard 1962).

Finally, in explanation of variations in c and μ_e, we can fall back on "slippage" (Beevers 1970; Neijssel and Tempest 1976). This includes not just the wasteful reoxidation of NADPH by O_2 rather than nitrate reductase, the excessive operation of the alternate oxidase, or the operation of futile cycles which act as ATPases; it can also extend to mismatches between the operation of reductant-generating and reductant-consuming reactions, or of energy-transducing and C-skeleton-generating reactions, either spatially or temporally, resulting in the "wasteful" oxidation of some potentially useful intermediate.

Dark Respiration — Conclusions

An analysis of dark respiration in microalgae in terms of running costs, capital costs, and safety will serve to summarize our discussion. The yield (ATP/quantum) of oxidative phosphorylation (calculated from the energy costs of carbohydrate synthesis in photosynthesis, and the ATP yield from the complete oxidation of carbohydrate is not more than 0.66. This value assumes not only complete coupling in photosynthetic and oxidative phosphorylation, but also that the cost of CO_2 fixation is 3 ATP and 2 NADPH per CO_2 (see above); this underestimates the cost in normal air when the RuBPo-PCOC and/ or CO_2 concentrating mechanism increase the energy required per CO_2 fixed. The maximum yield of pseudocyclic and cyclic photophosphorylation is 0.33 and 0.67, respectively, so oxidative phosphorylation has a similar efficiency to cyclic photophosphorylation and a better efficiency than pseudocyclic photophosphorylation. The direct use of photoproduced reductant is more efficient than the use of this reductant to generate carbohydrate with subsequent regeneration of NADPH in the oxidative PPP, as the direct use of NADPH yields, in addition, 1.33 ATP per NADPH in noncyclic photophosphorylation, while regeneration of NADPH from carbohydrate via the oxidative PPP involves the input of at least another 0.17 ATP per NADPH generated to give the minimal ATP required for CO_2 fixation. Fermentation as a source of ATP is some 20-fold less efficient than is the oxidative phosphorylation in terms of running costs. Thus the direct use of photoproduced reductant for growth processes is always favored over reductant generation by the oxidative PPP in terms of running costs, while the direct use of ATP generated in photophosphorylation has no such clear advantage.

The analysis of respiratory versus direct supply of ATP and NADPH for growth processes as a function of the capital invested requires cognizance to be taken of both the production and consumption costs of the cofactors. Clearly the capital costs of the direct use of cofactors are less than those involved in the use of photoproduced cofactors to fix CO_2 with subsequent regeneration of the cofactors in respiration; two further tiers of catalytic machinery are involved (the stromal CO_2 fixation system and the respiratory catalysts). However, a consideration of the energy-consuming reactions shows that more efficient use is made of unit synthetic machinery if the ATP and NADPH are supplied continuously (as is possible with respiratory energy supply) rather than intermittently (as is demanded by the direct use of photoproduced cofactors) (Raven 1976a, b; see above). Thus the relative advantages of direct versus respiratory generation of cofactors are difficult to analyze in terms of capital costs.

The final consideration is that of safety. Dark respiration involves the reduction of O_2, but the problem of O_2 radical generation is less severe than with photosynthetic processes (e.g. the Mehler reaction); the major superoxide and peroxide generator in respiration is the alternate oxidase (Rich et al. 1977). It is difficult to see how dark respiration can serve to prevent photoinhibition by consuming more excitation energy, as short-term feedback effects of photosynthate concentration on the rate of photosynthesis are poorly documented; thus additional consumption of photosynthate by dark respiration would not necessarily increase the rate of energy consumption by CO_2 fixation (cf. Fogg 1975). In any case, the extra respiration would presumably be via the alternate oxidase which would itself (like the Mehler reaction) generate toxic radicals.

In wider safety and survival terms, the presence of a substantial respiratory capacity may be useful in permitting the acquisition of scarce nutrients (e.g. phosphate, fixed nitrogen) over the whole 24-h cycle. This would be particularly advantageous in migratory organisms which can spend the day in a location optimal for light absorption and the night in regions optimal for nutrient acquisition; this behavior has been documented for Dinophyceae (Eppley et al. 1968), which have (as has been discussed earlier) high respiration rates (cf. Raven 1976a, b, 1980a). Similar considerations apply to the energy supply required to adapt to stresses which can occur in the dark as well as in the light: a good example is changes in osmolarity, where the rate of adaptation is similar in light and in darkness (Kirst 1975; Kirst and Keller 1976; Brown and Hellebust 1978).

An efficient respiratory supply of ATP for maintenance is important for dark survival of phytoplankton organisms which are likely to be subjected to prolonged darkness by dropping out of the euphotic zone (e.g. Antia and Cheng 1970; Smayda and Mitchell-Innes 1974; Antia 1976). Survival is improved by exposure to subcompensation irradiances which may work via photosynthesis or some partial reactions thereof serving to "spare" respiratory substrates. There seems to be no direct information relating respiratory capacity and efficiency to dark survival of microalgae; it would be expected that efficient respiration working on large reserves would lead to prolonged survival, as would a cell composition which needed less maintenance energy. In the dark in the absence of oxygen, the relatively inefficient process of fermentation is presumably used as a source of maintenance energy. Moss (1977) has demonstrated a positive correlation between the ability to survive dark anaerobiosis and likelihood of the organism encountering dark anaerobiosis in nature for a number of (nonplanktonic) microalgae. Kessler (1973) has suggested that the possession of hydrogenase, with a corresponding ability to produce less toxic fermentation products, can favor dark-anaerobic survival in microalgae (cf. the possible role of hydrogenase in energy dissipation under conditions of high light input–low redox acceptor availability as discussed above).

Conclusions

The respiratory processes of microalgae have been considered here in terms of their contributions to the efficiency of growth (from the point of view of running costs and capital investment) and to the safety and survival aspects of the organism's existence. "Dark" respiration has clear survival value from the viewpoint of the generation of essential C skeletons, and in generating ATP and NADPH for growth and maintenance processes in the dark. Efficiency and capital cost considerations may be involved in the evolutionary determination of how much of the conversion of immediate (mainly carbohydrate) products of photosynthesis into "cell material" occurs in the light when the direct use of photoproduced cofactors is possible as a supplement to the use of respiratory ATP and NADPH for these "growth" processes. The wide variation in the dark respiratory rate as a fraction of growth rate between different algal classes suggests that the selective balance between respiratory generation of cofactors and the direct use of cofactors from photosynthesis is struck at different points and for unknown reasons in different algae. The wide variations in dark respiratory rate between algae, and environmental influences on these rates, are not amenable to detailed explanation at the moment; clearly a process which consumes between 5 and 50% of gross photosynthate must be better understood before any comprehensive mechanistic analysis of the energetics and kinetics of phytoplankton growth is possible.

The photorespiratory processes (Mehler reaction, and RuBPo and its appendages) are best regarded as unavoidable consequences of the generation of photosynthetic reductant, of the operation of RuBPc-o, in "natural" CO_2 and O_2 concentrations; their survival value is primarily, on this view, that the alga has to carry out the processes of which they are necessary concomitants if it is to survive

as a phototroph. This is not to say that the processes cannot be modulated or made to serve other desirable ends; the Mehler reaction can function (via pseudo-cyclic photophosphorylation) to generate ATP, while both the Mehler reaction and RuBPo may be involved in the dissipation of excess, and possibly harmful, excitation energy in the photosynthetic apparatus. This "energy-dissipating" role of RuBPo activity under low CO_2–high O_2 conditions is perhaps not as significant in most microalgae as in C_3 higher plants, as many microalgae have a "CO_2 concentrating mechanism" which substantially suppresses RuBPo activity under natural conditions. Either the operation or the suppression of RuBPo is a costly procedure, with respect to running costs and to the production of the catalytic machinery, and this must be taken into account in considering the growth energetics and kinetics of algae which lack overt photorespiratory CO_2 production as well as those which possess it.

These physiological considerations can be applied to ecology. The competitive dominance of *Oscillatoria agardhii* in cultures or in shallow lakes at low irradiances (below $10 \text{ W} \cdot \text{m}^{-2}$) and of *Scenedesmus protuberans* at higher irradiances is clearly related to the lower specific maintenance coefficient of *Oscillatoria* and to the higher light-saturated specific growth rate and resistance to photoinhibition of *Scenedesmus* (Mur and Beijdorf 1978). However, we do not know the mechanisms behind the low maintenance requirement in the cyanophytes, or th relation of the Mehler reaction and RuBPo–PCOC activity to the higher irradiances required for photoinhibition in the chlorophyte.

Acknowledgments

We are grateful to the Science Research Council for supporting our work (and that of Dr S. M. Glidewell) by Grants B/RG/1403, B/RG/91966, and GR/A/69896. We dedicate this paper to Professor Jack Myers, Zoologist Extraordinary.

References

ANDREWS, T. J., AND G. H. LORIMER. 1978. Photorespiration — still unavoidable? FEBS Lett. 90: 1–9.

ANTIA, M. J. 1976. Effects of temperature on the darkness survival of marine microplanktonic algae. Microb. Ecol. 3: 41–54.

ANTIA, N. J., AND J. Y. CHENG. 1970. The survival of axenic cultures of marine planktonic algae from prolonged exposure to darkness at 20°C. Phycologia 9: 179–183.

APPLEBY, G., J. COLBECK, E. S. HOLDSWORTH, AND H. WADMAN. 1980. The β-carboxylation enzymes in marine phytoplankton and isolation and purification of pyruvate carboxylase from *Amphidinium carterae* (Dinophyceae). J. Phycol. 16: 290–295.

AP REES, T. 1974. Pathways of carbohydrate breakdown in higher plants, p. 89–128. *In* D. H. Northcote [ed.] M.T.P. International reviews of science, biochemistry series one. Vol. II. MTP Press.

ASADA, K., AND Y. NAKANO. 1978. Affinity for oxygen in photoreduction of molecular oxygen and scavenging of H_2O_2 in spinach chloroplasts. Photochem. Photobiol. 28: 917–920.

BADGER, M. R. 1980. Kinetic properties of RuBPc-o from *Anabaena variabilis*. Arch. Biochem. Biophys. 207: 247–254.

BADGER, M. R., A. KAPLAN, AND J. A. BERRY. 1977. The internal CO_2 pool of *Chlamydomonas reinhardtii*: response to external CO_2. Carnegie Inst. Wash. Yearb. 76: 362–366.

1978. A mechanism for concentrating CO_2 in *Chlamydomonas reinhardtii* and *Anabaena variabilis* and its role in photosynthetic CO_2 fixation. Carnegie Inst. Wash. Yearb. 77: 251–261.

1980. The internal inorganic carbon pool of *Chlamydomonas reinhardtii*: evidence for a CO_2 concentrating mechanism. Plant Physiol. 66: 407–413.

BADOUR, S. S., AND E. R. WAYGOOD. 1971a. Glyoxylate carboligase activity in the unicellular green alga *Gloeomonas* sp. Biochim. Biophys. Acta 242: 493–499.

1971b. Excretion of an acid semialdehyde by *Gloeomonas*. Phytochemistry 10: 967–976.

1972. Evidence for the operation of the glycerate pathway in *Chlamydomonas segnis*. Plant Physiol. 50: 572.

BANSE, K. 1976. Rates of growth, respiration and photosynthesis of unicellular algae as related to cell size — a review. J. Phycol. 12: 135–140.

BEALE, S. I. 1978. Aminolaevulinic acid in plants: its biosynthesis, regulation and role in plastid development. Annu. Rev. Plant Physiol. 29: 95–120.

BEARDALL, J., AND I. MORRIS. 1975. Effects of environmental factors on photosynthesis patterns in *Phaeodactylum tricornutum*. II. Effect of oxygen. J. Phycol. 11: 430–434.

1976. The concept of light intensity adaptation in marine phytoplankton: some experiments with *Phaeodactylum tricornutum*. Mar. Biol. 37: 377–388.

BEARDALL, J., D. MUKERJI, H. E. GLOVER, AND I. MORRIS. 1976. The path of carbon in photosynthesis by marine phytoplankton. J. Phycol. 12: 409–417.

BEARDALL, J., AND J. A. RAVEN. 1981. Transport of inorganic carbon and the CO_2 concentrating mechanism in *Chlorella emersonni* (Chlorophyceae). J. Phycol. 17: 134–141.

BEEVERS, H. 1970. Respiration in plants and its regulation, p. 209–214. *In* Measurement of photosynthetic productivity. PUDOC, Wageningen.

BENEDICT, C. R. 1978. Nature of obligate photo-autotrophy. Annu. Rev. Plant Physiol. 29: 67–93.

BERRY, J. A., AND G. BOWES. 1973. Oxygen uptake *in vitro* by RuDP carboxylase of *Chlamydomonas reinhardtii*. Carnegie Inst. Wash. Yearb. 72: 405–407.

BERRY, J. A., J. BOYNTON, A. KAPLAN, AND M. BADGER. 1976. Growth and photosynthesis of *Chlamydomonas reinhardtii* as a function of CO_2 concentration. Cargenie Inst. Wash. Yearb. 75: 423–432.

BIDWELL, R. G. S. 1977. Photosynthesis and light and dark respiration in freshwater algae. Can. J. Bot. 55: 809–818.

BIRMINGHAM, B. C., AND B. COLMAN. 1979. Measurement of carbon dioxide compensation points of freshwater algae. Plant Physiol. 64: 892–895.

BRAND, M. D. 1979. Stoichiometry of charge and proton translocation in mitochondria: steady-state measurement of charge/O and P/O ratios. Biochem. Soc. Trans. 7: 874–880.

BRAND, M. D., W. G. HARPER, D. G. NICHOLLS, AND W. J. INGELDEW. 1978. Unequal charge separation by different coupling spans of the mitochondrial electron transport chain. FEBS Lett. 95: 125–129.

BRANDEN, R. 1978. Ribulose bisphosphate carboxylase and oxygenase from green plants are two different enzymes. Biochem. Biophys. Res. Commun. 81: 539–546.

BROWN, A. H., AND D. WEIS. 1959. Relation between respiration and photosynthesis in the green alga *Ankistrodesmus braunii*. Plant Physiol. 34: 224–234.

BROWN, D. L., AND E. B. TREGUNNA. 1967. Inhibition of respiration during photosynthesis by some algae. Can. J. Bot. 45: 1135–1143.

BROWN, L. M., AND J. A. HELLEBUST. 1978. Ionic dependence of deplasmolysis in the euryhaline diatom *Cyclotella crytica*. Can. J. Bot. 56: 408–412.

BROWN, R. H. 1978. A difference in N use efficiency in C_3 and C_4 plants and its implications for adaptation and evolution. Crop Sci. 18: 93–98.

BUETOW, D. E. 1968. The biology of Euglena. Vol.I and II. Academic Press, New York, NY.

BULLOCK, K. W., T. R. DEASON, AND J. C. O'KELLEY. 1979. Occurrence of glycolate dehydrogenase and glycolate oxidase in some coccoid, zoospore-producing green algae. J. Phycol. 15: 142–146.

BUNT, J. S. 1965. Measurements of photosynthesis and respiration in a marine diatom with the mass spectrometer and with C14. Nature (London) 207: 1373–1375.

1971. Levels of dissolved oxygen and carbon fixation by marine microalgae. Limnol. Oceanogr. 16: 564–566.

BUNT, J. S., O. van H. OWENS, AND G. HOCH. 1966. Exploratory measurements on the physiology of a psychrophilic marine diatom. J. Phycol. 2: 96–100.

BURRIS, J. E. 1977. Photosynthesis, photorespiration and dark respiration in eight species of algae. Mar. Biol. 39: 371–379.

CHRISTEN, P., AND A. GASSER. 1980. Production of glycolate by oxidation of the 1,2 dihydroxyethylthiamin-diphosphate intermediate of transketolase with hexacyanoferrate (III) or H_2O_2. Eur. J. Biochem. 107: 73–77.

CODD, G. A., AND M. MERRETT. 1971a. Photosynthetic products of division synchronized cultures of *Euglena*. Plant Physiol. 47: 635–639.

1971b. The regulation of glycolate metabolism in division synchronized cultures of *Euglena*. Plant Physiol. 47: 640–643.

CODD, G. A., AND G. H. SCHMID. 1972. Serological characterization of the glycolate-oxidizing enzymes from tobacco, *Euglena gracilis* and a yellow mutant of *Chlorella vulgaris*. Plant Physiol. 50: 769–773.

CODD, G. A., AND A. K. J. SELLAL. 1978. Glycolate oxidation by thylakoids of the Cyanobacteria *Anabaena cyclindrica, Nostoc muscorum* and *Chlorogloea fritschii*. Planta 139: 177–182.

CODD, G. A., AND W. D. P. STEWART. 1973. Pathways of glycolate metabolism in the blue-alga *Anabaena cyclindrica*. Arch. Mikrobiol. 94: 11–28.

——— 1974. Glycolate oxidation and utilization by *Anabaena cylindrica*. Plant Sci. Lett. 3: 199–205.

COHEN, D., AND H. PARNAS. 1976. An optimal policy for the metabolism of storage materials in unicellular algae. J. Theor. Biol. 56: 1–18.

COLEMAN, J. R., AND B. COLMAN. 1980a. Effect of oxygen and temperature on photosynthetic carbon assimilation in two microscopic algae. Plant Physiol. 65: 980–983.

——— 1980b. Demonstration of C$_3$-photosynthesis in a blue-green alga, *Coccochloris peniocystis*. Planta 149: 318–320.

COLLINS, N., AND M. J. MERRETT. 1975. The localization of glycolate-pathway enzymes in *Euglena*. Biochem. J. 148: 321–328.

COOK, J. R. 1961. *Euglena gracilis* in synchronous division. II. Biosynthetic rates over the life cycle. Biol. Bull. 121: 277–289.

COUGHLAN, S. 1977. Glycolate metabolism in *Thalassiosira pseudonana*. J. Exp. Bot. 28: 78–83.

DAVIES, D. D., J. GIOVANELLI, AND T. AP REES. 1964. Plant biochemistry. Blackwell Scientific Publications, Oxford.

DIMON, B., AND R. GERSTER. 1976. Incorporation d'oxygène dans le glycolate excrété à la lumière par *Euglena gracilis*. C. R. Acad. Sci. Paris Ser. D 283: 507–510.

DOOLITTLE, W. F., AND R. A. Singer. 1974. Mutational analysis of dark endogenous metabolism of the blue-green bacterium *Anacystis nidulans*. J. Bacteriol. 119: 677–683.

DROOP, M. R. 1974. Heterotrophy of carbon, p. 530–559. *In* W. D. P. Stewart [ed.] Algal physiology and biochemistry. Blackwell Scientific Publications, Oxford.

DUNSTAN, W. H. 1973. A comparison of the photosynthesis-light intensity relationship in phylogenetically different marine microalgae. J. Exp. Mar. Biol. Ecol. 13: 181–187.

EGLE, K., AND W. SCHENK. 1952. Untersuchungen über die Reassimilation der Atmungkohlensaure bei der Photosynthese der Pflanzen. Beitr. Biol. Pflanz. 29: 75–105.

ELSTNER, E. F., AND J. KONZE. 1976. Wege der Sauerstoffaktivierung in verschedien Kompartimenten von Pflanzenzellen. Ber. Dtsch. Bot. Ges. 89: 335–348.

EPPLEY, R. W., O. HOLM-HANSEN, AND J. D. H. STRICKLAND. 1968. Some observations on the vertical migration of dinoflagellates. J. Phycol. 4: 333–340.

ERECINSKA, M., D. F. WULSON, AND K. NISHIKI. 1978. Homeostatic regulation of cellular energy metabolism: experimental characterization *in vivo* and fit to a model. Am. J. Physiol. 234: C82–C89.

FALKOWSKI, P. G., AND T. G. OWENS. 1978. Effects of light intensity on photosynthesis and dark respiration in six species of marine phytoplankton. Mar. Biol. 45: 289–295.

FARQUHAR, G. D., S. VON CAEMMERER, AND J. A. BERRY. 1980. A biochemical model of photosynthetic CO$_2$ fixation in leaves of C$_3$ plants. Planta 149: 78–90.

FERGUSSON, S. J., M. C. SORGATO, D. B. KELL, AND P. JOHN. 1979. Comparative aspects of the energetics of oxidative phosphorylation in bacteria and mitochondria. Biochem. Soc. Trans. 7: 870–873.

FINDENEG, G. R., AND E. FISHER. 1978. Apparent photorespiration of *Scenedesmus obliquus*: decrease during adaptation to low CO$_2$ level. Z. Pflanzenphysiol. 89: 363–371.

FLOYD, G. L., AND J. L. SALISBURY. 1977. Glycolate dehydrogenase in primitive green algae. Am. J. Bot. 64: 1294–1296.

FOCK, H. P., M. R. BADGER, D. T. CANVIN, AND S. C. WONG. 1981. Mass spectrometric determination of oxygen evolution and uptake in *Chlamydomonas reinhardtii*. (In preparation)

FOGG, G. E. 1975. Biochemical pathways in unicellular plants, p. 437–457. *In* J. P. Cooper [ed.] Photosynthesis and production in different environments. Cambridge University Press, Cambridge.

FOY, R. H., C. E. GIBSON, AND R. V. SMITH. 1976. The influence of daylength, light intensity and temperature on the growth rates of planktonic blue-green algae. Br. Phycol. J. 11: 151–163.

FOY, R. H., AND R. V. SMITH. 1980. The role of carbohydrate accumulation in the growth of planktonic *Oscillatoria* species. Br. Phycol. J. 15: 139–150.

FOYER, C. H., AND D. O. HALL. 1980. Oxygen metabolism in the active chloroplast. Trends Biochem. Sci. 5: 188–191.

FREDERICK, S. E., P. GRUBER, AND N. E. TOLBERT. 1973. The occurrence of glycolate dehydrogenase and glycolate oxidase in green plants. Plant Physiol. 52: 318–323.

FRENCH, C. S., AND D. C. FORK. 1960. Two primary photochemical reactions in photosynthesis driven by different pigments. Carnegie Inst. Wash. Yearb. 60: 351–357.

GARLAND, P. B. 1977. Energy transduction and transmission in microbial systems. Symp. Soc. Gen. Microbiol. 27: 1–21.

GERSTER, R., AND P. TOURNIER. 1977. Metabolic pathway of oxygen during photorespiration: incorporation of ^{18}O into glycolate, glycine and serine, p. 129–130. *In* Abstracts of the Fourth International Congress on Photosynthesis, Reading, September, 1977, U.K. ISES, 21 Albemarle St., London.

GIMMLER, H. 1977. Photophosphorylation *in vivo*, p. 448–472. *In* A. Trebst and M. Avron [ed.] Encyclopedia of plant physiology, new series. Vol. 5. Part I: Photosynthetic electron transport and photophosphorylation. Springer-Verlag, Berlin.

GLIDEWELL, S. M., AND J. A. RAVEN. 1975. Measurements of simultaneous oxygen uptake and evolution in *Hydrodictyon africanum*. J. Exp. Bot. 26: 479–488.

——— 1976. Photorespiration: RuDP oxygenase or hydrogen peroxide? J. Exp. Bot. 27: 200–204.

GOLDMAN, J. C., J. J. MCCARTHY, AND D. PEAVEY. 1979. Growth rate influence on the chemical composition of phytoplankton in oceanic waters. Nature (London) 279: 210–215.

GOVINDJEE, O. van H. OWENS, AND G. E. HOCH. 1963. A mass spectroscopic study of the Emerson enhancement effect. Biochim. Biophys. Acta 75: 281–284.

GRAHAM, D., AND M. L. REED. 1971. Carbonic anhydrase and the regulation of photosynthesis. Nature (London) 231: 81–83.

GRODZINSKI, B. 1979. A study of formate production and oxidation in leaf peroxisomes during photorespiration. Plant Physiol. 63: 289–293.

GRODZINSKI, B., AND B. COLMAN. 1975. The effect of osmotic stress on the oxidation of glycolate by the blue-green alga Anacystis nidulans. Planta 124: 125–134.

GRUBER, P. J., S. E. FREDERICK, AND N. E. TOLBERT. 1974. Enzymes related to lactate metabolism in green algae and lower land plants. Plant Physiol. 53: 167–170.

GUILLARD, R. R. L., AND P. KILHAM. 1977. The ecology of marine planktonic diatoms, p. 372–469. In D. Werner [ed.] The biology of diatoms. Blackwell Scientific Publications, Oxford.

GUILLARD, R. R. L., AND J. H. RYTHER. 1962. Studies on marine planktonic diatoms. I. Cyclotella nana Hustedt and Detonula confervacea (Cleve) Gran. Can. J. Microbiol. 8: 229–239.

HALLIWELL, B. 1974. Superoxide dismutase, catalase and glutathione peroxidase: solutions to the problem of living with oxygen. New Phytol. 73: 1075–1086.

——— 1978. The chloroplast at work. A review of modern developments in our understanding of chloroplast metabolism. Prog. Biophys. Mol. Biol. 33: 1–54.

HARTMANN, T., AND A. EHMKE. 1980. Role of mitochondrial glutamic dehydrogenase in the reassimilation of ammonia produced by the glycine-serine transformation. Planta 149: 207–208.

HEBER, U., AND G. H. KRAUSE. 1980. What is the physiological role of photorespiration? Trends Biochem. Sci. 5: 32–34.

HEBER, U., AND D. A. WALKER. 1979. The chloroplast envelope — barrier or bridge? Trends Biochem. Sci. 4: 252–256.

HENRY, H. F., AND E. J. NYNS. 1975. Cyanide-insensitive respiration. An alternative mitochondrial pathway. Sub-Cell. Biochem. 4: 1–66.

HOBSON, L. A., F. A. HARTLEY, AND D. E. KETCHUM. 1979. Effects of variation in daylength and temperature on net rates of photosynthesis, dark respiration and excretion by Isochrysis galbana Parke. Plant Physiol. 63: 947–951.

HOCH, G. E., O. van H. OWENS, AND B. KOK. 1963. Photosynthesis and respiration. Arch. Biochem. Biophys. 101: 171–180.

HOCHACHKA, P. W., AND J. M. TEAL. 1964. Respiratory metabolism in a marine dinoflagellate. Biol. Bull. 126: 274–281.

HOGETSU, D., AND S. MIYACHI. 1977. Some effects of CO₂ concentration during growth on subsequent photosynthetic CO₂ fixation in Chlorella. Plant Cell Physiol. 18: 347–352.

——— 1979. Role of carbonic anhydrase in photosynthetic CO₂ fixation in Chlorella. Plant Cell Physiol. 20: 747–756.

HUMPHREY, G. F. 1975. The photosynthesis: respiration ratio of some unicellular marine algae. J. Exp. Mar. Biol. Ecol. 18: 111–119.

——— 1979. Photosynthetic characteristics of algae grown under constant illumination and light-dark regimes. J. Exp. Mar. Biol. Ecol. 40: 63–70.

JACKSON, W. A., AND R. J. VOLK. 1970. Photorespiration. Annu. Rev. Plant Physiol. 21: 385–432.

JAKOBSSON, E. 1980. Interaction of cell volume, membrane potential and membrane transport parameters. Am. J. Physiol. 238: C196–C206.

KAPLAN, A., M. R. BADGER, AND J. A. BERRY. 1980a. Photosynthesis and the intracellular inorganic carbon pool in the blue-green alga Anabaena variabilis: response to external CO₂ concentration. Planta 149: 219–226.

KAPLAN, A., U. SCHREIBER, AND M. AVRON. 1980b. Salt-induced metabolic changes in Dunaliella salina. Plant Physiol. 65: 810–813.

KESSLER, E. 1973. Effect of anaerobiosis on photosynthetic reactions and nitrogen metabolism of algae with and without hydrogenase. Arch. Mikrobiol. 93: 91–100.

KEYS, A. J., I. F. BIRD, M. J. CORNELIUS, P. J. LEA, AND R. M. WALLSGROVE. 1978. Photorespiratory nitrogen cycle. Nature (London) 275: 741–743.

KIRST, G. O. 1975. Beziehungen unterschiedlicher Konzentrationen von NaCl und anderen osmotisch wirksamen substanzen auf die CO₂-Fixierung der einzelligen alge Platymonas subcordiformis. Oecologia 20: 237–254.

KIRST, G. O., AND H. J. KELLER. 1976. Der Einfluss unterschiedlicher NaCl-Konzentrationen auf die Atmung der enizelligen Alge Platymonas subcordiformis Hazen. Bot. Mar. 19: 241–244.

——— 1980. Phosphate transport in Platymonas subcordiformis after osmotic shock. Z. Pflanzenphysiol. 97: 289–297.

KLINGENBERG, M. 1979. The ADP, ATP shuttle of the mitochondrion. Trends Biochem. Sci. 4: 249–252.

KRATZ, A. W., AND J. MYERS. 1955. Photosynthesis and respiration of blue-green algae. Plant Physiol. 30: 257–280.

KREBS, H. A., AND R. L. VEECH. 1969. Equilibrium relations between pyridine nucleotides and adenine nucleotides and their roles in the regulation of metabolic processes. Adv. Enzyme Regul. 7: 397–413.

LAING, W. A., W. L. OGREN, AND R. H. HAGEMANN. 1974. Regulation of soybean net photosynthetic CO₂ fixation by the interaction of CO₂, O₂ and ribulose 1,5 diphosphate carboxylase. Plant Physiol. 54: 678–685.

LAWFORD, H. G., AND P. B. GARLAND. 1972. Proton translocation coupled to quinone reduction by reduced NAD in rat liver and ox heart mitochondria. Biochem. J. 130: 1029–1044.

LAWS, E. A. 1975. The importance of respiration losses in controlling the size distribution of marine phytoplankton. Ecology 56: 419–426.

LAWS, E. A., AND T. T. BANNISTER. 1980. Nutrient and light-limiting growth of Thalassiosira fluviatilis in continuous culture, with implications for phytoplankton growth in the ocean. Limnol. Oceanogr. 25: 457–473.

LAWS, E. A., AND J. CAPERON. 1976. Carbon and nitrogen metabolism by *Monochrysis lutheri*: measurement of growth-rate-dependent respiration rates. Mar. Biol. 36: 85–97.

LAWS, E. A., AND D. C. L. WONG. 1978. Studies of carbon and nitrogen metabolism by three marine phytoplankton species in nitrate-limited continuous cultures. J. Phycol. 14: 406–416.

LEX, M., J. B. SILVESTER, AND W. D. P. STEWART. 1972. Photorespiration and nitrogenase activity in the blue-green alga, *Anabaena cyclindrica*. Proc. R. Soc. London Ser. B 180: 87–102.

LLOYD, D. 1974a. The mitochondria of micro-organisms. Academic Press, London.

———— 1974b. Dark respiration, p. 505–529. *In* W. D. P. Stewart [ed.] Algal physiology and biochemistry. Blackwell Scientific Publications, Oxford.

LLOYD, D., AND G. TURNER. 1980. Structure, function, biogenesis and genetics of mitochondria. Symp. Soc. Gen. Microbiol. 30: 143–150.

LLOYD, N. D. H., D. T. CANVIN, AND D. A. CULVER. 1977. Photosynthesis and photorespiration in algae. Plant Physiol. 59: 936–940.

LORD, J. M., AND R. H. BROWN. 1975. Purification and some properties of *Chlorella fusca* ribulose bisphosphate carboxylase. Plant Physiol. 55: 310–314.

LORD, J. M., AND M. J. MERRETT. 1970. The regulation of glycolic oxidoreductase with the photosynthetic capacity. Biochem. J. 119: 125–127.

———— 1971. The intracellular localization of glycolate oxidoreductase in *Euglena gracilis*. Biochem. J. 124: 175–181.

LORIMER, G. M., AND T. J. ANDREWS. 1973. Plant photorespiration — an inevitable consequence of the existence of atmospheric oxygen. Nature (London) 243: 359–360.

LORIMER, G. M., T. J. ANDREWS, AND N. E. TOLBERT. 1973. Ribulose diphosphate oxygenase. II. Further proof of reaction products and mechanism of action. Biochemistry 12: 18–23.

LORIMER, G. M., M. R. BADGER, AND T. J. ANDREWS. 1977. Ribulose bisphosphate carboxylase-oxygenase. Improved methods for the activation and assay of catalytic activities. Anal. Biochem. 78: 66–75.

LORIMER, G. M., K. C. WOO, J. A. BERRY, AND C. B. OSMOND. 1978a. The C_2 photosynthetic carbon oxidation cycle in leaves of higher plants: pathway and consequences, p. 311–322. *In* J. Coombs, D. O. Hall, and T. W. Goodwin [ed.] Photosynthesis 77. The Biochemical Society, London.

LORIMER, G. M., C. B. OSMOND, T. AKAZAWA, AND S. ASAMI. 1978b. On the mechanism of glycolate synthesis by *Chromatium* and *Chlorella*. Arch. Biochem. Biophys. 185: 49–56.

MCCURRY, S. D., N. P. HALL, J. PIERCE, C. PAECH, AND N. E. TOLBERT. 1978. Ribulose bisphosphate carboxylase-oxygenase from parsley. Biochem. Biophys. Res. Commun. 84: 895–900.

MCFADDEN, B. A., J. M. LORD, A. ROWE, AND S. DILKS. 1975. Composition, quarternary structure and catalytic properties of D-ribulose-1,5-bisphosphate

carboxylase from *Euglena gracilis*. Eur. J. Biochem. 54: 195–206.

MARRE, E. 1961. Phosphorylation in higher plants. Annu. Rev. Plant Physiol. 12: 195–219.

MEHLER, A. H., AND A. H. BROWN. 1952. Studies on reactions of illuminated chloroplasts. II. Simultaneous photoproduction and consumption of oxygen: studies with oxygen isotopes. Arch. Biochem. Biophys. 38: 365–371.

MERRETT, M. J., AND J. M. LORD. 1973. Glycolate formation and metabolism by algae. New Phytol. 72: 751–757.

MITCHELL, P. 1976. Possible molecular mechanisms of the protonmotive function of cytochrome systems. J. Theor. Biol. 62: 327–367.

MOLLOY, G. R., AND R. R. SCHMIDT. 1970. Studies on the regulation of ribulose 1,5 diphosphate carboxylase synthesis during the cell cycle of the eukaryote *Chlorella*. Biochem. Biophys. Res. Commun. 40: 1125–1133.

MOORE, A. L., C. JACKSON, B. HALLIWELL, J. E. DENCH, AND D. O. HALL. 1977. Intramitochondrial localization of glycine decarboxylase in spinach leaves. Biochem. Biophys. Res. Communs. 78: 483–491.

MOSHKIND, L. V. 1961. Photosynthesis by dinoflagellates of the Black Sea. Sov. Plant Physiol. 8: 129–132.

MOSS, B. 1977. Adaptations of epipelic and epipsammic freshwater algae. Oecologia 28: 103–108.

MOYLE, J., AND P. MITCHELL. 1978a. Cytochrome c oxidase is not a proton pump. FEBS Lett. 88: 268–272.

———— 1978b. Measurements of mitochondrial H/O quotients: effects of phosphate and N-ethylmaleimide. FEBS Lett. 90: 361–365.

MUJAJI, B. W. 1980. The pentose phosphate pathway revised. Biochem. Educ. 8: 76–78.

MUR, L. R., AND R. O. BEIJDORF. 1978. A model for the succession from green to blue-green algae based on light limitation. Verh. Int. Verein. Limnol. 20: 2314–2321.

MYERS, J., AND J. R. GRAHAM. 1961. On the mass culture of algae. III. Light diffusors: high versus low temperature Chlorellas. Plant Physiol. 36: 342–346.

NEIJSSEL, O. H., AND D. W. TEMPEST. 1976. Bioenergetic aspects of aerobic growth of *Klebsiella aerogenes* NCTC in carbon-limited and carbon-sufficient chemostat cultures. Arch. Microbiol. 107: 215–222.

NEILSON, A. H., AND R. R. LEWIN. 1974. The uptake and utilization of organic carbon by algae: an essay in comparative biochemistry. Phycologia 13: 227–264.

NELSON, E. B., AND S. J. SURZYCKI. 1976a. A mutant strain of *Chlamydomonas reinhardtii* exhibiting altered ribulose diphosphate carboxylase. Eur. J. Biochem. 61: 465–474.

———— 1976b. Characterization of oxygenase activity in a mutant of *Chlamydomonas reinhardtii* exhibiting altered ribulose diphosphate carboxylase. Eur. J. Biochem. 61: 465–474.

NELSON, E. B., AND N. E. TOLBERT. 1969. The regulation of glycolate metabolism in *Chlamydomonas reinhardtii*. Biochim. Biophys. Acta 184: 263–270.

NELSON, E. B., A. CENEDELLA, AND N. E. TOLBERT. 1969. Carbonic anhydrase levels in *Chlamydomonas*. Phytochemistry 8: 2305–2306.

NICHOLLS, D. G. 1979. Brown adipose tissue mitochondria. Biochim. Biophys. Acta 549: 1–29.

ODUM, H. T., AND R. C. PINKERTON. 1955. Time's speed regulator: the optimum efficiency for maximum power output in physical and biological systems. Am. Sci. 43: 331–343.

OGAWARA, T., T. FUJII, AND S. AIBA. 1980. Effect of oxygen on the growth (yield) of Chlorella vulgaris. Arch. Microbiol. 127: 25–31.

OKABE, K. I., G. A. CODD, AND W. D. P. STEWART. 1979. Hydroxylamine stimulates carboxylase activity and inhibits oxygenase activity of cyanobacterial ribulose bisphosphate carboxylase-oxygenase. Nature (London) 279: 525–527.

OLSEN, L. F., A. TELFER, AND J. BARBER. 1980. A flash spectroscopic study of the kinetics of the electrochromic shift, proton release and the redox behaviour of cytochromes f and b-563 during cyclic electron flow. FEBS Lett. 118: 11–17.

OWENS, O. van H., AND G. E. HOCH. 1963. Enhancement and de-enhancement effects in Anacystis nidulans. Biochim. Biophys. Acta 75: 183–186.

PALMER, J. M. 1979. The 'uniqueness' of plant mitochondria. Trans. Biochem. Soc. 7: 246–252.

PARROTT, L. M., AND J. H. SLATER. 1980. The DNA, RNA and protein composition of the cyanobacterium Anacystis nidulans grown in light and carbon dioxide-limited chemostats. Arch. Microbiol. 127: 53–58.

PATTERSON, C. O. P., AND J. MYERS. 1973. Photosynthetic production of H₂O₂ by Anacystis nidulans. Plant Physiol. 51: 104–109.

PAUL, J. S., C. W. SULLIVAN, AND B. E. VOLCANI. 1975. Photorespiration in diatoms. II. Mitochondrial ttcolate dehydrogenase in Cylindrotheca fusiformis and Nitzschia alba. Arch. Biochem. Biophys. 169: 153–159.

PAUL, J. S., AND B. E. VOLCANI. 1974. Photorespiration in diatoms. I. The oxidation of glycolic acid in Thalassiosira pseudonana (Cyclotella nana). Arch Microbiol. 101: 115–120.

1975. Photorespiration in diatoms. III. Glycolate: cytochrome c reductase in the diatom Cylindrotheca fusiformis. Plant Sci. Lett. 5: 281–285.

1976a. A mitochondrial glycolate: cytochrome c reductase in Chlamydomonas reinhardtii. Planta 129: 59–61.

1976b. Photorespiration in diatoms. IV. Two pathways of glycolate metabolism in synchronized cultures of Cylindrotheca fusiformis. Arch. Microbiol. 110: 247–252.

PELLEGRINI, M. 1980. Three-dimensional reconstruction of organelles in Euglena gracilis Z. I. Qualitative and quantitative changes of chloroplasts and mitochondrial reticulum in synchronous photoautotrophic culture. J. Cell Sci. 43: 137–166.

PELROY, R. A., AND J. A. BASSHAM. 1973. Efficiency of energy conversion by aerobic glucose metabolism in Aphanocapsa 6714. J. Bacteriol. 115: 937–942.

PELROY, R. A., M. R. KIRK, AND J. A. BASSHAM. 1976. Photosystem two regulation of macromolecule synthesis in the blue-green alga Aphanocapsa 6714. J. Bacteriol. 128: 623–632.

PENNING DE VRIES, F. W. T. 1975. The cost of maintenance processes in plant cells. Ann. Bot. 39: 77–92.

PENNING DE VRIES, F. W. T., A. H. M. BRUNSTING, AND M. M. VAN LAAR. 1974. Products, requirements and efficiency of biosynthesis: a quantitative approach. J. Theor. Biol. 45: 339–377.

PESCHEK, G. A. 1980. Electron transport reactions in respiratory particles of hydrogenase-induced Anacystis nidulans. Arch. Microbiol. 125: 123–133.

PESCHEK, G. A., AND E. BRODA. 1973. Utilization of fructose by a unicellular blue-green alga, Anacystis nidulans. Naturwissenschaften 60: 479–480.

PESCHEK, G. A., AND G. SCHMETTERER. 1978. Reversible photooxidative loss of pigments and of intracellular membranes in the blue-green alga Anacystis nidulans. FEMS Microbiol. Lett.3: 295–297.

PIRT, S. J., Y. K. LEE, A. RICHMOND, AND M. W. PIRT. 1980. The photosynthetic efficiency of Chlorella biomass growth with reference to solar energy utilization. J. Chem. Tech. Bioeng. 30: 25–34.

POWLES, S. B. 1979. The role of carbon assimilation and photorespiratory carbon cycling in the avoidance of photoinhibition in intact leaves of C₃ and C₄ plants. Ph.D. thesis, Australian National University, Canberra.

PRÉZELIN, B. B. 1981. Light reactions in photosynthesis. Can. Bull. Fish. Aquat. Sci. 210: 1–43.

PRÉZELIN, B. B., AND R. S. ALBERTE. 1978. Photosynthetic characteristics and organization of chlorophyll in marine dinoflagellates. Proc. Natl. Acad. Sci. Wash. 75: 1801–1804.

PRÉZELIN, B. B., AND B. M. SWEENEY. 1978. Photoadaptation of photosynthesis in Gonyaulax polyedra. Mar. Biol. 48: 37–35.

PRITCHARD, G. G., C. P. WHITTINGHAM, AND W. J. GRIFFIN. 1961. Effect of isonicotinyl hydrazide on the path of carbon in photosynthesis Nature (London) 191: 553–554.

1963. The effect of isonicotinyl hydrazide on the photosynthetic incorporation of radioactive CO₂ into ethanol-soluble compounds in Chlorella. J. Exp. Bot. 14: 281–289.

RADMER, R. J., AND B. KOK. 1976. Photoreduction of O₂ primes and replaces CO₂ fixation. Plant Physiol. 58: 336–340.

RADMER, R. J., B. KOK, AND O. OLLINGER. 1978. Kinetics and apparent Kₘ of O₂ cycle under conditions of limiting carbon dioxide fixation. Plant Physiol. 61: 915–917.

RADMER, R. J., AND O. OLLINGER. 1980. Light-driven uptake of oxygen, carbon dioxide and bicarbonate by the green alga Scenedesmus. Plant Physiol. 65: 723–729.

RAVEN, J. A. 1971. Energy metabolism in green cells. Trans. Bot. Soc. Edinb. 41: 219–225.

1972a. Endogenous inorganic carbon sources in plant photosynthesis. I. Occurrence of dark respiratory pathways in illuminated green cells. New Phytol. 71: 227–247.

1972b. Endogenous inorganic carbon sources in plant photosynthesis. II. Comparison of total CO₂ production in the light with measured CO₂ evolution in the light. New Phytol. 71: 995–1014.

1976a. Division of labour between chloroplasts and cytoplasm, p. 403–443. In J. Barber [ed.] The intact chloroplast. Elsevier, Amsterdam.

1976b. The quantitative role of 'dark' respiratory processes in heterotrophic and photolithotrophic plant growth. Ann. Bot. 40: 587–602.

1976c. Transport in algal cells, p. 129–188. In U. Lüttge and M. G. Pitman [ed.] Encyclopedia of plant physiology. New Series. Vol. 2A. Transport in Cells and Tissues. Springer-Verlag, Berlin.

1977. Ribulose bisphosphate carboxlyase activity in terrestrial plants: significance of O_2 and CO_2 diffusion. Curr. Adv. Plant Sci. 9: 579–590.

1980a. Nutrient transport in microalgae. Adv. Microb. Physiol. 21: 47–226.

1980b. Chloroplasts of eukaryotic micro-organisms. Symp. Soc. Gen. Microbiol. 30: 181–205.

1981. Nutritional strategies of submerged benthic plants: The acquisition of C, N and P by rhizophytes and haptophytes. New Phytol. 86: 1–30.

RAVEN, J. A., AND J. BEARDALL. 1981. The intrinsic permeability of biological membranes to H^+: significance for the efficiency of low rates of energy transformation. FEMS Microbiol. Lett. 10: 1–7.

RAVEN, J. A., AND S. M. GLIDEWELL. 1975a. Sources of ATP for active phosphate transport in Hydrodictyon africanum: evidence for pseudocyclic photophosphorylation in vivo. New Phytol. 75: 197–204.

1975b. Photosynthesis, respiration and growth in the shade alga Hydrodictyon africanum. Photosynthetica 9: 361–371.

1978. C_4 characteristics of photosynthesis in the C_3 alga Hydrodictyon africanum. Plant Cell Environ. 1: 185–197.

1981. Processes limiting photosynthetic conductance, p. 109–136. In C. B. Johnson [ed.] Physiological processes limiting crop yield. Butterworths, London.

RAVEN, J. A., F. A. SMITH, AND S. M. GLIDEWELL. 1979. Photosynthetic capacities and biological strategies of giant-celled and small-celled macro-algae. New Phytol. 83: 299–309.

REED, M. L., AND D. G. GRAHAM. 1977. Carbon dioxide and the regulation of photosynthesis: activities of photosynthetic enzy   and carbonate dehydratase (carbonic anhydrase) .. Chlorella after growth or adaptation in different carbon dioxide concentrations. Austr. J. Plant Physiol. 4: 87–98.

RICH, P. R., A. L. MOORE, W. J. INGLEDEW, AND W. D. BONNER JR. 1977. EPR studies of higher plant mitochondria. I. Ubisemiquinone and its relation to alternative respiratory oxidations. Biochim. Biophys. Acta 462: 501–514.

RIED, A. 1970. Energetic aspects of the interaction between photosynthesis and respiration, p. 231–246. In Measurement of photosynthetic productivity, PUDOC, Wageningen.

RIED, A., I. MULLER, AND C. J. SOEDER. 1962. Wirkung von Stoffwechselinhibitoren auf den respiratorischen Gaswechsel verschiedener Entwicklungsstadien von Chlorella pyrenoidosa. Vortr. Gesamtgeb. Bot. Dtsch. Ges. 1: 187–194.

RIED, A., AND B. REINHARDT. 1980. Distribution of excitation energy between photosystem two and photosystem one in red algae. III. Quantum requirements of the induction of a State 2–State 1 transition. Biochim. Biophys. Acta 592: 76–86.

RIED, A., C. J. SOEDER, AND I. MULLER. 1963. Uber die Atmung synchron kultivierter Chlorella. I. Veranderingen des respiratorisches Gaswechsels im Laufe des Entwicklungscyclus. Arch. Mikrobiol. 45: 343–358.

ROSA, L. 1979. The ATP/2e ratio during photosynthesis in intact Spinacia chloroplasts. Biochem. Biophys. Res. Commun. 88: 154–162.

RYTHER, J. H., AND R. R. L. GUILLARD. 1962. Studies of marine planktonic diatoms. III. Some effects of temperature on respiration of five species. Can. J. Microbiol. 8: 447–453.

SARGENT, D. F., AND C. P. S. TAYLOR. 1972. Terminal oxidases of Chlorella pyrenoidosa. Plant Physiol. 49: 775–778.

1975. On the respiratory enhancement in Chlorella pyrenoidosa by blue light. Planta 127: 171–175.

SAYRE, P. T., AND P. H. HOMANN. 1979. Correlation between photorespiratory activity and hydrogenase content in Chlorella strains. Plant Physiol. 63: 153s.

SCOTT, J. M. 1980. Effect of growth rate of the food alga on the growth/ingestion efficiency of a marine herbivore. J. Mar. Biol. Assoc. U.K. 60: 681–702.

SENGER, H., AND P. FLEISCHENHACKER. 1978. Adaptation of Scenedesmus to light intensities. Physiol. Plant 43: 35–42.

SHARPLESS, T. K., AND R. A. BUETOW. 1970. An inducible alternate oxidase in Euglena gracilis mitochondria. J. Biol. Chem. 245: 58–70.

SHELP, B. J., AND D. T. CANVIN. 1980a. Utilization of exogenous inorganic carbon species in photosynthesis by Chlorella pyrenoidosa. Plant Physiol. 65: 774–779.

1980b. Photorespiration and oxygen inhibition of photosynthesis in Chlorella pyrenoidosa. Plant Physiol. 65: 780–784.

SHIMAZAKI, K., K. TAKAMIYA, AND M. NISHIMURA. 1978. Studies on electron transfer systems in the marine diatom Phaeodactylum tricornutum. II. Identification and determination of quinones, cytochromes and flavoproteins. J. Biochem. Tokyo 83: 1639–1642.

SLEIGH, M. A. [ed.] 1974. Cilia and flagella. Academic Press, London.

SMAYDA, T. J., AND B. MITCHELL-INNES. 1974. Dark survival of autotrophic, planktonic marine diatoms. Mar. Biol. 25: 195–202.

SMILLIE, R. M. 1963. Formation and function of soluble proteins in chloroplasts. Can. J. Bot. 41: 123–154.

SOEDER, C. J., I. MULLER, AND A. RIED. 1962. Uber der Einfluss von Salzkonzentration und Nitratangebout auf die RQ und das N-reduzierten-System von vollsynchroner Chlorella pyrenoidosa. Vortr. Gesamtgeb. Bot. Dtsch. Ges. 1: 195–200.

SOMERVILLE, C. R., AND W. L. OGREN. 1979. A phosphoglycolate phosphatase-deficient mutant of Arabidopsis. Nature (London) 280: 833–836.

1980. Photorespiration mutants of Arabidopsis thaliana deficient in serine-glyoxylate aminotransferase activity. Proc. Natl. Acad. Sci. Wash. 77: 2684–2687.

SPALDING, M. H., AND W. L. OGREN. 1980. Properties of the "CO_2 pump" in Chlamydomonas. Plant Physiol. 65: 69a.

STABENAU, H. 1974a. Vereilung von Microbody-Enzymen aus *Chlamydomonas* in Dichtegradienten. Planta 118: 35–42.

———. 1974b. Localization of enzymes of glycolate metabolism in the alga *Chlorobium elongatum*. Plant Physiol. 54: 921–924.

———. 1975. Zur localization von Glycolsaure-oxidase in *Spirogyra*. Ber. Dtsch. Bot. Ges. 88: 469–472.

———. 1977. Einfluss von CO_2-Konzentration auf Wachstum und Stoffwechsel von *Chlorogonium elongatum*. Biochem. Physiol. Pflanz. 171: 449–454.

———. 1980. Enzymes of glycolate metabolism in the alga *Mougeottia*. Plant Physiol. 65: 15a.

STEWART, R., AND G. A. CODD. 1980. Glycolate and glyoxylate excretion by the green alga *Sphaerocystis shroeteri*. Abstracts International Phycological Union Symposium, Glasgow, August 1980, p. 48.

STEWART, K. D., AND K. R. MATTOX. 1975. Comparative cytology, evolution and classification of the green algae with some consideration of the origin of other organisms with chlorophylls *a* and *b*. Bot. Rev. 41: 104–135.

STITT, M., AND T. AP REES. 1979. Capacities of pea chloroplasts to catalyse the oxidative pentose phosphate pathway and glycolysis. Phytochemistry 18: 1905–1912.

———. 1980. Estimation of the activity of the oxidative pentose phosphate pathway in pea chloroplasts. Phytochemistry 19: 1583–1585.

SYRETT, P. J. 1955. The assimilation of ammonia and nitrate by nitrogen-starved cells of *Chlorella vulgaris*. I. The assimilation of small quantities of nitrogen. Physiol. Plant 8: 924–929.

———. 1981. Nitrogen metabolism of microalgae. Can. Bull. Fish. Aquat. Sci. 210: 182–210.

THOMAS, W. H. 1955. Heterotrophic nutrition and respiration in *Gonyaulax polyedra*. J. Protozool. 2: 2s–3s.

TOLBERT, N. E. 1974. Photorespiration, p. 474–504. *In* W. D. P. Stewart [ed.] Algal physiology and biochemistry. Blackwell Scientific Publications, Oxford.

TOMAS, C. R. 1980. *Olisthodiscus luteus* (Chrysophyceae). IV. Effects of light intensity and temperature on photosynthesis and cellular composition. J. Phycol. 16: 1–15.

TROXLER, R. F., AND C. D. OFFNER. 1979. δ-Aminolaevulinic acid synthesis in a *Cyanidium caldarium* mutant unable to make chlorophyll *a* and phycobiliproteins. Arch. Biochem. Biophys. 195: 53–65.

VANDERLEYDEN, J., E. VAN DEN FYNDE, AND H. VERACHTENT. 1980a. Nature of the effect of adenosine-5'-monophosphate on the cyanide-insensitive respiration in mitochondria of *Moniliella tomentosa*. Biochem. J. 186: 309–316.

VANDERLEYDEN, J., C. PEETERS, H. VERACHTENT, AND H. BERTRAND. 1980b. Stimulation of the alternative oxidases of *Neurospora crassa* by nucleoside phosphates. Biochem. J. 188: 141–144.

VAN GEMERDEN, H. 1980. Survival of *Chromatium vinosum* at low light intensities Arch. Microbiol. 125: 115–121.

VAN LIERE, L., AND L. R. MUR. 1979. Growth kinetics of *Oscillatoria agardhii* Gomont in continuous culture, limited in its growth by light energy supply. J. Gen. Microbiol. 115: 153–160.

VAN LIERE, L., L. R. MUR, C. E. GIVSON, AND M. HERDMAN. 1979. Growth and physiology of *Oscillatoria agardhii* Gomont cultivated in continuous culture and with a light-dark cycle. Arch. Microbiol. 123: 315–318.

VENNESLAND, B., AND K. JETSCHMANN. 1976. The effect of cyanide and some other carbonyl binding reagents on glycolate excretion by *Chlorella vulgaris*. Planta 128: 81–84.

WARNCKE, J., AND C. L. SLAYMAN. 1980. Metabolic modulation of stoichiometry in a proton pump. Biochem. Biophys. Acta 591: 224–233.

WEIS, D., AND A. H. BROWN. 1959. Kinetic relationships between photosynthesis and respiration in the algal flagellate *Ochromonas malhamensis*. Plant Physiol. 34: 235–239.

WERNER, D. [ed.] 1977. The biology of diatoms. Blackwells Scientific Publications, Oxford.

WHITTENBURY, R., AND D. P. KELLY. 1977. Autotrophy: a conceptual phoenix. Symp. Soc. Gen. Microbiol. 27: 121–149.

WHITTINGHAM, C. P. 1952. Rate of photosynthesis and concentration of carbon dioxide in *Chlorella*. Nature (London) 170: 1017–1018.

WIKSTROM, M., AND K. KRAB. 1979. Mechanism and stoichiometry of redox-linked proton translocation in mitochondria. Biochem. Soc. Trans. 7: 880–886.

WISKICH, J. T. 1977. Mitochondrial metabolite transport. Annu. Rev. Plant Physiol. 28: 45–69.

WOO, K. C., AND C. B. OSMOND. 1976. Glycine decarboxylation in mitochondria isolated from spinach leaves. Aust. J. Plant Physiol. 3: 771–785.

YADER, J. A. 1979. Effect of temperature on light-limited growth and chemical composition of *Skeletonema costatum* (Bacillariophyceae). J. Phycol. 15: 362–370.

YAMANAKA, T., AND K. FUJII. 1980. Cytochrome a-type terminal oxidase derived from *Thiobacillus novellus*. Molecular and enzymatic properties. Biochem. Biophys. Acta 591: 53–62.

ZENVIRT, D., A. KAPLAN, AND L. REINHOLD. 1980. Accumulation of inorganic C in *Dunaliella salina*. Plant Physiol. 65: 70a.

ZIEM-HANCK, U., AND U. HEBER. 1980. Oxygen requirement of photosynthetic CO_2 assimilation. Biochim. Biophys. Acta 591: 266–274.

Photosynthetic Products, Physiological State, and Phytoplankton Growth

IAN MORRIS[1]

Marine Program, University of New Hampshire, Durham, NH 03824, USA

Introduction

The ultimate end-product of photosynthesis by phytoplankton is the synthesis of new cell material that permits the component cells to increase in mass and leads, eventually, to an increase in the number of cells in the population. The nature of the newly synthesized cell material will depend on the balance between the various metabolic reactions occurring in the cell. The nature of such a balance might be expected to be regulated by the environmental conditions prevailing at any given time and the physiological state of the algae that make up the phytoplankton population.

In this broad view of photosynthesis, it is difficult to make any clear distinctions between those reactions specific for the photosynthetic process and those of other aspects of cellular metabolism. Yet this broad view of photosynthesis is the approach of this paper. Thus, the discussion will be concerned with the overall end-products of photosynthesis — the major storage products and those essential polymers required for cell growth. Emphasis will be placed on the way in which the distribution of fixed carbon between the various types of products and the resulting chemical composition of the algae might be related to the environmental factors that control the growth and distribution of phytoplankton in the oceans.

Some Boundaries

It is clearly neither possible, nor desirable, to consider the entire field of algal metabolism in the way suggested by the opening remarks. It is necessary to draw some boundaries (albeit artificial) around the subject. Therefore, the following constraints have been put on the subject matter to be discussed:

1) No consideration is given to the production of small-molecular-weight metabolites such as the individual amino acids, fatty acids, sugars, nucleotides, etc.

2) Similarly, no consideration is given to the detailed chemical composition of the various end-products — the amino acid composition of proteins, the fatty-acid components of lipids, the nature of the polysaccharide material, etc.

3) Little consideration is given to the assimilation of elements other than carbon. A proper understanding of the factors that control the chemical composition of phytoplankton and the ultimate end-products of synthesis depends on understanding the assimilation of elements such as N, P, Si, S, etc., as well as C. Because this paper is part of a session on "photosynthesis," and consideration of other elements is the concern of other papers, emphasis is placed on C assimilation.

4) Finally, little mention is made of the pigment composition of phytoplankton. Clearly, this aspect is of profound importance in distinguishing the major groups of algae and in any understanding of the response of cells to varying illumination. However, few data permit one to consider the pigments as end-products of phytosynthetic C assimilation and their consideration would be inappropriate here.

As a result of such constraints, emphasis can be defined more precisely. It attempts to examine the relative synthesis of lipid, polysaccharide, and protein during the photosynthetic assimilation of inorganic carbon by marine phytoplankton. The concept that such an examination might be of relevance to the physiological ecology of phytoplankton depends on the assumption that the synthesis of essential growth materials such as proteins, in comparison with that of "storage" products such as lipid and polysaccharide, might be an important variable. This assumption is not based entirely on a priori reasoning, but depends, also, on empirical data obtained from studies with algal cultures.

Before continuing, it is worth emphasizing that by limiting the discussion to the overall products of C assimilation, several approaches to the physiological state of phytoplankton that have attracted considerable attention in recent years will be omitted. For example, a hyperbolic relationship between the cellular content of a limiting nutrient and the growth rate has been observed for a number of different systems (Fuhs 1969; Caperon and Meyer 1972; Paasche 1973; Droop 1974). Thus, the reasoning suggests, measurement of the cellular content of a particular nutrient might indicate its possible role as a limiting factor in the environment. Similarly, the kinetics of uptake of such nutrients might be expected to be a useful indicator of the factor that controls phytoplankton growth. Other examples of attempts to measure the physiological state of phytoplankton

[1] Present address: Center for Environmental & Estuarine Studies, University of Maryland, P.O. Box 775, Cambridge, MD.

include measurements of C:chlorophyll ratios (Steele and Baird 1961), carotenoid:chlorophyll ratios (Yentsch and Vaccaro 1958), adenylate energy charge (Falkowski 1977), and cellular content of such parameters as chlorophyll a, ATP, N, C, and P (e.g. Sakshaug and Holm-Hansen 1977; Sakshaug 1977).

Thus, an approach that emphasizes the relative importance of selected end-products of C assimilation is only one of several possible methods of relating characteristics of cell chemistry and metabolism to the controlling environmental factors. Lack of consideration of the other approaches is not to deny their importance. It merely recognizes the context into which this particular paper fits, as well as the restriction of space.

The Approach

The paper is divided into four basic parts:
1) A consideration of early work with *Chlorella*.
2) Some discussion of data from cultures of other algae, notably marine diatoms.
3) A summary of the major factors that influence photosynthetic products in algal cultures.
4) An analysis of available data from natural populations of marine phytoplankton.

In each part, two aspects of the data are considered: (a) the chemical composition of the cells and (b) the biochemical characteristics of the photosynthetic process, as revealed by the products of C assimilation. The cellular composition of the cells represents the "true" end-product of all synthetic reactions (including those of photosynthesis) in which the cell integrates the various processes over time periods equivalent to generation times. Studies of the biochemical characteristics of photosynthetic C assimilation can be viewed as attempts on the part of the scientist to understand some reactions (generally measured over relatively short times) that contribute to the integrated picture presented by the cellular composition. Perhaps surprisingly, there are few studies in which both the chemical composition and the patterns of C assimilation have been included in the same investigation. Also, there are many more data on the chemical composition of algae, particularly with natural populations, than on the products of C assimilation. Thus, precise comparisons are difficult. However, it will be seen that the juxtaposition of chemical composition and biochemical aspects of C assimilation raises important questions and such questions will become a central theme for the paper.

Early Work with *Chlorella*

It is popular for present-day phytoplanktologists to doubt the validity of considering results obtained with the "laboratory weed" *Chlorella*. Differences in algal types, densities of suspensions, concentrations of essential nutrients, etc., make such doubts understandable. However, failure to recognize the earlier work with this important alga can lead to an embarrassing announcement of a discovery made three decades earlier. The papers of Spoehr and Milner (1949), Myers (1949), Myers and Johnston (1949), and Myers and Cramer (1948) are examples of work with *Chlorella* that formed the starting point for later studies.

CHEMICAL COMPOSITION

The work of Spoehr and Milner (1949) established the essential characteristics of metabolism in *Chlorella*, i.e. that the alga is, in essence, a protein-synthesizing organism and that its metabolism can vary considerably with changing environmental conditions. A typical elementary composition of organic matter in *Chlorella* is 53% C, 7.5% H, 28.5% O, and 10.8% N. As Myers (1962) points out, 8–10% N implies a protein content of 50–60%. This predominantly protein-synthesizing type of metabolism can be forced into a form involving synthesis of non-N-containing compounds such as carbohydrate or lipid. This can be achieved by prolonged N depletion, or by transferring cells that grow at low light intensities to higher intensities.

Myers (1962) pointed to an anomaly in the history of biology, i.e. that "an essentially protein-synthesizing organism, *Chlorella*, was selected as a standard organism for study of photosynthesis, a process thought to be an exclusive synthesis of carbohydrate."

PHOTOSYNTHETIC CHARACTERISTICS

The predominant synthesis of protein in healthy growing cells of *Chlorella*, and the variability of such a phenomenon with changing environmental conditions, are confirmed by studies of certain characteristics of the photosynthetic process. The work of Myers (1949) illustrates the amount of information that can be inferred from a simple measurement of the assimilatory quotient (A.Q. = CO_2 absorbed/O_2 evolved). Table 1 summarizes such data and illustrates how the previous history of the cell and environmental conditions control the relative synthesis of carbohydrate and protein.

One other point emerges from the early work of Myers (1946a, b, 1949). Growth of *Chlorella* saturates at a lower light intensity than does photosynthesis. This observation puzzled Myers and it continues to be of relevance to phytoplankton growth and photosynthesis in the sea.

Thus, this early work with *Chlorella* established the essential features of algal photosynthesis. It also

TABLE 1. Some characteristics of photosynthesis in *Chlorella*. (From Myers 1949.)

Balanced equations for growth with:

Nitrate

$$1.0\ NO_3^- + 5.7\ CO_2 + 5.4\ H_2O \rightarrow C_{5.7}H_{9.8}O_{2.3}N + 8.5\ O_2 + 1.0\ OH^-$$

$$A.Q. = -0.69$$

and *Ammonium*

$$1.0\ NH_4^+ + 5.7\ CO_2 + 3.4\ H_2O \rightarrow C_{5.7}H_{9.8}O_{2.3}N + 6.25\ O_2 + 1.0\ H^+$$

$$A.Q. = -0.91$$

Previous history	A.Q. (CO_2/O_2)		Cho/N (inferred)
	low light	high light	
Grown low light	−0.68	−0.88	normal
4 h high light	−0.4	−	> normal
3 d dark	−0.91	−0.96	< normal
Normal		−0.86	
N-deficient + NO_3'		−0.74	
N-deficient − NO_3		−0.99	

initiated an awareness of the close links between C and N assimilation, an awareness that continues to be prominent in present-day studies of the physiological ecology of marine phytoplankton.

Other Species

After the initial work with *Chlorella*, it became important to establish the extent to which the major observations also apply to other types of algae, notably those that might be more important constituents of phytoplankton populations.

CHEMICAL COMPOSITION

Tables 2 and 3 reproduce data that support the idea that the prominent synthesis of protein observed with *Chlorella* can also be measured in other microalgae from several different groups. Data such as these

TABLE 2. Chemical composition of various species of marine phytoplankton. The algae were harvested in exponential phase. ("Continuous" light, 18°C, harvested during exponential growth, g's between 8 and 36 h.) (After Parsons et al. 1961.)

		% dry wt.	
	Protein	carbohydrate	Fat
Chlorophyceae			
Tetraselmis maculata	52	15.0	2.9
Dunaliella salina	57	31.6	6.4
Chrysophyceae			
Monochrysis lutheri	49	31.4	11.6
Syracosphaera catterae	56	17.8	4.6
Bacillariophyceae			
Chaetoceros sp.	35	6.6	6.9
Skeletonema costatum	37	20.8	4.7
Coscinodiscus sp.	17	4.1	1.8
Phaeodactylum tricornutum	33	24.0	6.6
Dinophyceae			
Amphidinium carteri	28	30.5	18.0
Exuviella sp.	31	37.0	15.0
Myxophyceae			
Agmenellum quadriplicatum	36	31.5	12.8

TABLE 3. Lipid, carbohydrate, and protein content of diatoms (expressed as a percentage of the ash-free "dry" weight). (After Lewin and Guillard 1963.)

Organism	Fat	Carbohydrate	Protein
Rhabdonema adriaticum (from plankton)	44.16	13.6	13.25
Chaetoceros decipiens (from plankton)	27.94	13.2	21.50
Chaetoceros sp. (unialgal culture, growing exponentially)	9.5	9.2	48.6
Skeletonema costatum (unialgal culture, growing exponentially)	7.7	34.1	60.6
Coscindiscus sp. (unialgal culture, growing exponentially)	4.2	9.5	39.5
Phaeodactylum tricornutum (unialgal culture, growing exponentially)	7.1	25.9	35.7
Phaeodactylum tricornutum (fusiform cells from 16-d pure culture)	38.6	2.2	46.5
Phaeodactylum tricornutum (oval cells from 16-d pure culture)	26.6	21.1	37.7
Cerataulina bergonii (unialgal culture, grown 2–4 wk)	14.76	26.72[a]	58.52
Chaetoceros lauderi (unialgal culture, grown 2–4 wk)	16.46	21.10[a]	62.44
Skeletonema costatum (unialgal culture, grown 2–4 wk)	21.93	34.55[a]	43.52
Leptocylindrus danicus (unialgal culture, grown 2–4 wk)	20.73	33.02[a]	46.25

[a]By difference.

form the basis for the idea that species differences are not significant in determining the gross chemical composition of the cells. Possible uncertainty surrounds the question of lipid synthesis in diatoms. It has sometimes been suggested that diatoms synthesize fats rather than carbohydrates as storage products (references cited in Lewin and Guillard 1963). In young exponentially growing cultures of diatoms, there is little evidence to support this generalization. However, it appears valid for certain species of diatoms (Lewin and Guillard).

The same variability of metabolism described earlier for *Chlorella* has been observed in cultures of other types of algae. Thus, prolonged growth in batch cultures under conditions that create severe N deficiency cause an increased synthesis of non-N-containing compounds (lipids or carbohydrates) at the expense of protein. Collyer and Fogg (1955) described the reciprocal relationship between protein and fat content during batch growth of six species belonging to the Chlorophyceae, Euglenophyceae, Xanthophyceae, and Bacillariophyceae. Table 4 describes the observations of Myklestad (1974) on the changing protein:carbohydrate ratio during batch growth of seven species of marine diatoms (a result also observed by Myklestad and Haug 1972). Other data on the changing nutritional patterns of algae are reviewed by Fogg (1959, 1965).

TABLE 4. The protein:carbohydrate ratios of seven species of marine diatoms grown for various periods in batch culture. (After Myklestad 1974.)

	Days of growth			
	0	2	6	12
Chaetoceros debilis	2.40	1.10	0.63	0.53
Chaetoceros curvisetus	1.36	1.24	0.88	0.58
Chaetoceros affinis var *willei*	2.16	1.51	0.31	0.23
Chaetoceros socialis	1.61	1.26	0.42	0.40
Thalassiosira gravida	2.31	1.59	0.83	0.55
Skeletonema costatum	1.86	1.21	0.34	0.18
Thalassiosira fluviatilis	0.60	0.39	0.16	0.11

Healey (1975) provides an extensive review of literature that deals with the physiological indicators of nutrient deficiency in algae. Part of that review considered the cellular contents of protein and carbohydrate. Healey recognized an overlap between nutrient-sufficient and nutrient-deficient algae in their protein or carbohydrate contents. However, use of the protein:carbohydrate ratio reduced this overlap considerably. Healey also recognized that use of the protein:carbohydrate ratio as an indicator of nutrient deficiency can be unreliable when considering algae that store lipid (rather than carbohydrate) under nutrient deficient conditions, so that a ratio of protein:carbohydrate and lipid reduced the overlap still further.

PHOTOSYNTHETIC CHARACTERISTICS

Few studies have considered the question of whether the changes in chemical composition described above are paralleled by comparable changes in photosynthetic characteristic measured over relatively short time periods. Fogg (1956) observed prominent incorporation of ^{14}C (supplied as [^{14}C]bicarbonate) into protein by actively growing cells of *Navicula pelliculosa*, and that this was replaced by incorporation into lipid in N-deficient algae. Few other studies have considered such aspects of photosynthesis and these are considered later, in a more detailed analysis of the effects of environmental factors on the products of photosynthesis.

Summary of Major Effects of Environmental Factors on Photosynthetic Products

Information in the previous two sections provides a basic description of the central features of the photosynthetic products in algae. In essence, microscopic algae are protein-synthesizing organisms with a capacity for metabolic diversity that allows extensive variability to be superimposed on this predominant synthesis of protein. The nature of this variability is regulated by the environmental conditions and the physiological state of the cell. In particular, high light intensities and N depletion appear to impose an enhanced synthesis of non-N-containing storage products such as carbohydrates or lipids. This effect of environmental factors appears to be more important than any effects of species differences.

This section considers more precise effects of specific environmental factors, in order to establish some basic framework of understanding from cultures that can be used to analyze data with natural populations. The variables affecting the nature of the photosynthetic products to be considered are the following: nutrient status, light, and temperature.

NUTRIENT STATUS

The only nutrient to be considered here is nitrogen (N). This restriction is not intended to deny the importance of studies of other nutrients, notably P and Si. It simply reflects the fact that studies of the effects of nutritional status on photosynthetic products have tended to emphasize N.

The effects of N depletion on the products of photosynthesis presented earlier is an over simplification. The pronounced synthesis of carbohydrate and lipid (at the expense of protein) under conditions of N deficiency depends on relatively prolonged N starvation. The effects of more moderate, short-term N depletion are less clear. For example, several observations report little change in protein content during batch growth of a number of different algae (e.g. *Skeletonema obliquus*, Thomas and Krauss 1955; *Nitzschia*, Badour and Gergis 1965; and *Skeletonema costatum*, Handa 1969). Also, in studies of nitrate reductase activities in *Chlorella*, I. Morris (unpublished data) observed little change in the protein content of cell-free extracts during the first 24 h after transfer to N-free medium. It appears that changes in soluble, nonprotein N might be expected to reflect initial or mild N deficiency (compare data with Syrett (1953) on the patterns of metabolism during the recovery from N deficiency.

Glover (1974) measured the photosynthetic assimilation of [^{14}C]bicarbonate into the major end-products during N starvation of *Phaeodactylum triconutum*. The proportion of ^{14}C incorporated into protein increased in the 2 d immediately following transfer to N-free medium (Table 5). This increase was most marked when a N source was provided during the assimilation of ^{14}C but also occurred to some extent in the absence of such a source. Thus, during the initial stages of N deficiency, there appears to be an atempt to conserve the synthesis of protein at the expense of storage (soluble?) N, so the dramatic changes observed with prolonged N starvation cannot be extrapolated immediately to less severe conditions.

The original work on the effects of N depletion generally involved starvation of batch cultures. In essence, this represents an unbalanced situation. This might be of relevance to cerain conditions in natural phytoplankton populations, for example, the transient conditions that occur immediately after a spring bloom and the accompanying depletion of N from the water. Of relevance to other situations, however, might be the balanced growth that occurs in N-limited chemostat continuous cultures. Studies of the effects of increasing N limitation on the chemical composition of cells growing in chemostats have tended to emphasize the C:N ratio. Increases in this ratio with increasing N limitation have been reported widely (see references, Goldman et al. 1979). The extent to which changes in the N content can be equated with changing protein contents is uncertain. The possible importance of stored soluble N compounds under conditions of N sufficiency and any tendency to conserce protein synthesis during moderate N limitation makes such a practice. Despite this danger, it seems reasonable to assume that part of the changing N content with different degrees of limitation is related to changing protein levels. For example, Glover (1974) observed a reduction of

TABLE 5. Pattern of photosynthesis following transfer of *Phaeodactylum tricornutum* to nitrogen-free medium (d 3). Cells were resuspended in fresh, nitrogen-free, and old media before the addition of radioactive bicarbonate. Results are expressed as a percentage of the total carbon incorporated. (From Glover 1974.)

	Nitrogen-free medium				
Days	3	5	7	11	15
Ethanol soluble	54.6	46.9	52.9	48.2	64.4
Polysaccharide	30.3	34.4	28.2	45.2	25.9
Protein	15.1	18.7	18.9	6.6	9.7
	Old medium				
Days	3	5	7	11	15
Ethanol soluble	38.9	35.0	53.2	42.4	55.5
Polysaccharide	44.6	44.1	21.2	42.7	32.4
Protein	16.5	20.9	25.6	14.9	12.1
	Fresh medium				
Days	3	5	7	11	15
Ethanol soluble	49.9	52.6	40.4	56.2	61.0
Polysaccharide	40.0	21.1	31.8	20.3	30.5
Protein	10.1	26.3	27.8	23.5	8.5

75% in protein content (per cell) with a 10-fold decrease in growth rate of *Phaeodactylum tricornutum* growing in NO_3^--limited chemostats.

Morris et al. (1974) examined changes in the products of [^{14}C]bicarbonate assimilation with increasing degrees of N limitation of *P. tricornutum* growing in a NO_3^--limited chemostat. These workers emphasized the way in which the proportion of ^{14}C incorporated into protein increased with increasing N limitation. However, a N source was present during ^{14}C assimilation and thus reflects the pattern of photosynthesis accompanying addition of a N source to N-limited algae. Konopka and Schnur (1980b) reported that N-deficient chemostats of a cyanobacterium *Merismopedia tenuissima* showed a reduced proportion of $^{14}C_2$ incorporated into protein when compared with cultures grown at maximum growth rate in nutrient-sufficient conditions. Unlike the experiments of Morris et al. (1974), the measurements of Konopka and Schnur (1980b) were made in the absence of added N. Interestingly, increasing degrees of P, S, or C deficiency had little or no effect on the proportion of ^{14}C incorporated into protein. Also, Glover (1977) observed increased proportions of ^{14}C incorporated into protein with increasing Fe limitation in *Phaeodactylum tricornutum* and *Isochrysis galbana*.

LIGHT

Three aspects of light availability influence the nature of the photosynthetic products in cultures of algae: alternating light/dark periods, effects of light intensity, and influence of light quality.

Alternating light/dark periods — Changing chemical composition and products of photosynthesis during the life cycle of *Chlorella ellipsoidea* synchronized in light/dark cycles have been studied extensively by Tamiya's group (e.g. review of Tamiya 1957). Increasing ratios of carbohydrates to proteins during the light period appear to be general. The dark period is a time when carbohydrates are transformed into a number of cell materials, including proteins. The changes in carbohydrate:protein ratio do not appear to result from any significant changes in the protein content (per cell), but result from increasing carbohydrate content when the light is superimposed on a more-or-less constant protein level (Kanazawa 1964). Comparable data have been reported by Darley et al. (1976) for synchronized cultures of *Navicula pelliculosa*.

A simplistic assumption states that this synthesis of storage products during the day occurs because of an excess of energy supply over the immediate requirements of the cells for growth. Cohen and Parnas (1976) doubted this assumption. Rather, they suggested that the production of storage material is a tightly regulated phenomenon, linked directly to future requirements and designed to produce an optimal policy for the metabolism of storage materials. For the most part, their arguments are theoretical and lead to the expression of a model (related to the more general model for reserve materials in all microorganisms (Parnas and Cohen 1976). Although Cohen and Parnas provide supporting evidence from experiments with cultures of *Chlamydomonas reinhardii*, it is uncertain how general are their conclusions. In particular, their model predicts (and their experimental data confirm) (1) that the synthesis of the storage product (starch) occurs towards the end of the light period and (2) that the duration of starch synthesis decreases with increasing light intensity. The authors recognize the fact that such observations conflict with others (e.g. Cook 1966).

Light intensity — Most works on the effect of light intensity on photosynthesis have emphasized changes in pigment content and physiological characteristics of the photosynthetic process. Less information is available on how light intensity modifies the overall synthesis of the end-products of photosynthesis. Myers (1946a, b, 1949) reports the way in which higher light intensities cause enhanced synthesis of carbohydrate to be superimposed on the predominantly protein-synthesizing metabolism of *Chlorella*. Cook (1963) observed the same phenomenon in *Euglena* (Table 6, Fig. 1). This effect of high light intensity can be observed by measuring both the chemical composition of cells grown at different light intensities and from measurements of the biochemical characteristics of photosynthesis (e.g. assimilation quotients in Myers 1949, and products of ^{14}C assimilation in Cook 1963). Comparable results were reported by Morris et al. (1974) for *Phaeodactylum tricornutum*. This last named work emphasized the fact that the proportion of fixed ^{14}C incorporated into the

TABLE 6. Effect of light intensity on the cellular composition of *Eglena* cells harvested in the logarithmic phase of growth. (After Cook 1963.)

Light intensity (foot candles)	pg/cell			
	Protein	Paramylum	Lipids	Protein/ paramylum
65	178	38	188	4.67
120	234	27	176	8.65
190	242	64	158	3.78
400	246	194	159	1.27
1200	235	378	158	0.62
3000	236	377	112	0.62

protein fraction increased at reduced light intensities. An alternative way to state the same fact is to say that protein synthesis saturates at lower light intensities than does total photosynthesis. Comparable data showing lower irradiances required to saturate incorporation of $^{14}CO_2$ into protein than that into a "polysaccharide and nucleic acid" fraction have been reported for a freshwater cyanobacterium *Merismopedia tenuissima* (Konopka and Schnur 1980a). Interestingly, this increased proportion of ^{14}C incorporated into protein at reduced irradiances could not be observed with nutrient-deficient cultures (cf. later discussion with natural populations). Myers (1949) pointed out the interesting puzzle that growth of *Chlorella* saturated at a lower light intensity than did photosynthesis. Beardall and Morris (1976) reported the same observation for *Phaeodactylum tricornutum*

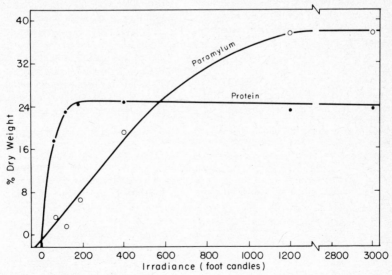

FIG. 1. Effect of light intensity on the paramylum and protein contents of *Euglena gracilis*. (After Cook 1963.)

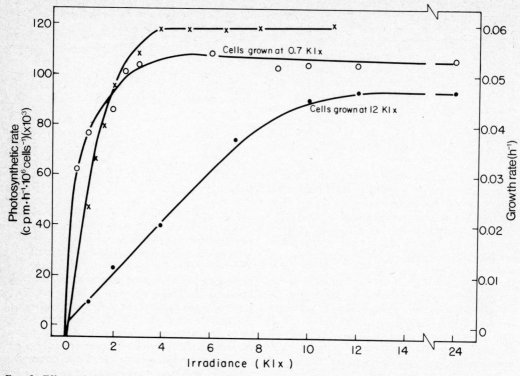

FIG. 2. Effects of light intensity on photosynthesis (●, ○) and growth (x) of *Phaeodactylum tricornutum*. (After Beardall and Morris 1976.)

(Fig. 2). To some extent, this difference between the light saturation curve for photosynthesis and that for growth depends on the light history of the cells. The difference is greatest when photosynthesis is measured with cells previously grown at high light intensities (Fig. 2). Previous growth at low light intensities reduces the saturating intensity for photosynthesis and the curve for carbon assimilation resembles that for growth (Fig. 2).

Light quality — The stimulatory effect of blue light on protein synthesis has been observed for a number of different algae (Hauschild et al. 1962a, b; Wallen and Geen 1971a). Some of the data from Wallen and Geen's work are presented in Table 7. Experiments with different light qualities are not as straightforward as might be supposed. Ensuring equal energy availability and absorption is not sufficiently rigorous to rule out the possibility that apparent effects of the spectral quality of light are related more to the amounts of light energy absorbed. It is unlikely that such doubts modify interpretation of results such as those of Table 7, but they do make it difficult to extrapolate from such data to natural populations.

TABLE 7. Effect of light on the distribution of ^{14}C in *Dunaliella tertiolecta* and *Cyclotella nana*. (After Wallen and Geen 1971a.)

	Spectral quality of light	%total ^{14}C fixed		% ^{14}C in ethanol-insoluble	
		EtOH-sol	EtOH-insol	Protein	Carbohydrate
D. tertiolecta	white	89.9	10.1	92.0	6.8
	blue	28.8	71.2	96.1	1.3
	green	33.2	66.8	95.9	1.8
C. nana	white	67.3	32.7	92.6	5.4
	blue	35.9	64.1	95.3	1.3
	green	39.8	60.2	98.8	1.2

Most studies of the effects of temperature on the chemical composition of algae and on the products of photosynthesis originate with the papers of Jørgensen and Steemann Nielsen (1965), Steemann Nielsen and Jørgensen (1968), and Jørgensen (1968). These workers proposed that algae adapt to suboptimal temperatures by synthesizing more of the enzymes required for photosynthesis. The evidence was indirect and was apparently supported by the fact that cells of *Skeletonema costatum* grown at 7°C contained more protein than did those grown at 20°C (Jørgensen 1968). This observation was apparently confirmed by Morris and Farrel (1971) with *Phaeodactylum tricornutum* and *Dunaliella tertiolecta*. Later, however, the observations of Morris and Glover (1974) suggested that the reported differences between algae grown at suboptimal temperatures and those from higher temperatures resulted from the changes that occur during batch growth. Parameters such as photosynthetic ability and enzyme activities were maximal early in batch growth at higher temperatures. Apparent enhanced activities in cells grown at lower temperatures resulted from the comparison made late in exponential growth. When earlier peaks at higher temperatures were taken into account, the apparent effects of reduced temperatures were not observed.

Morris et al. (1974) reported how temperature affected the assimilation of [^{14}C]bicarbonate into the major end-products of photosynthesis (Table 8). The proportion of ^{14}C incorporated into protein was greater at the higher temperatures used in the experiment. However, cells previously grown at the lower temperatures incorporated a higher proportion of ^{14}C into protein than did those algae previously grown at higher temperatures. These changes in the proportion of ^{14}C incorporated into protein were accompanied by reciprocal changes in either poly-saccharide synthesis or in the incorporation of radioactivity into an ethanol-soluble fraction (containing lipids) (Table 8).

Natural Phytoplankton Populations

SUMMARY OF CONCLUSIONS FROM CULTURES

The work with laboratory cultures described earlier forms the basis for measurements of photosynthetic products in natural populations of marine phytoplankton. The essential characteristics may be summarized thus:

1) Algae such as those that constitute phytoplankton populations are protein-synthesizing microorganisms.

2) There is a potential for considerable metabolic diversity and the nature of this is determined by environmental factors and the physiological state of the cells.

3) High light intensities and prolonged N depletion can impose excessive synthesis of storage materials (lipids or polysaccharides) in addition to the essential synthesis of protein.

4) The effect of short-term or moderate N depletion is less clear. There is some evidence that the synthesis of essential proteins is conserved so the proportion of fixed C incorporated into protein increases during moderate N deficiency.

5) Species differences appear to be less important than environmental factors and the physiological state of the cells.

Most of the relevant work with natural population has been concerned with the chemical composition of particulate matter in the oceans. Much less emphasis has been placed on following the fixation of [^{14}C]bicarbonate into the major end-products of photosynthesis.

CHEMICAL COMPOSITION

Most work on the chemical composition of suspended matter in the oceans has been concerned with the major elements, in particular, the C:N:P ratio (the so-called Redfield ratio). The recent paper of Goldman et al. (1979) documents the literature on this subject. These authors make the interesting point that over wide areas of the oceans the ratio approximates to 100:16:1 (C:N:P) and that this ratio is characteristic of algae growing at or near their maximum growth rate. Such observations raise the interesting possibility that phytoplankton growing in the nutrient-poor surface layers of many parts of the open ocean may be growing at, or near, their maximum growth rate. Other observations have also failed to find physiological indications of nutrient (particularly N) deficiency among phytoplankton of subtropical oceanic regions (e.g. Morris et al. 1971).

TABLE 8. Effects of temperature on the products of photosynthetic [^{14}C]bicarbonate assimilation by *Phaeodactylum tricotnutum*. The results are expressed as % of total ^{14}C fixed. (After Morris et al. 1974.)

Growth temperature, °C	Experimental temperature, °C	% ^{14}C fixed		
		Ethanol-soluble	Hot-TCA-soluble	Protein
18	18	45.2	33.5	21.3
	12	42.8	41.8	16.1
	7	34.9	55.8	9.3
7	18	44.2	22.7	33.1
	12	46.8	26.1	27.1
	7	58.1	20.9	21.0

Goldman et al. (1979) recognized that such physiological indices as the Redfield ratio can only indicate the relative growth rates. Organisms with widely different absolute values of μ max can show similar C:N:P ratios when growing near those maximum growth rates. This is a specific example of how an emphasis on the physiological state of phytoplankton fails to address the problem of the absolute rate at which the population is growing.

There have been fewer studies of the chemical composition of phytoplankton populations at more detailed levels than the elementary composition. Handa et al. (1972) reported the way in which the protein and carbohydrate contents of particulate carbon varied along a transect that extended from 48°N to 68°S in the Pacific Ocean. The proportion of particulate carbon found in carbohydrate did not vary significantly. However, the proportion that occurred as protein was greatest at the higher latitudes (lower temperatures). Packard and Dorch (1975) reported the way particulate protein N varied between oceanic and upwelling regions in the North Atlantic. The ratio of protein N:chlorophyll was higher at the oceanic stations (2.83) than at the upwelling stations (0.54). These authors calculated that only 20% of the sestonic protein N at the oceanic stations was associated with phytoplankton. The comparable figure at the upwelling stations was 65%. Hitchcock (1977) described the changes in particulate carbohydrate in an upwelling zone off West Africa. The concentration of particulate carbohydrate in the surface waters was directly proportional to the concentration of chlorophyll and the carbohydrate:chlorophyll ratio decreased with depth in the euphotic zone. Handa (1975) also observed marked diurnal changes in the carbohydrate content of particulate matter that appeared in the day and disappeared at night in Mikawa Bay. This author did not measure protein.

Few of these studies have tried to link such distributions of particular constituents to the physiological state of the phytoplankton. Haug et al. (1973) and Sakshaug and Myklestad (1973) observed a decrease in the protein:carbohydrate ratio when natural phytoplankton populations in Trondheimsfjord became N or P deficient. In an upwelling area off South Africa, Barlow (1980) also observed a declining ratio of protein:carbohydrate when a diatom bloom collapsed after nutrient depletion. Also, Maita and Yanada (1978) reported changing ratios of particulate protein C to total particulate carbon during seasonal changes in waters off Hokkaido. The ratio was highest during early spring, late fall, and winter, when the standing stock (measured either as chlorophyll or as particulate C) was least. In other words, the concentration of particulate protein changed less than did that of total C. These authors also calculated

turnover times for both total C and protein C. The latter values were generally less than the former but the values were comparable. Later in this review, there will be further discussion of protein turnover times. For the time being, it is worth noting that Maita and Yanada did not measure incorporation of ^{14}C into protein (contrast later). Rather, they measured total C assimilation and, from the measured protein C:total C ratio calculated the rates of protein synthesis; therefore, agreement between the two types of turnover values might be expected.

PATTERNS OF C ASSIMILATION IN NATURAL POPULATIONS OF MARINE PHYTOPLANKTON

C and N assimilation ratios — Goldman et al. (1979) emphasized the way in which the C:N composition ratios of phytoplankton populations varied over a small range of values (generally between 5:1 and 9–10:1). The variability in the measured C:N assimilation ratios is much greater. Table 9 summarizes some reported values for C:N assimilation ratios (cited by Slawyk et al. 1978). It is clear that the range of values is much greater than that observed for the C:N composition ratios. For example, in the work of Slawyk et al., C:N assimilation ratios from 4–45:1 occurred in a region where the composition ratio only varied from 5.4–9.1:1 (integrated over the euphotic zone). Also, observed changes in the assimilation ratios did not parallel those in the composition ratios. For example, Eppley and Renger (1974) noted that the C:N composition ratios of natural phytoplankton populations were lowest at the highest growth rates. The reverse trend was noted for the C:N assimilation ratio. Eppley and Renger pointed out that part of the reason for such a discrepancy lies in the methodology.

TABLE 9. Some examples of C:N assimilation ratios from natural populations of marine phytoplankton. (Cited by Slawyk et al. 1978.)

C:N assimilation ratio	Location	Reference
0–12:13–2	Discontinuity layer in Pacific Ocean	Goering et al. (1970)
12:40	Off S California	McCarthy (1972)
12:76	Various eutrophic and oligotrophic waters	MacIsaac and Dugdale (1972)
0.2:18	Central Gyre, N Pacific	Eppley et al. (1973)
4:45	NW African upwelling region	Slawyk et al. (1978)

The ^{14}C technique for measuring C assimilation is a genuine tracer technique. Use of ^{15}N, however, can perturb the system in the sense that carrier N is added with the isotope. The extent of this perturbation is greatest in those waters where the ambient concentrations of the appropriate N compounds are lowest. Under such conditions, addition of carrier N can result in observed rates of ^{15}N assimilation that are greater than those at ambient N concentrations.

Assimilation of C into major end-products of photosynthesis — Little work is available on the patterns of ^{14}C assimilation by natural populations of phytoplankton. The papers of Olive and Morrison (1967), Olive et al. (1969), Wallen and Geen (1971b), Morris et al. (1974), Morris and Skea (1978), Hitchcock (1978), Smith and Morris (1980a, b), and Morris et al. (1981) present most of the available data. Also, Li et al. (1980) made such measurements with *Oscillatoria (Trichodesmium) thiebautii* in the Caribbean Sea. This section summarizes the main findings from such observations, as well as some unpublished observations from our laboratory.

The broad aim of such work on photosynthetic products of natural phytoplankton populations is to question whether such measurements can (1) describe the physiological state of the populations, (2) identify those environmental factors that control phytoplankton growth, and (3) comment on the

relationship between rates of C assimilation and the growth rates of the phytoplankton populations. At the basis of such questions, is a comparison between observations with natural populations and those made with laboratory cultures, where the effects of particular environmental conditions can be identified under controlled conditions. It is convenient to consider the way in which the products of photosynthetic C assimilation are influenced by the three major environmental factors: light, temperature, and nutrient availability.

Light — Three aspects of the role of light can be considered: (a) diurnal changes, (b) light intensity, and (c) light quality.

a) Diurnal patterns of ^{14}C assimilation

Morris and Skea (1978) described the time courses for [^{14}C]bicarbonate incorporation into natural phytoplankton populations from the temperate waters of the Gulf of Maine. Incorporation into protein continued during both the light and dark periods; the assimilation into protein in the dark was paralleled by loss from the polysaccharide fraction. Thus, the proportion of ^{14}C incorporated depends on the length of incubation and increases after the period in darkness. Comparable results were obtained in the oligotrophic waters of the Sargasso Sea (Fig. 3), although the

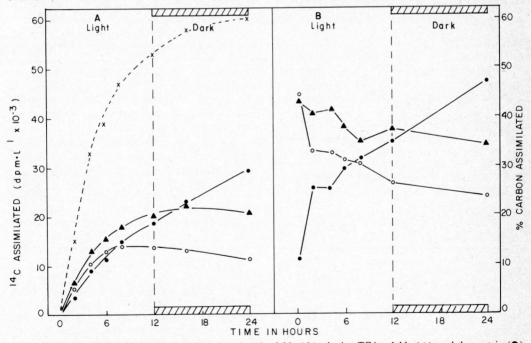

FIG. 3. Incorporation of [^{14}C]bicarbonate into the ethanol-soluble (○), the hot-TCA-soluble (▲), and the protein (●) fractions when surface phytoplankton populations from the southern Sargasso Sea (27°00'N, 64°00'W; July 27–30, 1976) are incubated under natural light for 24 h. (A) Radioactivity in each fraction and the total incorporation (x); (B) data expressed as percentages of the total ^{14}C assimilated.

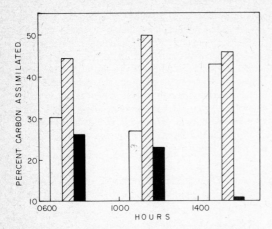

FIG. 4. Proportion of ^{14}C assimilated to ethanol-soluble (□), hot-TCA-soluble (▨), and protein (■) fractions when surface phytoplankton (the same station as in Fig. 3) were incubated for 4 h at different times of day.

disappearance of radioactivity from the polysaccharide fraction during the dark was less marked than that observed by Morris and Skea (1978).

In another type of experiment, surface populations from the Sargasso Sea were harvested at different times of the day and incubated for a constant time (4 h). The proportion of ^{14}C incorporated into protein was greatest early in the morning and decreased during the afternoon (Fig. 4). This decrease was accompanied largely by increasing proportion of ^{14}C incorporated into the ethanol-soluble fraction (also containing lipid material). In such experiments, changes due to diurnal fluctuations in the metabolism of phytoplankton are superimposed on effects of light intensity. It is unlikely that changes in irradiances during the day can explain wholly the results in Fig. 4. If the reduced proportion of ^{14}C incorporated into protein was caused solely by elevated light intensities, one might have expected to observe a similar difference between midday and the end of the day.

b) Effects of light intensity

Work with both cultures and natural populations (Morris et al. 1974; Morris and Skea 1978) has confirmed the generalization that incorporation of [^{14}C]bicarbonate into protein saturates at a lower light intensity than does incorporation into storage products such as polysaccharides. Thus, in such experiments the *proportion* of ^{14}C incorporated into protein increases at reduced light intensities.

Li et al. (1980) observed similar effects of suboptimal and supraoptimal light intensities on the patterns of ^{14}C assimilation by the marine cyanobacterium *Oscillatoria thiebautii* (*Trichodesmium*). In this organism, the proportion of ^{14}C incorporated into polysaccharide is greatest at the optimal irradiance levels and is reduced at both lower and higher levels. The proportion incorporated into protein, low-molecular-weight metabolites and (to a lesser extent) lipid showed the reverse trend, being lowest at the optimal intensities and increasing at both lower and higher levels.

Morris and Skea (1978) emphasized the way in which such an effect of light intensity depends on the nutrient status of the cells. That is, enhancement of the relative incorporation of ^{14}C into protein by reduced light intensities was less marked with summer populations from the Gulf of Maine (sampled from surface layers after the establishment of stratification and depletion of nutrients from the surface waters) than with populations sampled before the spring bloom; Fig. 5 and 6 present a similar observation for coastal and oceanic regions of tropical waters. These figures describe data from two different cruises and compare stations off the mouth of the Orinoco River with oceanic stations from the Caribbean Sea (Fig. 5) or the Western Atlantic Ocean (Fig. 6). Stimulation of the proportion of ^{14}C incorporated into protein by reduced light intensities was observed at the coastal stations but was not significant at the oceanic stations. Possibly, the physiological state of phytoplankton populations from oceanic regions might be revealed by emphasizing this effect of light intensity rather than the direct measurements of the patterns of ^{14}C assimilation (see below).

In waters that show the stimulating effect of reduced irradiances on the proportion of ^{14}C incorporated into protein, the observation can be made by incubating a single sample at a range of light intensities or in simulated in situ experiments, in which samples from different depths are incubated at light intensities corresponding to the depth from which they were taken.

It is interesting to question whether light intensities influence the time course of ^{14}C incorporation into different products during a 24-h light/dark cycle. Earlier, I commented on the hypothesis of Cohen and Parnas (1976) in proposing that, in unicellular algae that grow in light/dark cycles, synthesis of storage products such as polysaccharide during a light period was a regulated process. These authors proposed that synthesis of such storage products would occur late in the light period and that higher light intensities would reduce the period over which synthesis of storage products would occur. We have observed no such phenomenon in natural phytoplankton populations. For example, Fig. 7 describes the way in which the light intensity of incubation influences the proportion of ^{14}C incorporated into the various products but does not appear to alter the "shape of the curve" for incorporation during the light period.

94

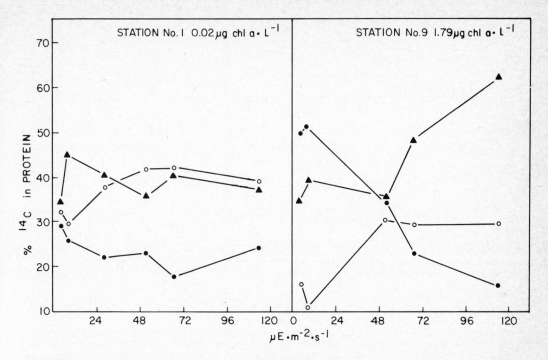

FIG. 5. Effect of irradiance on the proportion of [^{14}C]bicarbonate incorporated into protein (●), polysaccharide (▲), and ethanol-soluble material (○) when surface populations from two stations were incubated for 4 h in an incubator illuminated with warm white fluorescent tubes. Data were collected on a cruise of the *RV Eastward* between Feb. 14 and 19, 1974. Station 1 was south of Puerto Rico (17°18′N, 65°00′W) and station 9 at the mouth of the Orinoco River (09°33′N, 60°31′W).

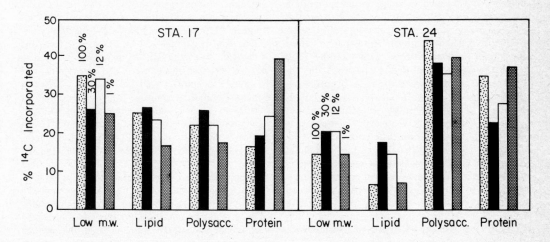

FIG. 6. Effect of irradiance on the proportion of [^{14}C]bicarbonate incorporated into the major end-products of photosynthesis at two stations during cruise EN-034 of the *RV Endeavor*. Station 17 is at the mouth of the Orinoco River (5.69 μg chl $a \cdot L^{-1}$) and station 24 (0.07 μg chl $a \cdot L^{-1}$) ~ 200 km NNE of station 17. Samples collected from a depth corresponding to 30% of surface irradiance were incubated at the range of intensities.

95

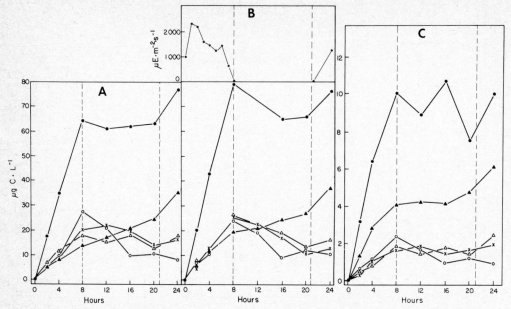

FIG. 7. Time courses of incorporation of [^{14}C]bicarbonate into polysaccharide (broken line), protein (▲), lipid (x), and low-molecular-weight metabolites (○); (●) shows total incorporation. Water samples were taken from a depth corresponding to 30% of surface irradiance and incubated at (A) 100%, (B) 30%, and (C) 1% of this surface value. The top part of Fig. 8 shows the changing irradiances during the period of incubation. Experiments were performed at station 17 (9°33.3′N, 60°42.7′W) of EN-034 cruise of the *RV Endeavor*, Apr. 5, 1979.

c) Light quality

The pattern of [^{14}C]bicarbonate assimilation also changes with depth in the water column. Figure 8 illustrates the increasing proportion of ^{14}C incorporated into protein with increasing depth. This is generally accompanied by a decreasing proportion incorporated into polysaccharide. The experiments described in Fig. 8 involved incubating surface water at the various depths. Comparable data are obtained with in situ incubations when water sampled from a particular depth is incubated at that depth (Fig. 9).

The effects of incubating samples at increasing depths described in Fig. 8 and 9 resemble those obtained by alterations in light intensities achieved with neutral density filters. Work in our laboratory has not detected any significant difference between the two approaches. From such work, therefore, it might be suggested that changing patterns of photosynthesis with depth are related solely to changes in light intensity and not to light quality. The opposite conclusion was reached by Wallen and Geen (1971b). These authors observed increasing proportions of [^{14}C]-bicarbonate being incorporated into ethanol-insoluble compounds (mainly protein) with increasing depth in Saanich Inlet and Indian Arm, B.C. Comparisons with their earlier work with laboratory cultures (Wallen and Geen 1971a) led them to emphasize light quality and not light intensity.

Temperature — It is difficult to identify precise and direct effects of temperature on the patterns of photosynthesis. Temperature changes with geography, or with time in temperature waters, are generally accompanied by changes in the degree of stratification and, thus, in nutrient availability. One of the most interesting effects of temperature has been reported by Smith and Morris (1980a, b) for phytoplankton populations from the Southern Atlantic Ocean. At locations with extremely low ambient temperatures ($< -1.0°C$) and low incident irradiance levels (maximum, 0.2 ly·min^{-1}) as much as 80–90% of the [^{14}C]bicarbonate assimilated during an 8-h day was incorporated into lipid. At such stations, there was insignificant incorporation into protein. At other locations with "higher" temperatures ($\sim 0°C$) the pattern of photosynthesis resembled that observed in other regions of the oceans, with prominent incorporation into polysaccharide and significant synthesis of protein.

The significance of such a striking synthesis of lipid material at the extremely low temperatures of polar regions is unknown. Populations that showed such a phenomenon did not show high lipid content in the particulate matter. Thus, incorporation of ^{14}C into lipid material might reflect synthesis of specialized lipids (possibly associated with membranes) or the synthesis of lipid which is degraded at night.

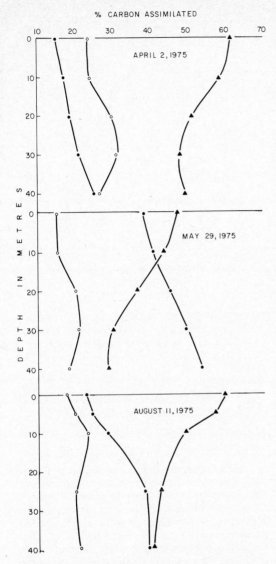

% CARBON ASSIMILATED

APRIL 2, 1975

MAY 29, 1975

AUGUST 11, 1975

DEPTH IN METRES

FIG. 8. Proportion of [¹⁴C]bicarbonate incorporated into the ethanol-soluble fraction (○), the polysaccharide fraction (▲), and protein (●) when surface water from a station in the Gulf of Maine (43°42′N, 69°39′W) was incubated for 4 h at various depths.

Nutrient status — It is attractive to consider the possibility that measurements of the flow of C into the major end-products of photosynthesis might be a means of detecting nutrient deficiency among phytoplankton populations. It is clear from the earlier discussion that the nutritional status of algae in laboratory culture has a profound effect on the products of photosynthesis. However, immediate extrapolation from such work with cultures to natural populations is not as straight-

forward as might be supposed. Earlier, it was emphasized that a shift from protein synthesis to excessive synthesis of non-N-containing compounds such as lipid and carbohydrate accompanied N deficiency. However, the result depends on extreme N starvation. During more moderate N deficiency, it appeared that the cellular content (and rates of synthesis) of nonprotein N might be more affected than that of protein. Also, enhanced synthesis of materials such as lipids and polysaccharides at the expense of protein appears to be specific for N deficiency. Deficiency of other nutrients (e.g. Fe, P, etc.) appears to be accompanied by a conservation of protein synthesis so that, under such conditions, the proportion of C incorporated into protein can be enhanced.

Attempts to relate patterns of C assimilation to the nutritional status of natural phytoplankton populations have generally been of two kinds: (a) studies of seasonal changes in temperate waters and (b) geographical comparisons of coastal and oceanic regions. Both types of studies are complicated by changes in the species composition of the phytoplankton populations. That is, observed changes may be related to changes in the dominant algae of the population and not to a changing environemental variable such as nutrient availability. However, the earlier discussion of data from laboratory cultures emphasized the way in which differences between species appeared to be less important than effects of physiological state. It therefore seems reasonable to relate measured changes in patterns of C assimilation to the physiological state of the phytoplankton.

a) Seasonal studies

The papers of Hitchcock (1978) and Morris and Skea (1978) present the few available data on seasonal changes in the products of [¹⁴C] bicarbonate assimilation. Hitchcock observed increasing proportions of ¹⁴C being incorporated into ethanol-soluble material during the development of a spring diatom bloom in lower Narragansett Bay. This increase was accompanied by a decrease in the proportion incorporated into both the polysaccharide and protein fractions. These changes could be correlated with a decline of nutrients (notably N) and a reduction in the protein:carbohydrate ratio in the particulate matter. The data of Morris and Skea (1978) are less clear. In their studies at a coastal station in the Gulf of Maine, Morris and Skea could not detect any increased incorporation of ¹⁴C into ethanol-soluble or polysaccharide material with the decline of nutrients from the surface waters. Indeed, these authors emphasized the way in which the proportion of ¹⁴C incorporated into protein was higher in the summer populations. They also detected a transient and striking increase in the proportion incorporated into

97

% CARBON ASSIMILATED INTO PROTEIN

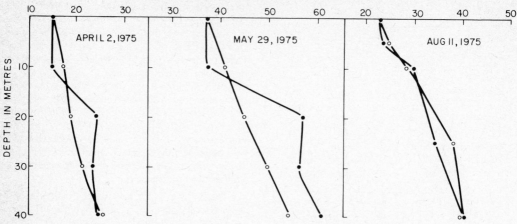

Fig. 9. The proportion of [^{14}C]bicarbonate incorporated into protein when surface water (●) and water from the various depths (○) were incubated for 4 h throughout the euphotic zone; same station location as in Fig. 8.

protein after the collapse of the first (of two) spring blooms. The authors questioned whether this increased relative incorporation into protein might indicate nutrient limitation.

b) Geographical comparisons of coastal and oceanic regions

To date, the only measurements of this kind are those pursued in the author's laboratory. The present section summarizes the data from the paper of Morris et al. (1981) and emphasizes the coastal and oceanic regions of the Caribbean Sea as well as the adjacent regions of the Western Atlantic. Table 10 summarizes the main observations on the proportion of [^{14}C]bicarbonate incorporated into the main end-products of photosynthesis. At the inshore stations (showing higher chlorophyll concentrations and measurable levels of inorganic nutrients in the surface layers) there was approximately equal incorporation over an 8-h light period into all four fractions studied.

Moving offshore was accompanied by a reduction in the proportion incorporated into lipid and (to a lesser extent) low-molecular-weight metabolites. Accompanying this change was an increase in the proportion of ^{14}C appearing in protein and polysaccharide (64–72%). The significance of these changes is unknown and cannot be related too immediately to observations from laboratory cultures.

PRODUCTS OF PHOTOSYNTHESIS AND PHYTOPLANKTON GROWTH

Elsewhere in this Bulletin, Eppley points out the impossibility of extrapolating from measured rates of assimilation of an element (e.g. carbon) to growth rates (doubling times) of the algae constituting the phytoplankton population. The reason most commonly recognized for this difficulty is the difficulty of measuring phytoplankton biomass, separate from other particulate matter (including detritus). However,

TABLE 10. Rates of photosynthesis and major end-products of [^{14}C]bicarbonate assimilation at coastal (17 and 15) and oceanic regions of the Caribbean Sea (28) and the Western Atlantic Ocean (24). All measurements were made on samples taken from depth corresponding to 30% of surface light and incubated at that intensity for 8 h. Data were collected on cruise EN-034 of *RV Endeavor* (Mar. 22–Apr. 14, 1979). (After Morris et al. 1981.)

Station	Chl a	Photosynthesis		% total ^{14}C assimilated			
		$\mu g\ C \cdot L^{-1} \cdot h^{-1}$	$\mu g\ C \cdot \mu g\ Chl^{-1} \cdot h^{-1}$	Low m.w.	Lipid	Polysacc.	Protein
17	5.69	10.0	1.76	26.4	27.1	26.5	20.0
15	2.05	2.70	1.32	27.7	24.1	24.9	23.3
24	0.07	0.67	10.4	21.1	17.9	41.0	23.0
28	0.09	0.36	4.0	19.2	8.9	41.1	30.8

Eppley describes an alternative (and fundamental) difficulty. Eppley recognizes "unbalanced growth" when at any one time, the relative rates of assimilation of elements or of the synthesis of various cellular components can differ from their relative proportions in the cell. The particular problem centers around the fact that algae of the phytoplankton population grow and divide in an environment of alternating light/dark periods. Under such conditions, rates of processes measured over relatively short periods in the light might not reflect net rates occurring over a 24-h (or longer) light/dark cycle. Eppley also identified other conditions under which phytoplankton populations may exhibit unbalanced growth.

The rates of synthesis of the different end-products of photosynthesis might be expected to indicate the conditions under which measurements of C assimilation during the light period might more or less closely reflect growth rates of the algal population. Thus, conditions promoting enhanced synthesis of storage products might yield rates of C assimilation that greatly overestimate the growth rates. Under conditions of reduced synthesis of storage products, the rate of C assimilation might reflect more closely the synthesis of those essential polymers required for growth and division.

The data from studies of Smith and Morris (1980b) in the waters around Antarctica illustrate such a problem (Table 11). At stations 13 and 18 significant incorporation of ^{14}C into lipid was observed. Such stations show higher assimilation ratios (C fixed per unit chlorophyll) than do stations 23 and 29 where there is no such marked incorporation into lipid. Thus, measurements of phytoplankton

biomass as chlorophyll and the rates of C assimilation might suggest that the growth of phytoplankton was comparable at both types of stations. Yet the "skewed" pattern of C assimilation with little detectable protein synthesis and dominant incorporation into lipid at certain stations makes such an extrapolation from C fixation to growth untenable. Indeed, the stations at which significant lipid synthesis occurred showed lower C-specific rates of C assimilation than did the others (Table 11). The PC:chl ratios were abnormally high at such stations and would normally be interpreted as indicating the influence of non-phytoplankton carbon in the measurement of PC. However, an abnormal C metabolism might also lead to such unusual PC:chl ratios.

The difficulty in extrapolating from rates of C assimilation to growth rates of the phytoplankton population introduces the question of whether rates of C incorporation into selected polymers might be a closer indication of growth rate. That is, if one of the reasons for a discrepancy between total rates of C assimilation and doubling times is in the variable synthesis of storage products during the light period, measurement of C incorporated into a compound more closely linked to growth and division might be expected to be a closer measure of growth rates. From our studies in coastal and oceanic regions of the Caribbean Sea and Western Atlantic Ocean we have attempted calculations of turnover times based on C incorporation into the various products (Table 12). Such calculations are difficult and the results must be interpreted as preliminary and with caution. Assumptions about the C-content of the lipid, polysaccharide, and protein of the particulate matter

TABLE 11. Characteristics of photosynthesis at four stations from the Southern Atlantic Ocean. (After Smith and Morris 1980b.)

	Biomass			Rates of photosynthesis (8 h)			% of total ^{14}C fixed (8 h)		
Station	Chl a (μg·L^{-1})	PC	PC:chl a	Per volume (g C^{-1}·h^{-1})	Assimilation No. (g C·g chl^{-1}·h^{-1})	C specific (h^{-1})	Lipid	Protein	"Polysacc/ metabolite"
13	0.04	167.8	4195	0.25	5.70	0.002	70.3	3.7	26.0
18	0.21	328.0	1433	0.92	4.44	0.003	48.6	9.7	41.7
23	0.85	196.2	231	1.80	2.11	0.009	4.2	11.9	83.9
29	0.62	144.3	233	1.03	1.67	0.007	25.1	17.9	57.0

				Rates of photosynthesis (24 h)			% of total ^{14}C fixed (24 h)		
				Per volume	Assimilation No.	C specific	Lipid	Protein	"Polysacc/ metabolite"
13				0.11	2.53	0.001	88.9	2.8	8.3
18				0.37	1.77	0.001	79.2	5.8	15.0
23				0.75	0.87	0.004	13.6	21.2	65.2
29				0.67	1.09	0.005	6.3	26.9	66.8

TABLE 12. Carbon-specific rates of [^{14}C]bicarbonate assimilation by phytoplankton populations at two coastal stations (15 and 17) and two oceanic stations in the Caribbean Sea (28) and the Western Atlantic (24). Rates of incorporation into particulate matter ("total") and into the various end-products were normalized to particulate C or to the C content of the various fractions (particulate protein, polysaccharide, and lipid were measured colorimetrically and the C contents estimated from published chemical compositions of laboratory cultures of marine algae). Further details are in legend to Table 10. (After Morris et al. 1981.)

Station	Time of incubation,	Assimilation rates (h^{-1})			
		Total	Lipid	Polysaccharide	Protein
15	8	0.021	0.003	0.009	0.001
17	8	0.051	0.028	0.012	0.002
24	8	0.015	0.009	0.042	0.007
28	8	0.006	0.003	0.029	0.004
15	20	0.014	0.014	0.032	0.005
17	20	0.017	0.066	0.030	0.013
24	20	0.006	0.003	0.014	0.006
28	20	0.002	0.001	0.008	0.001

were based on values from the literature for various cultures of marine algae (see Morris et al. 1981 for details). Also, distinguishing phytoplankton–protein, phytoplankton–lipid, etc., from nonphytoplankton material in the particulate matter is not possible. Although, therefore, the precise values presented in Table 12 are open to considerable question, the discrepancy between rates calculated from incorporation into protein and those from total C assimilation is interesting. Not only are the calculated turnover times for particulate protein longer than those for particulate C, the direction of change in comparing coastal and oceanic locations is opposite. Calculations based on total C assimilation show expected higher turnover times at the inshore stations. The reverse is true when rates of C incorporation into protein are normalized to particulate protein C. This similar reverse trend is also apparent (but with much shorter doubling times) when incorporation into polysaccharide is used as a basis for the calculations.

It might be argued that measurements of C assimilation over 24 h might reduce some of the discrepancy between such assimilation and growth rates. If the discrepancy results from the "unbalanced" synthesis of storage products in the light period, inclusion of the dark period in the time over which assimilation is measured might be expected to "cancel out" this effect. Data from 20 or 24 h are included in Tables 11 and 12, and some basic questions raised above remain. During the last 20–30 yr, there has been a growing awareness of the need to measure "instantaneous" rates and to avoid enclosing water samples for measurements over periods as long as 24 h. Being forced to consider 24-h incubations, therefore, is a dramatic illustration of the way in which measurements of productivity in terms of [^{14}C] bicarbonate assimilation

have failed to approach the problems of growth and division of a population of microbes growing in an environment of alternating light/dark periods.

However, from Table 12, it is apparent that the turnover times calculated from incorporation into protein are more comparable to those calculated from total ^{14}C incorporation when an incubation time of 20 h (includes the dark period) is considered.

Acknowledgments

The work associated with the author's laboratory was undertaken while he was at the Bigelow Laboratory for Ocean Sciences, West Boothbay Harbor, Maine, USA 04575. Colleagues who participated in the work and to whom I am grateful are H. E. Glover, A. E. Smith, W. Skea, J. C. Laird, and W. Li. The work was supported by NSF grants OCE 75-15104, OCE 75-21128, OCE 77-18722, and DPP 78-23833.

References

BADOUR, S. S., AND M. S. GERGIS. 1965. Cell division and fat accumulation in continuously illuminated mass cultures. Arch. Microbiol. 51: 94–102.

BARLOW, R. G. 1980. The biochemical composition of phytoplankton in an upwelling region off South Africa. J. Exp. Mar. Biol. Ecol. 45: 83–93.

BEARDALL, J., AND I. MORRIS. 1976. The concept of light intensity adaptation in marine phytoplankton: some experiments with Phaeodactylum tricornutum. Mar. Biol. 37: 377–387.

CAPERON, J., AND J. MEYER. 1972. Nitrogen limited growth of marine phytoplankton. I. Changes in population characteristics with steady-state growth rate. Deep-Sea Res. 19: 601–618.

COHEN, D., AND M. PARNAS. 1976. An optimal policy for the metabolism of storage products in unicellular algae. J. Theor. Biol. 56: 1–18.

COLLYER, D. M., AND G. E. FOGG. 1955. Studies on fat accumulation by algae, I. Exp. Bot. 6: 256–275.

COOK, J. R. 1963. Adaptations in growth and division in *Euglena* effected by energy supply. J. Protozool. 10: 436–444.

———. 1966. Photosynthesis activity during the division cycle in synchronized *Euglena gracilis*. Plant Physiol. 41: 821–825.

DARLEY, W. M., C. W. SULLIVAN, AND B. E. VOLCANI. 1976. Studies on the biochemistry and fine structure of silica shell formation in diatoms. Planta 130: 159–167.

DROOP, M. R. 1974. The nutrient status of algal cell in continuous culture. J. Mar. Biol. Assoc. U.K. 54: 825–855.

EPPLEY, R. W., AND E. M. RENGER. 1974. Nitrogen assimilation of an oceanic diatom in nitrogen limited continuous culture. J. Phycol. 10: 15–23.

EPPLEY, R. W., J. M. SHARP, E. H. RENGER, M. J. PERRY, AND W. G. MORRISON. 1977. Nitrogen assimilation by phytoplankton and other microorganisms in the surface waters of the central North Pacific Ocean. Mar. Biol. 39: 111–120.

FALKOWSKI, P. G. 1977. The adenylate energy charge in marine phytoplankton: the effect of temperature on the physiological state of *Skeletonema costatum* (Grev.) Cleve. J. Exp. Mar. Biol. Ecol. 27: 37–45.

FOGG, G. E. 1956. Photosynthesis and formation of fats in a diatom. Ann. Biol. London N. S. 20: 265–285.

———. 1959. Nitrogen nutrition and metabolic patterns in algae. Symp. Soc. Exp. Biol. 13: 106–125.

———. 1965. Algal cultures and phytoplankton ecology. Univ. Wisconsin Press, Madison, Milwaukee, and London. p. 11–126.

FUHS, G. W. 1969. Phosphorus content and rate of growth in the diatoms *Cyclotella nana* and *Thalassiosira fluviatilis*. J. Phycol. 5: 312–321.

GLOVER, H. E. 1974. Studies on the biochemistry and physiology of *Phaeodactylum tricornutum*, Ph. D. thesis, London. 195 p. Univ. London,

———. 1977. Effects of iron deficiency on *Csochrysis galbana* (Chrysophyceae) and *Phaeodactylum tricornutum* (Bacillariophyceae). J. Phycol. 13: 208–212.

GOERING, J. J., D. D. WALLEN, AND R. M. NANNAN. 1970. Nitrogen uptake by phytoplankton in the discontinuity layer of the eastern subtropical Pacific Ocean. Limnol. Oceanogr. 15: 789–796.

GOLDMAN, J. C., J. J. MCCARTHY, AND D. G. PEAVEY. 1979. Growth rate influence on the chemical composition of phytoplankton in oceanic waters. Nature (London) 279: 210–215.

HANDA, N. 1969. Carbohydrate metabolism in the marine diatom *Skeletonema costatum*. Mar. Biol. 4: 208–214.

———. 1975. The diurnal variation of organic constituents of particulate matter in coastal water, p. 125–132. *In* S. Mori and G. Yamamoto [ed.] ITBP synthesis. Univ. Tokyo Press.

HANDA, N., K. YANAGI, AND K. MATSUNAGA. 1972. Distribution of detrital materials in the Western Pacific Ocean and their biological nature. Mem. Ist. Ital. Idrobial. 29 Suppl. 53–71.

HAUG, A., S. MYKLESTAD, AND E. SAKSHAUG. 1973. Studies on the phytoplankton ecology of the Trondheimsfjord. I. The chemical composition of phytoplankton populations. J. Exp. Mar. Biol. Ecol. 11: 15–26.

HAUSCHILD, A. H. W., C. D. NELSON, AND G. KROTKOV. 1962a. The effect of light quality on the products of photosynthesis in *Chlorella vulgaris*. Can. J. Bot. 40: 179–189.

———. 1962b. The effect of light quality on the products of photosynthesis in green and blue-green algae and in photosynthetic bacteria. Can. J. Bot. 40: 1619–1630.

HEALEY, F. P. 1975. Physiological indicators of nutrient deficiency in algae. Res. Dev. Dir. Freshwater Inst. Tech. Rep. 585: 00–00.

HITCHCOCK, G. 1977. The concentration of particulate carbohydrate in a region of the West Africa upwelling zone during March 1974. Deep-Sea Res. 24: 83–93.

HITCHCOCK, G. L. 1978. Labelling patterns of carbon-14 in net plankton during a winter-spring bloom. J. Exp. Mar. Biol. Ecol. 31: 141–153.

JØRGENSEN, E. G. 1968. The adaptation of plankton algae II. Aspects of temperature adaptation of *Skeletonema costatum*. Physiol. Plant. 21: 423–427.

JØRGENSEN, E. G., AND E. STEEMANN NIELSEN. 1965. Adaptation in plankton algae. Mem. Ist. Ital. Idrobiol. 18: 37–46.

KANAZAWA, T. 1964. Changes of amino acid composition of *Chlorella* cells during their life cycle. Plant Cell Physiol. 5: 333–354.

KONOPKA, A., AND M. SCHNUR. 1980a. Effect of light intensity on macromolecular synthesis in cyanobacteria. Microbiol. Ecol. 6: 291–301.

———. 1980b. Biochemical composition and photosynthetic carbon metabolism of nutrient-limited cultures of *Merismopedia tenuissima* (Cyanophyceae). J. Phycol. (In press)

LEWIN, J. C., AND R. R. L. GUILLARD. 1963. Diatoms. Annu. Rev. Microbiol. 17: 373–414.

LI, W. K. W., M. E. GLOVER, AND I. MORRIS. 1980. Physiology of carbon photoassimilation by *Oscillatoria thiebautii* in the Caribbean Sea. Limnol. Oceanogr. 25: 447–456.

MACISAAC, J. J., AND R. C. DUGDALE. 1972. Interactions of light and inorganic nitrogen in controlling nitrogen uptake in the sea. Deep-Sea Res. 19: 209–232.

MAITA, Y., AND M. YANADA. 1978. Particulate protein in coastal waters, with special reference to seasonal variation. Mar. Biol. 44: 329–336.

MCCARTHY, J. J. 1972. The uptake of urea by natural populations of marine phytoplankton. Limnol. Oceanogr. 17: 738–748.

MORRIS, I., AND K. FARRELL. 1971. Photosynthetic rates, gross patterns of carbon dioxide assimilation and activities of ribulose diphosphate carboxylase in marine algae grown at different temperatures. Physiol. Plant 25: 372–377.

MORRIS, I., AND H. E. GLOVER. 1974. Questions on the mechanisms of temperature adaptation in marine phytoplankton. Mar. Biol. 24. 147–154.

MORRIS, I., AND W. SKEA. 1978. Products of photosynthesis in natural populations of marine phytoplankton from the Gulf of Maine. Mar. Biol. 47: 303–312.

MORRIS, I., A. E. SMITH, AND H. E. GLOVER. 1981. Products of photosynthesis in phytoplankton off the Orinoco River and in the Caribbean Sea. Limnol. Oceanogr. (In press)

MORRIS, I., C. M. YENTSCH, AND C. S. YENTSCH. 1971. The physiological state of phytoplankton from low-nutrient sub-tropical water with respect to nitrogen as measured by the effect of ammonium on dark carbon dioxide fixation. Limnol. Oceanogr. 16: 859–868.

MORRIS, I., H. E. GLOVER, AND C. S. YENTSCH. 1974. Products of photosynthesis by marine phytoplankton: the effect of environmental factors on the relative rates of protein synthesis. Mar. Biol. 27: 1–9.

MYERS, J. 1946a. Culture conditions and the development of the photosynthetic mechanism III. Influence of light intensity on cellular characteristics of *Chlorella*. J. Gen. Physiol. 29: 419–427.

    1946b. Culture conditions and the development of the photosynthetic mechanism IV. Influence of light intensity on photosynthetic characteristics of *Chlorella*. J. Gen. Physiol. 29: 429–440.

    1949. The pattern of photosynthesis in *Chlorella*, p. 349–364. *In* J. Franck and W. E. Loomis [ed.] Photosynthesis in plants. Am. Soc. Plant Physiol. Iowa State College Press.

    1962. Variability of metabolism in algae. Dtsch. Bot. Ges. Nene. Folge Nr. 1: 13–19.

MYERS, J., AND M. CRAMER. 1948. Nitrate reduction and assimilation in *Chlorella*. J. Gen. Physiol. 32: 93–102.

MYERS, J., AND J. A. JOHNSTON. 1949. Carbon and nitrogen balance of *Chlorella* during growth. Plant Physiol. 24: 111–119.

MYKLESTAD, S. 1974. Production of carbohydrates by marine planktonic diatoms, I. Comparison of nine different species in culture. J. Exp. Mar. Biol. Ecol. 15: 261–274.

MYKLESTAD, S., AND A. HAUG. 1972. Production of carbohydrates by the marine diatom *Chaetoceros affinis* var *willei* (gran) Mustedt. I. Effect of the concentration of nutrients in the culture medium. J. Exp. Mar. Biol. Ecol. 9: 137–144.

OLIVE, J. D. M., D. M. BENTON, AND J. KISHLER. 1969. Distribution of C-14 products of photosynthesis and its relationship to phytoplankton composition and rate of photosynthesis. Ecology 50: 380–386.

OLIVE, J. D. M., AND J. M. MORRISON. 1967. Variations in distribution of ^{14}C in cell extracts of phytoplankton living under natural conditions. Limnol. Oceanogr. 13: 383–391.

PAASCHE, E. 1973. Silicon and the ecology of marine plankton diatoms. II. Silicate uptake kinetics in five diatom species. Mar. Biol. 19: 262–269.

PACKARD, T. T., AND Q. DORTCH. 1975. Particulate protein–nitrogen in North Atlantic surface waters. Mar. Biol. 33: 347–354.

PARNAS, H., AND D. COHEN. 1976. The optimal strategy for the metabolism of reserve materials in microorganisms, J. Theor. Biol. 56: 19–55.

PARSONS, T. R., K. STEPHENS, AND J. D. M. STRICKLAND. 1961. On the chemical composition of eleven species of marine phytoplankton. J. Fish. Res. Board Can. 18: 1001–1016.

SAKSHAUG, E. 1977. Limiting nutrients and maximum growth rates for diatoms in Narragansett Bay. J. Exp. Mar. Biol. Ecol. 28: 109–123.

SAKSHAUG, E., AND O. HOLM-HANSEN. 1977. Chemical composition of *Skeletonema costatum* and *Pavlova (Monchrysis) lutheri* as a function of nitrate- phosphate- and iron-limited growth. J. Exp. Mar. Biol. Ecol. 29: 1–34.

SAKSHAUG, E., AND S. MYKLESTAD. 1973. Studies on the phytoplankton ecology of the Trondheimsfjord III. Dynamics of phytoplankton blooms in relation to environmental factors, bioassay experiments and parameters for the physiological state of populations. J. Exp. Mar. Biol. Ecol. 11: 157–188.

SLAWYK, G., Y. COLLOS, M. MINAS, AND J-R. GRALL. 1978. On the relationship between carbon to nitrogen composition ratios of the particulate matter and growth rate of marine phytoplankton from the northwest African upwelling area. J. Exp. Mar. Biol. Ecol. 33: 119–131.

SMITH, A. E., AND I. MORRIS. 1980a. Synthesis of lipid during photosynthesis of phytoplankton of the Southern Ocean. Science (Washington, D.C.) 207: 197–199.

    1980b. Pathways of carbon assimilation in phytoplankton from the Antarctic Ocean. Limnol. Oceanogr. 25: 865–872.

STEELE, J. H., AND I. E. BAIRD. 1961. Relations between primary production, chlorophyll and particulate carbon. Limnol. Oceanogr. 6: 68–78.

SPOEHR, H. A., AND H. W. MILNER. 1949. The chemical composition of *Chlorella*; effect of environmental conditions. Plant Physiol. 24: 120–149.

STEEMANN NIELSEN, E., AND E. G. JØRGENSEN. 1968. The adaptation of plankton algae. I. General Part. Physiol. Plant 21: 401–403.

SYRETT, P. J. 1953. The assimilation of ammonia by nitrogen-starved cells of *Chlorella unlgaris*. Ann. Bot. London N.S. 17: 1–18.

TAMIYA, H. 1957. Synchronous cultures of algae. Annu. Rev. Plant Physiol. 8: 309–334.

THOMAS, W. H., AND R. W. KRAUSS. 1955. Nitrogen metabolism in *Scenedesmus* as affected by environmental changes. Plant Physiol. 30: 113–122.

WALLEN, D. G., AND G. H. GEEN. 1971a. Light quality in relation to growth, photosynthetic rates and carbon metabolism in two species of marine plankton algae. Mar. Biol. 10: 34–43.

    1971b. The nature of the photosynthate in natural phytoplankton populations in relation to light quality. Mar. Biol. 10: 157–168.

YENTSCH, C. S., AND R. F. VACCARO. 1958. Phytoplankton nitrogen in the oceans. Limnol. Oceanogr. 3: 443–448.

Photosynthesis Measurements on Natural Populations of Phytoplankton: Numerical Analysis

CHARLES L. GALLEGOS AND TREVOR PLATT

Department of Fisheries and Oceans, Marine Ecology Laboratory,
Bedford Institute of Oceanography,
Dartmouth, N.S. B2Y 4A2

Introduction

In this paper we shall consider the numerical analysis of the data from that kind of experiment in which a natural phytoplankton assemblage from a particular depth is incubated at various light intensities in the presence of radioactive bicarbonate such that a curve can be constructed describing the relationship between photosynthetic rate and available light for that particular sample. The principles involved will also be applicable to photosynthesis–light measurements made on cultures by means of the oxygen electrode.

Experiments of the type described can be used to map geographic distributions of assimilation number, or in models for computing production under a square metre of ocean surface. However, our emphasis is on the physiological content of the models. In that respect, we gain the maximum information when the light-saturation experiments are used to test hypotheses, for example, about the relative values of physiological parameters of populations sampled from different physical environments (e.g. within versus below surface mixed layers) or about the effects on parameter values of some imposed treatment (e.g. temperature variations). Numerical analysis therefore involves choosing a mathematical model of the photosynthesis–light relationship; choosing a parameterization of the model that is consistent with the way the measurements are made; objectively estimating the parameters of the model and their confidence regions from experimental data; and interpreting the parameter values in terms of what is known about their physiological basis.

Choosing the Model

We have to select a mathematical description for data of the kind shown in Fig. 1 (from Platt and Gallegos 1980), where the range of light intensities is from zero to the maximum that can occur under natural circumstances. Figure 1a is a composite schematic showing the various possibilities that can occur. Depending on how the measurements are made, there may be a small, negative assimilation at zero light intensity, usually interpreted as the magnitude of the dark respiration. At low light intensities, the photosynthesis–light relationship is linear. The curve exhibits its maximum slope here (the initial slope). At some higher value of light intensity, the curve usually attains an upper bound (light saturated), where the slope has fallen to zero. At still higher light intensities, the rate of change of photosynthesis with light may become negative (the photoinhibited range). When photoinhibition is observed, the peak in the curve may be sharply defined, Fig. 1b, or relatively broad, Fig. 1c. Sometimes, no photoinhibition is observed over this range of light intensities, Fig. 1d.

Selection of a suitable model will depend on the light range over which the measurements are made. Many workers will be interested in working in a restricted range of light intensities where photoinhibition is unlikely ever to occur. In this case the models can be relatively simple compared with those necessary to represent photoinhibition.

Mathematical representation of the photosynthesis–light curve below the onset of photoinhibition is dealt with in Jassby and Platt (1976), Platt and Jassby (1976), and Platt et al. (1977). Models expanded to admit the possibility of photoinhibition are treated in Platt et al. (1980) and Platt and Gallegos (1980). It is important to note that these models are of the empirical kind rather than the mechanistic kind. That is, they each describe a family of curves according to a certain equation, with particular members of the family being specified by particular sets of the parameter values. The basic equation describing each family is constructed, not from physiological arguments, but from application of mathematical intuition to find a curve that matches typical data.

This being the case, the criterion of merit has to be the relative success with which a particular family of curves can describe experimental data. Stated another way, that equation representing a family of curves that describe the results of an experiment with the least residual variance when averaged over a large number of experimental trials will be the equation of choice. In this way, Jassby and Platt (1976) found that the hyperbolic tangent equation was a consistently successful description of their experiments:

$$(1) \qquad P(I) = P_m \tanh (\alpha I / P_m)$$

where P is the ^{14}C assimilation at light level I, P_m is the assimilation at saturating light, and α is the initial slope.

Following such a routine for the selection of an equation to describe a particular set of experiments presupposes an objective method for fitting the equations to the data. This will be dealt with in detail below.

Again, we emphasize that this hyperbolic tangent equation was used as no more than an empirical description, and that its initial trial (Jassby and Platt 1976) was based on no more sophisticated arguments than that it was known to describe a saturation-type equation. However, recent work by Chalker (1980) has shown that, if the photosynthesis–light curve is represented as a generalized expansion in P, then the only possible solution for the quadratic approximation is the hyperbolic tangent equation. This will be taken up in detail below.

Choosing the Parameters

Selection of the appropriate parameters for a photosynthesis–light model has been dealt with by Platt et al. (1977) and by Platt and Gallegos (1980). The number of parameters that are required will depend on the degree of complexity that is sought in the description. For example, referring again to Fig. 1, the dependance at low light can be described by a single parameter, the initial slope α:

$$(2) \qquad \alpha \equiv \left. \frac{\partial P^B}{\partial I} \right|_{I \to 0}$$

Here the superscript B implies that the value of ^{14}C assimilation (P) has been normalized to chlorophyll a. The adequacy of this one-parameter description breaks down if $P \neq 0$ at $I = 0$. In other words, if it is required to allow for the dark respiration, an additional parameter R^B, equal to the magnitude of the intercept, will have to be carried as an additive term.

A linear description is justified only at low light levels. Otherwise, the curvature must be allowed for through another parameter. A good choice is the height of the plateau P_m^B. This is not the only choice. One could equally use the light level at which the straight line with slope α cuts the plateau

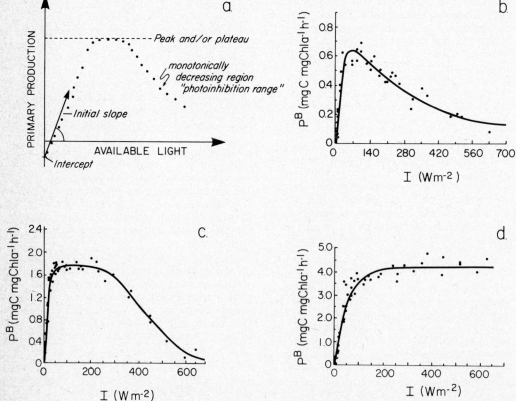

FIG. 1. (a) A generalized photosynthesis–light curve; (b–d) curves from experiments on natural assemblages of marine phytoplankton.

(I_k) or the light level at which $P = \frac{1}{2} P_m$ (half-saturation constant). Once the parameters are fitted, these alternatives may be found, one from the other, through simple identities.

To describe experimental data on photoinhibition, at least one additional parameter is required. This can be β, a parameter independant of α, describing the negative slope at high irradiances. Those curves that show an extended plateau before the onset of photoinhibition (Fig. 1c) require a final parameter I_T to describe the irradiance at which the slope of the curve becomes negative.

These summarize the minimum parameter sets necessary at each level of description. In every case, more parameters could be added and a better fit obtained. But the additional or superfluous parameters would have no biological meaning and no further information could be gained. Also, the curves should be fitted by an objective method to a data set containing sufficient points that reasonably precise estimates can be made for each of the parameters. This is the subject of the next section.

Estimating the Parameters and Confidence Regions

The fitting problem is to find the set of parameters that yield the "best" (in some sense) description of the data in terms of the chosen model formulation and parameterization. Measurements of production always contain errors, so that we may represent the observed data

$$(3) \qquad P_j^B = f(I_j; P_m^B, \alpha, \ldots) + e_j$$

where P_j^B is the measured production, $f(I_j; P_m^B, \alpha, \ldots)$ is the functional form of the light-saturation curve written in terms of irradiance, I_j, and P_m^B, α, and one or more photoinhibition parameters, and/or respiration; e_j is an error term that accounts for any effects not incorporated in the model, as well as measurement error. The choice of the functional form, $f(I_j; P_m^B, \alpha, \ldots)$ has been discussed previously, but we note that the model formulation and parameter estimation problems are not entirely independent (see below). It is the statistical distribution of the error term, e_j, that determines the details of the fitting procedure.

In the simplest case in which the errors are independent and normally distributed with a constant variance, the best parameters are those that minimize the sum of squared residuals (Bard 1974; Smith 1979)

$$(4) \qquad J = \sum_j [P_j^B - f(I_j; \hat{P}_m^B, \hat{\alpha}, \ldots)]^2$$

where $\hat{P}_m^B$ and α are the best estimates of their "true" values. If the errors are normally distributed but not of constant variance, then the weighted sum of squared residuals

$$(5) \qquad J = \sum_j \frac{1}{\sigma_j^2} [P_j^B - f(I_j; \hat{P}_m^B, \hat{\alpha}, \ldots)]^2$$

where σ_j^2 is the variance associated with the measured P_j^B, is the appropriate criterion to minimize (Bevington 1969). When the P_j^B are means of replicate samples, the computed variances may be used for σ_j^2. However, uniform light fields are difficult to produce, and minor differences in light intensity can produce large variations in P^B, particularly at low light, such that true replicates may be difficult to obtain. It is possible that this problem may be circumvented by modulating the position of replicate bottles relative to the light field, thereby exposing all bottles to the same average light during the course of an incubation. When replicates are not available, some assumption about the variances of the e_j must be made. Usually it is assumed either that they are constant, or that they are proportional to the observed value of P_j^B. In either case the appropriateness of such an assumption should be examined at the conclusion of the fitting exercise, for example, by forming a plot of the residuals as a function of predicted value (Draper and Smith 1966).

In an earlier paper (Platt et al. 1980) we gave some attention to whether or not a weighted sum of squared residuals should be minimized when fitting parameters of light-saturation models. We displayed a figure showing the standard deviation of estimated production (from in situ estimates) plotted against the mean. The relationship was roughly linear, but when a linear weighting function was used to fit the parameters, the fitting routine failed to converge on stable parameter estimates. The reason seems to be that, across a large number of experiments, the variance in estimated production is roughly correlated with P^B, but that within any given experiment, the variance is independent of P for all except the very lowest values. Figure 2 illustrates this point. In most instances an unweighted sum of squared residuals can probably be used provided the model is a good descriptor at the low light level.

Many algorithms have been developed for performing the sum of squares minimization in nonlinear parameter estimation problems. We shall not enter a detailed discussion of the mathematics of these techniques, but instead refer the reader to Smith (1979) and Bard (1974) for a comprehensive survey of the field. Basically all of the techniques are iterative, requiring initial or trial estimates of the parameters from which a search is conducted until the

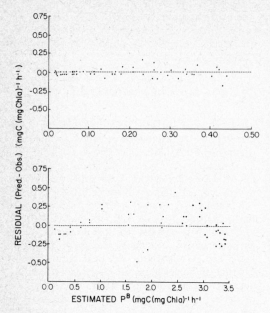

FIG. 2. Residuals about two fitted curves as a function of predicted P^B. Variance is larger for curve with larger P_m^B, but for both curves, the variance is roughly independent of P^B over most of the domain.

parameter set yielding a minimum of the objective function is located. The major difference among the algorithms is in the method of choosing the updated parameter set at each iteration. The simplest algorithms, both conceptually and computationally, are the pattern search techniques which employ only information about present and past values of the objective function and parameter estimates. These are simple to program, and several examples of FORTRAN subroutines are given by Bevington (1969). More sophisticated are the so-called descent methods, which employ the first (and sometimes higher) derivatives of the objective function with respect to the parameters in updating the parameter estimates. For electronic computers, various packaged routines are available to minimize the sum of squared residuals by these methods, and a list of programs available has been compiled by Bard (1974). We have found that the modified Gauss – Newton method performs satisfactorily, fitting up to at least four parameters simultaneously (see e.g. Fig. 1ç).

Packaged routines have the advantage that minimal programming effort is required of the user. Also, it is reasonably certain that a minimum sum of squared residuals will be found in an efficient (in the sense of minimal computation time) manner. However, a certain amount of checking, at least in a pilot analysis, should be done. It is advisable to ascertain that the fitted parameters indeed yield a minimum of the error criterion, and that the minimum is unique within the region of reasonable parameter estimates.

If a relatively small number of experiments is to be fitted, it may be simplest to write a short routine that computes the sum of squared residuals while stepping through a grid of trial estimates, and search for the minimum interactively (Silvert 1979). This is the crudest of the pattern search techniques but has the advantage that it is simple to write, can be implemented on relatively unsophisticated computers or programable calculators, and also provides information that is useful for determining confidence regions about the parameter estimates (see below).

Silvert (1979) presented two methods for determining confidence regions for parameters in general, nonlinear, biological models. We now discuss the application of these methods to a model of the light-saturation curve of photosynthesis.

The first method is a Monte Carlo approach, which is applicable when a packaged routine is used to obtain the parameter estimates. The procedure has been described by Bard (1974) and Smith (1979) and is implemented as follows. The best parameter estimates are obtained from a set of measurements of photosynthesis and irradiance. Those parameter estimates and measured irradiance values are used in the chosen model of the light-saturation curve to generate a set of simulated P^B values. The simulated values are "noise-corrupted" by adding a random error term having the distribution (known or assumed) in the original analysis. If the errors are of constant variance, then an estimate of the variance, s^2, is given by (Silvert 1979).

$$(6) \qquad s^2 = J/(n - m)$$

where J is given by Eq. (4), m is the number of parameters, and n is the number of data points. The fitting routine is then used to estimate the parameters of the light-saturation model using the simulated, noise-corrupted data. This procedure is repeated enough times (~ 100) to obtain a distribution of errors in the parameter estimates, from which confidence regions can be determined. A drawback of this procedure in the context of light-saturation models is that the procedure implicitly assumes that the model formulation is a perfect description of the process. In models that are based on mechanistic assumptions (e.g. physical models in which the equations are derived from Newton's laws) this is not a serious drawback. However, the models of the light-saturation curve are mainly geometric in their formulation. The Monte Carlo approach does not account for any systematic tendencies for the equations to over- or under-estimate production in certain regions of the curve. Failure of this approach to account for such trends can cause the computed confidence limits to be spuriously narrow.

The second method discussed by Silvert (1979) for computing confidence regions about parameter estimates is to determine contours of parameter combinations that yield a sum of squared residuals less than some critical value. The critical value is given by (Smith 1979)

$$(7) \qquad J_c = J_0 \left[1 + \left(\frac{m}{n-m} \right) F^\gamma_{m, \, n-m} \right]$$

where J_c is the critical sum of squared residuals, J_0 is the minimum, m and n are as given above, and $F^\gamma_{m, \, n-m}$ is the upper γ point of the F-distribution with m and $(n-m)$ degrees of freedom.

We illustrate the procedure below with data collected from the Labrador Sea. Equation (1), including an intercept term, R^B, was fitted to 43 pairs of production and irradiance estimates.

Contours of the sum of squared residuals were computed by first holding α and P^B_m constant well below their estimated values, and stepping through values of R^B, below and above its estimated value, and computing the sum of squared residuals at each combination of parameters. This was repeated for a range of values of α and P^B_m, until a three-dimensional space was defined, centered about the best estimates of the parameters, with the ranges of the trial parameters as principal axes. All combinations of parameters yielding sums of squared residuals less than the critical value are within the $(1-\gamma)$ confidence regions of the best estimates. As we noted above, this search procedure can be used in an interactive way, to locate the minimum sum of squared residuals and define confidence regions at the same time.

Figure 3 shows two-dimensional sections or slices through the confidence region of the parameters. In Fig. 3a the region is oblique to the axes because errors in P^B_m and R^B are correlated. The confidence regions about R^B extend 50% on either side of its estimated value, whereas the corresponding precision on P^B_m is roughly $\pm$ 5%, and $\pm$ 10% for α. The confidence regions about the parameter estimates allow us not only to make statements regarding the significance of differences observed among samples, but also to identify those parameters for which further study is warranted. For example, we might anticipate that there would be little to gain from an experimental program designed to improve our understanding of the term, R^B, until improvements were made in the precision with which it can be estimated.

A Case Study

The purpose of numerical analysis of light saturation experiments is to gain insight about the physiological mechanisms regulating growth of phytoplankton populations. It is at the interpretation stage of numerical analysis that we advance our understanding of the physiology of the organisms: nevertheless we have tried to emphasize that the use of objective procedures at every step of the analysis is a prerequisite that must be met before interpretation can be of much value. We illustrate the practical application of these procedures below, with data collected off the continental shelf of Nova Scotia.

One aspect of the photosynthesis–light relationship that has been of much interest is the vertical variation in the parameters of the $P - I$ curve. One way of examining this variation with natural phytoplankton populations is by sampling from widely different optical depths in areas where the populations are separated by a density gradient. We wish

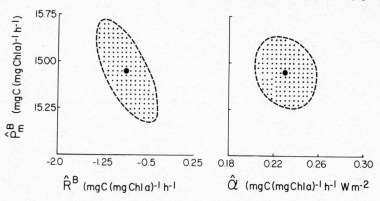

FIG. 3. Two-dimensional sections through the 95% joint confidence regions for the parameters P^B_m, α, and R^B. Errors in P^B_m and R^B are highly correlated. Precision of P^B_m is roughly $\pm$ 5%, $\pm$ 10% for α, and $\pm$ 50% for R^B.

107

to interpret the results in terms of the effect of light history on photosynthetic parameters; this requires that we first identify those parameters that show *significant* variations with depth.

Deciding on a model and parameters, and estimating the parameters is an iterative process in which we first try one formulation, evaluate the results after fitting the parameters, and increase the complexity of the model formulation if necessary. The first step is to examine $P - I$ plots of the data (Fig. 4). The points in Fig. 4a were taken from 5 m, the depth of penetration of 50% of surface irradiance, and the sample in Fig. 4b was taken from 35 m, or the 1% light-depth. It is immediately apparent that different levels of complexity will be required to fit the two experiments because the deep sample exhibits obvious photoinhibition at high irradiance, whereas photoinhibition is lacking in the near-surface sample. Although photoinhibition is outside the scope of our main discussion, we include it here because it illustrates a situation in which the choice of model formulation is not trivial.

For the near-surface sample, an equation just for light saturation seems sufficient, so we choose first the formulation and parameterization of Eq. (1). Objective estimation of the parameters P_m^B, α, and R^B requires initial estimates. In our experience, it has been possible to obtain initial estimates of sufficient accuracy by visual inspection of the curves. Based on Fig. 4a we used 2.0 mg C·(mg Chl a)$^{-1}$·h^{-1} as an initial estimate of P_m^B. Alpha is more difficult to estimate by inspection, but by extrapolating the initial slope, it appears to intersect P_m^B at $I_k \approx 40$ W·m^{-2}, which by the identity $I_k = P_m/\alpha$ gives 0.05 mg C·(mg Chl a)$^{-1}$·h^{-1}·W^{-1}·m^2 as an initial estimate for α. We use 0.0 as an initial estimate for R^B. These initial estimates are then entered into whatever fitting procedure is being used. With the modified Gauss-Newton procedure we obtained final estimates $P_m^B = 2.22$, and $\alpha = 0.045$, and $R^B = -0.19$.

It is apparent that some formulation including photoinhibition is necessary to describe the data of Fig. 4b. In the interest of parsimony we first

a. SCOTIAN SHELF 5m

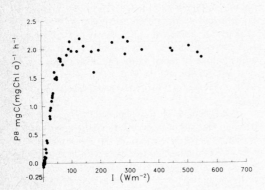

b. SCOTIAN SHELF 5m

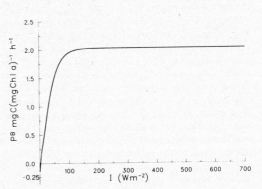

c. SCOTIAN SHELF 35m

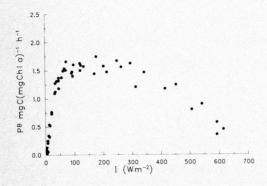

d. SCOTIAN SHELF 35m

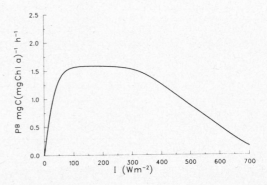

FIG. 4. (a–b) Photosynthesis–light experiment for station off the continental shelf of Nova Scotia from (a) 5 m and (b) 35 m; (c–d) empirical light-saturation models fit to data in (a) and (b).

tried the three parameter photoinhibition equation given in Platt et al. (1980). Trial estimates of the initial slope and maximum were chosen as before; we have found that it is sufficient to use a very small number (about 10^{-4}) as an initial estimate of β, the parameter controlling the strength of photoinhibition. However, if a grid search technique is being used to estimate the parameters it may be worthwhile to obtain a closer initial estimate of β. This can be done by noting that the intensity, I_b, at which the initial slope of the photoinhibited portion of the curve extrapolates to 0 is given by the identity $I_b = P_s/\beta$ (see Platt et al. 1980). From visual inspection of the curve we might estimate $I_b \approx 700$ $W \cdot m^{-2} = 1.5 / \beta$, so that $\beta = 0.0021$ mg $C \cdot$ (mg Chl $a)^{-1} \cdot h^{-1} \cdot W^{-1} \cdot m^2$ would be a reasonable initial estimate. Objective fitting of the parameters using the modified Gauss-Newton routine gave $P_s = 2.50$, $\alpha = 0.042$, and $\beta = 0.0052$ as final estimates.

It is necessary to evaluate the fit of the models by examining the residuals, i.e. the difference between predicted and observed values. In doing so we are examining both the validity of our assumption about the constancy of the variance, and the adequacy of the model formulation. We discussed the test of the error variance previously (Fig. 2). Testing the adequacy of the model formulation involves plotting the residuals as a function of irradiance (Fig. 5). In Fig. 5a we see that positive and negative residuals occur at all regions of the curve, whereas in Fig. 5b there is a noticeable curvature to the residuals, i.e. there is a tendency for residuals of a certain algebraic sign to be concentrated in certain regions of the I axis. We determine if the curvature is sufficient to warrant increasing the level of complexity in the formulation by testing if there is significant parabolic dependence in the residuals as a function of irradiance. An alternative procedure for analysis of Fig. 5 is the runs test (Platt and Gallegos 1980), but we believe the parabolic curvature analysis given here is a more powerful test. The procedure is as follows. Fit a second-order polynomial to the n residuals, with irradiance as the independent variable; form J_2, the sum of squared residuals about the polynomial regression, and J_0, the original sum of squared residuals (Eq. 4). Further complexity is warranted if the statistic

$$F = \frac{J_0 - J_2}{J_2/(n - 2)}$$

is greater than the critical value of the F-distribution with 1 and $n - 2$ degrees of freedom (Bevington 1969). We recommend using the 99% significance level in making this decision, because estimating an additional parameter should not be undertaken without very strong indications.

We applied this test to the residuals in Fig. 5. The computed F for the near-surface sample was 1.73, well below the critical value of 7.2 needed to reject the model formulation. For the deep sample, the computed F was 8.09, indicating that increasing the level of complexity in the model formulation is worthwhile to reduce the systematic error.

This means that we must return to the model formulation stage of the numerical analysis procedure. We note that the systematic trend in the residuals for the deep sample occurs at high irradiances, indicating that an equation permitting an extended plateau before the onset of photoinhibition is required to eliminate the trend; Platt and Gallegos (1980) presented an equation with that property. The model is parameterized in terms of the intensity I_b' at which photoinhibition reduces the value to half the maximum rate, and the intensity I_T' such that $I_b' - I_T' = I_T$, the intensity at which photoinhibition begins. Since the revised model formulation contains two parameters that are characteristic intensities, there may be some value to substituting I_k for α, using the identity given above; the range of intensities from I_k to I_T can be considered an optimal "window" for photosynthesis (Platt and Gallegos 1980), which may provide a useful way to compare the two samples.

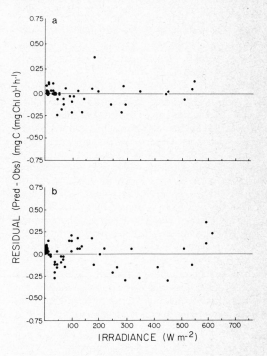

FIG. 5. Residuals about the fitted curves as a function of irradiance for samples off the continental shelf of Nova Scotia, (a) from 5 m (hyperbolic tangent equation) and (b) from 35 m (three-parameter photoinhibition equation of Platt et al. 1980).

109

Also, the characteristic intensities are invariant under a change in vertical scaling, which is advantageous should it be decided at a later stage of the analysis to normalize photosynthesis to cell number, cell volume, etc. We therefore made this change in parameterization for both experiments.

Following the reformulation we again estimate the parameters and evaluate the fit as above. At this iteration we found that the model formulations were sufficient and thus we may accept the parameter estimates as final. The fitting routine gave $P_m^B = 2.22$, $I_k = 49.9$, and $R^B = -0.19$ for the near-surface sample; for the deep sample we obtained $P_m^B = 1.59$, $I_k = 41.4$, $I_b' = 522$, and $I_T = 312$. The final fitted curves are shown next to the observed data point in Fig. 4c–d.

It is now appropriate to determine confidence intervals for the parameters. We illustrated above the procedure based on determining contours of critical sums of squared residuals. This procedure could be applied equally well to the present example. However, the deep sample required four parameters to obtain an adequate fit; if we were to compute confidence intervals by stepping through a grid of 10 values for each parameter, we would have 10^4 parameter combinations, and six 2-dimensional "slices" to examine. In a case like this it is much more convenient to use the Monte Carlo approach. Examination of the residuals revealed no systematic errors in the model formulations, so that the Monte Carlo approach should not give seriously biased confidence intervals.

The Monte Carlo procedure involves simulating data sets with residual errors distributed like those in the experimental data. The sum of squared residuals was 0.613 for the shallow sample, and 0.501 for the deep sample. There were 52 data points for each curve, so that the standard deviations were 0.111 and 0.102, respectively. We used the estimated parameter sets and measured irradiance values for each curve to generate 100 sets of pseudo-data. Each data point was noise-corrupted by adding a normal random variable with zero mean and the estimated standard deviation. Parameters for each of the 100 sets of pseudo-data were then estimated using the fitting routine.

Confidence limits are computed from the mean and standard deviation obtained by averaging over the replicate estimates from the simulated data. The confidence limits for a given parameter, say P_m^B, are given by

$$P_m^B \pm t_{\gamma/2} S_{P_m} / \sqrt{n - m}$$

where S_{P_m} is the standard deviation of the parameter and $t_{\gamma/2}$ is from a table of Student's t-distribution. The number of degrees of freedom associated with

the t value is $(n - m)$, not the number of cases of pseudo-data generated in the Monte Carlo procedure (Smith 1979).

In comparing the two samples, we are comparing models with different numbers of parameters. Both model formulas use the hyperbolic tangent function to describe the curve up to the threshold of photoinhibition, so that P_m^B and I_k are directly comparable. Observed differences between those parameters were statistically significant. The equation used for photoinhibition includes a derived parameter for the threshold of photoinhibition which, for the deep sample, fell within the 95% confidence interval $305 \leq I_T \leq 320$ W·m^{-2}. For the shallow sample we can say only that the threshold is greater than the highest light intensity used, 550 W·m^{-2}; in a one-tailed test of significance, the parameter I_T for the deep sample is significantly below that value. Similar remarks hold for I_T', the intensity at which $P^B = 0.5 \, P_m^B$.

Interpretation of the results is now in order. We can see that isolation below the density gradient in temperate waters results in a lower rate of light-saturated photosynthesis and lower irradiances required both to saturate and inhibit photosynthesis. Complete interpretation in terms of adaptation to low light or response to physiological stress would involve examination of species composition of the samples, as well as a suite of other environmental and biological covariates. Other questions of interest include the time required for the differences to develop, but these sorts of queries are beyond the scope of our paper.

Physiological Content of the Models

Although the modeling of photosynthesis–light curves is still stuck in the empirical stage, the ultimate aim of the work is a mechanistic description. For the range of light intensities below the onset of photoinhibition (which will satisfy the interests of most workers), Chalker (1980) provided a bridge between the empirical and the informed representation. Suppose that the rate of change of P and I is a function of P, $dP/dI = f(P)$ and expand $f(P)$ as a power series

$$(8) \quad \frac{dP}{dI} = a_0 + a_1 P + a_2 P^2 + a_3 P^3 + \dots .$$

Apply what is known about the photosynthesis–light curve to determine the coefficients in this expansion. For example in the linear approximation

$$(9) \quad \frac{dP}{dI} = a_0 + a_1 P$$

we know that at $P = 0$, $dP/dI = \alpha$, the initial slope, which can also be written as $\alpha = P_m/I_k$.

(10) $$\therefore \quad a_0 = P_m/I_k$$

We also know that as $P \to P_m$, $dP/dI = 0$. In Eq. (9) we then find

$$0 = \frac{P_m}{I_k} + a_1 P_m$$

(11) $$\therefore \quad a_1 = -\frac{1}{I_k}$$

Then

$$\int \frac{dP}{P_m - P} = \frac{\alpha}{P_m} \int dI$$

which leads, under the condition $P = 0$ at $I = 0$, to the solution

(12) $$P = P_m(1 - e^{-\frac{\alpha I}{P_m}})$$

This is an equation previously published by Webb et al. (1974).

The quadratic approximation of Eq. (8) is

(13) $$\frac{dP}{dI} = a_0 + a_1 P + a_2 P^2$$

As before, we find the constant term to be of magnitude $\alpha = P_m/I_k$. The condition that $dP/dI = 0$ at $P = P_m$ yields

(14) $$a_1 = -(\frac{1}{I_k} + a_2 P_m)$$

In Eq. (13), this gives

(15) $$\frac{dP}{dI} = \frac{1}{I_k}(P_m - P) - a_2 P(P_m - P)$$

Integration of (15) yields

(16) $$P = P_m \frac{1 - e^{(\frac{1}{I_k} - a_2 P_m)I}}{P_m I_k a_2 - e^{(\frac{1}{I_k} - a_2 P_m)I}}$$

Now let $y = dP/dI$ and calculate

(17) $$\frac{dy}{dP} = -\frac{1}{I_k} - a_2 P_m + 2a_2 P$$

For the maximum slope dP/dI, we must have $dy/dP = 0$. Substituting (14) into (17), we see that this occurs at

(18) $$P = -a_1/2a_2$$

In Eq. (15) we find

(19) $$(\frac{dP}{dI}) \max = \frac{P_m}{I_k} + \frac{a_1^2 P_m}{4(a_1 + \frac{1}{I_k})}$$

Now we know that the maximum slope of the photosynthesis–light curve is $\alpha = P_m/I_k$. This implies that $a_1 = 0$. Also we know that the maximum quantum yield, and therefore the maximum slope, occur at $P = 0$, which, from (18) implies that $-a_1/2a_2 = 0$ or $a_1 = 0$.

Thus, from (14), we can write

(20) $$a_2 = -\frac{1}{P_m I_k}$$

Substituting this into Eq. (16) gives us the final result

(21) $$P = P_m \frac{e^{\frac{2I}{I_k}} - 1}{e^{\frac{2I}{I_k}} + 1}$$

which is identical to

(22) $$P = P_m \tanh(\frac{\alpha I}{P_m})$$

Thus the hyperbolic tangent equation is the only possible outcome from this analysis. Further, one could say that the result $a_1 = 0$ is a natural consequence of the fact that only two parameters, in this case a_0 and a_2, are required to fix a curve below the onset of photoinhibition.

The leading parameters α and P_m have the following interpretation. The initial slope α is related directly to the maximum quantum yield (Rabinowitch and Govindjee 1969; Platt and Jassby 1976) and is scaled by the magnitude of the quantum requirement. The plateau height P_m (called the assimilation number P_m^B when normalized to chlorophyll a) is related to the processing time of the dark reactions (Rabinowitch and Govindjee 1969; Falkowski 1980). The processing time is scaled to the size of the photosynthetic unit to yield the observed value of P_m^B:

(23) $$P_m^B = \frac{1}{t_e} \frac{Chl_0}{2500}$$

where t_e is the handling time required for one substrate molecule (~ 0.02 s), Chl_0 is the concentration of photosynthetic pigment, and 2500 is a number derived from flashing light experiments, which is also scaled to the quantum requirement (Rabinowitch and Govindjee 1969).

Thus, when observing changes in P_m in the field, we may be seeing, for example, changes in the photosynthetic unit size. It is even possible that through a direct normalization to Ch$l a$, such important changes in size of the photosynthetic unit may be hidden, without parallel measurements on the reaction center chlorophyll P700. For a mechanistic model, parameterization in terms of photosynthetic unit size could perhaps be more informative than chlorophyll a. However, it is important to be realistic about the practical, operational observables and to recognize that P700 is not accessible to routine measurement in the field with the present state-of-the-art.

Similarly, changes in P_m could be mediated by changes in t_e, accessible perhaps through activity assays on the photosynthetic enzymes, when a quantitative interpretation of such results is formulated.

In the scheme that we have suggested for the numerical analysis of photosynthesis–light data, the effect of other environmental variables is best handled through their effect on the photosynthetic parameters themselves (Platt et al. 1977). Thus, for example, adaptation to a new light regime with an adjustment of photosynthetic unit size would be treated as effect of light history on P_m^B. A similar approach is used to handle the effect of temperature.

It is possible, however, that some of the subtlety of these adjustments will not be made clear until a mechanistic treatment is used which distinguishes between the two photosystems. Working with freshwater field communities of phytoplankton, Vincent (1979) has observed directly the redistribution of excitation energy (spill over) with adaptation to various light levels within the water column. The time-scale for this redistribution is of order minutes. Kok et al. (1970) has achieved new insights into the dynamics of photosynthesis through a model in which photosystem II is represented as a linear series of reactions involving four distinct time constants.

To conclude, we might summarize by saying that a numerical analysis based on semiempirical models can still be a useful vehicle for organizing data on photosynthesis–light relationships. It is a fully objective procedure for reducing many observations to a few parameters capable of physiological interpretation. For a more complete understanding, we need to keep moving towards a mechanistic representation. It may turn out, however, that viable mechanistic models will contain terms for which there is no operational technique for measurement in the field.

References

BARD, Y. 1974. Nonlinear parameter estimation. Academic Press, New York, NY. 332 p.

BEVINGTON, P. R. 1969. Data reduction and error analysis for the physical sciences. McGraw Hill, New York, NY. 336 p.

CHALKER, B. E. 1980. Modelling light saturation curves for photosynthesis: An exponential function. J. Theor. Biol. 84: 205-215.

DRAPER, N. R., AND H. SMITH. 1966. Applied regression analysis. John Wiley & Sons, Inc., New York, NY. 407 p.

FALKOWSKI, P. 1980. Light-shade adaptation in marine phytoplankton, p. 99–119. In P. Falkowski [ed.] Primary productivity of the sea. Plenum Press, New York, NY.

JASSBY, A. D., AND T. PLATT. 1976. Mathematical formulation of the relationship between photosynthesis and light for phytoplankton. Limnol. Oceanogr. 21: 540–547.

KOK, B., B. FORBUSH, AND M. MCGLOIN. 1970. Cooperation of charges in photosynthetic O_2 evolution 1. A linear 4-step mechanism. Photochem. Photobiol. 11: 457–475.

PLATT, T., AND A. D. JASSBY. 1976. The relationship between photosynthesis and light for natural assemblages of coastal marine phytoplankton. J. Phycol. 12: 421–430.

PLATT, T., AND C. L. GALLEGOS. 1981. Modelling primary production, p. 339–362. In P. Falkowski [ed.] Primary productivity in the sea. Plenum Press, New York, NY.

PLATT, T., C. L. GALLEGOS, AND W. G. HARRISON. 1980. Photoinhibition of photosynthesis in natural assemblages of marine phytoplankton. J. Mar. Res. 38: 687–701.

PLATT, T., K. L. DENMAN, AND A. D. JASSBY. 1977. Modelling the productivity of phytoplankton, p. 807–856. In E. D. Goldberg [ed.] The sea: ideas and observations on progress in the study of the seas. Vol. VI. John Wiley, New York, NY.

RABINOWITCH, E., AND GOVINDJEE. 1969. Photosynthesis. Wiley, New York, NY. 273 p.

SILVERT, W. 1979. Practical curve fitting. Limnol. Oceanogr. 24: 767–773.

SMITH, W. R. 1979. Parameter estimation in nonlinear models of biological systems. Fish. Mar. Tech. Rep. 889. 90 p.

WEBB, W. L., M. NEWTON, AND D. STARR. 1974. Carbon dioxide exchange of Alnus rubra: a mathematical model. Oecologia (Berl.) 17: 281–291.

VINCENT, W. G. 1979. Mechanisms of rapid photosynthetic adaptation in natural phytoplankton communities. I. Redistribution of excitation energy between photosystems I and II. J. Phycol. 15: 429–434.

Tracer Kinetic Analysis Applied to Problems in Marine Biology

DAVID F. SMITH AND S. M. J. HORNER

CSIRO, Division of Fisheries and Oceanography,
P.O. Box 20, Marmion, W.A. 6020
Australia

Introduction

"To be conscious that you are ignorant of the facts is a great step to knowledge."

BENJAMIN DISRAELI
1804–81

The proposition that marine bioscientists are largely ignorant of the body of theory required to successfully employ radioisotopes is a proposition that marine bioscientists might, justifiably, greet with some scepticism. However, we suggest that this proposition is true and present a brief historical resume of tracer kinetic analysis to support this contention and demonstrate that the present situation was almost inevitable.

Technological advances of the 1940s resulted in large quantities of certain isotopes being made generally available for research. In particular, the availability of ^{14}C, with its very long half-life, opened up areas of research which were previously inaccessible. Earlier studies employing ^{11}C as tracer had to be conducted at the site of production of the radioisotope because of its very short (20.3 min) half-life. Thus, prior to the availability of ^{14}C, isotopic carbon studies were as limited as those which today employ ^{13}N. The availability of large quantities of many new isotope species resulted in a rapid expansion in employment of isotopes, which in turn stimulated interest in the theory of tracer kinetic analysis.

The burst of activity in development of a general analytic treatment of data arising from tracer experiments probably can be said to have begun with the publication by Sheppard and Householder (1951) and continued with the simultaneous publications of Berman and Schoenfeld (1956), Berman et al. (1962a, b), Hart (1955, 1957, 1958, 1960, 1965a, b, 1966, 1967), Hart and Sondheimer (1970), Hart and Spencer (1976), Rescigno and Segre (1964), Mann and Gurpide (1969a, b), and culminating in the middle 1960s with the publications of Bergner (1964, 1965).

These publications, which collectively cover almost in entirety the present body of theory relating to interpretation of tracer kinetic data, appeared in the following journals: Bull. Math. Biophys., J. Appl. Phys., Biophys. J., and J. Theor. Biol. Thus, even the choice of journals tended to isolate most marine scientists from the theoretical basis of tracer kinetic analysis. Moreover, many of us would have been intimidated by the rigorous mathematical treatment demanded by the topic. Consider even an explanatory footnote found in such a paper (Hearon 1969).

"Choose A_1 to be irreducible. Then by lemma 2, there is a b such that $A_1 + bI$ has a real root $\alpha_1 + b$ where α_1 is the maximum real root of A_1. Further (Gantmacher 1959b), there is a positive eigenvector Z such that $(A_1 + bI)Z = (\alpha_1 + b)Z$ and clearly $A_1Z = \alpha Z$. Thus we choose $\alpha = \alpha_1$ and $\nu_1 = Z$. C can be chosen nonsingular and such that the real parts of the roots of C are less than α. Then the real parts of the roots of $C - \alpha I$ are negative and (Hearon 1963, 1968) the matrix $-(C - \alpha I)^{-1}$ is nonnegative."

The applications of tracer kinetic analysis were, like the theoretical development, published in journals that would rarely be read by the community of marine bioscientists. The most frequently encountered journals containing the results of applying tracer kinetic analysis were J. Clin. Invest., J. Clin. Endocrinol. Metab., Circ. Res., Physiol. Rev., and Radiat. Res.

This historical association between tracer kinetics and medical studies was to continue almost to the exclusion of other research areas for several years, broadening out to include pharmacokinetics and, finally, basic biological research.

One of the very earliest explicit references to the works of the theoretical tracer kineticists to appear in the literature of marine science was by Conover and Francis (1973). Thus, 17–20 yr after first appearing in press, the publications of some early theoreticians began to be cited in the literature of marine science.

We have not mentioned the work of Steemann Nielsen (1952) as contributing to the general framework of tracer kinetic theory; it was never intended to contribute to that body of knowledge. It should be clearly pointed out, however, that Steemann Nielsen's work is, in its entirety, consistent with tracer kinetic theory. It was necessary for Steemann Nielsen to place certain restrictions on the experimental systems employed to obtain the unambiguous interpretations of data that he demonstrated were possible. Had subsequent workers employed his

113

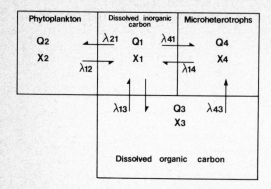

Phytoplankton	Dissolved inorganic carbon	Microheterotrophs
Q2 X2	$\lambda 21$ ⟵ Q1 $\lambda 41$ ⟶ X1 $\lambda 12$	Q4 X4 $\lambda 14$

$\lambda 13$ Q3 $\lambda 43$
X3

Dissolved organic carbon

FIG. 1. A model of ^{14}C fluxes in a water sample. If, in two experiments, radioisotope is added first as DI^{14}C to a seawater sample being incubated in the light and the time-varying compartmental radioactivities are measured, it is generally possible to estimate all the intercompartmental transport rates. The incorporation of radioactivity into DOC from labeled DIC is light dependent and mediated by the phytoplankton compartment. The DOC radioactivity, however, does not necessitate labeling phytoplankton carbon to obtain a radioactive precursor.

original protocol there would have been far fewer erroneous statements and confusion about what had been measured in labeling experiments.

Tracer kinetic analysis circumnavigates the frequent confusion about what is being measured in a radioisotope experiment. This is achieved, not by imposing experimental constraints, but rather by extending the analysis.

Figure 1 diagrammatically presents the information that can be obtained by applying a tracer kinetic analysis to the data arising from radioisotope incorporation experiments.

In this example a known quantity (in tracer amounts) of radioactive inorganic carbon is introduced to a water sample which is then incubated under constant environmental conditions. Portions of the sample are removed with time and freed of particulate matter by filtration. A portion of each filtrate is assayed for radioactivity and concentration of total dissolved inorganic carbon (DIC). Another portion of each filtrate is freed of DIC before being assayed for radioisotope content. Finally, the radioactivity of each filter is measured.

The tracer kinetic analysis of such experimental data permit one to estimate the rates of production of particulate organic carbon (POC) without resorting to any physical separation of phytoplankton from microheterotrophs. The analysis yields a measure of the rate of DIC production through respiration during the course of the experiment, as well as the rates of production of dissolved organic carbon (DOC) and rates of incorporation and respiration of DOC by

microheterotrophs. Finally, consideration of the DIC specific activity permits calculation of the moles carbon present in each compartment appearing in the diagram.

Multicompartmental Analysis: Theoretical Basis

The analyses currently employed to treat data arising from tracer kinetic experiments fall into three broad categories. These differ in complexity and, in an inverse fashion, in the number of restrictions that must be placed on the experimental system.

The first of these is exemplified by the analysis described by Berman and Schoenfeld (1956). This is a differential equation approach and requires that the system be in steady state over the course of the experiment and that the tracer and traced substance be homogenously mixed. Each and every inter-compartmental transfer can be elucidated and the associated rates measured solely by tracer experiments only if each and every compartment is accessible to tracer addition and to sampling. This latter restriction assumes that any n-compartment system has the maximum number, $n(n-1)$, interconnections and that all transfer rates between compartments are nonzero (Fig. 2). In practice, this restriction, i.e. accessibility of all compartments, is not nearly as severe as it might first seem. The number of accessible compartments required can be decreased by incorporating independently gained information about the system interconnections when analyzing the tracer kinetic data. This analysis is by far the most frequently employed and the easiest to employ due to later efforts of Berman et al. (1962a, b), who produced the SAAM series of programs. These programs are extremely efficient in parametric

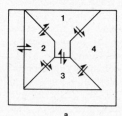 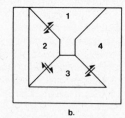

a.   b.

FIG. 2. Generally connected n-compartment system. (a) The maximum number of interconnections between a system of n compartments is $n(n-1)$. (b) Multicompartmental analysis permits one to proceed from the generally connected model to a specific one such as the closed catenary system. If every compartment is accessible to labeling and sampling, no information other than that obtained from tracer kinetic experiments is needed to define and measure all the transfer rates.

114

estimation employing multiple nonlinear regressions, fitting experimental data directly to a compartmental model or the defining differential equations, and can be obtained gratis as they were produced under the auspices of NIH. (Mathematical Research Branch, National Institute of Arthritis and Metabolic Diseases, National Institutes of Health, Bethesda, MD 20014, USA. Requests for SAAM 27 should be accompanied by a 7 track magnetic tape.)

The second method of tracer kinetic analysis is essentially that proposed by Hart (1955) and requires only that the experimental system be in steady state and that tracer and traced substance are in well-mixed compartments. The results obtained by applying this technique are always consistent with those obtained by the differential equation approach described above. In addition, a complete solution yielding all the transfer rates can be obtained if all compartments are accessible to sampling and a suitable number available for introduction of tracer. The increased generality is paid for by an increase in complexity of the procedure to obtain the solutions to the system equations that are integrodifferential in form.

The third broad category of data analysis is that proposed by Bergner (1964). This approach, which is obtained from maximum likelihood theory, requires a steady-state system but has relaxed the requirement of intimate mixing of tracer and "tracee."

The latter advantage gives one a powerful tool with which to conduct a special class of tracer kinetic experiments, i.e. "tag-recapture" experiments. Tag-recapture experiments, as most frequently conducted today, are merely tracer kinetic experiments as they were conducted before these three approaches to multicompartmental analysis were published.

Before presenting the theoretical basis of each approach in detail it might be worthwhile to comment on two of the shared constraints, i.e. the requirement of both a "steady state" and intimate mixing of tracer and traced substance.

In spite of the oft-heard statement, "Real world systems are probably never in a steady state!" this constraint is probably only rarely violated in a primary production estimate. The formal requirement, that the system be in steady state during the tracer experiment, can be met by making the duration of incubation only a few percent of the turnover time of the fastest compartment that is not in steady state. Furthermore, the compartmental analysis either furnishes or predicates a model which defines a set of equations. The equations will explicitly relate compartment sizes and rates; thus any deviation from steady state large enough to compromise the tracer kinetic analysis can also be used to calculate the maximum and minimum value of the rates measured during a period of growth or depletion of a compartment.

Furthermore, the SAAM 27 program now includes the option of incorporating time-varying coefficients in the system differential equations allowing one to solve for rate estimates in systems patently not in steady state during the experiment.

The second frequently encountered problem of intimate mixing of tracer and "tracee" can be entirely circumnavigated by choice of experimental technique. For example, to obtain a set of time-varying samples, do not add tracer to a large seawater sample and then remove aliquots with time. Instead, dispense a set of replicate samples, add to each the same quantity of tracer then, noting the elapsed time, filter the entire amount of the subsample. As shown in Fig. 3 this technique obviates the need for homogeneity in regard to added tracer or even the need to ensure that the "replicates" are equal in volume if the original water sample was homogenous at the time subsamples were removed.

In the remainder of this section a summary of the three general classes of tracer kinetic analysis provides insight into their differences. A complete

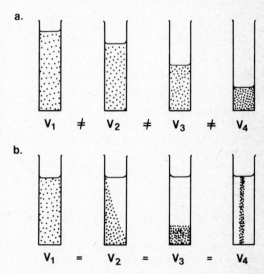

FIG. 3. Invariance in radioisotope incorporation. A set of replicate subsamples is dispensed from a single homogenous seawater sample and the same quantity of tracer $NaH^{14}CO_3$ is added to each replicate. If the replicates are incubated under identical conditions for the same period of time, then filtered, each filter will have precisely the same quantity of radioactivity. Neither the volumes dispensed, nor the degree of mixing the tracer with the sample, affects the total radioisotope incorporation. Any deviation in sample volume must result in equal but inverse deviations in both the total $NaHCO_3$ content and the total number of phytoplankton. The total radioisotope incorporation into POC is inversely related to $NaHCO_3$ content, through specific activity, and directly proportional to the number of phytoplankton. The two effects must always precisely cancel.

115

presentation of the theory is provided in the References.

TRACER KINETIC ANALYSIS
I: DIFFERENTIAL EQUATIONS APPROACH

The following presentation is essentially that of Berman and Schoenfeld (1956) and Berman et al. (1962a).

There is an experimental system that can be described by a set of n communicating compartments which are accessible to sampling and to addition of tracer. (Compartments may be chemical ($CO_2 \rightleftharpoons H_2CO_3 \rightleftharpoons HCO_3^{1-} \rightleftharpoons CO_3^{2-}$) or physical as in the case of the Donnan equilibrium.) If the system is in steady state and tracer is injected into one compartment, the time-varying distribution of label throughout the system is given by the set of differential equations

$$(1) \quad \begin{bmatrix} \dot{f}_1(t) \\ \dot{f}_2(t) \\ \cdot \\ \cdot \\ \cdot \\ \dot{f}_n(t) \end{bmatrix} \begin{bmatrix} -\lambda_{11} + \lambda_{12} + \ldots + \lambda_{1n} \\ \lambda_{21} - \lambda_{22} + \ldots + \lambda_{2n} \\ \cdot \quad \cdot \quad \quad \cdot \\ \cdot \quad \cdot \quad \quad \cdot \\ \cdot \quad \cdot \quad \quad \cdot \\ \lambda_{n1} + \lambda_{n2} + \ldots - \lambda_{nn} \end{bmatrix} \begin{bmatrix} f_1(t) \\ f_2(t) \\ \cdot \\ \cdot \\ \cdot \\ f_n(t) \end{bmatrix}$$

where
$$\dot{f}_i(t) = \frac{d[f_i(t)]}{dt}$$

$f_i(t)$ = time-varying radioactivity, or specific activity, of ith compartment (dpm or dpm$\cdot$mol^{-1})
λ_{ij} = fractional turnover rates from the jth to the ith compartment (min^{-1})

$$\lambda_{ii} = - \sum_{i=0}^{n} \lambda_{ki} \quad i \neq k$$

and λ_{0i} = transport from the ith compartment to outside the system.

For constant λ_{ij}, the solutions of equations (1) are always sums of exponentials.

$$(2) \quad f_i(t) = \sum_{j=1}^{n} A_{ij}e^{-\alpha_j t} \quad (i = 1, 2, \ldots n)$$

The $-\alpha_j$ are eigenvalues of the matrix $[\lambda_{ij}]$, the A_{ij} are elements of the eigenvectors. In matrix notation . . .

$$(3) \quad \lambda = A \begin{bmatrix} \alpha_1 & 0 & \ldots & 0 \\ 0 & \alpha_2 & \ldots & 0 \\ \cdot & \cdot & & \cdot \\ \cdot & \cdot & & \cdot \\ \cdot & \cdot & & \cdot \\ 0 & 0 & \ldots & \alpha_n \end{bmatrix} A^{-1}$$

Thus, in a tracer kinetic experiment data points are obtained that are measures of the different $f_i(t)$; each data set is then fitted to a sum of exponential terms. If n terms are required to fit the data we assume initially the system is composed of at least n compartments. If we were to lack all other information about the system but could take samples from all compartments during a tracer experiment we should still be able to obtain the n, A_{ij}'s and the n, α_j's and, therefore, estimate each and every λ_{ij} by the relations[1]

$$(4) \quad \lambda = A \alpha A^{-1}$$

Typically we cannot access all compartments; however we usually can bring independent knowledge about the system to assist in the analysis.

TRACER KINETIC ANALYSIS
II: INTEGRODIFFERENTIAL EQUATION APPROACH

The following is a description of the approach which was investigated intensively by Hart (1955, 1957, 1958, 1960, 1965a, b, 1966, and 1967). The advantage of this technique lies in the fact that it supplies a formal way to manipulate tracer data to test assumptions of compartmental contiguity. As an example, in numerous published experiments the separation of phytoplankton and microheterotrophs has been attempted with membrane filters and a judicious selection of pore size. If one does not employ a tracer kinetic analysis, this separation is required if only phytoplankton production of particulate carbon is to be measured in the presence of primary DOC production which, in turn, is incorporated by microheterotrophs.

The integrodifferential equation analysis can be applied to the data in the manner described by Hart as an alternative to physical separation of the autotrophic and heterotrophic components.

By way of illustration consider the three-compartment system in Fig. 4. This figure diagrammatically represents the distribution of tracer with time in compartment 1 (DOC), compartment 2 (DIC), and compartment 3 (POC). The POC compartment cannot conveniently be used to introduce label, but its radioactivity can be measured after introducing tracer as DIC or DOC (Wiebe and Smith 1977a).

---

[1] Frequently there are only $n(n-1)$ independent A_{ij}'s because, in an experiment, tracer can usually be introduced into a single compartment; as the initial conditions regarding radioisotope are known clearly only $(n-1)$ independent A_{ij}'s exist because

$$f_i(0) = \sum_{j=1}^{n} A_{ij}$$

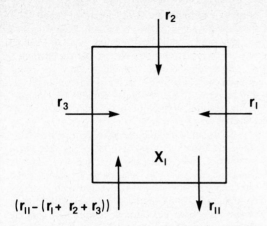

r_2

r_3 → ← r_1

X_1

$(r_{11} - (r_1 + r_2 + r_3))$ ↓ r_{11}

FIG. 4. Integrodifferential equation analysis of the single-compartment re-entry function. This analytical method is extremely powerful when applied to systems wherein only some compartments are accessible to tracer addition and to sampling. In the experimental system illustrated, at $t = 0$, tracer $NaH^{14}CO_3$ is added to a water sample containing X_1 mol of $NaH^{12}CO_3$. Radioisotope is lost by incorporation into nonrespired cell material and DOC. Radioisotope is returned to the DIC pool via respiration of DOC and of labeled phytoplankton and microheterotroph cell material. Even though these sources have differing specific activities and time lags, their cumulative re-entry (by respiration) and the size of the fixed $NaH^{12}CO_3$ pools can be obtained by only monitoring the radioactivity of the DIC pool. X_1, quantity of DIC in the sample (mol); r_{11}, fractional loss rate of DIC (min^{-1}); r_1, r_2, r_3, fractional respiration rates of carbon fixed as phytoplankton, microheterotrophs, and DOC (min^{-1}).

We obtain the rate of incorporation of radio-isotope due to all the POC trapped on a membrane filter. We then wish to know if the POC compartment is labeled solely through autotrophic DIC incorporation or also through microheterotrophic POC, which is not contiguous with DIC but receives its label via the DOC compartment. The rationale of this analysis is as follows:

The POC and DOC compartments receive label from phytoplankton at rates $\dot{Q}_h(t)$ and $\dot{Q}_i(t)$ which depend on the radioactivity of the DIC, $Q_j(t)$. The POC compartment also receives label in the form of microheterotrophs labeled via the DOC compartment; therefore, the rate of labeling microheterotrophs, $\dot{Q}_q(t)$, depends not on the DIC at time t, but on an earlier time $(t - \tau)$.

If equation (1) of the last section is rewritten to correspond to the nomenclature used by Hart we have

(5) $\dot{f}_i(t) - \sum_{j=1}^{n} a_{ij}f_j(t) = 0$ for $i = 1$ to n

These equations can be generalized to treat non contiguous compartmental systems by replacing each $a_{ij}f_j(t)$ by $\int_o^t a_{ij}^o (t - \tau) f_j(\tau) d\tau$ to give . . .

(6) $\dot{f}_i(t) - \sum_{j=1}^{n} \int_o^t a_{ij}^o (t - \tau) f_j(\tau) d\tau = 0$

for $i = 1 \ldots n$

By applying the Laplace transform $\mathscr{L}$, the integrodifferential equations (6) can be simplified to give a set of algebraic equations:

Letting $\mathscr{L}[\dot{f}_i(t)] \equiv Y_i(s)$
$\mathscr{L}[f_j(\tau)] \equiv X_j(s)$
and $\mathscr{L}[a_{ij}^o(t - \tau)] \equiv A_{ij}(s)$

then

(7) $$\begin{bmatrix} Y_1(s) \\ Y_2(s) \\ \cdot \\ \cdot \\ \cdot \\ Y_n(s) \end{bmatrix} = \begin{bmatrix} -A_{11}(s) + A_{12}(s) + \ldots + A_{1n}(s) \\ A_{21}(s) - A_{22}(s) + \ldots + A_{2n}(s) \\ \cdot \\ \cdot \\ \cdot \\ A_{n1}(s) + A_{n2}(s) + \ldots - A_{nn}(s) \end{bmatrix} \begin{bmatrix} X_1(s) \\ X_2(s) \\ \cdot \\ \cdot \\ \cdot \\ X_n(s) \end{bmatrix}$$

If we carry out a tracer experiment by adding label to compartment 2 (DIC) we can solve for each $X_j(t)$ (or express them as $X_j(s)$) of each measured compartment and write the numerical form of equation (7) as

(8) $\sum_{i=1}^{n} X_{j2}(s) A_{2j}(s) + [sX_{i2}(s) - X_{j2}(0)] = 0$

If the Wronskians (see Appendix I) of equation (8) do not all vanish (i.e. in the case of the POC compartment) there is no completely contiguous representation of the system; hence in the POC radioactivity we will find a contribution that did not come directly from DIC.

If the equation for DOC radioactivity is examined and the Wronskian $\omega\{X_{12}(s), [sX_{12}(s) - X_{12}(0)]\} = 0$ the DIC and DOC compartments are contiguous and constant A_{ij}'s will be found.

TRACER KINETIC ANALYSIS
III: INDICATOR EQUIVALENCE THEOREM

The following is a description of the basis for the tracer kinetic analysis described by Bergner (1964).

Given a steady-state compartment containing b^o moles of an element then the total input rate for that element, ζ^o, is related to the mean transit time for the element, θ^o, by . . .

117

(9)
$$b^o = \zeta^o\,\theta^o$$

If tracer is introduced to the system at $t = 0$ and $b(t)$ is the amount of tracer in the compartment at time t, then

(10)
$$\theta^o = \int_0^\infty \frac{b(t)}{b_s(0)}\,dt$$

where $b_s(0)$ is the total amount of tracer supplied to the whole system at $t = 0$.

Letting the amount of tracer present in the whole system be given by $b_s(t)$, and the specific activity, $a(t)$, given by the relation . . .

(11)
$$a(t) \equiv b(t)/b^o$$

then the quantity of the element in the whole system is

(12)
$$b^o s = \frac{\int_0^\infty b_s(t)\,dt}{\int_0^\infty a(t)\,dt}$$

Multicompartmental Analysis: Practical Applications

It would be foolhardy to believe that the preceding section is more than the barest outline, or

presents more than the most superficial treatment of theoretical tracer kinetics. Any individual interested in applying multicompartmental analysis should refer to the References as well as current literature.

Superficial though it might be, any discussion of a theoretical problem in physics necessitates the employment of mathematical notation so compact as to become cryptic to one unfamiliar with its routine use.

So as not to entomb the utility of tracer kinetics, alongside the experimentalist, inside its theoretical framework, two examples of actual experiments, data, and analysis will be presented. Much of the same material is covered as in the preceding section but numerical values in the appendices replace most of the functional notation. In addition to quieting the fear of unfamiliar mathematical expressions shared by many of us, this section explicitly states some problems and pitfalls not easily derived from solely theoretical considerations.

Example 1 — Labeling compounds with precursor–successor relationships during a constant infusion experiment — The curves of time-varying radioactivities (Fig. 5) were obtained by introducing tracer as an iodide-131 solution to a suspension of human thyroid cells. At varying times, portions of the cell suspension were removed and the compounds of interest isolated (for experimental details see Smith and Holmes 1970). This particular experi-

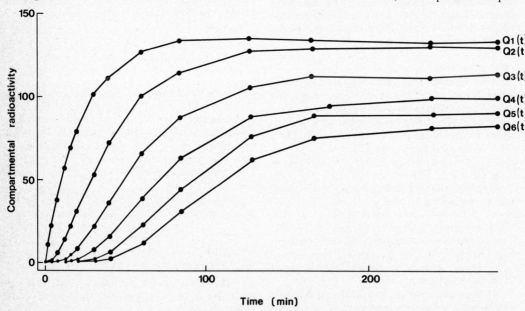

FIG. 5. Radioactivities of thyroxine pathway members following introduction of $^{131}I^{1-}$ to a thyroid cell suspension. After addition of radioiodide, portions of the cell suspension were removed at noted times and frozen in liquid nitrogen. The organic compounds of interest were extracted from each sample, then isolated from one another by chromatography. The radioactivity of each spot was measured and plotted versus sampling time. Analysis of these curves permits one to determine pool sizes, forward and reverse reaction rates, and precursor–product relationships.

mental system is one of special interest as it is an exact analogue of the one encountered in primary productivity experiments. One compartment, iodide or bicarbonate, is present in an enormous quantity relative to any other compartment or turnover rate of the system. Furthermore, it is into this compartment that label is introduced to the experimental system. In such a system the labeled compartment approximates a constant quantity of tracer present at constant specific activity during the course of the experiment. Compounds being formed from such a reactant will increase in total radioactivity until their specific activities equal that of the source of tracer. Thereafter, if the system of compartments remains in steady state in regard to the moles of compounds present, the quantity of radioactivity in each compartment also remains constant.

Curves of time-varying radioactivities arising from such an experimental system are, as noted earlier, graphs of sums of exponential terms. These curves, however, contain a term having a unique property. The exponential coefficient of this term is zero; hence the term is a constant. The origin of this constant term lies in the introduction of tracer via the extraordinarily large compartment of the system.

The classic approach to the analysis of data as in Fig. 5 begins with finding the number of exponential terms present in each curve and obtaining initial estimates of the exponents. To do this we first estimate the radioactivity maximum of each curve (i.e. the plateau each curve approaches as a limiting value).

Next, divide each data point of a curve by the radioactivity maximum. After dividing, change the sign of the quotient and add 1. This new quantity $R(t)$ is then plotted against time on semilogarithmic graph paper.

In theory we have eliminated the constant; the plot of $R(t)$ may be curvilinear near the origin, but at larger values of time it becomes straight as it contains contributions from only the term with the smallest exponent. In theory, we use the $R(t)$ values taken at the largest values of time to find the constant slope of the $R(t)$ plot by the relation

(13) $\qquad \lambda = \ln [R(t_2)/R(t_1)]/(t_1 - t_2)$

Figure 6 shows why this is rarely a good practice. The values at the largest values of time are the smallest quotients after division by the maximum radioactivity. Any error in either the estimation of numerator or denominator accentuates the scatter in the region of the linear portion of the graph.

The experimentalist has to judge the region of the graph that will yield the best approximation for the smallest exponent, i.e. the first to be found,

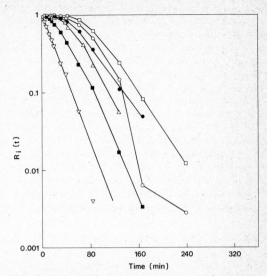

FIG. 6. Radioactivity curves obtained by transforming the experimental data. The data from experiment 1 were transformed by the relation $y_i = 1 - Q_i(t)/Q_i(t \rightarrow \infty)$. This transformation plus data point error preclude the arbitrary selection of the smallest values to obtain the initial λ_i estimates. The region of each curve which best approximates a straight line segment is used to obtain an initial estimate of the smallest λ in the sum of exponentials.

the exponent of the term that dies away most slowly in time.

After obtaining an initial estimate of the first exponent, λ_1, the value of the coefficient A_1 is obtained by substitution in the relation:

(14) $\qquad A_1 = R(t_k)/e^{-\lambda_1 t_k}$

The values of $R(t)$ and t employed are those used in obtaining λ_1 and an average value of A_1 is determined.

Once A_1 and λ_1 are obtained, $A_1 e^{-\lambda_1 t}$ can be calculated for each sample time and the difference taken between $A_1 e^{-\lambda_1 t}$ and $R(t)$ to give $R'(t)$. The function $R'(t)$ should lack $A_1 e^{-\lambda_1 t}$ and its graph can be employed to find $A_2 e^{-\lambda_2 t}$ as the new term having the smallest exponent. This process is repeated until each exponential term present in the original sum has been estimated. The decision as to whether or not to stop trying to extract additional exponential terms can be based on statistical constraints imposed by the data, on a priori knowledge about the system, and most importantly, on the experience of the researcher.

The detailed steps of this portion of the analysis are given in Appendix II and should be consulted before proceeding further.

Having obtained initial estimates of the exponents of each data set, the data sets are independently

119

fitted by a program employing multiple nonlinear regression and the values of the exponents obtained by an iterative process.

Exponents similar to each other in numerical value are tested to determine if they represent the same exponent appearing in different curves. This is accomplished by fitting all the data sets simultaneously and causing a λ_1 of one tracer curve to be equal to the λ_1 of another tracer curve. The final sums of squares for each data set should approach a minimum if the λ_1 is common.

Using the results obtained from the fitting of compartments E, F, and B in Appendix II, we can continue the analysis from the stage at which tracer curves are expressed as sums of exponentials. The global fitting provided the equations . . .

$$(15) \quad Q_E(t) = 134.51\,(1-1.003e^{-0.0454t})$$

$$(16) \quad Q_F(t) = 129.52\,(1-5.803e^{-0.0454t} + 4.801e^{-0.0553t})$$

$$(17) \quad Q_B(t) = 113.30\,(1-1.524e^{-0.0454t} + 0.524e^{-0.0352t})$$

The matrix A, of equation (4) is then . . .

$$(18) \quad A = \begin{bmatrix} 1.0 & 0 & 0 \\ 5.803 & -4.801 & 0 \\ 1.524 & 0 & -0.524 \end{bmatrix}$$

The inverse of A which is A^{-1} is calculated to be . . .

$$(19) \quad A^{-1} = \begin{bmatrix} 1 & 0 & 0 \\ 1.208 & -0.2083 & 0 \\ 2.907 & 0 & -1.909 \end{bmatrix}$$

The matrix, $\propto$, is taken from equations (15)–(17). . .

$$(20) \quad \propto = \begin{bmatrix} 0.0454 & 0 & 0 \\ 0 & 0.0553 & 0 \\ 0 & 0 & 0.0352 \end{bmatrix}$$

The intercompartmental transfer rates will be found by the relation given in equation (4).

$$(21) \quad \lambda = A \propto A^{-1} =$$

$$\begin{bmatrix} 1 & 0 & 0 \\ 5.803 & -4.801 & 0 \\ 1.524 & 0 & -0.524 \end{bmatrix}$$

$$\begin{bmatrix} 0.0454 & 0 & 0 \\ 0 & 0.0553 & 0 \\ 0 & 0 & 0.0352 \end{bmatrix}$$

$$\begin{bmatrix} 1 & 0 & 0 \\ 1.208 & -0.2083 & 0 \\ 2.907 & 0 & 1.909 \end{bmatrix}$$

and . . .

$$(22) \quad \lambda = \begin{bmatrix} 0.0454 & 0 & 0 \\ 0.0523 & 0.0552 & 0 \\ 0.0308 & 0 & 0.0352 \end{bmatrix}$$

Thus, compartment E receives no tracer from B or F, compartment F receives tracer only from E, and compartment B receives tracer only from E.

The fractional rates of transfer of material are given by each of the elements of λ and the absolute values can be found from the total radioisotope content of each compartment divided by the specific activity of the iodide supplied as tracer.

Example 2 — Estimating rates of DOC production by phytoplankton — Attempts to employ $DI^{14}C$ incorporation to measure the rates of DOC production by phytoplankton can only succeed if tracer kinetic experiments are used. Data from two such experiments (Table 1) plotted against time give curves similar to that of $Q_E(t)$ seen in the previous example.

Curves of this shape invariably result when seawater samples are incubated in the light and tracer is introduced as $DI^{14}C$ (Mague et al. 1980; Wiebe and Smith 1977a) or the complementary curves are seen during incubations in which tracer is introduced as labeled DOC (Wiebe and Smith 1977a, b). The shape of the DOC radioactivity curves as well as rate of production are apparently invariant, even under experimental conditions producing dramatic changes in the POC production rate (Smith and Wiebe 1976).

TABLE 1. Time-varying radioactivities obtained during light incubations of seawater samples with $DI^{14}C$.

Experiment 1		Experiment 2	
Time (min)	DO^{14}C content (Bq)	Time (min)	DO^{14}C content (Bq)
0	0	0	0
25	154.36	1.28	1.190
50	257.38	2.78	2.144
100	367.70	5.83	4.286
150	419.25	6.39	6.430
200	443.33	13.33	9.050
250	463.26	19.72	10.954
		23.33	12.859
		26.39	13.098
		29.06	13.336
		35.28	13.003
		38.89	14.288

Isotope incorporation experiments that employ a control sample and a single experimental sample processed after some arbitrary incubation period cannot estimate rates of DOC production.

Such an approach assumes that a constant rate of DOC production will be reflected by a constant rate of radioisotope accumulation in the DOC compartment. This is demonstrably not true and is an error that originates from failure to distinguish between radioisotope flux and carbon flux.

If the DOC compartment is in steady state with respect to carbon, then the DOC compartment is of constant size relative to carbon, i.e. the rate of DOC production is exactly equal to its rate of loss.

If a constant supply of tracer is introduced to the input of such a compartment, then the compartmental radioactivity will increase at a continuously decreasing rate, until the specific activity of the compartment is equal to that of its inputs. Thereafter, the compartment will be at steady state with respect to both isotope and carbon content.

Thus, isotope incubations employing only a single measurement in time must give smaller and smaller production rate estimates with longer and longer incubation periods. This is an artifact arising from division of a constant quantity of radioisotope, which is equal to the DOC compartment size divided by the DIC radioactivity, by an incubation period of arbitrarily long duration.

The analysis of the data of Table 1 shows DOC isotope incorporation curves to be described by the relation . . .

$$Q(t) = A_1(1 - e^{-\lambda_1 t})$$

The presence of only a single exponential can only mean that the DIC and DOC compartments are contiguous. This does not imply that $DI^{14}C$ does not have to enter the cell before being converted to $DO^{14}C$, but it does demonstrate that label in $DO^{14}C$ does not arise from labeled POC material.

"Nobody's perfect! Even I once made a mistake!
. . . I thought I'd made an error, and I hadn't."
ANON.

MULTICOMPARTMENTAL ANALYSIS: EXPERIMENTAL TECHNIQUE

Tracer kinetic experiments and the subsequent data analysis allow only one independent variable, time. Therein lies both the analytical power of the technique and the demand for rigor in the experimental portion of the work.

The investigator is responsible for ensuring that measurements on a given water sample reflect properties of that sample and are not artifacts. Super-

imposed on this responsibility is avoiding the introduction of systematic errors by dispensing subsamples from a nonhomogenous sample, or by altering the sample through mechanical stirring. Subsequently, all that is required is that each and every replicate has exactly the same history throughout the experiment. The degree of culpability regarding the first of these three pitfalls may never be resolved. The latter two can be almost entirely eliminated by methodically ensuring that replicates receive identical treatment.

Some idea of efficiency of this approach can be gleaned from the performance of a group of cell physiologists working under Professor F. C. Neidhardt at the University of Michigan, USA. A majority of the problems in which they were interested required precise estimates of the intrinsic growth rates of bacterial cultures. Their procedure was to remove an aliquot of a bacterial suspension, growing at approximately 37°C, and transfer the live cell suspension to a spectrophotometer cuvette. One then walked a distance of perhaps 10 m to the spectrophotometer, room temperature $\approx$ 20°C, and read the absorbancy of the cell suspension. The growth rate of the culture was estimated from the slope of the semilogarithmic plot of absorbancy versus time. In the course of a year, several thousands of such growth rate estimates were obtained, yet the entire range of variation of growth rate estimates made under the same culture conditions was less than 0.8%. Similar results can be obtained with less care in tracer kinetic experiments if a rigid experimental protocol has been devised.

Some specific suggestions and techniques to assist in tracer kinetic experiments will be given, but we will attempt to avoid giving any arbitrary values for universal employment. That is, we know of few experimental techniques that can be transferred from one experimental system to another without careful modification. Therefore, we would be loathe to recommend any specific values as "safe" pressure differentials and sample volumes which one might universally employ without testing. Instead, we would strongly recommend that each filtration manifold be equipped with an automatic pressure relief valve. The valve is adjusted to give the maximum pressure differential with all manifold ports closed. During all subsequent sample filtrations, although the number of ports open to vacuum flasks will vary from 10 to 1, the pressure differential will never rise above the maximum for which the valve has been set.

Purification of $DI^{14}C$ – Commercially available preparations of $Ba^{14}CO_3$ can have as much as 11% of the total radioactivity present in a form that is nonvolatile even from highly acid, boiling solutions. Moreover, the energy spectrum obtained from such a solution is complex and certainly is not the spectrum of ^{14}C.

Any tracer experiment that has not employed a $DI^{14}C$ preparation previously isolated from the commercially supplied material must be considered suspect. Any measure of DOC production rate must be made with radioisotope that was converted to a gas by addition of a nonvolatile acid to an aqueous solution. Only in this way can one hope to quantitatively remove $DI^{14}C$ at the end of an incubation.

Employment of carrier – Quantitative removal of a radioisotopically labeled element from an experimental system generally demands scrubbing the system with the unlabeled element in carrier form. To be a carrier for a tracer only the isotopes can be different. In a radiotracer experiment the only carrier for $H^{14}CO_3^{1-}$ is $H^{13}CO_3^{1-}$ or $H^{12}CO_3^{1-}$. There is no a priori means of guaranteeing that adding a nonvolatile acid to a water sample, then sparging with N_2, Ar, or air will quantitatively dilute out the $DI^{14}C$ present to background levels.

Estimation of sample radioactivity — It has already been mentioned that the only permissible variation between the samples originating from a tracer kinetic experiment is the length of the incubation period.

It follows then, that the precision associated with each radioactivity measurement should be the same. To ensure this, each sample must be counted until the same number of counts has been accumulated. Systematic error is guaranteed if one counts samples for the same length of time instead of to the same number of counts.

Transformation of data — Having paid strict attention to each portion of the experimental procedure and taken care to estimate properly sample radioactivity, it is still possible to snatch defeat from the jaws of victory.

As innocuous a procedure as a linear regression can sow the seeds of despair if transformed data points are employed and the ramifications of the transformation are unappreciated.

Heterotrophic potential experiments afford us with an excellent example. In these experiments, water samples are incubated with a labeled organic compound and the rate of incorporation estimated at varying concentrations of that compound. The incorporation rate is assumed to follow Michaelis-Menten kinetics and frequently the data are transformed to obtain a straight line for purposes of parameter estimation. Numerous examples of such transformed data that consist of not one but two straight line segments have been reported, the segment at higher substrate concentrations having the lesser slope. Unfortunately, this has been widely

interpreted as uptake by phytoplankton as opposed to microheterotrophs.

The truth is such plots occur if the radiochemical has not been purified just prior to use, if a background obtained by accumulating less counts than the samples is subtracted, or if the samples have not been counted to the same number of counts.

It cannot be too strongly emphasized that if the experimental data, y, has an associated uncertainty, σ, and one fits the transformed data $f(y)$ the uncertainties must be likewise compensated to give σ_f, by the relation,

$$\sigma_f = \frac{df(y)}{dy} \sigma$$

There is a desperate need for reviewers and editors to demand that manuscripts describing results that depend on curve fitting and parameter estimations include in the methods reported, the techniques and convergence criteria of the numerical analyses.

References

Not all references have been cited in the text.

BERGNER, P-E. E. 1964. Tracer dynamics and the determination of pool-sizes and turnover factors in metabolic systems. J. Theor. Biol. 6: 137–158.

——— 1965. Exchangeable mass: determination without assumption of isotopic equilibrium. Science (Washington, D.C.) 150: 1048–1050.

BERMAN, M., AND R. SCHOENFELD. 1956. Invariants in experimental data on linear kinetics and the formulation of models. Appl. Phys. 27: 1361–1370.

BERMAN, M., E. SHAHN, AND M. F. WEISS. 1962a. The routine fitting of kinetic data to models: a mathematical formalism for digital computers. Biophys. J. 2: 275–287.

BERMAN, M., M. F. WEISS, AND E. SHAHN. 1962b. Some formal approaches to the analysis of kinetic data in terms of linear compartmental systems. Biophys. J. 2: 289–316.

CONOVER, R. J., AND V. FRANCIS. 1973. The use of radioactive isotopes to measure the transfer of materials in aquatic food chains. Mar. Biol. 18: 272–283.

ESTREICHER, J., C. REVILLARD, AND J-R. SCHERRER. 1978. Compartmental analysis-I: Linde, a program using an analytical method of integration with constituent matrices. Comput. Biol. Med. 9: 49–65.

FLECK, G. M. 1972. On the generality of first-order rates in isotopic tracer kinetics. J. Theor. Biol. 34: 509–514.

GURPIDE, E., J. MANN, AND S. LIEBERMAN. 1965. Estimation of secretary rates of hormones from the specific activities of metabolites which have multiple secreted precursors. Bull. Math. Biophys. 27: 389–406.

HALL, S. E. H., R. GOEBEL, I. BARNES, G. HETENYI JR., AND M. BERMAN. 1977. The turnover and conversion to glucose of alanine in newborn and grown dogs. Fed. Proc. Fed. Am. Soc. Exp. Biol. 36 (2): 239–244.

HART, H. E. 1955. Analysis of tracer experiments in non-conservative steady-state systems. Bull. Math. Biophys. 17: 87–94.

———— 1957. Analysis of tracer experiments: II. Non-conservative non-steady-state systems. Bull. Biophys. 19: 61–72.

———— 1958. Analysis of tracer experiments: III. Homeostatic mechanisms of fluid flow systems. Bull. Math. Biophys. 20: 281–287.

———— 1960. Analysis of tracer experiments: IV. The kinetics of general N compartment systems. Bull. Math. Biophys. 22: 41–52.

———— 1965a. Analysis of tracer experiments: V. Integral equations of perturbation-tracer analysis. Bull. Math. Biophys. 27: 417–429.

———— 1965b. Analysis of tracer experiments: VI. Determination of partitioned initial entry functions. Bull. Math. Biophys. 27: 329–332.

———— 1966. Analysis of tracer experiments: VII. General multicompartment systems imbedded in non-homogeneous inaccessible media. Bull. Math. Biophys. 28: 261–282.

———— 1967. Analysis of tracer experiments: VIII. Integrodifferential equation treatment of partly accessible, partly injectable multicompartment systems. Bull. Math. Biophys. 29: 319–333.

HART, H. E., AND J. H. SONDHEIMER. 1970. Discrete formulation and error minimization in applying the integro-differential equation approach to mono-compartment data. Comput. Biol. Med. 1: 59–74.

HART, H. E., AND H. SPENCER. 1976. Vascular and extravascular calcium interchange in man determined with radioactive calcium. Radiat. Res. 67: 149–161.

HEARON, J. Z. 1969. Interpretation of tracer data. Biophys. J. 9: 1363–1370.

HETENYI, G. JR., AND K. H. NORWICH. 1974. Validity of the rates of production and utilization of metabolites as determined by tracer methods in intact animals. Fed. Proc. Fed. Am. Soc. Exp. Biol. 33: 1841–1848.

JACQUEZ, J. A. 1970. A global strategy for nonlinear least squares. Math. Biosci. 7: 1–8.

JENNRICH, R. I. 1979. Fitting nonlinear models to data. Annu. Rev. Biophys. Bioeng. 8: 195–238.

LEVY, G., M. GIBALID, AND W. J. JUSKO. 1969. Multi-compartment pharmacokinetic models and pharmacologic effects. Pharm. Sci. 58: 422–424.

MAGUE, T. H., E. FRIBERG, D. J. HUGHES, AND I. MORRIS. 1980. Extracellular release of carbon by marine phytoplankton; a physiological approach. Limnol. Oceanogr. 25: 262–279.

MANN, J., AND E. GURPIDE. 1969a. Interpretation of tracer data: significance of the number of terms in specific activity functions. Biophys. J. 9: 810–821.

———— 1969b. Interpretation of tracer data: some factors which reduce the number of terms in the specific activity functions in n-pool systems. Bull. Math. Biophys. 31: 473–486.

MYHILL, J. 1968. Some effects of data error in the analysis of radiotracer data. Acta Radiol. Ther. Phys. Biol. 7: 443–452.

PERL, W. 1960. A method for curve-fitting by exponential functions. Int. Appl. Radiat. 8: 212–222.

PERL, W., R. M. EFFROS, AND F. P. CHINARD. 1969. Indicator equivalence theorem for input rates and regional masses in multi-inlet steady-state systems with partially labeled input. J. Theor. Biol. 25: 297–316.

PROVENCHER, S. W. 1976a. A Fourier method for the analysis of exponential decay curves. Biophys. J. 16: 27–41.

———— 1976b. An eigenfunction expansion method for the analysis of exponential decay curves. Chem. Phys. 64: 2772–2777.

RESCIGNO, A., AND G. SEGRE. 1964. On some topological properties of the systems of compartments. Bull. Math. Biophys. 26: 31–38.

SHEPPARD, C. W., AND A. S. HOUSEHOLDER. 1951. The mathematical basis of the interpretation of tracer experiments in closed steady-state systems. J. Appl. Phys. 22: 510–520.

SMITH, D. F. 1974a. Quantitative analysis of the functional relationships existing between ecosystem components. I. Analysis of the linear intercomponent mass transfers. Oecologia 16: 97–106.

———— 1974b. Quantitative analysis of the functional relationships existing between ecosystem components. II. Analysis of the nonlinear relationships. Oecologia 16: 107–117.

———— 1975. Quantitative analysis of the functional relationships existing between ecosystem components. III. Analysis of ecosystem stability. Oecologia 21: 17–29.

———— 1977. Primary productivities of two foraminifera: zooxanthellae symbionts. Proc. Third Int. Symp. Coral Reefs. p. 593–597.

SMITH, D. F., AND R. A. HOLMES. 1970. Kinetics of allosteric inhibition in vivo: a quantitative analysis with synchronous cultures of *Blastocladiella emersonii*. J. Bacteriol. 104: 1223–1229.

SMITH, D. F., AND W. J. WIEBE. 1976. Constant release of photosynthate from marine phytoplankton. Appl. Environ. Microbiol. 32: 75–79.

———— 1977. Rates of carbon fixation, organic carbon release and translocation in a reef-building foraminifer, *Marginopora vertebralis*. Aust. J. Mar. Freshw. Res. 28: 311–319.

STEEMANN NIELSEN, E. 1952. The use of radioactive carbon (^{14}C) for measuring organic production in the sea. J. Cons. Perm. Int. Explor. Mer. 18: 117–140.

THAKUR, A. K. 1972. On the stochastic theory of compartments: I. A single-compartment system. Bull. Math. Biophys. 34: 53–63.

———— 1973. On the stochastic theory of compartments: II. Multi-compartment systems. Bull. Math. Biol. 35: 263–271.

THAKUR, A. K., AND A. RESCIGNO. 1978. On the stochastic theory of compartments: III. General time-dependent reversible systems. Bull. Math. Biol. 40: 237–246.

THOMASSON, W. M., AND J. W. CLARK JR. 1974. Analysis of exponential decay curves: a three-step scheme for computing exponents. Math. Biosci. 22: 179–195.

WIEBE, W. J., AND D. F. SMITH. 1977a. Direct measurements of dissolved organic carbon release by phytoplankton and incorporation by microheterotrophs. Mar. Biol. 42: 213–223.

———. 1977b. ^{14}C-labelling of the compounds excreted by phytoplankton for employment as a realistic tracer in secondary productivity measurements. Microb. Ecol. 4: 1–8.

Appendix I

After injecting label into a single compartment we obtain tracer kinetic curves and these are expressed as sums of exponentials, $Q_1(t)$, $Q_2(t)$ ... $Q_n(t)$.

Take the first, second, and finally the $(n-1)$th derivative of each $Q(t)$ and order them as in the matrix . . .

$$\begin{bmatrix} Q_1(t) & Q_2(t) & \cdots \\ \dfrac{d(Q_1(t))}{dt} & \dfrac{dQ_2(t)}{dt} & \cdots \\ \vdots & \vdots & \\ \dfrac{d^{n-1}(Q_1(t))}{d^{n-1}t} & \dfrac{d^{n-1}(Q_2(t))}{d^{n-1}t} & \cdots \end{bmatrix}$$

$$\begin{bmatrix} Q_i(t) & \cdots & Q_n(t) \\ \dfrac{dQ_i(t)}{dt} & \cdots & \dfrac{d(Q_n(t))}{dt} \\ \vdots & & \vdots \\ \dfrac{d^{n-1}(Q_i(t))}{d^{n-1}t} & \cdots & \dfrac{d^{n-1}(Q_n(t))}{d^{n-1}t} \end{bmatrix}$$

The Wronskian, ω, we seek is simply the number obtained by finding . . .

$$\det A = \omega$$

As an example, suppose $Y_1(t) = \sin(t)$, $Y_2(t) = \cos(t)$, $Y_3(t) = \cos(t + \pi/3)$. Because we have three functions we will need the first and second derivatives to evaluate the Wronskian.

The first derivatives are:

$$\frac{dY_1}{dt} = \cos(t) \qquad \frac{dY_2}{dt} = -\sin(t)$$

$$\frac{dY_3}{dt} = -\sin(t + \pi/3)$$

The second derivatives are:

$$\frac{D^2Y_1}{dt^2} = -\sin(t) \qquad \frac{d^2Y_2}{dt^2} = -\cos(t)$$

$$\frac{d^2Y_3}{dt^2} = -\cos(t + \pi/3)$$

The matrix to be assembled from the above equation is:

$$A = \begin{bmatrix} \sin(t) & \cos(t) & \cos(t + \pi/3) \\ \cos(t) & -\sin(t) & -\sin(t + \pi/3) \\ -\sin(t) & -\cos(t) & -\cos(t + \pi/3) \end{bmatrix}$$

$$\begin{aligned} \det A = {} & [(\sin(t) \cdot \sin(t) \cdot \cos(t + \pi/3)) \\ & + (\cos(t) \cdot \sin(t + \pi/3) \cdot \sin(t)) \\ & - (\cos(t + \pi/3) \cdot \cos(t) \cdot \cos(t))] \\ & - [(\sin(t) \cdot \sin(t) \cdot \cos(t + \pi/3)) \\ & - (\cos(t) \cdot \cos(t) \cdot \cos(t + \pi/3)) \\ & + (\sin(t) \cdot \cos(t) \cdot \sin(t + \pi/3))] \end{aligned}$$

Simplifying,

$$\begin{aligned} \det A = {} & W = \\ & [\sin^2(t) \cdot \cos(t + \pi/3) + \sin(t) \cdot \cos(t) \cdot \sin(t + \pi/3) \\ & - \cos^2(t) \cdot \cos(t + \pi/3) - \sin^2(t) \cdot \cos(t + \pi/3) \\ & + \cos^2(t) \cdot \cos(t + \pi/3) - \sin(t) \cdot \cos(t) \cdot \sin(t + \pi/3)] \end{aligned}$$

and $\omega \equiv 0$.

Appendix II

Three sets of data arising from tracer kinetic experiments have been included in this appendix to supply realistic numerical values and associated errors for practice in peeling exponential terms.

One must be warned, however, that each of the three data sets contains a trap for the unwary. Some compartmental radioactivity curves are described by a sum of exponentials containing two terms whose exponents differ by less than a factor of two. Classic curve peeling techniques are not applicable in cases where the exponential sum contains a λ_1 and a λ_2 such that

$$\lambda_2/\lambda_1 < 2$$

If a curve peeling procedure is to be done routinely one would, of course, write a simple program for calculator or computer. None the less, the exercise of graphical analysis often provides insight into the experimental results that is impossible to obtain any other way.

To illustrate the procedure by which we obtain initial estimates of the exponents present in the sum of exponentials we will employ the data of experiment 1 at the end of this appendix.

Inspection of the data from experiment 1 or the graphs in Fig. 5 indicate that tracer accumulates most rapidly in compartment E. The graph shows no inflection point and no discernible lag, which suggests that compartment E is contiguous with the source of tracer supply, the iodide compartment. To test this assumption and to initiate the analysis we obtain an estimate of the constant term by averaging the last four values of $Q_E(t)$ to obtain $Q_{MAX} = 133.574$.

EXPERIMENT 1. Tracer kinetic data.

Compartment A		Compartment B		Compartment C	
Time (min)	Total radioactivity (M cpm)	Time (min)	Total radioactivity (M cpm)	Time (min)	Total radioactivity (M cpm)
5.13	0.001 3485	0.7	0.000 338	4.85	0.007 556
8.57	0.003 166	2.47	0.014 98	8.30	0.068 02
13.37	0.060 588	4.64	0.127 99	13.12	0.420 88
17.05	0.192 615	8.00	0.685 55	16.77	1.074 4
21.13	0.498 598	12.84	2.689 9	20.85	2.189 8
31.45	2.539 46	16.50	4.865 8	31.22	7.785 0
40.75	6.689 56	20.59	8.616 9	40.50	15.920 7
61.52	22.731 14	30.95	22.112	61.23	38.556 6
85.18	44.360 24	40.25	35.781	84.90	63.003 2
128.38	75.878 87	60.94	66.075	128.1	88.326 9
166.89	88.524 24	84.62	87.162	166.59	94.156 8
239.02	88.838 50	127.5	106.075	238.72	99.025 1
285.75	89.901 68	166.28	112.585	285.27	98.967 9
		238.42	110.889		
		284.90	113.314		

Compartment D		Compartment E		Compartment F	
Time (min)	Total radioactivity (M cpm)	Time (min)	Total radioactivity (M cpm)	Time (min)	Total radioactivity (M cpm)
13.62	0.007 973	0.15	0.632 07	0.43	0.010 9
17.32	0.031 080	1.95	10.910 96	2.22	0.479 4
21.42	0.107 804	4.10	22.723 4	4.40	2.089
31.72	0.948 847	7.47	37.475 3	7.75	6.005
41.03	2.529 95	12.22	56.848 4	12.52	14.06
61.82	11.765 41	15.90	69.392 7	16.20	21.75
85.48	30.951 18	20.03	79.213 3	20.30	30.92
128.70	61.866 36	30.38	101.414	30.70	52.97
167.17	75.124 19	39.69	110.747	40.00	71.70
239.35	80.905 48	60.37	126.558	60.38	99.71
286.11	82.893 01	84.05	133.661	84.37	114.4
		126.79	134.739	127.18	127.3
		165.64	134.197	165.97	129.1
		237.75	132.420	238.12	130.2
		284.2	132.940	284.57	129.3

EXPERIMENT 2. Tracer kinetic data.

Compartment A		Compartment B		Compartment C	
Time (min)	Specific activity (cpm/μmol)	Time (min)	Specific activity (cpm/μmol)	Time (min)	Specific activity (cpm/μmol)
0.12	3 595.52	0.43	97.90	0.77	
1.94	96 626	2.27	4 958.18	2.53	
3.89	174 994	4.13	16 964.18	4.43	
6.87	293 934	7.20	47 298	7.53	166.84
11.08	421 890	11.35	103 878	11.60	1 004.12
15.00	555 810	15.32	178 846	15.62	3 117.18
19.10	629 634	19.38	247 934	19.72	7 686.14
29.12	778 110	29.43	453 066	29.69	30 356
39.23	891 906	39.50	596 150	39.80	75 310
59.15	1004 978	59.42	836 998	59.70	222 758
80.00	1041 374	80.32	984 638	80.64	437 666
122.27	1055 662	122.60	1076 218	122.92	781 166
164.33	1074 026	164.60	1053 406	164.90	962 554
234.30	1064 774	234.65	1079 570	234.97	1064 478
273.95	1086 286	274.32	1036 828	274.67	1082 842

Compartment D		Compartment E		Compartment F	
Time (min)	Specific activity (cpm/μmol)	Time (min)	Specific activity (cpm/μmol)	Time (min)	Specific activity (cpm/μmol)
2.89	150.26	3.17	100.02		
4.70	667.82	5.00	778.78		
7.87	3 522.82	8.18	3 619.06	8.53	237.88
11.87	12 691.80	12.15	12 384	12.47	1 136.32
15.89	29 474	16.22	28 802	16.52	3 402.16
20.00	52 870	20.33	51 850	20.62	8 057.78
29.95	143 142	30.20	135 518	30.48	29 710
40.08	255 170	40.35	236 998	40.65	74 946
60.02	493 322	60.28	476 462	60.62	225 162
80.92	721 118	81.22	708 314	81.50	413 894
123.22	930 866	123.50	915 430	123.82	751 106
165.20	1045 386	165.53	1050 050	165.90	950 998
235.27	1084 226	235.59	1085 798	235.92	1056 738
275.02	1123 734	275.30	1071 978	275.64	1071 754

Compartment A		Compartment B		Compartment C	
Time (min)	Specific activity (cpm/μmol)	Time (min)	Specific activity (cpm/μmol)	Time (min)	Specific activity (cpm/μmol)
		6.25	636	1.27	22 438
		9.58	2 510	2.50	47 748
14.47	1 440	14.73	8 894	6.57	126 176
19.65	4 744	19.95	20 572	9.92	182 352
30.68	21 332	31.05	64 048	15.03	279 424
43.45	63 036	43.82	134 296	20.25	330 516
65.90	181 232	66.22	289 732	31.33	462 800
86.38	306 848	86.75	422 892	44.18	571 156
126.83	524 020	127.17	617 748	66.52	735 764
167.33	701 940	167.68	755 756	87.13	766 184
205.07	788 804	205.47	803 452	127.55	839 976
233.92	799 900	234.28	849 048	168.03	832 372
				205.80	871 476
				234.65	872 304

Compartment D		Compartment E		Compartment F	
Time (min)	Specific activity (cpm/μmol)	Time (min)	Specific activity (cpm/μmol)	Time (min)	Specific activity (cpm/μmol)
				0.90	14 898
2.83	1 424	1.87	562	2.15	40 992
6.88	10 328	3.12	1 816	3.42	65 740
10.25	22 894	7.23	10 680	7.58	147 616
15.33	49 908	10.57	23 270	10.92	197 552
20.62	82 256	15.63	47 540	15.98	282 228
31.62	166 380	20.92	81 052	21.27	349 432
44.50	263 756	31.92	164 768	32.32	463 612
66.87	442 804	44.80	257 828	45.15	572 124
87.50	552 776	67.20	429 472	67.53	709 832
127.93	720 012	87.85	541 332	88.22	752 892
168.35	806 652	128.33	712 040	128.70	816 432
206.17	833 564	168.67	780 908	169.05	847,640
235.03	830 288	205.52	820 124	206.87	851 928
		235.37	830 604	235.70	876 028

TABLE A1. Initial estimates of exponents from data of experiment 1.

Compartment E		Compartment F			
Time (min)	$R_E(t)$	Time (min)	$R_F(t)$	$\dfrac{R_F(t)}{e^{-0.0454t}}$	$[5.8\,e^{-0.0454t}$ $-R_F(t)]$
0.15	0.995	0.43	0.9999	1.02	4.688
1.95	0.918	2.22	0.9963	1.102	4.276
4.10	0.830	4.40	0.9839	1.2	3.7659
7.47	0.719	7.75	0.9536	1.356	3.126
12.22	0.574	12.52	0.8914	1.574	2.3949
15.90	0.481	16.20	0.8320	1.736	1.9478
20.03	0.407	20.30	0.7612	1.913	1.5465
30.38	0.241	30.70	0.5910	2.382	0.8482
39.69	0.171	40.00	0.4463	2.744	0.4972
60.37	0.053	60.38	0.2300	3.566	0.1440
84.05	−0.001	84.37	0.1166	5.373	0.0093
126.79	−0.010	127.18	0.0170	5.47	0.0010
165.64	−0.005	165.97	0.0031	5.80	0.0000
237.75	0.009	238.12	−0.0054	—	—
284.20	0.005	284.57	0.0015	612.27	—

Each data point is divided by Q_{MAX} and the fraction subtracted from 1 to give $R(t)$ values shown in Table A1. Values of $R(t)$ obtained after $t \geqslant 84.05$ are of no value as they represent only statistical fluctuations (negative values have no physical meaning so they and all later values are not employed). The remaining values of $R_E(t)$ plotted on semilog paper give a straight line that passes through even the earliest points indicating that $R_E(t)$ consists of only a single exponential term and that our hypothesis concerning compartment E's relationship to the iodide compartment was correct.

To obtain the initial estimate of the first exponent choose several points on the line and apply the relationship, given in equation (13).

$$\ln(0.918/0.995)/(0.15-1.95) = 0.0447$$
$$\ln(0.830/0.918)/(1.95-4.10) = 0.0469$$
$$\ln(0.719/0.830)/(4.10-7.47) = 0.0426$$
$$\ln(0.574/0.719)/(7.47-12.22) = 0.0474$$

Although this simple graphical analysis has given a range of λ estimates, the average, $\bar{\lambda}_1 = 0.0454$, is quite adequate as an initial estimate for the subsequent parameter estimations.

Next, using the average value of λ_1 we find the coefficient A_1 by equation (14).

$$0.995\,e^{(0.0454)\,(0.15)} = 1.002$$
$$0.918\,e^{(0.0454)\,(4.10)} = 1.003$$
$$0.830\,e^{(0.0454)\,(4.10)} = 1.000$$
$$0.719\,e^{(0.0454)\,(7.47)} = 1.009$$

The average value, $A_1 = 1.003$, is further evidence that our original hypothesis concerning the compartmental relationships was correct because for that to be true requires $Q_E(t)$ to be of the form

$$Q_E(t) = A_E\,(1-1e^{-\lambda_1 t})$$

Before considering the next compartment it is worthwhile to note again a relationship between all A_{nj}'s. Because at $t = 0$ all $Q_j(0) = 0$, and because $e^{\lambda o} \equiv 1$, it follows that the A_{nj} must sum to zero, i.e. in the case of constant infusion (and primary productivity) experiments

$$1 + A_{n1} + A_{n2} + \ldots + A_{nm} = 0$$

Considering the data set which was employed and that

$$1 - A_1 = 1 - 1.003 = -0.003$$

search for a further exponential term would be naive.

Data from experiment 1 show compartment F to be accumulating tracer at the next greatest rate. Dividing each data point by the average of the last three values, 129.5, we obtain $R_F(t)$ values given in Table A1. The plot of $R_F(t)$ in Fig. 6 shows why the larger values of time, although most nearly associated with a single exponent, are not, in practice, of great value in estimating exponents. The scatter is simply greater than the information content. Just as much to be avoided, however, are those points obviously in the curvilinear region which obviously contain more than one exponential term.

At this point we deviate from orthodoxy which would have us proceed in the same fashion as we did for the curve $Q_E(t)$. Our rationale for the departure is based on three facts. First, it can be shown in theory and in practice that one cannot resolve two exponential terms if the ratio of the exponents is less than 2. Second, we know the curve $Q_E(t)$ contains at least two exponents. Third, because our system is one of interconnecting compartments, the exponent associated with one compartment (i.e. 0.0454 with $Q_E(t)$) may appear in the sum of exponentials associated with another compartment (i.e. $Q_F(t)$).

Having tabulated the values of $R_F(t)$, divide each by $e^{-0.0454t}$. If this term is present in $R_F(t)$ we obtain a limiting value at large values of t approximately equal to A_{1F}. This plateau value 5.8 (see Table A1) occurs because $R_F(t)$ can be written as . . .

$$R_F(t) = \sum_{j=1}^{k} A_j e^{-\lambda jt} = \sum_{j=1}^{k-1} A_j e^{-\lambda jt} + A_k e^{-\lambda kt}$$

Dividing $R_F(t)$ by $e^{-\lambda kt}$ gives . . .

$$\frac{R_F(t)}{e^{-\lambda kt}} = \sum_{j=1}^{k-1} A_j e^{-(\lambda_j - \lambda_k)t} + A_k$$

The graph of this equation approaches the value A_k at large values of time.

Having obtained A_1 we can take the difference $R_F(t)$ and $A_1 e^{-0.0454t}$ and plot the difference as shown in Fig. A1. A straight line extending to the origin indicates that only a single term remains. We find the exponent and coefficient of the term in the manner previously employed.

$$\ln(4.276/4.688)/(0.43-2.22) = 0.0514$$
$$\ln(3.7659/4.276)/(2.22-4.40) = 0.0583$$
$$\ln(3.126/3.7659)/(4.40-7.75) = 0.0556$$
$$\ln(2.3939/3.126)/(7.75-12.52) = 0.0559$$
$$\lambda_2 = 0.0553$$

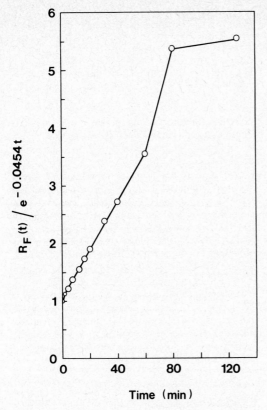

The remaining parameter A_2 is found as before . . .

$$
\begin{aligned}
4.688/e^{-0.0553(0.43)} &= 4.8008 \\
4.276/e^{-0.0553(2.22)} &= 4.8345 \\
3.7659/e^{-0.0553(4.4)} &= 4.8033 \\
3.126/e^{-0.0553(7.75)} &= 4.7986 \\
\overline{A_2} &= 4.8093
\end{aligned}
$$

The sum describing the original $Q_F(t)$ is

$$Q_F(t) = 129.5 \,(1-5.8e^{-0.0454t} + 4.8e^{-.0553t})$$

Note that the signs associated with the coefficients of each term are determined by $1 + A_1 + A_2 + \ldots + A_N = 0$.

This process is continued with the data from compartment B whose radioactivity curve is found to be described by . . .

$$Q_B(t) = 113.30 \,(1-1.524e^{-0.0454t} + 0.524e^{-0.0553t})$$

FIG. A1. Graphs of functions containing one less exponential than the original data. The difference between the smallest exponential term, $A_i e^{-\lambda_i t}$, and $R_i(t)$ is taken and plotted against time. This graph is then used to obtain the second smallest exponent present in the original data.

Cell-Cycle Events in Unicellular Algae

S. PUISEUX-DAO

*Laboratoire de Biologie cellulaire végétale, Tour 53, Université Paris VII,
C.N.R.S. — ERA n° 325. 2, Place Jussieu — 75005 Paris, France*

Introduction

In nature, circadian rhythms of cell division have been observed in some marine dinoflagellates as early as 1958 (Sweeney and Hastings). However, in natural conditions, the percentage of cells dividing simultaneously is generally low, and various attempts have been made to increase it in culture populations.

Apart from the selection of cells at a given stage in a population (separation of small cells or of dividing cells that do not swim), most other techniques for synchronizing cell division are based on the following principle: cells in an unsynchronized population progress at different rates through interphase and mitosis; if they could therefore be blocked at some definite stage of the progression, then all those which accumulate at this particular stage would recover when the applied blockage was lifted, and would resume their progression in parallel, at least for some time.

Devices for accumulating cells at a given physiological stage include temperature shocks, inhibitor treatments, deprivation of necessary nutrients, and, for plant cells, dark periods. For unicellular algae, suitable light–dark (LD) cycles are most frequently used, sometimes associated with temperature cycles (see in Zeuthen 1964; Cameron and Padilla 1966).

The best domesticated unicellular algae are either freshwater species like *Chlamydomonas*, *Euglena*, and *Chlorella*, or brackish and marine phytoplankton like *Dunaliella* (Volvocales), various dinoflagellates (*Gonyaulax*, *Amphidinium*), some Chrysophyceae like *Olisthodiscus luteus*, Prasinophyceae of the genus *Platymonas*, or diatoms like *Cylindrotheca fusiformis*.

This report describes the main findings resulting from an analysis of cell life in synchronized cultures of unicellular algae, with particular emphasis, where possible, on marine species.

MAIN EVENTS OF THE CELL CYCLE IN EUCARYOTIC CELLS

In procaryotic as well as in eucaryotic cells, cell division is easily detectable and has always been considered as the chief criterion of cell life. This event gives rise to two daughter cells, each of which carries a normal genome issuing from a semiconservative distribution of the parent DNA molecules. The process implies that at some previous time, DNA replication should have occurred.

By measuring the DNA content per cell and by labeling cultures with radioactive DNA precursors, preferably in synchronized cells, it has been shown that DNA synthesis takes place during the interphase between two divisions. In rapidly growing procaryotes, the DNA replication lasts throughout the time interval between two successive divisions. But in eucaryotes, the duration of nuclear DNA synthesis (S period) is shorter than this time interval, and the periods between the mitosis (M) and the nuclear DNA replication have been called gaps: G_1 occurs just after the cell division, G_2 just after DNA synthesis (Fig. 1). Such a cell cycle thus comprises four stages: G_1, S, G_2, and M. In fact, cell metabolism is very active during the two gap periods, but this activity does not concern the structure and quantity of the nuclear DNA itself.

It is well-known that cell metabolism can decline when living conditions become unsuitable. The cells enter dormancy and this step is called G_0. Most of the occasions when this occurs, cells pass into G_0 from G_1, but G_2 cells are also known to become dormant (G_0 or G_2') (Fig. 1). As soon as the environment is favorable, cells recover and resume their normal course through the four usual stages.

Three events of the cycle have a particular significance; they are the S phase and, during mitosis, the prophase and telophase. They indeed correspond to *irreversible* transitions of cell life. Once DNA has replicated, it is inconceivable for the same cell to revert to a state where the quantity of DNA is reduced to that before replication; when chromosomes have divided, no return to a single complement of chromosomes in that cell is possible; when one cell has given rise to two daughter cells, the new situation is normally irreversible (except under very particular experimental conditions, as in cell fusion).

It appears to be very clear that all these irreversible processes are linked to the need for DNA molecules to be equally distributed among the progeny. On the contrary, G_1 and G_2 consist of reversible steps because all molecules, except DNA, can be destroyed (in general enzymatically) and replaced by new ones when signals are received for the transcription and translation of the relevant information coded in the genome (Puiseux-Dao 1979).

130

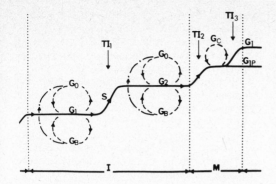

FIG. 1. Diagram showing the irreversible transitions of the cell cycle. TI_1, S phase; TI_2, chromosome division; TI_3, formation of the division membranes. During G_1 or G_2 the cells can enter dormancy (G_0) or they can return to a previous stage (G_B: wounded or intoxicated cells which digest part of their contents). G_0 and G_B are reversible stages, but the cells do not follow exactly the opposite path when they progress through the division cycle and when they pass to G_0 or G_B. This gives hysteresis cycles, G_0 and G_B corresponding to bifurcations in mathematical catastrophe theory. During mitosis, another hysteresis cycle can appear when the cells are treated with colchicine or by low temperatures. When the blockage is over, then the cells can progress normally to G_1 or they can become polyploid (G_{1P}). I, interphase; M, mitosis (after Puiseux-Dao 1979).

Main Biochemical Events of the Cell Cycle in Unicellular Eucaryotic Algae

DNA Syntheses

Most of the cellular DNA ($\geqslant$ 85%; see Boardman et al. 1971) is found in the nucleus; however, small quantities exist in the mitochondria ($\approx$ 1–4%) and in plant cells, chloroplasts can contain up to 14% of the total DNA (in very peculiar algae like *Acetabularia*, the plastid DNA is even predominant due to the fact that the cell has one nucleus but can possess several millions of chloroplasts).

The syntheses of nuclear and extranuclear DNAs would have to be examined separately.

Identification of the nuclear and extranuclear DNAs — DNA molecules are identified according to the physicochemical criteria of molecular weight, configuration, and base composition from determinations of the buoyant density (ρ) after centrifugation in a CsCl gradient, thermal denaturation temperature, and so on.

Table 1 gives some data reported in the litterature of DNA density in some unicellular algae which can be used for their identification.

In general (Fig. 2), in algae, nuclear DNA corresponds to 85–90% of the extracted DNA whereas the chloroplastic DNA represents 3–10%. Proof of the identity has been obtained by several means: extracting DNA from isolated organelles (nucleus or plastid fractions, Brawerman and Eisenstadt 1964); labeling with tritiated thymidine that in some species (*Euglena*, Sagan 1965; *Chlamydomonas*, Swinton and Hanawalt 1972; *Chlorella*, Dalmon et al. 1975b; *Dunaliella*, Marano 1979) preferentially labels plastid DNA; and analyzing the DNA of bleached cells when possible (Schiff and Epstein 1966). One practical difficulty is immediately recognizable, namely that mitochondrial DNA is not easy to study as it can be easily confounded with plastid DNA. Results obtained for *Euglena gracilis* have not been ambiguous in this respect because this alga loses its

TABLE 1.

	Nucleus		Chloroplast		chl DNA	
	ρ	%G.C	ρ	%G.C	Total	DNA
Dunaliella bioculata	1.707	48%	1.696	36%	10–15%	
Chlamydomonas reinhardtii	1.723	64%	1.695	36%	6–12%	
Euglena gracilis						
— var. *bacillaris*	1.702	43%	1.685	26%	—	
— var. Z	1.708	51%	1.684	25%	2–5%	
Chlorella pyrenoidosa:						
— var. Emerson	1.715	56%	1.689	30%	12%	
— var. 211/8b	1.710	51%	1.687	30%	10%	
Acetabularia mediterranea	1.697	38%	1.705	45%	—	

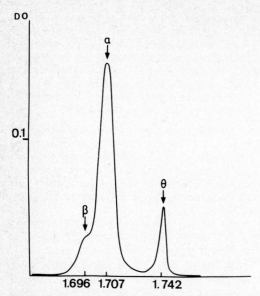

FIG. 2. The two nuclear (α: 1.707) and chloroplastic DNA (β: 1.696) of *Dunaliella bioculata* after analytic ultracentrifugation in a CsCl gradient. (Marker, ϕE DNA; θ, 1.742 g/cm^3). DO, optical density (after Marano 1979).

chloroplasts when cultivated in the dark. In normal dark–light cycles this species shows a main band of bulk nuclear DNA (ρ = 1.707–1.709) with a shoulder at 1.691 and a well-defined peak at 1.686;

the peak 1.686 disappears when cells are cultured in darkness so that it can be attributed to plastid DNA, whereas the shoulder at 1.691 that persists can be considered to correspond to mitochondrial DNA (see in Richards and Ryan 1974).

In some species, the fractions of nuclear and chloroplastic genomes that code for their respective ribosomal RNAs have been detected by techniques of hybridization of DNA with the relevant labeled ribosomal RNA; they are GC rich in *Euglena* (Stutz and Vaudrey 1971). The nuclear ribosomal DNA could possibly be the AT rich DNA fraction in some other species like *Dunaliella* (Marano 1980).

Nuclear DNA synthesis — When the DNA content per cell is followed in samples of synchronized cultures collected at successive stages of the life cycle, an increase is observed during interphase and a decrease following mitosis.

If similar samples are labeled for a definite time interval with PO_4^{3-}, or a radioactive base or nucleoside with the restriction reported above for thymidine, one observes that the algal nuclear DNA becomes significantly labeled only during the period of increasing DNA content (Fig. 3) that corresponds as stated above to the S phase.

Frequently in algae, the S phase takes place just before cell division and the G_2 period seems to be absent. It can be short and difficult to detect for two reasons: first, even an efficient synchro-

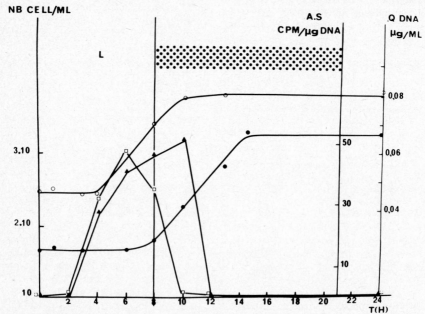

FIG. 3. The cell division cycle of *Dunaliella bioculata*. Abcissa: time in hours. Ordinates: ●—● number of cell per millilitre; ○—○ total DNA (μg/mL of culture); □—□ specific activity of nuclear DNA (cpm/μg DNA); ▲—▲ specific activity of chloroplastic DNA. L, light period; ⊠, dark period (after Marano 1979).

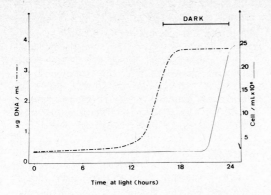

FIG. 4. Increase of DNA content and cell concentration in a synchronized *Chlorella* culture (after Wanka 1975).

nization of >95% shows a certain variability; second, many phytoplanktonic algae follow primitive mechanisms of division that last longer than the classical mitosis of higher organisms and in which cell furrowing becomes visible before or at the very beginning of nuclear changes.

Another peculiarity is that several unicellular algae can produce more than two daughter cells when dividing: for example, in *Chlorella* the number of daughter cells frequently reaches 16 and, in this case, during the resting phase the DNA content (Fig. 4) undergoes four successive doublings (Chiang and Sueoka 1967b; Wanka et al. 1970).

At least in some dinoflagellates, the rate of DNA synthesis decreases in the cultures long before the growth has reached a plateau (Galleron and Durrand 1979) and a loss of DNA has been observed in stationary phase cells (Allen et al. 1975).

Chloroplast DNA synthesis — Various results have been obtained showing either that extranuclear DNA replication takes place during the S phase or that it is not concomitant with nuclear DNA synthesis. In fact, it is possible that the correlation between the chloroplast (ct) and nuclear DNA replications depends on the number of plastids per cell and the number of daughter cells formed at each division.

In the simplest case, where one cell contains a unique chloroplast and gives two daughter cells, for example, in *Dunaliella bioculata* or *Amphidinium carterae*, nuclear and extranuclear DNA syntheses occur simultaneously, with or without a slight shift (Marano 1979; Galleron and Durrand 1979; Fig. 3 and 5).

In cells that contain one single plastid at the beginning of the cell cycle, but give in general four (or more) daughter cells, ct DNA replication has been shown to occur twice before the two successive nuclear DNA syntheses (*Chlamydomonas*, Chiang

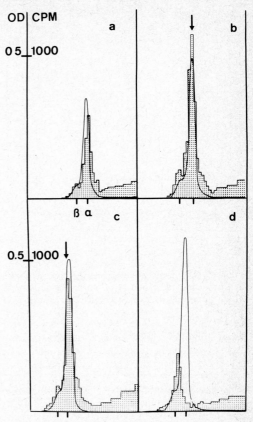

FIG. 5. DNA labeling of synchronized *Dunaliella* cultures. Identical samples have been labeled for 2 h with $^{32}PO_4^{3-}$ at different times of the cycle. (a) time 4 h of Fig. 3; (b) time 6 h; (c) 8 h; (d) 10 h, and the extracted DNA (α, nuclear; β, chloroplastic) has been ultracentrifuged. OD, optical density at 254 nm; ▨, (CPM) specific radioactivity (after Marano 1979).

and Sueoka 1967a; *Chlorella*, Dalmon et al. 1975a; Fig. 6 and 7).

When several plastids are observable in the cells during at least the first half of the interphase, various results have been reported that could be linked to the particular strains used and to the culture conditions. The best-known case of *Euglena gracilis*, strain Z, is complicated by the fact that the chloroplast content is influenced by the dark–light treatments. Therefore, the ct DNA may vary from ≈ 0 (in bleached cells) to ≈ 15% of the total DNA, the most frequent value being about 3–5% of the cellular DNA. Moreover, under usual growth conditions, Manning and Richards (1972) have observed that ct DNA may undergo $1^1/_2$ rounds of replication per round of nuclear DNA synthesis. Yet the mean amount of chloroplast DNA per cell remains stable. In such conditions, the ct DNA content is the result of a balance between destructive mechanisms prepon-

133

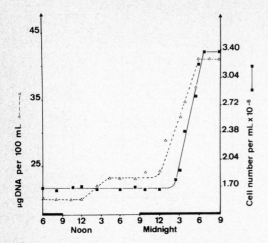

FIG. 6. DNA synthesis in a vegetative division cycle of *Chlamydomonas reinhardtii*. Abcissa: time in hours. Two periods of DNA increase are visible; the first was shown to correspond to the chloroplast DNA replication, the second to the nuclear DNA synthesis (after Chiang and Sueoka 1967a).

derant in the dark and a synthetic activity linked to light. Moreover, in illuminated cells this balance is related to the growth. These considerations may explain why some authors (Richards and Manning 1972) have observed a ct DNA replication limited to the S phase while others (Cook 1966; Brandt 1975) have reported two ct DNA synthetic periods, one when light is given and the second concomitant with nuclear DNA replication.

Mitochondrial DNA synthesis — As reported above, the case of *Euglena* is the only properly studied one. In bleached cells, mitochondrial (mt) DNA is detectable and seems to replicate at the same time as nuclear DNA. This replication is not inhibited by cycloheximide, an antibiotic intervening at the level of translation on 80*S* ribosomes, although nuclear DNA replication is (Richards and Ryan 1974; Ledoigt and Calvayrac 1979; Fig. 8).

RNA SYNTHESES

Characterization of the different RNAs — The main bulk (≈80%) of cellular RNAs is comprised of the ribosomal RNAs (rRNAs). In cells they are constituents of the ribosomes which are found in the cytoplasm, in chloroplasts, and in mitochondria. The different types of ribosomes are characterized by a sedimentation coefficient (in Svedberg units) measured in precise conditions of centrifugation and are made of two subunits, each containing one long RNA chain (Table 2).

The mitochondrial ribosomes have properties similar to chloroplastic ribosomes which themselves resemble procaryotic ribosomes, but in general, in studies concerning algal cells, either they are not differentiated from plastid ribosomes or they are not considered at all, the attention being focused on chloroplasts.

Cytoplasmic rRNAs come from the nucleus; except for the small 5*S* molecule, they are synthesized at the level of the nucleolus as larger precursors (45*S*–30*S*) and are split later on.

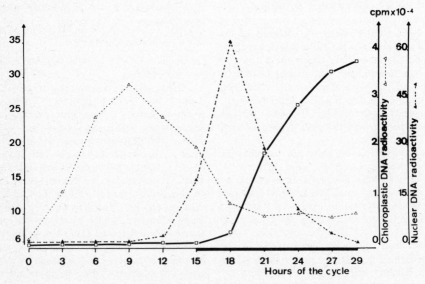

FIG. 7. Incorporation of labeled phosphate (pulse labeling) into the nuclear and chloroplast DNA in synchronized cultures of *Chlorella*. □—□ cell number per millilitre × 10⁶ (after Dalmon et al. 1975).

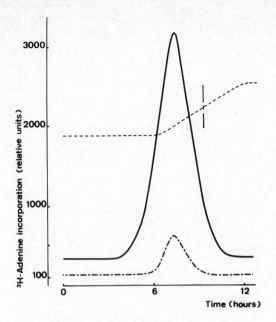

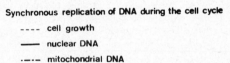

Synchronous replication of DNA during the cell cycle

---- cell growth

——— nuclear DNA

.—.— mitochondrial DNA

FIG. 8. Replication of nuclear DNA (———) and mito-chondrial DNA (— . — . — .) in synchronized cultures of *Euglena gracilis* (pulse labeling with radioactive adenine) (after Ledoigt and Calvayrac 1979).

TABLE 2.

	Cytoplasmic ribosomes	Chloroplastic ribosomes
Sedimentation coefficient	80S	70S
Two subunits	60S	50S
	40S	30S
rRNAs of large subunit	25S–28S + 5S	23S + 5S
small subunit	17–19S	16S

Messenger RNAs, at least part of them, are recognized by the poly A sequence attached to them. They have a very variable molecular weight.

Transfer RNAs ($\approx 5S$) are detected among other small RNAs (natural or resulting from the degra-dation of larger molecules) by their capacity to bind a specific radioactive amino acid.

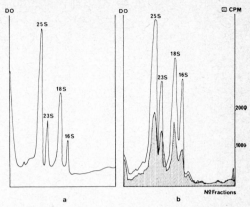

FIG. 9. (a) Ribosomal RNAs from *Dunaliella bioculata*. Cytoplasmic rRNAs 25S and 18S; chloroplast rRNAs 23S and 16S; (b) after 1-h labeling with $^{32}PO_4^{3-}$. DO, optical density; ▨, (CPM) specific radioactivity (after Marano 1980).

RNA syntheses — Of course, for quantitative reasons, most data concern the ribosomal RNAs. Their syntheses have been followed by labeling suc-cessive samples from synchronized cultures with radioactive PO_4^{3-}, uracil, or uridine and then sepa-rating the different rRNAs by centrifugation or elec-trophoresis (Fig. 9).

In general, the algal cultures are synchronized by dark–light cycles: rRNA content increases in the light, mainly chloroplastic rRNAs, and this corre-sponds to an active precursor incorporation as is shown in Fig. 10 for *Dunaliella*. Similar data have been described in *Chlorella* (Galling 1973, 1975), *Euglena* (Heizmann 1970), *Chlamydomonas* (Wilson and Chiang 1977), and *Dunaliella* (Marano 1980). Both cytoplasmic and chloroplastic rRNAs are syn-thesized in parallel in illuminated cells, whereas in the dark rRNA labeling is lower (Galling 1973; Wilson and Chiang 1977), and may correspond to a simple turnover because there is no rRNA weight increase (Cattolico et al. 1973; Wilson and Chiang 1977; Marano 1980). Moreover, in *Dunaliella*, rRNA synthesis is high during the first part of the S phase and declines during the second half. The replicating DNA is the lighter fraction during this second period, and might correspond to rDNA as in *Chlorella*; the replicating activity at the level of rDNA possibly inhibits the ribosomal transcription (Marano 1980).

The light dependence results in a cyclic activity of rRNA synthesis in algal cells which differs from that occurring in yeasts or animal cells. Yet in *Euglena gracilis*, grown on lactate medium, RNA synthesis was shown to be discontinuous in the light as well as in darkness. Heavy RNAs (40S, 35S, 30S) are labeled during the cell division, and chase

135

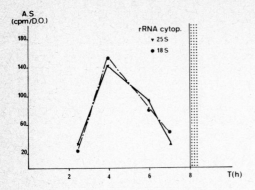

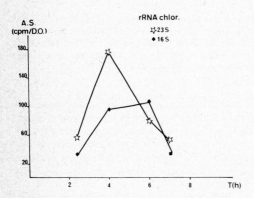

FIG. 10. Evolution of the synthetic activity of ribosomal RNAs in *Dunaliella bioculata* during the cell division cycle. Abcissa: time in hours; ordinates: specific activity (A.S) of the ribosomal RNA extracted from samples pulse labeled with $^{32}PO_4^{3-}$. Light, 8 h; dark ▨ , 16 h (after Marano 1980).

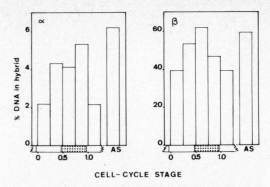

FIG. 11. Extent of RNA–DNA hybrid formation with RNA samples taken at different times of the cell cycle. ▭ light; ▨ dark. Percent DNA in hybrid at saturation was determined for nuclear DNA (α) and chloroplast DNA (β). % DNA in hybrid corresponds to the value observed at each stage compared with values obtained from asynchronous cultures (A.S) (after Howell 1975).

PROTEIN SYNTHESES

In general, in exponentially growing cells, the total protein content doubles during interphase; for algae, this doubling (which can mask a higher rate of synthesis associated with a rapid turnover) takes place during the light period. Of course each protein should have its own synthesis progression and this has been studied by two methods. On the one hand, single types of proteins have been followed during all the cell division cycle: this is possible for enzymes, cytochromes, or tubulins because these molecules are easily detectable by their activity (see in Wanka 1975), their absorption spectrum, or their migration on one- or two-dimensional electrophoretic gel. On the other hand, all the polypeptides of the cells have been studied at different stages of the cycle and the electrophoresis patterns have been compared (Howell et al. 1977). A similar polypeptide analysis has also been conducted on plastid fractions (Bourguignon and Palade 1976).

For all proteins studied, as predicted, the data show a quantitative or labeling specific evolution through the cell cycle: this is the case in *Euglena* or *Chlorella* for enzymes (see in Wanka 1975; Fig. 12) or cytochromes (see in Ledoigt and Calvayrac 1979), for many of polypeptides in *Chlamydomonas* (Howell et al. 1977; Fig. 13), and for tubulin in *Chlamydomonas* (Weeks and Collis 1979).

Therefore, such a cyclic timing of the protein synthesis implies coordinated regulation of processes at the level of both transcription and translation. This regulation is influenced by some external signals, mainly light and dark, as shown for microbody and mitochondrial enzymes in *Euglena*; for example, fumarate and succinate dehydrogenase syntheses are repressed by light acting on transcription at the

experiments suggest that they could be precursors of cytoplasmic rRNAs (Ledoigt and Calvayrac 1975).

Poly A mRNAs, which are synthesized in the nucleus as well as in plastids (Milner et al. 1979), appear preferentially when light is given to the cell (Howell 1975). As might be expected, transcripts of nuclear and chloroplast DNAs vary along the cell cycle. This could be determined from RNA–DNA reassociation at RNA excess, at least in *Chlamydomonas reinhardtii* (Howell 1975). Whereas only about 12% of the nuclear genome seems to be homologous to vegetative cell RNA, 60% of the single-strand chloroplast DNA is homologous to vegetative cell RNA. In such conditions possibly the entire chloroplast DNA could be transcribed. But as RNA transcript complexity was observed to change during the cell cycle, the hypothesis of variations of genome messages along the life cycle is likely to be valid (Howell 1975; Fig. 11).

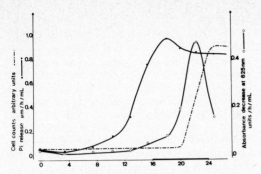

FIG. 12. Phosphorylase (●—●) and amylase (O—O) activities in synchronized cultures of *Chlorella* (after Wanka 1975).

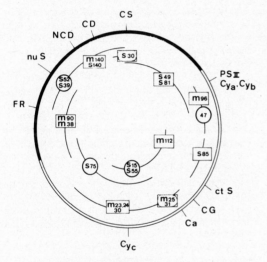

m : membrane polypeptides
s : soluble polypeptides
◯ : ³H- Arginine labeling
▢ : ³⁵S -labeling
▣ : ³H-Arginine and ³⁵S -labeling

FIG. 13. Cell-cycle map of labeling of some polypeptides in synchronous cultures of *Chlamydomonas reinhardtii*. Inner arcs show labeling periods for some membrane (m) or soluble (s) polypeptides as suggested by experiments with different precursors. Cell-cycle events are indicated on outer circle. (L.D., 12–12; light-bar, light period; dark bar, dark period). PS II, Cy_a, and Cy_b, increasing photosystem II, cytochrome 553, and cytochrome 559; ct S, chloroplast DNA synthesis; CG, competent gametogenesis; Ca, increasing chlorophyll and carboxydismutase activity; Cy_c, increasing cytochrome 563; FR, flagellar regression; nu S, nuclear DNA synthesis; NCD, nuclear and chloroplast divisions; CD, cell divisions; CS, cell separation (after Howell et al. 1977).

beginning of the light phase and exerting a post-transcriptional control at a later stage (Merrett 1975).

Moreover, the coordination involves the three genomes and the different translating machineries of the cytoplasm, the chloroplasts, and the mitochondria which cooperate in synthesizing organelle 70S ribosomal proteins (Bogorad et al. 1975), thylakoid membranes (Hoober 1970; Apel and Schweiger 1972; Eytan and Ohad 1972), or enzymes like RUBP carboxylase (Iwanij et al. 1975).

OTHER METABOLIC ACTIVITIES

There is no doubt that many of the physiological activities should behave with a typical periodicity during the division cycle as the cell enzymes themselves show a periodic evolution. This is the case for photosynthesis, and all the associated metabolic pathways, including the mitochondrial or microbody physiology. All these problems have been extensively studied for *Euglena*, *Chlorella*, *Scenedesmus*, and *Chlamydomonas*, and are discussed by others in this bulletin or elsewhere (see in Lefort-Tran and Valencia 1975; Edmunds 1978). This is also the case for nutrient uptake, mineral nutrients (PO_4^{3-}, Chisholm and Stross 1976a, b; $Si(OH)_4$, Chisholm et al. 1978), as well as for organic nutrients (Pedersed et al. 1975) and for adenine nucleotide content (Weiler and Karl 1979).

Main Morphological Events of the Cell Division Cycle

The simplest morphological events are an increase in size during interphase and, for swimming cells, a lower motility during the cell division with a flagellar regression observed in some species (Fig. 13). In *Chlamydomonas*, this regression is followed by a significant tubulin synthesis (Weeks and Collis 1979) probably useful for building the microtubules involved in mitosis, but also in the flagellar morphogenesis of the daughter cells.

When measuring the surface of the different organelles in electron micrographs, Marano (1980) could show in *Dunaliella* (Fig. 14) that except for the vacuoles, all other organelles followed a parallel size evolution.

NUCLEAR EVOLUTION

In plates I and II, one easily sees that in *Dunaliella* (L–D: 8 h–16 h) the nuclear and nucleolar structures change over the cycle during the non-dividing period: at the end of the dark phase, the chromatin and the nucleolus, fibrillar at that time, appear very compact (closed). When the light is given, those structures become less dense (open)

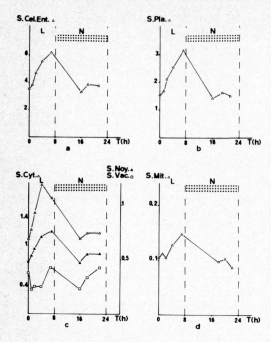

FIG. 14. Evolution of the mean surface (arbitrary units) of organelles in *Dunaliella bioculata* during the cell cycle. S.Cel Ent., surface of the entire cell; S. Pla., chloroplast surface; S. Cyt., cytoplasm surface; S. Noy., nucleus surface; S. Vac., vacuole surface; S. Mit., mitochondrial surface; L, light; N, night; T(h), time in hours. Measurements have been made on micrographs of longitudinal axial sections (after Marano 1980).

and the number of preribosomal-type granules increases inside and around the nucleolus. The loose chromatin aspect corresponds to the S phase, whereas the formation of particles by the nucleolus is concomitant with a high level of rRNA synthesis. Then the structures return to the closed configuration of the dark period (Marano 1980).

A similar evolution has been described in *Euglena* (Frayssinet et al. 1975) as well as in *Astasia* (Chaly et al. 1977).

In most of the unicellular algae, mitosis does not proceed exactly as in higher organisms. In general the mitoses are enclosed within a persistant nuclear membrane, more or less complete, and different types of mechanisms exist which are linked to various microtubule structures which are extranuclear in dinoflagellates (see Matthys-Rochon 1979), intranuclear among volvocales (see Marano 1980), and of a very particular configuration in diatoms (Pickett-Heaps et al. 1979a, b). An extensive study of the so-called "primitive mitoses" has been described by Pickett-Heaps' group.

CHLOROPLAST EVOLUTION

In algae grown in light–dark cycles, the thylakoid development is strongly influenced by light. At the end of the dark period, in the green algae studied so far (*Chlorella*, Atkinson et al. 1974; *Euglena*, Cook et al. 1976; *Dunaliella*, Marano 1980), the plastid lamellae are thin, short, and often form stacks similar to grana although the storage content is low. In *Euglena* (see in Leedale 1967; Buetow 1968) or in the Y-1 mutant of *Chlamydomonas reinhardtii* (Ohad et al. 1967), when the dark period is long, the lamellae can disappear entirely (as can the chloroplasts themselves in bleached *Euglena*). As soon as the cells receive light, the thylakoids become longer and thicker; they associate in pairs; the storage grains increase in number and size (Pl. III). A decrease takes place again in the next dark phase. Such figures fit adequately with the biochemical data concerning the influence of light on the thylakoid chlorophyll and polypeptide syntheses (Hoober 1970; Eytan and Ohad 1970, 1972; Bourguignon and Palade 1976).

In algae which contain one single chloroplast, its division proceeds in parallel with the cell division (*Chlamydomonas*, Osafume et al. 1972; *Chlorella*, Atkinson et al. 1974; *Dunaliella*, Marano 1980).

On the contrary, when several chloroplasts are observed in the cells, the chloroplast division is not strictly linked to the cell division. The organelles divide before the cell division or may even do so without any cell division during the stationary culture phase (*Olisthodiscus*, Cattolico et al. 1973). In *Euglena*, fusion of small plastids that takes place before their division has been described (Lefort-Tran 1975).

MITOCHONDRIAL EVOLUTION

In the electron micrographs, sections of mitochondria are generally small. However, in *Chlamydomonas* (Osafume et al. 1972; Arnold et al. 1972), *Chlorella* (Atkinson et al. 1974), or *Euglena* (Calvayrac et al. 1974; Lefort-Tran 1975), observations of serial sections, under the light and the electron microscope, have suggested that a true mitochondrial cycle exists. Small mitochondria observed after the cell division fuse forming a giant organelle which fragments or divides irregularly just prior to mitosis (Pl. IV).

Regulation of the Cell Division Cycle

The regulation of the cell division cycle (cdc) has been extensively studied on animal cells in cancer research; much data have also been obtained on yeast and on unicellular algae, for which light plays a

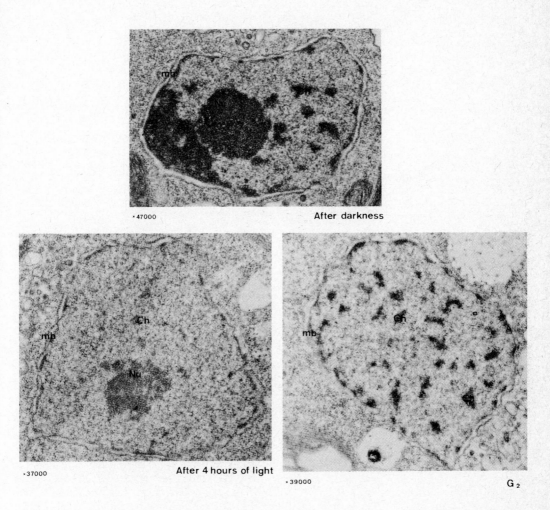

×47000   **After darkness**

×37000   **After 4 hours of light**

×39000   **G₂**

PLATE I. The nucleus of *Dunaliella bioculata* at different times of the day in synchronized cultures (L–D: 8–16 h). Nu, nucleolus; ch, chromatin; mb, nuclear membrane (after Marano 1980). Magnification indicated before print reduction to 46%.

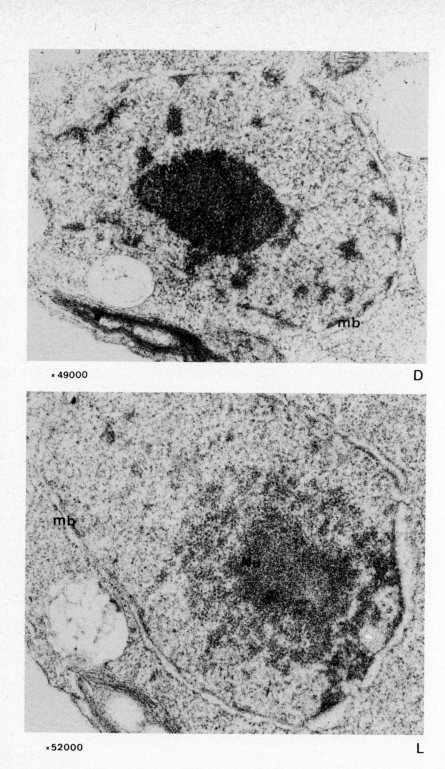

×49000 D

×52000 L

PLATE II. Closed aspect of the nucleolus in the nucleus of *Dunaliella* in the dark (D); open aspect in the light (L) (after Marano 1980). Magnification indicated before print reduction to 70%.

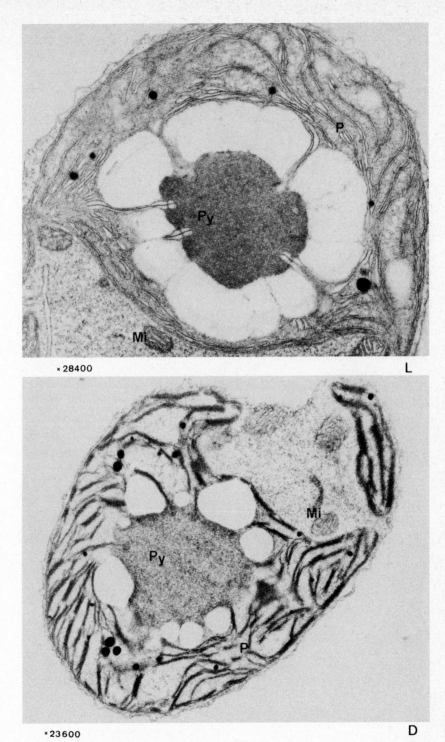

×28400   **L**

×23600   **D**

PLATE III. The chloroplast of *Dunaliella bioculata* in synchronized cultures (L–D: 8–16 h). L, after 4-h light; D, at the end of the dark period; P, chloroplast; Py, pyrenoid; Mi, mitochondria (after Marano 1980). Magnification indicated before print reduction to 68%.

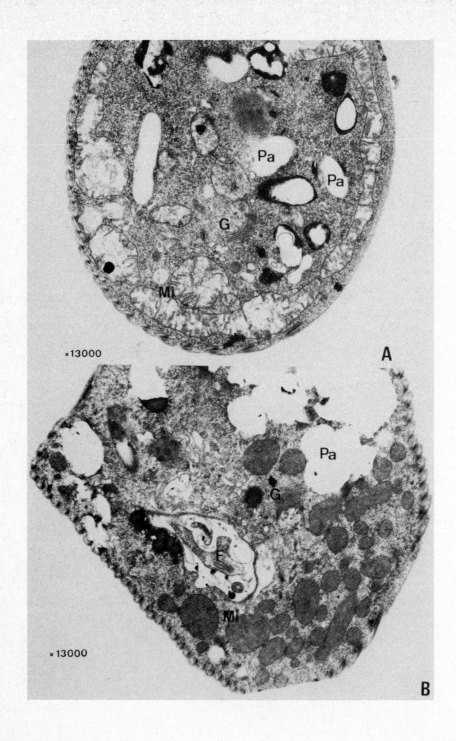

PLATE IV. The mitochondria of *Euglena gracilis* in synchronized cultures (A) during interphase and (B) during cell division. Pa, paramylon; F, flagellum; G, dictyosome; Mi, mitochondrion (by courtesy of Calvayrac). Magnification indicated before print reduction to 75%.

central role. Despite the apparent difficulties in discussing examples from such diverse sources, we find sufficient similarity for our purposes to justify this approach.

CELL-CYCLE PHENOMENA AND THE CELL DIVISION CYCLE

In exponentially growing *Saccharomyces* or *Euglena* many physiological functions have been shown to take place with a definite periodicity: for example, bud initiation in the yeast and photosynthetic capacity in algae. These rhythmic activities persist even when the cells do not divide; this has been observed in temperature-sensitive *Saccharomyces* mutants transferred to a temperature that inhibits mitosis but not budding, which then initiates periodically; this is typical of *Euglena* cultures in the stationary phase where many metabolic pathways can function with a periodicity, in general circadian (see Edmunds 1975, 1978). Though interrelations do exist between the network of metabolic pathways leading to mitosis rhythms and the network responsible for other periodic cellular events, we shall try to limit this discussion to the cell division cycle consisting of G_1, S, G_2, and M in eucaryotes, plus G_0.

Two properties are to be emphasized: (1) the cdc is sensitive to environmental conditions (nutrients, temperature, light for plant cells) that are able to impose their own periodicity (entraining conditions); yet (2) the cdc can persist, at least for a certain time, when the environmental conditions become constant (free-running conditions).

The easiest way to attack the problem is to analyze what occurs when resting cells are engaged in a new run of successive division cycles. This takes place when nutrients are added to the medium of stationary cultures. This is also observed after fertilization of dormant female gametes or when lymphocyte cultures are given a lectin. In this last case, it has been shown that the attachment of the lectin to the lymphocyte plasma membrane induces several very rapid reactions: ion transport change and acceleration of phospholipid turnover concomitant with an increase in the membrane lipid fluidity (Whitney and Sutherland 1972; Hui et al. 1979; Holian et al. 1979; Segel et al. 1979). Various membrane enzymatic activities are then enhanced (cyclases, ATPases, methyltransferases, phospholipases) (Hadden et al. 1974; Hirata et al. 1980). On the other hand, fertilization has been demonstrated to trigger a very rapid and precise program of ion exchanges between the cells and the surrounding medium (Epel 1977). Therefore, inducing mitotic activity seems to be linked to changes in the plasma membranes with consequences at this level on lipid fluidity, ion transport, and enzyme function. Cells which remained in the metabolically "dormant" mode are turned to a new physiological program by events occurring at the level of the external membrane.

A similar situation has been described for some animal cells whose physiology is directed by peptidyl hormones (see Robison et al. 1971; Greengard et al. 1972; Koch and Leffert 1979; Rubin et al. 1979). But in this case, the membrane modifications are under the hormonal influence which activates at least adenyl cyclase, and have been shown to result in a higher cAMP content inside the cells and, as a consequence, in a higher phosphorylating kinase activity which induces or inhibits precise metabolic pathways.

For microorganisms living in relatively simple media, nutrients likely play the same role as the specific molecules mentioned above. Indeed changes in the physiological programs occur when the cells are transferred to depleted solutions: this is well-known for bacterial sporulation in *Bacillus*, ascospore formation in *Saccharomyces*, or cell sexualization in *Chlamydomonas*. At least in *Bacillus subtilis* and *Saccharomyces*, the new metabolic activities seem to be linked to a new type of phosphorylation pattern (see in Rhaese et al. 1979). Moreover, simple modifications of the external ion concentration can induce cells to choose a new metabolic orientation. For example, in *Blastocladiella* motile zoospores transform into a sessile growing germling with a high degree of synchrony when K^+ is added to the medium; the transformation involves retraction and disassembly of the flagellum, fragmentation of the single mitochondrion, dispersal of the ribosomes from the nuclear cap through the cytoplasm, and de novo synthesis of a chitinous cell wall, changes that take place in 1 min and do not require protein synthesis (Soll and Sonneborn 1972; Van Brunt and Harold 1980).

Another fact of interest is that all cells are able to modify their movements (animal cells) or cytoplasmic streaming (plant cells) very rapidly. This is due to the following property: the structures involved in the cytoplasm hydrodynamics, such as microtubules, can appear and disappear in seconds when the environment (ion content, temperature) is changed. Each type of structure has its own environmental reactions, but all need ATP or GTP and phosphorylations for building and functioning. Moreover, in *Acetabularia*, one could observe that cellular streaming, when arrested by darkness, recovers after a few seconds of light, blue light being much more efficient than red light; this response controls RNA transport from the nuclear basal part towards the apical growth zone (Puiseux-Dao et al. 1980; Dazy et al. 1981) and chloroplast transport which shows a circadian rhythm correlated with the diurnal periodicity of electrophysiological activity (Broda et al. 1979; Schweiger et al. 1981; Dazy et al. 1980).

143

In *Euglena*, Schiff (1975) described two photo-controls of chloroplast development: one is blue-light dependent and influences nuclear DNA transcription, in particular to form cytoplasmic ribosomal RNA necessary for the translation of some plastid proteins; on the other hand chloroplast ribosomal RNA synthesis is regulated by both blue and red light, implicating another type of receptor (protochlorophyll or protochlorophyllide or the like). A similar double photocontrol has also been proposed for the regulation of chloroplast DNA content in *Euglena* (Srinivas and Lyman 1980).

When analyzing the data on *Euglena* and *Acetabularia* together, it seems possible to propose at least in green algae that two photocontrols can co-exist: one is very sensitive to blue light and responsible for cytoplasmic reactions (among the more rapid responses, one finds the acceleration of cytoplasmic streaming which in turn can activate the metabolism by the way of ion, molecule, and organelle transport); the second takes place inside chloroplasts and directs the plastid physiology with secondary consequences for the cytoplasm.

Turning back to animal cells or *Blastocladiella*, changes of the metabolic program are observed when information is received at the level of the plasma membrane from ions, nutrients, or other external molecules. Then enzymes (cyclases, ATPases) of the plasmalemma modify their activity which, in turn, influences ion transport and the phosphorylating pattern of the cells. This should, of course, be enough to transform by degrees all the cellular biochemical reactions which depend upon ions and phosphorylation. But the architectural components, such as microfilaments and microtubules, are also very sensitive to ions and phosphorylation; they may respond (cf. the rapid loss of the flagellum in *Blastocladiella* after the addition of K^+ to the medium) from nucleation centers on the plasma membrane itself, accelerating or inhibiting cellular streaming. This control on cytoplasmic streaming amplifies the cellular response, which would be slow if diffusion alone were responsible for transporting biochemical materials.

Therefore, we have proposed (Puiseux-Dao 1979) that the physiological signals acting on the plasmalemma (on proteins or lipids) are transformed into ionic messages and phosphorylating capabilities with consequences first on the membrane enzymes, then on the cell hydrodynamics, and then on all the internal biochemical reactions. This is also valuable for the membranes containing at least one photoreceptor, which is the case of the thylakoids, which are known to produce ion exchanges and ATP in light.

Under such conditions it is clear that external information can drive the cell from one physiological program to another, for example, during differentia-

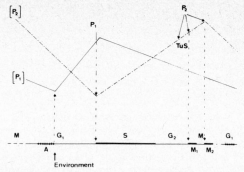

FIG. 15. Diagram showing our model for the cell-cycle regulation. In G_1, external conditions influence the synthesis (at least) of a plasma membrane protein P_1 whose level modifies the cell permeability to ions (and water). At a given level of P_1, the ion pattern ("ionic spectrum") inside the cell that influences phosphorylation and other biochemical processes becomes suitable for DNA synthesis and at a *correlated* time for the synthesis of another protein (P_2) of the plasma membrane. P_2 synthesis does not necessarily begin exactly when DNA replication starts. When the level of P_2 is high enough (associated with the decrease of P_1 due to the depletion of the specific mRNAs), the new ion balance inside the cell favors tubulin synthesis (TuS) and progressively but rapidly the evolution of mitosis. At the end of mitosis, mRNAs for P_2 are depleted, so the level of this protein decreases while synthesis of new membrane proceeds. This model is based on modifications of the plasma membrane permeability to ions (and water), which change the internal range of ion content. Driven by the ion content, the cell machinery works, at least for each of the two considered proteins (minimal hypothesis), with successive waves of mRNA and protein syntheses. When external signals are given to the cell (light, hormones), the internal ion pattern is adjusted in the convenient range (entrained rhythm in the case of plant cells). When the cell does not receive signals from outside, the periodic functioning of the cell machinery can go on until the progressive shift of the internal "ion spectrum" (linked to a slow down of protein synthesis) has become too large (decreasing free-running rhythm).

tion. But this type of control can also work for the regulation of the cell cycle as proposed in Fig. 15. This proposal is based on the experimental evidence that practically all molecules are always present in the cell, but they do or do not always function.

In our hypothesis (the most economical one), after mitosis and under usual conditions the cells enter a resting period (A) that lasts until a start signal is given by the environment, which in general for algae is light. This information induces a new definite ion composition ("ionic spectrum") inside the cell which in turn can achieve the possibility of synthesizing a short-lived protein (P_1) of the plasma membrane. As the P_1 level increases, the plasmalemma permeability may change and at a given time becomes available for nuclear DNA replication and at a correlated time for the synthesis of another short-lived protein (P_2) of the plasma membrane. The cessation of P_1 synthesis, probably due to the depletion of the specific mRNA, occurs more or less simultaneously. When the plasma membrane content in of P_1 and P_2 reaches certain precise values, then the "ionic spectrum" can allow prophase (M_1) to begin and for other values, telophase (M_2) can take place. Then the mRNAs for P_2 may be used up or at least at too low a level and P_2 synthesis ceases. The cells which have accumulated mRNAs for P_1 during the second part of the described cell cycle can wait in A for a new environmental signal.

The existence of a short-lived protein involved in the regulation of G_1 traverse has been recently suggested from pulse experiments with cycloheximide (see Shilo et al. 1979).

In fact our hypothesis shall be modified to include the various experimental situations described in the literature. First, it is necessary to explain why part of the rhythmic activity of the cells (see budding in *Saccharomyces*, photosynthesis in *Euglena*) can be disconnected from the cell division. This part might be linked to the environmental signal and to P_1 synthesis, but not to P_2 synthesis that could not take place when the P_1 level does not reach a certain value (depleted medium) or when the temperature is not suitable (temperature-sensitive mutant). The periodic metabolism would be due to the use of the mRNA stock for P_1 and its replacement.

The hypothesis must also account for circadian rhythms which persist though declining for about 2 wk in free-running conditions. Our model is based on the alternation of two opposite waves of translation and transcription concerning P_1, which influence the cell permeability and in turn may induce delayed but similar waves of translation and transcription for P_2. The starting signal, which comes from the environment and functions in G_1, is necessary for resting cells, but once given it probably serves not only for one unique cycle but for several because the oscillating machinery can function in a range of ionic composition and has its own inertia; in the absence of a new impulse from the outside, it will cease working after some cycles (whose number may depend upon the cell type and external conditions) after the "ionic spectrum" is shifted, by degrees, out of the convenient range. In Fig. 16, the model predicts that in free-running conditions, the cell division should be the first event to cease, then the G_2 period, then the S phase, then G_1. This could explain why in stationary cultures, no mitosis takes place while rhythms of the photosynthetic activity are still observable. This also fits with the fact that in general, cells enter dormancy

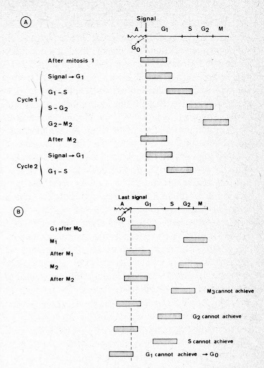

FIG. 16. (A) Hypothetical evolution of the cell internal "ionic spectrum" ▨ during the cell division cycle. The external signal (light for example) sets the shifted "ionic spectrum" to the right position after each cycle and G_1 starts progressing normally. (B) Free-running conditions. After the first mitosis, the ionic spectrum has shifted a little from the optimum range. However, G_1 can still start and the cell cycle can progress. At each round, in the absence of resetting by an external signal, the position of the ionic spectrum is more and more shifted, the traverse through the cell cycle becomes progressively slowed, and even the last events (mitosis, then G_2, then S) disappears one after the other. Then G_1 itself cannot take place and the cells enter G_0. Of course, the rate of disappearance of events occurring during the cell cycle might depend on the cell type and the external conditions. However, it is clear from experimental data that the cell division stops before other processes like photosynthesis which normally increases in G_1 and that except in precise conditions (intoxications for example), the cells enter G_0 from G_1.

from G_1. Of course, the shift of the internal "ionic spectrum" might be variable with the cell type and environmental factors. From the experimental data, which mainly concern the cell division and the photosynthetic activity, we can be assured that the second part of the cell cycle disappears before the first, that is G_1. However, the possibility of obtaining polyploid cells has to be considered because the S phase can occur without any cell division.

In our hypothesis, the biological clock is linked to alternate waves of transcription and translation

145

of at least two short-lived membrane proteins. But the model must account for some specific properties of the biological clock: (1) it may be temperature independent; (2) at least for plant cells, it may not function under bright illumination. As the plasma membrane is the fundamental structure implied in our model (coupled with chloroplast membranes in plant cells), we have to look for properties which are rapidly modified at that level when the temperature is changed. In fact, in animal cells the lipid composition of membranes can adapt almost instantaneously with an increase of unsaturated fatty acid chains at low temperatures and on the contrary a high content of saturated fatty acids at high temperatures. Under such conditions, rapid modifications of this type, similar to the changes observed when a lectin attaches to the lymphocyte external membrane, maintain the fluidity of the membranes at a constant level. Such an explanation has already been proposed by Njus et al. (1974) for explaining the temperature independence of the biological clock.

The loss of rhythm in bright illumination observed in plant cells is probably due to the effects of high light intensities on the cell permeability and the behavior of the cytoskeleton. In *Acetabularia*, we have seen that under such conditions, mainly in dark-treated algae transferred to light, large movements of water, and probably mineral ions, occur which induce plasmolysis and even rupture of the cytoplasm and the vacuole; but also the thin strands of cytoplasm break one after the other (Puiseux-Dao et al. 1980).

Another fact has to be explained: the phased growth described at least for some dinoflagellates (see Chisholm 1981). This type of growth concerns cultures in which, every day, a portion of the cells divide at a precise time, which is always the same; therefore the cell division is synchronized in relation to the time of day, but does not take place in all cells. It seems that at the beginning of each light period, the algae have been reset to a "start position," even when they have not achieved the preceding cell division cycle. In our hypothesis such resetting could be simply due to a shift back of the internal "ion spectrum" of the cells. This could be induced possibly by the light–dark transition. In *Acetabularia*, each time the light is turned off, an action potential takes place involving transmembrane ion movements (Rogatykh et al. 1979). Under such conditions, at least for some dinoflagellates, both light–dark and dark–light transitions would be able to modify the "ionic spectrum" which could explain why Weiler and Eppley (1979) could relate the time division of *Ceratium* both to the onset of dark and of light.

Another problem should be discussed: the lag period observed in growth curves when, for example, algae are transferred from stationary conditions (leading to G_0) to new conditions suitable for growth recovery. In fact we must remember that in the model, the progression through G_1 is linked to the synthesis of a protein P_1 from a stock of mRNA accumulated in the preceding cell division cycle. We can assume that during the resting stage or at least the stationary period, this stock of specific mRNA slowly decreases in such a way that in the cell population when the transfer to good conditions takes place, some cells would be unable to recover, others would recover very slowly, and others more rapidly depending upon the rest of mRNA still present.

Of course, this model is the simplest we could propose based on our hypothesis, which emphasizes the rapid response of the plasma membrane or membrane containing photoreceptors to environmental messages. It will probably be modified, in the future, but it calls attention to the regulatory role of ions which can influence all macromolecule configuration and functioning. In nature, pollutants that are lipophilic molecules or metals may interfere with this type of regulation.

References

ALLEN, J. R., T. M. ROBERTS, A. R. LOEBLICH III, AND L. C. KLOTZ. 1975. Characterisation of the DNA from the dinoflagellate *Cryptothecodinium cohnii* and its implication for nuclear organization. Cell 6: 161.

ALTKINSON, A. W., P. C. L. JOHN, AND B. E. S. GUNNING. 1974. The growth and division of the single mitochondrion and other organelles during the cell cycle of *Chlorella*. Protoplasma 81: 77.

APEL, K., AND H. G. SCHWEIGER. 1972. Nuclear dependency of chloroplast proteins in *Acetabularia*. Eur. J. Biochem. 25: 229.

ARNOLD, C. C., O. SCHIMMER, F. SCHOTZ, AND M. BATHELT. 1972. The mitochondria of *Chlamydomonas reinhardtii*. Arch. Mikrobiol. 81: 50.

BOARDMAN, N. K., A. W. LINNANE, AND R. M. SMILLIE [ed.]. 1971. Autonomy and biogenesis of mitochondria and chloroplasts. North-Holland. Publ. Co., Amsterdam and London.

BOGORAD, L., J. N. DAVIDSON, M. R. HANSON, AND L. J. METS. 1975. Genes for proteins of chloroplast ribosomes and evolution of eucaryotic genomes, p. 111. In S. Puiseux-Dao [ed.] Molecular biology of nucleocytoplasmic relationships. Elsevier, Amsterdam and New York.

BOURGUIGNON, L. Y. W., AND G. E. PALADE. 1976. Incorporation of polypeptides into thylakoid membrane of *Chlamydomonas reinhardtii*. J. Cell Biol. 69: 327.

BRANDT, P. 1975. Zwei Maxima plastidärer DNA-Synthese mit unterschiedlicher Lichtabhängigkeit im Zellcyclus von *Euglena gracilis*. Planta 124: 105.

BRAWERMAN, G., AND J. M. EISENSTADT. 1964. Deoxyribonucleic acid from the chloroplasts of *Euglena gracilis*. Biochim. Biophys. Acta 91: 477.

BRODA, H., G. SCHWEIGER, H. U. KOOP, R. SCHMID, AND H. G. SCHWEIGER. 1979. Chloroplast migration: a method for continuously monitoring a circadian rhythm in a single cell of *Acetabularia*, p. 163. *In* S. Bonotto, V. Kefeli, and S. Puiseux-Dao [ed.] Developmental biology of *Acetabularia*. Elsevier-North Holland, Amsterdam, New York, and Oxford.

BUETOW, D. E. [ed.]. 1968. The biology of *Euglena*. Academic Press, New York and London.

CALVAYRAC, R., O. BERTAUX, M. LEFORT-TRAN, AND R. VALENCIA. 1974. Généralisation du cycle mitochondrial chez *Euglena gracilis* (Z) en cultures synchrones, hétérotrophe et phototrophe. Protoplasma 80: 355.

CAMERON, I. L., AND G. M. PADILLA [ed.]. 1966. Cell synchrony: studies in biosynthetic regulation. Academic Press, New York and London.

CATTOLICO, R. A., J. W. SENNER, AND R. F. JONES. 1973. Changes in cytoplasmic and chloroplast ribosomal ribonucleic acid during the cell cycle of *Chlamydomonas reinhardtii*. Arch. Biochem. Biophys. 156: 58.

CHALY, N., A. LORD, AND J. G. LAFONTAINE. 1977. A light and electron microscope study of nuclear structure throughout the cell cycle in the euglenoid *Astasia longa*. J. Cell Sci. 27: 23.

CHIANG, K. S., AND N. SUEOKA. 1967a. Replication of chloroplast DNA in *Chlamydomonas reinhardtii* during vegetative cell cycle: its mode and regulation. Proc. Natl. Acad. Sci. 57: 1506.

1967b. Replication of chromosomal and cytoplasmic DNA during mitosis and meiosis in the eucaryote *Chlamydomonas reinhardtii*. J. Cell. Physiol. 70 Suppl. 1: 89.

CHISHOLM, S. W. 1981. Temporal patterns of cell division in unicellular algae. Can. Bull. Fish Aquat. Sci. 210: 150–181.

CHISHOLM, S. W., F. AZAM, AND R. W. EPPLEY. 1978. Silicic acid incorporation in marine diatoms on light:dark cycles: use as an assay for phased cell division. Limnol. Oceanogr. 23: 518.

CHISHOLM, S. W., AND R. G. STROSS. 1976a. Phosphate uptake kinetics in *Euglena gracilis* (Z) (Euglenophyceae) grown in light–dark cycles. I. Synchronized batch cultures. J. Phycol. 12: 210.

1976b. Phosphate uptake kinetics in *Euglena gracilis* (Z) (Euglenophyceae) grown in light–dark cycles. II. Phased P.O.$_1$-limited cultures. J. Phycol. 12: 217.

COOK, J. R. 1966. The synthesis of cytoplasmic DNA in synchronized *Euglena*. J. Cell Biol. 29: 369.

COOK, J. R., H. SMITH, AND P. HARRIS. 1976. Cyclic changes in chloroplast structures in synchronized *Euglena gracilis*. J. Protozool. 23: 368.

DALMON, J., M. BAYEN, AND R. GILET. 1975a. Periodic synthesis of DNA from *Chlorella pyrenoidosa* (strain 211/8B and strain Emerson). *In* Les cycles cellulaires et leur blocage chez quelques Protistes. Colloques CNRS, France 240. p. 179.

DALMON, J., M. BAYEN, AND A. RODE. 1975b. Incorporation of radioactive precursor into the desoxyribonucleic acid of *Chlorella pyrenoidosa*, Strain Emerson. Z. Pflanzen Physiol. 74: 189.

DAZY, A. C., H. BORGHI, AND Y. PICHON. 1980. Activité bioélectrique spontanée chez l'algue unicellulaire *Acetabularia mediterranea*. C.R. Acad. Sci. 291: 637.

DAZY, A. C., S. PUISEUX-DAO, M. DURAND, AND A. SANTA MARIA. 1981. The effects of blue and red light on streaming recovery and RNA transport after dark treatment in *Acetabularia mediterranea*. Protoplasma 105: 356.

EDMUNDS, L. N. JR. 1975. Temporal differentiation in *Euglena*: Circadian phenomena in non-dividing populations and in synchronously dividing cells. *In* Les cycles cellulaires et leur blocage chez quelques Protistes. Colloques CNRS, France 240. p. 53.

1978. Clocked cell cycle clocks: implications towards chronopharmacology and aging, p. 125. *In* H. V. Samis and S. Capobianca [ed.] Aging and biological rhythms. Plenum Publishing Corp., New York, NY.

EPEL, D. 1977. The program of fertilization. Sci. Am. 237: 128.

EYTAN, G., AND I. OHAD. 1970. Biogenesis of chloroplast membranes. J. Biol. Chem. 245: 4297.

1972. Biogenesis of chloroplast membranes. J. Biol. Chem. 247: 112.

FRAYSSINET, C., O. BERTAUX, AND R. VALENCIA. 1975. Noyau et nucléole chez *Euglena* au cours du cycle cellulaire. *In* Les cycles cellulaires et leur blocage chez quelques Protistes. Colloques CNRS, France 240. p. 291.

GALLERON, C., AND A. M. DURRAND. 1979. Cell cycle and DNA synthesis in a marine dinoflagellate *Amphidinium carterae*. Protoplasma 100: 155.

GALLING, G. 1973. Synthesis of chloroplast ribosomes during the development cycle of the *Chlorella* cell. Biochem. Physiol. Pflanz. 164: 575.

1975. RNA synthesis in synchronous cultures of unicellular algae. *In* Les cycles cellulaires et leur blocage chez quelques Protistes. Colloques CNRS, France 240. p. 225.

GREENGARD, P., R. PAOLETTI, AND G. A. ROBISON [ed.]. 1972. Physiology and pharmacology of cyclic AMP. Raven Press, New York, NY.

HADDEN, J. W., E. M. HADDEN, AND N. D. GOLDBERG. 1974. Cyclic GMP and cyclic AMP in lymphocyte metabolism and proliferation, p. 237. *In* W. Braun, L. M. Lichtenstein, and C. W. Parker [ed.] Cell growth and the immune response. Springer Verlag, New York, NY.

HEIZMANN, P. 1970. Propriétés des ribosomes et des RNA ribosomiques d'*Euglena gracilis*. Biochim. Biophys. Acta 224: 144.

HIRATA, F., S. TOYOSHIMA, J. AXELROD, AND M. WAXDAL. 1980. Phospholipid methylation: a biochemical signal modulating lymphocyte mitogenesis. Proc. Natl. Acad. Sci. 77: 862.

HOLIAN, A., C. J. DEUTSH, S. K. HOLIAN, R. P. DANIELE, AND D. F. WILSON. 1979. Lymphocyte response to phytohaemagglutinin: intracellular volume and intracellular (K$^+$). J. Cell. Physiol. 98: 137.

HOOBER, J. K. 1970. Sites of synthesis of chloroplast membrane polypeptides in *Chlamydomonas reinhardtii* y-1. J. Biol. Chem. 254: 4327.

HOWELL, S. H. 1975. Changing expression of the nuclear and chloroplast genomes during the cell cycle in *Chlamydomonas reinhardtii*. *In* Les cycles cellulaires et leur blocage chez quelques Protistes. Colloques CNRS, France 240. p. 159.

HOWELL, S. H., J. W. POSAKONY, AND K. R. HILL. 1977. The cell cycle program of polypeptide labelling in *Chlamydomonas reinhardtii*. J. Cell Biol. 72: 223.

HUI, D. Y., G. L. BEREBITSKY, AND J. A. K. HARMONY. 1979. Mitogen-stimulated calcium ion accumulation by lymphocytes. J. Biol. Chem. 254: 4666.

IWANIJ, V., N. H. CHUA, AND P. SIEKEVITZ. 1975. Synthesis and turnover of ribulose biphosphate carboxylase and its subunits during the cell cycle of *Chlamydomonas reinhardtii*. J. Cell Biol. 64: 572.

KOCH, K. S., AND H. L. LEFFERT. 1979. Increased sodium ion influx is necessary to initiate rat hepatocyte proliferation. Cell 18: 153.

LEDOIGT, G., AND R. CALVAYRAC. 1975. Synthèses périodiques, d'ARN chez *Euglena gracilis* en culture synchrone. *In* Les cycles cellulaires et leur blocage chez quelques Protistes. Colloques CNRS, France 240. p. 241.

——— 1979. Phénomènes périodiques, métaboliques et structuraux chez un Protiste, *Euglena gracilis*. J. Protozool. 26: 632.

LEEDALE, G. F. [ed.]. 1967. Euglenoid flagellates. Prentice-Hall, Inc., Englewood Cliffs, NJ.

LEFORT-TRAN, M. 1975. Mitochondries et chloroplastes chez *Euglena* en culture synchrone. *In* Les cycles cellulaires et leur blocage chez quelques Protistes. Colloques CNRS, France 240. p. 297.

LEFORT-TRAN, M., AND R. VALENCIA [ed.]. 1975. Les cycles cellulaires et leur blocage chez quelques Protistes. Colloques CNRS, France 240.

MANNING, J. E., AND O. C. RICHARDS. 1972. Synthesis and turnover of *Euglena gracilis* nuclear and chloroplast desoxyribonucleic acid. Biochemistry 11: 2036.

MARANO, F. 1979. Biosynthèse des DNA nucléaire et chloroplastique chez une Volvocale sans paroi. Biol. Cell. 36: 65.

——— 1980. Synchronisation et cycle cellulaire du *Dunaliella bioculata*, Utilisation de ce modèle expérimental pour l'étude du mode d'action de l'acroléine. Thèse d'état, Université Paris VII.

MATTHYS-ROCHON, E. 1979. Évolution d'un dinoflagellé libre au cours du cycle cellulaire. Biol. Cell. 35: 313.

MERRETT, M. J. 1975. The temporal expression of microbody and mitochondrial enzymes in division-synchronized *Euglena* cultures. *In* Les cycles cellulaires et leur blocage chez quelques Protistes. Colloques CNRS, France 240. p. 123.

MILNER, J. J., C. L. HERSHBERGER, AND D. E. BUETOW. 1979. *Euglena gracilis* chloroplast DNA codes for polyadenylated RNA. Plant Physiol. 64: 818.

NJUS, D., F. SULZMAN, AND J. W. HASTINGS. 1974. Membrane model for the circadian clock. Nature (London) 248: 116.

OHAD, I., P. SIEKEVITZ, AND G. E. PALADE. 1967. Biogenesis of chloroplast membranes. I. Plastid dedifferentiation in a dark-grown algal mutant (*Chlamydomonas reinhardtii*). J. Cell Biol. 35: 521.

OSAFUME, T., S. MIHARA, E. HASE, AND I. OHKURO. 1972. Electron microscope studies on the vegetative cellular cycle of *Chlamydomonas reinhardtii* in synchronous culture. Plant Cell Physiol. 13: 211.

PEDERSED, A. G., R. PETTERSEN, AND G. KNUTSEN. 1975. Uptake and metabolism of uracil, guanine and phenylanine by synchronized *Chlorella fusca*. *In* Les cycles cellulaires et leur blocage chez quelques Protistes. Colloques CNRS, France 240. p. 203.

PUISEUX-DAO, S. 1979. Mouvements cytoplasmiques et morphogenèse chez l'*Acetabularia mediterranea*. Biol. Cell. 34: 83.

PUISEUX-DAO, S., A. C. DAZY, M. DURAND, F. MARANO, C. BRUN, D. HOURSIANGOU-NEUBRUN, AND A. SANTA-MARIA. 1980. Régulation par la lumière et la teneur en Ca^{2+} du milieu des mouvements cytoplasmiques et du transport des RNA chez l'*Acetabularia*. Biol. Cell. 39: 11a.

PICKETT-HEAPS, J. D., D. H. TIPPIT, AND J. A. ANDREOZZI. 1979a. Cell division in the pennate diatom *Pinnularia*, I and II. Biol. Cell. 33: 71 and 79.

——— 1979b. Cell division in the pennate diatom *Pinnularia*, III and IV. Biol. Cell. 35: 195 and 199.

RHAESE, H. J., R. SCHECKEL, R. GROSCURTH, AND G. STAMMINGER. 1979. Studies on the control of development. Highly phosphorylated nucleotides (HPN) are correlated with ascopore formation in *Saccharomyces cerevisiae*. Mol. Gen. Genet. 170: 57.

RICHARDS, O. E., AND J. E. MANNING. 1975. Replication of chloroplast DNA in *Euglena gracilis*. *In* Les cycles cellulaires et leur blocage chez quelques Protistes. Colloques CNRS, France 240. p. 25.

RICHARDS, O. C., AND R. S. RYAN. 1974. Synthesis and turnover of *Euglena gracilis* mitochondrial DNA. J. Mol. Biol. 82: 57.

ROBISON, G. A., G. G. NAHAS, AND L. TRINER [ed.]. 1971. Cyclic AMP and cell function. Ann. N.Y. Acad. Sci. 185.

ROGATYKH, N. P., V. G. MELKUMYAN, AND T. N. ZUBAREV. 1979. Action potential signals and cell morphogenesis in *Acetabularia*. *In* S. Bonotto, V. Kefeli, and S. Puiseux-Dao [ed.] Developmental biology of *Acetabularia*. Elsevier-North Holland, Amsterdam, New York, and Oxford.

RUBIN, A. H., M. TERASAKI, AND H. SANUI. 1979. Major intracellular cations and growth control: correspondence among magnesium content, protein synthesis and the onset of DNA synthesis in BALB/C_3T_3 cells. Proc. Natl. Acad. Sci. 76: 3917.

SAGAN, L. 1965. Unusual pattern of tritiated thymidine incorporation in *Euglena*. J. Protozool. 12: 105.

SCHIFF, J. A. 1975. The control of differentiation in *Euglena*. *In* Les cycles cellulaires et leur blocage chez quelques Protistes. Colloques CNRS, France 240. p. 79.

SCHIFF, J. A., AND H. T. EPSTEIN. 1966. The continuity of the chloroplast DNA in *Euglena*, p. 131. *In* M. Locke [ed.] Reproduction: cellular, subcellular and molecular. Academic Press, New York, NY.

SCHWEIGER, H. G., H. BRODA, AND D. WOLFF. 1981. Simultaneous recording of two circadian rhythms in an individual cell of *Acetabularia*. International workshop on morphogenesis in *Acetabularia*. Protoplasma 105: 357.

SEGEL, G. B., W. SIMON, AND M. A. LICHTMAN. 1979. Regulation of sodium and potassium transport in phytohemagglutin-stimulated human blood lymphocytes. J. Clin. Invest. 64: 834.

SHILO, B., V. G. H. RIDDLE, AND A. B. PARDEE. 1979. Protein turnover and cell-cycle initiation in yeast. Exp. Cell Res. 123: 221.

SOLL, D. R., AND D. R. SONNEBORN. 1972. Zoospore germination in the water mold. *Blastocladiella emersonii*. IV. Ion control over cell differentiation. J. Cell Sci. 10: 315.

SRINIVAS, U., AND H. LYMAN. 1980. Photomorphogenic regulation of chloroplast replication in *Euglena*. Plant Physiol. 66: 295.

STUTZ, E., AND J. P. VAUDREY. 1971. Ribosomal DNA satellite of *Euglena gracilis* chloroplast DNA. FEBS Lett. 17: 277.

SWEENEY, B. M., AND J. W. HASTINGS. 1958. Rhythmic cell divisions in populations of *Gonyaulax polyedra*. J. Protozool. 5: 217.

SWINTON, D. C., AND P. C. HANAWALT. 1972. *In vivo* labelling of *Chlamydomonas* chloroplast DNA. J. Cell Biol. 54: 592.

VAN BRUNT, J., AND F. M. HAROLD. 1980. Ionic control of germination of *Blastocladiella emersonii* zoospores. J. Bacteriol. 130: 249.

WANKA, F. 1975. Possible role of the pyrenoid in the reproductional phase of the cell cycle of *Chlorella*. *In* Les cycles cellulaires et leur blocage chez quelques Protistes. Colloques CNRS, France 240. p. 131.

WANKA, F., H. F. P. JOOSTEN, AND W. J. DEGRIP. 1970. Composition and synthesis of DNA in synchronously growing cells of *Chlorella pyrenoidosa*. Arch. Mikrobiol. 75: 25.

WEEKS, D. P., AND P. S. COLLIS. 1979. Induction and synthesis of tubulin during the cell cycle and life of *Chlamydomonas reinhardtii*. Dev. Biol. 69: 400.

WEILER, C. S., AND R. W. EPPLEY. 1979. Temporal pattern of division in the dinoflagellate genus *Ceratium* and its application to the determination of growth rate. J. Exp. Mar. Biol. Ecol. 39: 1.

WEILER, C. S., AND D. M. KARL. 1979. Diel changes in phased-dividing cultures of *Ceratium furca* (Dinophyceae): nucleotide triphosphates, adenylate energy charge, cell carbon, and patterns of vertical migration. J. Phycol. 15: 384.

WHITNEY, R. B., AND R. M. SUTHERLAND. 1972. Enhanced uptake of calcium by transforming lymphocytes. Cell Immunol. 5: 137.

WILSON, R., AND K. S. CHIANG. 1977. Temporal programming of chloroplast and cytoplasmic ribosomal RNA transcription in the synchronous cell cycles of *Chlamydomonas reinhardtii*. J. Cell Biol. 72: 470.

ZEUTHEN, E. [ed.]. 1964. Synchrony in cell division and growth. Wiley-Intersciences, New York, Sydney, and London.

Temporal Patterns of Cell Division
in Unicellular Algae

SALLIE W. CHISHOLM

Ralph M. Parsons Laboratory
Massachusetts Institute of Technology
Cambridge, MA 02139

Introduction

The study of the growth of unicellular algae on light/dark cycles is "housed" in three separate subdisciplines of biology with distinctly different motivations for interest in the subject. These subdisciplines include cell biology (where interest lies in the mechanisms of cell cycle control), chronobiology (where interest is in revealing the mechanism of circadian clocks), and ecology (where the goal is to understand the temporal interactions between organisms and their environment. The forum for this review, and the motivation behind it, involves the third goal, but much of the material covered will be drawn from the cell cycle and clock literature. It is hoped that this synthesis will provide a new perspective for future studies of the physiological responses and adaptations of phytoplankton to the most predictable selective force in their environment — the 24-h light/dark cycle.

BACKGROUND

The methodologies and the terminology dealing with cell division synchrony originated in the cell biology school, where the precise goal is to create populations of cells that express the behavior of a single cell. To this end, culture systems have been developed in which the generation times of the individual cells in populations are aligned as tightly as possible to result in simultaneous division.

There are several ways this synchrony in cell division can be achieved (Prescott 1976). "Natural" synchrony (termed "natural" because it is spontaneous) exists in many cell types from plants (Erikson 1964) and animals (Agrell 1964). The initial cell divisions of fertilized sea urchin eggs (Mazia and Dan 1952) are synchronous, for example, as are nuclear divisions in slime molds (Rusch 1969), and in the anthers of liliaceous plant genera (Hotta et al. 1966).

In experimentally derived synchrony, simultaneity of events is achieved by mechanical selection of cells at the same stage of the cell cycle (selection synchrony) or by bringing all the cells of an asynchronous culture to a single point in the cell cycle by manipulation of culture conditions (induction synchrony). Strictly speaking, cell division synchrony achieved by the selection method is termed "synchronous," whereas that achieved by induction is called "synchronized" (Abbo and Pardee 1960; James 1966). The distinction between these two terms will not be strictly observed in this review. The use of induction synchrony for the study of cell cycle events has often been criticized (see Zeuthen 1974) as distorting the natural timing of events, because cells are most often subjected to periodic stresses such as temperature shocks, amino acid deprivation, and thymidine blocks to bring them into synchrony.

Cultures of unicellular algae grown on 24-h light/dark cycles express a special type of induction synchrony. What distinguishes this group of organisms from all heterotrophic microorganisms is that they have evolved in an environment where the supply of energy for cellular growth is periodic. The regularity and inevitability of the natural photocycle must have, through natural selection, imposed a need for coordination and temporal order among synthetic and reproductive events in the cells. The result, for most species at least, is a "preferred" alignment (phase relationship) between the biosynthetic processes, the cell division cycle, and the environmental light/dark cycle. When cells in a population of unicellular algae assume this optimal or preferred relationship, the cell cycles in the population become temporally phased by the photocycle. When the cell division cycles of all the cells in a population are aligned such that all cells divide each day, the population is termed "synchronous." When only a portion of the cells divides each day, but does so in a restricted gate, the population is "phased." This is a natural and fundamental property of growth in phytoplankton populations, and should not be viewed as induction synchrony in the artificial sense. We can, and must, assume that the temporal sequence of cell cycle processes and cell division patterns expressed by phytoplankton populations grown on 24-h photocycles are adaptive, and that they reflect the optimized alignment of cellular processes to a naturally periodic energy supply. The mechanisms by which this alignment is achieved and maintained and the extent to which it varies among and between various phytoplankton species are critical aspects of the adaptive physiology of phytoplankton (Sournia 1974).

The Eukaryotic Cell Cycle

The generalized cell division cycle for eukaryotic cells is usually viewed as 4 discrete sequential intervals: G_1–S–G_2–D (Fig. 1). G_1 and G_2 are the gaps separating DNA synthesis (S) and cell division (D, or M for mitosis). S and D periods are well defined and identifiable for most cell types. The precise biochemical events that comprise and define the two gap phases are not at all well understood (Prescott 1976).

The time it takes to traverse one cell division cycle is the generation time of the cell. The duration of the various stages varies with cell type. For example, a mammalian cell with a generation time of 16 h will typically spend 5 h in G_1, 7 h in S, 3 h in G_2, and 1 h in division (Prescott 1976). The dinoflagellate *Amphidinium carteri* has a very short (usually unmeasurable) G_1 phase, a 6- to 9-h S phase, and a 5- to 6-h G_2 phase (Galleron and Durrand 1979). In *Chlorella* grown with a 20-h generation time, the G_1 is about 10 h long, G_2 is absent, S is 6 h in duration, and the division process takes about 5 h (John et al. 1973).

The G_o state (Fig. 1) is one in which the cell cycle is arrested in G_1, i.e. withdrawn from the cell division cycle (Prescott 1976). This arrest is reversible for most cell types in which the G_o state has been identified, which include plant embryos (dormant seeds), cells in various tissues (such as kidney, liver, and pancreas), and nonrenewing tissues (neurons and skeletal muscle cells). Little, if anything, is known about the G_o state in algae, but it probably exists in dormant cysts and conceivably plays a role in the maintenance of vegetative cells in resource-limited "stationary phase."

The traverse time of the cell cycle in genetically identical cells in a uniform environment is not a constant. The distribution of generation times in most clonal populations of cells is described by a normal distribution skewed in favor of the shorter generation times (e.g. Prescott 1959; Cook and Cook 1962). This distribution dictates the degree of synchrony (the duration of the division burst) expressed by a population of cells after one generation, beginning with cells aligned at the beginning of G_1. It also dictates the rate at which a synchronized population will become asynchronous when released from the synchronizing force (Peterson and Anderson 1964; Spudich and Koshland 1976). Early attempts to explain this variability in generation times maintained that the G_1–S–G_2–M sequence was sufficiently complex that small biochemical variabilities along the way would be magnified to result in a rather large difference in intermitotic times. More recently, Smith and Martin (1973) attempted to explain the distribution with a cell cycle model in which the exit from G_1 is probabilistic (the probability of the transition from G_1 to S is a constant, regardless of how long a cell has been in G_1), whereas traversing the sequence S–G_2–M is deterministic.

Klevecz (1976) observed that the distribution of generation times in mammalian cell lines appears to be "quantized," such that cell generation times tend to occur as integer multiples of 3–4 h. To explain this distribution he has proposed a cell cycle model in which the G_1 interval has been replaced by a loop (G_q) whose traverse time is equal to the interval between the quantized peaks in generation times. Here, G_q is viewed as a subcycle from which the cells may make a gated exit into the remainder of the cell cycle. The exit of a particular cell from G_q is probabilistic in the sense that it depends on environmental factors, but the cell can only exit from G_q after completely traversing the subcycle one or more times. This "gated" entry into the division process is analogous to the gating mechanism proposed for the circadian clock, which is known to play a key role in regulating the timing of division in certain phytoplankton species.

The Circadian Clock

The underlying biochemical nature of the endogenous biological clock is not known, but this timekeeping mechanism appears to be essential to the creation and maintenance of temporal order in eukaryotic organisms and in the ecological systems which

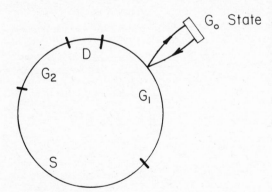

FIG. 1. Diagrammatic view of the cell cycle. The cycle begins after division, D, with the G_1 (gap) phase. It proceeds through DNA synthesis, S, through another gap (G_2), after which division occurs. Some cells can go into a reversible cell cycle arrest (G_0) while in G_1. (After Prescott 1976.)

they comprise (for books and symposia treating the subject see Aschoff 1965; Bünning 1967; Sweeney 1969; Menaker 1971; Hastings and Schweiger 1975; Palmer 1976; Suda et al. 1979; Scheving and Halberg 1980; and references therein). Many descriptors have been used to refer to "the clock," and they will be used interchangeably here: endogenous clock, biological clock, circadian clock, innate oscillator, and circadian pacemaker. In all eukaryotic organisms including unicellular algae, the clock can function (1) to create internal temporal order in cellular processes, (2) to properly phase these processes to natural (external) periodicities, and, in some organisms, (3) to measure the passage of time (as in sun compass behavior or photoperiodic time measurement). Various physiological processes that are known to be under the control of circadian clocks in algae are shown in Table 1.

My purpose here is not to document the evidence that circadian clocks exist, but rather to clearly define the general properties of the clock and clock-controlled processes, to provide a framework for the interpretation of clock-coupled cell division patterns in unicellular algae. Experimental documentation of the clock properties described below will be presented for specific phytoplankton species in subsequent sections.

The clock can be viewed as an endogenous self-sustaining oscillator whose natural period length is close to (but not equal to) 24 h. The innate "pacemaker" can be coupled to a multitude of physiological processes (see Table 1) and results in an overt or observed rhythm in these processes. The overt rhythm (i.e. the one we can measure) is often viewed as the "hands of the clock," because it reflects the properties of the clock, but is independent of, and distinct from, the mechanism itself.

Clock-controlled rhythms are entrainable. That is, they will assume the period length of an exogenous oscillator (the "Zeitgeber") and maintain a fixed phase relationship to it. The Zeitgeber of interest to ecologists (which, no doubt, molded the evolution of the clock) is the natural light/dark cycle. It entrains the clock, and in turn the overt rhythm, to a period length of exactly 24 h. It is most important to recognize that the role of the light/dark cycle is not to drive or create rhythmicity but to couple with the biological rhythm, i.e. set its phase relative to local time.

When an organism is released from entrainment, for example by placing it under conditions of constant darkness or constant dim light, endogenous rhythms will "free-run" with a period length close to 24 h. This free-running rhythm will persist indefinitely with remarkable precision in individual organisms. Although the rhythm may damp out after some time in populations of unicellular organisms, this must be recognized as reflecting slight differences in the free-running period lengths in individual cells. This results in eventual loss of synchrony between the individual cells and should not be interpreted as a loss of clock control in the individual cells under the free-running condition.

Although temperature changes can entrain an endogenous rhythm and ambient temperatures can

TABLE 1. Circadian rhythms in algae.

Species	Rhythm	Reference
Acetabularia sp.	Photosynthetic capacity	Sweeney and Haxo 1961
Chlamydomonas reinhardtii	Cell division Phototaxis	Bruce 1970
Gonyaulax polyedra	Cell division Luminescence Glow Photosynthetic capacity	Sweeney and Hastings 1958 Hastings and Sweeney 1958 Hastings 1960 Hastings et al. 1960
Ceratium furca	Cell division Photosynthetic capacity	Meeson pers. comm. Prezelin et al. 1977
Euglena gracilis	Alanine dehydrogenase activity Cell division Amino acid incorporation Settling Photosynthetic capacity	Sulzman and Edmunds 1972 Edmunds 1966 Feldman 1968 Terry and Edmunds 1970 Lonergan and Sargent 1978
Euglena obtusa	Vertical migration	Palmer and Round 1965
Oedogonium cardiacium	Sporulation	Bühnemann 1955
Phaeodactylum tricornutum	Photosynthetic capacity	Palmer et al. 1964
Hantzschia virgata	Vertical migration	Palmer and Round 1967

affect the amplitude of the rhythm, the period length of the rhythm is not dependent on temperature. This "temperature-compensation" is one of the most remarkable and essential characteristics of the clock mechanism. It is remarkable in that most known physiological processes of cells are quite temperature dependent (the most fundamental being growth rate), and it is essential in that it is difficult to conceive of a "chronometer" that could function properly unless its time-keeping property were insensitive to temperature.

An entrained endogenous rhythm can be viewed as three oscillators, the Zeitgeber, the clock, and the overt rhythm, which, under the proper conditions (see the section that follows for exceptions), are tightly coupled. One of the few ways to dissect the phase dependence of the three oscillators, and expose characteristics of the pacemaker itself, is to allow the rhythm to free run in constant conditions and then subject it to a short stimulus (e.g. light pulse in constant darkness) at various times during the cycle. Depending on when the pulse is given, a characteristic phase shift (either an advance or a delay) will occur in the overt rhythm. When the results of such an experiment are plotted as the difference between the phase of the shifted rhythm and its original phase, as a function of the phase of the oscillation when the pulse was given, a phase response curve (PRC) results. The PRC can be viewed as a plot of the changing sensitivity of the endogenous oscillator to the light phase, which is the essential property underlying the mechanism of entrainment (detailed discussion and analysis of PRCs and their utility in revealing properties of the clock can be found in Enright 1965; Aschoft 1965; Pittendrigh 1975, 1979).

The phase response curve is a "fingerprint" of pacemaker properties for a given species in that its shape is the same regardless of the overt rhythm that was monitored to construct it (Pittendrigh 1975). For example, although the rhythms in cell division, stimulated luminescence, glow, and photosynthesis in *Gonyaulax polyedra* have peaks at different times relative to each other on a light/dark cycle and when released from entrainment (McMurry and Hastings 1972), the phase response curve for each of these rhythms is identical (Hastings 1960; Sweeney 1969; McMurry and Hastings 1972; Pittendrigh 1975). The conservative detailed form of the PRC serves as the clearest evidence that the clock is independent of the processes it drives, and uniquely responsive to the environment that entrains it (Pittendrigh 1975). The fact that any of the overt rhythms can be destroyed by inhibitors (e.g. DCMU on photosynthesis) and the coupling between the pacemaker and the other rhythms is not disturbed (Hastings 1960) confirms the autonomy of the clock.

This discussion would not be complete without at least addressing the question of the underlying physical mechanism of the clock, and whether the hypothetical mechanism is indeed the same in all organisms. Several recent symposia (e.g. Hastings and Schweiger 1976; Suda et al. 1979) have been devoted to these questions, as is most of the current research in this field. The general feeling from these recent accounts is that a common molecular basis in all organisms is unlikely — i.e. that the universal features of circadian rhythms could easily result from convergent evolution under the strong selective pressure of the same external cycles (Hastings 1975). Nonetheless, many features of circadian rhythms from different organisms may be accommodated by one or parts of three classes of models (Edmunds 1976). (1) Metabolic feedback loop models in which the oscillatory behavior is maintained via biochemical feedback systems analogous to short-period glycolytic oscillations well documented in yeast (see Chance et al. 1973). (2) "Tape reading" transcription models that propose that the distance between genes and, thus, the time it takes to transcribe the DNA "tape," could be used to measure biological time (Ehret and Trucco 1967; Ehret 1974). (3) Membrane models, in which the oscillatory mechanism is derived from the interaction between membrane configurations, ion distribution, and membrane bound ion transport channels (Njus et al. 1974).

One of the most promising developments in the efforts to reveal the clock mechanism has been the isolation of clock mutants in *Drosophila* (Konopka and Benzer 1971), *Neurospora* (Feldman and Hoyle 1973), and *Chlamydomonas* (Bruce 1972). In *Neurospora*, for example, several mutants have been isolated that have dramatically altered free-running period lengths. Each mutant segregates as a single nuclear gene; thus it is likely that the mutations are in the basic timing mechanism itself (Edmunds 1976).

Infradian and Ultradian Growth

The premise of circadian regulation of cellular events runs into difficulty in populations that are doubling more than once each day, because in such cases the average cell division cycle is shorter than the circadian period length. Wille and Ehret (1968) were the first to formalize this problem, and Ehret and Wille (1970), Ehret (1974), Ehret and Dobra (1977), and Ehret et al. (1977) have developed a unified theory (complete with an entirely new vocabulary) to describe this apparently schizophrenic existence in eukaryotic microorganisms.

They first define the two fundamental growth modes. One is the fast exponential or "ultradian" growth mode in which the generation times of the cells are shorter than 1 d, and the other is the slow or "infradian" growth mode in which the average cell generation times are much longer than 1 d. The basic axiom of their formalization is the "eukaryotic–circadian principle" (that all eukaryotic organisms have the capacity for circadian timekeeping), and its corollary is the "circadian–infradian rule" (that a cell must be in the infradian mode to have circadian outputs). This rule was dubbed the G–E–T effect (*Gonyaulax–Euglena–Tetrahymena*) because these three organisms were thought to best demonstrate the phenomenon of light-synchronizable division patterns with circadian period lengths in cultures growing in infradian mode (Ehret and Wille 1970). It should be noted here that *Gonyaulax polyedra* has never been reported to exhibit generation times less than 1 d; thus it is not an appropriate species from which to launch such a theory.

Although the formalism and terminology surrounding the ultradian/infradian growth mode phenomenon are perhaps excessive, the concept and distinction are very important, particularly for fast-growing phytoplankton species that must frequently switch between these two modes. What is emphasized in recent discussions (Ehret et al. 1977) is that cell cycle time and cell generation time are not equivalent. Although this has been stressed repeatedly in a variety of contexts (e.g. Hartwell 1971, 1974; Gotham 1977; Edmunds 1978; Mitchison 1971, 1973, 1974) it becomes particularly significant in the context of circadian control. According to the infradian/circadian rule, when cells are growing in the fast (ultradian) mode, the cell cycle is tightly coupled to the cell division cycle, so that the period lengths of the two processes are functionally related (Fig. 2) and they are both temperature dependent. When cell generation times are slowed down to infradian mode by some limiting resource, the cell cycle becomes uncoupled from the cell division cycle, assumes a circadian period length (Fig. 2), and becomes temperature independent (Ehret et al. 1977). At the limit of infradian mode is the "stationary-phase" of growth, which is classically viewed as a population of non-dividing cells, or cells that are "arrested" in G_1 (or possibly G_o). Ehret stresses that such a view, unfortunately, projects the image that when cells do not divide they do not cycle, which is not the case. He further suggests that the "absolutist" concept of stationary-phase cells as nondividing cells should be replaced by one in which the cells are viewed as having a finite (though small) probability of division.

The temporal order of cellular processes that cycle independently of the cell division cycle, the "circadian chronotype" (Ehret et al. 1977; Ehret and Dobra, 1977), can be considered the temporal analogue of the phenotype, and is useful for comparing physiological aspects of various phyla. The chronotype of a species can be elucidated by forcing popula-

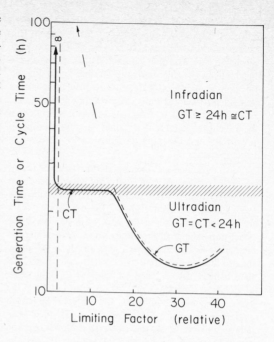

FIG. 2. Diagrammatic view of the relationship between cell generation time (*GT*) and cell cycle time (*CT*) in infradian and ultradian growth modes controlled by a growth-limiting factor. In ultradian mode, *CT* is a function of *GT*. They are uncoupled in infradian mode, where *CT* becomes circadian and *GT* assumes values that are integral multiples of 24 h. Only in lethal environments (to the left of the broken vertical line) does the period of *CT* exceed circadian values. (Modified from Ehret and Dobra 1977; Gotham 1977.)

tions of cells into infradian growth mode and entraining their cell cycles with a Zeitgeber such as light/dark cycles or temperature cycles. This entrainment serves to bring all the cell cycles in phase so the population of cells will express chronotypic patterns.

Chronotypes for *Euglena* and *Gonyaulax* have been assembled in Fig. 3. Unfortunately, the various activities measured for these two organisms show very little overlap; thus comparisons are limited. What is important here is to recognize that the chronotype is a conservative property of a species. In *Gonyaulax*, for example, the phase relationship between the rhythms in glow, stimulated luminescence, photosynthetic capacity, and cell division is preserved throughout a phase shift induced by interrupting the continuous light regime with a dark interval (McMurry and Hastings 1972). Of equal importance is recognition that many cellular processes are rhythmic regardless of whether or not the cell division cycle is proceeding toward mitosis.

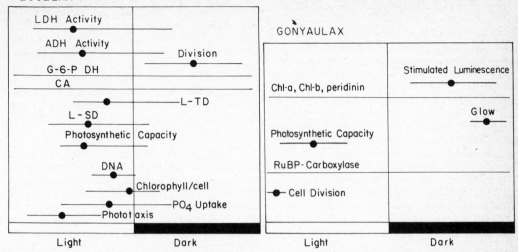

FIG. 3. Chronotypes for *Euglena gracilis* and *Gonyaulax polyedra*. Solid circles mark the peak in activity and lines mark the interval of the peak in the rhythm. All rhythms except DNA synthesis and cell division were measured in infradian cells.

Euglena

ADH	= alanine dehydrogenase activity	Sulzman and Edmunds 1972
LDH	= lactic dehydrogenase activity	Edmunds 1974
L-TD	= L-threonine deaminase activity	Edmunds 1974
L-SD	= L-serene deaminase activity	Edmunds 1974
G-6-P	= glucose-6-phosphate dehydrogenase activity	Lonergan and Sargent 1978
CA	= carbonic anhydrase activity	Lonergan and Sargent 1978
Photoaxis		Bruce and Pittendrigh 1956
PO_4 uptake		Chisholm and Stross 1976
Chlorophyll/cell		Laval-Martin et al. 1979
Photosynthetic capacity		Laval-Martin et al. 1979
DNA synthesis		Edmunds 1965b
Cell division		Cook 1961a

Gonyaulax

Stimulated luminescence	Hastings and Sweeney 1958
Glow	Hastings 1960
Photosynthetic capacity	Hastings et al. 1960
Cell division	Sweeney and Hastings 1958
Chlorophyll *a*, *c*, peridinin	Prezelin and Sweeney 1977
RuBP carboxylase activity	Bush and Sweeney 1972

The question of the behavior of the cell cycle when the cell division cycle is in ultradian mode remains. Ehret and Dobra (1977) claim that the cell cycle (and the circadian clock) assumes the frequency of the cell division cycle (Fig. 2), which represents a fundamental change in temporal order within the cell and reflects very "unclocklike" properties. Klevecz (1976) offers an alternative, with a model that allows for strict temporal control in ultradian and infradian growth modes. As discussed previously, the G_q subcycle in his model has a traverse time that is necessarily shorter than the generation time and must be cycled through at least twice before mitosis can occur. The possible values of generation times that can result from such control must then be "quantized" and (assuming $G_q < 12$ h) allow for ultradian or infradian growth. In mammalian cells, where G_q appears to have about a 4-h duration, various enzyme activities have been observed to oscillate at a corresponding frequency regardless of the *GT* values of the population, and the rhythms are temperature compensated (Klevecz 1969, 1975). From this, the inference is that G_q is a clock of sorts, but with a shorter period length than the circadian clock. The latter could be a special case ($G_q = 24$ h) or the circadian frequency might reflect several passes through the high frequency G_q loop. This, however, is all in the realm of speculation.

Euglena: An Example of Clock-Coupled Division

Of all autotrophic unicellular algae, *Euglena* is the best understood in terms of the characteristics and mechanisms of phasing the cell cycle to light/dark cycles. Work on synchrony in this genus was pioneered by Leedale (1959), Cook (1961a, b, 1963, 1971), Cook and Cook (1962), and Cook and James (1960) and systematically pursued by Edmunds and co-workers (see Edmunds 1974, 1978) who have firmly established that the cell cycle in this species is coupled to a circadian clock. Although this genus is not ideal for ecological extrapolation, it is presented here as a "model system" exemplifying the basic characteristics of clock-coupled cell cycles in unicellular algae. These characteristics should, in principle, be manifested in all species with the capacity for circadian control of cell division.

When cultured in continuous light under optimum conditions (25°C; 7000 lx) *Euglena* grows with an average generation time of ~ 11 h (Cook 1963; Edmunds 1965a). In an exponentially growing culture with an average generation time of 13.4 h, the generation times of individual cells range from 9.5 to 23.7 (Cook and Cook 1962). The minimum number of hours a cell must be exposed to saturating light intensities to undergo division has been estimated to range from 10 h (Edmunds and Funch 1969b) to 14 h (Padilla and Cook 1964; Edmunds 1965a).

When grown on an appropriate light/dark cycle, populations of *Euglena* become synchronized so that all the cells divide during a restricted time interval (the division gate) during the dark period (Table 2). For example, on L:D 10:14 (Fig. 4a) the division burst begins 12–13 h after the onset of the light period, continues for about 10–11 h, and results

TABLE 2. Summary of the growth and periodicity parameters for *Euglena gracilis* Z grown on various photoperiodic regimes.

Photoperiodic regime	Light I	L:D photo-period	Average step size	Equivalent[a] photoperiod	Beginning of division burst (hours after lights on)	Period length (h)	Reference
24-h periods	3500 lx	16:8	2.03		11–14 h	24	Edmunds 1965a
	800 lx	14:10	1.14		14 h	24	Edmunds 1966
	3500 lx	14:10	2.02		13–14 h	24	Edmunds 1966
	8000 lx	12:12	2.00		–	24	Edmunds and Funch 1969a
	8000 lx	10:14	1.97		12–13 h	24	Edmunds and Funch 1969b
	8000 lx	8:16	1.68		12 h	24	Edmunds and Funch 1969b
Skeleton photo-periods	8000 lx	4,4,4:12	1.50	8:16	12 h	24	Edmunds and Funch 1969a
	8000 lx	3,6,3:12	1.31	6:18	13 h	24	Edmunds and Funch 1969a
Constant L:D ratio	8000 lx	10:10	1.81			20	Edmunds and Funch 1969a
	8000 lx	8:8	2.02			33	
	8000 lx	6:6	(Random division)			—	
	8000 lx	5:5	2.4			32	
	8000 lx	4:4	> 2			30–40	
High frequency	8000 lx	0.25:0.50	1.68	8.16		30	Edmunds and Funch 1969a
	8000 lx	0.50:1	1.22	8:16		26	
	8000 lx	1:2	1.48	8:16		26	
	8000 lx	1:3	1.20	6:18		24	
	8000 lx	2:4	1.47	8:16		27	
	8000 lx	2:6	1.41	6:18		28	
Random	8000 lx	Random	1.67	8:16		27	Edmunds and Funch 1969a
Continuous low light	800 lx	Continuous (following 12:12)	1.17			24.2	Edmunds 1966
Low frequency	8000 lx	12:24	1.74			36	Edmunds 1971
	8000 lx	12:36	1.79			48	Edmunds 1971

[a]Total number of hours of light and dark per 24-h period.

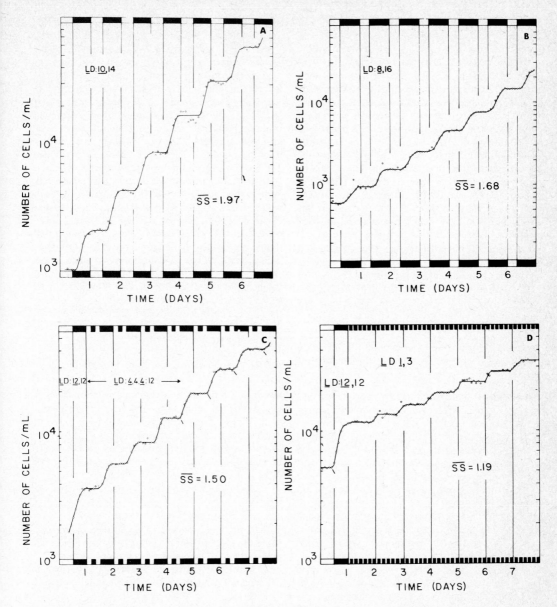

FIG. 4. Patterns of entrained cell division in *Euglena gracilis* grown on various photocycles. The average step size ($\overline{ss}$) is the relative increase in the number of cells during each 24-h period. In all photocycles shown, the period length of the division rhythm is 24 h. (Adapted from Edmunds 1978; see also Table 2.)

in a doubling of cell numbers (step size = 1.97). The distribution of generation times reflected by the duration of the division burst is consistent with the distribution of generation times observed in exponentially growing cultures under optimal conditions (Cook and Cook 1962).

If the photoperiod is shortened to L:D 8:16 (Fig. 4b) cell division in the population becomes phased so that division is still restricted to the division gate (6–10 h) but all the cells do not divide every 24 h (step size = 1.68). Here, the doubling time of the population is 36 h as is the average generation time of the cells. Because of the restriction imposed by the division gate, however, the generation times of individual cells must be discontinuously distributed with modes at 24 and 48 h (Edmunds 1978). This type of population response is suggestive of clock-controlled phasing.

Lengthening the photoperiod beyond 10 h does not significantly affect the synchrony in the population, provided light intensities are reduced for the longer photoperiods (Table 2). Note that L:D 10:14 and 12:12 (8000 lx) and L:D 14:10 and 16:8 (3500 lx) yield approximately the same synchrony patterns, with step sizes close to 2 and the onset of division beginning between 11 and 14 h after the onset of the light period. If photoperiod is lengthened beyond 12 h (e.g. L:D 14:10, 16:8, 18:10) while maintaining high light intensities (8000 lx), the step size increases above 2 indicating that some cells are dividing twice during each division burst (Edmunds and Funch 1969b). Although the division gate is apparently preserved to some extent in this ultradian growth mode, there is a tendency towards asynchrony, which becomes complete in LL.

Continuous illumination during the photoperiod is not essential to maintain the phasing of cell division in *Euglena* (Fig. 4c, d). When the photoperiod of an L:D 12:12 regime is interrupted by 4 (Fig. 4c) or 6 (L:D 3,6,3:12) h of darkness, gated cell division continues, although the step size is reduced because of the reduced energy input (Table 2).

All light/dark regimes discussed thus far have resulted in synchronized or phased division patterns that have period lengths equal to that of the entraining cycle, i. e. 24 h. To reveal the free-running period of the putative clock mechanism, many light regimes may be employed. The most straightforward demonstration that the cell cycle in *Euglena* can be coupled to an endogenous clock is to entrain the population to L:D 12:12 and then place it in continuous dim (800 lx) light (Edmunds 1966). Under such conditions rhythmic cell division will persist for at least 10 d (for weeks in continuous culture) with a period length between bursts of 24.2 h, and a step size of about 1.17 (Fig. 5a). Although the average individual cell cycle in this experiment has a duration of 134 h, a population rhythmicity is expressed with a period length of 24.2 h, reflecting the gated division time.

Various "exotic" (Edmunds 1974) photocycles also reveal the underlying clock mechanism. High-frequency light/dark cycles with periods that are integral submultiples of 24 h all invoke free-running cell division patterns with period lengths ranging from 24 to 30 h and step sizes ranging from 1.20 to 1.68 (Table 2; Fig. 4d). It should be noted that populations taken from continuous bright light (7500 lx) and placed in similar high-frequency light/dark cycles will express the same rhythmicity as those taken from L:D 12:12; thus prior entrainment to a 24-h period is not necessary for the free-running rhythm to be expressed.

Light/dark regimes of somewhat longer period lengths that are not integral submultiples of 24 h (with an L:D ratio of 1) invoke a variety of responses in the division rhythm (Table 2). On L:D 10:10, the populations entrain directly to the 20-h period length of the light/dark cycle. This appears to be the lower limit of entrainment for this organism as further reduction of the entraining period to L:D 8:8 results in an uncoupled division rhythm with an average period length of 33 h. The fact that this period length is about twice the duration of the entraining cycle suggests that "frequency demultiplication" has occurred. Curiously enough, all attempts to entrain *Euglena* to L:D 6:6 have failed (Edmunds and Funch 1969b). On this regime, the population ignores the L:D cycle completely and increases exponentially with a generation time of 28 h. Higher frequency cycles (L:D 5:5 and 4:4) result in long period division bursts with step sizes greater than 2 (Table 2). The pattern on L:D 4:4 is particularly interesting in that the period lengths are reportedly cyclical (Edmunds and Funch 1969b). Duplicate experiments have shown successive periods of 28, 38, 40, and 32 h in one culture and 30, 36, 40, and 30 h in another. This behavior, in conjunction with step sizes greater than 2, could be interpreted as rhythmicity in ultradian growth mode, and is reminiscent of patterns seen in marine diatoms (see below).

The ultimate "exotic" light/dark cycle employed by Edmunds and Funch (1969a, b) was a "random" one, in which (i) the total duration of light was 8 h per 24 h, (ii) the total duration of darkness during that inerval was 16 h, and (iii) the lengths of the light periods were between 0.25 and 1.0 h, and the dark periods between 0.5 and 1.5 h. The division pattern resulting from this regime appears to be truly "free-running" with an average period length of 27.5 h and step size of 1.67 (Fig. 5b).

Various low-frequency light/dark regimes have also been employed to examine the mechanism of synchronization in *Euglena* (Edmunds 1971). When grown on L:D 12:24 or L:D 12:36, the cells directly entrain to the period of the light/dark cycle (Table 2). Step sizes of 2 are not achieved (even though 12 h light should be sufficient) presumably because of the metabolic "tax" imposed during the extended dark period.

It is somewhat puzzling that the step sizes resulting from the various photoperiods show little relationship to the total amount of light seen by the cells during each 24-h period (Table 2). Note, for example, that even though L:D 1/4:1/2 and 1/2:1 both receive the equivalent of an 8:16 photocycle, the step sizes are dramatically different. Similarly, cells on L:D 1:3 and 2:6 receive 6 h of light per 24 h yet the population receiving 2-h "parcels" of light seems to grow more efficiently. In fact this population grows faster than one maintained on L:D 1/2:1 which receives 2-h more of light per 24-h period (Table 2). In contrast, the "random" regime,

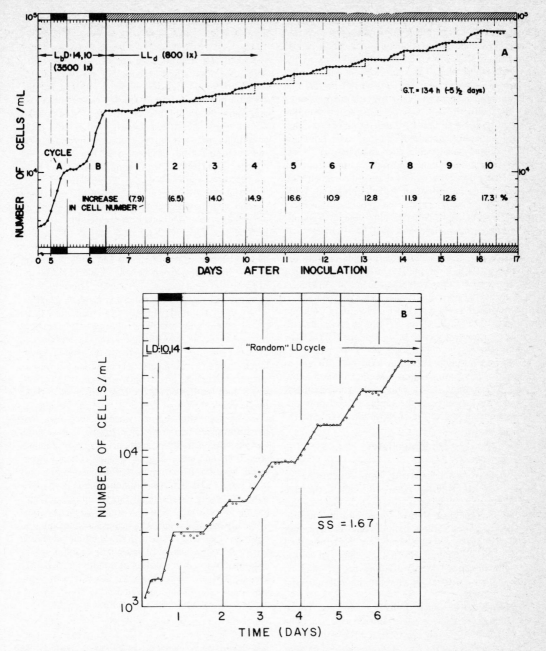

FIG. 5. Free-running, clock-coupled, cell division rhythms in *Euglena gracilis*. (A) In continuous dim light, the average period length is 24.0 h, step sizes are extremely small, and the average generation time is 5.5 d. (B) On a "random" light/dark cycle the rhythm has a period length of 27.5 h and an average step size of 1.67. (Adapted from Edmunds 1978.)

L:D 1/4:1/2, and L:D 8:16, all with the same amount of light and dark per 24 h, yielded identical step sizes (albeit different period lengths). Precisely why cells can "process" certain light/dark regimes more efficiently than others is not at all clear.

The data presented thus far for autotrophically grown *Euglena* strongly support the contention that the mechanism of synchronization in this species must involve an endogenous clock that restricts cell division to a certain "gate" in the entraining cycle.

It would be difficult to invoke light- or dark-inhibited cell cycle block points (see Spudich and Sager 1980 and the section on green algae below) to explain all the observed patterns, particularly the free-running rhythm. The interpretation of these types of results, however, is complicated by the fact that the entraining agent (light) is also an energy source for the cells. In this regard, it is significant that various mutant strains of *Euglena* that are either photosyntheticly impaired (Jarrett and Edmunds 1970) or permanently bleached (Mitchell 1971) behave very similarly to the autotrophic strains. Furthermore, these mutants provide a dramatic demonstration of the Circadian-Infradian Rule (Ehret and Wille 1970). When the P_4 Zul mutant (blocked in the electron transport chain between photosystem I and II) is grown in organic medium on L:D 10:14 at 25°C it grows exponentially with a generation time of 10 h, clearly in ultradian growth mode (Jarrett and Edmunds 1970). If one then lowers the growth temperature to 19°C, thus reducing the mean generation time to 24 h, the culture becomes synchronized to the light/dark cycle with a period length of 24 h and a step size of 1.96. The rhythm in division will persist for several weeks in continuous darkness or continuous bright light (9000 lx) (Edmunds et al. 1971) and a single L:D transition is sufficient to entrain an exponential culture and elicit a free-running rhythm (Edmunds 1974). This is a clear demonstration of clock control of the timing of cell division, and an uncoupling of the clock in ultradian growth.

Dinoflagellates

Because of the inherently slow growth rates of dinoflagellates and the ease with which division stages can be recognized, division rhythms in this group are usually examined by monitoring the frequency of paired cells or paired nuclei in light/dark phased cultures. Strict phasing has been observed in all species examined. That is, there is always an interval during which dividing cells cannot be detected or there is no increase in cell numbers (Table 3).

The time at which division occurs relative to the light/dark cycle varies between species. The most common trend, documented in cultures of *Gonyaulax polyedra*, *G. sphaeroidea*, *Ceratium furca*, *Cachonina niei*, and *Prorocentrum* sp., is maximum division frequencies appearing near the dark to light transition (Table 3). In several species, however, the division process spans the dark period (*Amphidinium carteri*, *Gymnodinium splendens*, and *Scrippsiella trochoidea*), or begins in the middle of the light period and is completed by the onset of darkness (*Scrippsiella sweeneyi* and *Prorocentrum micans*).

The rhythm in cell division in *G. polyedra* is known to be endogenous (Sweeney and Hastings 1958). As mentioned above, cell division in this species is restricted to a 5-h period during the light/dark transition. When an entrained culture is transferred to continuous bright light (10 000 lx) the division phasing is lost within 4–6 d. In continuous dim light (1000 lx), however, division in the population remains phased for at least 14 d. Under these conditions, the interval between division bursts (the free-running period) is close to 24 h, and does not change significantly with temperature (i.e. it is temperature compensated).

The only dinoflagellate species that has been studied systematically with regard to division timing on different photoperiods and temperature regimes is *Ceratium furca* (Weiler and Eppley 1979). The timing of the onset of division seems to be independent of temperature (on L:D 12:12) and photoperiod (at 20°C), and always occurs between 9 and 11 h after the beginning of the dark period (Table 3). This is in direct contrast with the division pattern in *Euglena gracilis*, where the onset of division seems to maintain a fixed phase relationship relative to the onset of the light period (see Table 2). Although there is good evidence that in *Ceratium*, as in *Euglena*, division is under clock control (Meeson personal communication), it is clear that the phase angles between the clock, the cell cycle, and the light/dark cycle are different in these two species.

It is of extreme importance to recognize that the differences in the division timing between the various species could be influenced by experimental conditions and what stage of division is being monitored. Meeson, for example, has shown that in *Ceratium furca*, although the duration of the "early division" stages are independent of temperature and light, the duration of the "late division" stages are not. The early division stage, which consists of the interval between the time at which the oblique cleavage furrow becomes visible to the middle of cytokinesis, lasts for about 2 h regardless of conditions, whereas the late division stage, from the last stages of cytokinesis to cell separation, can last 12 h on a light/dark cycle and up to 48 h in continuous light.

Green Algae

CHLORELLA

Studies of cell synchrony and the cell cycle of *Chlorella* have been dominated over the years by Japanese and German researchers (e.g. Tamiya et al. 1953; Lorenzen 1957; Pirson and Lorenzen 1958). Extensive reviews have been written on the subject (Tamiya 1964; John et al. 1973; Schmidt 1966) and

TABLE 3. Division patterns of *Dinoflagellate* species cultured on light/dark cycles. The intervals during which division was occurring (subjectively determined) are indicated with an x. Each x is 1 h and the blackened interval represents the dark period of a 24-h light/dark cycle.

Species	Reference	Temp., °C	Light intensity	Variable measured	Division pattern
Amphidinium carteri (Amphi)	Chisholm and Brand 1980	16	$40\ \mu E \cdot m^{-2} \cdot s^{-1}$	cell no.	xxxxxxxxxxxx
Gymnodinium splendens	Hastings and Sweeney 1964	—	—	% paired	xxxxxxxxxxxx
Scrippsiella trochoida (Peri)	Nelson and Brand 1979	20	$5 \times 10^{-2}\ ly \cdot min^{-1}$	cell no.	xxxxxxxxxx
Scrippsiella sweeneyi	Sweeney and Hastings 1964		—	cell no.	xxxx
Prorocentrum micans	Hastings and Sweeney 1964	—	—	% paired	xxxxxxxxxx
Gonyaulax polyedra	Sweeney and Hastings 1958	20	1400 ft can.	cell no.	xxxxxx
				% paired	xx ... xxxx
	Sweeney and Hastings 1964	—		cell no.	xx ... xxxxxx
				% paired	xxxxxx
Gonyaulax sphaeroidia	Hastings and Sweeney 1964	—	—	% paired	xxxxx ... xxxxx
Cachonina niei	Loeblich 1977	24	1000 ft can.	cell no.	xxxx
Prorocentrum sp. (Exuv)	Chisholm and Brand 1980	16	$40\ \mu E \cdot m^{-2} \cdot s^{-2}$	cell no.	xxxxxx ... xxxxx
Ceratium furca	Weiler and Eppley 1979	15	$3 \times 10^{16}\ quanta \cdot cm^{-2} \cdot s^{-1}$	% paired[a]	xxxx ... xx
		10	$3 \times 10^{16}\ quanta \cdot cm^{-2} \cdot s^{-1}$		xx ... xx
		25	$3 \times 10^{16}\ quanta \cdot cm^{-2} \cdot s^{-1}$		x ... xx
		20	$3 \times 10^{16}\ quanta \cdot cm^{-2} \cdot s^{-1}$		xxx
		20	$3 \times 10^{16}\ quanta \cdot cm^{-2} \cdot s^{-1}$		x ... xxx
		20	$3 \times 10^{16}\ quanta \cdot cm^{-2} \cdot s^{-1}$		xx ... xx
		20	$3 \times 10^{16}\ quanta \cdot cm^{-2} \cdot s^{-1}$		xxxx
		20	$3 \times 10^{16}\ quanta \cdot cm^{-2} \cdot s^{-1}$		xxx

[a] Reflects interval when division frequency was $\geq 1/2$ maximal.

many reviews of synchrony in algae in general are dominated by examples from the *Chlorella* literature (e.g. Tamiya 1966; Lorenzen 1970; Pirson and Lorenzen 1966). Given these extensive reviews, my purpose here is simply to examine certain aspects of the synchrony in *Chlorella* as they relate to and compare with those of other key species analyzed thus far.

The approach of the Tamiya school (see e.g. Tamiya 1964; Morimura 1959; Hase et al. 1957) has been to dissect the cell cycle by classifying the various stages according to their responsiveness to illumination or darkness after certain preconditioning. They have relied extensively on selection synchrony for this dissection. The detailed description of the cell cycle that has resulted from their work is structured around a distinction between two types of cells: dark cells (D) and light cells (L) (Fig. 6). The former are small, highly pigmented cells with relatively high quantum efficiency of photosynthesis and low respiratory activity, which turn into light cells when illuminated. These light cells in turn ripen and ultimately divide into a number of autospores, which become dark cells.

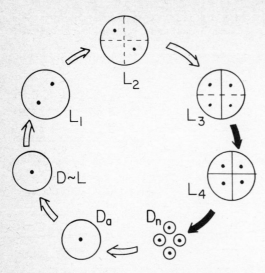

FIG. 6. The *Chlorella* cell cycle. The cycle begins with "nascent dark cells" (D_n) which become "active dark cells" (D_a) when illuminated, and the growth stage (D_n to L_2) is initiated. D ~ L marks the transition to the "ripening" stage. "Unripened light cells" (L_1) are large but cannot divide when placed in the dark; ripened light cells (L_3) can divide completely when placed in the dark; and L_4 cells are just about to divide. The dark arrows indicate those transitions that do not require light. (After Tamiya et al. 1961.)

The division process is not only independent of light in *Chlorella* but is actually retarded by it. If a L:D synchronized culture is released into continuous light, the division burst that would have occurred takes 8–9 h in the light rather than the usual 3- to 4-h span observed in the dark (Sorokin and Krauss 1959). Thus, in cultures grown in continuous light, D_n cells (see Fig. 6) do not emerge from the mother cells as such, but remain inside the mother cell and emerge as D_a or D ~ L cells at some later time (Morimura 1959). Although the growth process continues while the D cells are inside the mother cell, it seems likely that the growth efficiency is not the same as that of illuminated D_n cells. This explains the higher growth rates obtained in light/dark synchronized cultures (Sorokin and Krauss 1959).

According to Morimura (1959) the time required for the growth and ripening stages of the cell cycle (Fig. 6) are independent of light intensity, but dependent on temperature at saturating light intensities. In contrast, the number of autospores produced is independent of temperature but increases with increasing light intensity. In other words, the cells respond to reduced light intensities by producing fewer daughter cells at the same rate, whereas they respond to lowered temperatures by extending the growth and ripening periods appropriately to produce

the same number of daughter cells at the various temperatures. The latter response is not what we would expect for a clock-controlled species but it must be stressed that these experiments were done by monitoring the synchronous development of D_a cells isolated by fractional centrifugation. The population was not entrained by a light/dark cycle.

The results of the German workers, who tended to use programmed light/dark cycles to induce synchronous division, show characteristics that are in keeping with a clock-coupled mechanism for phasing. As early as 1957, Lorenzen noted that when *Chlorella pyrenoidosa* was grown on various light/dark cycles, the onset of division appeared to occur a fixed number of hours (16–20) after the onset of the light period, regardless of the L:D regime (Table 4). Pirson and Lorenzen (1958) extended this observation to include changes in temperature and light intensity as well as photoperiod, and noted again that although growth rate (Schub number) was dependent on these environmental parameters the onset of division was always gated to occur 20 h after the onset of the light period. These authors suggested at the time that the onset of the light period acted as a Zeitgeber to some "endogenous machinery" (Tamiya 1964). Subsequently, Hesse (1971) has shown conclusively that the cell cycle in *Chlorella* can be clock controlled.

CHLAMYDOMONAS

There are many similarities between *Chlamydomonas* and *Chlorella* in terms of their responses to light/dark regimes. *Chlamydomonas* exhibits some of the tightest synchrony patterns observed for unicellular algae. Zoospore production is restricted to a 2-h gate at the end of the dark period (Bernstein 1960, 1964) on both L:D 12:12 and 10:14 (Mihara and Hase 1971). Thus, this genus is ideal for cell cycle studies, and the conditions for optimizing synchrony of all cell cycle parameters have been extensively examined (Lien and Knutsen 1979).

Mihara and Hase (1971) have shown that when *Chlamydomonas reinhardtii* (IAM C-9) is grown on L:D 12:12 and released into continuous bright light (5000 lx), the liberation of zoospores occurs at the same time as in the light/dark cycle, although other cellular events such as nuclear and chloroplast division, and cytokinesis tend to lose synchrony (see also Bruce 1970). During the second cycle of continuous light zoospore liberation begins earlier than usual and synchrony begins to deteriorate. These authors have shown that zoospore liberation is timed relative to the beginning of the light period, and that dim light (700 lx) is not sufficient to set the timing. Furthermore, as in *Chlorella* (Morimura 1959), the timing of zoospore liberation is not affected by light intensity on L:D 12:12 (although the number of zoospores is) but is quite delayed at reduced tempe-

TABLE 4. The timing of cell division in *Chlorella pyrenoidosa* grown on various light/dark cycles, at 22°C and 6000 lx. Intervals when division was occurring are marked with an x; darkness is indicated by a solid bar. (From Lorenzen 1957.)

L:D

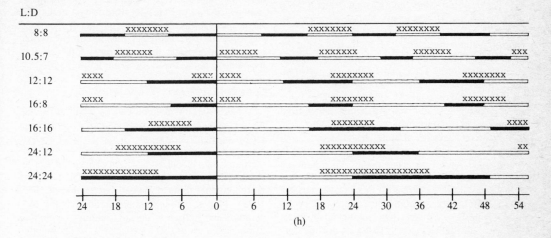

ratures in LL. The temperature effect on the timing of zoospore liberation in cells grown on L:D 12:12, however, is minor, with a 2-h shift in timing between 25 and 30°C. It is noteworthy that the development and release of zoospores in *Chlamydomonas* is not inhibited (or delayed) by light as is reportedly the case for *Chlorella* (Sorokin and Krauss 1959).

In direct contrast with the results of Mihara and Hase (1971), Bruce (1970) has shown that the rhythm in zoospore release in *C. reinhardtii* does persist for at least 14 d in continuous light, strongly suggesting that the timing of zoospore release is regulated by clock coupling. Bruce used a different strain (RS strain) of this species and used a continuous culture apparatus rather than the daily dilution technique of Mihara and Hase (1971). Temperatures and light intensities used in the two studies were comparable, but the growth rates of the cultures in Bruce's experiments were much slower (mean population doubling times of 30–44 h vs. 12 h for Mihara and Hase). These slow growth rates were attributed to light limitation because of self-shading, but the cell densities in Bruce's experiments were of the same order of magnitude as those reported by Mihara and Hase. Whatever the reason for the slower growth rates in Bruce's experiments, the evidence is strong for endogenous control and it is tempting to argue that the infradian growth mode promoted the expression of the circadian rhythm in zoospore release. Whether or not the growth rates in Mihara and Hase's experiments can be called ultradian, however, is not clear, as distinction may not be appropriate for cells that divide into more than two daughter cells. This whole issue needs clarification.

We are left then with two conflicting views of the mechanism of synchronization in *Chlamydomonas*, which have been recently recast by Spudich and Sager (1980). The first view maintains that the synchrony results from light/dark cycles driving the cell cycle, i.e. from dark or light inhibition of certain metabolic steps (Bernstein 1964). The second view proposes that the cell cycle is clock coupled and entrained by the light/dark cycle (Bruce 1970). Spudich and Sager (1980) have identified two transition points in the *Chlamydomonas* cell cycle (not unlike the D and L cell transition in *Chlorella*), which they believe explain synchronization and thus support the first hypothesis. Both of these points are in G_1. At the primary arrest point A, the progression of the cell cycle becomes light dependent until the second point, T, is reached and the completion of the cycle becomes independent of light. If exponentially growing populations of cells are placed in the dark (or subjected to the photosystem II inhibitor DCMU) before they reach point T, they remain viable but do not progress through their cycles. Under the condition of the experiments, 6 h of light exposure is required for the cell to progress from A to T. Regardless of how long cells are arrested between A and T by a dark block (at least to 48 h), the cells always take the same amount of time in the light to complete division. Thus, the cells are all blocked at the same point and are not cycling in the dark. Although cells in dark arrest are viable and metabolically active, they do not mobilize available carbohydrate reserves to provide energy to complete the cycle. These reserves are not utilized until after the cycle passes the transition point, T.

163

At this time endogenous respiration shows a sharp increase, presumably to provide the energy necessary to progress through the cell division cycle from T to A.

The results of the Spudich and Sager (1980) study show that if one grows *Chlamydomonas* on L:D 6:12 or on L:D 6:48 one gets exactly the same division pattern. As shown in Table 2, this is not the case for *Euglena*. When the minimum light requirement for division is 12 h, and *Euglena* is grown on L:D 12:12, 12:34, 12:36, the step size is smaller for the extended dark periods (Edmunds 1971; Table 2), suggesting that reserves are being metabolized for maintenance requirements.

Clearly, the results of Spudich and Sager (1980) are consistent with a synchronization mechanism that operates via a dark arrest point. When exposed to darkness, all cells between A and T do not progress through their cycle, whereas all those that are past T progress to A. Thus, within a few light/dark cycles the cell cycles of all cells will be aligned in phase with the light/dark cycle. Whether or not the data are inconsistent with a clock-entrained model, however, is not clear. The clock can be reset on exposure to bright light after periods of darkness (see Aschoff 1965; Palmer 1976); thus, the apparent noncycling in the dark followed by simultaneous division in the light in *Chlamydomonas* is not problematical. The equivalent actions of darkness and DCMU, however, are more difficult to explain in the context of a clock-controlled model. Spudich and Sager (1980) offer an interesting discussion of the alternative hypotheses regarding mechanisms of synchrony, and conclude that light/dark synchrony of both photosynthetic and nonphotosynthetic algae (e.g. photosynthetic mutants of *Euglena*) results from forced periodicity in the availability of high-energy metabolites from electron transport. Whether this proximate mechanism would exclude the possibility of the ultimate mechanism being the clock is not entirely clear.

SCENEDESMUS AND DUNALIELLA

Fairly tight synchrony can be achieved in cultures of *Scenedesmus obliquus* and *S. quadricauda* grown on light/dark cycles (Table 5), with division restricted to a short interval in the dark period. Furthermore, in a pleomorphic strain of *S. quadricauda*, photoperiod is a significant determinant of the morphological form of the cells (Steenbergen 1975, 1978). Under the appropriate conditions of temperature and nutrients, unicell-yielding populations can be achieved in L:D 14:10, but if the photoperiod is shortened (e.g. L:D 3:21) the coenobial morph predominates.

Unlike other green algae, division in L:D synchronized *Dunaliella tertiolecta* does not appear to be totally restricted to the dark period and the division gate can be fairly broad, especially for short and long photoperiods (Table 5). The synchrony can be enhanced somewhat and shifted to later in the dark

TABLE 5. Patterns of cell division in various species of green algae grown on light/dark cycles. The interval where division occurs is marked by x; the dark period is indicated by the solid bar. Total interval is 24 h and each x represents 1 h.

Species	Reference	Temp., °C	Light	Division pattern
Scenedesmus obliquus	Lafeber and Steenbergen 1967	30	~15 000 lx	xxxx
Scenedesmus quadricauda	Komárek and Simmer 1965	—	—	xxxx
Dunaliella tertiolecta	Eppley and Coatsworth 1966	20	0.05 cal·cm⁻²·min⁻¹	xxxxxxxxxx
	Eppley and Coatsworth 1966	20	0.05 cal·cm⁻²·min⁻¹	xxxxxxxxxx
	Eppley and Coatsworth 1966	20	0.05 cal·cm⁻²·min⁻¹	xxxxxxxx
	Eppley and Coatsworth 1966	20	0.05 cal·cm⁻²·min⁻¹	xxxxxxxxxxxx
	Eppley and Coatsworth 1966	20	0.05 cal·cm⁻²·min⁻¹	xxxxxxxxxxxxxxxx
Dunaliella tertiolecta	Wegmann and Metzner 1971	40/20	8000 lx	xxxxxx
Chlamydomonas reinhardtii	Mihara and Hase 1971	25	5000 lx	xx
Chlamydomonas moewusii	Bernstein 1960	25	8000 lx	xx
Chlorella pyrenoidosa	Lorenzen 1957	22	6000 lx	xx ... xxxxx

period, if a temperature cycle (L:D 40°C:20°C) is superimposed on the L:D cycle (Wegmann and Metzner 1971). This is attributed to the fact that the temperature optimum for photosynthesis is 35°C in this species whereas the optimum for growth (increase in population cell number) is 20°C. Cell division will not occur at 40°C.

Other Taxonomic Groups

An overview of the division patterns in all other groups of phytoplankton that have been studied (Table 6) reveals quite clearly that there is a preference for nighttime division. The exception in this group is *Platymonas striata*, but the timing of division (as determined by the time course of cell numbers) in this species is misleading in regard to the timing of cytokinesis (Ricketts 1979). It appears that after the formation of daughter cells inside the parental theca, which normally occurs in the light period, there must be a maturation period of about 6 h before they can be released. The escape of the daughter cells from the theca is triggered by light; thus tight synchrony results in which increases in cell number occur early in the light period. Only under conditions of low temperature, or high growth rates induced by long photoperiods, are any of the daughter cells released in the dark (Table 6).

Of the group of species presented in Table 6, only *Emeliania huxleyi* has been systematically studied in terms of its response to photoperiod (Paasche 1967). Although it is difficult to separate the effects of the variable light intensities, it appears that the timing of division is determined primarily by the onset of the previous photoperiod, which is similar to the case for *Euglena*, but opposite to the pattern for *Ceratium* (see Weiler and Eppley 1979 and discussions above). A more distinctive trend is the fact that the degree of synchrony is not strongly influenced by photoperiod and/or light intensity and tends to be tightest in the populations grown under long photoperiods of low light intensity. As Paasche (1967) recognized, this is different from the case for diatoms, where short photoperiods of high light intensity significantly enhance the synchrony.

It is somewhat difficult to address the question of growth rates for this group of species, because the data are not easily extracted from some of the studies. Paasche's data for *E. huxleyi* are all for populations doubling once per day, and the species examined by Chisholm and Brand (1980) were all in infradian growth (generation times ≥ 1 d). As far as can be deduced from the Nelson and Brand (1979) data, those species were also doubling close to once per day. In clear cases of ultradian growth, such as *P. striata* grown under long photoperiods, multiple division bursts can be seen. We have observed a similar phenomenon for *Hymenomonas carterae* grown in a cyclostat at 20°C on L:D 14:10 (Chisholm and Costello 1980). At an average population growth rate of 1.5 doublings/d there is a major division burst at the beginning of the dark period, followed by a second peak at the dark/light transition. It is logical and necessary that such patterns should emerge under conditions of rapid growth, and it is interesting that they have never been systematically studied in terms of the distribution of generation times in the population and in the context of cell cycle phasing. This is undoubtedly because most research on algae grown on light/dark cycles has been directed towards achieving and understanding the mechanisms of synchrony, rather than understanding how populations respond to a 24-h light/dark cycle in general. A mix of goals and approaches would be helpful here.

Cyanobacteria

The cyanobacterium *Anacystis nidulans* has been synchronized and studied intensively using a variety of induction synchrony methods such as L_{bright}: L_{dim}:D 2.5:0.5:5 and alternating temperature cycles (26°C:32°C, 8:6 h) (Herdman et al. 1970; Lorenzen and Kaushik 1976; Venkataraman and Lorenzen 1969; Csatorday and Horvath 1977; Lorenzen and Venkataraman 1969), but the division patterns of cyanobacteria have rarely been examined on 24-h photocycles. In search of circadian rhythmicity in prokaryotic organisms, Taylor (1979) grew several species of cyanobacteria on L:D 12:12 at 20°C, which produced infradian growth rates. Unfortunately, however, he did not measure cell number, but rather optical density of the cultures; thus division timing cannot be deduced from these data. Taylor concluded from a variety of measurements, however, that there was no evidence of a circadian clock in the species he examined.

Recently, S. Lohrenz (unpublished data) monitored the cell division patterns in the marine cyanobacterium *Synecococcus* sp., grown in a cyclostat in infradian growth mode. Although the patterns are not clear-cut, peak division rates appear to occur in the light period reaching a maximum towards the end and declining during the dark period (Fig. 7). The impression one gets (with little justification) is that the observed pattern reflects a cessation of population growth in the dark rather than a phasing of cell cycles. The increase in optical density in the late dark period, however, is difficult to explain, as are the negative division rates (cell death?) that occur regularly each day. This latter phenomenon appears to be a common occurrence in light/dark grown cultures of nondiatoms. Chisholm and Costello (1980) have seen similar "negative" division rates in cyclostat-grown cultures of *Hymenomonas carterae*, and Shifrin (personal communication) observed them in the fresh-

TABLE 6. Division patterns of various species of phytoplankton cultured on light/dark cycles. The intervals during which division was occurring (subjectively determined) are indicated with an x. Each x is 1 h and the blackened interval represents the dark period of a 24-h light/dark cycle.

Species	Clone	Reference	Temp., °C	Light intensity	Division pattern
Emeliania huxleyi (ex-Coccolithus huxleyi) (Haptophyceae)		Paasche 1967	21	0.07 cal·cm^{-2}·min^{-1}	xxxxxxxx
			21	0.028 cal·cm^{-2}·min^{-1}	xxxxxxxxx
			21	0.015 cal·cm^{-2}·min^{-1}	xxxxxxxx
			21	0.011 cal·cm^{-2}·min^{-1}	xxxxxx
Emeliania huxleyi (ex-Coccolithus huxleyi) (Haptophyceae)	BT6	Nelson and Brand 1979	20	5×10^{-2} ly·min^{-1}	xxxxx xxxxxxxxx
	G4	Nelson and Brand 1979	20	5×10^{-2} ly·min^{-1}	xxxxxx xxxxxxxxxx
	92A	Nelson and Brand 1979	20	5×10^{-2} ly·min^{-1}	xxxxxx xxxxxxxxxx
	WHA	Nelson and Brand 1979	20	5×10^{-2} ly·min^{-1}	xxxx xxxxxxxxxx
	MCH	Nelson and Brand 1979	20	5×10^{-2} ly·min^{-1}	xxxx xxxxxxxxxx
	MCH	Chisholm and Brand 1980	16	40 μE·m^{-2}·s^{-1}	xxxx xxxxxxxxxx
	451B	Nelson and Brand 1979	20	5×10^{-2} ly·min^{-1}	xx xxxxxxxxxx
	451B	Chisholm and Brand 1980	16	40 μE·m^{-2}·s^{-1}	xx xxxxxxxxxx
Hymenomonas carterae (Haptophyceae)	CoccoII	Nelson and Brand 1979	20	5×10^{-2} ly·min^{-1}	xxxxxxxxxx
		Chisholm and Brand 1980	16	40 μE·m^{-2}·s^{-1}	xxxxxxxxxx
Prymesium parvum (Haptophyceae)	Prym	Chisholm and Brand 1980	16	40 μE·m^{-2}·s^{-1}	xxxxxxxxxx
Chroomonas salina (Cryptophyceae)	3C	Nelson and Brand 1979	20	5×10^{-2} ly·min^{-1}	xxxxxxxxxx
Isochrysis galbana (Chrysophyceae)	Iso	Nelson and Brand 1979	20	5×10^{-2} ly·min^{-1}	xxxxx xxxxxxxxxx
Pavlova lutheri (ex-Monochrysis lutheri) (Chrysophyceae)	Mono	Nelson and Brand 1979	20	5×10^{-2} ly·min^{-1}	xxxx xxxxxxxxxx
Olisthodiscus sp. (Xanthophyceae)	Olistho	Chisholm and Brand 1980	16	40 μE·m^{-2}·s^{-1}	xxxxxxx xxxx
Pyramimonas sp. (Prasinophyceae)	Pyr-1	Chisholm and Brand 1980	16	40 μE·m^{-2}·s^{-1}	xx xxxxxxxxxx
Platymonas striata (Prasinophyceae)		Ricketts 1979	20	6500 lx	xxxx
			25	6500 lx	xxxx
			15	6500 lx	xxxx xxxxxx
			20	6500 lx	xxxx xxxxxx
			20	6500 lx	xxxx xxxx

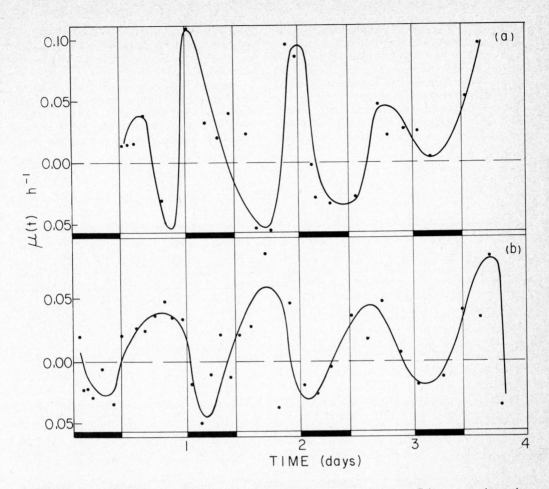

FIG. 7. Patterns of cell division in *Synecococcus sp.* grown on light/dark cycles in a cyclostat. Culture was nutrient replete and maintained at 16°C on L:D 14:10 with a light intensity of 70 $\mu E \cdot m^{-2} \cdot s^{-1}$ and a dilution rate of 0.02 h^{-1}. $\mu(t)$ was calculated directly from (a) cell density data and (b) measurements of absorption by the cell suspension at 750 nm. It is the rate of change of these parameters. (S. Lohrenz unpublished data.)

water green algae *Oocystis polymorpha*. In continuous cultures, these negative rates could reflect error in the dilution rate measurements, but the fact that Nelson and Brand (1979) observed the same thing in batch cultures of several species makes us doubt that this is the explanation. Thus, the decrease in cell number right before the onset of the division burst must either reflect cell death (and disintegration), or sticking of some cells to the walls of the container so samples collected underestimate the population density. We have been unable to find evidence to support either of these hypotheses; thus the phenomenon remains a mystery.

Diatoms

The patterns of cell division expressed by diatoms grown on light/dark cycles appear to be fundamentally different from those of other groups of phytoplankton. The arguments buttressing this view, as well as a thorough survey of the literature on phased division in diatoms, are presented in a recent paper (Chisholm et al. 1980) so only a brief history and the essence of the argument will be covered here.

Interest in growth patterns in diatoms on light/dark cycles began early (Rieth 1939; Braarud 1945; Subrahmayan 1945; von Denffer 1949). A series of papers 20 yr later began revealing that the responses of diatoms grown on light/dark cycles were not clear-cut. Palmer et al. (1964) reported that division occurred in the last half of the dark period in *Phaeodactylum tricornutum*, while Jorgensen (1966) observed the exact opposite pattern in *Skeletonema costatum*, and Glooschenko and Curl (1968) found no evidence of phasing at all in the latter species. Eppley et al. (1967), Paasche (1968), and Chisholm et al. (1978) found similar patterns in *Ditylum bright-wellii* with division occurring mainly in the light period, while Richman and Rogers (1969) found division to be restricted to the dark in this species. More recent evidence (Chisholm et al. 1980) confirms early suspicions that many of these differences were due to differences in the experimental temperatures or light intensities used in the various studies. *Ditylum*, for example, appears to divide primarily during the night at 15°C and during the day at 20°C (compare panels E and F in Fig. 9).

Recently, Nelson and Brand (1979) and Chisholm and Costello (1980) noted that several species of diatoms, when grown on L:D 14:10 or 12:12, exhibit division patterns characterized by multiple bursts in population division rate (μ_t) that appear

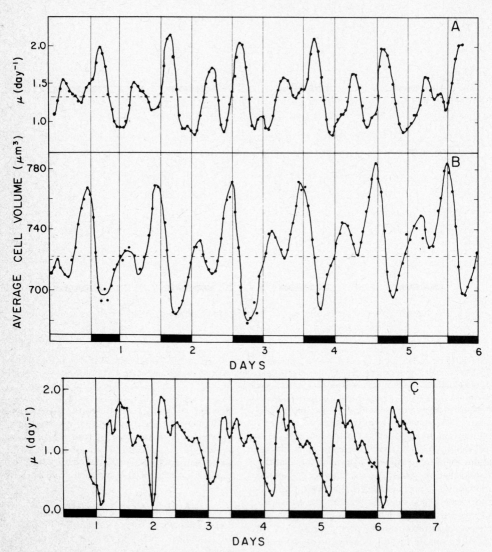

FIG. 8. Division patterns of *Thalassiosira weissflogii* grown in a cyclostat (data from Chisholm and Costello 1980). $\mu(t)$ was calculated from a smoothed function fitted to the cell density data and is the first derivative of that function. (A) Specific division rate $\mu(t)$ as a function of time for a culture grown on L:D 14:10, 190 $\mu E \cdot m^{-2} \cdot s^{-1}$, at 20°C at an average population growth rate of 1.31 d^{-1} (broken line). (B) Average cell volume (as determined with an electronic particle counter) as a function of time for the population in (A). Broken line indicates daily average cell volume. (C) Specific division rate as a function of time for a culture grown on L:D 10:14, 190 $\mu E \cdot m^{-2} \cdot s^{-1}$, at 20°C at an average population growth rate of 1.06 d^{-1}.

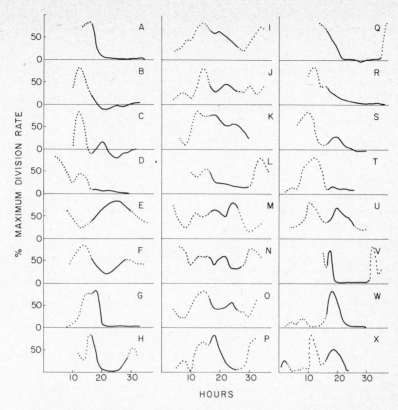

FIG. 9. Relative cell division patterns of various species of diatoms. When the data
were not in the form of $\mu(t)$, they were smoothed and converted using the formula of
Nelson and Brand (1979). All $\mu(t)$ patterns are normalized to the maximum division
rate per 24-h period. Solid lines indicate the dark period, and dotted lines indicate the
light period. Species names, experimental conditions, and references for each pattern
are given in Table 7.

to repeat themselves with a 24-h period length and
by division rates that are positive at all times throughout the light/dark cycle. A typical example of such
a pattern for *Thalassiosira weissflogii* (ex. *T. fluviatilis*) is shown in Fig. 8.

If we normalize and summarize all data on the
division patterns of diatoms (Fig. 9), we find that
patterns such as that displayed by *T. weissflogii* appear
to be the rule rather than the exception. The exceptions
(at least those in the minority) in Fig. 9 are in fact
those patterns which reflect what might be considered
"typical" synchrony patterns, i.e. containing an
interval where no change in cell numbers occurs
($\mu_t = 0$) and a single burst of division each day
(see panels A, B, C, G, Q, R, and V, Fig. 9). All
these cases except V (for which there were no data
points during the interval where $\mu_t = 0$) reflect
situations in which relatively short photoperiods of
high light intensity were used to synchronize the
cultures. It is noteworthy also that in our study of

the effects of environmental conditions on the division patterns in *T. weissflogii* (Chisholm and Costello
1980) the tightest degree of phasing was observed
on L:D 8:16, which was the shortest photoperiod
used. Based on these observations, it was proposed
that the cell cycle in diatoms is not entrained by or
phased to the light/dark cycle in the manner of most
other taxonomic groups (Chisholm et al. 1980). The
"synchrony" observed in some cases on short photoperiod light/dark cycles is analogous to silicon-
starvation synchrony (Lewin et al. 1966; Busby and
Lewin 1967; Coombs et al. 1967), and synchrony
induced by pulses of other nutrients. In such cases,
light is acting as a limiting resource which, when
supplied periodically, synchronizes (but does not
entrain) the cell division cycles of the population.

There is one flaw in the argument presented
above, and that is the question of ultradian vs. infradian growth modes. Many (if not most) of the growth
conditions used in the experiments in Fig. 9 promote

169

Panel	Species	Clone	L:D cycle	Temperature, °C	Light intensity	Reference
A	*Ditylum brightwellii*	Dit	8:16	20	0.032 cal·cm^{-2}·min^{-1}	Paasche 1968
B			4.5:19.5	20	0.120 cal·cm^{-2}·min^{-1}	
C			8:16	20	0.011 cal·cm^{-2}·min^{-1}	
D			14:10	20	0.015 cal·cm^{-2}·min^{-1}	
E			12:12	15	0.030 cal·cm^{-2}·min^{-1}	Chisholm et al. 1980
F			12:12	21	0.030 cal·cm^{-2}·min^{-1}	
G			8:16	20	0.050 cal·cm^{-2}·min^{-1}	Eppley et al. 1967
H			10:14	18	0.030 cal·cm^{-2}·min^{-1}	Chisholm et al. 1978
I	*Thalassiosira weissflogii*	SA	14:10	20	0.050 ly·min^{-1}	Nelson and Brand 1979
J		Actin	14:10	20	0.050 ly·min^{-1}	
K		Actin	10:14	20	190 μE·m^{-2}·s^{-1}	Chisholm and Costello 1980
L	*Thalassiosira pseudonana*	66A	10:14	20	0.030 cal·cm^{-2}·min^{-1}	Chisholm et al. 1978
M		13-1	14:10	20	0.050 ly·min^{-1}	Nelson and Brand 1979
N		W	14:10	20	0.050 ly·min^{-1}	Nelson and Brand 1979
O	*Phaeodactylum tricornutum*	Pet Pd	14:10	20	0.050 ly·min^{-1}	Nelson and Brand 1979
P	*Chaetoceros simplex*	Bbsm	14:10	20	0.050 ly·min^{-1}	Nelson and Brand 1979
Q	*Nitzschia turgidula*		5:19	20	0.069 cal·cm^{-2}·min^{-1}	Paasche 1968
R			8:16	20	0.022 cal·cm^{-2}·min^{-1}	
S			12:12	20	0.013 cal·cm^{-2}·min^{-1}	
T			16:8	20	0.009 cal·cm^{-2}·min^{-1}	
U	*Cyclotella cryptica*	WT-1-8	14:10	20	0.050 ly·min^{-1}	Nelson and Brand 1979
V	*Skeletonema costatum*		12:12	20	0.060 cal·cm^{-2}·min^{-1}	Jorgensen 1966
W	*Navicula ostrearea*		16:8	14	3500 lx	Neuville and Daste 1977
X	*Nitzschia palea*		12:12	?	118 μE·m^{-2}·s^{-1}	Hunding 1978

ultradian (generation times shorter than 1 d) growth. Thus, we should not expect to see entrainment in the classical sense. The question then becomes whether we would see entrainment of cell cycles if we forced the populations into infradian mode by some form of growth limitation. The answer (for one species at least) is no. When the growth rate of populations of *T. weissflogii* is reduced to less than one doubling per day by lowered temperatures or nutrient limitation, entrainment does not result (Fig. 10b, c). Moreover, the degree of phasing to the light/dark cycle (although difficult to quantify) appears to be weaker than in the ultradian case (compare with Fig. 10a). This is not characteristic of clock-coupled cell division, and can only be interpreted as a forced, rather than entrained, periodicity.

Nutrient-Limited Cyclostat Growth

Most of our understanding of nutrient-limited growth in phytoplankton is a result of continuously lit, steady-state chemostat cultures. Although many investigators have recognized the extremely unnatural nature of such systems (e.g. Jannasch 1974), the ease with which steady-state chemostats can be sampled and described mathematically usually overrides the logic of using light/dark cycles. Only in a few investigations (e.g. Eppley et al. 1971; Chisholm et al. 1975; Gotham 1977; Williams 1971; Malone et al. 1975; Chisholm and Costello 1980) have nutrient-limited growth and the phasing of cell cycles in phytoplankton been studied simultaneously, usually in cyclostat systems (Chisholm et al. 1975) that are (physically at least) nothing more than a chemostat on a light/dark cycle.

A complete mathematical description of the growth of phytoplankton cyclostats has been developed by Gotham (1977) and Frisch and Gotham (1977, 1978) and recently reviewed by Rhee et al. (1981). Unfortunately, the data base for the theory comes exclusively from *Euglena gracilis*, because this is the only species for which periodic components have been exhaustively studied in a cyclostat system. Caution must be exercised in generalizing from this

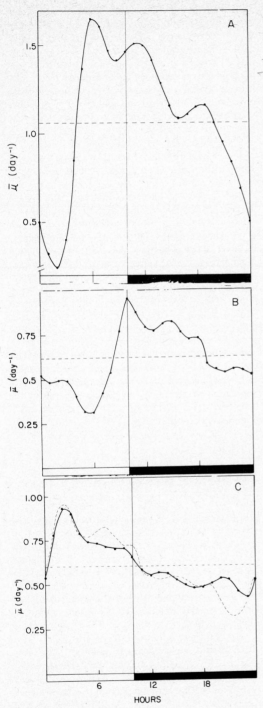

species in particular, because it is so tightly clock controlled.

The nutrient-limited growth of algae in a cyclostat can be described by a set of equations not unlike those developed for chemostats (Frisch and Gotham 1977, 1978; Rhee et al. 1981) except that they consider time dependency. When cells are grown on a 24-h light/dark cycle in such a system, only the period average of the derivatives of residual limiting nutrient concentration (S), cell number (X), nutrient uptake rate (V), and instantaneous division rate (μ) are independent of time such that:

$$\text{(1)} \qquad <\mu>_T = <VX>_T / <QX>_T =$$
$$<VX>_T / (S_o - <S>_T)$$

$$\text{(2)} \qquad <V>_T = <\mu Q>_T$$

where $<\ldots>_T = \dfrac{1}{T} \displaystyle\int_0^T \ldots \, dt$ (or period average), $T = 24$ h, Q is the amount of limiting nutrient per cell, and S_o is the influent concentration of the limiting nutrient.

From these equations:

$$\text{(3)} \qquad DT = \int_0^T \mu(t) \, dt$$

where DT is the integrated specific growth over the period, T, and is equivalent numerically to the dilution rate, D, of the cyclostat.

The relationship between nutrient cell quotas and growth rates is well established for chemostat-grown cultures (Droop 1973) and has been documented for average values in some cyclostat studies (Chisholm et al. 1975; Eppley et al. 1971). Gotham (1977) has shown that the period averaged growth rate in P-limited *Euglena gracilis* grown in a cyclostat is a function of the minimum cell quota per 24-h period (Q_c) for a given dilution rate:

$$\text{(4)} \qquad <\mu>_T = \frac{<\hat{\mu}_m>_T (Q_c - Q_{co})}{K_{qc} + (Q_c - Q_{co})}$$

where $Q_{co} = Q_c$ for $<\mu>_T = 0$, $<\hat{\mu}_m>$ is the theoretical maximum growth rate, and K_{qc} is a constant. An example of the temporal patterns be-

FIG. 10. Average division patterns of *Thalassiosira weissflogii* grown in a cyclostat under various conditions (data from Chisholm and Costello 1980). $\bar{\mu}(t)$ time courses were calculated as described in Fig. 8 and averaged for

several days. (A) Ultradian growth mode with nutrient-replete conditions at 20°C and an average growth rate of 1.06 d^{-1} (data are the average of those in Fig. 8C). (B) Infradian growth mode imposed by lowered temperature (15°C). Average population growth rate was 0.62 d^{-1} (0.89 doublings/d). (C) Infradian growth mode imposed by PO$_4^-$ limitation. Average growth rate was 0.61 d^{-1} (0.88 doublings/d). Broken function is the $\mu(t)$ pattern from (B), phase shifted by 8 h for comparison. (See Chisholm and Costello 1980.)

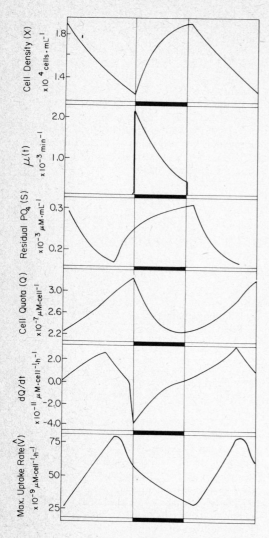

FIG. 11. Time courses of measured variables from PO_4^- limited *Euglena gracilis* grown in a cyclostat on L:D 14:10 with a dilution rate of 0.68 d^{-1}. X = cell density showing washout when there is no division and an increase when division is occurring. μ = the instantaneous division rate. Q = cell quota or the amount of P per cell. $\hat{V}$ = maximum capacity for P uptake at saturating concentrations of P. (Modified from Gotham 1977.)

tween $Q(t)$, $dQ/dt(t)$, $X(t)$, $\mu(t)$, $S(t)$, and $\hat{V}(t)$ for a given average growth rate are shown in Fig. 11. One hour after the beginning of the light period $Q(t) = Q_c$ and $\mu(t)$ is zero; $\mu(t)$ remains equal to zero throughout the light period because this is outside the division gate, but $Q(t)$ increases from minimum to a maximum value during this period.

At the beginning of the dark phase of the photocycle, $\mu(t)$ jumps dramatically to a peak as cell division begins and $Q(t)$ begins declining due to net loss to daughter cells. Plots of $\mu(t)$ as a function of $Q(t)$ for any given dilution rate (growth rate) in the cyclostat describe closed trajectories (Fig. 12). If the cyclostat were placed in continuous light these trajectories would spiral into a family of $\mu(Q)$ values that describe a Droop hyperbola (Droop 1973). The capacity of the cells to take up PO_4 also changes over the 24-h light/dark cycle (Fig. 11).

It should be clear from this analysis that for species like *Euglena*, the basic functional relationships derived from the period averages in the cyclostat do not deviate from our understanding of nutrient/growth relationships derived from chemostat studies (Rhee et al. 1980). The time courses of nutrient uptake, $Q(t)$ and $\mu(t)$, take on significance, however, when more than one species or fluctuation in the nutrient environment are considered. Although quantitative analyses have been done (Chisholm and Nobbs 1975; Frisch and Gotham 1978; Rhee et al. 1980), one needs only to ponder the problem in a qualitative sense to realize that consideration of only the daily averaged behavior of organisms cannot predict the results of a dynamic competitive interaction among species and between species and their environment. One can apply this same reasoning at the cellular level, i.e. the average behavior of a population of cells does not necessarily reflect the behavior of the individual cells that comprise that population (Chisholm et al. 1980).

Patterns of Division Observed in Situ

The first observations of synchronized mitosis in phytoplankton in situ were reported near the turn of the century (Gough 1905; Apstein 1911; Jorgensen 1911; Gran 1912) for the members of the genus *Ceratium*. Since that time, this genus and other dinoflagellates have been the object of numerous investigations into the phasing of phytoplankton cell division in situ because of the easily identified division stages.

In *Ceratium*, division stages are usually restricted to the late night–early morning hours (Elbrachter 1973; Doyle and Poore 1974; Heller 1977; Weiler and Chisholm 1976; Weiler and Eppley 1979; Weiler 1980) although dividing cells have been observed in midday (Lanskaya 1963; Pavlova and Lanskaya 1969). A typical pattern for this genus is shown in Fig. 13. Weiler (1980) found that the timing of maximum division frequency varied by only 2 h among 51 different *Ceratium* species in

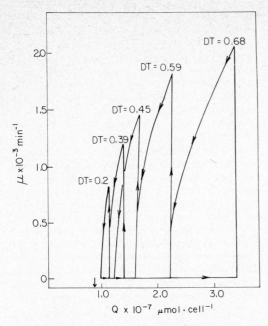

FIG. 12. Phase loop trajectories from experimental data for instantaneous growth rate, $\mu(t)$, as a function of phosphate quota, $Q(t)$ in *Euglena gracilis* grown in a cyclostat. Arrow marks the subsistence quota (below which no growth occurs). DT is the average specific growth rate of the culture (d^{-1}). (Redrawn from Gotham 1977.)

the central Pacific (photoperiods of 10.5–14.0 h), always occurring around 04:00. The timing and duration of division in the field populations agreed well with laboratory cultures grown under similar conditions (Weiler and Eppley 1979). The width of the division gate in this genus is apparently variable. Reported values range from 2 h (Doyle and Poore 1974) to about 12 h (Heller 1977), but are commonly on the order of 5–7 h (Weiler and Eppley 1979; Elbrachter 1973). The maximum proportion of cells observed dividing, which reflects the population growth rate (see below), has been found to range from 1 to 40% (Elbrachter 1973), but usually is between 10 and 20%.

The in situ division patterns of other dinoflagellates are not as well studied as those of *Ceratium*, but data exist for several species. Weiler and Eppley (1979) observed that in six species of *Ornithocercus* division frequency was maximal (14% dividing cells) at dawn, but dividing cells were observed throughout the 24-h period indicating a broad division gate. This contrasts with the data for *O. magnificus* reported by Doyle and Poore (1974) in which dividing cells (8% of the total) were observed only at 05:00. In the latter study, paired cells of *Peridinium* sp. were only observed at 03:00 and *Ceratocorys horrida*

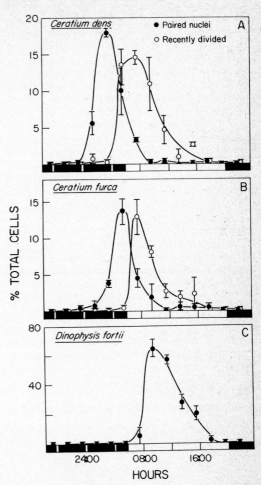

FIG. 13. The frequency of paired nuclei of various dinoflagellate species observed as a function of time of day in samples collected in Santa Monica Bay, CA. Open circles are ¹/₂ the recently divided cells. (From Weiler and Chisholm 1976.)

divided between 04:00 and 06:00. *Pyrocystis noctiluca* and *P. fusiformis* show maximal production of reproductive cells during the latter part of the night (Swift and Durbin 1972), but the gate appears to span the entire dark interval. In contrast, division in fast-growing field populations of *Dinophysis fortii* has been noted to span the entire day, with the maximum frequency of paired cells occurring soon after sunrise (Weiler and Chisholm 1976). The freshwater dinoflagellate *Peridinium cinctum* divides primarily between 02:00 and 04:00 regardless of the season (Pollingher and Serruya 1976).

Although the patterns of in situ division phasing in dinoflagellates can be characterized generally by a late night or early morning division gate, with a significant interval over the day when no dividing cells are observed, this is not the case with diatoms (Smayda 1975; Lewin and Rao 1975; Chisholm et al. 1978; Williamson 1980). Cells can be observed in the division process at all times of the day or night, but the frequency of dividing cells usually shows one or more peaks during each 24-h period.

In early studies (Allen 1922; Savage and Wimpenny 1936; Wimpenny 1938), the highest frequencies of dividing cells in diatom populations were detected at night. More recently, Smayda (1975) observed that percentage of dividing cells was also maximal in the night in natural populations of *Ditylum brightwellii* and *Biddulphia mobiliensis* from the Gulf of California (Fig. 14). Lewin and Rao (1975) on the other hand, found the maximum frequency of dividing cells to occur during the day in the surf-zone diatom *Chaetoceros armatum*, and this timing was independent of the time of year. The various species examined by Williamson (1980) exhibited all possible patterns: no rhythmicity (*Chaetoceros vanheurckii*), dominant daytime peak (*Thalassiothrix nitzschioides* and *Tropidoneis antarctica*), or dominant nighttime peak (*Thalassiosira rotula*).

In an effort to avoid the tedium of scoring percent dividing cells for monitoring division in diatoms, Chisholm et al. (1978) attempted to take advantage of the coupling between frustule deposition and cell division (Lewin et al. 1966) and tried to assay the timing of division in natural diatom assemblages by following the time course of silicic acid incorporation into frustules. Our hypothesis was that if there was a clear preference for day- or nighttime division in diatoms, this should be reflected in the silicon incorporation patterns of the whole water sample. Typical time courses observed (Fig. 15) indicated that division (Si incorporation) was occurring all the time, with bursts appearing both during the day and night. As we were dealing with mixed populations, the patterns could be interpreted in two ways: either different species were dividing at different times, or all species were dividing continuously, with preferred division times both night and day. At the time, the former interpretation seemed most plausible, but in view of the more recent evidence from culture work discussed above, the latter now seems more likely. The entire rationale behind this shift in interpretation is discussed in detail in Chisholm and Costello (1980) and Chisholm et al. (1980).

Two reports of in situ synchrony have been made for freshwater green algae. Simmer and Sodomkova (1968) observed division in *Scenedesmus acumenatus* (cultivated in large outdoor cultures) to be concentrated in the dark period. Stayley (1971), who has made the only direct observation of cell division timing in nature, actually imersed a microscope in a small pond and photographed the growth and cell division in attached chlorelloid algae over the day. Most of the size increase in the cells occurred during the day and division at night. Growth rates of the cells ranged from 1.3 to 1.8 doublings/d.

Measurements of the frequency of division stages in natural populations of phytoplankton can be used to calculate in situ growth rates of the populations. Various formulae have been used for this calculation, which depend on either the maximum frequency of paired division stages (Swift and Durbin 1972; Elbrachter 1973; Lewin and Rao 1975; Smayda 1975; Swift et al. 1976; Weiler and Chisholm 1976) or the sum of the frequency of paired stages observed, over a 24-h period (Weiler and Chisholm 1976; Heller 1979; Weiler and Eppley 1979), for the growth rate calculation. The expressions that have been used are diverse, often of unclear origin, and vary in degree of correctness and in underlying assumptions.

McDuff and Chisholm (1981) have reviewed the various formulations used in the past, and present a derivation of the appropriate expressions from first principles. As noted by others (Swift et al. 1976; Weiler and Chisholm 1976; Weiler and Eppley 1979), in situations where the maximum frequency of paired division stages (f_{max}) observed in a 24-h period is a measure of all the cells that are dividing in that interval, the expression

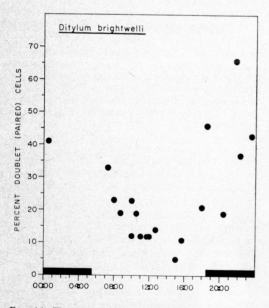

FIG. 14. The percentage of doublet (paired) cells of *Ditylum brightwellii* in net tows as a function of time of day. Samples were collected in the Gulf of California. (From Smayda 1975.)

$$(5) \qquad \mu = \frac{1}{t}\ln(1 + f_{max})$$

174

$$(6) \qquad \mu = \frac{1}{n\,t_d} \sum_{i=1}^{n} \ln\,(f_i + 1)$$

where n is the number of samples taken and t_d is the duration of the division stage. When division is phased or synchronous, the sampling period ($n\,t_s$) must be an even multiple of 24 h to obtain an accurate estimate of the average daily growth rate.

The critical parameter in equation (6) is the duration of the paired division stage, t_d. This can be estimated from the interval between the peaks in division frequency and frequency of recently divided cells (if identifiable). Alternatively, it can be calculated from data from laboratory cultures in which the increase in cell number (N) is followed along with the frequency of paired division stages. Since

$$(7) \qquad \mu = \ln\,(N_t/N_o)/\Delta t$$

substituting into equation (6) we find that

$$t_d = \frac{\Delta t}{n\,\ln\,(N_t/N_o)} \sum_{i=1}^{n} \ln\,(f_i + 1)$$

Measuring the frequency of division stages in natural populations of phytoplankton is perhaps one of the best (surely the most direct) tools to estimate the growth rates of phytoplankton in the sea. The accuracy of this method, however, is critically dependent on the following factors: (i) that there is no differential mortality between the various division stages (and there may be for some species (Richman and Rogers 1969)) and (ii) that either the duration of the division stage monitored is precisely known and an appropriate sampling interval is chosen or (iii) all the cells undergoing division in a given day can be observed doing so at one time.

Adaptive Significance and Ecological Implications

It is clear from this review that phytoplankton species differ in their growth patterns on light/dark cycles. The discussion would not be complete without some attempt at considering the selective pressures that may have resulted in the observed patterns of division.

In clock-controlled species, the timing of division is phase restricted, i.e. cells can only divide when the division gate is open. The possible selective advantage of such rigid control over the timing of the cell cycle has been discussed repeatedly in recent years (e.g. Smayda 1975; Starkweather 1975; Chisholm et al. 1978; Weiler 1978). Interesting

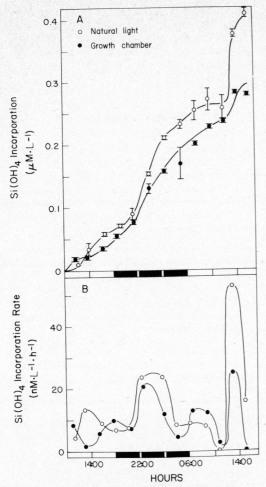

FIG. 15. (A) Time course of Si(OH)$_4$ incorporation into diatom frustules in a surface seawater sample collected 3 km off La Jolla, CA, incubated under natural conditions, and in a growth chamber at 17°C on L:D 12:12. Initial Si(OH)$_4$ concentration was 3.5 μM. (B) Data from (A) converted to rates of Si(OH)$_4$ incorporation for each inverval between measurements. Negative rates are plotted as zero. (From Chisholm et al. 1978.)

where $t = 1$ d, correctly describes the specific growth rate of the population per day. The use of this expression is only correct when the duration of the paired division stage is long relative to the width of the division gate, or when recently divided cells can be recognized (Weiler and Chisholm 1976; McDuff and Chisholm 1981).

For the more general case, which includes exponential growth, one must calculate the average of μ from sequential observations of the frequency of paired division stages (f) over a 24-h period to obtain a daily averaged growth rate hypotheses suggesting the avoidance of grazing pressure (McAllister 1970; Starkweather 1975; Chisholm et al. 1978) or the reduction of competition (Williams 1971; Eppley et al. 1971; Stross et al. 1973; Doyle and Poore 1974; Chisholm and Nobbs 1976; Chisholm et al. 1978) have been advanced, but they are difficult, if not impossible, to test. It seems likely that part of the selective advantage at least must involve the optimization and maintenance of the temporal order of cellular events (Gotham 1977; Chisholm et al. 1980). In other words, clock control of division timing could simply serve to insure that the cell division cycle is optimally phased to the periodic supply of energy to the cell.

In some species, in particular certain diatoms, the timing of division is not phase restricted (Chisholm et al. 1980); thus the advantage of strict temporal ordering does not appear to be universal. Division rhythms expressed by diatom populations appear to be forced oscillations rather than entrained. Strict cell division phasing occurs only when the cells are subjected to a strong forcing oscillation such as short photoperiods or nutrient pulses (Chisholm et al. 1980). Under most growth conditions and photoperiods, division occurs at all times during the photocycle; thus individual cells in the population are not responding to the light/dark cycle in the same manner (Chisholm and Costello 1980). Each cell "processes" environmental inputs as it experiences them rather than aligning the cell cycle to the environmental periodicities by "waiting" for the division gate.

It has been suggested that the flexibility in the division patterns of diatom cells grown on light/dark cycles reflects extensive nongenetic (phenotypic) variability in the populations (Chisholm et al. 1980), particularly in terms of the distribution of generation times. This necessarily results in asynchronous division, unless a forcing oscillation in a limiting substance is strong enough to align the cell cycles.

The relative selective advantages of these two growth "strategies" (i.e. strict phasing of cell cycles versus the absence of phase-restricted division) have been discussed in a variety of contexts in recent years (Spudich and Koshland 1976; Gotham 1977; Chisholm et al. 1980). Although difficult to prove, it seems logical that species with strict, clock-coupled temporal ordering might be selected for in stable, predictable environments, whereas those species with less rigid cell cycle timing would thrive in environments where the population is subjected to widely varying conditions. The difficulty in examining this hypothesis in more detail is in defining predictable and unpredictable environments, particularly on the space and time scales experienced by single cells. Until we know more about the temporal and spatial distribution of the key environmental parameters a cell experiences, as well as the distribution of properties among cells comprising populations, it is difficult to do more than speculate on the selective pressures that have resulted in the patterns of division expressed by phytoplankton populations.

Acknowledgments

This work was supported in part by NSF-OCE-7708999, by the MIT Sea Grant College Program under grant No. NA-79AA-D-00101 from the Office of Sea Grants, National Oceanic and Atmospheric Administration, U.S. Department of Commerce, and by funds awarded to S.W.C. as Doherty Professor of Ocean Utilization.

References

ABBO, F. E., AND A. B. PARDEE. 1960. Synthesis of macromolecules in synchronously dividing bacteria. Biochim. Biophys. Acta 39: 478–485.

AGRELL, I. 1964. Natural division synchrony and mitotic gradients in metazoan tissues, p. 39–70. In E. Zeuthen [ed.] Synchrony in cell division and growth. Interscience, New York.

ALLEN, W. E. 1922. Quantitative studies on marine phytoplankton at LaJolla in 1919. Univ. Calif. Berkeley, Publ. Zool. 22: 329–347.

APSTEIN, C. 1911. Biologische studie uber Ceratium tripos var. subsalsa Ostf. Wiss. Meeresunters. N.F. Bd. 12 (S): 137–162.

ASCHOFF, J. 1965. Response curves in circadian periodicity, p. 95–111. In J. Aschoff [ed.] Circadian clocks. North Holland Publ. Co., Amsterdam.

BERNSTEIN, E. 1960. Synchronous division in Chlamydomonas moewusii. Science (Washington, D.C.) 131: 1528–1529.

——— 1964. Physiology of an obligate photoautotroph (Chlamydomonas moewusii). I. Characteristics of synchronously and randomly reproducing cells and a hypothesis to explain their population curves. J. Protozool. 11(1): 56–74.

BRAARUD, T. 1945. Experimental studies on marine plankton diatoms. Nor. Vidensk. Akad. Oslo I. Mat. Naturvidensk. Kl. No. 10.

BRUCE, V. G. 1970. The biological clock in Chlamydomonas reinhardtii. J. Protozool. 17: 328–334.

——— 1972. Mutants of the biological clock in Chlamydomonas reinhardtii. Genetics 70: 537–548.

BRUCE, V. G., AND C. S. PITTENDRIGH. 1956. Temperature independence in a unicellular "clock." Proc. Natl. Acad. Sci. U.S.A. 42: 676–682.

BÜHNEMANN, F. 1955. Die rhythmische sporenbildung von Oedogonium cardiacium. Zentralbl. Wittr. Biol. 74: 1–54.

BÜNNING, E. 1967. The physiological clock. Springer-Verlag, New York. 167 p.

BUSBY, W. F., AND J. LEWIN. 1967. Silicate uptake and silica shell formation by synchronously dividing cells of the diatom *Navicula pelliculosa* (Bréb) Hilse. J. Phycol. 3: 127–131.

BUSH, K. J., AND B. M. SWEENEY. 1972. The activity of ribulose diphosphate carboxylase in extracts of *Gonyaulax polyedra* in the day and the night phases of the circadian rhythm of photosynthesis. Plant Physiol. 50: 446–451.

CHANCE, B., E. K. PYE, A. K. GHOSH, AND B. HESS. 1973. Biological and biochemical oscillators. Academic Press, New York. 374 p.

CHISHOLM, S. W., F. AZAM, AND R. W. EPPLEY. 1978. Silicic acid incorporation in marine diatoms on light/dark cycles: use as an assay for phased cell division. Limnol. Oceanogr. 23: 518–529.

CHISHOLM, S. W., AND L. E. BRAND. 1980. Persistence of cell division phasing in marine phytoplankton in continuous light after entrainment to light/dark cycles. J. Exp. Mar. Biol. Ecol. 51: 107–118.

CHISHOLM, S. W., AND J. C. COSTELLO. 1980. Influence of environmental factors and population composition on the timing of cell division in *Thalassiosira fluviatilis* (Bacillariophyceae) grown on light/dark cycles. J. Phycol. 16: 375–383.

CHISHOLM, S. W., F. M. M. MOREL, AND W. S. SLOCUM. 1980. The phasing and distribution of cell division cycles in marine diatoms, p. 281–300. *In* P. Falkowski [ed.] Primary productivity in the sea. Brookhaven Symp. Biol. 31.

CHISHOLM, S. W., AND P. A. NOBBS. 1976. Simulation of algal growth and competition in a phosphate-limited cyclostat, p. 337. *In* R. P. Canale [ed.] Modeling biochemical processes in aquatic ecosystems. U. Mich. Ann Arbor Science Publ.

CHISHOLM, S. W., AND R. G. STROSS. 1976. Phosphate uptake kinetics in *Euglena gracilis* (Z) (Euglenophyceae) growth on light/dark cycles. II. Phased, PO_4-limited cultures. J. Phycol. 12: 217–222.

CHISHOLM, S. W., R. G. STROSS, AND P. A. NOBBS. 1975. Light/dark phased cell division in *Euglena gracilis* (Z) (Euglenophyceae), in PO_4 limited cultures. J. Phycol. 77: 367–373.

COOK, J. R. 1961a. *Euglena gracilis* in synchronous division. I. Dry mass and volume characteristics. Plant Cell Physiol. 2: 199–202.

1961b. *Euglena gracilis* in synchronous division. II. Biosynthetic rates over the life cycle. Biol. Bull. Woods Hole Mass. 121: 277–289.

1963. Adaptations in growth and division in *Euglena* effected by energy supply. J. Protozool. 10: 436–444.

1971. Influence of culture pH and phosphate on synchrony of *Euglena gracilis*. Exp. Cell Res. 69: 207–211.

COOK, J. R., AND B. COOK. 1962. Effects of nutrients on the variation of individual generation times. Exp. Cell Res. 28: 524–530.

COOK, J. R., AND T. W. JAMES. 1960. Light-induced division synchrony in *Euglena gracilis* var. bacillaris. Exp. Cell Res. 21: 583–589.

COOMBS, J., C. SPANIS, AND B. E. VOLCANI. 1967. Studies on the biochemistry and fine structure of silica shell formation in diatoms. Photosynthesis and respiration in silicon-starvation synchrony of *Navicula pelliculosa*. Plant Physiol. 42: 1607–1611.

CSATORDAY, K., AND G. HORVATH. 1977. Synchronization of *Anacystis nidulans*: oxygen evolution during the cell cycle. Arch. Microbiol. 111: 245–246.

DENFFER, D. VON. 1949. Die planktische massenkultur pennater Grunddiatomeen. Arch. Mikrobiol. 14: 159–202.

DOYLE, R., AND R. V. POORE. 1974. Nutrient competition and division synchrony in phytoplankton. J. Exp. Mar. Biol. Ecol. 14: 201–210.

DROOP, M. R. 1973. Some thoughts on nutrient limitation in algae. J. Phycol. 9: 264–272.

EDMUNDS, L. N. JR. 1965a. Studies on synchronously dividing cultures of *Euglena gracilis* Klebs (Strain Z). I. Attainment and characterization of cell division. J. Cell. Comp. Physiol. 66: 147–158.

1965b. Studies on synchronized dividing cultures of *Euglena gracilis* Klebs (Strain Z). II. Patterns of biosynthesis during the cell cycle. J. Cell. Comp. Physiol. 66: 159–182.

1966. Studies on synchronously dividing cultures of *Euglena gracilis* Klebs (Strain Z). III. Circadian components of cell division. J. Cell. Physiol. 67: 35–44.

1971. Persisting circadian rhythm of cell division in *Euglena*: Some theoretical considerations and the problem of intercellular communication, p. 594–611. *In* M. Menaker [ed.] Biochronometry. Natl. Acad. Sci. USA.

1974. Circadian clock control of the cell developmental cycle in synchronized cultures of *Euglena*, p. 287–297. *In* R. L. Bieleski, A. R. Ferguson, and M. M. Cresswell [ed.] Mechanisms of regulation of plant growth. R. Soc. N.Z. Bull. 12.

1976. Models and mechanisms for endogenous timekeeping, p. 280–361. *In* J. D. Palmer [ed.] An introduction to biological rhythms. Academic Press, New York.

1978. Clocked cell cycle clocks: implications toward chronobiology and aging, p. 125–184. *In* H. V. Samis and S. Capobianco [ed.] Aging and biological rhythms. Adv. Exp. Med. Biol. Vol. 108.

EDMUNDS, L. N. JR., L. CHUANG, R. M. JARRETT, AND W. O. TERRY. 1971. Long-term persistence of free-running circadian rhythms of cell division of *Euglena* and the implication of autosynchrony. J. Interdiscip. Cycle Res. 2(2): 121–123.

EDMUNDS, L. N., AND R. R. FUNCH. 1969a. Circadian rhythm of cell division in *Euglena*: effects of a random illumination regimen. Science (Washington, D.C.) 165: 500–503.

1969b. Effects of "skeleton" photoperiods and high frequency light/dark cycles on the rhythm of cell division in synchronized cultures of *Euglena*. Planta 87: 134–163.

EHRET, C. F. 1974. The sense of time: evidence for its molecular basis in the eukaryotic gene-action system. Adv. Biol. Med. Phys. 15: 47–77.

EHRET, C. F., AND K. W. DOBRA. 1977. The infradian eukaryotic cell: a circadian energy-reserve escapement, p. 563–570. Proceedings of XII International Conference, International Society for Chronobiology

(Section on Cellular and Metabolic Mechanisms). Casa Editrice "Il Ponte," Milano.

EHRET, C. F., J. C. MEINERT, K. R. GROH, K. W. DOBRA, AND G. A. ANTIPA. 1977. Circadian regulation: growth kinetics of the infradian cell, p. 62–64. In B. Drewinko and R. M. Humphrey [ed.] Growth kinetics and biochemical regulation of normal and malignant cells. Williams and Wilkins Co., Baltimore.

EHRET, C. F., AND E. TRUCCO. 1967. Molecular models for the circadian clock. 1. The chronon concept. J. Theor. Biol. 15: 240–262.

EHRET, C. F., AND J. J. WILLE. 1970. The photobiology of circadian rhythms in protozoa and other eukaryotic microorganisms, p. 369–416. In P. Halladal [ed.] Photobiology of microorganisms. Wiley-Interscience, London, New York, Sydney, and Toronto.

ELBRACHTER, M. 1973. Population dynamics of Ceratium in coastal waters of the Kiel Bay. Oikos Suppl. 15: 43–48.

ENRIGHT, J. T. 1965. Synchronization and ranges of entrainment, p. 113–124. In J. Aschoff [ed.] Circadian clocks, North Holland Publ. Co., Amsterdam.

EPPLEY, R. W., AND J. L. COATSWORTH. 1966. Culture of the marine phytoplankter, Dunaliella tertiolecta, with light/dark cycles. Arch. Mikrobiol. 55: 66–80.

EPPLEY, R. W., R. W. HOLMES, AND E. PAASCHE. 1967. Periodicity in cell division and physiological behavior of Ditylum brightwellii, a marine plankton diatom, during growth in light/dark cycles. Arch. Mikrobiol. 56: 305–323.

EPPLEY, R. W., J. N. ROGERS, J. J. McCARTHY, AND A. SOURNIA. 1971. Light/dark periodicity in nitrogen assimilation of the marine phytoplankters Skeletonema costatum and Coccolithus huxleyi in N-limited chemostat culture. J. Phycol. 7: 150–154.

ERIKSON, R. O. 1964. Synchronous cell and nuclear division in tissues of the higher plants, p. 11–37. In E. Zeuthen [ed.] Synchrony in cell division and growth. Interscience, New York.

FELDMAN, J. F. 1968. Circadian rhythmicity in amino acid incorporation in Euglena gracilis. Science (Washington, D.C.) 160: 1454–1456.

FELDMAN, J. F., AND M. N. HOYLE. 1973. Isolation of circadian clock mutants of Neurospora crassa. Genetics 75: 605–613.

FRISCH, H. L., AND I. J. GOTHAM. 1977. On periodic algal cyclostat populations. J. Theor. Biol. 66: 665.
1978. A simple model for periodic cyclostat growth of algae. J. Math. Biol. 7: 149–169.

GALLERON, C., AND A. M. DURRAND. 1979. Cell cycle and DNA synthesis in a marine dinoflagellate, Amphidinium carteri. Protoplasma 100: 155–165.

GLOOSCHENKO, W. A., AND H. CURL. 1968. Obtaining synchronous cultures of algae. Nature (London) 218: 573–574.

GOTHAM, I. J. 1977. Nutrient limited cyclostat growth: a theoretical and physiological analysis. Ph. D. thesis, New York State Univ., Albany, NY. 222 p.

GOUGH, L. H. 1905. Report on the plankton of the English Channel in 1903. Rep. (S. Area) Fish. Hydrogr. Invest. N. Sea 1: 325–377.

GRAN, H. H. 1912. Pelagic plant life, p. 307–386. In J. Murray and J. Hjort [ed.] The depths of the ocean. Macmillan and Co., London.

HARTWELL, L. H. 1971. Genetic control of the cell division cycle in yeast. II. Genes controlling DNA replication and its initiation. J. Mol. Biol. 59: 183–194.
1974. Saccharomyces cerevisiae cell cycle. Bacteriol. Rev. 38: 164–198.

HASE, E., Y. MORIMURA, AND H. TAMIYA. 1957. Some data on the growth physiology of Chlorella studied by the technique of synchronous culture. Arch. Biochem. Biophys. 69: 149.

HASTINGS, J. W. 1960. Biochemical aspects of rhythms: Phase shifting by chemicals. Cold Spring Harbor Symp. Quant. Biol. 25: 131–143.

HASTINGS, J. W. 1975. Basic features: group report 1, p. 49–62. In J. W. Hastings and H.-G. Schweiger [ed.] The molecular basis of circadian rhythms. Report of the Dahlem Konferenzen, Berlin, Life Sci. Res. Rep. 1.

HASTINGS, J. W., AND B. M. SWEENEY. 1958. A persistant diurnal rhythm of luminescence in Gonyaulax polyedra. Biol. Bull. 115: 440–458.

HASTINGS, J. W., L. ASTRACHAN, AND B. M. SWEENEY. 1960. A persistent daily rhythm in photosynthesis. J. Gen. Physiol. 45: 69–76.

HASTINGS, J. W., AND H.-G. SCHWEIGER. 1976. The molecular basis of circadian rhythms. Rep. Dahlem Workshop, Abakon Ver. Berlin. 461 p.

HASTINGS, J. W., AND B. M. SWEENEY. 1964. Phased cell division in the marine dinoflagellates, p. 307–321. In E. Zeuthen [ed.] Synchrony in cell division and growth. Interscience Publ., New York.

HELLER, M. D. 1977. The phased division of the freshwater dinoflagellate Ceratium hirundinella and its use as a method of assessing growth in natural populations. Freshwater Biol. 7: 527–533.

HELLMAN, W. S. 1976. Biological rhythms and physiological timing. Annu. Rev. Plant Physiol. 27: 159–179.

HERDMAN ET AL. 1970. Synchronous growth and genome replication in the blue-green alga, Anacystis nidulans. Arch. Mikrobiol. 73: 238–249.

HESSE, M. 1971. Endogene schwankungen der produktionsfahigkeit bei Chlorella und ihre beeinflussung durch licht sehr niedriger intensitat und durch tiefe temperatur. Dissertation, Gottingen. p. 1–84.

HOTTA, Y., M. ITO, AND H. STERN. 1966. Synthesis of DNA during meiosis. Proc. Natl. Acad. Sci. U.S.A. 56: 1184–1191.

HUNDING, C. 1978. Growth cycle of a freshwater diatom. Mitt. Int. Ver. Limnol. 21: 136–146.

JAMES, T. W. 1966. Cell synchrony, a prologue to discovery, p. 1–13. In I. L. Cameron and G. M. Padella [ed.] Cell synchrony. Academic Press, New York, NY.

JANNASCH, H. W. 1974. Steady-state and the chemostat in ecology. Limnol. Oceanogr. 19: 716.

JARRETT, R. M., AND L. N. EDMUNDS JR. 1970. Persisting circadian rhythm of cell division in a photosynthetic mutant of Euglena. Science (Washington, D.C.) 167: 1730–1733.

JOHN, P. C. L., W. McCULLOUGH, A. Q. ATKINSON, B. G. FORD, AND B. E. S. GUNNING. 1973. The cell cycle in *Chlorella*, p. 61–76. *In* M. Balls and F. S. Bellett [ed.] The cell cycle in development and differentiation. Cambridge Univ. Press, Cambridge, MA.

JØRGENSEN, E. G. 1911. Die *Ceratien*, eine kurze monographie der gattung *Ceratium* Schrank. Int. Rev. Gesamten Hydrobiol. Hydrogr. Biol. Suppl. Ser. 2: 1–124.

1966. Photosynthetic activity during the life cycle of synchronous *Skeletonema* cells. Physiol. Plant. 19: 789–799.

KLEVECZ, R. R. 1969. Temporal order in mammalian cells. I. The periodic synthesis of lactate dehydrogenase in the cell cycle. J. Cell Biol. 43: 207–219.

1975. Molecular manifestations of the cellular clock, p. 1–19. *In* J. C. Hampton [ed.] The cell cycle in malignancy and immunity. 13th Annu. Hanford Biol. Symp.

1976. Quantized generation time in mammalian cells as an expression of the cellular clock. Proc. Natl. Acad. Sci. U.S.A. 73: 4012–4016.

KOMÁREK, J., AND J. SIMMER. 1965. Synchronization of the cultures of *Scenedesmus quadricauda* (TURP.) Breb. Biol. Plant. 7: 409.

KONOPKA, R. J., AND S. BENZER. 1971. Clock mutants of *Drosophila melanogaster*. Proc. Nat. Acad. Sci. U.S.A. 68: 2112–2116.

LAFEBER, A., AND C. L. M. STEENBERGEN. 1967. Simple device for obtaining synchronous cultures of algae. Nature (London) 213: 527–528.

LANSKAYA, L. A. 1963. Fission rate of plankton algae of the Black Sea in cultures, p. 127–132. *In* C. A. Oppenheimer [ed.] Symposium on marine microbiology. Charles C. Thomas, Publisher, Springfield, IL.

LAVAL-MARTIN, D. L., D. J. SHUCH, AND L. N. EDMUNDS JR. 1979. Cell cycle related and endogenously controlled circadian photosynthetic rhythms in *Euglena*. Plant Physiol. 63: 495–502.

LEEDALE, G. F. 1959. Periodicity of mitosis and cell division in the *Euglenineae*. Biol. Bull. 116: 162–174.

LEWIN, J. C., AND V. N. R. RAO. 1975. Blooms of surf-zone diatoms along the coast of the Olympic Peninsula, Washington. VI. Daily periodicity phenomena associated with *Chaetoceros armatum* in its natural habitat. J. Phycol. 11(3): 330–338.

LEWIN, J. C., B. E. REIMANN, W. F. BUSBY, AND B. E. VOLCANI. 1966. Silica shell formation in synchronously dividing diatoms, p. 169–188. *In* I. L. Cameron and G. M. Padilla [ed.] Cell synchrony. Academic Press, New York, NY.

LIEN, T., AND G. KNUTSEN. 1979. Synchronous growth of *Chlamydomonas reinhardtii* (Chlorophyceae): a review of optimal conditions. J. Phycol. 15: 191–200.

LOEBLICH, A. R. 1977. Studies on synchronously dividing populations of *Cachonina niei*, a marine dinoflagellate. Bull. Jpn. Soc. Physiol. 25: 119–126.

LONERGAN, T. A., AND M. L. SARGENT. 1978. Regulation of the photosynthesis rhythm in *Euglena gracilis*. I. Carbonic anhydrase and glyceraldehyde-3-phosphate dehydrogenase do not regulate the photosynthesis rhythm. Plant Physiol. 61: 150–153.

LORENZEN, H. 1957. Synchrone zellteilungen von *Chlorella* bei verschiedenen Licht-Dunkel-Wechseln. Flora (Jena) 144: 473.

1970. Synchronous cultures, p. 187–212. *In* P. Halldal [ed.] Photobiology of microorganisms. Wiley-Interscience, London.

LORENZEN, H., AND B. D. KAUSHIK. 1976. Experiments with synchronous *Anacystis nidulans*. Ber. Dtsch. Bot. Ges. 89: 491–498.

LORENZEN, H., AND G. S. VENKATARAMAN. 1969. Synchronous cell divisions in *Anacystis nidulans* Richter. Arch. Mikrobiol. 67: 251–255.

MCALLISTER, C. D. 1970. Zooplankton rations, phytoplankton mortality and the estimation of marine production, p. 419–457. *In* J. Steele [ed.] Marine food chains. Oliver and Boyd, Edinburgh.

MCDUFF, R., AND S. W. CHISHOLM. 1981. The calculation of *in situ* growth rates of phytoplankton populations from fractions of cells undergoing mitosis: a clarification. Limnol. Oceanogr. (In press)

MCMURRY, L., AND J. W. HASTINGS. 1972. No desynchronization among four circadian rhythms in the unicellular alga, *Gonyaulax polyedra*. Science (Washington, D.C.) 175: 1137–1139.

MALONE, T. C., C. GARSIDE, K. C. HAINES, AND O. A. ROELS. 1975. Nitrate uptake and growth of *Chaetoceros* sp. in large outdoor continuous cultures. Limnol. Oceanogr. 20: 9–19.

MAZIA, D., AND K. DAN. 1952. The isolation and biochemical characterization of the mitotic apparatus of dividing cells. Proc. Natl. Acad. Sci. U.S.A. 38: 826–838.

MENAKER, M. 1971. Biochronometry. Natl. Acad. Sci. USA. 662 p.

MIHARA, S., AND E. HASE. 1971. Studies on the vegetative life cycle of *Chlamydomonas reinhardtii* Dangeard in synchronous culture. I. Some characteristics of the cell cycle. Plant Cell Physiol. 12: 225–236.

MITCHELL, J. L. A. 1971. Photoinduced division synchrony in permanently bleached *Euglena gracilis*. Planta 100: 244–257.

MITCHISON, J. M. 1971. The biology of the cell cycle. Cambridge Univ. Press, Cambridge, MA. 313 p.

1973. Differentiation in the cell cycle, p. 1–11. *In* M. Balls and F. S. Billet [ed.] The cell cycle in development and differentiation. Cambridge Univ. Press, Cambridge.

1974. Sequences, pathways and timers in the cell cycle, p. 125–142. *In* G. M. Padilla, I. L. Cameron, and A. Zimmerman [ed.] Cell cycle controls. Academic Press, New York, NY.

MORIMURA, Y. 1959. Synchronous culture of *Chlorella*. I. Kinetic analysis of the life cycle of *Chlorella ellipsoidea* as affected by changes of temperature and light intensity. Plant Cell Physiol. 1: 49.

NELSON, D. M., AND L. E. BRAND. 1979. Cell division periodicity in 13 species of marine phytoplankton on a light/dark cycle. J. Phycol. 15: 67–75.

NEUVILLE, D., AND P. DASTE. 1977. Premiers essais de synchronisation des divisions cellulaires chez la diatomée *Navicula ostrearia* (Gaillon) bory en culture axenique. C.R. Acad. Sci. Paris Ser. D 284: 761–764.

NJUS, D., F. SULZMAN, AND J. W. HASTINGS. 1974. Membrane model for the circadian clock. Nature (London) 248: 116–120.

PAASCHE, E. 1967. Marine plankton algae grown with light/dark cycles. I. *Coccolithus huxleyi*. Physiol. Plant. 20: 946–956.

——— 1968. Marine plankton algae grown with light/dark cycles. II. *Ditylum brightwellii* and *Nitzschia turgidula*. Physiol. Plant. 21: 66–77.

PADILLA, G. M., AND J. R. COOK. 1964. The development of techniques for synchronizing flagellates, p. 521–535. *In* E. Zeuthen [ed.] Synchrony in cell division and growth. Interscience, New York, NY.

PALMER, J. D. 1976. An introduction to biological rhythms. Academic Press, New York, NY. 375 p.

PALMER, J. D., L. LIVINGSTON, AND D. ZUSY. 1964. A persistent diurnal rhythm in photosynthetic capacity. Nature (London) 203: 1087–1088.

PALMER, J. D., AND F. E. ROUND. 1965. Persistent vertical migration rhythms in the benthic microflora. I. The effect of light and temperature on the rhythmic behavior of *Euglena obtusa*. J. Mar. Biol. Assoc. U.K. 45: 567–582.

——— 1967. Persistent, vertical migration rhythms in benthic microflora. VI. The tidal and diurnal nature of the rhythm in the diatoms *Hantzschia virgata*. Biol. Bull. Woods Hole Mass. 132: 44–55.

PAVLOVA, E. V., AND L. A. LANSKAYA. 1969. Energy expenditures for movement in some Black Sea dinoflagellates. Prog. Protozool. III: 174–175.

PETERSON, D. F., AND E. C. ANDERSON. 1964. Quantity production of synchronized mammalian cells in suspension culture. Nature (London) 203: 642–643.

PIRSON, A., AND H. LORENZEN. 1958. Ein endogener zeitfaktor bei der teilung von *Chlorella*. Z. Bot. 46: 53.

——— 1966. Synchronized dividing algae. Annu. Rev. Plant Physiol. 17: 439–457.

PITTENDRIGH, C. S. 1975. Circadian clocks: what are they?, p. 11–48. *In* J. W. Hastings and H.-G. Schweiger [ed.] The molecular basis of circadian rhythm. Life Sci. Res. Rep. 1.

——— 1979. Some functional aspects of circadian pacemakers, p. 3–12. *In* M. Suda, O. Haysaishi, and H. Nakagawa [ed.] Biological rhythms and their central mechanism. Elsevier/North Holland Biomedical Press, Amsterdam.

POLLINGHER, U., AND C. SERRUYA. 1976. Phased division of *Peridinium cinctum* F. Westii (Dinophyceae) and development of the Lake Kinneret (Israel) bloom. J. Phycol. 12: 162–170.

PRESCOTT, D. M. 1959. Variations in the individual generation times of *Tetrahymena geleii* HS. Exp. Cell Res. 16: 279.

——— 1976. Reproduction of eukaryotic cells. Academic Press, New York, NY. 177 p.

PREZELIN, B. B., B. W. MEESON, AND B. M. SWEENEY. 1977. Characterization of photosynthetic rhythms in marine dinoflagellates. I. Pigmentation photosynthetic capacity and respiration. Plant Physiol. 60: 384–387.

PREZELIN, B. B., AND B. M. SWEENEY. 1977. Characterization of photosynthetic rhythms in marine dinoflagellates. II. Photosynthesis-irradiance curves and *in vivo* Chlorophyll a fluorescence. Plant Physiol. 60: 388–392.

RHEE, G. Y., I. J. GOTHAM, AND S. W. CHISHOLM. 1981. Use of cyclostat cultures to study phytoplankton ecology, p. 159–186. *In* P. Calcott [ed.] Continuous cultures of cells. Vol. II. CRC Press. (In press)

RICHMAN, S., AND J. N. ROGERS. 1969. The feeding of *Calanus helgolandicus* on synchronously growing populations of the marine diatom *Ditylum brightwellii*. Limnol. Oceanogr. 14: 701–709.

RICKETTS, T. R. 1979. The induction of synchronous cell division in *Platymonas striata* Butcher (Prasinophyceae). Br. Phycol. J. 14: 219–223.

RIETH, A. 1939. Photoperiodizität bei zentrischen diatomeen. Planta 30: 294–296.

RUSCH, H. P. 1969. Some biochemical events in the growth cycles of *Physarum polycephalum*. Fed. Proc. Fed. Am. Soc. Exp. Biol. 28: 1761–1770.

SAVAGE, R. E., AND R. S. WIMPENNY. 1936. Phytoplankton and the herring. Part II. 1933 and 1934. Fish. Invest. G.B. Ser. II, 15(1). 88 p.

SCHEVING, L. E., AND F. HALBERG. 1980. Chronobiology. Sijthoff Intl. Publ., Netherlands. 312 p.

SCHMIDT, R. 1966. Intracellular control of enzyme synthesis and activity during synchronous growth of *Chlorella*, p. 189–235. *In* I. L. Cameron and G. M. Padilla [ed.] Cell synchrony. Academic Press, New York, NY.

SIMMER, J., AND M. SODOMKOVA. 1968. Synchronization of natural populations of *Scenedesmus acuminatus* (Lagerh) Chod. induced by rhythmical changes in the environment. Acta Univ. Carol. Biol. 1967: 251–254.

SMAYDA, T. J. 1975. Phased cell division in natural populations of the marine diatom *Ditylum brightwellii* and the potential significance of diel phytoplankton behavior in the sea. Deep-Sea Res. 22: 151–165.

SMITH, J. A., AND L. MARTIN. 1973. Do cells cycle? Proc. Natl. Acad. Sci. U.S.A. 70: 1263–1267.

SOROKIN, C., AND R. W. KRAUSS. 1959. Maximum growth rates in synchronized cultures of green algae. Science (Washington, D.C.) 129: 1289.

SOURNIA, A. 1974. Circadian periodicities in natural populations of marine phytoplankton. Adv. Mar. Biol. 12: 325–389.

SPUDICH, J. L., AND D. E. KOSHLAND, JR. 1976. Nongenetic individuality: chance in the single cell. Nature (London) 262: 467–471.

SPUDICH, J., AND R. SAGER. 1980. Regulation of the *Chlamydomonas* cell cycle by light and dark. J. Cell Biol. 85: 136–145.

STARKWEATHER, P. L. 1975. Diel changes in the feeding behavior of *Daphnia pulex* Leydig (Crustacea: Branciopoda). Ph.D. thesis, Dartmouth College, Hanover, NH. 190 p.

STAYLEY, J. T. 1971. Growth rates of algae determined *in situ* using an immersed microscope. J. Phycol. 7: 13–17.

STEENBERGEN, C. L. M. 1975. Light-dependent morphogenesis of unicellular stages in synchronized cultures of *Scenedesmus quadricauda*. Acta Bot. Neerl. 24: 391–396.

——— 1978. Pleomorphism of *Scenedesmus quadricauda* (Turp.) (Chlorophyceae) in synchronized cultures. Mitt. Int. Ver. Theor. Angew. Limnol. 21: 216–223.

STROSS, R. G., S. W. CHISHOLM, AND T. A. DOWNING. 1973. Causes of daily rhythmicity in photosynthetic rates of phytoplankton. Biol. Bull. 145: 200–209.

SUBRAHMANYAN, R. 1945. On the cell division and mitosis in some South Indian diatoms. Proc. Indian Acad. Sci. Ser. B 22: 331–354.

SUDA, M., O. HAYAISHI, AND H. NAKAGAWA. 1979. Biological rhythms and their central mechanism. Elsevier/North Holland Biomedical Press, Amsterdam. 265 p.

SULZMAN, F. M., AND L. N. EDMUNDS. 1972. Persisting circadian oscillations in enzyme activity in non-dividing cultures of Euglena. Biochem. Biophys. Res. Commun. 47: 1338–1344.

SWEENEY, B. M. 1969. Rhythmic phenomena in plants. Academic Press, New York and London. 147 p.

SWEENEY, B. M., AND J. W. HASTINGS. 1958. Rhythmic cell division in populations of Gonyaulax polyedra. J. Protozool. 5: 217–224.

——— 1964. The use of the electronic cell counter in studies of synchronous cell division in dinoflagellates, p. 579–587. In E. Zeuthen [ed.] Synchrony in cell division and growth. Interscience, New York, NY.

SWEENEY, B. M., AND F. T. HAXO. 1961. Persistence of a photosynthetic rhythm in enucleated Acetabularia. Science (Washington, D.C.) 134: 1361–1363.

SWIFT, E., AND E. G. DURBIN. 1972. The phased division- and cytological characteristics of Pyrocystis spp. can be used to estimate doubling times of their populations in the sea. Deep-Sea Res. 19: 189–198.

SWIFT, E., M. STUART, AND V. MEUNIER. 1976. The in situ growth rates of some deep-living oceanic dinoflagellates: Pyrocystis fusiformis and Pyrocystis noctiluca. Limnol. Oceanogr. 21: 418–426.

TAMIYA, H. 1964. Growth and cell division in Chlorella, p. 247–305. In E. Zeuthen [ed.] Synchrony in cell division and growth. Interscience, New York, NY.

——— 1966. Synchronous cultures of algae. Annu. Rev. Plant Physiol. 17: 1–26.

TAMIYA, H. Y., Y. MORIMURA, M. YOKOTA, AND R. KUNIEDA. 1961. Mode of nuclear division in synchronous cultures of Chlorella: comparison of various methods of synchronization. Plant Cell Physiol. 2: 383.

TAMIYA, H., K. SHIBATA, T. SASA, T. IWAMURA, AND Y. MORIMURA. 1953. Effect of diurnally intermittant illumination on the growth and some cellular characteristics of Chlorella. Carnegie Inst. Washington Publ. 600: 76.

TAYLOR, W. R. 1979. Studies on the bioluminescent glow rhythm of Gonyaulax polyedra. Ph.D thesis, Univ. Michigan, Ann Arbor, MI. 260 p.

TERRY, O. W., AND L. N. EDMUNDS. 1970. Rhythmic settling induced by temperature cycles in continuously stirred autotrophic cultures of E. gracilis (Z strain). Planta 93: 128–142.

VENKATARAMAN, G. S., AND H. LORENZEN. 1969. Biochemical studies on Anacystis nidulans during its synchronous growth. Arch. Mikrobiol. 69: 34–39.

WEGMANN, K., AND H. METZNER. 1971. Synchronization of Dunaliella cultures. Arch. Mikrobiol. 78: 360–367.

WEILER, C. S. 1978. Phased cell division in the dino-flagellate genus Ceratium: temporal pattern, use in determining growth rates, and ecological implications. Ph. D. thesis, Univ. California San Diego, La Jolla, CA. 126 p.

——— 1980. Population structure and in situ division rates of Ceratium in oligotrophic waters of the North Pacific central gyre. Limnol. Oceanogr. 25: 610–619.

WEILER, C. S., AND S. W. CHISHOLM. 1976. Phased cell division in natural populations of marine dino-flagellates from shipboard cultures. J. Exp. Mar. Biol. Ecol. 25: 239–247.

WEILER, C. S., AND R. W. EPPLEY. 1979. Temporal pattern of division in the dinoflagellate genus Ceratium and its application to the determination of growth rate. J. Exp. Mar. Biol. Ecol. 39: 1–24.

WILLE, J. J., AND C. F. EHRET. 1968. Light synchronization of an endogenous circadian rhythm of cell division in Tetrahymena. J. Protozool. 5: 785–789.

WILLIAMS, F. M. 1971. Dynamics of microbial populations, p. 197–267. In B. C. Patten [ed.] Systems analysis and simulation in ecology. Vol. I. Academic Press, New York, NY.

WILLIAMSON, C. E. 1980. Phased cell division in natural and laboratory populations of marine phytoplankton diatoms. J. Exp. Mar. Biol. Ecol. 43: 271–279.

WIMPENNY, R. S. 1938. Diurnal variation in the feeding and breeding of zooplankton related to the numerical balance of the zoo-phytoplankton community. J. Cons. Perm. Int. Explor. Mer. 13: 323–337.

ZEUTHEN, E. 1974. A cellular model for repetitive and free-running synchrony in Tetrahymena and Schizo-saccharomyces, p. 1–30. In G. M. Padella, I. L. Cameron, and A. Zimmerman [ed.] Cell cycle controls. Academic Press, New York, NY.

Nitrogen Metabolism of Microalgae

P. J. SYRETT

*Department of Botany and Microbiology, University College of Swansea,
Swansea, Wales, UK*

Introduction

Study of the nitrogen metabolism of algae may be said to have started some 60 years ago when Warburg and Negelein (1920), following Warburg's introduction of the use of the alga *Chlorella* for studying photosynthesis, showed that light stimulated nitrate reduction by this organism. Since then studies of algal nitrogen metabolism have been published at an ever-increasing rate. The topics studied have diversified and just as Warburg's initial work with *Chlorella* led to an understanding of the fundamentals of photosynthesis so have later studies on algal nitrogen metabolism thrown light on fundamental cellular processes.

Along with the diversification of topics has been a great increase in the number of different species that have been studied. It remains true, however, that there are few detailed laboratory studies of truly planktonic algae and this is largely because biochemical physiologists prefer to work with organisms that can be grown readily and *axenically* in laboratory culture. These conditions still impose a considerable limitation on the variety of algae that can be used. For these reasons therefore this article is about the nitrogen metabolism of microalgae, rather than of phytoplankton only, and one presumes that some of our knowledge of the nitrogen metabolism of algae such as *Chlorella*, *Chlamydomonas*, *Phaeodactylum*, and *Anacystis* will apply to their much less studied oceanic cousins.

After carbon and excluding hydrogen and oxygen that can come from water, nitrogen is quantitatively the most important single element contributing to the dry matter in algal cells. The proportion of nitrogen as a percentage of dry weight can vary from 1 to 10%. It is low in diatoms where the silica in the cell wall makes a substantial contribution to dry matter and in nitrogen-deficient organisms that have accumulated large amounts of carbon compounds such as oils or polysaccharides (Fogg and Collyer 1953). But in an exponentially growing non-diatomaceous microalga, nitrogen is about 7–10% of the dry matter and carbon about 50% (Vaccaro 1965). The C:N ratio is therefore around 5. As estimates put the primary productivity of the oceans at 3.1×10^{10} t per annum due to phytoplankton photosynthesis (Platt and Subba Rao 1975), this suggests that the total amount of nitrogen assimilated by oceanic phytoplankton must be of the order of 6×10^9 t per annum (Fogg 1978).

Nitrogen Sources for Algal Growth

GASEOUS NITROGEN

Microscopic algae include both procaryotes and eucaryotes although many would now regard the procaryotes, the blue-green organisms (Cyanophyceae or Cyanobacteria) as bacteria. The ability to fix gaseous nitrogen is confined to procaryotes and, among algae, only some blue-greens are able to do so. Fogg (1978) has recently reviewed nitrogen fixation in the oceans. It is not known with certainty how much occurs but it cannot be very great because nitrogen-fixing microorganisms are not abundant in oceans. The best-known planktonic blue-green alga which almost certainly fixes nitrogen is *Trichodesmium (Oscillatoria)* which can form extensive blooms in tropical waters. Nevertheless Fogg's very tentative estimate of the quantity of gaseous nitrogen fixed in the oceans is 0.1×10^9 t per annum or about 1% of the total annual N incorporation by phytoplankton. Even this estimate may be too high and it is not clear what has limited the development of autotrophic marine nitrogen-fixing organisms.

Biochemically, nitrogen fixation takes place by reduction of N_2 to NH_4^+, the reaction being catalyzed by nitrogenase. Six electrons are required for each N_2 molecule reduced; these are derived from a low potential reductant such as reduced ferredoxin. ATP is also required, most probably 12 molecules for each N_2 molecule (Mortenson and Thorneley 1979). In blue-green algae both reduced ferredoxin and ATP can probably be generated either by photochemical reactions or by dark respiratory reactions (Gallon 1980).

COMBINED INORGANIC NITROGEN

Almost all chlorophyll-containing algae studied in culture will grow with either nitrate (NO_3^-), nitrite (NO_2^-), or ammonium (NH_4^+) as a nitrogen source. Care has to be taken to avoid large changes in pH and the toxic effects of high concentrations of NO_2^-, and sometimes of NH_4^+. Maximum growth rates are generally much the same with either NO_3^- or NH_4^+ as N source (see Table 1) but a careful study by

TABLE 1. Comparison of the growth rates of some algae cultured on various N sources (from Leftley 1980).

Organism	Specific growth rate constant (k) ($\log_{10}$ units $\cdot$ d^{-1})			Concentration of N (mmol $\cdot$ L^{-1})			Reference
	NH$_4^+$	NO$_3^-$	Urea	NH$_4^+$	NO$_3^-$	Urea	
Cyanophyta							
Agmenellum quadruplicatum	3.3	3.0	1.7	0.6	variable	4.3	Kapp et al. (1975)
Anabaena variabilis	0.69	0.69	0.81	3.0	10.0	1.0	Kratz and Myers (1955)
Nostoc muscorum	0.48	0.50	0.54	"	"	"	" " "
Chlorophyta							
Chlorella ellipsoidea	—	0.50	0.40	—	12.0	66.0	Samejima and Myers (1958)
Chlorella pyrenoidosa	0.5	0.45	0.47	13.0	"	"	" " "
Chrysophyta							
Amphiphora alata	1.14	1.30	1.30	0.1	0.1	0.1	Carpenter et al. (1972)
Chaetoceros simplex	1.54	1.58	1.35	"	"	"	" " "
Chaetoceros sp.	0.96	1.30	1.03	"	"	"	" " "
Chrysochromulina sp.	1.12	1.14	1.35	"	"	"	" " "
Cyclotella cryptica	0.57	0.57	0.49	0.1	0.9	0.2	Liu and Hellebust (1974)
Skeletonema sp.	1.41	1.66	0.99	0.1	0.1	0.1	Carpenter et al. (1972)
Stephanopyxis costata	1.23	1.35	1.58	"	"	"	" " "

Paasche (1971) established that *Dunaliella tertiolecta* grows 10–30% faster on NH$_4^+$ than on NO$_3^-$. The difference may partly reflect the greater need for reductant (ultimately photogenerated) for assimilation of NO$_3^-$ but the NH$_4^+$-grown cells also have higher ribulose biphosphate carboxylase activities. Although laboratory algae grow well on NO$_3^-$, Antia et al. (1975) point out that this may be partly a consequence of the fact that they have almost always been isolated from natural populations by selective growth on media containing NO$_3^-$. Indeed Antia et al. (1975) showed that one marine species, *Hemiselmis virescens*, that had been isolated by Droop in a medium containing glycine and purines, was exceptional among the 26 planktonic species they studied in being unable to utilize NO$_3^-$ or NO$_2^-$.

AMIDES AND AMINO ACIDS

Thomas (1968) has compiled useful tables summarizing the information that was available up to then about the utilization of organic N by freshwater and marine algal species. Additional studies with marine forms have been carried out by Wheeler et al. (1974), Antia et al. (1975), and Neilson and Larsson (1980). In general, the amides, urea, glutamine, and asparagine are good sources of nitrogen for algal growth. For example, Antia et al. found that 23 of the 26 marine species they studied could grow with urea. Guillard (1963) found that of 16 marine centric diatoms and 3 coccolithophorids, 16 grew on glutamine and 12 on urea. Growth rates in urea are generally similar to those in NO$_3^-$ or NH$_4^+$ (Table 1). Glutamine contains two N atoms and *Chlorella* can utilize *both* for growth although unable to grow on glutamic acid (Lynch and Gillmor 1966). The explanation appears to be that glutamine can enter the cells of this *Chlorella* strain and hence be metabolized whereas glutamic acid cannot. The alga *Monodus* may be somewhat exceptional in producing an extracellular glutaminase which hydrolyzes glutamine to NH$_4^+$ and glutamic acid; the organism uses the NH$_4^+$ released for growth but not the glutamic acid (Belmont and Miller 1965).

Amino acids, particularly glycine, serine, alanine, glutamic acid, and aspartic acids, also serve as N sources for the growth of some algae, although of the diatoms studied by Wheeler et al. (1974) it was nearshore species of *Nitschia* and *Phaeodactylum* that most readily grew on these compounds. Uptake mechanisms for some amino acids, of high affinity (i.e. half saturation at less that 10 μM), have been demonstrated in pennate diatoms and in *Platymonas* (Hellebust and Lewin 1977; Wheeler et al. 1974). This suggests an ecological significance for amino acid utilization but sometimes an organism will take up an amino acid rapidly while not being able to grow on it, e.g. *Thalassiosira* with lysine (Wheeler et al. 1974).

PURINES AND PYRIMIDINES

Study of the use of purines as nitrogen sources is hindered by their low solubility in water. Nevertheless uric acid, xanthine, guanine, or adenine can be used as sole N sources by some blue-greens, chlorophytes, and diatoms (Van Baalen 1962; Birdsey and Lynch 1962; Cain 1965). Antia and Landymore (1974) point to the instability of uric acid and xanthine in seawater which means that in nature it may be degradation products of these compounds that are used. Antia et al. (1975) tested the more stable purine, hypoxanthine, and found that 17 out of 26 marine strains tested grew well on it, although some did so only after a very long lag period (e.g. about 30 d with *Isochrysis*).

Pyrimidines appear to be much less utilizable as N sources for growth (Cain 1965). Nevertheless the soil alga *Chlorella* has an active mechanism for the uptake of uracil (Knutsen 1972).

GLUCOSAMINE

Mention should be made of this compound Antia et al. (1975) found to be used as a N source for growth by several marine phytoplankters although none grew well on it.

TAXONOMIC DIFFERENCES

There appears to be no clear relationship between the ability to use a particular group of nitrogen compounds and taxonomic class. The work of Antia et al. (1975) shows that within both the chlorophytes and diatoms some species (e.g. *Tetraselmis maculata* and *Nitzschia acicularis*) show ability to utilize a wide range of organic N sources while other species (e.g. *Nannochloris oculata* and *Cyclotella cryptica*) cannot do so. Possibly, as Naylor (1970) suggests, more extensive studies will reveal evolutionary relationships but it may well be that ability to utilize, or lack of it, depends on rather small genetic differences.

OXIDATION STATES

The nitrogen sources for algal growth occur in widely different states of oxidation (Table 2). Thus, if nitrogen gas is regarded as an oxidation state of zero, NO_3' is the most oxidized inorganic form (oxidation state, $+5$) and NH_4^+ the most reduced (oxidation state, -3); this means that eight electrons are necessary to reduce a nitrogen atom in the form of NO_3' to NH_4^+. Amide N can also be regarded as at an oxidation state of -3 since no oxido/reduction occurs in the formation of an amide from NH_4^+. However, the formation of an amino acid from an oxo-acid and NH_4^+ is a reductive reaction which requires two electrons per N atom incorporated. To

TABLE 2. Nitrogen sources for algal growth with oxidation states ($\pm$ one electron is required to change the oxidation state of one N atom by 1 unit).

		Oxidation state
Nitrate ions	NO_3'	$+5$
Nitrite ions	NO_2'	$+3$
Nitrogen gas	N_2	0
Ammonium ions Urea	NH_4^+ }	-3
Glutamine		-4 (see text)
Amino acids Purines	}	-5 (see text)

emphasize this in Table 2, amino acids (and purines in which the N is derived from amino N) are shown at an oxidation state of -5 although, overall, amino acids, like alanine, are at the same oxidation level as carbohydrate plus NH_4^+.

Sources of Combined Nitrogen in Seawater

Parsons et al. (1977) summarize naturally occurring concentrations of combined nitrogen compounds in seawater as $NO_3' < 0.01-50$ μM, $NO_2' < 0.01-5$ μM, $NH_4^+ < 0.1-5$ μM, urea $< 0.1-5$ μM, and amino acids $< 0.2-2$ μM. In the North Atlantic, alanine was the amino acid present in highest concentration and the most widely distributed (Pocklington 1971). It is obvious that there must be considerable variation in the concentrations of nitrogenous compounds both in space and in time. Higher concentrations, sometimes much higher, are likely around coasts and when rates of phytoplankton metabolism are low. Information about concentrations of purines in seawater appears to be lacking although their ready utilization by several algal species makes them of interest.

Assimilation of Nitrogen Compounds

Figure 1 depicts a much idealized algal cell setting out some of the major features of nitrogen assimilation that will be discussed in more detail later. The diagram shows all nitrogen sources crossing the cell wall and outer cell membrane (the plasmalemma) to enter the cytoplasm. For all the com-

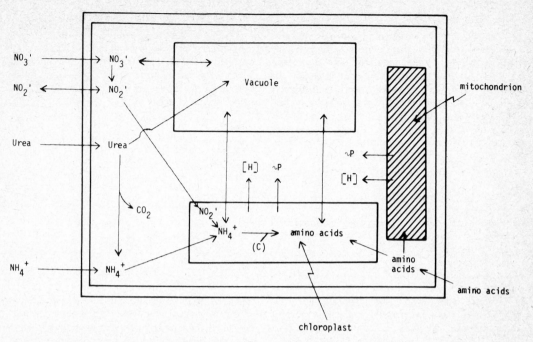

FIG. 1. Main features of nitrogen assimilation in a eucaryotic algal cell. See text for discussion.

pounds depicted, there is evidence for active uptake systems dependent on metabolism although there may be passive entry by free diffusion as well. The diagram shows exchange between the compounds in the cytoplasm and compounds in the vacuole. It also shows the involvement of the chloroplast and, to a lesser extent, of the mitochondrion. One of our main areas of ignorance about the nitrogen metabolism of microalgae is that we do not know, with any certainty, exactly where in the cells the various metabolic reactions are located nor, indeed, where the metabolic "pools" are. We do not know, therefore, what part the internal membranes surrounding the vacuole, chloroplast, and mitochondrion play in the regulation of metabolism but we suspect it may be an important one.

The figure contains a number of assumptions which will not be discussed again. The first is that nitrate transport across the membrane(s) and nitrate reduction in the cytoplasm are separate events; in contrast, Butz and Jackson (1977) have argued that the enzyme nitrate reductase is located in cellular membranes and has the dual functions of both transport and reduction of nitrate. Second, the nitrogen in nitrate, nitrite, and urea is shown as being converted into NH_4^+ before being assimilated into organic N compounds. There have been suggestions of a partial reduction of nitrate and nitrite to the level of hydroxylamine followed by combination with an organic acid to form an oxime that is then further

metabolized (Czygan 1965); firm evidence for such reactions is lacking. Similarly there are suggestions for a direct incorporation of urea N into organic compounds (Kitoh and Hori 1977); again the bulk of the evidence is against this. Third, the vacuole is depicted as containing a metabolically inactive solution into and from which solutes pass. But in higher plant cells the vacuole contains hydrolytic enzymes (Boller and Kende 1979). Whether such enzymes are present in algal vacuoles and, if so, whether they affect nitrogen metabolism is unknown.

Assimilation of Ammonium (NH_4^+)

FORMATION OF GLUTAMIC ACID

Studies of NH_4^+ assimilation have been much aided by the use of nitrogen-deficient *Chlorella* cultures. Cultures that are deprived of nitrogen go on accumulating polysaccharides by photosynthesis. When such cultures are supplied with NH_4^+ ions, they are taken up rapidly and converted to organic N compounds. At the same time the accumulated polysaccharide in the cells disappears, partly because of a greatly increased role of respiration during the rapid assimilation of NH_4^+, but largely because it is converted into organic N compounds (Syrett 1953a, b; Hattori 1958; Reisner et al. 1960). During the first 15 min of NH_4^+ assimilation the greatest increases of organic N are in glutamine and alanine with other amino acids showing smaller increases (Reisner et al. 1960) and, in experiments in which $^{15}NH_4^+$ was fed, after 1 min the greatest incorporation was into the amide group of glutamine (36.8 atom% excess), followed by the amino groups of glutamine and glutamic acid (16% atom% excess), with alanine showing lower labeling (6.5% atom% excess) (Baker and Thompson 1961).

At the time these experiments were carried out they were interpreted as being consistent with the then accepted mechanism of ammonium assimilation by plants. The key compound was glutamic acid which was formed from NH_4^+ and α-oxoglutaric acid by the reductive reaction catalyzed by glutamic dehydrogenase (GDH) namely:

(1)

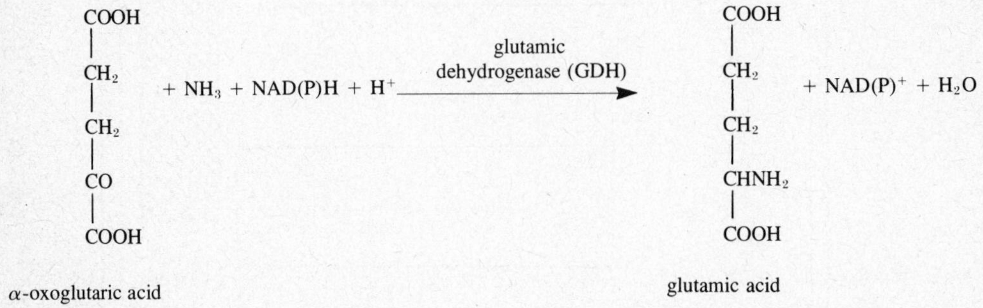

$$
\begin{array}{c}
\text{COOH} \\
| \\
\text{CH}_2 \\
| \\
\text{CH}_2 \\
| \\
\text{CO} \\
| \\
\text{COOH}
\end{array}
+ NH_3 + NAD(P)H + H^+
\xrightarrow[\text{dehydrogenase (GDH)}]{\text{glutamic}}
\begin{array}{c}
\text{COOH} \\
| \\
\text{CH}_2 \\
| \\
\text{CH}_2 \\
| \\
\text{CHNH}_2 \\
| \\
\text{COOH}
\end{array}
+ NAD(P)^+ + H_2O
$$

α-oxoglutaric acid

glutamic acid

Other amino acids, including alanine, were regarded as being formed from glutamic acid by transamination and glutamine by the further addition of NH_4^+ to the γ-carboxyl group of glutamic acid, a reaction requiring ATP and catalyzed by the enzyme glutamine synthetase (GS) (reaction 2 below). All the necessary enzymes were known to be present in *Chlorella* (Baker and Thompson 1961).

However, in the early 1970s work by Brown and his colleagues with bacteria revealed an alter-

native pathway of NH_4^+ assimilation (Tempest et al. 1970; Brown et al. 1974) and Miflin and Lea (1976) showed that the pathway could also operate in leaves of higher plants and in blue-green and green algae. In this pathway, glutamine rather than glutamic acid is the first product of NH_4^+ assimilation and the NH_4^+ incorporated into the amide group of glutamine is then transferred to α-oxoglutaric acid in a reductive reaction from which two molecules of glutamic acid result; thus

(2)

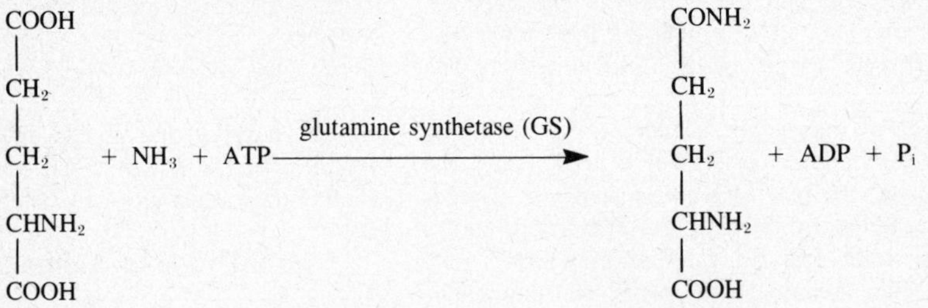

$$
\begin{array}{c}
\text{COOH} \\
| \\
\text{CH}_2 \\
| \\
\text{CH}_2 \\
| \\
\text{CHNH}_2 \\
| \\
\text{COOH}
\end{array}
+ NH_3 + ATP
\xrightarrow{\text{glutamine synthetase (GS)}}
\begin{array}{c}
\text{CONH}_2 \\
| \\
\text{CH}_2 \\
| \\
\text{CH}_2 \\
| \\
\text{CHNH}_2 \\
| \\
\text{COOH}
\end{array}
+ ADP + P_i
$$

glutamic acid ⟵   ⟶ glutamine

GOGAT

(3)

$$
\begin{array}{c}
\text{COOH} \\
| \\
\text{CH}_2 \\
| \\
\text{CH}_2 \\
| \\
\text{CHNH}_2 \\
| \\
\text{COOH}
\end{array}
\qquad [2H] \qquad
\begin{array}{c}
\text{COOH} \\
| \\
\text{CH}_2 \\
| \\
\text{CH}_2 \\
| \\
\text{CO} \\
| \\
\text{COOH}
\end{array}
$$

glutamic acid

α-oxoglutaric acid

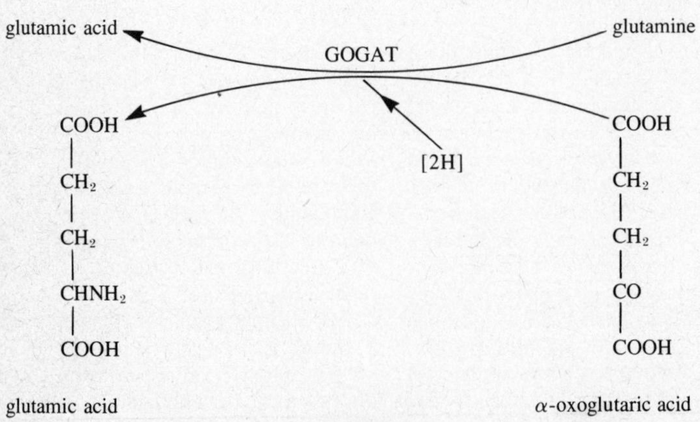

The enzyme catalyzing reaction (3) is glutamine-oxoglutarate aminotransferase or glutamate synthase; it is often called GOGAT. GOGAT catalyzes a reductive reaction and, in higher plants and algae, the reductant can be either NADH or reduced ferredoxin. By reactions (2) and (3) operating in sequence, NH_4^+ is assimilated into glutamic acid by combination with α-oxoglutaric acid but GDH is not involved. The overall reaction is still reductive, as is reaction (1), but it also requires ATP which reaction (1) does not. It is particularly attractive to think of reaction (2) as being the major reaction responsible for the incorporation of NH_4^+ into organic combination because GS has a much higher affinity for ammonium than does GDH (Miflin and Lea 1976). In a number of marine phytoplankters, for example, the apparent K_m (concentration supporting half maximum velocity of reaction) of GDH for NH_4^+ was 4 500–10 000 μM (Ahmed et al. 1977). For *Skeletonema*, Falkowski and Rivkin (1976) found a K_m for GDH of 28 000 μM; for GS it was only 29 μM which is similar to the value for higher plant enzymes (Miflin and Lea 1976).

GDH OR GS/GOGAT?

Much work has now been done with higher plants and some with algae to discover whether NH_4^+ assimilation mainly takes place through GDH or through the GS/GOGAT reactions. One approach has been to make use of inhibitors. L-Methionine-DL-sulphoximine (MSO or MSX) forms an analogue of the γ-glutamyl phosphate enzyme complex of GS and is a powerful inhibitor of GS. Azaserine is an analogue of glutamine and inhibits GOGAT. These substances do not inhibit GDH (Miflin and Lea 1976). If ammonium assimilation is primarily by the GS/GOGAT pathway it should be possible to inhibit it substantially with these inhibitors. That this is so has been shown for the blue-green alga *Anacystis*, where azaserine and MSO at 1 mM concentration caused 90% inhibition of NH_4^+ assimilation by illuminated cells (Ramos et al. 1980a). MSO-treated *Anacystis* reduced nitrate almost quantitatively to NH_4^+ which accumulated because it could not be assimilated (Ramos et al. 1980b). MSO at a concentration of 2.0 μM MSO was sufficient to prevent growth with NO_3^-, NH_4^+, glutamate, or alanine as N source; normal growth occurred in the presence of 2.0 μM MSO and 1 mM glutamine (Ramos et al. 1980a). When illuminated *Anabaena*, which fixes N_2, was treated with MSO, the nitrogen fixed accumulated as NH_4^+ (Stewart and Rowell 1975). Meeks et al. (1978) showed with three other species of blue-green algae that 1 mM MSO almost completely inhibited incorporation of $^{13}NH_3$ (^{13}N is a short-lived radioactive isotope).

Rigano et al. (1979, 1980) have made similar observations with the eucaryotic alga *Cyanidium*

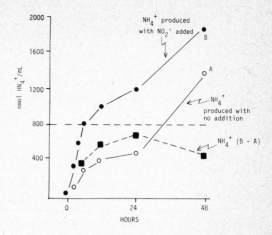

FIG. 2. Ammonium production by illuminated MSO-(1 mM)-treated *Chlamydomonas*. Cell density, 1.3×10^7 cells/mL. The horizontal broken line shows the quantity of NH_4^+ expected from the complete reduction of the NO_2^- added to B (unpublished data of C. R. Hipkin, T. A. V. Rees, and S. A. Everest).

caldarium, where NH_4^+ assimilation is inhibited by either MSO or azaserine and again, in the presence of MSO, NO_3^- is reduced quantitatively to NH_4^+ which accumulates. Inhibition of GS activity and of NH_4^+ assimilation by MSO also occurs in *Chlamydomonas* (Cullimore and Sims 1981; C.R. Hipkin, T. A. V. Rees, and S. A. Everest unpublished data). But here a new phenomenon is seen, namely a substantial production of NH_4^+ in the presence of MSO in the absence of any added nitrogen source; NH_4^+ production is increased on addition of NO_2^- (Fig. 2).

The other approach that has been used is to survey algae for the presence of the key enzymes, GDH, GS, and GOGAT, and to estimate their activities. These studies can sometimes be misleading because an enzyme activity may appear to be absent or low in cell-free extracts because of failure to establish optimal conditions for assay. At present such studies are few. Substantial GS and GOGAT activity has been measured in *Platymonas* (Edge and Ricketts 1978), *Chlorella fusca* (Lea and Miflin 1975), and *Chlamydomonas reinhardii* (Cullimore and Sims 1981; S. A. Everest unpublished data). In *Platymonas* and *Chlamydomonas*, GDH activities, in contrast, were very low. In other algae, e.g. *Chlorella fusca*, GDH is present with a high activity which is higher in NH_4^+-grown cells than in NO_3^--grown ones and highest of all in N-deficient cells (Morris and Syrett 1965). This strain of *Chlorella* (8p) contains only a NADP- dependent GDH. Shatilov et al. (1978) have shown the presence in a thermophilic strain of *Chlorella* 82T of two glutamic dehydrogenases, one that is constitutive and functional with either NADH or

187

NADPH, and another that is present only in NH_4^+-grown cells and specific for NADPH. The Russian authors favor the view that in *Chlorella* assimilation of NH_4^+ at high concentrations is mainly through glutamic dehydrogenase while at low concentrations or in NO_3'-grown cells it is through GS/GOGAT (Shatilov et al. 1978). Conclusive evidence for this view is lacking.

ALANINE DEHYDROGENASE

Of other pathways of NH_4^+ assimilation, the direct formation of alanine from NH_4^+ and pyruvic acid is significant in some blue-green algae, those that lack GDH activity (Neilson and Doudoroff 1973). Rowell and Stewart (1976) characterized the enzyme from *Anabaena cylindrica*; they suggest that because of its high K_m (> 8 mM) it is likely to be of less importance in overall ammonium assimilation than GS. It is interesting that of three species of blue-greens studied by Meeks et al. (1978), incorporation of $^{13}NH_3$ into alanine was inhibited greatly by MSO in two species but not at all in the third, *Cylindrospermum licheniforme*, suggesting that in this organism alanine is formed directly and not via the GS/GOGAT pathway as in the two inhibited species. Alanine dehydrogenase is also present in *Chlamydomonas* where, during the life cycle, its activity changes in an inverse way to that of glutamic dehydrogenase (Kates and Jones 1964).

CARBAMYL PHOSPHATE

Another subsidiary pathway of NH_4^+ assimilation is that which results in carbamyl phosphate and hence incorporation into citrulline (and then arginine), pyrimidines (including thiamine), and biotin; it is probable that in plants the ammonia for carbamyl phosphate synthesis is derived from the amide group of asparagine or glutamine rather than from free NH_4^+ ions (Beevers 1976).

Assimilation of Nitrate (NO_3') and Nitrite (NO_2')

Assimilation of NO_3' takes place by reduction of NO_3' to NO_2' followed by a reduction of NO_2' to NH_4^+ which is then converted to organic compounds. The first step requires two electrons and the second, six.

$$NO_3' \xrightarrow[\text{nitrate reductase}]{2e} NO_2' \xrightarrow[\text{nitrite reductase}]{6e} NH_4^+$$

$$\text{(NR)} \qquad\qquad \text{(NiR)}$$

NITRATE REDUCTION

There are two types of nitrate reductase known in algae. The first, and better known enzyme, is

found in eucaryotic algae; it resembles higher plant nitrate reductases in many respects. It is found in the soluble portion of cell-free extracts and although there have been suggestions for an association of it with chloroplasts, possibly in between the inner and outer membranes (Grant et al. 1970), convincing evidence is lacking.

The enzyme catalyzes:

$$NO_3' + NAD(P)H + H^+ \xrightarrow{\text{nitrate reductase}}$$
$$NO_2' + NAD(P)^+ + H_2O$$

The most highly purified and best characterized algal enzyme is from *Chlorella* (Solomonson et al. 1975; Solomonson 1979; Giri and Ramadoss 1979) but it has also been studied in detail after 200-fold purification from the diatom, *Thalassiosira* (Amy and Garrett 1974). The *Chlorella* enzyme has a molecular mass of about 350 000 and a complex structure. It contains molybdenum, haem, and flavin adenine dinucleotide, most probably two molecules of each in each molecule of enzyme. Molybdenum appears to be at or close to the site at which NO_3' is reduced and the enzyme works by molybdenum being reduced by electrons derived from NADH, possibly to Mo^{IV}, and then reoxidized, possibly to Mo^{VI}, by NO_3' which is consequently reduced to NO_2'. Substitution of molybdenum by tungsten produces an enzyme which cannot reduce NO_3' but still retains its ability to reduce cytochrome c (see below) (Vega et al. 1971; Paneque et al. 1972). Growth of algae on a medium with tungstate present to produce an inactive nitrate reductase has proved a most useful experimental tool (e.g. Solomonson and Spehar 1977; Serra et al. 1978b). With the higher plant enzyme there is evidence that the molybdenum is contained in a small complex (molar mass less than 30 000) that can be fairly easily separated from the bulk of the enzyme (Notton and Hewitt 1979). Haem is probably present as a b-type cytochrome which is reduced by NADH and reoxidized by NO_3'; cyanide stops its reoxidation by NO_3' but not its reduction by NADH (Solomonson 1979). Solomonson's tentative picture of the structure of *Chlorella* nitrate reductase is shown in Fig. 3 although this does not show molybdenum in a component of fairly small molecular weight. This figure shows a characteristic feature of nitrate reductase from eucaryotic cells, namely, that it

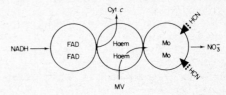

FIG. 3. Structure of *Chlorella* nitrate reductase according to Solomonson (1979).

TABLE 3. Pyridine nucleotide specificity of nitrate reductase from eucaryotic algae. (*All* enzymes studied can utilize NADH for nitrate reduction. The table therefore lists those able or not able to utilize NADPH.)

	Utilizes NADPH	Does not utilize NADPH
Rhodophyceae	*Cyanidium caldarium*[a]	*Porphyridium aerugineum* (1380/2)[b] *Porphyridium cruentum* (1380/12)[c]
Haptophyceae		*Isochrysis* (927/1)[c] *Coccolithus huxleyi*[d]
Dinophyceae		*Gonyaulax polyedra*[d]
Prasinophyceae		*Platymonas subcordiformis* (161/12)[c]
Bacillariophyceae		*Phaeodactylum tricornutum* (1052/6)[c] *Cyclotella nana*[d] *Ditylum brightwellii*[d] *Thalassiosira pseudonana*[e] *Skeletonema costatum*[f] (NADPH used poorly)
Chlorophyceae	*Chlorella variegata* (211/10a)[c] *Chlorella variegata* (211/10d)[c] *Ankistrodesmus braunii* (202/7c)[c] *Chlamydomonas reinhardii* (2192)[c] *Dunaliella primolecta* (11/34)[c] *Dunaliella tertiolecta* (19a)[c] *Dunaliella parva*[g]	*Chlorella* (211/8p)[c] *Chlorella fusca* (211/15)[c] *Chlorella vulgaris* (211/11b)[c] *Chlorella stigmatophora* (211/20)[c] *Scenedesmus obliquus* (276/3a)[c] *Scenedesmus obliquus* (276/3b)[c]

[a]Rigano (1971); [b]Rigano et al. (1979b); [c]Hipkin et al. (1979); [d]Eppley et al. (1969a); [e]Amy and Garrett (1974); [f]Serra et al. (1978c); [g]Heimer (1976).

has three enzymic activities that can be measured and distinguished experimentally. The first is the ability to reduce nitrate with NAD(P)H; this activity requires the full functional enzyme. The second is the ability to reduce NO_3' with electron donors such as reduced methyl viologen or reduced flavin mononucleotide (FMN). The third is cytochrome c reductase activity, i.e. the ability to reduce cytochrome c with NAD(P)H. In some mutants of *Chlamydomonas* the enzyme has lost the ability to utilize NAD(P)H but it can still reduce NO_3' with methyl viologen or FMN (Nichols et al. 1978). However, such mutants cannot grow with NO_3' as a N source which suggests that, in vivo, the enzyme functions only with NAD(P)H as electron donor for nitrate reduction.

The pyridine nucleotide specificity of the enzyme differs in different algae (Table 3). It can be seen that the enzyme is always active with NADH as electron donor and, in many algae, only with this. But in *Cyanidium* and in several species of Chlorophyceae it is also active with NADPH and for some, e.g. *Chlamydomonas* and *Dunaliella*, one suspects that NADPH may be the natural physio-

logical electron donor. There is no convincing evidence that, in algae, bispecificity of pyridine nucleotide utilization is due to the presence of two different nitrate reductases as is so in some higher plants (Campbell 1976). Attempts to separate the two activities in extracts of *Dunaliella parva* were unsuccessful (Heimer 1976).

The second type of nitrate reductase is found in procaryotic cells and, in the algae, in the blue-greens (Cyanophyceae). In broken cell preparations of blue-green algae the enzyme is associated with chlorophyll-containing particles but it can be solubilized and purified (Manzano et al. 1978; Losada and Guerrero 1979). The enzyme is smaller than the eucaryotic one, with a molecular mass of about 75 000. It contains molybdenum but not flavin or cytochrome (Losada and Guerrero 1979). The important difference from the enzyme of eucaryotes is that it does not use pyridine nucleotide as electron donor but reduced ferredoxin. It therefore catalyzes the reaction:

$$NO_3' + 2Fd_{red} + 2H^+ \rightarrow NO_2' + 2Fd_{ox} + H_2O$$

The reduction of NO_2' to NH_4^+ is catalyzed by ferredoxin nitrite reductase. This enzyme appears to be much the same in algae and in leaves of higher plants. It is a small molecule with a molecular mass of 60 000–70 000. In algae it has now been studied in *Anabaena* (Hattori and Uesugi 1968), *Dunaliella* (Grant 1970), *Ditylum* (Eppley and Rogers 1970), *Chlorella* (Zumft 1972), *Porphyra* (Ho et al. 1976), and *Skeletonema* (Llama et al. 1979). The enzyme contains sirohaem which is an iron tetrahydroporphyrin (Murphy et al. 1974) and where NO_2' probably attaches, it also contains an iron–sulphur center which participates in electron transport (Losada and Guerrero 1979). The reaction catalyzed is:

$$NO_2' + 6Fe_{red} + 8H^+ \xrightarrow{\text{nitrite reductase}}$$
$$NH_4^+ + 6Fe_{oxid} + 2H_2O$$

With the purified enzymes reduced methyl viologen will also act as an electron donor but pyridine nucleotides are inactive. Despite the reduction of NO_2' to NH_4^+ requiring six electrons per NO_2' ion, no intermediates have been detected in this reaction.

In the leaves of higher plants, nitrite reductase appears to be located in the chloroplasts (Miflin 1974); information about its localization in algal cells is lacking but the quenching of chlorophyll fluorescence following addition of NO_2' (but not of NO_3') to cells of *Chlorella* and *Ankistrodesmus* (Kessler and Zumft 1973) suggests a close linkage between nitrite reduction and the photochemical reactions in the chloroplasts.

Metabolism of Urea

Urea is an excellent nitrogen source for algae in culture and may well be an important natural source in seawater (McCarthy 1972). Nitrogen makes up almost half of the mass of the urea molecule, $CO(NH_2)_2$. The work of Allison et al. (1954) on feeding [^{14}C]urea to *Nostoc* suggested that carbon from urea was assimilated by algae only after its conversion to CO_2 and most subsequent workers agree with this view (e.g. Hattori 1960). There are, however, suggestions that urea N may be assimilated into organic N without prior conversion to NH_3^+ (Kitoh and Hori 1977).

Two enzymes which metabolize urea are now known in algae. The first is *urease*, an enzyme which is widespread in the plant kingdom. It catalyzes:

$$CO(NH_2)_2 + H_2O \longrightarrow CO_2 + 2NH_3$$

A number of algae that grow well on urea do not contain this enzyme. Instead they contain a urea carboxylase and also allophanate hydrolase. Together these enzymes catalyze:

$$urea + ATP + HCO_3' \xrightarrow[\text{urea carboxylase}]{Mg^{2+} K^+}$$
$$allophanate + ADP + P_i$$

$$allophanate \xrightarrow{\text{allophanate hydrolase}} 2NH_3 + 2CO_2$$

The overall reaction catalyzed is:

$$CO(NH_2)_2 + ATP + H_2O \longrightarrow$$
$$CO_2 + 2NH_3 + ADP + P_i$$

This result is the same as that achieved by the urease reaction but at the expense of a molecule of ATP per molecule urea. The overall reaction is referred to as the urea amidolyase (UAL-ase) reaction. After its initial description by Roon and Levenberg (1968) it has been studied in detail in yeast (Whitney and Cooper 1972, 1973), *Chlorella* (Thompson and Muenster 1971, 1974), and *Chlamydomonas* (Hodson et al. 1975).

The reaction catalyzed by urea carboxylase is a biotin-dependent carboxylation which, like other such carboxylations, is inhibited in cell-free preparations by avidin: the inhibition is relieved by addition of biotin. This reaction is not much inhibited by hydroxyurea whereas the urease reaction is. These differences in inhibition properties, together with the requirement of the UAL-ase reaction for ATP, allows the UAL-ase and urease reactions to be distinguished in crude cell-free extracts and using these methods Leftley and Syrett (1973) and Bekheet and Syrett (1977) surveyed the distribution of the urea-degrading enzymes in a number of algae. The result is fairly clear-cut. If an alga can metabolize urea it has one enzyme or the other, not both, although it must be said that the methods would not detect a low activity of one enzyme in the presence of the other. The occurrence of UAL-ase is restricted to certain orders of the Chlorophyceae namely the Volvocales, Chlorococcales, Chaetophorales, and Ulotrichales. The other chlorophytes examined contained urease as did members of all the other algal classes. As far as phytoplankton is concerned a generalization based on the limited evidence available at present is that the chlorophytic phytoplankters are likely to contain UAL-ase and the others, urease.

The hydrolytic reaction catalyzed by urease goes to completion and it is not clear what biological advantage, if any, is gained by using ATP to accomplish the same overall reaction. Leftley showed that whole cells of *Phaeodactylum* (containing urease) could metabolize urea at low concentrations just as well as cells of *Dunaliella* (with UAL-ase): both had a half-saturation value of about $1.5 \mu M$ urea (Syrett and Leftley 1976). One advantage would be if the intermediate allophanate could be assimilated into metabolism but evidence for this is lacking. Another possibility is that UAL-ase levels can be regulated more readily than those of urease. Certainly in the few algae that have been examined UAL-ase behaves as an inducible/repressible enzyme in a way that urease does not (Syrett and Leftley 1976).

It has recently been shown that purified urease from jack bean contains nickel (Dixon et al. 1975). Rees and Bekheet (unpublished results) have shown a strong dependence on nickel for the development of urease activity in *Phaeodactylum* and *Tetraselmis*. In the absence of nickel these organisms appear to overproduce a urease protein because the restoration of nickel after a period of deprivation leads to a very rapid "overproduction" of urease activity (Fig. 4).

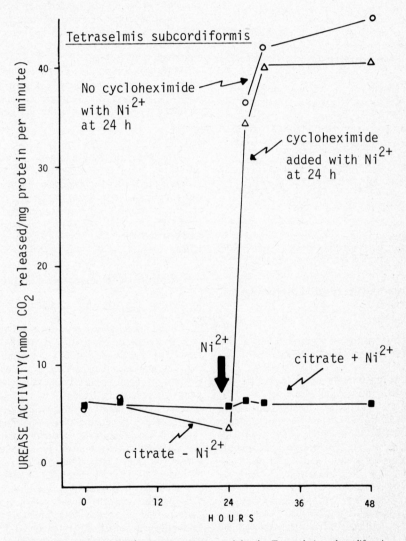

FIG. 4. The effect of Ni^{2+} ions on urease activity in *Tetraselmis subcordiformis*. Cultures were grown with added citrate and either $\pm Ni^{2+}$. After 24 h Ni^{2+} was added to a $-Ni^{2+}$ culture. Urease activity was determined in cell-free extracts at the times shown. Note that addition of cycloheximide with Ni^{2+} after 24 h had no effect on the marked and rapid increase in urease activity (I.A. Bekheet and T. A. V. Rees unpublished data).

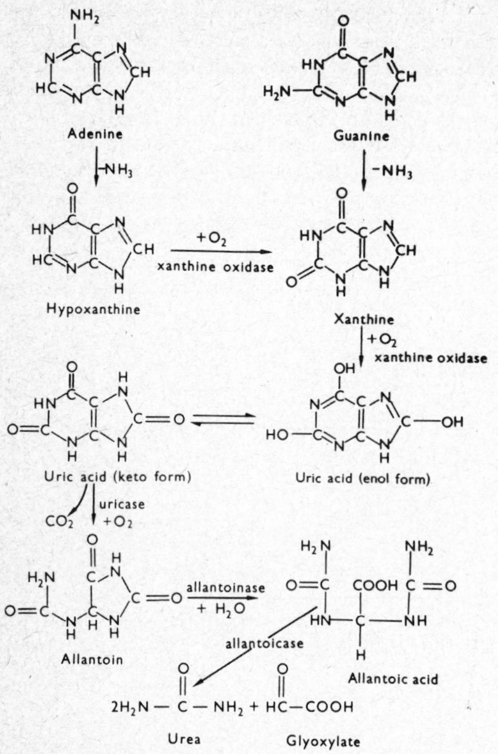

FIG. 5. Biochemistry of purine breakdown in aerobic microorganisms (from Beevers 1976).

Metabolism of Purines and Pyrimidines

PURINES

The aerobic pathway of purine degradation appears to be much the same in animals and microorganisms (Vogels and van der Drift 1976). It is summarized in Fig. 5. Although it is possible that an alga might gain nitrogen only from the side $-NH_2$ of adenine or guanine, this restricted metabolism of purines is not known to occur. The best evidence for the occurrence of the reactions of Fig. 5 in algae comes from the studies of Lynch and her co-workers. *Chlorella* cells took up uric acid, xanthine, hypoxanthine, or adenine (the latter two only after long lag periods). Uric acid and xanthine were initially taken up faster than they were utilized so that they accumulated in the cells (Ammann and Lynch 1964). When utilization commenced analysis showed the presence of the expected intermediates. Thus hypoxanthine was produced from adenine, xanthine from hypoxanthine, and uric acid and allantoin from xanthine. The associated enzymes were not studied in detail but uricase was shown to be very active. The enzyme, allantoinase, which converts allantoin to allantoic acid is widely distributed in algae (Villeret 1955, 1958). Two enzymes are known in animals and bacteria, which metabolize allantoic acid. One is allantoicase catalyzing the conversion of allantoic acid to one molecule of urea and one of ureidoglycolate; the other is allantoate amidohydrolase which catalyzes the formation of $2NH_3$, $1CO_2$, and 1 ureidoglycolate. The enzyme ureidoglycolase converts ureidoglycolate into urea plus glyoxylic acid. Little is known of these enzymes in algae. Villeret's studies (1955, 1958) suggested a rather limited distribution of allantoicase among algae.

In fungi some of these enzymes, e.g. uricase and allantoinase, are inducible and their formation is repressed by NH_4^+ (Vogels and van der Drift 1976). Information is lacking for algae about regulation of these enzymes but the long periods of adaptation necessary before some algae can grow on hypoxanthine (Antia et al. 1975) strongly suggests that induction of new enzyme systems is necessary.

PYRIMIDINES

These are not good nitrogen sources for algal growth but uracil is degraded by *Chlorella* to CO_2 and β-alanine with dehydrouracil and β-ureidopropionic acid as intermediates (Knutsen 1972). These are the intermediates expected from the reductive route of pyrimidine degradation as established in some bacteria and fungi (Vogels and van der Drift 1976).

Uptake of Nitrogenous Compounds

NECESSITY FOR UPTAKE MECHANISMS

The concentrations of nitrogenous compounds in seawater are often low, i.e. 0–10 μM. More than 10 yr ago, Dugdale (1967), with natural populations of marine phytoplankton, and Eppley et al. (1969b), with pure cultures, showed that when rate of nitrate (or ammonium) uptake was plotted against concentration of nitrate (or ammonium) the result was a hyperbolic curve resembling the familiar Michaelis–Menten velocity/substrate curve for an enzyme-catalyzed reaction. Moreover, they showed that the concentration of nitrate (or ammonium), generally called the K_s value, that supported half the maximum rate of nitrate (or ammonium) uptake was 0.1–10 μM with the lower values being more characteristic of species from open oceans where environmental concentrations are lowest. These half-saturation concentrations are considerably lower than the concentrations necessary to half-saturate the enzyme, nitrate reductase, where K_m is often about 150 μM although it may be lower (about 50 μM) in some marine phytoplankters (Packard 1979). Even the K_m for glutamine synthetase (20–30 μM) looks

TABLE 4. Some examples of uptake systems for nitrogenous compounds in microalgae which result in substantial accumulation of substrate within the cells.

Organism	Compound	K_s (μM)	Inhibition by DNP, CCCP, or FCCP	References
Chlorella fusca	Phenylalanine	5.0	+	Pedersen and Knutsen (1974)
"	Uracil	0.25	+	Knutsen (1972)
"	Guanine	1.0	+	Pettersen and Knutsen (1974)
Chlorella pyrenoidosa	Methylammonium	4.0	N.T.[a]	Pelley and Bannister (1979)
Chlamydomonas reinhardii	Urea	5.1	+	Williams and Hodson (1976)
Cyclotella cryptica	Arginine	3.2	+	Liu and Hellebust (1974)
	Glutamic acid	36.0	+	"
	Methylammonium	5.0	N.T.[a]	Wheeler (1980)
Ditylum brightwellii	NH_4^+	1.1	N.T.[a]	Eppley and Rogers (1970)
	NO_2^-	4.0	N.T.[a]	"
	NO_3^-	0.6	N.T.[a]	"
Phaeodactylum tricornutum	Urea	0.6	+	Rees and Syrett (1979)
	NO_3^-	10.0	+	Cresswell and Syrett (1981)
	Methylammonium	30.0	+	Wright (unpublished)

[a]N.T. = not tested.

somewhat high against natural concentrations of NH_4^+ in seawater. A similar situation exists for urea metabolism where McCarthy (1972) found K_s values for uptake in several species of marine phytoplankton ranged from 0.2 to 0.8 μM whereas the K_m of urease is considerably higher, e.g. 460 μM for the urease from Phaeodactylum (Syrett and Leftley 1976). These findings clearly suggest the existence at the surface of the cells of uptake mechanisms with a high affinity for the substrate which will lead to the concentration of the substrate within the cell. Such mechanisms for the uptake of ammonium, nitrite, nitrate, urea, amino acids, pyrimidines, and purines have now been studied in algae. Some of them are listed in Table 4.

STUDY OF UPTAKE MECHANISMS

The more detailed study of uptake mechanisms has been much aided by the use of radioactive compounds. With nitrogenous compounds, radioactivity can usually be introduced only when the compound is organic; thus [14C]urea and 14C-labeled amino acids have proved useful. It is also helpful to use an analogue of the compound which is not metabolized in the cells. The uptake and accumulation of the analogue can then readily be measured, particularly if it is radioactive. [14C]Thiourea has been used to study urea uptake (Syrett and Bekheet 1977) and [14C]methylammo-

nium has been much used in the study of ammonium uptake mechanisms, e.g. in yeast (Dubois and Grenson 1979), in Chlorella (Pelley and Bannister 1979), in Phaeodactylum (Wright and Syrett unpublished data), and in Cyclotella (Wheeler 1980). A particularly interesting finding is the great increase in the rate of [14C]methylammonium transport which occurs when cells of Chlorella (Pelley and Bannister 1979), Cyclotella (Wheeler 1980), or Phaeodactylum (Fig. 6) are deprived of nitrogen for growth.

A radioactive analogue of nitrate that has been used in a limited way is [36Cl]chlorate (Tromballa and Broda 1971; Shehata 1977). Chlorate competes with nitrate for both the uptake mechanism and for nitrate reductase. In Chlorella with which it has been used, much of the chlorate is reduced to chlorite but in organisms known to accumulate nitrate, it might be an effective tool for measurement of the uptake system.

Several of the uptake systems listed in Table 4 share common features. First, the substrate is accumulated within the cells sometimes reaching a concentration 10^2 or 10^3 higher than the external concentration. Second, the uptake is inhibited by substances such as 2,4-dinitrophenol (DNP), carbonyl cyanide m-chlorophenyl hydrazone (CCCP), or p-trifluoromethoxy carbonyl cyanide phenylhydrazone (FCCP).

193

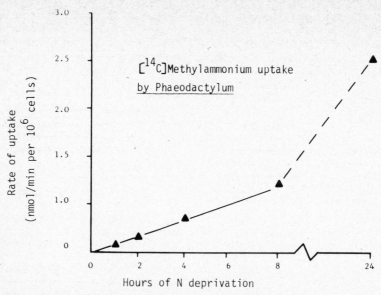

FIG. 6. Increase in rate of uptake of [^{14}C]methylammonium by *Phaeodactylum* as a consequence of N deprivation. The culture (2×10^6 cells/mL) was suspended in N-free medium, illuminated, and aerated with air containing 0.5% CO_2. Samples were removed at the times shown for measurement of [^{14}C]methylammonium uptake (S. Wright unpublished data).

A MODEL SYSTEM — HEXOSE UPTAKE

The best indication of how such uptake systems may work in microalgae comes from Tanner and Komor's detailed study of the mechanism of hexose-sugar uptake by *Chlorella*. The uptake system is inducible, i.e. it develops during 1-h incubation with glucose or with nonmetabolizable sugars such as 3-*O*-methylglucose or 6-deoxyglucose. Nonmetabolizable sugars may be taken up and concentrated in the cells by as much as 1600×. The uptake can be driven by cyclic photophorylation (i.e. it takes place in illuminated anaerobic cells in which O_2 evolution has been inhibited by DCMU) and it is inhibited by 50 μM FCCP. At pH 6.0–6.5 the K_s for uptake of glucose (and deoxyglucose) is 0.3 mM (Komor and Tanner 1971) but at higher pH values, the uptake system shifts to one of lower affinity, e.g. with a K_s of about 30 mM at pH 8.4 (Komor and Tanner 1975). The simultaneous occurrence of dual uptake systems for the same substrate, one of high affinity and one of low affinity, has often been noted (Nissen 1974). When deoxyglucose is added to induced cells at pH 6.5 it is immediately taken up and at the same time the external medium becomes more alkaline; the transient pH rise lasts for about 60 s and the stoichiometry is such that one OH^- ion is produced for each molecule of deoxyglucose taken up (Komor 1973).

These results are consistent with a mechanism of uptake in which hexose transport is linked to a co-transport of protons (H^+) (or a counter transport of OH^- ions) as proposed by Mitchell (1967). In this proposal the driving force for uptake is a proton gradient across the cell boundary which is maintained by metabolism; the theory can be represented diagrammatically as in Fig. 7 (Eddy 1978). On the left of Fig. 7 is an ATP-ase whose function is to pump out protons with a stoichiometry of m H^+ per ATP hydrolyzed and on the right a cotransport mechanism in which the transport of one substrate molecule, S, is linked to the cotransport of n protons. In the glucose uptake system $n = 1$.

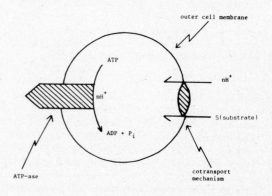

FIG. 7. Model for substrate (S) uptake by proton-linked cotransport (Eddy 1978). See text for explanation.

194

If the transported complex is indeed S - H$^+$ as shown in Fig. 7, then the complex is charged and the driving force for its movement can have two components: (i) the pH gradient across the membrane and (ii) the difference in charge across the membrane, i.e. the membrane potential. The role of ATP which is generated by metabolic reactions is to maintain these gradients across the membrane. Komor and Tanner (1974, 1976) have estimated both the pH gradient and the membrane potential of *Chlorella* by measuring equilibrium distributions between cells and medium of radioactive dimethyloxazolidinedione (distribution determined by difference in pH) or radioactive tetraphenylphosphonium (distribution determined by difference in potential). With an external pH of 6.0, they find an internal pH of 7.1 and a membrane potential of -135 mV (i.e. cell interior is negatively charged with respect to external medium). Moreover, the membrane potential is shown to rise (i.e. become *less* negative) when FCCP is added. It also rises when 6-deoxyglucose is added and taken up as the theory depicted in Fig. 7 requires. Komor and Tanner (1976) calculated the free energy requirement to maintain a 1600-fold accumulation of 6-deoxyglucose. They also calculated that, of this energy requirement, the measured difference in pH can contribute about one-third and the membrane potential about two-thirds, giving a sufficent total to meet the free energy requirement.

The agreement between the measured pH and membrane potential gradients and those predicted by the Mitchell theory as necessary to maintain the measured concentration gradient of 6-deoxyglucose is impressive. It may be partly fortuitous for, after all, a *Chlorella* cell is a complex structure with organelles and small vacuoles: one does not know what internal gradients of pH or of membrane potential exist, nor does one know that the deoxyglucose is uniformly distributed within the cell; it seems unlikely that it is. Nevertheless the model depicted in Fig. 7 clearly has experimental support. One of its chief features is that the pump driven by ATP is not particularly closely linked to the uptake mechanism for the substrate. Rather, the role of metabolism, through ATP, is to maintain a differential between cell interior and the outside from which the uptake of the substrate follows. The system very much resembles that studied by Jacques (1938–39) many years ago where distribution of ammonium between seaweed cells and seawater was determined by differences in pH and the NH$_3$ was thought to combine with something in the cell surface which played a part in transport.

More work is needed to determine whether the model of Fig. 7 is correct. It does not explain the occurrence of a NO$'_3$, Cl$'$ stimulated ATP-ase in membrane preparations from *Skeletonema* and

Chroomonas (Falkowski 1975). If such ATP-ases are important in uptake and are specifically stimulated by substrates in cell-free preparations the linkage between the ATP-ase and the substrate uptake mechanism must be much closer than as depicted in Fig. 7.

H$^+$ AND Na$^+$ COTRANSPORT

Nevertheless, evidence is growing that the uptake of substrates other than sugars may be by a proton-linked cotransport (or OH$^-$-ion linked counter transport). For example, thiourea uptake by *Chlorella* is accompanied by a 1.1 uptake of protons (T. A. V. Rees unpublished data).

It has long been known that the uptake of nitrate and ammonium by algal cultures is accompanied by pH changes, the medium becoming alkaline when nitrate is used and acidic when ammonium is taken up. That such changes in H$^+$ and OH$^-$ must inevitably accompany the conversion of NO$'_3$ or NH$^+_4$ N into cellular nitrogen was well shown by the equations that Cramer and Myers (1948) were able to write for *Chlorella* growth. It is, however, only recently that the changes in pH have been linked mechanistically to the uptake of the ions by algae (Raven and De Michelis 1979; Ullrich 1979).

In animal cells transport of substrate apparently takes place by cotransport with Na$^+$ ions rather than with protons (Eddy 1978). It is possible that the same is true in microscopic marine plants. There are now a number of reports of sodium-dependent transport, e.g. of phosphate by the marine fungus *Thraustochytrium roseum* (Siegenthaler et al. 1967), of glucose, amino acids, and methylammonium by *Cyclotella* (Hellebust 1978; Wheeler and Hellebust 1981), and of urea and nitrate by *Phaeodactylum* (Rees et al. 1980). It is tempting to speculate that in such plants which live in an environment where the concentration of Na$^+$ is high but that of H$^+$ is low, substrate uptake may take place by systems resembling that of Fig. 7 but with Na$^+$ replacing H$^+$.

Regulation of Nitrate Reduction: Effects of Ammonium

It is now well known that during growth in batch culture with ammonium nitrate as N source, the NH$^+_4$ is assimilated first, and only when it has gone is NO$'_3$ utilized (Ludwig 1938; Harvey 1953). There are several reasons for this preferential assimilation of ammonium. Active nitrate reductase is not formed in the presence of NH$^+_4$ nor is the NO$'_3$ uptake system. And even if active nitrate reductase and an NO$'_3$ uptake system are present, the addition of NH$^+_4$ can lead to a rapid cessation of NO$'_3$ utilization. These effects of NH$^+_4$ have now been observed with a variety of micro algae and they have been subject to considerable laboratory investigation in recent years.

REGULATION OF NITRATE REDUCTASE FORMATION

Active nitrate reductase (NR) is not formed while NH_4^+ is present as a major source of nitrogen. Active NR is formed when NH_4^+-grown cells are transferred to nitrogen-free medium (Morris and Syrett 1965; Öesterheld 1971; Hipkin and Syrett 1977a). It has been argued that cells suspended in N-free medium produce small quantities of NO_3^- which then lead to induction of NR (Kessler and Öesterheld 1970; Spiller et al. 1976) but others dispute this (Syrett and Hipkin 1973). No NO_3^- formation could be detected in nitrogen-deprived cultures of a *Chlamydomonas* mutant lacking the ability to assimilate NO_3^- yet during nitrogen deprivation the cultures formed a modified form of NR (Hipkin et al. 1980). It seems most likely therefore that the major effect of nitrogen deprivation is to remove NH_4^+ repression of the formation of NR. It is unlikely that the repressor is NH_4^+ per se. In the fungus *Neurospora* where a rather similar control operates, there is good evidence that the repressor of NR formation is glutamine (Premakumar et al. 1979; Dunn-Coleman et al. 1979). Nevertheless although NR is formed in nitrogen-deprived algae in the absence of NO_3^-, addition of NO_3^- generally leads to more rapid production of NR and a greater maximum activity. This may be partly because the NO_3^- N is assimilated and used for protein synthesis including synthesis of NR. This cannot be the whole story, however, because with the *Chlamydomonas* mutant lacking NAD(P)H–NR, which is unable to reduce nitrate, although addition of nitrate has no effect on the initial formation of the altered NR activity that this mutant forms, it does have a large effect later, possibly by preventing degradation of the enzyme (Hipkin et al. 1980).

The formation of NR is inhibited by cycloheximide, an inhibitor of protein synthesis, but not by 6-methyl purine which inhibits RNA synthesis (Hipkin and Syrett 1977b). This suggests that the formation of a messenger RNA is not necessary. Moreover, it is now known that NH_4^+-grown cells of *Chlorella* contain substantial quantities of a protein which is immunologically very close to NR (Funkhouser and Ramadoss 1980). Thus formation of active NA after removal of NH_4^+ does not necessitate de novo synthesis of the whole NR molecule but only of part of it. As the formation of active enzyme is prevented by tungstate (Solomonson and Spehar 1977) it is probable that one part that has to be synthesized contains Mo; it may be that a small molecular weight Mo-containing peptide has to be formed and added to the preformed major protein.

The regulation of the formation of nitrite reductase has received much less attention. Like NR, its formation in diatoms (Eppley and Rogers 1970; Llama et al. 1979), *Platymonas* (Ricketts and Edge 1978), *Chlorella* (Losada et al. 1970), and *Chlamydomonas* (Herrera et al. 1972) is repressed in the presence of ammonium.

DISAPPEARANCE OF NR ACTIVITY

There are at least three mechanisms by which NR activity can disappear from cells. These include two sorts of reversible inactivation phenomena and an irreversible loss of the enzyme due, presumably, to degradation.

Losada et al. (1970) described an inactivation of NR after addition of NH_4^+ to *Chlorella* cells assimilating NO_3^-. Inactivation was almost complete in 90 min and was reversed following removal of NH_4^+ and its replacement by NO_3^-. In cell-free extracts, the inactivated NR still retains its cytochrome reductase activity (see Fig. 3) and the NR activity can be restored by incubation with the mild oxidant, potassium ferricyanide. At about the same time Vennesland and Jetschmann (1971) described an inactive nitrate reductase in another strain of *Chlorella*. The NR activity in cell-free extracts as normally prepared was only partial but full activity developed during storage of the extract at 4°C in phosphate buffer. Later studies showed that the cytochrome reductase activity was always fully developed and that full NR activity was restored by oxidation with ferricyanide (Pistorius et al. 1976). Much work has now been done by the Losada and Vennesland schools to elucidate the details of this reversible inactivation. Both agree that reduction of the enzyme, probably at the molybdenum site, is necessary for inactivation. The presence of NO_3^- protects the enzyme. The chief difference between their views is that the Losada group hold that reduction of the enzyme by NAD(P)H, with the involvement of oxygen and ADP, is sufficient to inactivate the enzyme in vitro (Losada and Guerrero 1979). The Vennesland group hold that a small amount of cyanide (10^{-3} μM) must also be present which combines with the enzyme (Lorimer et al. 1974; Pistorius et al. 1976).

The role of this reversible inactivation in vivo is not easy to assess. There is no doubt that the reversible inactivation of NR following NH_4^+ addition occurs but most workers find it less rapid and dramatic than as originally described by Losada et al. (1970) and Herrera et al. (1972) (e.g. Rigano and Violante 1972; Pistorius et al. 1978). Rigano's work is with *Cyanidium* where the NR after extraction is partially inactive with activity being fully restored by heat treatment; *Dunaliella* also has a heat-activated NR activity (Heimer 1975). The in vivo reversible inactivation seems greatest with high O_2 and low

CO$_2$ concentrations (Pistorius et al. 1976) and this suggests a link with photorespiration. Solomonson and Spehar (1977) have developed a model for the regulation of NR activity in vivo which suggests that intracellular cyanide plays an important part, it being formed by an interaction between glyoxylate (from photorespiration) and hydroxylamine (from NO$_2'$ reduction).

The other type of reversible inactivation is best seen in studies of *Chlorella* cultures synchronized by light/dark alternation (Hodler et al. 1972; Tischner 1976; Griffiths 1979). Activities of NR and nitrite reductase increase rapidly during the light period. The activities decrease during the dark period although they may begin to fall before the dark period starts. Tischner and Hütterman (1978) showed that the rapid increase of NR activity following illumination is due to conversion of a preformed macromolecule into active enzyme but the activation differs from the oxidation activation discussed above because it is inhibited in vivo by cycloheximide and cannot, in cell-free extracts, be brought about by oxidation with ferricyanide. Possibly part of the enzyme is synthesized during this process as appears to happen when the enzyme is induced in NH$_4^+$-grown cells (see above).

In addition, irreversible degradation of NR probably occurs when, for example, cells are given ammonium or darkened (e.g. Thacker and Syrett 1972b) but it is not clear how such losses of activity are related to the reversible type studied by Tischner and Hütterman.

EFFECTS OF AMMONIUM ON NITRATE UPTAKE

NO$_3'$ uptake by algal cells generally stops very quickly when NH$_4^+$ is added and recommences when the NH$_4^+$ has disappeared because of its assimilation (Syrett and Morris 1963; Eppley et al. 1969a; Conway et al. 1976). This inhibition by NH$_4^+$ is too rapid to be accounted for by the inactivation of nitrate reductase and there have been several suggestions that it is due to an effect on uptake. This effect is most readily demonstrated using diatoms where the appearance of NO$_3'$ in the cells can be measured (Fig. 8). Serra et al. (1978b) demonstrated similar NH$_4^+$ inhibition of NO$_3'$ uptake using *Skeletonema* grown with tungstate to produce inactive NR.

With highly carbon-deficient cells, NH$_4^+$ does not inhibit NO$_3'$ uptake; indeed NO$_3'$ is reduced to NH$_4^+$ which accumulates (Syrett and Morris 1963; Thacker and Syrett 1972a; Ullrich 1979). These findings suggest that it is not NH$_4^+$ that is the inhibitor but an organic product of NH$_4^+$ assimilation. Following the finding that GS plays a major role in the assimilation of NH$_4^+$, it has now been shown that algae incubated with MSO (an inhibitor of GS) show

no NH$_4^+$ inhibition of NO$_3'$ uptake and, as with C-deficient cells, NO$_3'$ is reduced to NH$_4^+$ which accumulates (Rigano et al. 1979a; Cullimore and Sims 1981). As MSO stops glutamine formation one might suggest that glutamine is the inhibitor of NO$_3'$ uptake. However, with *Anacystis*, NH$_4^+$ does not inhibit NO$_3'$ uptake in the presence of either MSO or azaserine which inhibits GOGAT and hence does not prevent glutamine formation (Flores et al. 1980). Hence, if the inhibitor is organic, it is not glutamine, but something formed from it. Conway et al. (1976) suggested that inhibition was caused by the total internal amino acid pool.

Another possibility is that the inhibition results not from an organic product of NH$_4^+$ assimilation but from the production of protons as NH$_4^+$ incorporation may be represented as:

$$NH_4^+ + \text{organic C} \longrightarrow \text{organic N} + H^+$$

(Raven and De Michaelis 1979)

Proton production inside the cells could interfere with NO$_3'$ uptake if this does take place by H$^+$- or Na$^+$-linked cotransport but it is difficult to see how such an inhibitory mechanism could be sufficiently selective. It is also unlikely because NO$_2'$ addition has the same inhibitory effect on NO$_3'$ assimilation (Thacker and Syrett 1972a).

The effects of addition of NH$_4^+$ to cells assimilating NO$_3'$ are thus complex. The first effect appears to be an inhibition of NO$_3'$ uptake but this is followed by loss of NR (and nitrite reductase) activities. The loss of NR activity will be partly due to a reversible inactivation, and partly due to irreversible loss of enzyme with the rate of proteolytic breakdown of NR possibly being greater in the presence of NH$_4^+$ (Hipkin et al. 1980). At the same time addition of NH$_4^+$ stops the synthesis of NR.

SIMULTANEOUS ASSIMILATION OF AMMONIUM AND NITRATE

Although NH$_4^+$ inhibition of NO$_3'$ assimilation by algae has often been demonstrated both with laboratory cultures and in field experiments (MacIsaac and Dugdale 1969, 1972) it is clear that algae that are highly nitrogen deficient or growing with a limiting nitrogen supply assimilate both NH$_4^+$ and NO$_3'$ simultaneously. This was shown nearly 50 yr ago by Urhan (1932) using nitrogen-starved *Chlorella* and *Scenedesmus*. Simultaneous assimilation has been demonstrated using nitrogen-limited chemostat cultures, e.g. Bienfang (1975) with *Dunaliella*, Caperon and Ziemann (1976) with *Pavlova (Monochrysis)*. In Bienfang's experiments the steady-state NH$_4^+$ concentration never exceeded 0.5 μM but in

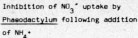
Inhibition of NO$_3^-$ uptake by
__Phaeodactylum__ following addition
of NH$_4^+$

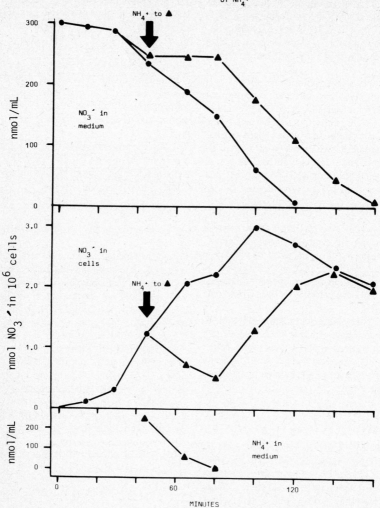

FIG. 8. Effect of NH$_4^+$ addition to a *Phaeodactylum* culture in a NO$_3^-$ medium on A (top), NO$_3^-$ disappearance from the medium; B (middle), NO$_3^-$ appearance in the cells; C (bottom) shows NH$_4^+$ disappearance from the medium; NO$_3^-$ uptake recommences after the NH$_4^+$ has gone (2 × 10^7 organisms/mL) (Cresswell and Syrett 1979).

the experiments with *Pavlova* cells taken from a nitrogen-limited chemostat, simultaneous uptake of NH$_4^+$ and NO$_3^-$ occurred with NH$_4^+$ concentrations of 4 μM.

NITROGEN STATUS OF ALGAL CULTURES

Algal cultures can exist in various states of nitrogen nutrition. With batch cultures these range, at one extreme, from cultures growing with an ample supply of NH$_4^+$ to cultures that are existing in a N-free medium at the other. In between, some cultures grow with N sources such as NO$_3^-$, urea, or amino acids which, while allowing close to maximal growth rates, nevertheless do not repress the formation of some enzymes as does NH$_4^+$. In chemostat cultures various states of nitrogen nutrition can also be arranged by limiting the N input in the medium. It may be, however, that nitrogen limitation by chemostat culture produces rather different metabolic states than does N starvation of batch cultures.

The effects of nitrogen deprivation are summarized in Table 5. Some of the more obvious effects are an accumulation of carbon compounds such as polysaccharides and fats, a reduction in the rate of photosynthesis, and, sometimes, a loss of chlorophyll. When supplied with NO_3', and more especially NH_4^+, the N compound is assimilated more rapidly than it is by normal-growing N-replete cells (see Table 6). Enzymic readjustments occur during N-deprivation. For example, in N-starved batch culture of *Ankistrodesmus*, there were increases in the activities of NR, nitrite reductase, GDH, GS, and the allophanate hydrolase component of urea amidolyase. In contrast, ribulose biphosphate carboxylase activity fell as did the rate of $^{14}CO_2$ incorporation but the activity of glucose-6-phosphate dehydrogenase increased (Hipkin and Syrett 1977a). In N-limited chemostat cultures similar adjustments are seen. For example, with *Thalassiosira* (Eppley and Renger 1974) increased N limitation, by reduction of the dilution rate, led to a fall in the rate of photosynthesis as measured by allowing samples to fix $^{14}CO_2$ at saturating light intensity, but to little change in chlorophyll. Increasing N limitation increased the maximum rates of NO_3' or NH_4^+ assimilation and NR activity per cell. In contrast, GDH activity fell markedly; GS activity was not measured. Not only the activities of metabolic enzymes change but also the activities of uptake mechanisms. Thus in *Phaeodactylum* even a short period of N deprivation leads to a marked increase in the rates of uptake of nitrate, urea, and methylammonium and in other diatoms and in *Platymonas* the activity of uptake systems for amino acids rises steeply (North and Stephens 1971; Liu and Hellebust 1974).

Conway et al. (1976) used N-limited cultures of *Skeletonema* to study the relationship between rate of uptake of NH_4^+ and NH_4^+ concentration. Rate of uptake increased with increasing NH_4^+ concentration up to a concentration at which the rate quite suddenly became maximal and higher NH_4^+ concentrations produced no further increase. The maximum rate of uptake was dependent on the N content of the cells, cells with the lowest N/cell giving the highest maximum rate. Conway et al. interpret these results as showing that rate of NH_4^+ uptake vs. NH_4^+ concentration follows Michaelis-Menten kinetics but only up to the point at which some internal factor

TABLE 5. Changes in algal cultures consequent upon nitrogen status.

Cultures grown on NH_4^+	Cultures grown on NO_3' or urea	Nitrogen-deficient cultures
		accumulation of C reserves
		decrease in rate of PS
		loss of RuBP carboxylase activity
		loss of chlorophyll
		increased proteolysis
repression of some N-assimilatory enzymes		increase in activity of N-assimilatory enzymes
repression of uptake systems for N compounds		increase in activity of uptake systems for N compounds
		induction of gamete formation

imposes a limitation on rate of uptake. This they suggest may be the concentration of the intracellular pool of amino acids (Sims et al. 1968). This may be so but it is clear that we are far from understanding the internal controls that regulate the metabolic readjustments that occur during N deprivation. Interest now focuses on the glutamine synthetase pathway. Glutamine may play an important regulatory role or the regulator may be, as in the bacterium *Klebsiella*, the glutamine synthetase protein itself (Tyler 1978).

Effects of Light on Nitrate Assimilation: Interaction with Carbon Metabolism

NECESSITY FOR A SUPPLY OF CARBON

Figure 9 and Table 6 show some results from work with *Chlamydomonas* which illustrate a number of points relating to NO_3' and NH_4^+ assimilation and their interrelationships with light and carbon metabolism. Essentially similar results have been found with *Dunaliella* and other algae (Grant 1967, 1968; Grant and Turner 1969). Figure 9 shows that with a "normal" culture of *Chlamydomonas* the assimilation of *both* NO_3' and NH_4^+ is dependent on photosynthesis: that is assimilation requires light + CO_2; removal of either of these prevents assimilation and

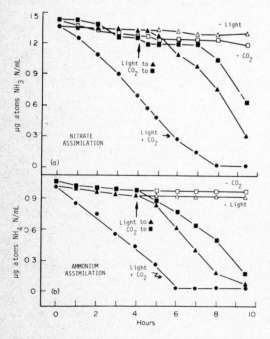

FIG. 9. Effect of darkness or removal of CO_2 on uptake of (a) NO_3', (b) NH_4^+ by *Chlamydomonas*. All cultures except the $-CO_2$ ones were aerated throughout with air containing 0.5% CO_2 (from Thacker and Syrett 1972).

TABLE 6. Rates of assimilation of NO_3' and NH_4^+ by *Chlamydomonas* (Thacker and Syrett 1972). (Rates are μg atoms $N \cdot (mg\ dry\ wt)^{-1} \cdot h^{-1}$.)

	NO_3'		NH_4^+	
	Normal cells	N-deprived cells	Normal cells	N-deprived cells
In darkness	0.013	0.14	0.000	0.58
In light	0.117	0.38	0.127	0.81
Stimulation by light (%)	800	170	∞	39

so does the addition of a low concentration of 3-(3,4-dichlorophenyl)-1',1'-dimethylurea (DCMU). Moreover, one notes that in light with CO_2, the rates of NH_4^+ and NO_3' assimilation are about the same. One might interpret these results as demonstrating an obligatory linkage between NO_3' or NH_4^+ assimilation and light. But that this is not so is shown by Table 6. In this experiment the *Chlamydomonas* cultures were allowed to photosynthesize overnight in a nitrogen-free medium; the cells then become nitrogen starved and accumulate polysaccharide. Such cultures now assimilate either NO_3' or NH_4^+ in darkness. NH_4^+ is assimilated some 4 times faster than nitrate but even NO_3' is assimilated faster than it is by "normal" photosynthesizing cells. Nevertheless even higher rates of NO_3' or NH_4^+ assimilation are attained when these nitrogen-starved cells are illuminated with CO_2 (Table 6).

One can conclude then that both NO_3' and NH_4^+ assimilation can take place in darkness provided that sufficient carbon reserves are available; the extent to which illumination will stimulate assimilation will depend on the metabolic state of the cells (Grant and Turner 1969).

Figure 9 shows that "normal" cells, when illuminated without CO_2, do nothing with NO_3', that is, they do not reduce it to NH_4^+ as do cells which are carbon-starved as well as being deprived of CO_2. This finding points to the operation of a feed-back control in "normal" cells when unable to photosynthesize, which prevents reduction of NO_3', possibly by stopping uptake. The control is absent from carbon-starved cells and probably works through levels of organic N compounds; it is removed when ample carbon is available (see Table 8 for summary).

PHOTOGENERATION OF REDUCTANT

The results of Fig. 9 illustrate one relationship between photosynthesis and nitrogen assimilation but ever since Warburg and Negelein's (1920) demonstration of a light stimulation of NO_3' reduction by *Chlorella* closer connections between nitrate assimilation and light have been sought.

It should be noted that NO_3' assimilation, like CO_2 assimilation, is a reductive process. Losada (1980) has emphasized that reduction of a N atom in NO_3' to a N atom in an amino acid requires 10 electrons. Reduction of one CO_2 molecule to (CH_2O) requires 4. As the C:N ratio of phytoplankton cells is about 5, the ratio of electrons required for CO_2 incorporation to those required for NO_3' N incorporation by growing cells is about $5 \times 4:10$ or $2:1$. This argument does not necessarily imply that the reductant for NO_3' assimilation is derived directly from photochemical reactions but it does illustrate that considerable amounts of reductant have to be generated for NO_3' N assimilation.

The physiological electron donors for NO_3' reduction to NH_4^+ are NADH (and NADPH in some algae) for eucaryotic NR, and reduced ferredoxin for the NR of blue-green algae and for all nitrite reductases. Reduced ferredoxin or NADH is also required for the GOGAT reaction of NH_4^+ assimilation. Neither NO_3' nor NO_2' reduction requires ATP whereas the assimilation of ammonium by the GS/GOGAT pathway does requires ATP to drive the synthesis of glutamine. Ferredoxin is well known as a component of the photochemical reactions in the chloroplast where it is reduced by electrons derived from Photosystem I. It is likely, therefore, that there will be a close connection between light and those reactions that require reduced ferredoxin to drive them. But we also note (Table 6) that NO_3' assimilation to organic N can occur in darkness; therefore there must be dark catabolic reactions that can lead to ferredoxin reduction just as there must be for the nitrogen fixation system of blue-green algae. In the chloroplast, electrons from reduced ferredoxin can be transferred and so reduce pyridine nucleotide. But the chloroplast pyridine nucleotide that is so reduced is NADPH. Although this can act as electron donor for some nitrate reductases, all eucaryotic algal nitrate reductases can use NADH as electron donor and some only utilize this (Table 3). Moreover, the major pathway for NADH reduction in cells is the TCA cycle reactions of the mitochondrion with the glycolytic triose phosphate dehydrogenase reaction (located in the cytoplasm) playing a subsidiary role.

With cell-free preparations of chloroplasts of chlorophyll-containing particles a photochemically driven reduction of NO_3' to NH_4^+ can be demonstrated (Paneque et al. 1969; Candau et al. 1976). Studies with whole cells are physiologically more relevant and with these a quantitative photochemical conversion of NO_3' to NH_4^+ can be demonstrated by preventing NH_4^+ assimilation either by rigorous exclusion of carbon (e.g. Syrett and Morris 1963 with *Chlorella* 8p.; Thacker and Syrett 1972 with *Chlamydomonas*; Ullrich 1979 with *Ankistrodesmus*) or by treatment with MSO (e.g. Ramos et al. 1980a with *Anacystis*). The result with *Chlorella* is worth noting because this strain of *Chlorella* contains an NADH-specific nitrate reductase so that presumably NADH must have been generated via the photochemical reactions in the chloroplasts. These experiments with whole cells are successful, however, only because the conditions of treatment, i.e. deprivation of carbon or treatment with MSO, somehow remove the normal inhibition of NO_3' assimilation by NH_4^+; possibly this is because the treatments prevent the formation of glutamine. They do not necessarily prove that in the normal growing algal cell, reductant for NO_3' reduction is generated by photochemical reactions. Perhaps the best evidence that it may be is the demonstration that at saturating light intensity, the rate of oxygen evolution by *Chlorella* was increased by addition of NO_3' while CO_2 assimilation was unchanged (van Niel et al. 1953). As the carbon dioxide reduction system was already working at full capacity, the evolution of extra O_2 when NO_3' was added could not be due to the assimilation of CO_2 produced during a dark reduction of NO_3'. This rather clear-cut result of van Niel et al. (1953) appears not to have been confirmed by workers with other algal species (Bongers 1958; Grant and Turner 1969). Generally, addition of NO_3' depresses CO_2 fixation. This depression could result from a direct competition between NO_3' (and NO_2' produced from it) and CO_2 for photochemically generated electrons or it could result from an increased rate of respiration coupled to NO_3' reduction. The extent of the depression of CO_2 fixation is, however, often too great, particularly with nitrogen-deficient cells (e.g. Thomas et al. 1976), to make the second alternative tenable.

There is more evidence for a direct photochemical reduction of nitrite in algae (Kessler 1957, 1964). Nitrogen-deficient cells, with C reserves, can, in low illumination or darkness, reduce NO_3' to NO_2' which accumulates because the photochemical reactions to reduce NO_2' further are lacking (Carlucci et al. 1970; Thomas et al. 1976).

Interrelationship with Mitochondrial Metabolism

The complexities of the relationship between light and NO_3' reduction are well illustrated by recent work with higher plant leaves. NO_3' reduction to NO_2' is strictly light dependent and normally ceases as soon as light is removed. However, NO_3' reduction continues in darkness under anaerobiosis or when the mitochondrial electron transport chain is inhibited with antimycin A (Canvin and Atkins 1974; Canvin and Woo 1979). The anaerobic dark reduction of nitrate is inhibited by malonate and the inhibition is removed by addition of fumarate; these observations imply that it is the TCA cycle that is supplying electrons for NO_3^- reduction (Ramaroa et al. 1980) and are consistent with the view that, in leaves, the NADH for nitrate reduction is generated in the mitochondrion by TCA-cycle reactions. Under aerobic conditions in darkness this NADH is not used for nitrate reduction but is reoxidized by molecular oxygen via the electron chain, i.e. it is used in normal aerobic respiration and ATP is generated by oxidative phosphorylation. If the transport of electrons down the mitochondrial electron transport chain to oxygen is prevented by (i) antimycin A or (ii) lack of oxygen or (iii) a high level of ATP coming from photophosphorylation, then the NADH is not reoxidized by oxygen but by NO_3^-. Thus the strict light dependence of NO_3^- reduction under aerobic conditions is explained although the reactions generating electrons for NO_3^- reduction are essentially dark respiratory ones (Sawhney et al. 1978). Whether such a regulatory mechanism for NO_3^- reduction occurs in algal cells is not known but it is clear that interrelationships between the cellular organelles may play a major part in metabolic control.

PHOTOGENERATION OF ATP

Light can have other effects on nitrate metabolism. For example, CCCP and FCCP are known to uncouple the formation of ATP from the electron transport reactions in the mitochondria and the chloroplasts and to decrease the charge difference across the plasma membrane; 10 μM CCCP inhibits both NO_3^- and NO_2^- reduction by illuminated *Ankistrodesmus* (Ullrich 1974) and 0.2 μM FCCP inhibits NO_3^- reduction and NO_2^- reduction by *Scenedesmus* at pH 6.5 (Andersson and Larrson 1980); at pH 5.0 NO_2^- reduction is much less inhibited by FCCP. The explanation here is that NO_3^- (and NO_2^- at pHs around neutrality) enters the cells by an active uptake mechanism requiring ATP which can come from photophosphorylation. Uncouplers which prevent ATP synthesis consequently stop NO_3^- reduction. This mechanism comes close to the suggestion of Warburg and Negelein (1920) that light stimulates NO_3^- reduction by *Chlorella* by increasing the rate of permeation into the cells.

LIGHT ACTIVATION/INACTIVATION OF ENZYMES

Another effect of light just becoming understood is its effect on enzyme activation and deactivation. Several of the enzymes of the Calvin cycle in the chloroplasts, e.g. ribulose biphosphate carboxylase and fructosebiphosphatase, are inactive in darkness but become active following illumination. Other enzymes of glycolysis (e.g. phosphofructokinase) and of the pentose phosphate pathway (e.g. glucose-6-phosphate dehydrogenase) are active in darkness but inactivated by light and, in some algae, ribulose biphosphate carboxylase becomes inactivated again at high light intensities (Codd and Stewart 1980). Part, at least, of the mechanism of light activation/inactivation involves the reduction of the enzyme by electrons derived from reduced ferredoxin and passed to the enzyme via a low molecular weight protein, thioredoxin (Buchanan 1980). Light may, however, activate enzymes more directly. One inactive form of *Chlorella* nitrate reductase can be reactivated in vitro in darkness by addition of the oxidant, ferricyanide: it can also be activated in vitro by illumination with blue light but *not* by red light (Aparacio et al. 1976). Yet another type of light activation of NR occurs in light/dark synchronized cultures of *Chlorella*; this has been discussed above. In these cultures not only NR but also glutamine synthetase and GOGAT show light activation (Tischner 1980).

EFFECTS OF LIGHT QUALITY ON PROTEIN SYNTHESIS

Another effect of light on algal nitrogen metabolism is that of light quality on the nature of the products of photosynthesis (see Kowallik 1970; Raven 1974). In general, blue light favors the production of amino acids and proteins rather than of carbohydrate with either NO_3^-, NH_4^+, or urea as N source. *Chlorella* has been much studied but so have the marine microalgae *Cyclotella nana* and *Dunaliella tertiolecta* (Wallen and Geen 1971); both these organisms grew faster in blue light than in white light of equal energy content, and a greater proportion of ^{14}C fixed went into protein. The underlying mechanism is not understood but the effect may be confined to eucaryotes and Kowallik points to a suggestion of Pirson that the explanation may lie in effects of light quality on intracellular transport of metabolites, across the chloroplast boundary, for instance.

SUMMARY

Table 7 summarizes some of the ways in which light can affect algal nitrogen assimilation and Table 8, the interaction between light and the metabolic state of the cells as these factors alter NO_3^- and NH_4^+ assimilation.

TABLE 7. Possible interactions of light with inorganic nitrogen metabolism of algae.

PHOTOSYNTHETIC (CHLOROPLAST) EFFECTS

(i) Generation of reduced ferredoxin which then:
    (a) reduces NO_2' (and N_2 and NO_3' in blue-greens).
    (b) reduces NAD(P)H and hence NO_3' in eucaryotic algae.
    (c) drives GOGAT reaction of NH_4^+ assimilation.
    (d) activates/inactivates enzymes via thioredoxin.

(ii) Generation of ATP through photophosphorylation which then:
    (a) is used for to drive transport mechanisms for NO_3', NO_2', NH_4^+.
    (b) drives GS reaction of NH_4^+ assimilation.
    (c) stops the reoxidation of mitochondrial NADH by O_2 so making this NADH available for NO_3' reduction.
    (d) drives N_2 fixation in blue-greens.

(iii) Photosynthetic fixation of CO_2 makes C acceptors available for NH_4^+ assimilation thus removing feed back inhibition by organic N compounds of NO_3' (NO_2') uptake.

OTHER EFFECTS

(i) Phytochrome (red light) effects?
(ii) Direct enzyme activation/inactivation by blue light possibly mediated through flavoproteins.
(iii) Effects of light quality on protein synthesis.

TABLE 8. Interaction of light and metabolic state in determining NH_4^+ or NO_3' assimilation by microalgae such as *Chlamydomonas* and *Dunaliella*.

		Metabolic state of cells	
	Carbon-starved $-CO_2$	Normal growth fast $+CO_2$	Nitrogen-starved
Storage C compounds	Nil	Very low	High
Rate of assimilation of			
NH_4^+ Light	0	+	+ + + +
NH_4^+ Dark	0	0	+ + +
NO_3' Light	+ ammonium accumulates	+	+ +
NO_3' Dark	0	0	+ nitrite accumulates
NH_4^+ inhibition of NO_3' uptake	0	+ [a]	± [a]

[a] With dependence on NH_4^+ concentration.

Relevance of Laboratory Investigations to Studies of Natural Populations

It is never easy to extend to natural populations the results of laboratory studies, carried out under defined conditions with pure cultures of organisms, often of little ecological significance. But there are several situations where analogies can be drawn and to conclude attention is drawn briefly to three examples.

First, the well-known diel periodicity of NR activity (and of NO_3' uptake) which has been observed with diatoms (Eppley et al. 1971) and with other phytoplankters in culture and in natural populations (Eppley et al. 1970) has a clear relationship to the light activation of NR that has been so well studied in synchronous *Chlorella* cultures.

Second, studies in the oceans of the assimilation of NH_4^+, urea, NO_2', and NO_3' which show preferential assimilation of NH_4^+ followed by urea, but simultaneous assimilation of all substrates when concentrations are low (McCarthy et al. 1977) must be considered in relationship to laboratory studies which reveal a variety of effects of ammonium on nitrate metabolism. (These studies also suggest that the extent of ammonium inhibition of nitrate assimilation will depend both on NH_4^+ concentration and on the metabolic state of the organisms.

Lastly, one can comment on the relationship of laboratory studies to the vertical distribution of nitrite (NO_2') in oceans. In late summer in the N. Pacific, NO_2' concentration is relatively low down to a depth of 100 m. It then rises sharply to a peak at 130 m depth and then declines again; this peak coincides with a maximum of chlorophyll. In contrast, NO_3' concentration remains low until 130 m, and then begins to rise markedly so that its concentration continues to increase down to 200 m and beyond (Kiefer et al. 1976). There are two major ways in which NO_2' may be formed. First, from NO_3' reduction by phytoplankton (Vaccaro and Ryther 1960); second, from bacterial oxidation of NH_4^+ (Wada and Hattori 1971). The relative importance of the two processes may well differ in different circumstances. Nevertheless, laboratory studies of algal cultures utilizing NO_3' show that among the conditions leading to NO_2' accumulation are (i) the presence of nitrogen-deficient organisms rich in C reserves and (ii) inhibition of photoreactions by either darkness or a chemical inhibitor (DCMU) (Carlucci et al. 1970; Thomas et al. 1976). Under these conditions NO_3' can be reduced to NO_2' by respiratory-linked reactions but as the further reduction of NO_2' is more closely linked to light reactions, NO_2' accumulates. It seems probable, therefore, as Kiefer et al. (1976) have argued, that the peak of NO_2' at 130 m in the N. Pacific is due to

203

carbon-rich organisms sinking to a position where illumination is low but NO_3^- concentration high.

When one reflects on advances in knowledge of the nitrogen metabolism of microalgae over the last 25 yr, one is indeed struck by how many fundamental studies have been undertaken, successfully, in attempts to explain ecological observations. Indeed, one suspects that microalgal studies may represent one of the best examples of close and fruitful cooperation between the closed environment of the laboratory and the open one outside.

Acknowledgments

I wish to thank the following members of my research group for permission to quote their unpublished results: Dr I. A. Bekheet, Ray Cresswell, Sue Everest, Nish Shah, and Sally Wright. I thank Drs Charles Hipkin and Alwyn Rees both for results and for helpful criticisms of the manuscript.

References

AHMED, S. I., R. A. KENNER, AND T. T. PACKARD. 1977. A comparative study of the glutamate dehydrogenase activity in several species of marine phytoplankton. Mar. Biol. 39: 93–101.

ALLISON, R. K., H. E. SKIPPER, M. R. REID, W. A. SHORT, AND G. L. HOGAN. 1954. Studies on the photosynthetic reaction. II. Sodium formate and urea feeding experiments with *Nostoc muscorum*. Plant Physiol. 29: 164–168.

AMMANN, E. C. B., AND V. H. LYNCH. 1964. Purine metabolism by unicellular algae. II. Adenine, hypoxanthine, and xanthine degradation by *Chlorella pyrenoidosa*. Biochim. Biophys. Acta 87: 370–379.

AMY, N. K., AND R. H. GARRETT. 1974. Purification and characterization of the nitrate reductase from the diatom, *Thalassiosira pseudonana*. Plant Physiol. 54: 629–637.

ANDERSON, M., AND C.-M. LARRSON. 1980. NO_3^- and NO_2^- dependent O_3 evolution in *Scenedesmus*: interactions with CO_2 reduction, p. 178–179. Conference proceedings. II. Congress of Federation of European Societies of Plant Physiology, Santiago.

ANTIA, N. J., B. R. BERLAND, D. J. BONIN, AND S. Y. MAESTRINI. 1975. Comparative evolution of certain organic and inorganic sources of nitrogen for phototrophic growth of marine microalgae. J. Mar. Biol. Assoc. U.K. 55: 519–539.

ANTIA, N. J., AND A. F. LANDYMORE. 1974. Physiological and ecological significance of the chemical instability of uric acid and related purines in sea water and marine algal culture medium. J. Fish. Res. Board Can. 31: 1327–1335.

APARACIO, P. J., J. M. ROLDÁN, AND F. CALERO. 1976. Blue light photoreactivation of nitrate reductase from green algae and higher plants. Biochem. Biophys. Res. Commun. 70: 1071–1077.

BAKER, J. E., AND J. F. THOMPSON. 1961. Assimilation of ammonia by nitrogen-starved cells of *Chlorella vulgaris*. Plant Physiol. 36: 208–212.

BEEVERS, L. 1976. Nitrogen metabolism in plants. Edward Arnold, London.

BEKHEET, I. A., AND P. J. SYRETT. 1977. Urea-degrading enzymes in algae. Br. Phycol. J. 12: 137–143.

BELMONT, L., AND J. D. A. MILLER. 1965. The utilization of glutamine by algae. J. Exp. Bot. 16: 318–324.

BIENFANG, P. K. 1975. Steady state analysis of nitrate-ammonium assimilation by phytoplankton. Limnol. Oceanogr. 20: 402–411.

BIRDSEY, E. C., AND V. H. LYNCH. 1962. Utilization of nitrogen compounds by unicellular algae. Science (Washington, D.C.) 137: 763–764.

BOLLER, T., AND H. KENDE. 1979. Hydrolytic enzymes in the central vacuole of plant cells. Plant Physiol. 63: 1123–1132.

BONGERS, L. H. J. 1958. Kinetic aspects of nitrate reduction. Neth. J. Agric. Sci. 6: 70–88.

BROWN, C. M., D. S. MACDONALD-BROWN, AND J. L. MEERS. 1974. Physiological aspects of microbial inorganic nitrogen metabolism. Adv. Microb. Physiol. 11: 1–52.

BUCHANAN, B. B. 1980. Role of light in the regulation of chloroplast enzymes. Annu. Rev. Plant Physiol. 31: 341–374.

BUTZ, R. G., AND W. A. JACKSON. 1977. A mechanism for nitrate transport and reduction. Phytochemistry 16: 409–417.

CAIN, BROTHER JOSEPH. 1965. Nitrogen utilization in 38 freshwater chlamydomonad algae. Can. J. Bot. 43: 1367–1378.

CAMPBELL, W. H. 1976. Separation of soybean leaf nitrate reductases by affinity chromatography. Plant Sci. Lett. 7: 239–247.

CANDAU, P., C. MANZANO, AND M. LOSADA. 1976. Bioconversion of light energy into chemical energy through reduction with water of nitrate to ammonia. Nature (London) 262: 715–717.

CANVIN, D. T., AND C. A. ATKINS. 1974. Nitrate, nitrite and ammonia assimilation by leaves: effects of light, carbon dioxide and oxygen. Planta 116: 207–224.

CANVIN, D. T., AND K. C. WOO. 1979. The regulation of nitrate reduction in spinach leaves. Can. J. Bot. 57: 1155–1160.

CAPERON, J., AND D. A. ZIEMANN. 1976. Synergistic effects of nitrate and ammonium ion on the growth and uptake kinetics of *Monochrysis lutheri* in continuous culture. Mar. Biol. 36: 73–84.

CARLUCCI, A. F., E. O. HARTWIG, AND P. M. BOWES. 1970. Biological production of nitrite in sea water. Mar. Biol. 7: 161–166.

CARPENTER, E. J., C. C. REMSEN, AND S. W. WATSON. 1972. Utilization of urea by some marine phytoplankters. Limnol. Oceanogr. 17: 265–269.

CODD, G. A., AND R. STEWART. 1980. Photoinactivation of ribulose bisphosphate carboxylase from green algae and cyanobacteria. FEMS Microbiol. Lett. 8: 237–240.

CONWAY, H. L., P. J. HARRISON, AND C. O. DAVIS. 1976. Marine diatoms grown in chemostats under silicate or ammonium limitation. II. Transient response of *Skeletonema costatum* to a single addition of the limiting nutrient. Mar. Biol. 35: 187–199.

CRAMER, M., AND J. MYERS. 1948. Nitrate reduction and assimilation in *Chlorella pyrenoidosa*. J. Gen. Physiol. 32: 93–102.

CRESSWELL, R. C., AND P. J. SYRETT. 1979. Ammonium inhibition of nitrate uptake by the diatom, *Phaeodactylum tricornutum*. Plant Sci. Lett. 14: 321–325.

——— 1981. Uptake of nitrate by the diatom, *Phaeodactylum tricornutum*. J. Exp. Bot. 32: 19–26.

CULLIMORE, J. V., AND A. P. SIMS. 1981. An association between photorespiration and protein catabolism: studies with *Chlamydomonas*. Planta. (In press)

CZYGAN, F. C. 1965. Zur Frage der Zwischenprodukte der Nitratreduktion bei Grünalgen. Planta 64: 301–311.

DIXON, N. E., C. GAZZOLA, R. L. BLAKELEY, AND B. ZERNER. 1975. Jack bean urease (EC 3.5.1.5). A metalloenzyme. A simple biological role for nickel? J. Am. Chem. Soc. 97: 4131–4133.

DUBOIS, E., AND M. GRENSON. 1979. Methylamine/ammonia uptake systems in *Saccharomyces cerevisiae*: multiplicity and regulation. Mol. Gen. Genet. 175: 67–76.

DUGDALE, R. C. 1967. Nutrient limitation in the sea: dynamics, identification, and significance. Limnol. Oceanogr. 12: 685–695.

DUNN-COLEMAN, N. S., A. B. TOMSETT, AND R. H. GARRETT. 1979. Nitrogen metabolite repression of nitrate reductase in *Neurospora crassa*: effect of the *gln-1a* locus. J. Bacteriol. 139: 697–700.

EDDY, A. A. 1978. Proton-dependent solute transport in microorganisms, p. 280–360. *In* F. Bronner and A. Kleinzeller [ed.] Current topics in membranes and transport. Vol. 10. Academic Press, New York and London.

EDGE, P. A., AND T. R. RICKETTS. 1978. Studies on ammonium-assimilating enzymes of *Platymonas striata* Butcher (Prasinophyceae). Planta 138: 123–125.

EPPLEY, R. W., J. L. COATSWORTH, AND L. SOLÓRZANO. 1969a. Studies of nitrate reductase in marine phytoplankton. Limnol. Oceanogr. 14: 194–205.

EPPLEY, R. W., T. T. PACKARD, AND J. J. MACISAAC. 1970. Nitrate reductase in Peru current photoplankton. Mar. Biol. 6: 195–199.

EPPLEY, R. W., AND E. H. RENGER. 1974. Nitrogen assimilation of an oceanic diatom in nitrogen-limited continuous culture. J. Phycol. 10: 15–23.

EPPLEY, R. W., AND J. N. ROGERS. 1970. Inorganic nitrogen assimilation of *Ditylum brightwellii*. J. Phycol. 6: 344–351.

EPPLEY, R. W., J. N. ROGERS, AND J. J. MCCARTHY. 1969b. Half saturation constants for uptake of nitrate and ammonia by marine phytoplankton. Limnol. Oceanogr. 14: 912–920.

EPPLEY, R. W., J. N. ROGERS, J. J. MCCARTHY, AND A. SOURNIA. 1971. Light/dark periodicity in nitrogen assimilation of the marine phytoplankters *Skeletonema costatum* and *Coccolithus huxleyi* in N-limited chemostat culture. J. Phycol. 7: 150–154.

FALKOWSKI, P. G. 1975. Nitrate uptake in marine phytoplankton: (nitrate–chloride)-activated ATP from *Skeletonema costatum* (Bacillariophyceae). J. Phycol. 11: 323–326.

FALKOWSKI, P. G., AND R. B. RIVKIN. 1976. The role of glutamine synthetase in the incorporation of ammonium in *Skeletonema costatum* (Bacillariophyceae). J. Phycol. 12: 448–450.

FLORES, E., M. G. GUERRERO, AND M. LOSADA. 1980. Short-term ammonium inhibition of nitrate utilization by *Anacystis nidulans* and other cyanobacteria. Arch. Microbiol. 128: 137–144.

FOGG, G. E. 1978. Nitrogen fixation in the oceans, p. 11–19. *In* V. Granhall [ed.] Environmental role of nitrogen fixing blue-green algae and asymbiotic bacteria. Ecol. Bull. 26. Swedish Natural Science Research Council.

FOGG, G. E., AND D. M. COLLYER. 1953. The accumulation of lipides by algae, chap. 12, p. 177–182. *In* J. S. Burlew [ed.] Algal culture: from laboratory to pilot plant. Carnegie Institution of Washington Publication 600, Washington, DC.

FUNKHOUSER, E. A., AND C. S. RAMADOSS. 1980. Synthesis of nitrate reductase in *Chlorella*. II. Evidence for synthesis in ammonia-grown cells. Plant Physiol. 65: 944–948.

GALLON, J. R. 1980. Nitrogen fixation by photoautotrophs, p. 197–238. *In* W. D. P. Stewart and J. R. Gallon [ed.] Nitrogen fixation. Annu. Proc. Phytochem. Soc. Europe, Vol. 18. Academic Press, London and New York.

GIRI, L., AND C. S. RAMADOSS. 1979. Physical studies on assimilatory nitrate reductase from *Chlorella vulgaris*. J. Biol. Chem. 254: 11703–11712.

GRANT, B. R. 1967. The action of light on nitrate and nitrite assimilation by the marine Chlorophyte, *Dunaliella tertiolecta*. J. Gen. Microbiol. 48: 379–389.

——— 1968. Effect of carbon dioxide concentration and buffer system on nitrate and nitrite assimilation in *Dunaliella tertiolecta*. J. Gen. Microbiol. 54: 327–336.

——— 1970. Nitrite reductase in *Dunaliella tertiolecta*: isolation and properties. Plant Cell Physiol. 11: 55–64.

GRANT, B. R., C. A. ATKINS, AND D. T. CANVIN. 1970. Intracellular location of nitrate reductase and nitrite reductase in spinach and sunflower leaves. Planta 94: 60–72.

GRANT, B. R., AND I. M. TURNER. 1969. Light stimulated nitrate and nitrite assimilation in several species of algae. Comp. Biochem. Physiol. 29: 995–1004.

GRIFFITHS, D. J. 1979. Factors affecting nitrate reductase activity in synchronous cultures of *Chlorella*. New Phytol. 82: 427–438.

GUILLARD, R. R. L. 1963. Organic sources of nitrogen for marine centric diatoms, p. 93–104. *In* C. H. Oppenheimer [ed.] Marine microbiology. C. C. Thomas, Springfield, IL.

HARVEY, H. W. 1953. Synthesis of organic nitrogen and chlorophyll by *Nitzschia closterium*. J. Mar. Biol. Res. Assoc. U.K. 31: 477–487.

HATTORI, A. 1958. Studies on the metabolism of urea and other nitrogenous compounds in *Chlorella ellipsoidea*. II. Changes in levels of amino acids and amides during the assimilation of ammonia and urea by nitrogen-starved cells. J. Biochem. (Tokyo) 45: 57–64.

———. 1960. Studies on the metabolism of urea and other nitrogenous compounds in *Chlorella ellipsoidea*. III. Assimilation of urea. Plant Cell Physiol. 1: 107–115.

HATTORI, A., AND I. UESUGI. 1968. Purification and properties of nitrite reductase from the blue-green alga *Anabaena cylindrica*. Plant Cell Physiol. 9: 689–699.

HEIMER, Y. M. 1975. Nitrate reductase of *Dunaliella parva*. Electron donor specificity and heat activation. Arch. Microbiol. 103: 181–183.

———. 1976. Specificity for nicotinamide adenine dinucleotide and nicotinamide adenine dinucleotide phosphate of nitrate reductase from the salt-tolerant alga *Dunaliella parva*. Plant Physiol. 58: 57–59.

HELLEBUST, J. A. 1978. Uptake of organic substrates by *Cyclotella cryptica* (Bacillariophyceae): effects of ions, ionophores and metabolic and transport inhibitors. J. Phycol. 14: 79–83.

HELLEBUST, J. A., AND J. LEWIN. 1977. Heterotrophy, chap. 6. *In* D. Werner [ed.] The biology of diatoms. Blackwell Scientific Publications, Oxford.

HERRERA, J., A. PANEQUE, J. M. MALDONADO, J. L. BAREA, AND M. LOSADA. 1972. Regulation by ammonia of nitrate reductase synthesis and activity in *Chlamydomonas reinhardii*. Biochem. Biophys. Res. Commun. 48: 996–1003.

HIPKIN, C. R., B. A. AL-BASSAM, AND P. J. SYRETT. 1980. The roles of nitrate and ammonium in the regulation of the development of nitrate reductase in *Chlamydomonas reinhardii*. Planta 150: 13–18.

HIPKIN, C. R., AND P. J. SYRETT. 1977a. Some effects of nitrogen-starvation on nitrogen and carbohydrate metabolism in *Ankistrodesmus braunii*. Planta 133: 209–214.

———. 1977b. Post-transcriptional control of nitrate reductase formation in green algae. J. Exp. Bot. 28: 1270–1277.

HIPKIN, C. R., P. J. SYRETT, AND B. A. AL-BASSAM. 1979. Some characteristics of nitrate reductase in unicellular algae, p. 309–312. *In* E. J. Hewitt and C. V. Cutting [ed.] Nitrogen assimilation of plants. Academic Press, London and New York.

HO, C-H., T. IKAWA, AND K. NISIZAWA. 1976. Purification and properties of a nitrite reductase from *Porphyra yezoensis* Ueda. Plant Cell Physiol. 17: 417–430.

HODLER, M., J-J. MORGENTHALER, W. EICHENBERGER, AND E. C. GROB. 1972. The influence of light on the activity of nitrate reductase in synchronous cultures of *Chlorella pyrenoidosa*. FEBS Lett. 28: 19–21.

HODSON, R. C., S. K. WILLIAMS, AND W. R. DAVIDSON. 1975. Metabolic control of urea catabolism in *Chlamydomonas reinhardii* and *Chlorella vulgaris*. J. Bacteriol. 121: 1022–1035.

JACQUES, A. G. 1938–39. The kinetics of penetration. XVI. The accumulation of ammonia in light and darkness. J. Gen. Physiol. 22: 501–520.

KAPP, R., S. E. STEVENS, AND J. L. FOX. 1975. A survey of available nitrogen sources for the growth of the blue-green alga, *Agmenellum quadruplicatum*. Arch. Microbiol. 104: 135–138.

KATES, J. R., AND R. F. JONES. 1964. Variation in alanine dehydrogenase and glutamate dehydrogenase during the synchronous development of *Chlamydomonas*. Biochim. Biophys. Acta 86: 438–447.

KESSLER, E. 1957. Untersuchungen zum Problem der photochemische Nitratreduktion in Grünalgen. Planta 49: 505–523.

———. 1964. Nitrate assimilation by plants. Annu. Rev. Plant Physiol. 15: 57–72.

KESSLER, E., AND H. ÖESTERHELD. 1970. Nitrification and induction of nitrate reductase in nitrogen-deficient green algae. Nature (London) 228: 287–288.

KESSLER, E. AND W. G. ZUMFT. 1973. Effect of nitrite and nitrate on chlorophyll fluorescence in green algae. Planta 111: 41–46.

KIEFER, D. A., R. J. OLSON, AND O. HOLM-HANSEN. 1976. Another look at the nitrite and chlorophyll maxima in the central North Pacific. Deep-Sea Res. 23: 1199–1208.

KITOH, S., AND S. HORI. 1977. Metabolism of urea in *Chlorella ellipsoidea*. Plant Cell Physiol. 18: 513–519.

KNUTSEN, G. 1972. Uptake of uracil by synchronous *Chlorella fusca*. Physiol. Plant. 27: 300–309.

KOMOR, E. 1973. Proton-coupled hexose transport in *Chlorella vulgaris*. FEBS Lett. 38: 16–18.

KOMOR, E., AND W. TANNER. 1971. Characterization of the active hexose transport system of *Chlorella vulgaris*. Biochim. Biophys. Acta 241: 170–179.

———. 1974. The hexose-proton cotransport system of *Chlorella*. J. Gen. Physiol. 64: 568–581.

———. 1975. Simulation of a high and low affinity sugar uptake system in *Chlorella* by a pH-dependent change in the K_m of the uptake system. Planta 123: 195–198.

———. 1976. The determination of the membrane potential of *Chlorella vulgaris*. Evidence for electrogenic sugar transport. Eur. J. Biochem. 70: 197–204.

KOWALLIK, W. 1970. Light effects on carbohydrate and protein metabolism in algae, p. 165–186. *In* P. Halldal [ed.] Photobiology of microorganisms. Wiley-Interscience, London and New York.

KRATZ, W. A., AND J. MYERS. 1955. Nutrition and growth of several blue-green algae. Am. J. Bot. 42: 282–287.

LEA, P. J., AND B. J. MIFLIN. 1975. The occurrence of glutamate synthase in algae. Biochem. Biophys. Res. Commun. 64: 856–859.

LEFTLEY, J. W. 1980. Studies on urea metabolism in some unicellular algae. Ph.D. thesis, University of Wales, Wales.

LEFTLEY, J. W., AND P. J. SYRETT. 1973. Urease and ATP: urea amidolyase activity in unicellular algae. J. Gen. Microbiol. 77: 109–115.

LIU, M. S., AND J. A. HELLEBUST. 1974. Uptake of amino acids by the marine centric diatom *Cyclotella cryptica*. Can. J. Microbiol. 20: 1109–1118.

LLAMA, M. J., J. M. MACARULLA, AND J. L. SERRA. 1979. Characterization of the nitrate reductase activity in the diatom *Skeletonema costatum*. Plant Sci. Lett. 14: 169–175.

LORIMER, G. H., H-S. GEWITZ, W. VÖLKER, L. P. SOLOMONSON, AND B. VENNESLAND. 1974. The presence of bound cyanide in the naturally inactivated form of nitrate reductase of *Chlorella vulgaris*. J. Biol. Chem. 249: 6074–6079.

LOSADA, M. 1980. The photosynthetic assimilation of nitrate, p. 112–113. Conference proceedings. II. Congress of Federation of European Societies of Plant Physiology, Santiago.

LOSADA, M., AND M. G. GUERRERO. 1979. The photosynthetic reduction of nitrate and its regulation, chap. 12, p. 366–408. *In* J. Barber [ed.] Photosynthesis in relation to model systems. Elsevier/North-Holland Biomedical Press.

LOSADA, M., A. PANEQUE, P. J. APARICIO, J. M. VEGA, J. CÁRDENAS, AND J. HERRERA. 1970. Inactivation and repression by ammonium of the nitrate reducing system in *Chlorella*. Biochem. Biophys. Res. Commun. 38: 1009–1015.

LUDWIG, C. A. 1938. The availability of different forms of nitrogen to a green alga (*Chlorella*). Am. J. Bot. 25: 448–458.

LYNCH, V. H., AND G. G. GILLMOR. 1966. Utilization of glutamine and glutamic acid by *Chlorella pyrenoidosa*. Biochim. Biophys. Acta 115: 253–259.

MCCARTHY, J. J. 1972. The uptake of urea by natural populations of marine phytoplankton. Limnol. Oceanogr. 17: 738–748.

MCCARTHY, J. J., W. R. TAYLOR, AND J. L. TAFT. 1977. Nitrogenous nutrition of the plankton in the Chesapeake Bay. 1. Nutrient availability and phytoplankton preferences. Limnol. Oceanogr. 22: 996–1011.

MACISAAC, J. J., AND R. C. DUGDALE. 1969. The kinetics of nitrate and ammonium uptake by natural populations of marine phytoplankton. Deep-Sea Res. 16: 45–57.

1972. Interactions of light and inorganic nitrogen in controlling nitrogen uptake in the sea. Deep-Sea Res. 19: 209–232.

MANZANO, C., P. CANDAU, AND M. G. GUERRERO. 1978. Affinity chromatography of *Anacystis nidulans* ferredoxin-nitrate reductase and NADP reductase on reduced ferredoxin-Sepharose. Anal. Biochem. 90: 408–412.

MEEKS, J. C., C. P. WOLK, W. LOCKAU, N. SCHILLING, P. W. SHAFFER, AND W-S. CHIEN. 1978. Pathways of assimilation of (^{13}N) N_2 and $^{13}NH_4^+$ by cyanobacteria with and without heterocysts. J. Bacteriol. 134: 125–130.

MIFLIN, B. J. 1974. The location of nitrite reductase and other enzymes related to amino acid biosynthesis in the plastids of root and leaves. Plant Physiol. 54: 550–555.

MIFLIN, B. J., AND P. J. LEA. 1976. The pathway of nitrogen assimilation in plants. Phytochemistry 15: 873–885.

MITCHELL, P. 1967. Active transport and ion accumulation, chap. IV, p. 167–198. *In* M. Florkin and E. H. Stotz [ed.] Comprehensive biochemistry, Vol. 22. Elsevier Publishing Company, Amsterdam, London, New York.

MORRIS, I., AND P. J. SYRETT. 1965. The effect of nitrogen starvation on the activity of nitrate reductase and other enzymes in *Chlorella*. J. Gen. Microbiol. 38: 21–28.

MORTENSON, L. E., AND R. N. F. THORNELEY. 1979. Structure and function of nitrogenase. Annu. Rev. Biochem. 48: 387–418.

MURPHY, M. J., L. M. SIEGEL, S. R. TOVE, AND H. KAMIN. 1974. Siroheme: a new prosthetic group participating in six-electron reduction reactions catalysed by both sulfite and nitrite reductases. Proc. Natl. Acad. Sci. U.S.A. 71: 612–616.

NAYLOR, A. W. 1970. Phytogenetic aspects of nitrogen metabolism in the algae. Ann. N.Y. Acad. Sci. 170: 511–523.

NEILSON, A. H., AND M. DOUDOROFF. 1973. Ammonia assimilation in blue-green algae. Arch. Mikrobiol. 89: 15–22.

NEILSON, A. H., AND T. LARSSON. 1980. The utilization of organic nitrogen for growth of algae: physiological aspects. Physiol. Plant. 48: 542–553.

NICHOLS, G. L., S. A. M. SHEHATA, AND P. J. SYRETT. 1978. Nitrate reductase deficient mutants of *Chlamydomonas reinhardii*. Biochemical characteristics. J. Gen. Microbiol. 108: 79–88.

NISSEN, P. 1974. Uptake mechanisms: inorganic and organic. Annu. Rev. Plant Physiol. 25: 53–79.

NORTH, B. B., AND G. C. STEPHENS. 1971. Uptake and assimilation of amino acids by *Platymonas*. 2. Increased uptake in nitrogen-deficient cells. Biol. Bull. 140: 242–254.

NOTTON, B. A., AND E. J. HEWITT. 1979. Structure and properties of higher plant nitrate reductase, especially *Spinacea oleracea*, p. 227–244. *In* E. J. Hewitt and C. V. Cutting [ed.] Nitrogen assimilation of plants. Academic Press, London and New York.

ÖESTERHELD, H. 1971. Das Verhalten von Nitratreductase, Nitritreductase, Hydrogenase und anderen Enzymen von *Ankistrodesmus braunii* bei Stickstoffmangel. Arch. Mikrobiol. 79: 25–43.

PAASCHE, E. 1971. Effect of ammonia and nitrate on growth, photosynthesis and ribulosediphosphate carboxylase content of *Dunaliella tertiolecta*. Physiol. Plant. 25: 294–299.

PACKARD, T. T. 1979. Half-saturation constants for nitrate reductase and nitrate translocation in marine phytoplankton. Deep-Sea Res. 26A: 321–326.

PANEQUE, A., P. J. APARICIO, J. CÁRDENAS, J. M. VEGA, AND M. LOSADA. 1969. Nitrate as a Hill reagent in a reconstituted chloroplast system. FEBS Lett. 3: 57–59.

PANEQUE, A., J. M. VEGA, J. CÁRDENAS, J. HERRERA, P. J. APARICIO, AND M. LOSADA. 1972. ^{185}W-labelled nitrate reductase from *Chlorella*. Plant Cell Physiol. 13: 175–178.

PARSONS, T. R., M. TAKAHASHI, AND B. HARGRAVE. 1977. Biological oceanographic processes, 2nd ed. Pergamon Press, Oxford, New York.

PEDERSEN, A. G., AND G. KNUTSEN. 1974. Uptake of L-phenylalanine in synchronous *Chlorella fusca*; characterization of the uptake system. Physiol. Plant. 32: 294–300.

PELLEY, J. L., AND T. T. BANNISTER. 1979. Methylamine uptake in the green alga *Chlorella pyrenoidosa*. J. Phycol. 15: 110–112.

PETTERSEN, R., AND G. KNUTSEN. 1974. Uptake of guanine by synchronised *Chlorella fusca*: characterization of the transport system in autospores. Arch. Mikrobiol. 96: 233–246.

PISTORIUS, E. K., E. A. FUNKHOUSER, AND H. VOSS. 1978. Effect of ammonium and ferricyanide on nitrate utilization by *Chlorella vulgaris*. Planta 141: 279–282.

PISTORIUS, E. K., H-S. GEWITZ, H. VOSS, AND B. VENNESLAND. 1976. Reversible inactivation of nitrate reductase in *Chlorella vulgaris in vivo*. Planta 128: 73–80.

PLATT, T., AND D. V. SUBBA RAO. 1975. Primary production of marine microphytes, p. 249–280. *In* J. P. Cooper [ed.] Photosynthesis and productivity in different environments. Cambridge University Press, Cambridge.

POCKLINGTON, R. 1971. Free amino-acids dissolved in North Atlantic ocean waters. Nature (London) 230: 374–375.

PREMAKUMAR, R., G. J. SORGER, AND D. GOODEN. 1979. Nitrogen metabolite repression of nitrate reductase in *Neurospora crassa*. J. Bacteriol. 137: 1119–1126.

RAMAROA, C. S., SRINIVASAN, AND M. S. NAIK. 1980. Origin of reductant for *in vivo* reduction of nitrate and nitrite in rice and wheat leaves. New Phytol.

RAMOS, J. L., E. FLORES, AND M. G. GUERRERO. 1980a. Glutamine synthetase – glutamate synthase: the pathway of ammonium assimilation in *Anacystis nidulans*, p. 579–580. Conference proceedings. II. Congress of Federation of European Societies of Plant Physiology, Santiago.

RAMOS, J. L., M. G. GUERRERO, AND M. LOSADA. 1980b. Photosynthetic production of ammonia by blue-green algae, p. 581–582. Conference proceedings. II. Congress of Federation of European Societies of Plant Physiology, Santiago.

RAVEN, J. A. 1974. Carbon dioxide fixation, chap. 15, p. 434–435. *In* W. D. P. Stewart [ed.] Algal physiology and biochemistry. Blackwell Scientific Publications, Oxford, London.

RAVEN, J. A., AND M. I. DE MICHELIS. 1979. Acid-base regulation during nitrate assimilation in *Hydrodictyon africanum*. Plant Cell Environ. 2: 245–257.

REES, T. A. V., AND P. J. SYRETT. 1979. The uptake of urea by the diatom *Phaeodactylum*. New Phytol. 82: 169–178.

REES, T. A. V., R. C. CRESSWELL, AND P. J. SYRETT. 1980. Sodium-dependent uptake of nitrate and urea by a marine diatom. Biochim. Biophys. Acta 596: 141–144.

REISNER, G. S., R. K. GERING, AND J. F. THOMPSON. 1960. The metabolism of nitrate and ammonia by *Chlorella*. Plant Physiol. 35: 48–52.

RICKETTS, T. R., AND P. A. EDGE. 1978. Nitrate and nitrite reductases in *Platymonas striata*, Butcher (Prasinophyceae). Br. Phycol. J. 13: 167–176.

RIGANO, C. 1971. Studies on nitrate reductase from *Cyanidium caldarium*. Arch. Mikrobiol. 76: 265–276.

RIGANO, C., V. DI MARTINO RIGANO, A. FUGGI, AND V. VONA. 1980. Control of the assimilatory nitrate reduction in a unicellular alga and the possible effector, p. 595–596. Conference proceedings. II. Congress

of Federation of European Societies for Plant Physiology, Santiago.

RIGANO, C., V. D. M. RIGANO, V. VONA, AND A. FUGGI. 1979a. Glutamine synthetase activity, ammonia assimilation and control of nitrate reduction in the unicellular red alga *Cyanidium caldarium*. Arch. Microbiol. 121: 117–120.

RIGANO, C., AND U. VIOLANTE. 1972. Effect of heat treatment on the activity *in vitro* of nitrate reductase from *Cyanidium caldarium*. Biochim. Biophys. Acta 256: 524–532.

RIGANO, C., V. VONA, V. DI MARTINO RIGANO, AND A. FUGGI. 1979b. Nitrate reductase and glutamate dehydrogenase of the red alga *Porphyridium aerugineum*. Plant Sci. Lett. 15: 203–209.

ROON, R. J., AND B. LEVENBERG. 1968. An adenosine triphosphate-dependent avidin-sensitive enzymatic cleavage of urea. J. Biol. Chem. 245: 4593–4595.

ROWELL, P., AND W. D. P. STEWART. 1976. Alanine dehydrogenase of the N_2-fixing blue-green alga, *Anabaena cylindrica*. Arch. Microbiol. 107: 115–124.

SAMEJIMA, H., AND J. MYERS. 1958. On the heterotrophic growth of *Chlorella pyrenoidosa*. J. Gen. Microbiol. 18: 107–117.

SAWHNEY, S. K., M. S. NAIK, AND D. J. D. NICHOLAS. 1978. Regulation of nitrate reduction by light, ATP and mitochondrial respiration in wheat leaves. Nature (London) 272: 647–648.

SERRA, J. L., M. J. LLAMA, AND E. CADENAS. 1978a. Nitrate utilization by the diatom *Skeletonema costatum*. I. Kinetics of nitrate uptake. Plant Physiol. 62: 987–990.

  1978b. Nitrate utilization by the diatom *Skeletonema costatum*. II. Regulation of nitrate uptake. Plant Physiol. 62: 991–994.

  1978c. Characterization of the nitrate reductase activity in the diatom *Skeletonema costatum*. Plant Sci. Lett. 13: 41–48.

SHATILOV, V. R., A. V. SOF'IN, T. M. ZABRODINA, A. A. MUTUSKIN, K. V. PSHENOVA, AND V. L. KRETOVICH. 1978. Ferredoxin-dependent glutamate synthase from *Chlorella*. Biokhimiya 43: 1492–1495.

SHEHATA, S. A. 1977. Mechanisms for the uptake and metabolism of nitrate by *Chlamydomonas*. Ph.D. thesis, University of Wales.

SIEGENTHALER, P. A., M. M. BELSKY, AND S. GOLDSTEIN. 1967. Phosphate uptake in an obligately marine fungus: a specific requirement for sodium. Science (Washington, D.C.) 155: 93–94.

SIMS, A. P., B. F. FOLKES, AND A. H. BUSSEY. 1968. Mechanisms involved in the regulation of nitrogen assimilation in microorganisms and plants, p. 91–114. *In* E. J. Hewitt and C. V. Cutting [ed.] Recent aspects of nitrogen metabolism in plants. Academic Press, London and New York.

SOLOMONSON, L. P. 1979. Structure of *Chlorella* nitrate reductase, p. 199–205. *In* E. J. Hewitt and C. V. Cutting [ed.] Nitrogen assimilation of plants. Academic Press, New York and London.

SOLOMONSON, L. P., G. H. LORIMER, R. L. HALL, R. BORCHERS, AND J. L. BAILEY. 1975. Reduced nicotinamide adenine dinucleotide-nitrate reductase of *Chlorella vulgaris*. Purification, prosthetic groups and molecular properties. J. Biol. Chem. 250: 4120–4127.

SOLOMONSON, L. P., AND A. M. SPEHAR. 1977. Model for the regulation of nitrate assimilation. Nature (London) 265: 373–375.

SPILLER, H., E. DIETSCH, AND E. KESSLER. 1976. Intracellular appearance of nitrite and nitrate in nitrogen-starved cells of Ankistrodesmus braunii. Planta 129: 175–181.

STEWART, W. D. P., AND P. ROWELL. 1975. Effects of L-methionine-DL-sulphoximine on the assimilation of newly fixed NH₃, acetylene reduction and heterocyst production in Anabaena cylindrica. Biochem. Biophys. Res. Commun. 65: 846–856.

SYRETT, P. J. 1953a. The assimilation of ammonia by nitrogen-starved cells of Chlorella vulgaris. I. The correlation of assimilation with respiration. Ann. Bot. (London) 17: 1–19.

——— 1953b. The assimilation of ammonia by nitrogen-starved cells of Chlorella vulgaris. II. The assimilation of ammonia to other compounds. Ann. Bot. (London) 17: 20–36.

SYRETT, P. J., AND I. A. BEKHEET. 1977. The uptake of thiourea by Chlorella. New Phytol. 79: 291–297.

SYRETT, P. J., AND C. R. HIPKIN. 1973. The appearance of nitrate reductase activity in nitrogen-starved cells of Ankistrodesmus braunii. Planta 111: 57–64.

SYRETT, P. J., AND J. W. LEFTLEY. 1976. Nitrate and urea assimilation by algae, p. 221–234. In N. Sunderland [ed.] Perspectives in experimental biology. Vol 2. Pergamon Press, Oxford and New York.

SYRETT, P. J., AND I. MORRIS. 1963. The inhibition of nitrate assimilation by ammonium in Chlorella. Biochem. Biophys. Acta 67: 566–575.

TEMPEST, D. W., J. L. MEERS, AND C. M. BROWN. 1970. Synthesis of glutamate in Acrobacter aerogenes by a hitherto unknown route. Biochem. J. 117: 405–407.

THACKER, A., AND P. J. SYRETT. 1972a. The assimilation of nitrate and ammonium by Chlamydomonas reinhardii. New Phytol. 71: 423–433.

——— 1972b. Disappearance of nitrate reductase activity from Chlamydomonas reinhardii. New Phytol. 71: 435–441.

THOMAS, R. J., C. R. HIPKIN, AND P. J. SYRETT. 1976. The interaction of nitrogen assimilation with photosynthesis in nitrogen deficient cells of Chlorella. Planta 133: 9–13.

THOMAS, W. H. 1968. Nutrient requirements and utilization; algae, p. 210–228. In P. L. Altman and D. S. Dittmer [ed.] Metabolism. Biological Handbooks. Federation of America Societies for Experimental Biology, Bethesda, MD, USA.

THOMPSON, J. F., AND A.-M. MUENSTER. 1971. Separation of the Chlorella ATP: urea amidolyase into two components. Biochem. Biophys. Res. Commun. 43: 1049–1055.

——— 1974. ATP-dependent urease: characteristics of a control in Chlorella; the search for it in higher plants. Bull. R. Soc. N. Z. 12: 91–97.

TISCHNER, R. 1976. Zur Induktion der Nitrat-und Nitritreduktase in vollsynchronen Chlorella Kulturen. Planta 132: 285–290.

——— 1980. The effect of light on nitrogen metabolism of Chlorella sorokiniana, p. 659–660. Conference proceedings. II. Congress of Federation of European Societies for Plant Physiology, Santiago.

TISCHNER, R., AND A. HÜTTERMAN. 1978. Light-mediated activation of nitrate reductase in synchronous Chlorella. Plant Physiol. 62: 284–286.

TROMBALLA, H. W., AND E. BRODA. 1971. Das Verhalten von Chlorella fusca gegenüber Perchlorat und Chlorat. Arch. Mikrobiol. 78: 214–223.

TYLER, B. 1978. Regulation of the assimilation of nitrogen compounds. Annu. Rev. Biochem. 47: 1127–1162.

ULLRICH, W. R. 1974. Der nitrat-und nitritäbhangige photosynthetische O₂-Entwicklung in N₂ bei Ankistrodesmus braunii. Planta 116: 143–152.

——— 1979. Die Nitritaufnahme bei Grünalgen und ihre Regulation durch äussere Faktoren. Ber. Dtsch. Bot. Ges. 92: 273–284.

URHAN, O. 1932. Beiträge zur Kenntis der Stickstoffassimilation von Chlorella und Scenedesmus. Jahrb. Wiss. Bot. 75: 1–44.

VACCARO, R. F. 1965. Inorganic nitrogen in sea-water, chap. 9, p. 365–408. In J. P. Riley and G. Skirrow [ed.] Chemical oceanography. Vol. 1. Academic Press, London and New York.

VACCARO, R. F., AND J. H. RYTHER. 1960. Marine phytoplankton and the distribution of nitrite in the sea. J. Cons. Cons. Perm. Int. Explor. Mer 25: 260–271.

VAN BAALEN, C. 1962. Studies on marine blue-green algae. Bot. Mar. 4: 129–139.

VAN NIEL, C. B., M. B. ALLEN, AND B. E. WRIGHT. 1953. On the photochemical reduction of nitrate by algae. Biochim. Biophys. Acta 12: 67–74.

VEGA, J. M., J. HERRERA, P. J. APARICIO, A. PANEQUE, AND M. LOSADA. 1971. Role of molybdenum in nitrate reduction by Chlorella. Plant Physiol. 48: 294–299.

VENNESLAND, B., AND C. JETSCHMANN. 1971. The nitrate reductase of Chlorella pyrenoidosa. Biochim. Biophys. Acta 227: 554–564.

VILLERET, S. 1955. Sur la présence des enzymes des uréides glyoxyliques chez les Algues d'eau douce. C. R. Acad. Sci. Ser. D: Sci. Nat. 241: 90–92.

——— 1958. Recherches sur la présence des enzymes des uréides glyoxyliques chez les Algues marines. C. R. Acad. Sci. Ser. D: Sci. Nat. 246: 1452–1454.

VOGELS, G. D., AND C. VAN DER DRIFT. 1976. Degradation of purines and pyrimidines by microorganisms. Bacteriol. Rev. 40: 403–468.

WADA, E., AND A. HATTORI. 1971. Nitrite metabolism in the euphotic zone of the Central Pacific ocean. Limnol. Oceanogr. 16: 766–772.

WALLEN, D. G., AND G. H. GEEN. 1971. Light quality in relation to growth, photosynthetic rates and carbon metabolism in two species of marine plankton-algae. Mar. Biol. 10: 34–43.

WARBURG, O., AND E. NEGELEIN. 1920. Über die Reduktion der Salpetersäure in grünen Zellen. Biochem. Z. 110: 66–115.

WHEELER, P. A. 1980. Use of methylammonium as an ammonium analogue in nitrogen transport and assimilation studies with Cyclotella cryptica (Bacillariophyceae). J. Phycol. 16: 328–334.

WHEELER, P. A., AND J. A. HELLEBUST. 1981. Uptake and concentration of alkylamines by a marine diatom: effects of H$^+$ and K$^+$ and implications for the transport and accumulation of weak bases. Plant Physiol. 67: 367–372.

WHEELER, P. A., B. B. NORTH, AND G. C. STEPHENS. 1974. Amino acid uptake by marine phytoplankters. Limnol. Oceanogr. 19: 249–295.

WHITNEY, P. A., AND T. G. COOPER. 1972. Urea carboxylase and allophanate hydrolase. Two components of adenosine triphosphate: urea amidolyase in *Saccharomyces cerevisiae*. J. Biol. Chem. 247: 1349–1353.

――― 1973. Urea carboxylase from *Saccharomyces cerevisiae*. Evidence for a minimal two-step reaction sequence. J. Biol. Chem. 248: 325–330.

WILLIAMS, S. K., AND R. C. HODSON. 1977. Transport of urea at low concentrations in *Chlamydomonas reinhardii*. J. Bacteriol. 130: 266–273.

ZUMFT, W. G. 1972. Ferredoxin: nitrite oxidoreductase from *Chlorella*. Purification and properties. Biochim. Biophys. Acta 276: 363–375.

The Kinetics of Nutrient Utilization

JAMES J. MCCARTHY

Museum of Comparative Zoology,
Harvard University,
Cambridge, MA 02138, USA

Assessment of Nutrient Uptake and Assimilation Kinetics

KINETIC MODELS AND THEIR BIOCHEMICAL AND PHYSIOLOGICAL BASES

An understanding of the kinetics of phytoplankton nutrient uptake has been the subject of numerous investigations in the last decade. This period of activity began with the nearly coincident papers of Dugdale (1967) and Eppley and Coatsworth (1968), which shed new light, both theoretical and empirical, on the potential role of nutrient uptake kinetics in phytoplankton physiological ecology. Dugdale used Harvey's (1963) data for *Phaeodactylum tricornutum* phosphate uptake, and Eppley and Coatsworth used results from nitrate uptake studies with *Ditylum brightwellii* to demonstrate that nutrient uptake (v) is a hyperbolic function of substrate concentration (S) with the half-saturation constant (K_s) equivalent to the concentration necessary to achieve half the maximal rate of uptake (V_{max}).

$$(1) \qquad v = V_{max} \frac{S}{K_s + S}$$

In studies that utilize ^{15}N-labeled substrates to determine rates of nutrient uptakes, v is usually expressed in dimensions of N taken up per unit particulate N per unit time, or simply reciprocal time.

The use of the rectangular hyperbola (Fig. 1) as an approximation of the observed relationship can be supported in theory, as carrier-mediated transport of nutrients across the plasmalemma might be expected to follow so-called Michaelis-Menten kinetics. The use of this model simplifies the analysis of the kinetics of uptake in that only two parameters, K_s and V_{max} need to be known in order to specify the rate of uptake for any given concentration of substrate.

In the Michaelis-Menten model, substrate (S) reversibly binds with enzyme (E) to form an enzyme-substrate complex (ES) that subsequently yields product (P) and free enzyme.

$$(2) \qquad S + E \underset{K_{-1}}{\overset{K_1}{\rightleftharpoons}} ES \overset{K_2}{\longrightarrow} E + P$$

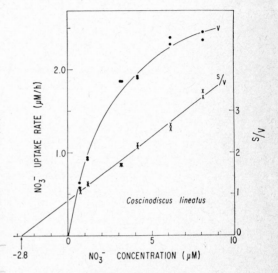

FIG. 1. NO_3^- uptake rate (v) as a function of NO_3^- concentration (S) for *Coscinodiscus lineatus* (●), and the Woolf plot linear transformation of S/v vs. S (x). (From Eppley et al. 1969.)

The derivation of Eq. (1) for the purposes of describing phytoplankton nutrient uptake requires the following primary assumptions:

1) There is only a single substrate or, in the case of multisubstrate reactions, the concentration of all other substrates are held constant.

2) Only truly *initial* rates of reaction (v) are measured at different starting concentrations of S, i.e. reaction rates are observed over a time interval sufficiently short to preclude both significant back reaction and feedback inhibition.

3) The medium is mixed sufficiently to prevent depletion of substrate at the cell surface.

It needs to be stated, however, that saturable kinetics do not necessarily imply product formation. Either a saturable transport or uptake system could result in kinetics that can be described by Eq. (1). For example, *Ditylum brightwellii* (*D. bright.*) was unable to grow on urea, but uptake of urea by NO_2^--grown culture followed saturation kinetics (Fig. 2).

211

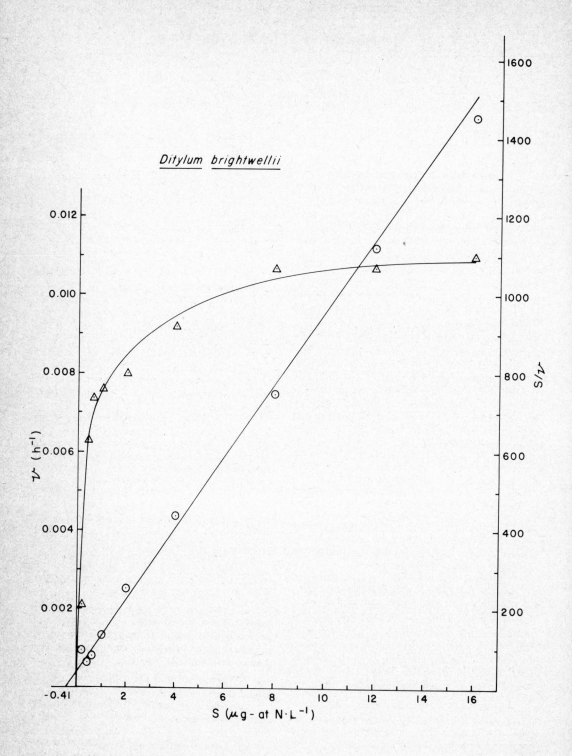

FIG. 2. Urea uptake rate (v) as a function of urea concentration (S) for *Ditylum brightwellii* ($\triangle$), and the Woolf plot linear transformation of S/v vs. S ($\bigcirc$). (From McCarthy 1972.)

In an alternate formulation used to describe nutrient-limited, steady-state growth (Droop 1974; Dugdale 1977), ρ and ρ_m are the rate of nutrient uptake and maximal rate of uptake per individual unit of the population (i.e. per cell), respectively. K_s is the same parameter represented in Eq. (1).

$$(3) \qquad \rho = \rho_m \frac{S}{K_s + S}$$

The chemostat is a steady-state, continuous culture system that permits the study of the relationship between the growth rate and the nutritional state of microorganisms in an aqueous medium. In balanced growth (Eppley 1981) the rate of nutrient uptake is comparable to the rate of synthesis of new organic material. Caperon's experimental work with continuous cultures heralded the introduction of the chemostat in studies of phytoplankton nitrogenous nutrition. The origin of the chemostat in microbiological studies can be traced to Monod (1942) and Novick and Szilard (1950), and its utility had previously been demonstrated for bacteria grown in media prepared so that the supply of organic carbon was growthrate limiting (see Herbert et al. 1956, for example). Under steady-state conditions the chemical composition of both the medium and the organisms, in addition to the physiological state of the population, can then be related to the growth rate.

In many studies of phytoplankton in nutrient-limited, chemostat culture, the specific growth rate of the population, $\mu(T^{-1})$ has been shown to be hyperbolically related to the cell quota, $Q(M\ cell^{-1})$, or concentration of the limiting nutrient per cell, where K_Q is the Q below which there is no population growth and $\bar{\mu}$ is the specific growth rate at which Q is infinite (Droop 1968).

$$(4) \qquad \mu = \bar{\mu} \frac{Q - K_Q}{Q}$$

In apparent contrast with the results reported above for the relationship between S and ν, Caperon (1967, 1968) observed that for chemostat-grown, nitrate-limited *Isochrysis galbana* the growth rate, and hence the nutrient uptake rate, was a function of the concentration of nitrogen within the individual cell rather than that of the growth media. Equation (4) has also provided an adequate fit to data from vitamin B_{12} (Droop 1968), phosphate (Droop 1974; Fuhs 1968; Goldman 1977; Rhee 1973), and iron (Davies 1970) limited chemostat cultures (see, for example, Fig. 3). In general, though, it has been considerably less useful in describing the kinetics of growth on silicic acid (Paasche 1973; Harrison et al. 1976) and nitrogen (Harrison et al. 1976; Goldman and McCarthy 1978). In each of these studies, Q was shown to vary with μ,

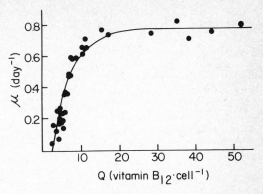

FIG. 3. Growth rate (μ) as a function of cell quota (Q) of vitamin B_{12} for *Pavlova (Monochrysis) lutheri*. (From Droop 1968.)

but for silicic acid and nitrogen the maximum growth rate attainable in chemostat culture ($\hat{\mu}$) was considerably less than the $\bar{\mu}$ of Eq. (4). As both Droop (1973) and Dugdale (1977) pointed out, the $\bar{\mu}$ of the Droop expression is not necessarily equivalent to the maximum growth rate attainable in culture. The $\bar{\mu}$ parameter is by definition the growth rate at which Q becomes infinite, and as such is never actually achieved in culture. As will be seen below, the degree of discrepancy between $\bar{\mu}$ and $\hat{\mu}$ is not the same for all elements.

The true maximum growth rate ($\hat{\mu}$) can be related to medium nutrient concentration by the Monod expression

$$(5) \qquad \mu = \hat{\mu} \frac{S}{K_\mu + S}$$

where K_μ is the half-saturation constant for growth, and definitions for other terms are as previously used. K_μ is not equal to the K_s value in Eq. (1) and (3).

Frequent failure to demonstrate empirically the relationship between chemostat population growth rates and nutrient concentration predicted by Eq. (5), or the Monod expression (see, for example, Caperon and Meyer 1972; Eppley and Renger 1974; Bienfang 1975), led to increasing use of Eq. (4), or the cell quota model. It has been shown, however, that the equations that formulate growth as functions of cellular content (Eq. (4)) and media nutrient concentration (Eq. (5)) are equally appropriate for describing steady-state growth kinetics (Goldman 1977; Dugdale 1977). Burmaster (1979) provides the algebraic analysis that demonstrates this strict equivalence.

The difficulties often reported in efforts to obtain data that conform to Eq. (5) apparently stem both from earlier expectations that K_μ would be equal to K_s and from an inability to measure pre-

213

cisely nutrient concentrations that approach K_μ. For example, Caperon (1968) interpreted his data for invariant residual nitrate concentrations in the growth chamber of a nitrate-limited chemostat culture of *I. galbana* over a six-fold range in population growth rates as evidence that growth rate is solely regulated by the quantity of nitrogen in an internal cellular pool. Similarly, Bienfang (1975) observed near order of magnitude variability in media nitrate and ammonium concentrations for replicate chemostat runs with *Dunaliella tertiolecta* at near maximal growth rates. As $\hat{\mu}$ is approached, the media concentration of the limiting nutrient can increase from undetectable to several μg-at·L^{-1} with a very small incremental increase in μ (Fig. 4), making it very difficult to define the precise shape of the μ vs. S relationship (Caperon and Ziemann 1976; Goldman and McCarthy 1978; Burmaster and Chisholm 1979). Implicit in the kinetic model for growth as a function

of nutrient concentration (Eq. (5)) is the assumption that the portion of the μ vs. S relationship that cannot be observed with conventional methods for measuring nutrients still follows the hyperbolic expression.

From considerations of typical elemental composition and the different structural and functional roles of various elements, the total cellular Q terms for major elemental constituents such as carbon, nitrogen, phosphorus, and, in the case of diatoms, silicon would be expected to have variable applicability in population growth models. Over the range of possible Q values it is evident that for different elements there are different strategies partitioning the elemental material. From several studies it is apparent that Q is less variable for N than for P, and it may be invariant for C. Goldman and McCarthy (1978) proposed that the ratio of minimum to maximum Q, K_Q/Q_m, was useful in approximating the degree to which the $\bar{\mu}$ in Eq. (3) overestimates $\hat{\mu}$

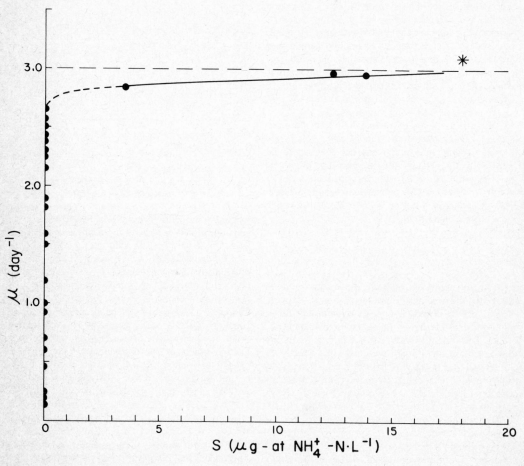

FIG. 4. Steady-state growth rate (μ) as a function of NH$_4^+$ concentration for *Thalassiosira pseudonana* (3-H). (From Goldman and McCarthy 1978.)

or the maximum growth rate, just short of washout in a chemostat culture,

$$(6) \qquad \hat{\mu} = \overline{\mu} \left[1 - \frac{K_Q}{Q_m} \right]$$

where Q_m is determined from a population at washout, or in batch culture during logarithmic growth. It was shown that for *Dunaliella tertiolecta* the $\hat{\mu}$ and Q_m values were identical in batch and chemostat cultures (Goldman and Peavey 1979). Data from numerous studies were compiled to demonstrate that the K_Q/Q_m values for vitamin B_{12}-, iron-, or phosphorus-limited cultures are approximately 0.01–0.03, whereas those silicon- or nitrogen-limited cultures are 0.20. Expressed another way, cultures for which the growth rate is limited by vitamin B_{12}, iron, or phosphorus can vary their cellular content of these elements over an order of magnitude range that is greater than can be realized for the cell quota of silicon- or nitrogen-limited cultures. Carbon-limited growth has been studied only in freshwater phytoplankton, and here data are few, but Q appears to be invariant over a wide range of growth rates; hence the K_Q/Q_m for carbon is $\sim$ unity and, correspondingly, $\overline{\mu}$ in Eq. (3) for carbon-limited growth is infinite.

Some studies have attempted to relate specific subunits of the total cellular Q term to growth or uptake potential characteristic of a given steady state, but few generalizations can be made. It is known that internal ammonium and nitrate can reach measurable levels (often up to a few percent of total cellular nitrogen) (Eppley and Rogers 1970; Conover 1975; Bhovichitra and Swift 1977) but for steady-state population there is no evidence that the concentration of either can be related to growth rate more usefully than the total Q. The model proposed by Greeney et al. (1973) partitions the uptake and growth processes as functions of extracellular nitrogenous nutrient concentration and intracellular amino acid concentrations, respectively. An internal compartmentalization approach was found to be practical for silicon (Davis et al. 1978). The utilization of silicon within the cell and the rate of population growth were independently modeled as functions of internal dissolved silicate pool size and silica content in the frustule, respectively.

Clearly, subdivision of the Q term has the potential of bringing additional insight and precision to the cell quota model. For example, DeManche (1980) noted that for *Skeletonema costatum* the amino acid pools were higher in well-nourished versus nitrogen-starved populations, but for *Thalassiosira aestivalis* pool sizes for amino acids were not correlated with nutritional history. His data show, however, the potential for rapid increase in pool size when a pulse of nutrient is added to a nitrogen-starved population.

The extent to which NO_3^- is accumulated intracellularly following a pulse of NO_3^- is obviously related to the degree of coupling between the processes of uptake and reduction.

RELATIONSHIP BETWEEN UPTAKE AND
ASSIMILATION CAPACITIES

The process of nutrient uptake is usually measured by the disappearance of substrate from the medium or the accumulation of total labeled elemental material within the cell. It represents transport of the substrate across the plasmalemma, and does not permit inference regarding metabolism of the substrate. Our understanding of the mechanisms responsible for transport and metabolism of nitrogen by phytoplankton is, however, insufficiently complete to permit convenient separation of the two processes in most cases. The activities of several enzymes involved in the metabolism of nitrogen have been identified in phytoplankton. Nitrate reductase, nitrite reductase, glutamate dehydrogenase, glutamine synthetase, and glutamate synthase appear to function similarly to enzymes that have long been subjects of biochemical investigations in fungi and higher plants (Syrett 1981). In contrast, however, we know much less regarding the process of transport across the plasmalemma into the cytoplasm. Furthermore, with the exception of glutamine synthetase in *Skeletonema costatum* (Falkowski and Rivkin 1976), the enzymes thought to regulate nitrogen assimilation in phytoplankton have high K_m values relative to typical environmental concentrations of the substrate. In the cases of nitrate reductase, nitrite reductase, and glutamate dehydrogenase in marine diatoms, this difference approaches 2–3 orders of magnitude, and it has led to the suggestion that internal pooling of substrate is necessary for the enzymes to function efficiently (Eppley and Rogers 1970).

An examination of recent literature on the subject of nitrate transport and metabolism in both microalgae and higher plants clearly points to the problem of distinguishing between transport and metabolic processes for the purpose of discussing kinetics. Falkowski (1975) presented evidence for a membrane-bound transferase, a nitrate and chloride-activated ATPase, in *Skeletonema costatum*. He reported a K_m of 0.9 μM NO_3^-, thus indicating that this enzyme could provide an effective transport system for nitrate at concentrations that occur naturally in marine waters. There is evidence, however, that both the transport of nitrate across the plasmalemma and its subsequent reduction to nitrite can be effected by a single enzyme associated with the plasmalemma in at least some higher plants and microalgae. The role of such a nitrate reductase in the regulation of nitrate uptake can be inferred from the data of Rao and Rains (1976) for barley and from that of Nichols et al. (1978) for *Chlamydomonas reinhardi*. Moreover, in both *Anabaena* (Hattori and Myers 1967) and *Platymonas* (Ricketts and Edge 1977) nitrate reductase activity was found to be associated with the particulate fraction of broken cells. Experiments with *Neurospora crassa* have, however, led to the conclusion that this organism has a nitrate transport system independent of the reduction of nitrate (Schloemer and Garrett 1974).

Butz and Jackson (1977) proposed the existence of a transmembrane enzyme that both transports and reduces NO_3^-. If both transport and reduction are functions of the same enzyme, then similar K_m values for the two processes might be expected. This has been found to be the case in some vascular plants (Butz and Jackson 1977) and a marine bacterium (Brown et al. 1975). Likewise, similarity would be expected in the half-lives for nitrate transport and reduction activities, but there are few data to either support or refute this hypothesis. For marine phytoplankton there is, however, a large difference between the K_s values for a nitrate uptake and the K_m values for nitrate reductase. Numerous studies with both laboratory cultures and natural assemblages (cf. Eppley et al. 1969; Carpenter and Guillard 1971; MacIsaac and Dugdale 1969) have reported K_s values $\leqslant 2~\mu M$, whereas the K_m values for nitrate reductase in laboratory clones of marine phytoplankton have ranged from 60 to 110 μM (Eppley et al. 1969; Eppley and Rogers 1970; Packard 1979), and those for several natural assemblages in the upwelled waters off Cape Blanc, Mauritania, ranged from 40 to 210 μM (Packard 1979). Because the nitrate concentrations in near surface waters of the sea are usually closer to the K_s values, it is reasonable to expect that a transport mechanism with greater substrate affinity than nitrate reductase is responsible for the translocation of this ion across the plasmalemma of marine phytoplankton.

Clearly then, in the case of one well-studied enzyme system it is at present either difficult or impossible to speak distinctly of transport and metabolic process for the purposes of understanding whole cell studies of nutrient uptake. If the rate of leakage for both the substrate and its products can be either estimated or assumed to be negligible during steady-state growth, then rates of metabolism for essential elements must equal rates of uptake.

As will be seen below, transient uptake phenomena may be an important adaptive strategy for phytoplankton in nature, and the steady-state condition that is easily established in laboratory continuous culture may for this reason be a poor analogue of nature. In spite of our incomplete understanding of the manner in which nutrient uptake and organism growth are coupled and regulated (Eppley 1981),

it is sufficient at this point to accept that for significant portions of a doubling period they may proceed at dramatically different instantaneous rates.

DETERMINATION OF KINETIC PARAMETERS

Nutrient uptake as a function of substrate concentration — The idea that the rate of nutrient uptake by phytoplankton can be expressed as the function of substrate concentration as described by Eq. (1) (Dugdale 1967; Eppley and Coatsworth 1968) led to multiple efforts to assess the kinetic parameters of this functionality for both laboratory-grown cultures and natural assemblages of phytoplankton. The hypothesis underlying much of this work was that for a specific habitat the indigenous species or races of phytoplankton would have been selected on the basis of their ability to compete for nutrients at concentrations characteristic of the habitat. It was thought that a certain pattern of uptake for a given species could be taken as a measure of fitness for a nutritional dimension of the habitat, and that this could be a contributing factor in the determination of the temporal succession of dominant species in environments that undergo seasonal changes in nutrient availability. Eppley et al. (1969) demonstrated that the K_s values for NO_3^- and NH_4^+ uptake were lower for oceanic than for neritic clones, and that there was a direct correlation between cell size and the K_s value. MacIsaac and Dugdale (1969) also offered evidence for the significance of the K_s value as a measure of environmental fitness in their demonstration that average values for natural mixed population assemblages differed between oligotrophic oceanic and eutrophic neritic waters. Carpenter and Guillard (1971) added further support to this notion with their observation that the pattern in K_s values for clones of a single species isolated from oceanic and neritic waters reflects the nutrient regime representative of the waters of origin for each clone.

The hypothetical potential for competitive advantage associated with paired K_s and V_m values proposed by Dugdale (1967) is shown in Fig. 5. The separate lines can be viewed as representative of a species or clone-specific response pattern to a nutrient such as NO_3^-. Uptake rate is in dimensions of mass of the element of nutritional significance, i.e. the nitrogen in NO_3^-, taken up per unit organism mass of the same element per unit time. Uptake is conveniently expressed in these dimensions, which reduce simply to reciprocal time, since it is then equivalent to a growth constant (Dugdale and Goering 1967), as will be seen below.

It became clear during these early studies of nutrient uptake kinetics that the V_m values obtained from short-term uptake studies following even a brief period of nutrient deprivation were elevated. When expressed in dimensions of reciprocal time, they

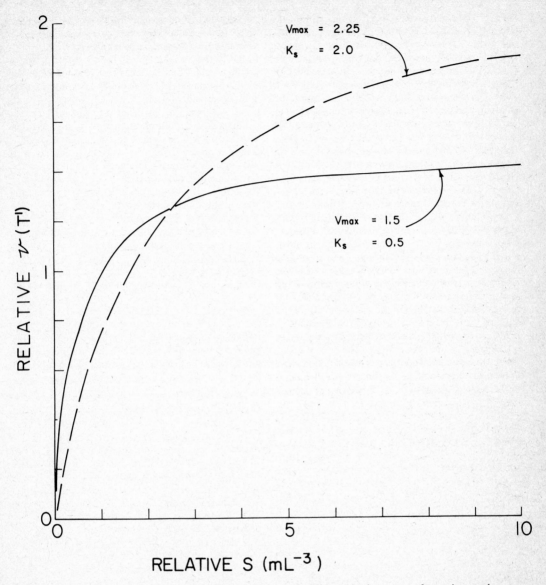

V_{max} = 2.25
K_s = 2.0

V_{max} = 1.5
K_s = 0.5

FIG. 5. Hypothetical competitive interaction between species with different kinetic constants for nutrient uptake.

were much greater than the maximum attainable growth constant for the clone under study (Eppley et al. 1969). As a consequence, estimates of competitive ability for different clones were derived from combinations of K_s values for nutrient uptake and maximum growth rates from batch culture. This represents a hybridization of Eq. (1) and (5) or, in other words, it assumes that the half-saturation constants for nutrient-limited uptake and growth are identical. This assumption seemed valid at the time, as Eppley and Thomas (1968) had found K_s and K_μ to be indistinguishable for *Chaetoceros gracilis*.

The most common procedure used in estimating K_s values for nutrient uptake requires observing the change in concentration over time for multiple concentrations of substrate added to aliquots of a culture that has been deprived of the nutrient of interest. The period of exposure to nutrient must be long enough to observe uptake, but at the same time brief enough to prevent a significant change in the initial nutrient concentration. A more sensitive variant of this approach is to use isotopically labeled nutrient and assay the amount of label incorporated by the organisms. Nutrient uptake data collected with both

217

these methods have usually been based on a single or terminal analysis, and they have been assumed to represent a constant rate of uptake over the period of incubation. If, however, the rate changes with time as a consequence of either substrate depletion or altered physiological response, then the kinetic parameters computed from such data cannot be determined accurately. An example of such a problem can be seen in a particular example of data for ammonium uptake by *Thalassiosira pseudonana* (3H) (Fig. 6). The linear transformation (S/ν vs. S) of the hyperbola fits the data well from 4 to 16 μg-at $NH_4^+-N \cdot L^{-1}$. Below this range, however, the transformed values are elevated relative to the extrapolation from higher concentrations. It is necessary to remember that the expectation of linearity presumes that uptake behaves according to saturation kinetics. A K_s value derived from uptake data has meaning only if this presumption is valid, and numerous data sets have been published for which the rectangular hyperbola provides an adequate approximation. The case discussed above for Fig. 6, however, demonstrates the difficulty that can be encountered in such an effort. This population was growing at 1.55 d^{-1}, or ~50% $\hat{\mu}$, and the uptake determinations were made during 5-min exposure to $^{15}NH_4^+$. The quantity of culture material used per uptake determination was the minimum required for the analysis of isotope

incorporation. Analyses of the data reveal that in the incubation flasks for concentrations <4 μg-at N $\cdot$ L^{-1} substantial depletion of the substrate occurred (>50%) in the 5-min period. This is a reasonably common problem, and if it is not taken into consideration, the resultant estimates of K_s are erroneously high and the confidence intervals are excessively broad.

An alternative procedure for estimating kinetic parameters is the disappearance study, in which the decrease in nutrient added at a high initial concentration is observed (Fig. 7). This approach has been used in both nitrogen and phosphorus uptake studies (cf. Caperon and Meyer 1972; Burmaster and Chisholm 1979). When this approach is used for steady-state chemostat populations, inaccurate approximations of K_s values would be expected if during the experiment there were significant physiological adjustment of the uptake process in response to the elevated nutrient concentration. In other words, the question needs to be asked as to whether a nutrient-limited chemostat population maintained at steady state would respond similarly both to the exposure to a low concentration of nutrient and to the exposure to a low concentration immediately following exposure to a high concentration. Numerous studies with both batch and continuous culture have shown that a ν at any values of S is enhanced in response to nutrient deprivation (Eppley et al.

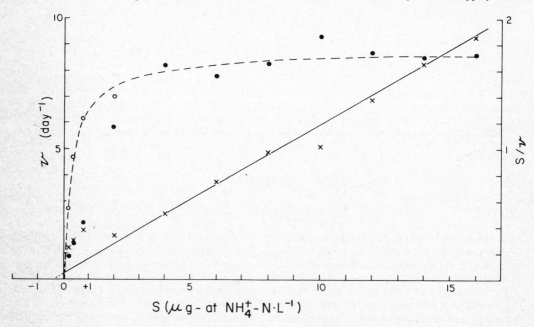

FIG. 6. NH_4^+ uptake (ν) as a function of NH_4^+ concentration (S) for *Thalassiosira pseudonana* (3-H) maintained in steady-state continuous culture at $\mu = 1.55$ d^{-1} ($\bullet$), and the Woolf plot linear transformation of S/ν vs. S (x). The hyperbolic form (broken line) is extrapolated at low values of S in the region for which the S/ν values are higher than expected from the linear transformation. Values for uptake (ν) at low values for S that would correspond to S/ν values coincident with the linear extrapolative ($\bigcirc$) are fit by the hyperbolic form. (From McCarthy 1981.)

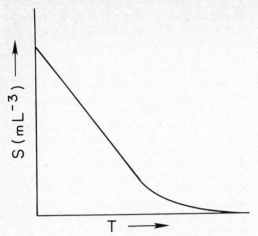

FIG. 7. Nutrient concentration (S) disappearance from the media with time (T) by phytoplankton uptake following a nutrient pulse.

1969; Perry 1972; Rhee 1973; Eppley and Renger 1974; Caperon and Ziemann 1976; Conway and Harrison 1977; McCarthy and Goldman 1979) and evidence for this has also been reported for natural assemblages (Glibert and Goldman 1981). For phosphate-limited *Pavlova (Monochrysis) lutheri*, Burmaster and Chisholm (1979) did demonstrate linearity in uptake rates as a function of time, and they found no statistically significant differences in K_s values determined by the multiple concentration and disappearance methods. Clearly, they were dealing with populations that maintained constant uptake capacity over the course of the experiment. The controls in this study were usually rigorous.

Another problem that some investigators have encountered in studies of nutrient kinetics for natural populations is that of overestimating the available nutrient. This can result from either contamination or lack of specificity in the nutrient analysis, and it has been shown to be a potentially serious problem for both the uptake of phosphorus in freshwater (Rigler 1966; Brown et al. 1978) and nitrogen both in freshwater (Liao and Lean 1978) and in the sea (Eppley et al. 1977). The effect is to overestimate rates of uptake at the lowest concentrations (Fig. 8). The artifact becomes obvious in data sets that include uptake rates for several concentrations, and conversely it can go undetected if uptake rate determinations are based on a single nutrient concentration.

The validity of the hyperbolic fit to nutrient kinetic data can be conveniently tested by the use of linear transformations (Dowd and Riggs 1964). For systems known to be described by Eq. (1), departures from linearity in transformed data due either to substrate depletion or overestimation of ambient nutrient will be readily apparent. Subtle departures can also arise for other reasons, such as

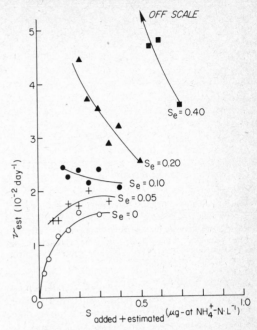

FIG. 8. Calculated effect of erroneously high estimates of ambient nutrient concentration (S_e) on rates of nutrient uptake (ν) determined by isotope techniques. (From Eppley et al. 1977.)

high variance in the K_s values for constituent populations of a natural assemblage (Williams 1973) or multiple uptake processes for the same nutrient.

In reviewing the literature on the kinetics of phytoplankton nutrient uptake, one frequently finds it difficult or impossible to ascertain whether or not appropriate controls were conducted. Unless time course data are available to demonstrate linearity in the uptake versus substrate response over the duration of the experiment, uptake data must remain suspect, and their utility questionable.

Nutrient uptake as a function of cellular composition — The rate of nutrient uptake is a function of substrate concentration (Eq. (1) and (3)), and the rate of population growth is a function of both cellular composition (Eq. (4)) and substrate concentration (Eq. (5)). During balanced growth $\nu = \mu$, but if the population is nutrient limited, then a potential for V_m can materialize that is in excess of the rate of nutrient uptake necessary to provide the needs of the population.

Dugdale (1977), in his analysis of the enhanced maximum uptake property, suggested that V_m' be used to denote the maximum "nutrient specific uptake rate" characteristic of a steady-state population and hypothesized that

(7)
$$V_m' = \frac{P_m}{Q}$$

219

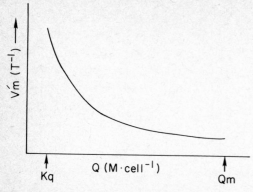

FIG. 9. Enhanced potential for maximum specific rate of nutrient uptake (V_m') as a function of cell quota (Q) assuming that the maximum rate of uptake per cell (ρ_m) is invariant with Q. K_Q and Q_m represent minimum and maximum values of Q for steady-state populations maintained in continuous culture.

where ρ_m is the maximum rate of cellular uptake ($M \cdot cell^{-1} \cdot T^{-1}$). In steady-state populations V_m' should then be a function of the growth rate and, furthermore, Dugdale proposed that if ρ_m is constant, then a plot of Q vs. V_m' should be hyperbolic (Fig. 9). There

are upper and lower limits for the range of Q and the lower limit of V_m' is that observed when the population has maximal Q or is at $\hat{\mu}$.

Data for nitrogen uptake by *Thalassiosira pseudonana* oceanic clone 13-1 (Eppley and Renger 1974) and for estuarine clone 3-H (McCarthy and Goldman 1979), in addition to phosphorus uptake by *Scenedesmus* sp. (Rhee 1973) (Fig. 10a, b, c), indicate, however, that ρ_m is not constant and, hence, the term ρ_m' is proposed to denote the maximum rate of uptake per cell for a population in steady state at a specific growth rate. One exception to this pattern is the data of Burmaster and Chisholm (1979) for *Pavlova (Monochrysis) lutheri* (Fig. 10d). In the results of Brown and Harris (1978) for *Selenastrum*, ρ can also be seen to decrease with increasing μ and increasing Q.

Over roughly similar relative growth rates, as % $\hat{\mu}$, the relationship between ρ_m' and % $\hat{\mu}$ is similar for three of the four studies (Fig. 10, Table 1). In the exception, the Burmaster and Chisholm (1979) study, both the ^{33}P uptake and phosphate disappearance experiments yielded similar data, and the authors suggest that the combined data appear to show an apparent maximum at intermediate growth rates.

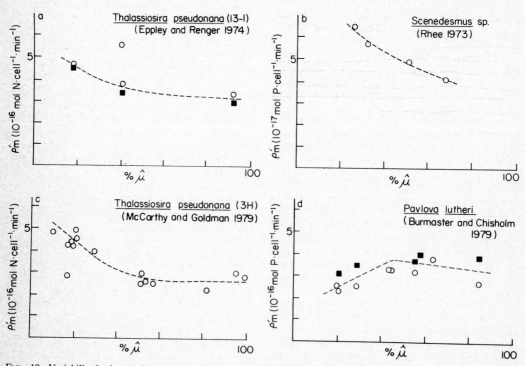

FIG. 10. Variability in the maximum rate of nutrient uptake per cell (hence ρ_m' rather than ρ_m) as a function of relative growth rate (% $\hat{\mu}$). (a) *Thalassiosira pseudonana* (13–1) (from Eppley and Renger 1974); (b) *Scenedesmus* sp. (from Rhee 1973); (c) *Thalassiosira pseudonana* (3–H) (from McCarthy and Goldman 1979); (d) *Pavlova (Monochrysis) lutheri* (from Burmaster and Chisholm 1979).

220

TABLE 1.

Nutrient	Growth rate region (% $\hat{\mu}$)	$\dfrac{\max \rho'_m}{\min \rho'_m}$	Range in Q	Organism	Study
NO₃⁻ or NH₄⁺	19–94	1.5	4 ×	*T. pseudonana* (13–1)	Eppley and Renger 1974
NH₄	20–95	1.6	3.8 ×	*T. pseudonana* (3–H)	Goldman and McCarthy 1978 McCarthy and Goldman 1979
PO₄	26–68	1.6	4 ×	*Scenedesmus* sp.	Rhee 1973
PO₄	20–85	—	4.3 ×	*Pavlova lutheri*	Burmaster and Chisholm 1979

It might be expected that the relationships between ρ'_m and Q would differ for nitrogen- and phosphorus-limited populations. Goldman and McCarthy (1978) proposed that the ratio of maximum to minimum cell quota (Q_m / K_Q) over the entire range of growth rates is >30 for phosphorus in phosphate-limited populations and ~5 for nitrogen in ammonium-limited populations. It is, however, not just the range, but the shape of the μ vs. Q relationship that is of importance. The studies cited above plus several others support the generalization that ~50% of Q_m for nitrogen is attained at 50% $\hat{\mu}$ under nitrogen-limited growth, whereas only 10–20% of the Q_m for phosphorus is attained at 50% $\hat{\mu}$ under phosphorus-limited growth.

Consequently, the slope of the μ vs. Q relationship at low growth rates is greater for phosphorus than for nitrogen. The ρ_m values for phosphorus-limited populations may remain uniformly high over a range of growth rates that extends from low to near maximal values. For the highest growth rate included in the Burmaster and Chisholm (1979) study (~85% μ), the average ρ_m (4.3 × 10⁻¹⁶ mol P·cell⁻¹·min⁻¹) was still near the maximum observed. However, Q for this population (4 × 10⁻¹⁵ mol·cell⁻¹) was less than 25% Q_m.

Of equal ecological significance is the relationship between V'_m and μ (Fig. 11). If ρ_m were constant then the expression derived by Dugdale (1977)

$$(8) \qquad V'_m = \rho_m \, \frac{1 - \dfrac{\mu}{\bar{\mu}}}{K_Q}$$

(substituting $\bar{\mu}$ for μ_m, the maximum μ in the Droop expression, in order to keep terms equivalent, and moving a misplaced parenthesis), would satisfactorily relate V'_m and μ. (It is important to note that $\bar{\mu}$, the unattainable μ in the Droop expression rather than $\hat{\mu}$, the true maximum growth rate, must be used in order for V'_m to remain finite at the maximum growth rate.) The effect of an enhancement in ρ'_m at low

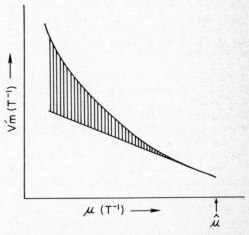

FIG. 11. Enhanced potential for maximum specific rate of nutrient uptake (V'_m) as a linear function of growth rate (μ) when ρ_m is assumed constant, and as a curvilinear function of μ when ρ'_m varies with μ as seen in Fig. 10.

values of Q and μ is to increase V'_m at low growth rates relative to that expected from Eq. (8) (Fig. 11). The concept of a variable ρ'_m needs to be studied further to express it adequately as a function of μ for both nitrogen and phosphorus. Only then can we present an accurate mathematical representation of V'_m as a function of μ.

The variable nature of the maximum rate of nutrient uptake (V'_m) permits phytoplankton populations to grow at near maximal rates at virtually undetectable levels of nutrient in the medium. This concept, which was discussed by Caperon and Ziemann (1976), allows for $K\mu \ll K_s$ and it can be easily demonstrated. Figure 6 represents a typical data set for NH₄⁺ uptake by a marine phytoplankter. As described above, because of the enhanced potential for uptake, accurate data at low values of S are particularly difficult to obtain. A smooth curve drawn through the measured values for uptake (solid circles) would give the impression that a concen-

221

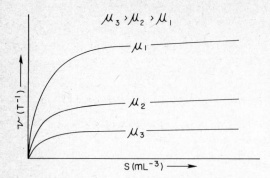

$$\mu_3 > \mu_2 > \mu_1$$

$\nu\,(\mathrm{T}^{-1})$ ⟶

$S\,(\mathrm{mL}^{-3})$ ⟶

FIG. 12. Proposed relationship between rate of nutrient uptake (ν) and nutrient concentration (S) for steady-state population maintained at three different growth rates (μ_1, μ_2, and μ_3). As seen in Fig. 11, the population with the lowest μ (μ_1) has the highest potential rate of nutrient uptake. The half-saturation constant for nutrient uptake (K_s) is assumed to be invariant with μ.

tration of approximately 0.5 μg–at NH_4^+–N·L^{-1} is necessary in order to maintain a V equivalent to the measured steady-state growth rate of 1.55 d^{-1}, whereas the observed growth chamber concentration was lower than expected by at least an order of magnitude. If, however, we agree to assume that the V vs. S relationship is hyperbolic, and then estimate V values for low S values by extrapolation from the linear transformation, one can see the possibility of attaining a V of ~1.55 d^{-1} at a concentration <0.03 μg–at N·L^{-1}. The discrepancy that appears to exist between data sets like those represented in Fig. 4 and 6 can be reconciled in such a manner if it is remembered that the former is a composite for multiple steady states and the latter is representative of a single steady state. A single species maintained at different growth rates will be capable of uptake response patterns that are unique for each growth rate (Fig. 12). Thus far the evidence seems to indicate that, whereas ν for a given substrate concentration is a function of $\mu/\hat{\mu}$, the K_s for uptake remains constant (Eppley and Renger 1974). It needs to be emphasized, though, that there are few reliable uptake data for very low growth rates.

Although an uncoupling between uptake and growth has been well documented for both phosphorus- and nitrogen-limited growth, it has not been seen for silicon. In several studies, the maximum rates of Si(OH)$_4$ uptake (V_m) are similar to the specific growth rates (μ) (Paasche 1973; Conway et al. 1976; Nelson et al. 1976) regardless of the state of nutrient deprivation. This generalization is utilized in the Davis et al. (1978) model that describes Si(OH)$_4$ uptake as functionally dependent on media Si(OH)$_4$ concentration (S), and independent of cellular silicon content (Q).

The family of curves representing the hypothetical ν vs. S responses for three populations at different steady-state growth rates (Fig. 12) illustrates the control of ν by both S and Q. When studies of uptake kinetics with nutrient-limited populations involve alteration of the steady-state nutrient concentrations, the population will shift from the balanced to unbalanced growth. Such a shift may, for practical purposes, be instantaneous, and an interpretation of the uptake data must take this into consideration.

Interactions between Uptake Processes for Multiple Nutrients

NUTRIENTS THAT SUPPLY THE SAME CELLULAR ELEMENTAL REQUIREMENT

For elemental needs that can be met with nutrient material in a variety of different forms, there is good reason to investigate the kinetics of interaction for the uptake and/or assimilation of the various substrates. In the case of silicon nutrition in diatoms, the source is believed to be exclusively limited to monomeric orthosilicic acid (Si(OH)$_4$). The phosphorus nutrition of phytoplankton can be met universally by orthophosphate (PO$_4^{3-}$), and in some cases by monophosphoesters (MPE). The kinetics of interaction between PO$_4^{3-}$ and MPE uptake and assimilation have been the subject of a few investigations with phytoplankton (Perry 1972; Taft et al. 1977). The general pattern that has been observed is that the induction of alkaline phosphatase activity associated with the cell surface is correlated with the depletion of inorganic phosphate in the growth medium. The phosphatases facilitate the utilization of organically bound phosphate by a hydrolysis that releases PO$_4^{3-}$ in the immediate vicinity of the cell surface. For nitrogenous nutrition, the nearly universal suitability of at least three forms of nitrogen for phytoplankton growth (NO$_3^-$, NO$_2^-$, and NH$_4^+$), in addition to the species or clone-specific potentiality to utilize urea and some amino acids, greatly increases the possibility of competitive interaction between the processes responsible for transport and assimilation of different forms of this element.

The importance of NO$_3^-$ as a source of nitrogenous nutrient in upwelling regions, coastal regions in temperature latitudes, and perhaps deep in the euphotic zone of oceanic waters is evident from many studies. The suppression of NO$_3^-$ uptake by NH$_4^+$ when both are present in the growth medium has been the subject of many laboratory and field studies. The generalization that has emerged from batch culture and field data is that NH$_4^+$ is preferentially utilized (Fig. 13), but the actual kinetics of this interaction have received relatively little attention

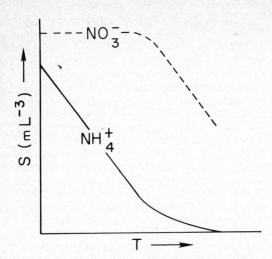

FIG. 13. Typical patterns of NO_3^- and NH_4^+ disappearance from culture media resulting from preferential uptake of NH_4^+.

(cf. Grant et al. 1967; Eppley et al. 1969; Eppley and Rogers 1970; Packard and Blasco 1974; McCarthy et al. 1977). In still other studies, however, the simultaneous utilization of both NH_4^+ and NO_3^- has been documented (Eppley and Renger 1974; Bienfang 1975; Caperon and Ziemann 1976). The findings of both preferential or apparently indiscriminant uptake are not contradictory, rather they serve to define the degree to which a given concentration of NH_4^+ will suppress the utilization of NO_3^-.

Again it becomes important to distinguish between results from relatively short-term uptake experiments and those from longer term growth experiments, as well as between nitrogen-limited and non-nitrogen-limited populations. With short-term experiments the uptake response may represent transient forms of behavior in the transport processes, whereas in long-term experiments the difference between supplied and residual nutrient in either a steady-state continuous culture or a batch culture integrated over a period of time equivalent to at least a few generations presumably reflects the growth requirements of the population.

In short-term uptake experiments with nitrogen-starved phytoplankton it is possible to observe simultaneously high rates of uptake for both NO_3^- and NH_4^+ (DeManche et al. 1979). Whether or not the NO_3^- taken up will be reduced or whether or not NO_3^- uptake will continue in the presence of NH_4^+ depends on whether the nitrate reductase system is active, which in turn is related to the sufficiency of the NH_4^+–N supply.

Results of several studies on the induction and repression of nitrate reductase have led to the suggestion that an inactive precursor protein for this enzyme is present in NH_4^+-grown cells. The induction process is thought to involve the synthesis of an "activator," which is in direct response to an exposure to NO_3^- and an absence of NH_4^+. The evidence for *Chlorella* is the following:

1) Cyclohexamide will suppress synthesis of the activator when the cells are treated simultaneously with exposure to NO_3^- (Funkhouser et al. 1980).

2) Deuterium labeling demonstrates that only a small fraction of increased activity can be attributed to de novo synthesis of enzyme following either transfer from NH_4^+- to NO_3^--enriched media or transfer from dark to light (Johnson 1979; Tischner and Hüttermann 1978, respectively).

3) NH_4^+ grown cells with almost no active enzyme contain a protein that cross reacts with nitrate reductase antibodies, thus indicating that the inactive precursor is immunologically related to purified nitrate reductase (Funkhouser and Ramadoss 1980).

Thacker and Syrett (1972) stated that "indeed it is not yet clear whether the inhibition of NO_3^- reduction (by NH_4^+) results from an inhibition of the enzymes of nitrate reduction or from prevention of NO_3^- uptake by the cells." Since that time numerous papers have contributed to our current understanding of the effect of NH_4^+ on NO_3^- utilization, but few have provided clear insight into the actual mechanism by which NH_4^+ suppresses either the uptake or the assimilation of nitrate. It has been argued by Chaparro et al. (1976), for example, that the similarity of the effects of both NH_4^+ and arsenate in promoting the reversible inactivation of nitrate reductase lends credence to the hypothesis that the inactivation occurs via uncoupling of photophosphorylation. It remains to be seen, however, how the proposed effect on photophosphorylation can inactivate nitrate reductase without having other serious consequences for cellular metabolism as well. Ohmori and Hattori (1978) refuted the uncoupling hypothesis by contending that the suppression of both NO_3^- utilization and N_2 fixation by the presence of NH_4^+ in the growth medium resulted from preferential routing of available ATP to the glutamine synthesis process, leaving insufficient reserves for uptake and assimilation of nitrogen by other pathways. A similar change in ATP levels has been detected in *Chlorella* (Akimova et al. 1977). However, a change in ATP levels cannot be the only effect of NH_4^+, because methylammonium, an NH_4^+ analogue that is transported into the cell but not metabolically assimilated, inhibits utilization of NO_3^- (Wheeler 1980) and inactivates nitrate reductase as effectively as do NH_4^+ and arsenate (Chaparro et al. 1976). Furthermore, the results with methylammonium generally support the argument that it is NH_4^+ rather than a product of NH_4^+ assimilation, such as glutamine, that inactivates nitrate reductase. It is clear from several studies

223

that even in the presence of NO_3^-, both NH_4^+ and methylammonium suppress all activities associated with the nitrate reductase complex NAD(P)H-NR, NAD(P)H-cytochrome-c reductase and $FMNH_2$ or MVH-NR (see, for example, Diez et al. 1977, for *Ankistrodesmus*).

The reduced rate of NO_3^- utilization in the presence of NH_4^+ has also been attributed to a reversible inactivation of nitrate reductase by cyanide (Solomonson 1974; Gewitz et al. 1974). Inactive enzyme preparations can be completely reactivated by reduction with ferricyanide (Jetschmann et al. 1972; Solomonson et al. 1973). Hydroxylamine has a similar effect on nitrate reductase, but higher concentrations are required than for cyanide (Solomonson and Vennesland 1972), and Solomonson and Spehar (1977) have based a model for the regulation of nitrate assimilation on a hydroxylamine and glyoxylate reaction that yields cyanide. A rather tenuous tenet of this model is that sufficient hydroxylamine accumulates during NH_4^+ assimilation to suppress nitrate reductase activity effectively.

Very few studies of the effect of NH_4^+ on NO_3^- uptake have used sufficiently controlled experiments to determine whether the presence of NH_4^+ in the growth media is actually suppressing NO_3^- transport across the plasmalemma. Pistorius et al. (1976) discovered that for *Chlorella* the degree of inactivation of the nitrate reductase in a culture deprived of nitrogen is not increased when NH_4^+ is added. Whereas reactivation is stimulated by NO_3^-, an addition of NO_3^- plus NH_4^+ yields a level of inactivation that is comparable to that attained with NH_4^+ alone. In a subsequent series of short-term time course experiments with *Chlorella*, Pistorius et al. (1978) observed that NO_3^- uptake ceases within 5 min following an addition of NH_4^+, whereas nitrate reductase is still highly active up to 60 min later. They interpreted these findings as additional evidence that the transport as well as the reduction of NO_3^- is suppressed by NH_4^+ in the growth medium. Moreover, Tischner and Lorenzen (1979) have demonstrated with *Chlorella* that NO_3^- uptake is totally suppressed within 1 min following an addition of NH_4^+ at concentrations as low as 12 μM, whereas an hour later the nitrate reductase activity had only decreased by 50%.

At this time it is not clear as to the degree to which the observations and ideas regarding an inactivation of nitrate reductase through oxidation, such as with cyanide, and those regarding an inactive constitutive precursor plus an inducible activator are consistent or compatible with each other. In the case of the former, no de novo protein synthesis is required to activate the enzyme, whereas in the latter a minor component of the enzyme complex must be synthesized.

Regardless of the precise nature of the means by which unicellular algae regulate their nitrate transport and reduction processes, it is clear from many batch culture studies that there is little evidence to suggest that NO_3^- in the growth medium will be utilized when the available NH_4^+ is sufficient to meet the nitrogen growth requirement (cf. Syrett 1962; Morris and Syrett 1963; Eppley et al. 1969; Thacker and Syrett 1972). In drawing this generalization, it is important to distinguish between the results obtained with batch culture, those with continuous culture at steady state, and those with continuous culture in which the steady-state coupling between nutrient uptake and population growth has been perturbed by a pulse of nutrient. During exponential growth in batch culture, NH_4^+ in the presence of NO_3^- may be utilized exclusively as long as the medium concentration is sufficiently high to saturate the NH_4^+ uptake system. Under these conditions nitrate reductase is inactive, and there is no net uptake of NO_3^-. Because ν approaches V_{max} asymptotically as a function of S (Fig. 1), the concentration of NH_4^+ required to suppress completely NO_3^- utilization is difficult to determine with high precision from kinetic analyses of uptake data. If for the sake of example one assumes that the K_s values for NH_4^+ and NO_3^- uptake by a certain species are identical, and that the maximum growth rates attainable on both forms of nitrogen are also identical, then the population can remain in an exponential growth phase at a constant μ as long as the sum of available NH_4^+ and NO_3^- is in excess of that necessary to saturate either uptake system. If there is a lag in NO_3^- uptake at the beginning of the transition from sole dependence on NH_4^+ to one of mixed dependence, possibly resulting from the time required for induction of the necessary enzymes, then the rates of uptake and population growth might be unequal for a short period. It is likely, however, that compensation for such a deficit in nitrogen uptake would arise if V_m for NH_4^+ became enhanced during the transition.

The simultaneous utilization of NH_4^+ and NO_3^- is well documented. In many cases for which nitrogen-limited chemostat populations have been grown in media containing both NH_4^+ and NO_3^-, the concentrations remained at less than the conventional limits of analytical detection (Eppley et al. 1971; Eppley and Renger 1974; Bienfang 1975; Caperon and Ziemann 1976). By incrementally increasing the dilution rate of the growth chamber to permit successively faster steady-state population growth rates, the nitrate concentration in the growth chamber will rise as $\hat{\mu}$, the maximum growth rate, is approached. Unfortunately, data are not available to quantify rigorously the kinetics of the interaction between NO_3^- and NH_4^+ uptake under these conditions. For the sake of simplicity, the patterns of

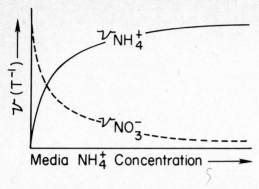

FIG. 14. Schematic approximation of the simultaneous rates of NO_3^- and NH_4^+ uptake as a function of NH_4^+ concentration. Several assumptions are discussed in the text.

NH_4^+ uptake and NO_3^- uptake over a growth rate limiting concentration of NH_4^+ and a saturating concentration of NO_3^- can be seen as a pair of complimentary hyperbolas that sum to the same ν for any concentration of NH_4^+ (Fig. 14). As stated above, however, this is only an accurate representation of the interaction if the uptake of each substrate has the same K_s value and if each substrate will support the same maximum growth rate. A consequence of departure from equality for either term would be an alteration of the paired hyperbolic representation in Fig. 14. If the maximum growth rate values were to differ such that NH_4^+ promoted more rapid growth, the sum of the ν values could be linear with a positive slope, but if the K_s values differed the sum need not be a linear function of concentration.

One useful approach in investigating the potential to discriminate between different forms of nitrogen is to follow the time course of nutrient uptake following a pulse delivery of nutrient. By observing nutrient concentrations after adding NH_4^+ to a NO_3^--grown culture of *Skeletonema costatum*, Conway (1977) was able to demonstrate a suppression of NO_3^- uptake at NH_4^+ concentration >1 μM. Time course data for both nutrient uptake and cellular nutrient content are needed in such studies to distinguish between utilization that includes assimilation and mere transport as DeManche et al. (1979) observed for NO_3^- in the presence of NH_4^+. With nutrient deprivation, the kinetics of interaction between the two substrates are further complicated by the enhancement of V_m'. If the regulators of enhancement in the two uptake systems are different, then the time courses for changes in activity during nutrient deprivation and following exposure to nutrient may also differ.

Several field studies with natural assemblages of phytoplankton in both marine and freshwater support the generalization from laboratory studies that NH_4^+ will be utilized in preference to NO_3^- (cf. Prochazkova et al. 1970; Brezonik 1972; Conway 1977; McCarthy et al. 1975, 1977; Eppley et al. 1979), while at least one has shown that this may not always be the case (Conover 1975). In one study with 120 different natural assemblages in the Chesapeake Bay (salinity 2–30‰, temperature 4–29°C) (McCarthy et al. 1975), the sum of NO_3^- plus NO_2^- uptake accounted for $<7\%$ of the phytoplankton nitrogen ration when NH_4^+ concentrations exceeded 1 μM with only three exceptions (Fig. 15). The pattern of these data is similar to the hyperbolic form for NO_3^- as a function of NH_4^+ concentration (Fig. 14). Clearly there is considerable range in the degree of suppression associated with a particular NH_4^+ concentration, and presumably this is a reflection of the diverse nature of the natural assemblages studied. For about 10% of the assemblages the degree of suppression was more extreme than the generalization given above.

Whereas the pattern for NH_4^+ suppression of NO_3^- utilization is similar for several species and natural assemblages, large species-specific differences are apparent in the kinetics of both the interaction between NO_3^- and NO_2^- utilization and in those involving urea. Typically, the concentration of NO_2^- in marine water is low. There are exceptions, however, such as at the base of the euphotic zone in oceanic regions of both the Atlantic and the Pacific. Nitrite has received relatively little attention as a source of phytoplankton nitrogen, and to some degree its importance in this regard is not always clear, as its primary source in the euphotic zone may be phytoplankton release (Carlucci et al. 1970; Harrison and Davis 1977; Olson et al. 1980). At times, however, it may be the dominant form of nitrogen in the nutrition of phytoplankton (McCarthy et al. 1977).

In a few studies designed to examine the interaction between NO_3^- and NO_2^- uptake and assimilation by phytoplankton, it has been noted that for *Ditylum brightwellii* both forms are utilized simultaneously at similar rates over wide ranging concentrations (Eppley and Rogers 1970), but for natural assemblages both were utilized only at low concentrations of NO_3^- (Harrison and Davis 1977). For another diatom, *Thalassiosira pseudonana* (66-A) from the central North Pacific gyre, Olson et al. (1980) have described the interaction of NO_3^- and NO_2^- uptake as quasi-competitive. Growth on NO_3^- was twice as rapid as that on NO_2^-, and the K_s for uptake of NO_3^- was about half of that for NO_2^-. These differences result in a marked preference for NO_3^-, regardless of substrate concentration, and results of short-term uptake experiments exhibit classical competitive inhibition kinetics. For *Chlamydomonas reinhardi*, however, the uptake of NO_3^- is inhibited

225

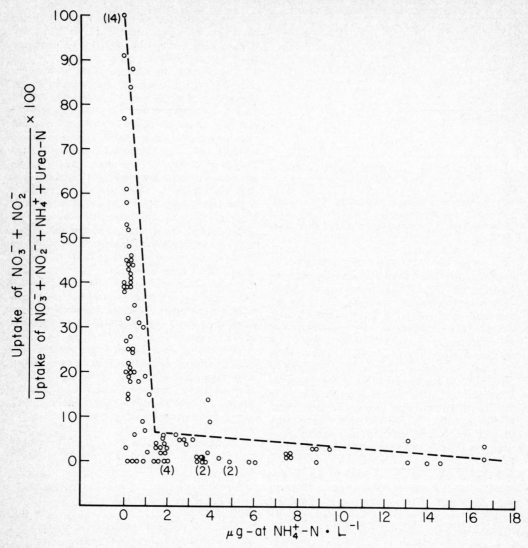

FIG. 15. Relationship between the fraction of the total nitrogen utilized by natural phytoplankton assemblages in Chesapeake Bay and the ambient NH_4^+ concentration. (From McCarthy et al. 1975.)

completely by the presence of NO_2^- (Thacker and Syrett 1972). The patterns in NO_2^- and NO_3^- preference when both were present in concentrations sufficient to saturate the uptake process are shown schematically in Fig. 16. Little attention has been given to the study of nitrite reductase in phytoplankton. Apparently, it is similar to nitrite reductase in higher plants in that it can be induced by both nitrate and nitrite in the culture medium, while nitrate, but not ammonium, suppresses activity in cell-free extracts (Syrett 1981).

Few data are available for generalization regarding the kinetics of interaction between the uptake of urea and that of other nitrogenous nutrients. Grant

et al. (1967) observed that for *Cylindrotheca* the order of nutritional preference proceeded from NH_4^+ to urea to NO_3^-. A similar order of preference can be seen in field studies in both Kaneohe Bay (Harvey and Caperon 1976) and Chesapeake Bay (McCarthy et al. 1977).

Not all phytoplankton can utilize urea (Guillard 1963), but for those able to transport and assimilate this substrate the kinetics of uptake can closely resemble those for NH_4^+ (McCarthy 1972). In one recent study it has been shown that a uniform high potential for urea uptake (V_m') is maintained by both *Thalassiosira pseudonana* and *Skeletonema costatum*

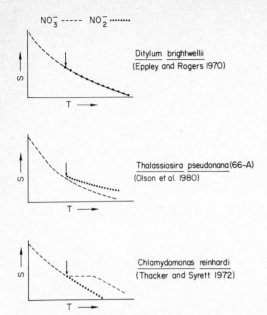

NO$_3^-$ ----- NO$_2^-$ ········

Ditylum brightwellii
(Eppley and Rogers 1970)

Thalassiosira pseudonana(66-A)
(Olson et al. 1980)

Chlamydomonas reinhardi
(Thacker and Syrett 1972)

FIG. 16. Schematic representation of the three patterns observed for NO$_3^-$ and NO$_2^-$ disappearance from culture media. Pulse addition of NO$_2^-$ equal in concentration to the media NO$_3^-$ concentration is indicated by an arrow on the abscissa.

while the nutritional state ranges from well nourished on NO$_3^-$ and NO$_2^-$ to nitrogen starved (Horrigan and McCarthy 1981). This rate of uptake can be ~15 times the rate at which NO$_3^-$ and NO$_2^-$ are being utilized for growth, and the period over which it is sustained is a function of the nutritional state: minutes for the well-nourished population versus several tens of minutes for the nitrogen-starved population.

In the Chesapeake Bay study, McCarthy et al. (1977) found that a relative preference index (RPI) calculated for each form of nitrogenous nutrient was useful in assessing the competitive interaction between suitable alternative substrates:

$$RPI_{N_i} = \frac{\dfrac{V_{N_i}}{\Sigma V_N}}{\dfrac{S_{N_i}}{\Sigma S_N}}$$

where N_i is a particular form of nitrogenous nutrient N, V is the rate of uptake, and S is the concentration. Through this approach it has been demonstrated that, when NO$_4^+$ availability is adequate to meet the entire nitrogenous demand of the constituent population, urea may or may not be utilized, while NO$_3^-$ is rejected. For Chesapeake Bay the NH$_4^+$ RPI values were never less than unity, indicating that NH$_4^+$ was never rejected, while those for NO$_3^-$ never exceeded

unity. Moreover, the RPI values for NO$^-_3$, NH$^-_4$, urea, and NO$_2^-$ all converged at values of unity when availability of the more preferred forms was insufficient to meet the nutritional needs of the organisms (Fig. 17). Data for Lake Kinneret (McCarthy et al. unpublished manuscript) show an extremely similar pattern to those of the Chesapeake for NH$_4^+$, NO$_3^-$, and urea. The same pattern for NH$_4^+$ and NO$_3^-$ is also seen in data for the Southern Ocean, although a high level of NO$_3^-$ persisted throughout the study (Glibert et al. unpublished manuscript). In a study of the California Current, Eppley et al. (1979) found NH$_4^+$ RPI values as low as 0.73, but 75% of their reported values were >0.95 (max. 13.8). Their NO$_3^-$ RPI values were all less than unity, and, as before, these values converged with those for NH$_4^+$ as the ambient nitrogenous nutrient concentration approached levels known to limit the rate of phytoplankton growth.

For the oceanic regions, which accommodate as much as 80% of the marine phytoplankton productivity, the concentrations of nutrients are too low to undertake similar studies of nutrient preference. In all likelihood, there is little discrimination between available forms of nitrogen at these low concentrations, except in the cases of particular species that cannot utilize certain forms of nitrogen such as urea or some amino acids.

NUTRIENTS THAT SUPPLY DIFFERENT CELLULAR ELEMENTAL REQUIREMENTS

A question often asked by aquatic ecologists is whether particular natural assemblages of phytoplankton are limited by single or multiple nutrients. Although numerous papers have been written on field efforts to identify *the* limiting nutrient in oceanic, neritic, estuarine, and lake studies, the data usually do not lend themselves to unequivocal interpretation. The purpose of the present discussion is not to review this large body of literature, but rather to examine the results from some studies of nutrient uptake for which there is a transition from one limiting nutrient to another. In most studies with natural systems, an interest in limiting nutrients has usually focused on nitrogen and phosphorus. Rhee (1974, 1978), Goldman et al. (1979), and Terry (1980) examined interactions between uptake capabilities for these two nutrients, and Droop (1974) studied interactions between phosphate and vitamin B$_{12}$.

Although some treatments of this subject have considered the possibility that population growth during transition from one nutrient-limited state to another is regulated in a multiplicative manner that involves both nutrients, recent data indicate that this is not the case for nitrogen and phosphorus (Rhee 1974, 1978; Terry 1980). Clearly, during such a transition there could be a range of growth rates

227

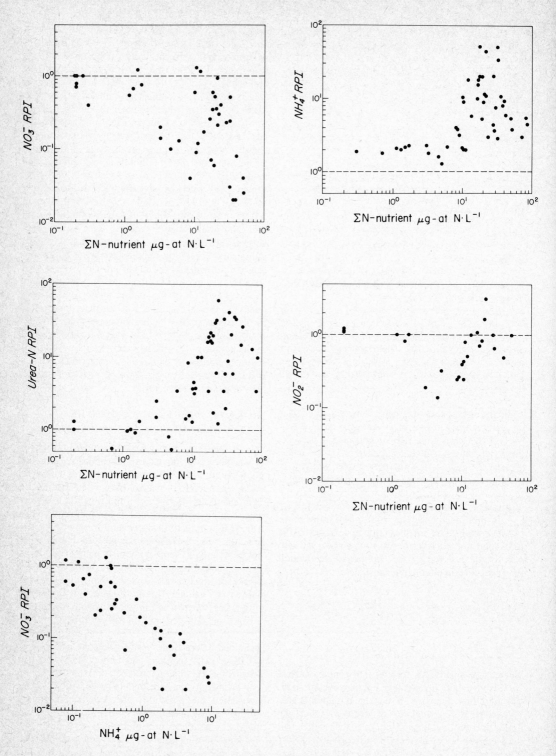

FIG. 17. Relationship between relative preference indices (RPI) for nitrogenous nutrients and the concentration of total available nutrient for Chesapeake Bay phytoplankton. (From McCarthy et al. 1977.)

for which control is multiplicative, but if it does exist it must represent less than a few percent of the entire range of growth rates.

Redfield (1958) called attention to the similarity in the elemental N:P content of both well-nourished plankton and the deep oceanic reserves of these elements in the form of dissolved ions. This typical elemental composition for well-nourished phytoplankton is often referred to as the "Redfield ratio." It averages approximately 16, by atoms, and it has found wide ranging application in models for plankton productivity that include terms for nutrient limitation.

Goldman et al. (1979) observed that at growth media N:P ratios $\leq$ 15:1 the phytoplankton N:P composition reflects the availability of these elements in the media. For an N:P ratio > 50, however, the phytoplankton N:P composition only reached values as high as the media at the lowest growth rates. Terry (1980) also observed a lack of correspondence between media and cellular elemental composition above a media N:P value of 50.

Rhee (1978) was able to show a very abrupt transition between nitrogen and phosphorus limitation at a media N:P ratio of about 30 for *Scenedesmus* (Fig. 18). These data are for a single growth rate, ~44% $\hat{\mu}$, and they clearly demonstrate that for both N and P it is the Q for the nutrient that limits growth that determines μ (Fig. 2). Neither μ nor Q are determined by the N:P ratio in the media. Of particular interest is the finding that some polyphosphate fractions, especially the acid-soluble component, occur in much higher cell concentration during nitrogen limitation than during phosphorus limitation at the same value for μ. Correspondingly, the maximum specific rate of P uptake at a given growth rate is as much as eightfold lower during nitrogen limitation than it is during phosphorus limitation.

The maximum potential for NO_3^- uptake, V'_m, is an inverse function of the cellular N:P ratio (Fig. 19). Under N limitation and for a single N:P ratio in the medium, V'_m is an inverse function of both μ

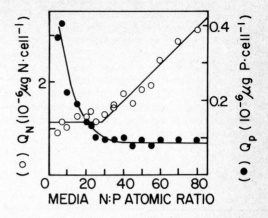

FIG. 18. Cell quotas for N and P determined at a single steady-state growth rate for *Scenedesmus* sp. grown with N:P nutrient ratios in the incoming media. (From Rhee 1978.)

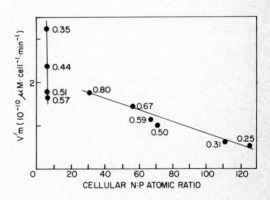

FIG. 19. Enhanced potential for nutrient uptake (V'_m) as a function of cellular N:P ratio for N-limited (N:P < 20) and P-limited (N:P > 20) populations of *Scenedesmus* sp. (From Rhee 1978.)

TABLE 2. (From Rhee 1974.)

Media N:P ratio	% $\hat{\mu}$	N/cell ($\times$ 10^{-16} mol/cell)	P/cell ($\times$ 10^{-16} mol/cell)	Cell N:P (atomic)
1.0 (N-limited)	0.12	455	110	4.1
	0.14	539	121	4.5
	0.52	863	117	7.4
1900 (P-limited)	0.26	2570	17.9	143
	0.32	2223	19.7	111
	0.52	2150	30.7	71
	0.69	2320	39.3	59
	0.83	2350	73.6	32

and the N-cell quota (Table 2, Fig. 19). Under P limitation, however, the V_m' for NO_3^- at a single media N:P ratio is independent of the N-cell quota although it is still inversely proportional to μ. Whereas the results for the N-limited state are like those seen before in studies of N-limited growth (McCarthy and Goldman 1979), those for the P-limited state represent another condition for which generalizations presented earlier regarding the regulation of V_m' for nitrogen do not apply.

Conclusions

As can be easily seen in an examination of the bibliography necessary to document many of the findings and concepts discussed in a review chapter such as this, much of our current understanding of nutrient kinetics is based on rather recent work. Laboratory studies with clones isolated from various estuarine, neritic, and oceanic regions have provided the substance for increased generalization from the principles of plant physiology to the study of plankton ecology. Moreover, studies with continuous cultures maintained at steady state have permitted us to examine with increasing precision the most dynamic aspects of nutrient uptake and assimilation. One potentially exciting avenue in the pursuit of a better understanding of the nature of the metabolic regulation of nutrient transport and assimilation involves the use of analogues and inhibitors (Syrett 1981).

In most field studies we are usually far too ignorant of the physiological characteristics of the species that constitute the natural assemblage to predict with confidence the community response to a change in nutrient availability. To better interpret field data, we need increased laboratory study with the organisms that are typical in natural assemblages. This will require more attention to the systematics of the phytoplankton, the nanoplankton in particular, and an increased effort to bring into culture more of the species that are commonly observed in nature but rarely maintained in our laboratories.

At this time there is considerable interest in deriving from laboratory experiments specific patterns in cellular elemental composition and physiological potential that have applicability in assessing the average nutritional state of the populations that naturally co-occur. The usual problem in drawing inference from elemental composition data collected in field studies is, however, the uncertainty regarding the relative contributions attributable to the phytoplankton, other biota, and detritus. Except in bloom conditions the detrital component may be the dominant one. On occasion an abundance of net plankton may permit the selective capture of large phytoplankters, but these typically constitute a small portion of the total phytoplankton biomass.

The greatest difficulty in extending laboratory analysis for nutrient uptake potential to field studies is that of processing the samples over sufficiently brief periods to observe a realistic time course response to nutrient pulses. Except in rich coastal or estuarine waters, the quantities of biomass are too low to permit the use of volumes of seawater that can be manipulated rapidly. Typically, the time period of interest (minutes) is considerably less than that necessary to terminate the experiment and collect the particulate material by gentle filtration. In one coastal study, however, such experiments have shown that natural populations do at times have the potential to take up NH_4^+ at enhanced rates following even trace additions of substrate (Glibert and Goldman 1981). By analogy to laboratory culture data, the field observations have been used to infer that the populations studied were nitrogen deficient.

A fuller understanding of the role of nutrients in regulating the primary productivity of the nutrient impoverished oceanic waters will also require improved methodology for quantifying the ambient nutrient. As seen above, some phytoplankters can attain near maximal growth rates in continuous steady-state cultures at nutrient concentrations that are below conventional limits of detection. As a consequence, the kinetics of nutrient uptake for such species cannot be defined for conditions that range from a moderate to a serious state of nutrient deprivation.

The body of information covered in this review reflects the roots of the investigators who have produced it. Most of it is the work of classically oriented but broad-minded physiologists, ecologists, and oceanographers. The future of the field of phytoplankton ecology lies in the hands of those who will be successful both in extending our knowledge within these subject areas and in closing the gaps between them.

References

AKIMOVA, N. I., Z. G. EVSTIGNEEVA, AND V. L. KRETOVICH. 1977. Regulation of the glutamine metabolism in *Chlorella pyrenoidosa*. Regulation of the glutamine synthetase activity by components of the adenylic system. Biochemistry (USSR) 42: 739–743.

BHOVICHITRA, M., AND E. SWIFT. 1977. Light and dark uptake of nitrate and ammonium by large oceanic dinoflagellates: *Pyrocystis noctiluca*, *Pyrocystis fusiformis*, and *Dissodinium lunula*. Limnol. Oceanogr. 22: 73–83.

BIENFANG, P. K. 1975. Steady state analysis of nitrate-ammonium assimilation by phytoplankton. Limnol. Oceanogr. 20: 402–411.

BREZONIK, P. L. 1972. Nitrogen: sources and transformation in natural waters, p. 1–47. *In* H. E. Allen and J. R. Kramer [ed.] Nutrients in natural waters. John Wiley, New York, NY.

BROWN, C. M., D. S. MACDONALD-BROWN, AND S. O. STANLEY. 1975. Inorganic nitrogen metabolism in marine bacteria: nitrate uptake and reduction in a marine pseudomonad. Mar. Biol. 31: 7–13.

BROWN, E. J., AND R. F. HARRIS. 1978. Kinetics of algal transient phosphate uptake and the cell quota concept. Limnol. Oceanogr. 23: 35–40.

BROWN, E. J., R. F. HARRIS, AND J. K. KOONCE. 1978. Kinetics of phosphate uptake by aquatic microorganisms: derivations from a simple Michaelis-Menten equation. Limnol. Oceanogr. 23: 26–34.

BURMASTER, D. E. 1979. The continuous culture of phytoplankton: mathematical equivalence among three steady-state models. Am. Nat. 113: 123–134.

BURMASTER, D. E., AND S. W. CHISHOLM. 1979. A comparison of two methods for measuring phosphate uptake by *Monochrysis lutheri* grown in continuous culture. J. Exp. Mar. Biol. Ecol. 39: 187–202.

BUTZ, R. G., AND W. A. JACKSON. 1977. A mechanism for nitrate transport and reduction. Phytochemistry 16: 409–417.

CAPERON, J. 1967. Population growth in micro-organism limited by food supply. Ecology 48: 715–722.

1968. Population growth response of *Isochrysis galbana* to nitrate variation at limiting concentrations. Ecology 49: 715–721.

CAPERON, J., AND J. MEYER. 1972. Nitrogen-limited growth of marine phytoplankton-II. Uptake kinetics and their role in nutrient limited growth of phytoplankton. Deep-Sea Res. 19: 619–632.

CAPERON, J., AND D. A. ZIEMANN. 1976. Synergistic effects of nitrate and ammonium ion on the growth and uptake kinetics of *Monochrysis lutheri* in continuous culture. Mar. Biol. 36: 73–84.

CARLUCCI, A. F., E. O. HARTWIG, AND P. M. BOWES. 1970. Biological production of nitrate in seawater. Mar. Biol. 7: 161–166.

CARPENTER, E. J., AND R. R. L. GUILLARD. 1971. Intraspecific differences in nitrate half-saturation constants for three species of marine phytoplankton. Ecology 52: 183–185.

CHAPARRO, A., J. M. MALDONADO, J. DIEZ, A. M. RELIMPIO, AND M. LOSADA. 1976. Nitrate reductase inactivation and reducing power and energy charge in *Chlorella* cells. Plant Sci. Lett. 6: 335–342.

CONOVER, S. A. M. 1975. Nitrogen utilization during spring blooms of marine phytoplankton in Bedford Basin, Nova Scotia, Canada. Mar. Biol. 32: 247–261.

CONWAY, H. L. 1977. Interactions of inorganic nitrogen in the uptake and assimilation by marine phytoplankton. Mar. Biol. 39: 221–232.

CONWAY, H. L., AND P. J. HARRISON. 1977. Marine diatoms grown in chemostats under silicate or ammonium limitation. IV. Transient response of *Chaetoceros debilis, Skeletonema costatum* and *Thalassiosira gravida* to a single addition of the limiting nutrient. Mar. Biol. 43: 33–43.

CONWAY, H. L., P. J. HARRISON, AND C. O. DAVIS. 1976. Marine diatoms grown in chemostats under silicate or ammonium limitation. II. Transient response of *Skeletonema costatum* to a single addition of the limiting nutrient. Mar. Biol. 35: 187–199.

DAVIES, A. G. 1970. Iron, chelation and the growth of marine phytoplankton. I. Growth kinetics and chlorophyll production in cultures of the euryhaline flagellate *Dunaliella tertiolecta* under iron-limiting conditions. J. Mar. Biol. Assoc. U.K. 50: 65–86.

DAVIS, C. O., N. F. BREITNER, AND P. J. HARRISON. 1978. Continuous culture of marine diatoms under silicon limitation. 3. A model of Si-limited diatom growth. Limnol. Oceanogr. 23: 41–51.

DEMANCHE, J. M. 1980. Variations in phytoplankton physiological parameters during transient nitrogen environments. Ph.D. thesis, Oregon State Univ., Corvallis, OR. 110 p.

DEMANCHE, J. M., H. C. CURL JR., D. W. LUNDY, AND P. L. DONAGHAY. 1979. The rapid response of the marine diatom *Skeletonema costatum* to changes in external and internal nutrient concentration. Mar. Biol. 53: 323–333.

DIEZ, J., A. CHAPARRO, J. M. VEGA, AND A. RELIMPIO. 1977. Studies on the regulation of assimilatory nitrate reductase in *Ankistiodesmus braunii*. Planta 137: 231–234.

DOWD, J. E., AND D. S. RIGGS. 1964. A comparison of estimates of Michaelis-Menten kinetic constants from various linear transformations. J. Biol. Chem. 240: 863–869.

DROOP, M. R. 1968. Vitamin B_{12} and marine ecology. IV. The kinetics of uptake, growth and inhibition in *Monochrysis lutheri*. J. Mar. Biol. Assoc. U.K. 48: 689–733.

DROOP, M. R. 1973. Some thoughts on nutrient limitation in algae. J. Phycol. 9: 264–272.

1974. The nutrient status of algal cells in continuous culture. J. Mar. Biol. Assoc. U.K. 54: 825–855.

DUGDALE, R. C. 1967. Nutrient limitation in the sea: dynamics, identification, and significance. Limnol. Oceanogr. 12: 685–695.

1977. Modeling, p. 789–806. *In* E. D. Goldberg et al. [ed.] The sea. Vol. 6. Wiley-Interscience, New York, NY.

DUGDALE, R. C., AND J. J. GOERING. 1967. Uptake of new and regenerated forms of nitrogen in primary productivity. Limnol. Oceanogr. 12: 196–206.

EPPLEY, R. W. 1981. Relations between nutrient assimilation and growth in phytoplankton with a brief review of estimates of growth rate in the ocean. Can. Bull. Fish. Aquat. Sci. 210: 251–263.

EPPLEY, R. W., AND J. L. COATSWORTH. 1968. Nitrate and nitrite uptake by *Ditylum brightwellii*. Kinetics and mechanisms. J. Phycol. 4: 151–156.

EPPLEY, R. W., J. L. COATSWORTH, AND L. SOLORZANO. 1969. Studies of nitrate reductase in marine phytoplankton. Limnol. Oceanogr. 14: 194–205.

EPPLEY, R. W., AND E. M. RENGER. 1974. Nitrogen assimilation of an oceanic diatom in nitrogen-limited continuous culture. J. Phycol. 10: 15–23.

EPPLEY, R. W., E. H. RENGER, W. G. HARRISON, AND J. J. CULLEN. 1979. Ammonium distribution in southern California coastal waters and its role in the growth of phytoplankton. Limnol. Oceanogr. 24: 495–509.

EPPLEY, R. W., AND J. N. ROGERS. 1970. Inorganic nitrogen assimilation of *Ditylum brightwellii*, a marine plankton diatom. J. Phycol. 6: 344–351.

EPPLEY, R. W., J. N. ROGERS, AND J. J. MCCARTHY. 1969. Half-saturation constants for uptake of nitrate and ammonium by marine phytoplankton. Limnol. Oceanogr. 14: 912–920.

EPPLEY, R. W., J. N. ROGERS, J. J. MCCARTHY, AND A. SOURNIA. 1971. Light/dark periodicity in nitrogen assimilation of the marine phytoplankton *Skeletonema costatum* and *Coccolithus huxleyi* in N-limited chemostat culture. J. Phycol. 7: 150–154.

EPPLEY, R. W., J. H. SHARP, E. H. RENGER, M. J. PERRY, AND W. G. HARRISON. 1977. Nitrogen assimilation by phytoplankton and other microorganisms in the surface waters of the central North Pacific Ocean. Mar. Biol. 39: 111–120.

EPPLEY, R. W., AND W. H. THOMAS. 1968. Comparison of half-saturation constants for growth and nitrate uptake of a marine phytoplankton. J. Phycol. 5: 375–379.

FALKOWSKI, P. G. 1975. Nitrate uptake in marine phytoplankton (nitrate, chloride) activated adenosine triphosphatase from *Skeletonema costatum* (Bacillariophyceae). J. Phycol. 11: 323–326.

FALKOWSKI, P. G., AND R. B. RIVKIN. 1976. The role of glutamine synthetase in the incorporation of ammonium in *Skeletonema costatum* (Bacillariophyceae). J. Phycol. 12: 448–450.

FUHS, G. W. 1968. Phosphorus content and rate of growth in the diatom *Cyclotalla nana* and *Thalassiosira fluviatilis*. J. Phycol. 5: 312–321.

FUNKHOUSER, E. A., T.-C. SHEN, AND R. ACKERMANN. 1980. Synthesis of nitrate reductase in *Chlorella*. I. Evidence for an inactive protein precursor. Plant Physiol. 65: 939–943.

FUNKHOUSER, E. A., AND C. S. RAMADOSS. 1980. Synthesis of nitrate reductase in *Chlorella*. II. Evidence for synthesis in ammonia-grown cells. Plant Physiol. 65: 944–948.

GEWITZ, H.-S., G. H. LORIMER, L. P. SOLOMONSON, AND B. VENNESLAND. 1974. Presence of HCN in *Chlorella vulgaris* and its possible role in controlling the reduction of nitrate. Nature (London) 249: 79–81.

GLIBERT, P. M., AND J. C. GOLDMAN. 1981. Rapid ammonium uptake by marine phytoplankton. Mar. Biol. Lett. 2: 25–31.

GOLDMAN, J. C. 1977. Steady state growth of phytoplankton in continuous culture: comparison of internal and external nutrient equations. J. Phycol. 13: 251–258.

GOLDMAN, J. C., AND J. J. MCCARTHY. 1978. Steady state growth and ammonium uptake of a fast-growing marine diatom. Limnol. Oceanogr. 23: 695–730.

GOLDMAN, J. C., J. J. MCCARTHY, AND D. G. PEAVEY. 1979. Growth rate influence on the chemical composition of phytoplankton in oceanic waters. Nature (London) 279: 210–215.

GOLDMAN, J. L., AND D. G. PEAVEY. 1979. Steady state growth and chemical composition of the marine chlorophyte *Dunaliella tertiolecta* in nitrogen-limited continuous cultures. Appl. Environ. Microbiol. 38: 894–901.

GRANT, B. R., J. MADGWICK, AND G. DAL PONT. 1967. Growth of *Cylindrotheca closterium* var. Californica (Mereschk.) Reimann and Lewin on nitrate, ammonia, and urea. Aust. J. Mar. Freshw. Res. 18: 129–136.

GREENEY, W. J., D. A. BELLA, AND H. C. CURL JR. 1973. Effects of intracellular nutrient pools on growth dynamics of phytoplankton. J. Water Pollut. Control Fed. 46: 1751–1760.

GUILLARD, R. R. L. 1963. Organic sources of nitrogen for marine centric diatoms, p. 93–104. *In* C. H. Oppenheimer [ed.] Symposium on marine microbiology. Charles C. Thomas, Springfield, IL.

HARRISON, P. J., H. L. CONWAY, AND R. C. DUGDALE. 1976. Marine diatoms grown in chemostats under silicate or ammonium limitation. I. Cellular chemical composition and steady state growth kinetics of *Skeletonema costatum*. Mar. Biol. 35: 177–186.

HARRISON, P. J., AND C. O. DAVIS. 1977. Use of the perturbation technique to measure nutrient uptake rates for natural phytoplankton populations. Deep-Sea Res. 24: 247–255.

HARVEY, H. W. 1963. The chemistry and fertility of sea waters. Cambridge Univ., London. 240 p.

HARVEY, W. A., AND J. CAPERON. 1976. The rate of utilization of urea, ammonium, and nitrate by natural populations of marine phytoplankton in a eutrophic environment. Pac. Sci. 30: 329–340.

HATTORI, A., AND J. MYERS. 1967. Reduction of nitrate and nitrite by subcellular preparations of *Anabaena cylindrica*. II. Reduction of nitrate to nitrite. Plant Cell Physiol. Tokyo 8: 327–337.

HERBERT, D., R. ELSWORTH, AND R. C. TELLING. 1956. The continuous culture of bacteria; a theoretical and experimental study. J. Gen. Microbiol. 14: 601–622.

HORRIGAN, S. G., AND J. J. MCCARTHY. 1981. Urea uptake by phytoplankton at various stages of nutrient depletion. J. Plankton Res. 3: 403–414.

JETSCHMANN, K., L. D. SOLOMONSON, AND B. VENNESLAND. 1972. Activation of nitrate reductase by oxidation. Biochem. Biophys. Acta (Amst.) 25: 276–278.

JOHNSON, C. B. 1979. Activation, synthesis and turnover of nitrate reductase controlled by nitrate and ammonium in *Chlorella vulgaris*. Planta 147: 63–68.

LIAO, C. F.-H., AND D. R. S. LEAN. 1978. Nitrogen transformations within the trophogenic zone of lakes. J. Fish. Res. Board Can. 35: 1102–1108.

MACISAAC, J. J., AND R. C. DUGDALE. 1969. The kinetics of nitrate and ammonia uptake by natural populations of marine phytoplankton. Deep-Sea Res. 16: 45–57.

MCCARTHY, J. J. 1972. The uptake of urea by marine phytoplankton. J. Phycol. 8: 216–221.

1981. Uptake of major nutrients by estuarine plants. *In* B. Neilson and G. Cronin [ed.] Effect of nutrient enrichment in estuaries. (In press)

MCCARTHY, J. J., AND J. C. GOLDMAN. 1979. Nitrogenous nutrition of marine phytoplankton in nutrient-depleted waters. Science (Washington, D.C.) 23: 670–672.

MCCARTHY, J. J., W. R. TAYLOR, AND J. L. TAFT. 1975. The dynamics of nitrogen and phosphorus cycling in the open waters of the Chesapeake Bay,

p. 664–681. *In* T. M. Church [ed.] Marine chemistry in the coastal environment. ACS Symp. Ser. 18.

———. 1977. Nitrogenous nutrition of the plankton in the Chesapeake Bay. I. Nutrient availability and phytoplankton preferences. Limnol. Oceanogr. 22: 996–1011.

MONOD, J. 1942. Recherches sur la croissance des cultures bactériennes. Hermann and Cie, Paris. 210 p.

MORRIS, I., AND P. J. SYRETT. 1963. The development of nitrate reductase in *Chlorella* and its repression by ammonium. Arch. Mikrobiol. 47: 32–41.

NELSON, D. M., J. J. GOERING, S. S. KILHAM, AND R. R. L. GUILLARD. 1976. Kinetics of silicic acid uptake and rates of silica dissolution in the marine diatom *Thlassiosira pseudonana*. J. Phycol. 12: 246–252.

NICHOLS, G. L., S. M. SHEHATA, AND P. J. SYRETT. 1978. Nitrate reductase deficient mutants of *Chlamydomonas reinhardii*. Biochemical characteristics. J. Gen. Microbiol. 108: 79–88.

NOVICK, A., AND L. SZILARD. 1950. Experiments with the chemostat on spontaneous mutations of bacteria. Proc. Natl. Acad. Sci. USA 36: 708.

OHMORI, M., AND A. HATTORI. 1978. Transient change in the ATP pool of *Anabaena cylindrica* associated with ammonia assimilation. Arch. Microbiol. 117: 17–20.

OLSON, R. J., J. B. SOOTOO, AND D. A. KEIFER. 1980. Steady-state growth of the marine diatom *Thalassiosira pseudonana*. Uncoupled kinetics of nitrate uptake and nitrite production. Plant Physiol. 66: 383–389.

PAASCHE, E. 1973. Silicon and the ecology of marine plankton diatoms. I. *Thalassiosira pseudonana* (*Cyclotella nana*) grown in a chemostat with silicate as the limiting nutrient. Mar. Biol. 19: 117–126.

PACKARD, T. T. 1979. Half-saturation constants for nitrate reductase and nitrate translocation in marine phytoplankton. Deep-Sea Res. 26A: 321–326.

PACKARD, T. T., AND D. BLASCO. 1974. Nitrate reductase activity in upwelling regions. 2. Ammonia and light dependence. Tethys 6: 269–280.

PERRY, M. J. 1972. Alkaline phosphatase activity in subtropical central North Pacific waters using a sensitive fluorometric method. Mar. Biol. 15: 113–119.

PISTORIUS, E. K., E. A. FUNKHOUSER, AND H. VOSS. 1978. Effect of ammonium and ferricyanide on nitrate utilization by *Chlorella vulgaris*. Planta 141: 279–282.

PISTORIUS, E. K., H.-S. GEWITZ, H. ROSS, AND B. VENNESLAND. 1976. Reversible inactivation of nitrate reductase in *Chlorella vulgaris* in vivo. Planta 128: 73–80.

PROCHAZKOVA, L., B. BLAZKA, AND M. KRALOVA. 1970. Chemical changes involving nitrogen metabolism in water and particulate matter during primary production experiments. Limnol. Oceanogr. 15: 797–807.

RAO, K. P., AND D. W. RAINS. 1976. Nitrate absorption by barley. II. Influence of nitrate reductase activity. Plant Physiol. 57: 59–62.

REDFIELD, A. C. 1958. The biological control of chemical factors in the environment. Am. Sci. 46: 205–221.

RHEE, G. 1973. A continuous culture study of phosphate uptake, growth rate and polyphosphate in *Scenedesmus* sp. J. Phycol. 9: 495–506.

———. 1974. Phosphate uptake under nitrate limitation by *Scenedesmus* and polyphosphate in *Scenedesmus* sp. J. Phycol. 10: 470–475.

———. 1978. Effects of N:P atomic ratios and nitrate limitation on algal growth, cell composition, and nitrate uptake. Limnol. Oceanogr. 23: 10–25.

RICKETTS, T. R., AND P. A. EDGE. 1977. The effect of nitrogen refeeding on starved cells of *Platymonas striata* Butcher. Planta 134: 169–176.

RIGANO, C., G. AHOTTA, AND U. VIOLANTE. 1974. Reversible inactivation by ammonia of assimilatory nitrate reductase in *Cyanidium caldarium*. Arch. Microbiol. 99: 81–90.

RIGLER, F. H. 1966. Radiobiological analysis of inorganic phosphorus in lake water. Int. Ver. Theor. Angew. Limnol. Verch. 16: 465–470.

SCHLOEMER, R. H., AND R. H. GARRETT. 1974. Nitrate transport system in *Neurospora crassa*. J. Bacteriol. 118: 259–269.

SOLOMONSON, L. P. 1974. Regulation of nitrate reductase activity by NADH and cyanide. Biochim. Biophys. Acta (Amst.) 334: 297–308.

SOLOMONSON, L. P., K. JETSCHMANN, AND B. VENNESLAND. 1973. Reversible inactivation of the nitrate reductase of *Chlorella vulgaris* Beijerinck. Biochim. Biophys. Acta (Amst.) 309: 32–43.

SOLOMONSON, L. P., AND A. M. SPEHAR. 1977. Model for regulation of nitrate assimilation. Nature (London) 265: 373–375.

SOLOMONSON, L. P., AND B. VENNESLAND. 1972. Nitrate reductase and chlorate toxicity in *Chlorella vulgaris* Beijerinck. Plant Physiol. 50: 421–424.

SYRETT, P. J. 1962. Nitrogen assimilation, p. 171–188. *In* R. A. Lewin [ed.] Physiology and biochemistry of algae. Academic Press, New York & London.

———. 1981. Nitrogen metabolism of microalgae. Can. Bull. Fish. Aquat. Sci. 210: 182–210.

SYRETT, P. J., AND C. R. HIPKIN. 1973. The appearance of nitrate reductase activity in nitrogen-starved cells of *Ankistrodesmus braunii*. Planta (Berl.) 111: 57–64.

TAFT, J. L., M. E. LOFTUS, AND W. R. TAYLOR. 1977. Phosphate uptake from phosphomonoesters by phytoplankton in Chesapeake Bay. Limnol. Oceanogr. 22: 1012–1021.

TERRY, K. L. 1980. Nitrogen and phosphorus requirements of *Pavlova lutheri* in continuous culture. Bot. Mar. 23: 757–764.

THACKER, A., AND P. J. SYRETT. 1972. The assimilation of nitrate and ammonium by *Chlamydomonas reinhardi*. New Phytol. 71: 422–433.

TISCHNER, R., AND A. HUTTERMAN. 1978. Light-mediated activation of nitrate reductase in synchronous *Chlorella*. Plant Physiol. 62: 284–286.

TISCHNER, R., AND H. LORENZEN. 1979. Nitrate uptake and nitrate reduction in synchronous *Chlorella*. Planta 146: 287–292.

WHEELER, P. A. 1980. Use of methylammonium as an ammonium analogue in nitrogen transport and assimilation studies with *Cyclotella cryptica* (Bacillariophyceae). J. Phycol. 16: 328–334.

WILLIAMS, P. J. L. 1973. The validity of the application of simple kinetic analysis to heterogenous microbial populations. Limnol. Oceanogr. 18: 159–164.

Adaptation of Nutrient Assimilation

R. C. Dugdale, B. H. Jones Jr., and J. J. MacIsaac

Department of Biological Science, Allan Hancock Foundation,
University of Southern California, Los Angeles, CA 90007, USA

and J. J. Goering

Institute for Marine Science, University of Alaska, College,
AK 99708, USA

Introduction

Nutrient uptake clearly is a key process in the growth of marine phytoplankton, and the ability of a species to integrate changes in the nutrient environment into its own synthetic process with minimal disruption may determine its success in relation to other species and groups of species. The objective of this paper is to assess current knowledge of the changes in nutrient uptake and assimilation that occur in response to changes in nutrient concentrations, irradiance, and temperature. Adaptation is used here in the sense that the organism responds, passively or actively, in some manner to circumvent or ameliorate the stress imposed by environmental changes linked to nutrient uptake and utilization. Adaptation, then, is the end result of a chain of events that occur with a range of time scales. Cognizance of these time scales and their relationship to the spectra of variability in marine environments is essential to an understanding of the significance of adaptation phenomena in marine phytoplankton, and further is often the key to effective communication between laboratory and field scientists, and even between groups of the latter. To the extent possible, these relevant time scales will be indicated throughout this communication.

Scientific Background

Dugdale (1967) suggested the use of the Michaelis-Menten expression to describe the uptake of a limiting nutrient by marine phytoplankton. The expression is:

$$(1) \qquad V = V_{max} \frac{S}{K_s + S}$$

where V_{max} is the nutrient-specific uptake rate, V, at infinite substrate concentration; S is the concentration of limiting nutrient; K_s is the half-saturation constant, the concentration of limiting nutrient at which $V = V_{max}/2$.

Evidence for Michaelis-Menten type kinetics has been obtained from experiments with natural populations of marine phytoplankton for ammonia and nitrate uptake using ^{15}N as a tracer (MacIsaac and Dugdale 1969) and for silicic acid using ^{29}Si (Goering et al. 1973) and ^{68}Ge (Azam and Chisholm 1976) as tracers. Perry (1976) observed a trend toward hyperbolic uptake using ^{33}P as a tracer. In the laboratory, Michaelis-Menten type kinetics have been obtained with various species of marine algae for inorganic nitrogen uptake (e.g. Eppley et al. 1969), for silicic acid uptake in diatoms (Paasche 1973a; Azam 1974; Nelson et al. 1976), for inorganic phosphate uptake (Rhee 1973; Perry 1976), and for carbon (Goldman et al. 1974; Caperon and Smith 1978).

Natural populations of marine phytoplankton have been shown to obey Michaelis-Menten kinetics also in relation to light intensity for uptake of ammonia and nitrate (MacIsaac and Dugdale 1972) and of silicic acid (Goering et al. 1973; Azam and Chisholm 1976). The same relationship has been shown in the laboratory for nitrogen uptake (MacIsaac et al. 1979). From these results and from our published results on nitrogen uptake it appears that both light- and substrate-limited uptake of nitrate and silicic acid follow virtually identical patterns. Lehninger (1971) points out that active transport through cell membranes often shows kinetics that are similar to enzyme kinetics, an observation amply borne out by the studies of phytoplankton nutrient uptake reported above. Moreover, active transport systems are considered to be composed of two major components, the specific carrier and the energy-transferring component. Losada and Guerrero (1979) reviewed the literature on nitrate reduction in relation to photosynthesis. These authors concluded that the enzyme system was simpler than that involved with carbon reduction with only two enzymes, nitrate reductase and nitrite reductase, using ferredoxin or pyridine nucleotide as the electron donor. Further, the enzymatic activity appears to be tightly bound to pigment-containing particles, with the evidence for a direct link much better for nitrite reduction than for nitrate reduction. From energetic considerations, Losada and Guerrero pointed out that nitrate assimilation can proceed at the energy level of ferredoxin or pyridine nucleotide in contrast with carbon reduction, which requires energy at a higher level, i.e. ATP. Regulation of nitrate assimilation appears to be targeted to nitrate reductase with ammonia as a key element. Most conclusions reached by Losada and Guerrero (1979) appear to be at least consistent with the laboratory and field results reported below.

Our view of nutrient interactions is essentially the same as that of Droop's (1974) threshold concept, i.e. only one nutrient is limiting at a given time. The uptake rate of the limiting nutrient is set externally by the concentration of that nutrient and the uptake rates of nonlimiting nutrients are controlled internally by the cell to correspond with the externally set, limiting-nutrient uptake rate. To distinguish the mode of control of uptake of a cellular component it is convenient to designate the externally controlled specific uptake rate as V_e and internally controlled specific uptake rate as V_i. Because light appears nearly identical with a limiting nutrient in its effect on nutrient uptake, the threshold concept may be applied to it also (Dugdale and MacIsaac 1971). The basic theory and our supporting experimental results concerning nutrient interactions and phytoplankton growth processes are presented below. A glossary of terminology and symbols is on p. 248.

Laboratory Observations

Studies of *Skeletonema costatum* (Greve.) Cleve grown under silicic acid and ammonia limitation were made in our laboratory and the research has been reported by Davis (1973), Harrison (1974), and Conway (1974). It has been standard practice in our experiments to measure all the primary nutrients, in contrast with most other studies of phytoplankton in continuous culture where only the limiting nutrient has been measured (Fuhs 1969; Carpenter 1970; Caperon and Meyer 1972; Paasche 1973b; Eppley and Renger 1974; Goldman and McCarthy 1978). Consequently, we have obtained some insight into the interactions between inorganic phosphorus, silicic acid, and inorganic nitrogen uptake under chemostat culture conditions (Harrison et al. 1976; Conway et al. 1976; Dugdale 1977).

LIMITING AND NONLIMITING NUTRIENT UPTAKE INTERACTIONS

Conway et al. (1976) were able to distinguish between uptake rates associated with external and internal control, as limitation shifted from one variable to another, and to observe the effect of this shift on

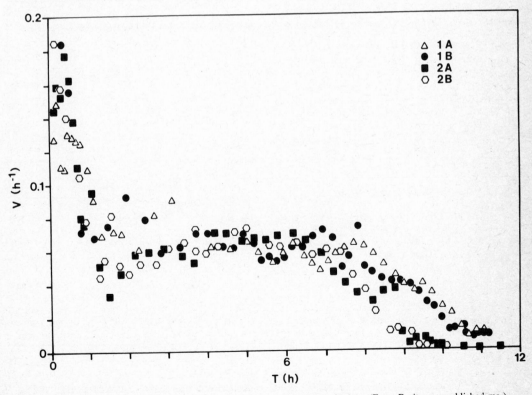

FIG. 1. Silicic acid uptake rate versus time from perturbation in four experiments. (From Breitner unpublished ms.)

uptake rates of nonlimiting nutrients. Their evidence was obtained from perturbation experiments in which a large amount of the limiting nutrient was added to a chemostat reactor, the subsequent decline with time observed, and the specific uptake rates calculated from the time series. The time course of uptake in four replicate experiments with *S. costatum* and silicic acid limitation (N. Breitner unpublished ms) is shown in Fig. 1. A high rate or "spike" of uptake occurs initially, followed by a period of reduced, but constant, uptake rate, V_i. Finally, nutrient-limited uptake, V_e, occurs when the substrate concentration has fallen to a sufficiently low level. The same uptake data are plotted against substrate concentration in Fig. 2, where the three phases of uptake can be distinguished clearly with the transition between V_e and V_i occurring at a silicic acid concentration of about $2 \mu g\text{-at} \cdot L^{-1}$.

From these results, and from ^{15}N uptake experiments made on ammonia-limited cultures of *S. costatum*, the limiting-nutrient uptake hyperbolas were shown to be truncated at the point where a transition between V_e and V_i for the limiting nutrient occurred, i.e. at the point where a new variable (probably light) became limiting (Fig. 3a). The substrate concentration at which the transition occurred is called S_T for convenience, and the resulting hyperbola referred to as truncated. These relationships are shown in Fig. 3b.

The perturbation experiments yielded values of V_i for the original limiting nutrient that were different from the values of V_i for the nonlimiting nutrients. Specifically, in Table 1, values of V_i for limiting silicic acid were about twice the dilution rate. The values of V_i for the nonlimiting nutrients, however, remained approximately equal to the initial dilution rate. The agreement between dilution rate and V_i for nonlimiting nutrient uptake indicates strong cellular control of these rates.

Perry (1976), using chemostat cultures of *Thalassiosira pseudonana* Hasle and Helmdal (formerly *Cyclotella nana*) clone 66-H, found that saturated phosphate uptake rates, on a per cell basis, were 10 times higher under phosphate limitation than under nitrogen limitation. Her observations and those of Rhee (1974) indicate that maximal phosphate uptake is controlled under limiting nitrogen in similar fashion to that shown above for limiting silicic acid control of maximal phosphate and nitrate uptake.

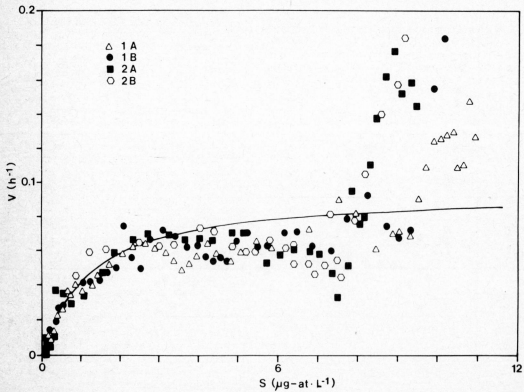

FIG. 2. Silicic acid uptake rate versus reactor silicic acid concentration in four experiments with overlaid weighted regression curve. (From Breitner unpublished ms.)

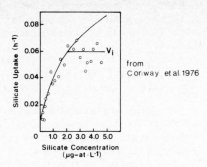

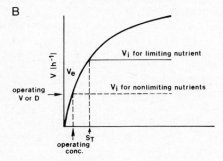

FIG. 3. The distinction between V_e and V_i shown by chemostat perturbation experiments (A) and schematically (B). The data points above the truncation point, S_T, give an estimate of V_i for the nutrient limiting the chemostat at the operating dilution rate, and those below are values of V_e. From steady-state chemostat theory and the concept of balanced growth, the dilution rate, D, is equivalent to growth, μ, and to V; and in the Conway et al. (1976) experiment, $D = 0.04$ h^{-1} and lies in the V_e range. Only the values of V_e are useful for estimating the K_s and V_{max} values of the full hyperbola.

TABLE 1. Mean uptake rates of phosphate, nitrate, and silicic acid during two silicic acid limited perturbation experiments. Number of observations in parentheses. (From Conway et al. 1976.)

Dilution rate (h^{-1})	$V_{i_{PO_4}}$ (h^{-1})	$V_{i_{NO_3}}$ (h^{-1})	$V_{i_{Si}}$ (h^{-1})
0.040	0.040 (15)	0.040 (15)	0.070
0.041	0.038 (15)	0.040 (15)	0.060

TABLE 2. Kinetic parameters obtained from perturbations conducted on the 30 and 100% light populations. V_{max} and K values are given ± 1 standard deviation.

Light level (ly·min^{-1})	V_{max} (h^{-1})	K_s (μg-at Si·L^{-1})	V_i (h^{-1})
0.14	0.101 $\pm$ 0.02	1.81 $\pm$ 0.89	0.074
0.04	—	—	0.055
0.14	0.127 $\pm$ 0.01	1.1 $\pm$ 0.2	0.088
0.04	—	—	0.051

Rhee (1973, 1974) suggested a physiological basis for the control of phosphate uptake in *Scenedesmus* sp. Under nitrate or phosphate limitation, phosphate uptake apparently is controlled by the intracellular concentration of inorganic, acid-soluble polyphosphate; noncompetitive inhibition kinetics are followed. An abrupt change occurred in the slope of the maximal phosphate uptake versus cellular P/N ratio for *Scenedesmus* sp. at a value of P/N of 0.033 where P limitation changed to N limitation and vice versa. In a later paper, Rhee (1978) suggested that the internal concentrations of free amino acids control nitrate uptake under phosphate limitation. On the basis of his studies of *Scenedesmus* sp. Rhee considers the threshold concept the most appropriate to describe the interaction between limiting nutrient and nonlimiting nutrient uptake.

INTERACTIONS OF LIGHT AND LIMITING SILICIC ACID UPTAKE

The strong cellular control of nonlimiting-nutrient uptake to levels that correspond to the existing limiting-nutrient uptake has been demonstrated above. Davis (1973, 1976) was able to show further that the limiting-nutrient (silicic acid) concentration at which truncation occurred, S_T, was determined by light intensity and suggested that the resulting values of V_i for silicic acid approximated light-limited maximal growth rates.

The silicic acid uptake kinetics obtained by Davis (1976) are summarized in Table 2. The V_i values give a saturation curve when plotted against light as shown in Fig. 4a. There was good agreement at all but the highest light intensity between these values of V_i and those for growth rate as a function of light intensity (Fig. 4b) as measured by McAllister et al. (1964).

The value of V_i measured for limiting silicic acid in Davis' (1976) perturbation experiments was 0.081 h^{-1}, set by the light intensity at which the culture was grown (Table 3). The values of V_i for

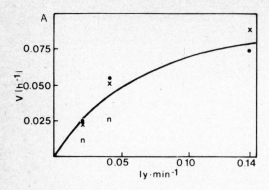

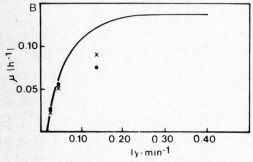

FIG. 4. (A) Maximal silicic acid uptake as a function of light intensity. Symbols denote different chemostat culture experiments and time periods within experiments. (B) Growth rate as a function of light intensity, with selected data from (A) plotted with the curve for growth from McAllister et al. (1964). All data for *S. costatum*. The lowest values were obtained under non-steady-state conditions by measuring washout rates. (From Davis 1976.)

TABLE 3. Nutrient uptake rates and growth rates from 9 h batch uptake experiments. Rates are per hour; samples taken from chemostats at steady state at $D = 0.04$ h^{-1} and light intensity indicated.

Source % light	Incub. % light	V_{PO_4}	V_{SiO_4}	V_{NO_3}	V_{NH_4}	V_{Σ_N}
100	100	0.043	0.081	0.049	0.011	0.060
	30	0.027	0.077	0.030	0.010	0.040
	15	0.032	0.078	0.022	0.019	0.041
	1	0.025	0.073	0.015	0.017	0.032

nonlimiting phosphate and nitrate for the full light intensity reactor were 0.043 h^{-1} and 0.049 h^{-1}, respectively, demonstrating again that the V_i values for the nonlimiting nutrients were controlled internally at the initial dilution rate, 0.04 h^{-1}. An additional feature of the data in Table 3 is the relative independence of the V_i for silicic acid on light intensity when the latter was reduced for short periods (9 h

in this case). On the same time scale the V_i for nitrate appeared to be strongly dependent on light intensity and the V_i for phosphate showed a similar relationship.

ADAPTATIONS TO NUTRIENT LIMITATION AND EFFECTS ON NUTRIENT UPTAKE KINETICS

A primary adaptation of marine phytoplankton species to nutrient limitation occurs through the reduction of growth rate, μ, and of cell quota, Q (cellular concentration of limiting nutrient). The variation in the cell quota of the limiting nutrient is related under some circumstances to the dilution (growth) rate in the chemostat at steady state by the expression (Droop 1968):

$$(2) \qquad \mu = \mu'_m \left(1 - \frac{K_Q}{Q} \right)$$

where K_Q is the subsistence cell quota of the limiting nutrient at zero growth rate, and μ'_m is an abstract maximum growth rate, different from the real μ_{max} of the cell. The maximum realizable growth rate is always less than μ'_m, as pointed out by Goldman and McCarthy (1978).

The reduction of cell quota with nutrient limitation has been documented in chemostats for vitamin B_{12} (Droop 1968), for nitrate (Caperon and Meyer 1972), for ammonia (Conway 1974), for phosphorus (Fuhs 1969; Rhee 1973), and for silicic acid (Paasche 1973b; Harrison 1974). One of the consequences of this response is a possible increase in the maximum specific uptake rate, V_{max} or V_i if truncation has occurred, of the limiting nutrient (Dugdale 1977). This result can be seen from the relationship between V and the cellular uptake rate, ρ:

$$V = \frac{\rho}{Q}$$

Similarly,

$$V_{max} = \frac{\rho_{max}}{Q}$$

where ρ_{max} is the maximum capacity of the cell to take up nutrient. The effect of decreasing Q is to increase the initial slope of the specific uptake hyperbola with decreasing nutrient concentrations, and thereby to hold up the specific uptake rate and growth rate at low concentrations. The effect may result in virtually undetectable limiting nutrient in the chemostat at all moderate dilution rates.

Using inorganic nitrogen as the example, if ρ_{max} remains constant V_{max} rises hyperbolically with decreasing Q_N. This effect was shown by Dugdale (1977) using data of Eppley and Renger (1974)

238

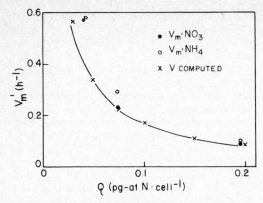

FIG. 5. Relationship between Q and V_{max} with constant ρ_{max}, data from Eppley and Renger (1974) as plotted with a computed curve of the relationship in Dugdale (1977). V_m' is the same as V_{max}.

for *Thalassiosira pseudonana* (13-1) under nitrogen limitation (Fig. 5). Using ^{15}N as a tracer in a more detailed study, McCarthy and Goldman (1979) obtained the same result, also with *T. pseudonana* (3 H). In both studies V_{max} tended to rise with decreasing Q_N, and the measured curves rose a little more steeply than that calculated with constant ρ_{max}.

Brown and Harris (1978) found, in *Nostoc* sp. and *Selenastrum capricornutum* grown in batch culture, that phosphate uptake per cell (ρ_P) varied inversely with the cell quota, Q_P, rising quite rapidly in the vicinity of K_Q. Rhee (1974) found in *Scenedesmus* sp. that an abrupt change in maximal phosphate uptake rate, $\rho_{max P}$, occurred with the onset of phosphate limitation; under these conditions of low cellular P/N ratio, $\rho_{max P}$, increased to 8 times over the value characteristic of nitrogen-limited growth. Under silicic acid limitation, *S. costatum* showed a different pattern, Fig. 6, with $\rho_{i si}$ decreasing with decreasing Q_{Si}; however, the net effect is still an increase in $V_{i si}$ with decreasing Q_{Si}.

MULTIPLE GROWTH PATTERNS

Another adaptive response to nutrient limitation observed in chemostats is that a species may show more than one pattern of growth. These patterns are readily distinguishable by the differing slopes, μ_m, and intercepts, K_Q, of their μQ vs. Q plots (the linearization of the Droop hyperbola, Eq. 2). Cells showing this response are described by Droop (1974) as "slow adapted" when exhibiting the lower values of μ_m and K_Q, and "fast adapted" with the higher μ_m and K_Q. This change in growth patterns was observed in our laboratory for *S. costatum* grown under silicic acid limitation (Harrison 1974) and under nitrogen limitation (Conway 1974; Harrison et al. 1976), and for *Monochrysis lutheri* under phosphorus and vitamin B_{12} limitation by Droop (1974). The μQ vs. Q plots for the two species are shown in Fig. 7 where it appears that a similar phenomenon was being observed.

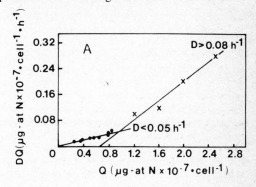

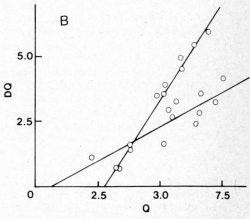

FIG. 7. Multiple growth patterns. (A) For *S. costatum*. Circles represent dilution rates $< 0.05 \, h^{-1}$, crosses represent dilution rates $> 0.08 \, h^{-1}$. (From Harrison et al. 1976) (B) For *M. lutheri*. $D = \mu$ under steady-state chemostat conditions. (From Droop 1974)

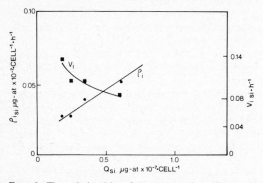

FIG. 6. The relationship of V_i and ρ_i for silicic acid uptake in *S. costatum* to cell quota, Q, for silicic acid. (Data from Harrison 1974, table 13.)

A phenomenon closely related or identical with that described above has been reported for bacteria (Herbert et al. 1956) and for yeast (Mian et al. 1969; Button et al. 1973). All these workers observed higher growth rates for these organisms in chemostat culture than the maximum growth rates found in batch culture. The terminology used to describe this mode of adaptation has varied. For example, Droop (1974) used "fast-adapted," Button et al. (1973) used "μ_{max}-adapted," and we (Harrison et al. 1976) used "shifted-up" to refer to cultures exhibiting this enhanced μ_{max} state. In the case of a marine yeast, D. Button (personal communication) found that μ_{max}-adapted cells resume their original slower growing state when the chemostat dilution rate is lowered appropriately. This evidence suggests that in his experiments the adaptation was a physiological response and not selection occurring within the chemostat.

The growth response characteristics of $M.$ $lutheri$ cells growing in the two modes were described by Droop (1974) and are paraphrased in the following: The state of adaptation will remain unchanged so long as the appropriate dilution rate is maintained. If the population has been maintained in one mode for a long time, it cannot adapt to a sudden large change in dilution rate across the threshold value that distinguishes the two states. On the other hand, if the population has undergone recent change in the state of adaptation, the population can adjust its mode almost immediately to a sudden change in dilution rate across the threshold value. It possibly is significant that the threshold dilution rate is similar to μ_m for the slow-adapted mode (a correspondence observed as well in our work with $S.$ $costatum$).

Some adaptations to low nutrient conditions known to occur in microorganisms are discussed by Tempest and Neijssel (1976). Among these are (1) synthesis of alternate high-affinity pathways for uptake and assimilation of the growth-limiting nutrient, (2) modulation of nonlimiting nutrient uptake, and (3) modulation of macromolecular synthesis to allow growth at submaximal rates. The Droop model has an empirical basis and has the serious drawback that physiological adaptations cannot be interpreted easily in terms of cell quota and vice versa. Nevertheless, it seems virtually certain that some or all adaptations mentioned above would be expressed as changes in the variables of the cell quota model.

Goldman and McCarthy (1978) found no evidence for such response in their data obtained with $Thalassiosira$ $pseudonana$ (3 H) grown under nitrogen limitation. It is not clear in the Goldman and McCarthy work that the slow change of dilution rate necessary for adjustment from one mode to the other (Button et al. 1973; Droop 1974) was a part of their experimental technique, and thus the characterization of $T.$ $pseudonana$ as a species not showing multiple states of adaptation might be premature.

The important feature exhibited by slow-adapted cells in the context of Dugdale (1977) is the large increase in maximal specific uptake rate that occurs and the resulting ability to grow relatively rapidly at very low nutrient concentrations; the disadvantage incurred is a reduced μ_{max}. For example, in the $S.$ $costatum$ data of Dugdale (1977, Fig. 8) the slow-adapted cells have a μ_{max} of 0.051 h^{-1} and the fast-adapted cells have a μ_{max} of 0.098 h^{-1}. These values of maximum realizable growth rate were calculated from an equation developed by solving the Droop hyperbolic equation (Eq. 7 in Dugdale 1977) for Q, and substituting the resultant expression with Eq. 13 in Dugdale; μ_{max} is taken as the value of μ when silicic acid concentration is infinitely large. The equation is:

$$(3) \qquad \mu = \left[\frac{K_Q}{\dfrac{\rho_{max}\,[Si]}{K_{Si} + [Si]}} + \frac{1}{\mu'_m} \right]^{-1}$$

The effect on the nutrient concentration versus growth rate curve calculated from the above equation for these two sets of parameters is shown in Fig. 8. The slow-adapted populations apparently can maintain respectable growth rates at concentrations of silicic acid of 0.05 μg-at·L^{-1} and less, and these growth rates are about twice those of the fast-adapted cells in this low nutrient range. (No allowance has been made in the calculations or Fig. 8 for an S_O, the silicic acid concentration observed in some experiments below, in which no uptake or growth takes place.)

Doyle (1975), in developing the case for selection of cells or cell lines under varying nutrient conditions, predicted that a given genetic line would have either low V_{max} and low K_s for low-nutrient environments, or high V_{max} and high K_s for high-nutrient environments. For selection to be effective then it is necessary that the growth (or uptake) rate–nutrient concentration curves cross each other. Thus, one type of organism is selected for under a low-nutrient regime and the other under a high-nutrient regime. The evidence shown above for $S.$ $costatum$ suggests that this organism maintains both options within a single clone (Fig. 8). There is the suggestion also that, in our experiments, selection in the chemostat may have been responsible for the appearance of populations exhibiting different growth states.

PHOTOSYNTHESIS, NUTRIENT UPTAKE, AND NUTRIENT LIMITATION

An understanding of the relationship between the photosynthetic rate, nutrient limitation, and

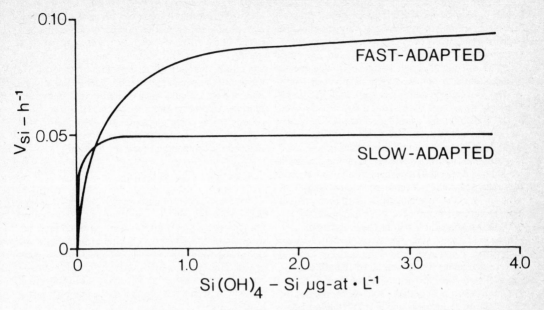

FIG. 8. Theoretical effect of different states of adaptation on the nutrient concentration versus growth rate curve.

nutrient uptake is essential to an understanding of the interaction between nutrient and light limitation. Many more data are available on the effect of light reduction under nutrient-limited growth on chlorophyll concentration and on maximum photosynthetic rates than for maximum nutrient uptake rates. Therefore, the discussion of laboratory results will be limited largely to this area. Some necessary definitions are (1) P_M^B, the assimilation number is the rate of photosynthesis at saturating light intensities (per unit chlorophyll, g C·g chl $a^{-1}·h^{-1}$) and (2) α, the initial slope of the photosynthesis per unit chlorophyll versus I curve.

Several investigators have explored the relationship between assimilation number and nutrient-limited growth but the published results do not show a clear pattern. Thomas and Dodson (1972) have shown that for *Chaetocerus gracilis* the assimilation number increases with increasing growth rate under nitrogen-limited growth. Senft (1978) has shown that the assimilation number increases with increasing cell quota for phosphorus in *Anabaena wisconsinense* and *Chlorella pyrenoidosa*. On the other hand, Eppley and Renger (1974) saw no relationship between the growth rate and the assimilation number for *Thalassiosira pseudonana* grown in a chemostat under nitrogen limitation. Laws and Wong (1978) did not observe an increase in the productivity index with increasing growth rate for *Monochrysis lutheri* and *Dunaliella tertiolecta*, but observed a decrease for *Thalassiosira allenii*, also grown in nitrogen-limited chemostats. Laws and Bannister (1980) grew *Thalassiosira fluviatilis* under nitrate, ammonia,

and phosphate limitation and found a single hyperbolic curve to describe the relationship between assimilation number and dilution rate. Chlorophyll per cell increased with dilution rate under each nutrient limitation.

Three generalizations about the photosynthetic response to nutrient limitation emerge from the above data: (1) the chlorophyll a/carbon ratio increases linearly with the growth rate, shown for nitrogen by Caperon and Meyer (1972) and Laws and Wong (1978), and for phosphorus by Rhee (1978); (2) the chlorophyll a/cell ratio increases more or less linearly with growth rate, shown for nitrogen by Caperon and Meyer (1972) and Thomas and Dodson (1972), and for phosphorus by Rhee (1978); *S. costatum* under silicic acid limitation showed no particular trend of chlorophyll a/cell with growth rate (Harrison 1974); (3) with nitrogen limitation, the assimilation number generally remains constant (Eppley and Renger 1974) or increases (Thomas and Dodson 1972) with increasing growth rate. The results of the last two generalizations indicate that the maximum photosynthetic rate per cell increases with increasing growth rate under nutrient limitation.

The results of studies of the assimilation number as a function of the light intensity at which the phytoplankton are grown have been more consistent than studies of the assimilation number as a function of nutrient-limited growth rate. Yentsch and Lee (1966) demonstrated with *Nannochloris atomus* in semicontinuous culture that the assimilation number increased with increasing mean light intensity. Using

241

Phaeodactylum tricornutum in a turbidostat culture, Beardall and Morris (1976) also showed that the assimilation number increased with increasing mean light intensity. In their experiments, the increased assimilation number resulted from both an increase in maximum rate of photosynthesis per cell and a decrease in chlorophyll *a* per cell with increased intensity. Laws and Bannister (1980) also showed with *T. fluviatilis* that assimilation number increased and chlorophyll per cell decreased with increasing light intensity under nutrient-saturated conditions. However, the curve of growth rate versus assimilation number had a very different shape from that obtained by the same authors for the nutrient-limited condition. As a result, the assimilation number of natural populations cannot be used as an index of growth rate unless the growth-limiting factor is known.

In the experiments by Davis (1976) to study the effect of reduced light intensity on limiting silicic acid uptake using chemostat cultures of *S. costatum* reduction of light intensity from 0.14 ly·min^{-1} to 0.042 ly·min^{-1} resulted in a doubling of silicic acid/cell and a reduction of $V_{i_{Si}}$ where adaptation took place slowly over a period of days. In one experiment, chlorophyll per cell increased by about 50%; in the other, where rapid adaptation occurred, an initially high chlorophyll/cell de-

creased. Such an increase in limiting nutrient per cell results in a specific uptake hyperbola with a lower initial slope as well as a lower V_{max}, with the result that with constant limiting nutrient concentration, the growth rate would be reduced. In the chemostat where growth rate is set by the dilution rate, the end result is an increase in the limiting nutrient concentration in the reactor. Harrison (1974) observed the same sequence of events also with *S. costatum* grown under silicate limitation when he reduced the temperature from 18 to 12°C.

THE TRUNCATION MODEL

Limiting light — The possible interrelationships between light intensity, limiting nutrient concentration, and nonlimiting nutrient concentration are illustrated for the condition of limiting silicic acid and suboptimal light intensity in Fig. 9. The maximum growth rate, μ_{max}, may be described by a saturation curve, as indicated in Fig. 9a, where the average light intensity is seen to set the specific net carbon uptake rate:

$$(4) \qquad V_c = V_{c\,max} \frac{\overline{I}}{K_I + I}$$

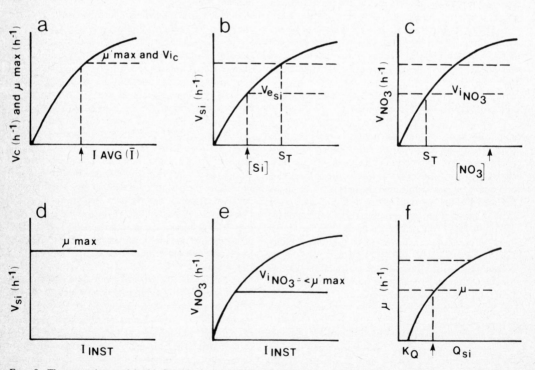

FIG. 9. The truncation model with figures arranged to illustrate interactions. See text for explanations.

The value of V_c corresponding to $\bar{I}$, shown by the arrow in Fig. 9a, is an internally controlled rate, V_{i_c}, in the sense that further increases in light in a short-term experiment would not result in an increase in photosynthetic rate (a definition of P_{max}). Because respiration would reduce the carbon available for growth, the μ'_{max} vs. I curve would fall somewhat below the V_c vs. I curve. (This area is complex and care must be taken in making definitions and measurements of the carbon variables. For the present it will suffice to note that a net V_{i_c} should be equivalent to the maximum realizable growth rate, μ'_{max}, and that it should be possible to calculate V_{i_c}, net, by subtracting respiration from the gross maximal photosynthetic rate.)

Limiting silicic acid — The point marked S_T in Fig. 9b is the truncation point for the uptake hyperbola, designating the boundary between external control expected in this case by average light intensity and internal control. At the silicic acid concentration indicated by the arrow,

$$(5) \qquad V_{Si} = V_{eSi} = \frac{V_{maxSi}\,[Si]}{K_{Si} + [Si]} = \mu,$$

the specific growth rate,

since in this example the concentrations of nitrate and phosphate (latter not illustrated) are set to be nonlimiting. If the concentration of limiting nutrient, S_i, is greater than S_T, then

$$V_{Si} = V_{iSi} = V_{i_c} = \mu'_{max}$$

Nonlimiting nutrient — The arrow on the abscissa in Fig. 9c designates the ambient concentration of nitrate in a silicic acid limited system. Under such conditions,

$$(6) \qquad \frac{V_{maxNO_3}\,[NO_3]}{K_{NO_3} + [NO_3]} > V_{eSi}$$

and $\qquad V_{NO_3} = V_{eSi} = V_{iNO_3}$

i.e. the V_{NO_3} vs. $[NO_3]$ curve is truncated at V_{eSi}. The same will be true for phosphorus. For balanced growth with silicic acid limitation,

$$\mu = V_{eSi} = V_{iNO_3} = V_{iPO_4}$$

and the nutrient-saturated uptake rates of nonlimiting nutrients, V_{iNO_3} or V_{iPO_4}, can be used as measures of V_{eSi}. The nitrate uptake kinetic constants are influenced by ammonia concentration (e.g. Conway 1977). For simplicity, the concentration of ammonia is assumed here to be 0.

Light and limiting silicic acid — Dependence of limiting silicic acid uptake on light intensity is weak or nonexistent as shown in Fig. 9d, and the values of V_{Si} obtained during silicic acid saturated perturbations at all light levels approximate $V_{iSi} = \mu'_{max}$.

Light and nonlimiting nutrient — Light dependence of nitrate uptake is hyperbolic, but truncated at $V_{iNO_3} \approx \mu$ as shown in Fig. 9e. The same pattern is expected to hold for phosphate uptake.

If Droop kinetics are followed, there is a hyperbolic relation at steady state between the growth rate and the cell quota, Fig. 9f, according to the expression

$$(7) \qquad \mu = \mu'_m \frac{(Q_{Si} - K_{QSi})}{Q_{Si}}$$

$$= V_{iNO_3} = V_{iPO_4} = V_{eSi}$$

Under silicic acid limitation, the arrow in Fig. 9f indicates the operating point for Q_{Si}. Because cell quota decreases with decreasing μ and

$V_{maxSi} = \dfrac{\rho_{maxSi}}{Q_{Si}}$, the shape of the limiting-nutrient hyperbola on a specific basis changes, rather than staying constant as shown in the diagrammatic representation of Fig. 9b. The growth rate is calculated from Eq. 3 rather than from Eq. 5.

Light and fixed limiting-nutrient concentration — The effect of light intensity on growth rate at fixed limiting-nutrient concentration is expressed in Eq. 3 through the value of μ'_m. From Eq. 3 an expression for μ'_{max} can be obtained by letting the silicic acid concentration become infinitely large:

$$\mu'_{max} = \left(\frac{K_Q}{\rho_{max}} + \frac{1}{\mu'_m} \right)^{-1}$$

and because we have equated μ'_{max} with V_{i_c},

$$(8) \quad V_{i_c} = V_{iSi} = \left(\frac{K_Q}{\rho_{max}} + \frac{1}{\mu'_m} \right)^{-1} = \mu'_{max}$$

There is insufficient information available to say whether light intensity and temperature influence μ'_m directly as suggested by Dugdale (1977) and whether K_Q and ρ_{max} are affected directly by changes in these variables. However, Eq. 8 can be solved for μ'_m to give:

$$(9) \qquad \mu'_m = \frac{1}{\dfrac{1}{V_{i_c}} - \dfrac{K_{QSi}}{\rho_{maxSi}}}$$

A reduction in I results in a decrease in μ'_m and a change in shape of the μ vs. Q_{Si} curve, Fig. 9f, and a new operating point at a higher Q would be established if $K_{Q_{Si}}$ and $\rho_{\max_{Si}}$ remain unchanged.

In any event, it appears from laboratory experiments that the shape of the μ vs. Q hyperbola is affected by changes in both temperature and light intensity, a reduction in either at fixed growth rate resulting in increased cell quota of the limiting nutrient (Harrison 1974; Davis 1973).

Field Observations

Nitrogen often is postulated to be the limiting nutrient in various parts of the marine environment (e.g. Ryther and Dunstan 1971; Eppley et al. 1972; Thomas et al. 1974; Perry 1976; Goldman 1976). However, limitation by other primary nutrients such as phosphorus (Perry 1976), silicic acid (Thomas and Dodson 1975; Azam and Chisholm 1976), or by light (Huntsman and Barber 1977) may occur and also can generate signals in the nitrogen uptake data, which may be interpreted in the framework of the truncation model described above. The following discussion of results from our work in the Peru upwelling system demonstrates sequences of events influencing the uptake of nitrate and assimilation number by changes in the stability of the water column and reductions in the ambient concentrations of silicic acid.

INORGANIC NITROGEN UPTAKE

A drogue was placed near the Peru coast at about 15°S on *Anton Bruun* 15 and followed for 5 d in March 1966. Although drogues cannot track a water mass faithfully in an upwelling area, they provide sampling targets related to the mean drift at the drogue depth. Ryther et al. (1970) described the evolution of the diatom bloom that occurred during this drogue experiment. The three most abundant species were *Chaetoceros debilis*, *C. lorenzianus*, and *C. socialis*. Specific inorganic nitrogen uptake rates were measured using ^{15}N on water taken from the 50% light-penetration depth. The ambient nitrate concentrations were nonlimiting, such that the uptake rates measured may be designated V_i. When plotted against nitrate, phosphate, and silicic acid concentrations, the specific nitrate uptake rates ($V_{i_{NO_3}}$) showed no likely relation to the first two, but gave a hyperbolalike curve with silicic acid (Dugdale and Goering 1970). The summed $V_{i_{NO_3}}$ and $V_{i_{NH_4}}$ (ammonia concentrations were brought to nonlimiting levels by additions of NH_4Cl) showed a positive correlation with silicic acid concentration, Fig. 10a (Dugdale 1972). For the same data set, the carbon assimilation number (P_M^B) also was correlated positively with silicic acid (Fig. 10b).

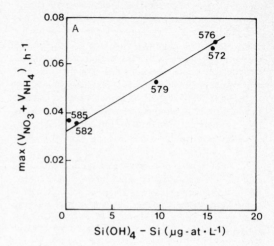

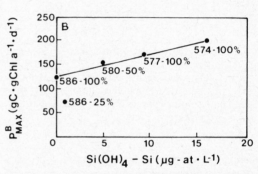

FIG. 10. Inorganic nitrogen and carbon uptake as functions of silicic acid concentration. Carbon, chlorophyll a, and silicic acid data were taken from Ryther (1966).

Two drogue experiments were made in the same region during the JOINT II expedition to Peru on the RV *Wecoma* in March 1977 and the results described by Brink et al. (1980). The first of these was initiated near the end of a calm period when diatom populations (primarily *Detonula pumilla* according to D. Blasco personal communication) and uptake rates were high. The values of $V_{i_{NO_3}}$ for samples from the 50% light-penetration depth are plotted together with those from *Anton Bruun* 15 in Fig. 11. The agreement between the two data sets is good, and these results suggest control of nonlimiting nitrate uptake by silicic acid concentrations of up to at least 10 μg-at·L^{-1}. The conditions for observing this interaction between silicic acid concentration and nitrate uptake during the *Wecoma* drogue 1 experiment were especially favorable: (1) winds remained low, contributing to stability in the

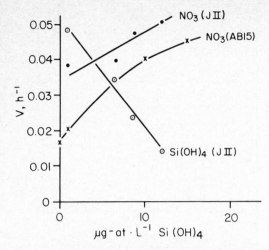

FIG. 11. Nitrate and silicic acid uptake in the Peruvian upwelling system as functions of silicic acid concentration. Open circles are silicic acid uptake from JOINT II; solid circles are nitrate uptake from JOINT II; X's are nitrate uptake from *Anton Bruun* 15.

water column and leading to high-average light conditions for near-surface populations, (2) ammonia concentrations were below levels where a significant suppression of nitrate uptake would be expected, and (3) the nitrate/silicic acid ratio has been shown to be high in the upper region of the pycnocline in Peru (Dugdale 1972), so that upwelling from this part of the pycnocline can be expected to result in surface waters characterized by excess nitrate in relation to silicic acid. The section at 15°S from the PISCO cruise (RV *Thomas G. Thompson*, March 1969), Fig. 12a, clearly shows vertical and horizontal gradients in the nitrate/silicic acid ratio; where upwelling is strongest, near stations 14 and 15, the ratio is about 1.6–1.8. The nitrate section, Fig. 12b, shows surface concentrations to be 15–20 μg-at$\cdot$L^{-1} with active upwelling; the silicate section, Fig. 12c, shows surface concentrations in the nearshore region to be about the same as for nitrate.

We routinely performed holdover experiments on shipboard to aid in the interpretation of temporal changes observed in nitrate uptake. Water from the 50% light-penetration depth was obtained on the 0800 productivity station and placed in two bottles with 50% light screens. One bottle was inoculated immediately with ^{15}N-labeled nitrate or ammonia, incubated for 6 h in a deck incubator, and filtered (MacIsaac and Dugdale 1972). The other bottle was held in the deck incubator until the next morning. At that time ^{15}N was added and the bottle returned to the incubator for 6 h before filtering. Although a number of changes may occur within the bottle during the 24-h preincubation, e.g. decrease in ammonia

concentration resulting in increased nitrate uptake rate or growth on the side of the bottle, the major "bottle effect" appeared to be simply the stabilization of the population at natural saturating light intensity. The characteristically low uptake rates observed off northwest Africa during the JOINT I cruise would increase significantly during a 24-h holdover when the samples were collected from a deeply wind-mixed water column.

The *Wecoma* drogue 1 experiments showed a decrease in $V_{i_{NO_3}}$ during the 24-h holdover (Fig. 13). Nutrient concentrations measured at the beginning and end of the 24-h period showed silicic acid to decline and the inorganic nitrogen concentrations to vary but little. The silicic acid concentrations decreased in the bottles just as occurred in nature. The data in Fig. 13 show that the 24-h holdover values predict accurately the direction of change in the value of $V_{i_{NO_3}}$ in the regular, nonholdover samples. Presumably, the nitrate uptake rates in the holdover bottles and along the drogue track were being set by limiting silicic acid uptake.

A second drogue experiment was initiated at the same point immediately following termination of the first. Strong upwelling occurred just prior to the experiment (Brink et al. 1980) flooding the area with nutrients; the diatom populations were replaced by small unidentified flagellates. Low values of $V_{i_{NO_3}}$ were obtained throughout the experiment and no relationship between them and silicic acid concentration could be seen. Further, the 24-h holdover experiments showed enhancement in $V_{i_{NO_3}}$ similar to that seen in the JOINT I experiments, reflecting the observed physical instability of the system during the drogue 2 experiment.

SILICIC ACID UPTAKE

Goering et al. (1973) obtained the first evidence for Michaelis-Menten kinetics for silicic acid uptake in natural populations using [29]Si as a tracer. (Two stable isotopes of silicon, [29]Si, and [30]Si, are available for use in tracer experiments; Goering has used both at different times and now uses [30]Si.) At station 51 of the PISCO cruise to Peru, they found $V_{max} = 0.075$ h^{-1} and $K_s = 2.93$ μg-at$\cdot$L^{-1}. During the JOINT II expedition, the results of a [30]Si K_s measurement at *Wecoma* station 124 gave a value for K_s of approximately 3 μg-at$\cdot$L^{-1} silicic acid and of V_{max}, approximately 0.08 h^{-1}. Azam and Chisholm (1976) obtained values of 1.59 and 2.53 μg-at$\cdot$L^{-1} silicic acid for K_s in two natural populations in the Gulf of California. Harrison (1974) summarized silicic acid kinetic observations from culture and reported a range of values for K_s of 0.7–3.37 μg-at $\cdot$L^{-1}. Azam (1974) found a K_s of 6.8 μg-at$\cdot$L^{-1} silicic acid for the nonpelagic diatom *Nitzschia alba* in culture. The range of values for both laboratory

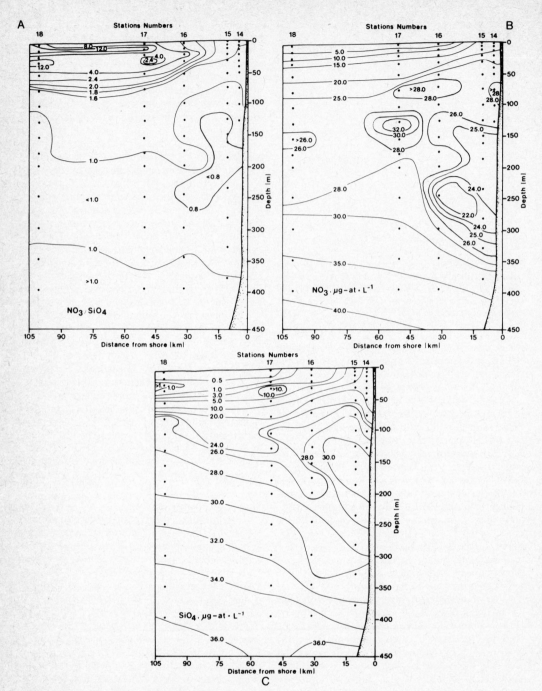

FIG. 12. Nitrate and silicic acid in the Peruvian upwelling system during the PISCO cruise. (A) Nitrate/silicic acid ratio; (B) nitrate; (C) silicic acid. (From Dugdale 1972.)

and field populations is strikingly small, and both the values and the range are similar to those reported for nitrogen and tabulated by Dugdale (1976).

The uptake of ^{30}Si was measured along with the ^{15}N experiments during the *Wecoma* drogue 1 experiment. The silicic acid enrichments used in

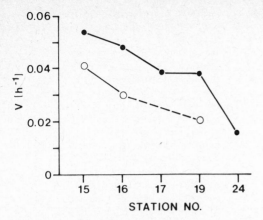

FIG. 13. Nitrate uptake as measured at sampling time (closed circles) and 24 h later (open circles), in samples collected at the same time from the *Wecoma* drogue 1 experiment in Peru. Stations were ~24 h apart.

the experiments were high enough to be nonlimiting, although even the highest ambient concentrations ($12 \ \mu g\text{-at} \cdot L^{-1}$) appeared to be limiting. Values of $V_{i_{Si}}$ for the 50% light-penetration depth populations are plotted against ambient silicic acid concentration in Fig. 11. Two possible explanations for the observed increase in $V_{i_{Si}}$ with decreasing silicic acid concentration are (1) changes in nonnutrient environmental variables leading to enhanced biological rates, and (2) decreasing silicon per cell (cell quota). The latter effect is consistent with decreasing growth rate, as implied by decreasing $V_{i_{NO_3}}$, with decreasing silicic acid concentration (Fig. 11).

Two curves of light versus silicic acid uptake, Fig. 14, also were obtained in the course of the *Wecoma* drogue 1 experiment. The large increase in dark uptake of silicic acid between the two experiments coincided with a decrease in ambient silicic acid concentration. This observation of light independence of limiting silicic acid uptake is consistent with the chemostat results of Davis (1976) and Nelson et al. (1976). Nitrate uptake as a function of light also was measured with the second of the light versus silicic acid experiments (station 19), and the results are shown in Fig. 14. Two features are of interest and indicate that nitrogen was nonlimiting: (1) dark uptake was low, and (2) reciprocal plot analysis of the kinetic parameters showed the curve to be truncated between 30 and 50% surface light.

A parameter $K_{\lim}$, the substrate concentration at which $V/V_{\max} = 0.9$, has been used (Nelson et al. 1976) to estimate the ambient silicic acid concentrations below which significant and observable reductions in uptake may be expected to occur. On this basis, the range of $K_{\lim}$ predicted from the field values of K_s given at the beginning of

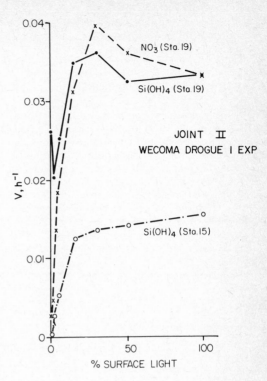

FIG. 14. Silicic acid (open circles, Sta. 15; solid circles, Sta. 19) and nitrate (X's, Sta. 19) uptake as a function of light, from two stations during the *Wecoma* drogue 1 experiment.

this section is $14.3 - 26.4 \ \mu g\text{-at} \cdot L^{-1}$; from the laboratory, the computed range is $4.32 - 52.7 \ \mu g\text{-at} \cdot L^{-1}$ (ignoring the value for *N. alba*). These calculations give results that are consistent with the field observations reported above that suggest observable effects on phytoplankton uptake processes with silicic acid concentrations up to at least $10 \ \mu g\text{-at} \cdot L^{-1}$. There is the possibility that uptake may cease at some nonzero value of silicic acid concentration, S_0 (Paasche 1973a, b), and in that case the values of $K_{\lim}$ calculated above should be increased by S_0 (no greater than $2 \ \mu g\text{-at} \cdot L^{-1}$ in Paasche's data); Nelson et al. (1976) did not observe an S_0.

Although the $K_{\lim}$ value should provide a good indicator of expected changes in the dynamics of nutrient uptake processes in phytoplankton populations as silicic acid concentrations fall, effects on growth rate may not be realized until lower concentrations are reached. For example, the K_s for silicic acid limited growth reported by Guillard et al. (1973), 0.19 and 0.98 $\mu g\text{-at} \cdot L^{-1}$ for two clones of *T. pseudonana*, compare with K_s values of 0.8 and 1.5 $\mu g\text{-at} \cdot L^{-1}$ for uptake in the same clones (Nelson et al. 1976). Paasche (1973b) found approximately the same relationship, and it appears that the ranges for K_{lim} for uptake given above may be divided by about 1.5–4.0 to obtain an estimate of K_{lim} for growth under silicic acid limitation.

Acknowledgments

This paper is based on Technical Report No. 51 (Dugdale et al. 1979) of the Coastal Upwelling Ecosystem Analysis program prepared under Grant No. OCE-7727006 from the National Science Foundation IDOE program. The assistance of D. Boisseau and G. Grunseich in conducting experiments and analyzing the samples for, respectively, the *Wecoma* ^{30}Si and ^{15}N work is deeply appreciated. Support for the present effort was provided also by the National Science Foundation under Grant No. OCE-8015705 from the IDOE program and under Grant No. OCE-7910112.

Symbols

V specific uptake rate (h^{-1})

$V = \dfrac{1}{S}\dfrac{dS}{dt}$ which, during balanced growth,

equals $\dfrac{1}{x}\dfrac{dx}{dt}$

where S is the phytoplankton particulate substrate concentration and x is the cell concentration (no. cells/unit volume)

V_{max} specific uptake rate at infinite substrate concentration (h^{-1})

V_e the externally controlled specific uptake rate (h^{-1})

V_i the internally controlled specific uptake rate (h^{-1})

S substrate concentration (μg-at·L^{-1})

S_T substrate concentration at which control of nutrient uptake switches from external to internal (μg-at·L^{-1})

D the dilution rate of the culture, equal to the flow rate of medium into and out of the chemostat divided by the culture volume (h^{-1})

$\bar{I}$ the mean light intensity in the culture (ly·min^{-1} or microeinsteins ·m^{-2}·s^{-1})

Q cell quota, the concentration of limiting nutrient per cell (μg-at·cell^{-1})

μ growth rate (h^{-1})

μ'_m maximum apparent growth rate obtained from plots of the linearized Droop hyperbola; an abstract variable, greater than μ_{max} (h^{-1})

μ_{max} the maximum (nutrient- and light-saturated) growth rate realizable under the given culture conditions (h^{-1})

μ'_{max} the maximum (nutrient-saturated) growth rate realizable under light limitation (h^{-1})

K_s half-saturation constant, substrate concentration at which $V = V_{max}/2$ (μg-at·L^{-1})

K_{lim} the limiting substrate concentration at which $V/V_{max} = 0.9$

K_I the light intensity at which the $\mu'_{max} = \mu_{max}/2$ (ly·min^{-1} or microeinsteins·m^{-2}·s^{-1})

K_Q subsistence quota for limiting nutrient at zero growth rate (μg-at·cell^{-1})

ρ absolute substrate transport rate, usually on a per cell basis (μg-at·cell^{-1}·h^{-1})

ρ_{max} absolute substrate transport rate at infinite substrate concentration (μg-at·cell^{-1}·h^{-1})

ρ_i constant, absolute substrate uptake rate following initial high uptake in a perturbation experiment (μg-at·cell^{-1}·h^{-1})

C phytoplankton carbon concentration (either μg C·cell^{-1} or μg C·L^{-1})

P^B the photosynthetic rate per unit phytoplankton biomass (usually g C·g chl a^{-1}·h^{-1})

P^B_M the assimilation number P^B at optimum light (usually g C·g chl a^{-1}·h^{-1})

P_{max} photosynthetic rate at saturating light (g C·cell^{-1}·h^{-1})

α the initial slope of the P^B vs. I curve (g C·g chl a^{-1}·h^{-1} vs. microeinsteins·m^{-2}·s^{-1})

P_{Si} the particulate silicon concentration (μg-at Si·L^{-1} or μg-at Si·cell^{-1})

References

AZAM, F. 1974. Silicic-acid uptake in diatoms studied with [68GE] germanic acid as tracer. Planta (Berl.) 121: 203–212.

AZAM, F., AND S. W. CHISHOLM. 1976. Silicic acid uptake and incorporation by natural marine phytoplankton populations. Limnol. Oceanogr. 21: 427–435.

BEARDALL, J., AND I. MORRIS. 1976. The concept of light intensity adaptation in marine phytoplankton: some experiments with *Phaeodactylum tricornutum*. Mar. Biol. 37: 377–387.

BRINK, K. H., B. H. JONES JR., J. C. VAN LEER, C. N. K. MOOERS, D. STUART, M. STEVENSON, R. C. DUGDALE, AND G. HEBURN. 1980. Physical and biological structure and variability in an upwelling center off Peru near 15° during March 1977. *In* F. Richards [ed.] Coastal upwelling-1980. American Geophysical Union.

BROWN, E. J., AND R. F. HARRIS. 1978. Kinetics of algal transient phosphate uptake and the cell quota concept. Limnol. Oceanogr. 23: 35–40.

BUTTON, D.K., S. S. DUNKER, AND M. L. MORSE. 1973. Continuous culture of *Rhodotorula rubra*: kinetics of phosphate-arsenate uptake, inhibition, and phosphate limited growth. J. Bacteriol. 113: 559–611.

CAPERON, J., AND J. MEYER. 1972. Nitrogen-limited growth of marine phytoplankton: changes in population characteristics with steady-state growth rate. Deep-Sea Res. 19: 601–618.

CAPERON, J., AND D. F. SMITH. 1978. Photosynthetic rates of marine algae as a function of inorganic carbon concentration. Limnol. Oceanogr. 23: 704–708.

CARPENTER, E. J. 1970. Phosphorus requirements of two planktonic diatoms in steady state culture. J. Phycol. 6: 28–30.

CONWAY, H. L. 1974. The uptake and assimilation of inorganic nitrogen by *Skeletonema costatum* (Greve) Cleve. Ph.D. thesis, Univ. Washington, Seattle. 125 p.

   1977. Interactions of inorganic nitrogen in the uptake and assimilation of nitrate by marine phytoplankton. Mar. Biol. 39: 221–232.

CONWAY, H. L., P. J. HARRISON, AND C. O. DAVIS. 1976. Marine diatoms grown in chemostats under silicate or ammonium limitation. II. Transient response of *Skeletonema costatum* to a single addition of the limiting nutrient. Mar. Biol. 35: 187–199.

DAVIS, C. O. 1973. Effects of changes in light intensity and photoperiod on the silicate-limited continuous culture of the marine diatom *Skeletonema costatum* (Greve) Cleve. Ph.D. thesis. Univ. Washington, Seattle. 122 p.

   1976. Continuous culture of marine diatoms under silicate limitation. II: Effect of light intensity on growth and nutrient uptake of *Skeletonema costatum*. J. Phycol. 12: 291–300.

DOYLE, R. W. 1975. Upwelling, clone selection, and the characteristic shape of nutrient uptake curves. Limnol. Oceanogr. 20: 487–489.

DROOP, M. R. 1968. Vitamin B-12 and marine ecology. IV: The kinetics of uptake, growth and inhibition in *Monochrysis lutheri*. J. Mar. Biol. Assoc. U.K. 48: 689–733.

   1974. The nutrient status of algal cells in continuous culture. J. Mar. Biol. Assoc. U.K. 54: 825–855.

DUGDALE, R. C. 1967. Nutrient limitation in the sea: dynamics, identification, and significance. Limnol. Oceanogr. 12: 685–695.

   1972. Chemical oceanography and primary productivity in upwelling regions. Geoforum 11: 47–61.

   1976. Nutrient cycles, p. 141–172. *In* D. H. Cushing and J. J. Walsh [ed.] The ecology of the sea. Blackwell, London.

   1977. Modeling, p. 789–806. *In* E. D. Goldberg et al. [ed.] The sea. Vol. 6. Ideas and observations on progress in the study of the seas. John Wiley & Sons, Inc., New York, NY.

DUGDALE, R. C., AND J. J. GOERING. 1970. Nutrient limitation and the path of nitrogen in the Peru current production. *Anton Bruun* Rep. 4: 3–8. Texas A & M Press.

DUGDALE, R. C., B. H. JONES JR., J. J. MACISAAC, AND J. J. GOERING. 1979. Interactions of primary nutrient and carbon uptake in the Peru current: a review and synthesis of laboratory and field results. Coastal Upwelling Ecosystems Analysis (CUEA) Program Tech. Rep. 51. 40 p.

DUGDALE, R. C., AND J. J. MACISAAC. 1971. A computation model for the uptake of nitrate in the Peru upwelling region. Invest. Pesq. 35: 299–308.

EPPLEY, R. W., ET AL. 1972. Evidence for eutrophication in the sea near Southern California coastal sewage outfalls — July, 1970. Calif. Coop. Oceanic Fish. Invest. Rep. 16: 74–83.

EPPLEY, R. W., AND E. H. RENGER. 1974. Nitrogen assimilation of an oceanic diatom in nitrogen-limited continuous culture. J. Phycol. 10: 15–23.

EPPLEY, R. W., J. H. ROGERS, AND J. J. MCCARTHY. 1969. Half-saturation constants for uptake of nitrate and ammonium by marine phytoplankton. Limnol. Oceanogr. 14: 912–20.

FUHS, W. G. 1969. Phosphorus content and rate of growth in the diatoms *Cyclotella nana* and *Thalassiosira fluviatilis*. J. Phycol. 5: 312–321.

GOERING, J. J., D. M. NELSON, AND J. A. CARTER. 1973. Silicic acid uptake by natural populations of marine phytoplankton. Deep-Sea Res. 20: 777–789.

GOLDMAN, J. C. 1976. Identification of nitrogen as a growth-limiting nutrient in wastewaters and coastal marine waters through continuous culture algal assays. Water Res. 10: 97–104.

GOLDMAN, J. C., AND J. J. MCCARTHY. 1978. Steady state growth and ammonium uptake of a fast-growing marine diatom. Limnol. Oceanogr. 23: 695–703.

GOLDMAN, J. C., W. J. OSWALD, AND D. JENKINS. 1974. The kinetics of inorganic carbon-limited algal growth. J. Water Pollut. Control Fed. 46: 554–574.

GUILLARD, R. L., P. KILHAM, AND T. A. JACKSON. 1973. Kinetics of silicon-limited growth in the marine diatom *Thalassiosira pseudonana* Hasle and Heimdal (= *Cyclotella nana* Hustedt). J. Phycol. 9: 233–237.

HARRISON, P. J. 1974. Continuous culture of the marine diatom *Skeletonema costatum* (Greve). Ph.D. thesis, Univ. Washington, Seattle. 140 p.

HARRISON, P. J., H. L. CONWAY, AND R. C. DUGDALE. 1976. Marine diatoms grown in chemostats under silicate or ammonium limitation. I: cellular composition and steady-state growth kinetics of *Skeletonema costatum*. Mar. Biol. 35: 177–186.

HERBERT, D., R. ELSWORTH, AND R. C. TELLING. 1956. The continuous culture of bacteria: a theoretical and experimental study. J. Gen. Microbiol. 14: 601–622.

HUNTSMAN, S. A., AND R. T. BARBER. 1977. Primary production off northwest Africa: the relationship to wind and nutrient conditions. Deep-Sea Res. 24: 25–33.

LAWS, E. A., AND T. T. BANNISTER. 1980. Nutrient- and light-limited growth of *Thalassiosira fluviatilis* in continuous culture, with implications for phytoplankton growth in the ocean. Limnol. Oceanogr. 25: 457–473.

LAWS, E. A., AND D. C. L. WONG. 1978. Studies of carbon and nitrogen metabolism by three species of marine phytoplankton in nitrate-limited continuous culture. J. Phycol. 14: 406–416.

LEHNINGER, A. L. 1971. Bioenergetics. Benjamin/Cummings. 245 p.

LOSADA, M., AND M. G. GUERRERO. 1979. The photosynthetic reduction of nitrate and its regulation, p.

365–408. *In* J. Barber [ed.] Photosynthesis in relation to model systems. Elsevier, Amsterdam.

MacIsaac, J. J., and R. C. Dugdale. 1969. The kinetics of nitrate and ammonia uptake by natural populations of marine phytoplankton. Deep-Sea Res. 16: 45–57.

1972. Interactions of light and inorganic nitrogen uptake in the sea. Deep-Sea Res. 19: 209–232.

MacIsaac, J. J., G. S. Grunseich, H. E. Glover, and C. M. Yentsch. 1979. Light and nutrient limitation in *Gonyaulax excavata*: nitrogen and carbon tracer results, p. 107–110. *In* D. Taylor and H. Seliger [ed.] Proceedings second conference on toxic dinoflagellate blooms. Elsevier, Amsterdam.

McAllister, C. D., N. Shah, and J. D. H. Strickland. 1964. Marine phytoplankton photosynthesis as a function of light intensity: a comparison of methods. J. Fish. Res. Board Can. 21: 159–181.

McCarthy, J. J., and J. C. Goldman. 1979. Nitrogenous nutrition of marine phytoplankton in nutrient-depleted waters. Science (Washington, D.C.) 203: 670–672.

Mian, F. H., Z. Fencl, and A. Prokop. 1969. Growth rate and enzyme activity in yeast *(Candida utilis)*, p. 105–115. *In* E. O. Powell et al. [ed.] Continuous culture of micro-organisms.

Nelson, D. M., J. J. Goering, S. S. Kilham, and R. L. Guillard. 1976. Kinetics of silicic acid uptake and rates of silica dissolution in the marine diatom *Thalassiosira pseudonana*. J. Phycol. 12: 246–252.

Paasche, E. 1973a. Silicon and the ecology of marine plankton diatoms. I. *Thalassiosira pseudonana (Cyclotella nana)* grown in a chemostat with silicate as limiting nutrient. Mar. Biol. 19: 117–126.

1973b. Silicon and the ecology of marine plankton diatoms. II. Silicate uptake dynamics in five diatom species. Mar. Biol. 19: 262–269.

Perry, M. J. 1976. Phosphate utilization by an oceanic diatom in phosphorus-limited chemostat culture and in the oligotrophic waters of the central north Pacific. Limnol. Oceanogr. 21: 88–107.

Rhee, G. 1973. A continuous culture study of phosphate uptake, growth rate and polyphosphate in *Scenedesmus* sp. J. Phycol. 9: 495–506.

1974. Phosphate uptake under nitrate limitation by *Scenedesmus* sp. J. Phycol. 10: 470–475.

1978. Effects of N:P atomic ratios and nitrate limitation on algal growth, cell composition, and nitrate uptake. Limnol. Oceanogr. 23: 10–25.

Ryther, J. H. 1966. Cruise report R/V *Anton Bruun*, cruise 15. Texas A & M Univ. Mar. Lab. Spec. Rep. 5. 53 p.

Ryther, J. H., and W. M. Dunstan. 1971. Nitrogen, phosphorus and eutrophication in the coastal marine environment. Science (Washington, D.C.) 171: 1008–1013.

Ryther, J. H., D. W. Menzel, E. M. Hulbert, C. J. Lorenzen, and N. Corwin. 1970. Production and utilization of organic matter in the Peru coastal current. Texas A & M Univ. *Anton Bruun* Rep. 5: 3–12.

Senft, W. H. 1978. Dependence of light-saturated rates of algal photosynthesis on intracellular concentrations of phosphorus. Limnol. Oceanogr. 23: 709–718.

Tempest, D. W., and O. M. Neijssel. 1976. Microbiological adaptation to low-nutrient environments, p. 283–296. *In* A. C. R. Dean et al. [ed.] Continuous culture 6: applications and new fields. Ellis Harwood Ltd., Chichester.

Thomas, W. H., and A. N. Dodson. 1972. On nitrogen deficiency in tropical Pacific oceanic phytoplankton. II. Photosynthetic and cellular characteristics of a chemostat-grown diatom. Limnol. Oceanogr. 17: 515–523.

1975. On silicic acid limitation of diatoms in near-surface waters of the eastern tropical Pacific Ocean. Deep-Sea Res. 22: 671–677.

Thomas, W. H., D. L. R. Seibert, and A. N. Dodson. 1974. Phytoplankton enrichment experiments and bioassays in natural coastal seawater and in sewage outfall receiving waters off Southern California. Est. Coast. Mar. Sci. 2: 191–206.

Yentsch, C. S., and R. W. Lee. 1966. A study of photosynthetic light reactions, and a new interpretation of sun and shade phytoplankton. J. Mar. Res. 24: 319–337.

Relations between Nutrient Assimilation and Growth in Phytoplankton with a Brief Review of Estimates of Growth Rate in the Ocean

R. W. EPPLEY

Institute of Marine Resources,
University of California, San Diego, La Jolla, CA 92093, USA

Nutrient Assimilation and Growth

THE CONCEPT OF BALANCED GROWTH

"Growth is balanced when the amounts of all cellular components increase exponentially at the same rate. Under these conditions, cellular composition remains fixed" (Shuter 1979). The assimilation of the various nutritional elements will then take place in the same proportion as they occur in the cellular composition. Measurement of the rate constant for any one of these elements will then be valid for all, including cell division (Eppley and Strickland 1968).

The concept of balanced growth is fundamental to the use of nutrient assimilation rates as measures of the rate constants of phytoplankton growth. The concept is not usually stated explicitly in texts and reviews on algal physiology although it is implied throughout. It is not likely to be a strange or new idea. Nevertheless, the conditions under which balanced growth can be expected are not very common, even in studies with laboratory cultures. It is doubtful that balanced growth of phytoplankton ever takes place in natural waters except under certain restricted definitions of balanced growth (to be discussed later).

Shuter (1979) pointed out that balanced growth is found only in totally asynchronous growing populations. Single cells do not display balanced growth "since the synthesis of individual components occurs at discrete intervals over the cell cycle." Balanced growth can only be a property of a population of cells growing asynchronously. Asynchronous population growth is to be expected only under strictly constant and uniform supply rates of all materials and energy sources required for growth. Algal cultures growing exponentially with excess nutrients (batch cultures) or with constant nutrient supply rate (continuous cultures) and with constant irradiance and temperature approach the ideal of balanced growth.

Neither cyclostats (Chisholm and Nobbs 1976), i.e. continuous cultures growing under periodic illumination, nor natural systems with periodicity or irregularity in light, temperature, or nutrient supply can be expected to show balanced growth; rather, periodicity in growth is imposed by the environmental conditions. Nevertheless, there is a special case in which growth in a cyclostat or in natural populations may be expected to be nearly balanced. That is when average rates of assimilation of the various nutritional elements are considered over the cell cycle imposed by the environment (Shuter 1979). The natural day–night cycle is a principal environmental forcing function that imposes periodicity on phytoplankton growth and elemental assimilation rates. Exponential growth of natural populations may be balanced if rates are averaged over this 24-h light cycle, unless temporal variations in nutrient supply rates are overriding or unless short-term variations in irradiance or temperature within the 24-h cycle are sufficiently large.

GROWTH IN THE OCEANS

Discontinuous supply — Sunlight is obviously discontinuous and periodic on both a daily and a seasonal basis. Entrainment of phytoplankton photosynthesis to the daily cycle results in circadian periodicity in photosynthesis (Doty and Oguri 1957) with the ratio between daily maxima and minima a function of latitude (Doty 1959) or, more precisely, of day length (Lorenzen 1963). Soeder (1965) concluded that microalgae tend toward synchrony in their activities under light–dark cycles whenever exponential growth is possible. Sournia (1974) reviewed the literature on such periodicity in several phytoplankton processes. We can expect discontinuous or periodic assimilation whenever illumination is discontinuous or periodic. Diel changes in dissolved carbohydrates in seawater have been observed in both coastal (Walsh 1965; Sellner 1980) and open ocean locations (Burney et al. 1979). Diel changes in oxygen (Tijssen 1979) and particulate organic carbon (Postma and Rommets 1979) also imply the 24-h cycle is important in phytoplankton dynamics.

Nutrient substances in the euphotic zone of the oceans are also subject to temporal and spatial variation in ambient concentrations and rate of supply. The source of the supply may be mixing with, or replacement by deeper ocean water, lateral advection of surface water from elsewhere, or from rivers or the atmosphere. Coastal upwelling generates spectacular differences in nutrient supply rate to the euphotic zone episodically. Winter–summer differences in nutrient concentration, related to seasonal differences in mixing/stratification, may also be extreme, especially in the coastal regions of temperate and boreal waters of the North Atlantic and North Pacific.

The kinds of variation in nutrient supply most important for the estimation of growth rate from rates of nutrient assimilation, however, are those which take place within the generation time of the phytoplankton. Variation in nutrient supply on a time scale of hours, where there is assurance the same parcel of water was being sampled, is not well documented.

Ryther et al. (1961) and Beers and Kelley (1965) measured day–night differences in the ambient concentrations of ammonium and other nutrients in the Sargasso Sea. Müller-Haeckel (1965) found a daily periodicity in silicic acid in a saline creek. The excretion of nutrients into the euphotic zone waters by zooplankton and fish would be expected to be greater by night than day if a significant fraction of the excretion was due to vertically migrating animals. Discontinuous supply may be a much more common and important phenomenon than we have considered in the past (Goldman et al. 1979; McCarthy and Goldman 1979).

Considering the spatial scale, Oviatt et al. (1972) found marked increases in the ammonium concentration in the wake of a menhaden school. Calculations suggest the ammonium concentration is probably doubled over ambient levels in southern California waters in the wake of an anchovy school (P. E. Smith and R. W. Eppley unpublished data). Such patches of elevated nutrient content would be expected to have a lifetime of minutes to hours, depending on ambient phytoplankton concentrations and assuming dispersal by eddy diffusion with a typical horizontal "mixing length" of about $1 \text{ km} \cdot \text{d}^{-1}$.

Nutrient patches brought about by schools of fish and individual large animals, such as sharks, seals, and whales, are likely important to phytoplankton in low nutrient waters (J. J. McCarthy personal communication). McCarthy and Goldman (1979) proposed that the nutrient patches in the wake of individual macrozooplankton may also be significant for phytoplankton nutrient uptake. Very short lifetimes are calculated for patches of such small size, however (Jackson 1980).

Discontinuous assimilation and cell division — In what follows I will argue for the validity of the hypothesis that measurement of nutrient assimilation rate per unit biomass does not provide an accurate measure of phytoplankton specific growth rate (μ). The evidence available suggests that periodicity in elemental uptake and assimilation and in cell division is the rule. Thus, measurements over the cell cycle

are required if specific nutrient assimilation rate (μ_C, μ_N, μ_P, etc.) is to be equivalent to μ for cell numbers and, therefore, the null hypothesis rejected. The cell cycle may usually be assumed to be linked to the 24-h illumination cycle, however. In that case average assimilation rates over 24 h may be equivalent to μ if the chemical composition and cell size remain constant between days.

Certain cell constituents vary greatly in magnitude over the 24-h day–night cycle. For example, the water-soluble carbohydrate content of the particulate matter in Mikawa Bay varied almost an order of magnitude whereas chlorophyll remained essentially constant (Handa 1975). This carbohydrate was produced in the light and respired by the phytoplankton at night. Its specific rate of increase in the light would exceed μ severalfold. ATP levels in a *Ceratium furca* culture showed similar light–dark variations, with the daytime ATP increase an order of magnitude greater than for cell division (Weiler and Karl 1979). The cellular nitrate content of phytoplankton in shipboard cultures also showed large day/night differences (Collos and Slawyk 1976).

Microscopic observations have revealed phased cell division (i.e. cell division restricted to a portion of the 24-h day) in a number of phytoplankters in natural samples. The large-celled dinoflagellates are best known in this respect. Recent observations include *Pyrocystis* spp. (Swift and Durbin 1972; Swift et al. 1976) and *Ceratium* spp. in coastal waters (Elbrächter 1973; Weiler and Chisholm 1976) and in the central North Pacific (Weiler 1980). Phased cell division was also noted in the large-celled diatom *Ditylum brightwellii* (Smayda 1975).

The diel periodicity in photosynthesis of phytoplankton in natural samples has been examined extensively. Malone (1971) noted differences in nanoplankton versus netplankton in this respect in samples of oligotrophic surface water. The nanoplankton showed a greater productivity index (milligrams C per milligram chlorophyll a per hour) in the morning than the afternoon whereas afternoon values for netplankton were the same or higher than morning values. Morning and afternoon values were similar for both size fractions in the more eutrophic California Current waters. Paerl and MacKenzie (1979) made similar observations in freshwater. Statistical analysis of many photosynthetic light curves indicated the diel periodicity was in the maximum photosynthetic rate (P_{max}^B); diel variation in the initial slope (α) of the curves was not statistically significant although α and P_{max}^B were correlated (MacCaull and Platt 1976).

Truly endogenous circadian rhythms are well-known for certain marine phytoplankters. What remains unclear is the extent of their modification by environmental factors such as ambient nutrient levels (Stross et al. 1973).

Diel periodicity in nutrient uptake by natural populations of phytoplankton is also well-known. Goering et al. (1964) found diel variations in ammonium and nitrate uptake in Sargasso Sea samples with maximum rates in the early morning. In richer waters off Peru the peak was near noon; the observations there were extended also to silicic acid uptake (Goering et al. 1973). In 200-L shipboard cultures off California diel periodicity was noted for nitrate, ammonium, urea, and phosphate uptake. Peak rates were near noon as for photosynthesis. Diatoms in the cultures divided in the afternoon and early evening (Eppley et al. 1971a).

Although photosynthesis is by definition restricted to daytime, several nutrient substances are also taken up, often at reduced rate, in darkness. Silicic acid uptake and incorporation in natural samples is not completely light dependent (Azam and Chisholm 1976; Goering et al. 1973). Neither is ammonium uptake, as noted above. MacIsaac and Dugdale (1972) prepared uptake rate versus irradiance curves indicating low half-saturating irradiances for nitrate uptake and even lower ones for ammonium uptake. Dark uptake rates of nitrate were much lower than those for ammonium in Kaneohe Bay, Hawaii (Harvey and Caperon 1976). Phosphate uptake took place at the same rate day and night in the oligotrophic central North Pacific (Perry 1976) yet showed diel periodicity in coastal waters (Harrison et al. 1977). Reshkin and Knauer (1979) provided phosphate uptake rate versus irradiance curves for natural samples of coastal plankton.

Falkowski and Stone (1975) made the interesting observation that adding 3 μM nitrate or ammonium to coastal British Columbia water samples resulted in a lowered maximum rate of photosynthesis (P_{max}^B) that persisted several hours. Presumably the additions brought about a temporary change in the C/N assimilation ratio of the phytoplankton (although N-assimilation rates were not measured).

These and many other observations indicate that uptake of various nutrient substances may be either in phase or somewhat out of phase with one another and with photosynthetic carbon assimilation. Cell division activity may peak at a totally different time, such as at dawn in *Ceratium* spp. (cf. Weiler and Chisholm 1976), an unlikely time for peak rates of photosynthesis and nutrient assimilation. These observations draw attention to the balanced growth concept and to the idea that only average values over the 24-h day could possibly give rates related to the rate of cell division and net growth.

It is particularly worrisome to those making uptake rate measurements of several nutrients in the same samples that the assimilation ratios, e.g. C uptake/N uptake, are not the same as the composition ratios of the particulate matter (and presumably of the phytoplankton). Departures from balanced growth during the experimental incubations may contribute appreciably to these discrepancies (G. A. Jackson and R. W. Eppley unpublished data).

CULTURE STUDIES: EXAMPLES OF UNBALANCED GROWTH

Experiments with laboratory cultures of phytoplankton provide many examples of discontinuous or phased assimilation of nutrient elements, including photosynthetic carbon assimilation. These further examples of unbalanced growth lend credence to the null hypothesis that rate measurements of nutrient elements will not usually provide accurate estimates of specific growth rate. Cellular periodicity and either nutrient deprivation or discontinuous supply result in most of these observations.

Cellular periodicity — It used to be common practice to maintain algal cultures in the north window. Here they were exposed to diffuse daylight and its natural light–dark cycle. The algae in such cultures often divided at night (Braarud 1945). In the late 1940s and early 50s, serious consideration was given to the mass culture of algae, greatly stimulating activity and research on the physiology of algae. The notion of synchronously dividing algal populations has its roots in those times (see the review of Tamiya 1966). In some cases it could be shown that the rhythmic cell division was endogenous and would persist, once established during growth on light–dark cycles, in continuous dim light (Sweeney and Hastings 1958).

Recently Nelson and Brand (1979) examined the periodicity in cell division in 26 clones (13 species) of marine phytoplankton. Phased cell division resulting simply from growth in light–dark cycles was found in 22 of the 26 strains. Cell division began in the light period in 10 clones of diatoms. Other taxa showed maximum cell division at night. These also showed slight decreases in cell number in the light period, a phenomenon not seen in the diatoms. Such spontaneous cell lysis has not been systematically observed in previous culture studies. The lysis resulted in negative rate constants for growth based on cell counts about -0.01 h^{-1} for periods of 4–8 h. Paasche (1968) showed that some diatoms display maximum growth rates on light–dark cycles. For example, *Ditylum brightwellii* grew faster with 16-h photoperiods than in continuous light. The significance and role of biological clocks in phytoplankton growth are reviewed by Chisholm (1981).

Cyclostats — The cyclostat is a continuous culture operated with a light–dark illumination cycle (Chisholm and Nobbs 1976). Cyclostat cultures typically show diel periodicity in cell division, photosynthetic rate, nutrient uptake rate (at high dilution rates approaching maximum growth rates), and in chemical composition. Thus, growth in cyclostats begins to approach the complexity we assume for the phytoplankton of the ocean. The cultures are homogeneous, however, and display steady states when rates and concentrations are averaged over the duration of the light–dark illumination cycle, usually 24 h. Examples of cyclostat results with marine phytoplankton can be found in Davis et al. (1973), Eppley et al. (1971b), Eppley and Renger (1974), Laws and Wong (1978), Laws and Bannister (1980), and in Malone et al. (1975).

These studies have made comparisons based on samples taken at a given time each day or on rates averaged over 12 or 24 h. To date, nutrient uptake rates for several elements have not been examined in detail as a function of time in the cell cycle. At low growth rates compared to μ_m, the growth-limiting nutrient (N) remained undetectable in the medium over the light–dark cycle (Malone et al. 1975; Eppley et al. 1971b) and its specific uptake rate varied with cell number and N/cell. (In continuous light the limiting nutrient in chemostats, either N or P, remained undetectable in the medium for $\mu < 0.85\ \mu_m$ (Goldman et al. 1979)). Assimilation of C and N were clearly out of phase in the cyclostat cultures as N uptake was continuous while C assimilation took place only in the light.

Most physiological processes of phytoplankton become entrained to some degree during growth on light–dark cycles. This has provided an experimental tool for probing many aspects of the timing of events in the cell cycle and of cellular biochemistry well beyond the scope of this review (see Sournia 1974; Mitchison 1973). Studies of rhythmic phenomena in unicellular algae began in the laboratory. Studies relative to understanding primary production and phytoplankton growth in the sea are more limited in history and scope. The diel periodicity in photosynthesis, nutrient assimilation, and cell division in natural samples discussed earlier has also been observed in cultures growing on light–dark cycles, as have several more subtle phenomena of interest to planktologists. Respiration is one of these; it varied over the cell cycle in *Chlorella* (Sorokin and Myers 1957).

Nutrient deprivation or discontinuous supply — A striking departure from balanced growth is provided when a batch culture approaches the stationary phase because of the depletion of a necessary nutrient. It is often observed that two or more cell divisions and considerable photosynthetic carbon assimilation may continue following the depletion of nitrogen from the medium. The N content of each cell then declines, being "diluted" by the subsequent cell division. Carbon assimilation measurement would

indicate rapid growth, yet N assimilation would be zero. Under this transient condition nutrient assimilation measurements cannot provide general measures of growth, which is rapidly approaching zero by any definition, and rate constants may even take negative values for cell constituents such as chlorophyll. Some earlier studies were reviewed with respect to growth models a decade ago (Eppley and Strickland 1968, p. 44–45).

Phytoplankton respond to environmental change by adjusting their chemical composition. ". . . phytoplankton have mechanisms for regulating uptake of each element and . . . these mechanisms are used to maintain composition and achieve balanced growth" (Laws and Bannister 1980). The direction of these adjustments tends to maximize growth rate under the new conditions (Shuter 1979). Shuter summarized the responses to increases in light, nutrient supply, and temperature and reviewed published examples showing changes in chlorophyll, RNA, carbon reserves, and growth rate. Droop's model (Droop 1970) clarifies these changes in cellular composition as functions of nutrient supply rate (McCarthy 1981). When nutrients are suddenly added to depleted cells the response is often a rapid uptake of the depleted nutrient. For example, when nitrogen was added to N-limited diatom cultures the nitrogen was taken up rapidly. Carbon assimilation was depressed (as Falkowski and Stone (1975) found with natural samples) such that the ratio of assimilation rate, V_c/V_N, was as low as 1.0 by atoms (Collos and Slawyk 1979). In balanced growth the assimilation ratio would be the same as the composition ratio: five or more.

Conway et al. (1976) and Conway and Harrison (1977) measured specific uptake rates of N, P, and Si at the same time using three diatom species growing in N-limited chemostat cultures. Silicic acid limited cultures were also studied as were cultures starved of nutrient for 72 h, and nutrient-sufficient batch cultures. Nutrient uptake rates were calculated from the decline in external concentrations measured chemically. The cultures were kept in continuous light and constant temperature. Departures from balanced growth in the exponentially growing, N-limited chemostat cultures reflected responses to pulse, 7–8 μM additions of ammonium. Not only were subsequent uptake rates of the ammonium-N higher than the steady-state growth rate, but phosphate and silicic acid uptake rates were depressed after the ammonium addition (Table 1).

This result is also reminiscent of the Falkowski and Stone (1975) observation and takes us back to earlier observations where adding ammonium (Syrett 1958) or silicic acid (Coombs et al. 1967) to N- or Si-depleted cells, respectively, resulted in a transient but spectacular decline in cell ATP content. Holm-

254

TABLE 1. Departures from balanced growth due to addition of 7 μM ammonium to an ammonium-limited chemostat culture of *Skeletonema costatum*. Flow was stopped upon the NH_4^+ addition. The dilution rate had been 0.040 h^{-1}, 18°C, irradiance 0.14 ly·min^{-1}, continuous. (From Conway et al. 1976.) Uptake rates are per weight of element in the algae.

Expt.	Ammonium uptake			Phosphate uptake		Silicic acid uptake	
	Surge rate (h^{-1})	Duration of surge (h)	Steady rate (h^{-1})	Lag (h)	Subsequent rate (h^{-1})	During lag (h^{-1})	Subsequent rate (h^{-1})
BMP-1	0.218	1.8	0.098	0.6	0.059	0.004	0.087
2	0.235	1.2	0.103	0.6	0.058	0.020	0.067
3	0.188	0.9	0.130	0.6	0.075	0.020	0.110

Hansen (1970) and Sakshaug and Holm-Hansen (1977) supply many dramatic examples of changing cellular composition when nutrients are resupplied to depleted cells. These results together suggest that if there is small-scale spatial and temporal patchiness in nutrients in the ocean, and if the phytoplankton are at all nutrient depleted, then the cells may indeed channel their available energy resources into the uptake and assimilation of the depleted nutrient. The time scale for recovery from depletion, as assessed by the time required for uptake rates to recover, was several hours (Conway and Harrison 1977). Whatever the time required it is clear that balanced growth was not taking place and that specific uptake rates would not be accurate measures of growth in that period.

Myers (1951) concluded that cells suddenly exposed to high irradiance, saturating for photosynthesis, show an abnormally high C/N assimilation ratio. On return to lower irradiances, below saturation for photosynthesis, the rate of N assimilation will be unusually high. Thus, changes in irradiance can mimic N limitation and pulsed N additions in their effects on C/N assimilation ratios.

The above lead us to inquire: what is the nutritional status of phytoplankton in the ocean? Is it apt to be uniform over the 24-h illumination cycle such that balanced growth can be expected as in cyclostat cultures, or is it forever fluctuating on a time scale of minutes to hours such that balanced growth can rarely be expected even over the 24-h cycle?

NUTRITIONAL STATUS OF PHYTOPLANKTON IN THE OCEAN

Geographical differences between biotic provinces — The major biotic provinces of the oceans are determined by the ocean boundaries and major current systems. For the most part, we can assume that ambient nutrient concentration at the surface, the depths at which measurable concentrations are first encountered, and the nutrient flux into the euphotic zone provide similar (qualitative) measures of primary production and the nutritional status of the phytoplankton. Sverdrup (1955) produced a rough map of global production based on general knowledge of such physical processes as vertical convection, upwelling, and turbulent diffusion which bring nutrients to the surface waters. Modern maps of primary production based on ^{14}C measurements are very similar to Sverdrup's map (Koblentz-Mishke et al. 1970). The provinces with the most depauperate euphotic zones are the anticyclonic central gyres of the North and South Atlantic and Pacific oceans. Antarctic waters, temperate and boreal coastal waters in winter, and offshore waters to the north and south of about 40°N and 40°S, respectively, have measurable surface nutrients the year around. Nutrient-limited growth of phytoplankton seems unlikely in those locations. Temporal and spatial variations in nutrient concentrations there may not be important for balanced growth if concentrations are sufficient to saturate the nutrient uptake mechanisms.

Nitrogen is the nutrient first depleted by phytoplankton growth in most locations examined (Ryther and Dunstan 1971). Silicic acid may be depleted before nitrate in the eastern South Pacific, however (Zentara and Kamykowski 1977), and phosphate may be the chief limiting nutrient in the Mediterranean (D. Bonin and S. Maestrini personal communication).

Various methods are in use for assessing the physiological state of the phytoplankton with respect to nutrients. Compositional ratios of the elements in the seston are a particularly powerful tool, especially in the present context of assessing balanced growth. Ratios of C/P have been determined, for example, in the central gyre of the North Pacific

(Perry 1976; Perry and Eppley 1980) and in lake waters (Peterson et al. 1974). The C/N ratio provides a relative measure of growth rate (Donaghay et al. 1978) and, thus, may provide a guide to growth reduction due to nutrient lack. The ratio of protein/carbohydrate in the seston is also a measure of physiological state of diatom populations (Myklestad and Haug 1972; Sakshaug and Mykelstad 1973). The acid-soluble fraction of carbohydrate containing the β-1, 3-glucan is the more likely carbohydrate fraction to be associated with living cells (Myklestad 1977). These observations from cultures and Trondheimsfjord have been extended to the cape upwelling area of South Africa where the protein/carbohydrate ratio of a large crop of diatoms fell to <1.0 as nutrients were depleted (Barlow 1980).

Most indicators of physiological state in phytoplankton suggest only marginal deprivation of N or P even in the most oligotrophic ocean waters. For example, the productivity index (PI) was examined for its potential value as such an indicator by Curl and Small (1965); low values, $1-3\,h^{-1}$ were indicative of regions of very low nutrient supply. Thomas (1970) found values about 5 where nitrate was measurable and about 3 where it was absent in the eastern tropical Pacific. Values of $3-5$ were found in regions "bordering on nutrient sufficiency" (Curl and Small 1965).

The effect of added ammonium on dark ^{14}C uptake also varies with the nitrogen status of the phytoplankton (Morris et al. 1971); Florida Strait plankton were N sufficient by this assay. Nitrogen deficiency was indicated, however, in Gulf of Maine phytoplankton at the end of the spring bloom (Yentsch et al. 1977).

PI values take on added significance as indicators of nutritional status since the report of Laws and Bannister (1980). They developed a mathematical relation for PI as a function of nutrient-limited growth rate common to phosphate, nitrate, or ammonium limitation (Fig. 1). The PI values are insensitive to μ at growth rates greater than about $0.25\,d^{-1}$. The PI ranged from >1 to ~ 5 for μ values $0-0.25\,d^{-1}$ in the model and experimental data, from a cyclostat culture of the diatom *Thalassiosira fluviatilis*. In reviewing the literature values of PI they concluded that phytoplankton in oligotrophic central ocean waters must be growing at rates $<0.25\,d^{-1}$. Such reduced rates must reflect nutrient limitation of growth. If so, nutrient assimilation ratios (C/N, N/P) would be affected and would be expected to depart from the Redfield ratio of 106C:16N:1P (Redfield et al. 1963). Addition of nutrients to such waters would be expected to cause transient changes in C/N and N/P assimilation ratios and cellular composition ratios as described earlier.

Unfortunately, in the ^{15}N stable isotope tracer methodology for measuring ammonium uptake,

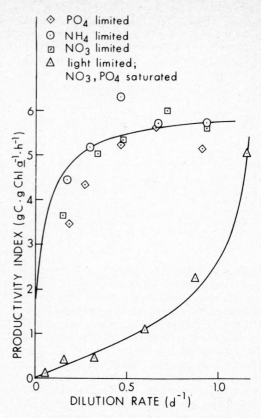

FIG. 1. Photosynthetic carbon assimilation rate per weight of chlorophyll *a* in *Thalassiosira fluviatilis*. Data (from Laws and Bannister 1980) are for nutrient- and light-limited continuous cultures grown on a 12:12 light–dark cycle. Curves were calculated from their growth model.

quantities of [^{15}N]ammonium must be added at concentrations equal to or exceeding ambient levels in oligotrophic waters. The measured N-uptake rates would then be high and not representative of previous N-uptake rates before ^{15}N addition (McCarthy 1981). Considerable agonizing over this problem resulted in tentative corrections for central North Pacific samples (Eppley et al. 1973, 1977). Even with the corrections, however, specific assimilation rates calculated for N exceeded those of C (Sharp et al. 1980). PI values for those samples were only a little greater than 1.0, on average, but varied directly with the N/C ratio of the seston (Sharp et al. 1980).

Glibert and Goldman (1980) examined short-term (5 min–2 h) [^{15}N]ammonium uptake of Vinyard Sound, MA, plankton. Specific uptake rates were low, compared with expected values of μ for coastal plankton. Perhaps this is due to unusually high levels of detrital-N. Nevertheless, the rates declined over time, when saturating concentrations of ammonium were added, as if the plankton in situ were N limited.

Temporal changes in nutrient status — McCarthy and Goldman (1979) have proposed that microscale patchiness of nutrients may be important for phytoplankton growth in nutrient-depleted regions of the oceans. Such patches could result from individual zooplankton and from organic particles colonized by bacteria. They calculated, for example, that small oceanic copepods may release enough ammonium in 5 s to bring the ammonium concentration up to 5 μM in a volume of water equal to the displacement volume of the animal. Their own N-limited chemostat culture data, and other data cited earlier, show quite clearly that the phytoplankton, if sufficiently N depleted, have the capacity to take up ammonium as much as 30 times faster than the steady-state growth rate when the cells are exposed briefly (5 min) to saturating ammonium concentrations (i.e. >1 μM). It is easy to calculate that about twenty 5-min exposures to saturating ammonium concentrations over 24 h would support a growth rate of 0.5 doublings d^{-1}. McCarthy and Goldman (1979) indicated that ammonium concentrations may be <0.03 μM in oligotrophic ocean waters, undetectable with present chemical methods. The postulated microscale patches, perhaps of only a few nanolitres volume, would also be undetectable by present methods.

Exposure of nutrient-deficient phytoplankton intermittently to discrete patches of ammonium or phosphate and the resulting episodes of nutrient uptake and assimilation would effectively uncouple nutrient uptake from photosynthesis and lead to unbalanced growth. The frequency of encountering the patches, as visualized, appears high, relative to the frequency of cell division, however, and the extent of departure from balanced growth might be relatively small. Storage of nutrient in inorganic form within the cells (DeManche et al. 1979) could result in fairly uniform protein synthesis rates over time, depending on the cells' storage capacity for the nutrient, the growth rate, and the frequency of nutrient encounters.

Jackson (1980) carried out an analysis of the effects of diffusion on such microscale patches and concluded the individual nutrient pulses from zooplankters decayed too quickly to serve as the main nutrient source for phytoplankton. Nevertheless, nutrient patches due to large animals and fish schools will persist longer than the postulated micropatches and surely must influence nutrient uptake by phytoplankton.

Perry (1972) used the cell-surface alkaline phosphate activity of the plankton of the central North Pacific as an indication of cellular P status. Activity developed over time when natural samples were incubated. The shortest times for appearance of activity, zero in some cases, were found late in the day, as if the cells became relatively P depleted over the light period and recovered at night.

The potential importance of temporal variation in nutrient availability is brought forth in a report by Turpin and Harrison (1979). They operated ammonium-limited chemostats which differed only in the time variation of ammonium input. One culture had a constant ammonium input, one had eight pulse additions per day, and a third culture had one ammonium addition per day. The total daily additions were the same, only the frequency of addition differed for the three cultures. Uptake rates of ammonium in the three cultures were quite different; rates varied directly with the time between ammonium additions. We can infer that uptake of C and P were uncoupled from N uptake in these experiments although 24-h averages would reflect balanced growth.

The coupling between carbon, nitrogen, and phosphate assimilation by phytoplankton may be altered, leading to departure from balanced growth, in yet another way. The phytoplankton cells, behaving as passive scalers, are carried over several metres in the vertical direction by the semidiurnal internal tide on the continental shelf. Depending on the phase relationship of the semidiurnal internal tide to the daily insolation, the phytoplankton may experience irradiance levels over the course of the day quite different than if the cells remained fixed at one depth in the euphotic zone (Kamykowski 1974). Differences in saturating irradiance for uptake of the different nutrients, C, N, P, Si, and the rates of dark uptake would determine the precise departures from balanced growth in any particular case. Higher frequency internal waves would cause qualitatively similar problems for balanced growth. I know of no detailed analysis of either phenomenon nor their likely importance for balanced growth.

Estimates of Growth Rate of Ocean Phytoplankton

It was easy to review the available estimates of phytoplankton specific growth rate in the ocean in 1972 as only a few were available (Eppley 1972). The early estimates from oligotrophic waters were less than 0.5 doublings per day while estimates for nutrient-rich waters were higher, about 1.0 doublings per day when averaged over the depth of the euphotic zone. Recently Goldman et al. (1979) compiled additional estimates (Table 2). They also proposed that rates in oligotrophic waters are probably high, approaching maximum expected rates, i.e. $\mu \rightarrow \mu_m$. The brief review of Koblentz-Mishke and Vedernikov (1976) also indicated high growth rates in oligotrophic central ocean waters of 6.6 doublings per day. Values were lower in mesotrophic and eutrophic waters, 2.3

257

TABLE 2. Summary of available phytoplankton growth rate data in doublings/day for natural marine waters compiled by Goldman et al. (1979).

Location	Growth rate (doublings / day)[a]	Reference
Sargasso Sea	0.26[b]	
Florida Strait	0.45[b]	
Carolina Coast	0.37[b]	Riley et al. (1949)
Montauk Pt., LI	0.35[b]	
S. California Coast	0.25–0.4[b]	Eppley et al. (1972)
S. California Coast	0.7[b]	Eppley et al. (1970)
N.W. Atlantic	0.2–1.7	Sutcliffe et al. (1970)
N. Pacific	0.2–0.4	Eppley et al. (1973)
Northern N. Pacific	0.36–0.89	Saino and Hattori (1977)
North Sea	0.67–1.33	Cushing (1971)
Sargasso Sea	0.05–0.14	
Tyrrhenian Sea	0.07–0.25	Swift and Durbin (1972)
Baja, California Coast	0.2–1.4	Smayda (1975)
Peru Current	0.67[b]	Strickland et al. (1969)
Peru Current	0.73[b]	Beers et al. (1971)
S.W. Africa Coast	1.0[b]	Hobson (1971)
W. Arabian Sea	>1.0[b]	Ryther and Menzel (1965)
Narragansett Bay, RI	0.4–1.94	Durbin et al. (1975)
Narragansett Bay, RI	<0.1–3.8	Smayda (1973)
Santa Monica Bay, CA	0.3–0.7	Weiler and Chisholm (1976)
Oligotrophic waters	6.6	
Mesotrophic waters	2.3	Koblentz-Mishke and Vedernikov (1976)
Eutrophic waters	0.14	

[a] Doublings/day $\times$ 0.693 = specific growth rate μ.
[b] Obtained from Table 2 in Eppley (1972).

and 0.14 doublings per day, respectively. Nearly all these estimates have been based upon ^{14}C photosynthetic rate and the phytoplankton biomass as carbon.

Actually the only growth rate estimate of Table 2 that appears high to me is the 6.6 divisions per day for oligotrophic, subtropical waters from Koblentz-Mishke and Vedernikov (1976). This estimate was based on photosynthesis rates of many surface samples. Those rates ranged from <0.1 to 10 mg $C \cdot m^{-3} \cdot d^{-1}$, with an average value of 1.0 mg $C \cdot m^{-3} \cdot d^{-1}$. They are essentially identical in range and average with those measured by my colleagues and I in the central gyre of the North Pacific (Eppley et al. 1973; Perry and Eppley 1980; Sharp et al. 1980). The difference in the two data sets is in the estimate of phytoplankton biomass.

Koblentz-Mishke and Vedernikov (1976) acknowledge that their carbon biomass estimates, derived from cell counts, are probably low by at least 50-fold, resulting from the loss of nanoplankton in the preserved samples. Their values ranged from 0.001 to 0.05 with a mean value of 0.01 mg $C \cdot m^{-3}$. Increasing these 50-fold to correct for nanoplankton would raise the average value from 0.01 to 0.5 mg $C \cdot m^{-3}$. This would reduce the growth rate estimate to 1.6 doublings d^{-1}, a rate still higher than their eutrophic

waters and the Scripps estimates of 0.1–0.2 doublings per day (averaged over the upper euphotic zone).

Our mean phytoplankton carbon estimate is about 10 mg $C \cdot m^{-3}$, still 20-fold higher than their value corrected for nanoplankton loss. The SIO values are based upon cell counts, POC, ATP, and chlorophyll a. The cell counts would be subject to nanoplankton losses also. On the other hand, the possible inclusion of heterotrophic flagellates would lead to overestimation of phytoplankton carbon (Beers et al. 1975).

Clearly the phytoplankton biomass estimation is as difficult as the physiological rate measurements. At present both are required for estimating the growth rate of the entire phytoplankton assemblage.

It is always fashionable to criticize existing views, especially if the standing outlook can be termed dogma. For example, "it is now essential to have unequivocal evidence as to what is being measured by the various techniques which can be employed in marine productivity work" was written by McAllister et al. (1964). Nevertheless, the evidence is still equivocal in spite of much careful work in the intervening years. In many cases the problems seem not to lie so much in the quality of the experimental data as in the conceptions and inter-

258

pretations of phytoplankton growth in the sea which guide the measurements.

Originally, it was my intent to review critically the available information on growth-rate measurement. I have been unable to do this constructively and suggest instead some criteria for experimental work and some comparisons that need to be made before drawing generalizations.

1) Published growth rates include values either for near-surface samples from a single depth, or alternatively, rates averaged over the depth of the euphotic zone. The former are usually much greater than the latter but the distinction is not always made clear.

2) Balanced growth and the 24-h light–dark cycle should be considered. Although it may not be feasible to measure rates over 24 h, nevertheless, both daytime and nighttime rates must be considered along with the expected periodicity in rate over the light hours of the day. Rates based upon brief incubations near midday can be expected to give very high values, not representative of balanced growth or of the actual growth of the phytoplankton assemblage in the sea.

3) Calculation of growth rate from nutrient assimilation rate also requires assessment of the elemental content of that nutrient in the phytoplankton. The phytoplankton biomass is just as important as the uptake rate for the growth rate calculation and should be given equal attention.

4) Some existing data sets are not internally consistent. Growth rates reported in one part of a publication may be inconsistent with, for example, productivity indices reported in another section. Internal consistency and corroborating evidence lead to reader confidence.

5) Geographical variation in the productivity index can take place along gradients which so far defy experimental definition in terms of ambient nutrient concentration, chlorophyll content, species composition, etc. For example, Bienfang and Gunderson (1977) found maximum PI values in the euphotic zone of about 3 mg C (mg Chl$a$)$^{-1} \cdot$ h^{-1} 25 km off Oahu in the central North Pacific, but only 1.3 and 1.1 at stations about 100 and 200 km offshore, respectively. Given equal carbon biomass, these PI values imply differences in μ at the three stations, which in other characteristics were nearly identical. Relatively small differences in growth rate could bring about such differences (Laws and Bannister 1980). Thus, it may be superficial to draw generalities for large portions of the oceans. It seems equally unwise to insist on growth rate values to be expected in the various biotic provinces until their horizontal, depth, and temporal variation is defined more fully in terms of phytoplankton dynamics.

Challenges for the Future

The paradigm that substantially complete food webs may operate within the volume of seawater in a productivity bottle, due to overlapping size categories of the planktonic primary producers, herbivores, and decomposers, stresses the need for new approaches in planktonic rate measurements (Sieburth 1977; Peterson 1980). Phytoplankton growth rate is best measured, and incubations in bottles avoided, by assessing the cell division rate in situ. To date this has been successful only with a few large-celled taxa. Primary production (P) would best be estimated as the sum of the product of the growth rate and biomass carbon (B) of each taxon of photoautotrophs

$$P = \sum_{n=1}^{N} (\mu_i \cdot B_i)$$

Such an ideal scheme would also provide the population dynamics of each taxon, information ideally suited for examination of species succession and its causes.

Given a less perfect ability than the ideal above, phytoplankton dynamicists must use other approaches in estimating growth rates under all but the most favorable circumstances. We need not remain content with carrying out incubations over finite time periods in containers of convenient volume, but we seem to be stuck with them for most routine work. If C, N, P, Si uptake and assimilation rate measurements prove unsuitable for growth rate estimation, even when average values over the 24-h light–dark cycle are used along with acceptable biomass measurements, then the only recourses for estimating μ for oceanic phytoplankton are (1) biochemical measurements which determine rates of processes associated with cell division (DNA, RNA, protein synthesis), (2) analysis of the cell cycle of individual taxa or size categories, or (3) to find compositional ratios that reflect absolute rather than relative values of μ.

The present state of the art is to make the rate measurements with several methods at once, for example, with ^{14}C, ^{15}N, and ^{33}P isotopes, and to evaluate temporal changes over the 24-h cycle.

State of the art biomass estimation includes, along with chemical measurements, microscopic measurement of cell dimensions and examination of fresh samples with the fluorescence microscope in order to recognize and differentiate between cells with chlorophyll (presumed to be photoautotrophs) and those without (presumed to be heterotrophs).

At the same time, the physiological state of the phytoplankton assemblage can be judged as an indication of whether growth rates should be high or low relative to the expected μ_m.

Greater understanding is needed also of the dynamics of water motions that bring nutrients into the euphotic zone, at least for those times and places where nutrient input rate is a strong regulator of phytoplankton production. The CUEA upwelling program was successful in combining physical and biological information in the study of upwelling regions. This merger of interest has not yet developed for studies of the most oligotrophic oceanic regions, however.

Chemical information can also be helpful for probing phytoplankton dynamics. Measurement of ambient nutrient levels and cell constituents is already a necessary aspect. Diel periodicity in dissolved materials released or consumed by organisms can provide boundaries on daytime production and night-time respiration. Particle interceptor traps (PITS) can provide, at least in the ideal, the loss rates of particulate materials to depth. The downward loss rate of particulate carbon and nitrogen from the euphotic zone provides a lower limit of primary production in the overlying euphotic zone. What few flux data exist were reviewed earlier (Eppley 1980).

Probably the best approach for the interim is to pursue multiple lines of investigation that bear on the magnitude of plant production, biomass, and growth rate and not to focus too intently on any one of the existing methods of estimating these. We have reason to mistrust all the published growth rate data for the oceans, except, perhaps, for those few data based on microscopic observations of cell division. Actually, the data for coastal waters are fairly harmonious; data are most conflicting for the oligotrophic central oceans.

Acknowledgments

This paper was prepared during a stay at, and with the financial support of, the Friday Harbor Laboratories, University of Washington, Friday Harbor, WA. I thank Doris Osborn for typing the manuscript.

References

AZAM, F., AND S. W. CHISHOLM. 1976. Silicic acid uptake and incorporation by natural marine phytoplankton populations. Limnol. Oceanogr. 21: 427–435.

BARLOW, R. G. 1980. The biochemical composition of phytoplankton in an upwelling region off South Africa. J. Exp. Mar. Biol. Ecol. 45: 83–93.

BEERS, J. R., AND A. C. KELLEY. 1965. Short-term variation of ammonia in the Sargasso Sea off Bermuda. Deep-Sea Res. 12: 21–25.

BEERS, J. R., F. M. H. REID, AND G. L. STEWART. 1975. Microplankton of the North Pacific Central Gyre Population structure and abundance, June 1973. Int. Rev. Gesamten Hydrobiol. 60: 607–638.

BIENFANG, P., AND K. GUNDERSEN. 1977. Light effects on nutrient-limited, oceanic primary production. Mar. Biol. 43: 187–199.

BRAARUD, T. 1945. Experimental studies on marine plankton diatoms. I. Mat. Naturv. Klasse No. 10. 15 p. Avh. norske VidenskAkad, Oslo.

BURNEY, C. M., K. M. JOHNSON, D. M. LAVOIE, AND J. M. SIEBURTH. 1979. Dissolved carbohydrate and microbial ATP in the North Atlantic: concentration and interactions. Deep-Sea Res. 26: 1267–1290.

CHISHOLM, S. W. 1981. Temporal patterns of cell division in unicellular algae. Can. Bull. Fish. Aquat. Sci. 210: 150–181.

CHISHOLM, S. W., AND P. A. NOBBS. 1976. Light/dark-phased cell division in *Euglena gracilis* (Z) (Euglenophyceae) on PO_4-limited continuous culture. J. Phycol. 11: 367–373.

COLLOS, Y., AND G. SLAWYK. 1976. Significance of cellular nitrate content in natural populations of marine phytoplankton growing in shipboard cultures. Mar. Biol. 34: 27–32.

1979. ^{13}C and ^{15}N uptake by marine phytoplankton. I. Influence of nitrogen source and concentration in laboratory cultures of diatoms. J. Phycol. 15: 186–190.

CONWAY, H. L., AND P. J. HARRISON. 1977. Marine diatoms grown in chemostats under silicate or ammonium limitation. IV. Transient responses of *Chaetoceros debilis*, *Skeletonema costatum*, and *Thalassiosira gravida* to a single addition of the limiting nutrient. Mar. Biol. 43: 33–43.

CONWAY, H. L., P. J. HARRISON, AND C. O. DAVIS. 1976. Marine diatoms grown in chemostats under silicate or ammonium limitation. III. Transient response of *Skeletonema costatum* to a single addition of the limiting nutrient. Mar. Biol. 35: 187–199.

COOMBS, J., P. J. HALICKI, O. HOLM-HANSEN, AND B. E. VOLCANI. 1967. Studies on the biochemistry and fine structure of silica shell formation in diatoms. II. Changes in concentration of nucleoside triphosphates in silicon-starvation synchrony of *Navicula pelliculosa* (Breb.) Hilse. Exp. Cell Res. 47: 315–328.

CURL, H. JR., AND L. F. SMALL. 1965. Variations in photosynthetic assimilation ratios in natural marine phytoplankton communities. Limnol. Oceanogr. 10 (Suppl.): 67–73.

DAVIS, C. O., P. J. HARRISON, AND R. C. DUGDALE. 1973. Continuous culture of marine diatoms under silicate limitation. I. Synchronized life cycle of *Skeletonema costatum*. J. Phycol. 9: 175–180.

DEMANCHE, J. M., H. C. CURL JR., D. W. LUNDY, AND P. L. DONAGHAY. 1979. The rapid response of the marine diatom *Skeletonema costatum* to changes in external and internal nutrient concentration. Mar. Biol. 53: 323–333.

DONAGHAY, P. L., J. M. DEMANCHE, AND L. F. SMALL. 1978. On predicting phytoplankton growth rates from carbon:nitrogen ratios. Limnol. Oceanogr. 23: 359–362.

DOTY, M. S. 1959. Phytoplankton photosynthetic periodicity as a function of latitude. J. Mar. Biol. Assoc. India 1: 66–68.

DOTY, M. S., AND M. OGURI. 1957. Evidence for a photosynthetic daily periodicity. Limnol. Oceanogr. 2: 37 –40.

DROOP, M. R. 1970. Vitamin B_{12} and marine ecology. V. Continuous culture as an approach to nutritional kinetics. Helgoland. Wiss. Meeresunters. 20: 629–636.

ELBRÄCHTER, M. 1973. Population dynamics of *Ceratium* in coastal waters of Kiel Bay. Oikos (Suppl.) 15: 43–48.

EPPLEY, R. W. 1972. Temperature and phytoplankton growth in the sea. Fish. Bull. (US) 70: 1063–1085.
——— 1980. Estimating phytoplankton growth rates in the central oligotrophic oceans. Brookhaven Symp. Biol. 31: 231–242.

EPPLEY, R. W., A. F. CARLUCCI, O. HOLM-HANSEN, D. KIEFER, E. VENRICK, AND P. M. WILLIAMS. 1971a. Phytoplankton growth and composition in shipboard cultures supplied with nitrate, ammonium, or urea and the nitrogen source. Limnol. Oceanogr. 16: 741–751.

EPPLEY, R. W., W. G. HARRISON, S. W. CHISHOLM, AND E. STEWART. 1977. Particulate organic matter in surface waters off Southern California and its relation to phytoplankton. J. Mar. Res. 35: 671–696.

EPPLEY, R. W., AND E. H. RENGER. 1974. Nitrogen assimilation of an oceanic diatom in nitrogen-limited continuous culture. J. Phycol. 10: 15–23.

EPPLEY, R. W., E. H. RENGER, E. L. VENRICK, AND M. M. MULLIN. 1973. A study of plankton dynamics and nutrient cycling in the central gyre of the North Pacific Ocean. Limnol. Oceanogr. 18: 534–551.

EPPLEY, R. W., J. N. ROGERS, J. J. McCARTHY, AND A. SOURNIA. 1971b. Light/dark periodicity in nitrogen assimilation of the marine phytoplankters *Skeletonema costatum* and *Coccolithus huxleyi* in N-limited chemostat culture. J. Phycol. 7: 150–154.

EPPLEY, R. W., AND J. D. H. STRICKLAND. 1968. Kinetics of marine phytoplankton growth, p. 23–62. *In* M. Droop and E. J. Ferguson Wood [ed.] Advances in microbiology of the sea. Vol. 1. Academic Press, London.

FALKOWSKI, P. G., AND D. P. STONE. 1975. Nitrate uptake in marine phytoplankton: energy sources and the interaction with carbon fixation. Mar. Biol. 32: 77–84.

GLIBERT, P. M., AND J. C. GOLDMAN. 1981. Rapid ammonium uptake by natural marine phytoplankton. Mar. Biol. Lett. 2: 25–31.

GOERING, J. J., R. C. DUGDALE, AND D. W. MENZEL. 1964. Cyclic diurnal variations in the uptake of ammonia and nitrate by photosynthetic organisms in the Sargasso Sea. Limnol. Oceanogr. 9: 448–451.

GOERING, J. J., D. M. NELSON, AND J. A. CARTER. 1973. Silicic acid uptake by natural populations of marine phytoplankton. Deep-Sea Res. 20: 777–790.

GOLDMAN, J. C., J. J. McCARTHY, AND D. G. PEAVEY. 1979. Growth rate influence on the chemical composition of phytoplankton in oceanic waters. Nature (London) 279: 210–215.

HANDA, N. 1975. The diurnal variation of organic constituents of particulate matter in coastal water, p. 125–132. *In* S. Mori and G. Yamamoto [ed.] JIBP synthesis. Univ. Tokyo Press 12.

HARRISON, W. G., F. AZAM, E. H. RENGER, AND R. W. EPPLEY. 1977. Some experiments on phosphate assimilation by coastal marine plankton. Mar. Biol. 40: 9–18.

HARVEY, W. A., AND J. CAPERON. 1976. The rate of utilization of urea, ammonium, and nitrate by natural populations of marine phytoplankton in a eutrophic environment. Pac. Sci. 30: 329–340.

HOLM-HANSEN, O. 1970. ATP levels in algal cells as influenced by environmental conditions. Plant Cell Physiol. 11: 689–700.

JACKSON, G. A. 1980. Phytoplankton growth and zooplankton grazing in oligotrophic oceans. Nature (London) 284: 439–441.

KAMYKOWSKI, D. 1974. Possible interactions between phytoplankton and semi-diurnal internal tides. J. Mar. Res. 34: 499–509.

KOBLENTZ-MISHKE, O. J., AND V. I. VEDERNIKOV. 1976. A tentative comparison of primary production and phytoplankton quantities at the ocean surface. Mar. Sci. Commun. 2: 357–374.

KOBLENTZ-MISHKE, O. J., V. V. VOLKOVINSKY, AND J. G. KABANOVA. 1970. Plankton primary production of the world ocean, p. 183–193. *In* W. Wooster [ed.] Scientific exploration of the South Pacific. NAS, Washington, DC.

LAWS, E. A., AND T. T. BANNISTER. 1980. Nutrient- and light-limited growth of *Thalassiosira fluviatilis* in continuous culture, with implications for phytoplankton growth in the ocean. Limnol. Oceanogr. 25: 457–473.

LAWS, E. A., AND D. C. L. WONG. 1978. Studies of carbon and nitrogen metabolism by three marine phytoplankton species in nitrate-limited continuous culture. J. Phyco!. 14: 406–416.

LORENZEN, C. J. 1963. Diurnal variation in phytosynthetic activity of natural phytoplankton populations. Limnol. Oceanogr. 8: 56–62.

McALLISTER, C. D., N. SHAH, AND J. D. H. STRICKLAND. 1964. Marine phytoplankton photosynthesis as a function of light intensity; a comparison of methods. J. Fish. Res. Board Canada 21: 159–181.

McCARTHY, J. J. 1981. The kinetics of nutrient utilization. Can. Bull. Fish. Aquat. Sci. 210: 211–233.

McCARTHY, J. J., AND J. C. GOLDMAN. 1979. Nitrogenous nutrition of marine phytoplankton in nutrient-depleted waters. Science (Washington, D.C.) 203: 670–672.

MacCAULL, W. A., AND T. PLATT. 1976. Diel variations in the photosynthetic parameters of coastal marine phytoplankton. Limnol. Oceanogr. 22: 723–731.

MacISAAC, J. J., AND R. C. DUGDALE. 1972. Interactions of light and inorganic nitrogen in controlling nitrate uptake in the sea. Deep-Sea Res. 19: 209–232.

MALONE, T. C. 1971. Diurnal rhythms in netplankton and nannoplankton assimilation ratios. Mar. Biol. 10: 285–289.

MALONE, T. C., C. GARSIDE, K. C. HAINES, AND O. A. ROELS. 1975. Nitrate uptake and growth of *Chaeto-*

ceros sp. in large outdoor continuous cultures. Limnol. Oceanogr. 20: 9–19.

MITCHISON, J. M. 1973. The biology of the cell cycle. Cambridge Univ. Press, London. 312 p.

MORRIS, I., C. M. YENTSCH, AND C. S. YENTSCH. 1971. The physiological state with respect to nitrogen of phytoplankton from low-nutrient subtropical water as measured by the effect of ammonium ion on dark carbon dioxide fixation. Limnol. Oceanogr. 16: 859–868.

MULLER-HAECKEL, A. 1965. Tagesperiodik des Siliciumgehaltes in einem Fliesswasser. Oikos 16: 232–233.

MYKLESTAD, S. 1977. Production of carbohydrates by marine planktonic diatoms. II. Influence of the N/P ratio in the growth medium on the assimilation ratio, growth rate, and production of cellular and extracellular carbohydrates by *Chaetoceros affinis* var. Willei (Gran) Hustedt and *Skeletenema costatum* (Grev.) Cleve. J. Exp. Mar. Biol. Ecol. 29: 161–179.

MYKLESTAD, S., AND A. HAUG. 1972. Production of carbohydrates by the marine diatom *Chaetoceros affinis* var. *willei* (Gran) Hustedt. I. Effect of concentration of nutrients in the culture medium. J. Exp. Mar. Biol. Ecol. 9: 125–136.

MYERS, J. 1951. Physiology of the algae. Annu. Rev. Microbiol. 5: 157–180.

NELSON, D. M., AND L. E. BRAND. 1979. Cell division periodicity in 13 species of marine phytoplankton on a light:dark cycle. J. Phycol. 15: 67–75.

OVIATT, C. A., A. L. GALL, AND S. W. NIXON. 1972. Environmental effects of Atlantic menhaden on surrounding waters. Chesapeake Sci. 13: 321–323.

PAASCHE, E. 1968. Marine plankton algae grown with light:dark cycles. II. *Ditylum brightwellii* and *Nitzschia turgidula*. Physiol. Plant. 21: 66–77.

PAERL, H. W., AND L. A. MACKENZIE. 1979. A comparative study of the diurnal carbon fixation patterns of nannoplankton and net plankton. Limnol. Oceanogr. 22: 732–738.

PERRY, M. J. 1972. Alkaline phosphatase activity in subtropical central North Pacific waters using a sensitive fluorometric method. Mar. Biol. 15: 113–119.

——— 1976. Phosphate utilization by an oceanic diatom in phosphorus-limited chemostat culture and in the oligotrophic waters of the central North Pacific. Limnol. Oceanogr. 21: 88–107.

PERRY, M. J., AND R. W. EPPLEY. 1980. Phosphate uptake by phytoplankton in the central North Pacific Ocean. Deep-Sea Res. 27: 39–49.

PETERSON, B. J. 1980. Aquatic primary productivity and the ^{14}C–CO_2 method: a history of the productivity problem. Annu. Rev. Ecol. Syst. 11: 359–385.

PETERSON, B. J., J. P. BARLOW, AND A. E. SAVAGE. 1974. The physiological state with respect to phosphorus of Cayuga Lake phytoplankton. Limnol. Oceanogr. 19: 396–408.

POSTMA, H., AND J. W. ROMMETS. 1979. Dissolved and particulate organic carbon in the North Equatorial Current of the Atlantic Ocean. Nether. J. Sea Res. 13: 85–98.

REDFIELD, A. C., B. H. KETCHUM, AND F. A. RICHARDS. 1963. The influence of organisms on the composition of seawater, p. 26–77. *In* M. N. Hill [ed.] The sea. Vol. 2. Interscience Publishers, New York, NY.

RESHKIN, S. J., AND G. A. KNAUER. 1979. Light stimulation of phosphate uptake in natural assemblages of phytoplankton. Limnol. Oceanogr. 24: 1121–1124.

RILEY, G. A., H. STOMMEL, AND D. F. BUMPUS. 1949. Quantitative ecology of the plankton of the western North Atlantic. Bull. Bingham Oceanogr. Coll. 12: 1–169.

RYTHER, J. H., AND W. M. DUNSTAN. 1971. Nitrogen, phosphorus and eutrophication in the coastal marine environment. Science (Washington, D.C.) 171: 1008–1013.

RYTHER, J. H., D. W. MENZEL, AND R. F. VACCARO. 1961. Diurnal variations in some chemical and biological properties of the Sargasso Sea. Limnol. Oceanogr. 6: 149–153.

SAKSHAUG, E., AND O. HOLM-HANSEN. 1977. Chemical composition of *Skeletonema costatum* (Grev.) Cleve and *Pavlova* (Monochrysis) *lutheri* (Droop) Green as a function of nitrate-, phosphate-, and iron-limited growth. J. Exp. Mar. Biol. Ecol. 29: 1–34.

SAKSHAUG, E., AND S. MYKLESTAD. 1973. Studies on the phytoplankton ecology of the Trondheimsfjord. III. Dynamics of phytoplankton blooms in relation to environmental factors; bioassay experiments and parameters for the physiological state of the populations. J. Exp. Mar. Biol. Ecol. 11: 157–188.

SELLNER, K. G. 1981. Primary productivity and the flux of dissolved organic matter in several marine environments. Mar. Biol. (In press)

SHARP, J. H., M. J. PERRY, E. H. RENGER, AND R. W. EPPLEY. 1980. Phytoplankton rate processes in the oligotrophic waters of the central North Pacific Ocean. J. Plankton Res. 2: 335–353.

SHUTER, B. 1979. A model of physiological adaptation in unicellular algae. J. Theor. Biol. 78: 519–552.

SIEBURTH, J. M. 1977. International Helgoland Symposium: Convenor's report on the informal session on biomass and productivity of microorganisms in planktonic ecosystems. Helgolander Wiss. Meeresunters. 30: 697–704.

SMAYDA, T. J. 1975. Phased cell division in natural populations of the marine diatom *Ditylum brightwellii* and the potential significance of diel phytoplankton behavior in the sea. Deep-Sea Res. 22: 151–165.

SOEDER, C. J. 1965. Some aspects of phytoplankton growth and activity, p. 47–59. *In* C. R. Goldman [ed.] Primary productivity in aquatic environments. Mem. Ist. Idrobiol. 18 (Suppl.).

SOROKIN, C., AND J. MYERS. 1957. The course of respiration in the life cycle of *Chlorella* cells. J. Gen. Physiol. 40: 579–592.

SOURNIA, A. 1974. Circadian periodicities in natural populations of marine phytoplankton. Adv. Mar. Biol. 12: 325–389.

STROSS, R. G., S. W. CHISHOLM, AND T. A. DOWNING. 1973. Cause of daily rhythms in photosynthetic rates of phytoplankton. Biol. Bull. 145: 200–209.

SVERDRUP, H. V. 1955. The place of physical oceanography in oceanographic research. J. Mar. Res. 14: 287–294.

SWEENEY, B. M., AND J. W. HASTINGS. 1958. Rhythmic cell division in populations of *Gonyaulax polyedra*. J. Protozool. 5: 217–224.

SWIFT, E., AND E. G. DURBIN. 1972. The phased division and cytological characteristics of *Pyrocystis* spp. can be used to estimate doubling times of the population in the sea. Deep-Sea Res. 19: 189–198.

SWIFT, E., M. STUART, AND V. MEUNIER. 1976. The *in situ* growth rates of some deep-living oceanic dinoflagellates: *Pyrocystis fusiformis* and *Pyrocystis noctiluca*. Limnol. Oceanogr. 21: 418–426.

SYRETT, P. J. 1958. Respiration rate and internal adenosine triphosphate concentration in *Chlorella*. Arch. Biochem. Biophys. 75: 117–124.

TAMIYA, H. 1966. Synchronous cultures of algae. Annu. Rev. Plant Physiol. 17: 1–26.

THOMAS, W. H. 1970. On nitrogen deficiency in tropical Pacific oceanic phytoplankton: photosynthetic parameters in poor and rich water. Limnol. Oceanogr. 15: 380–385.

TIJSSEN, S. B. 1979. Diurnal oxygen rhythm and primary production in the mixed layer of the Atlantic Ocean at 20°N. Nether. J. Sea Res. 13: 79–84.

TURPIN, D. H., AND P. J. HARRISON. 1979. Limiting nutrient patchiness and its role in phytoplankton ecology. J. Exp. Mar. Biol. Ecol. 39: 151–166.

WALSH, G. E. 1965. Studies on dissolved carbohydrate in Cape Cod waters. II. Diurnal fluctuations in Oyster Pond. Limnol. Oceanogr. 10: 577–582.

WEILER, C. S. 1980. Population structure and *in situ* division rates of *Ceratium* in oligotrophic waters of the North Pacific Central Gyre. Limnol. Oceanogr. 25: 610–619.

WEILER, C. S., AND S. W. CHISHOLM. 1976. Phased cell division in natural populations of marine dinoflagellates from shipboard cultures. J. Exp. Mar. Biol. Ecol. 25: 239–247.

WEILER, C. S., AND D. M. KARL. 1979. Diel changes in phased-dividing cultures of *Ceratium furca* (Dinophyceae): nucleotide triphosphates, adenylate energy charge, cell carbon and patterns of vertical migration. J. Phycol. 15: 384–391.

YENTSCH, C. M., C. S. YENTSCH, AND L. R. STRUBE. 1977. Variations in ammonium enhancement, an indication of nitrogen deficiency in New England coastal phytoplankton populations. J. Mar. Res. 35: 539–555.

ZENTARA, S.-J., AND D. KAMYKOWSKI. 1977. Latitudinal relationships among temperature and selected plant nutrients along the west coast of North and South America. J. Mar. Res. 35: 321–337.

Competition Among Phytoplankton Based on Inorganic Macronutrients

SERGE Y. MAESTRINI AND DANIEL J. BONIN

Station marine d'Endoume
Chemin de la Batterie des Lions
F 13007 Marseille, France

Introduction

Theories and tentative models of competition established to give a scientific basis to the "struggle for life" were stimulated first by observations made on animal species (Lotka 1920, 1934; Volterra 1926; Volterra and d'Ancona 1935). Since Gause (1932a, b), theories have been developed to describe the respective behavior of two or more species inhabiting the same niche and competing for the same food. They apply very well to microorganisms sharing the same pool of nutrients. All such models have been based on the assumption that, as a population becomes more dense, the conditions of life become more severe and increase the rate of mortality or decrease the rate of growth, or both. The particular mechanism by which an individual inhibits the growth of another of the same or of a different competing species is usually left vague, or interpreted in terms of resources. The rationale is that rates of growth decrease because the available food decreases as the population increases.

Because all algae require the same major nutrients (except silicon used in great amounts only by diatoms) which they take up from a common water resource pool, and because Liebig (1840) stated that plants are limited by the one nutrient that is least available relative to the plants requirements for growth, the models established from data on animals have implicitly been considered to be valid also for plant competition. It is demonstrative, for instance, that all the basic background cited by Hutchinson (1961) in his classic paper includes only such references. Thus, algal competition was also perceived to operate on the basis that the one species best able to obtain and assimilate the actual limiting nutrient should take the upper hand and outgrow the other competing species. Thus, by measuring the relevant uptake or/and growth parameters and comparing them to the nutrient contents of waters, one could hope to predict the species dominance and its succession in time and space. However, recently a few authors claimed to have evidence that natural oceanic phytoplankton is not nutrient limited. According to this new concept, nutrient competition should be considered as having little effect on the species competition and succession, which is then thought to be controlled by other processes, such as selective grazing, whose importance has previously been underestimated.

Trying to appreciate the arguments of both sides by criticizing the main contributions seems to us a sufficient goal for this review; an exhaustive listing of published papers is certainly useless here and most of the foremost knowledge on algal nutrition mechanisms is summarized in other chapters by R. Dugdale, R. Eppley, and J. McCarthy.

Resource-Based Competition Between Algae

THE PHYSIOLOGICAL BASIS

Monod (1942) presented a mathematical model expressing the fact that the growth rate of a microorganism increases with increasing concentrations of the nutrient limiting growth, but that there is a limit to this increase. The growth model is described by a rectangular hyperbola which is virtually identical with the one of Michaelis and Menten (1913) for representation of enzyme kinetics. Therefore, the constants used to represent the specific growth and uptake features are homologous. The so-called maximum specific growth rates and the specific half-saturation constants have come into common use in microbiology, including also the study of aquatic microheterotrophs since Parsons and Strickland (1962).

Efforts to extend the hyperbolic model to phytoplankton were attempted first by Droop (1961) who studied the uptake of vitamin B_{12} by the rock pool flagellate *Pavlova lutheri* (formerly *Monochrysis lutheri*). The kinetics he first recorded did not follow the model, but this was a result of inadequate technical approach (batch culture), as he demonstrated later using continuous culturing. On the contrary, Price and Carell (1964) obtained data from batch culture with *Euglena gracilis* that fit a hyperbola, but they did not discuss this feature. Then, Caperon (1967) discussed the applicability of the hyperbolic model to the growth of a nitrogen-limited flagellate, *Iso-*

chrysis galbana, and demonstrated it fits quite well. But emphasis and detailed discussion with respect to natural populations were the contributions of Dugdale (1967), whose article has become classic. The important point of his concept is that the concentration of a limiting nutrient is set by the magnitude of loss rate and by the Michaelis–Menten parameters of the natural phytoplankton. Thus, the system is considered as regulating itself through the interaction between algae and nutrients and these interactions are dynamic. Dugdale demonstrated the importance of the growth kinetic characteristics in the study of species competition and succession. He postulated that species characteristic of nutrient-poor waters are expected to show low values for maximum uptake rate and half-saturation constant, and species of nutrient-rich waters opposite values; this was fully demonstrated a little later.

Soon after Dugdale's stimulating theory, other authors demonstrated that the model was obeyed both by laboratory-cultured algae (Caperon 1968; Gates and Marlar 1968; Eppley and Coatsworth 1969) and by natural populations (MacIsaac and Dugdale 1969). The models based on a linear effect of nutrient concentration on growth (Steele 1959; Riley 1963) were definitively displaced. However, further contributions beginning with Caperon (1968) and Droop (1968) and reviewed by Dugdale (1977) pointed out that substitution of growth for nutrient uptake is valid only in the steady state of a continuous culture limited by organic carbon. That was the case in Monod's (1942) carbon-limited bacterial culture, but it does not generally occur in natural waters; with other limiting nutrients, growth and uptake are uncoupled. Price and Carell (1964) and Price and Quigley (1966) were the first to suggest the existence of an internal pool of nutrients, namely iron and zinc, in their study on *Euglena gracilis*, but their statement was not related to a general concept of growth and uptake. That was done by Caperon (1968) and Droop (1968) who hypothesized that growth rate is most likely related to the intracellular nutrient reservoir. In this case, the nutrient history of the phytoplankton becomes important. Ability of a cell to store nutrients is a considerable advantage, because a cell with high rate of uptake that spends only a brief time in a nutrient-rich deep water would have a very high growth potential when returning to lighted surface waters (Caperon 1968). Dinoflagellates that migrate below the thermocline during the nights and return to the surface during the days (Dugdale and Goering 1967; Holmes et al. 1967) are a fascinating example of this mechanism.

The introduction of a second compartment had already improved the concept of algal growth as a function of nutrient processes in natural waters. However, the two-compartment model does not specifically distinguish between intracellular storage issued from luxury uptake and elements that have been incorporated into the biochemically active cell material. That was done through the introduction of a three-compartment model by Grenney et al. (1973) who separated the extracellular pool of nutrients, the intracellular reservoir of inorganic nutrients, the intermediate organic compounds, and the constitutive molecules of the biomass.

At that time, supporters of the cell quota models (= two-compartment model) claimed that it is not necessary to consider the biochemical details of the cell processes as internal nutrient pools represent only a few percent of the total cell nutrients, and challenged supporters of the internal-pool model (= three-compartment model). The contention has produced abundant literature of comments and replies, from which it seems to us that the cell-quota models are fitted quite well to steady-state systems while the internal-pool models apply better to natural dynamic conditions. Hence, for predicting the behavior of two or more species competing for the same nutrients, the former are probably more useful in laboratory experiments and the latter in field observations. Yet, one should not forget that the nutrient reservoir, if any, may have been supplied by the parent cells of those studied, and the true competition may have taken place long before the observed situation.

Thus, the physiological processes of algal nutrition now appear to be considerably more complicated than one would have expected two decades ago. Yet, Droop (1974) suggested that the whole algal machinery might adapt to external conditions by shifting from "fast-adapted cells" to "slow-adapted cells," and vice versa. Therefore, the same species might show two sets of quite different kinetic constants. The fast-adapted cells, which appear only in nutrient-rich medium, have a high subsistence quota (Droop's k_Q); nevertheless, they divide very fast. The slow-adapted cells are the common cells; their k_Q is low, and their division rate also. Further researches reported by Harrison et al. (1976) and Conway et al. (1976) confirmed this hypothesis by demonstrating the diatom *Skeletonema costatum* can have two such physiological states. This is not unique among microorganisms, however, as an homologous mechanism has been already described for bacteria (Schaechter 1968; Bremer and Dennis 1975), under the name of "shift-up" and "shift-down" process; other algal species will probably show such a pattern when studied.

Otherwise, Law and Button (1977) criticized the rationale of expressing species-specific constants, because the K values are dependent on U_{max} and because their measurements lead to imprecise data ($\pm 100\%$). They proposed a new parameter: the "affinity" of an organism to a substrate, which pertains to microalgae as well as bacteria (Button 1978). They concluded that nutrients taken up and stored in the internal nutrient pool may leak back through the cell envelope because of excess accumulation, but that they are also transported to the cell deficient in macromolecules and assimilated. To summarize, affinity is "either a measure of effective collision between substrate and transport site, or a measure of the absolute substrate flux at low concentration normalized against substrate concentration and cell population." Button (1978) stressed the importance of affinity in evaluating the competitive ability of an organism in a nutrient-limited system, but available data on this parameter are rare.

NUTRIENT-BASED ALGAL COMPETITION: THEORIES, EXPERIMENTAL STUDIES

During the past two decades, the nutrition of individual species of algae has stimulated much research in the laboratory, which has led to several models, as summarized above. Natural populations have also been studied and modeled using the same approaches. Thence, it is surprising that little has been done to observe the concomitant behaviors of two or more species sharing the same nutrient pool in the same ecological niche or experimental vessel. It was also a surprise to us that we could not find a review fully and specifically dedicated to nutrient-based algal competition, and that the few articles dealing with this topic are introduced typically by such a sentence: "Classical ecological competition concept" without any citation, or by referring to one of the models established for single species growth. That concepts established for other organisms, especially bacteria, have been implicitly considered as also valid for algae is obvious. Nothing clear-cut was available until Titman (1976), who first associated the words "algae" and "resource-based competition" for a tentative prediction of a two-species experimental competition, but several authors had already included this idea in models established to describe the nutrient limitation of algal growth. Besides such particular contributions, several authors have referred to nutrient competition as a whole to explain some specific dominance in natural or experimental situations (e.g. Elbrächter 1977).

Use of single species nutrient-kinetic constants — Dugdale (1967) emphasized the ecological advantage given to an alga by the set of physiological adaptations represented by a low half-saturation constant (K) and a high maximum growth rate (μ_{max}). He discussed the question of whether the species with lower μ_{max} values also have lower K that would enable them to compete with species with high specific uptake rate (U_{max}) values, when living in oligotrophic waters. On the other hand, eutrophicated waters should be inhabited mostly by fast-growing species, because, as nutrients are more abundant, ability to take them up at low concentrations is not as important, and natural selection will tend to favor organisms capable of dividing rapidly. Although other adaptative processes like predator defense, ability to remain suspended in the photic layer, and growth responses to temperature and illumination variations contribute to the success of a species, Dugdale's hypothesis was complete in itself and stimulated research for almost a decade.

The simplest application of the model, i.e. the comparison of the K and U_{max} values of species competing for the same limiting nutrient, was done soon after Dugdale's paper. Eppley and Coatsworth (1968), Eppley and Thomas (1969), and Eppley et al. (1969) hypothesized that species involved sequentially in a seasonal succession of dominant species related to declining nutrient concentrations should be ordered by lower and lower K values. Then they measured the kinetic constant values of 16 cultured species of phytoplankton and made calculations by combining the K and U_{max} values for nitrogen with irradiance and temperature. Results obtained showed, as expected, that the coastal diatom, *Asterionella japonica*, has a higher K value for nitrate uptake (1.3 μg-at·L^{-1}) than an isolate of *Chaetoceros gracilis* from the open sea (0.3 μg-at· L^{-1}). In general terms, they remarked that algal K (NO$_3$) decreasing values paralleled a succession of aquatic natural niches, namely freshwater ponds, estuarines, and marine coastal waters and oceanic waters. This obviously reflects an adaptation to decreasing nitrogen richness of waters. They suggested that an alga like the coccolitophorid *Coccolithus huxleyi* is a good competitor when nitrogen concentration and irradiance are low. On the contrary, laboratory results predicted that the diatoms *Ditylum brightwellii* and *Skeletonema costatum* would grow faster than *C. huxleyi* at high irradiance and nitrogen available at a concentration higher than 1.5 μg-at–N·L^{-1}. Hence, in the California coastal waters studied, *C. huxleyi* would predominate over diatoms unless upwelling increased the nitrate concentration in surface water; then diatoms would fare better. This was actually observed and confirmed later by Estrada and Blasco (1979). Carpenter and Guillard (1971) and Guillard et al. (1973) also compared the kinetic constant values of nitrogen- and silicon-limited growth of estuarine and oceanic strains of the algae *Bellorochia* sp., *Fragilaria pinnata*, and *Thalassiosira pseudonana*. Data obtained demonstrated that clones isolated from oceanic low-nutrient area, i.e. Sargasso Sea, have K (NO$_3$) values ranging from 0.25 μg-at·L^{-1}, while those of the same species taken from estuarine or eutrophicated water have K values from 1.6 μg-at·L^{-1} to 6.8 μg-at·L^{-1}.

Isolates from continental shelf areas have intermediate or low K values. These differences between clones are paralleled by those observed in silica uptake kinetics, which are 5 times higher for K and 1.6 times higher for U_{max}. These authors concluded that physiological races of phytoplankton are adapted to high- or low-nutrient levels. Another similar supporting contribution is Qasim et al. (1973), who determined the phosphate and nitrate requirements of the diatom, *Biddulphia sinensis*, and the dinoflagellate, *Ceratium furca*, and showed that the diatom, which is a large-celled organism, has higher K values than the dinoflagellate for both elements. When comparing the seasonal variations in abundance and the averaged monthly concentrations of the two ions in the Cochin Backwater area, they remarked that at low nutrient concentration *C. furca* appears to be at an advantage. At slightly higher concentrations of the two nutrients, *B. sinensis* begins to predominate. When heavy rainfall and subsequent land runoff have enriched the coastal waters, *C. furca* is scarce enough not to be recorded while the diatom blooms. Natural populations seem to behave similarly according to MacIsaac and Dugdale (1969), who measured nitrogen uptake in varied seawaters. They reported that populations from oligotrophic areas show a $K = 0.2 \ \mu g\text{-at} \cdot L^{-1}$, in corresponding eutrophic regions $K = 1.0 \ \mu g\text{-at} \cdot L^{-1}$, and also K values measured in laboratory cultures correspond to those given for eutrophic regions.

Research devoted to the role of carbon is rare and usually focuses on freshwater species. Goldman et al. (1974) measured the inorganic carbon limited growths of *Selenastrum capricornutum* and *Scenedesmus quadricauda*. On the basis of kinetic values obtained, they predict that, in a mixed culture, *S. quadricauda* will eliminate *S. capricornutum*. An experiment done in continuous culture proved this prediction correct. After 7 d, the dominant species represented 86–93% of the total biomass, when initial respective biomasses were equivalent. King and Novak (1974), who discussed these data, demonstrated that inorganic carbon would never be rate limiting for algal growth. However, they suggested that a succession of algal types can occur, when species capable of existing on progressively lower concentrations of CO_2 are present, with an ultimate dominance of cyanophyta, apparently the algae (= cyanobacteria) best able to use very low concentrations of inorganic carbon. Such a statement is also defended by Pruder and Bolton (1979). However, since they reported that the advantage given to some species by their capability to directly take up HCO_3^-, or by having a functional carbonic anhydrase, will appear only below $2 \ \mu M\text{-}CO_2 \cdot L^{-1}$ (= 0.088 mg $CO_2 \cdot L^{-1}$), the so-called advantage is certainly rarely acting. Alhgren (1977) also re-corded the kinetic constant values of the cyanophyta, *Oscillatoria agardhii*, and remarked the μ_{max} he obtained was consistent with the turn over times of carbon in lake waters where this organism is strongly dominant. Then, by comparing these values with those of the green alga, *Selenastrum capricornutum*, he predicted the cyanophyta would out-compete the green alga when nutrient reserve decreases below $0.2 \ \mu g\text{-at-N} \cdot L^{-1}$ and $0.03 \ \mu g\text{-at-P} \cdot L^{-1}$. Brown and Harris (1978) and Brown and Button (1979) examined in detail the ability of *S. capricornutum* to compete for orthophosphate when P limits algal growth (frequently the case in fresh waters), and concluded that it will not be growth-competitive with some other common aquatic autotrophs such as *Nostoc* sp. They also reported some peculiar kinetic features that will be discussed.

Thus, it seems to be well established that specific kinetic constants reflect quite well the algal ability to compete for nutrient partition, and that natural populations are nutrient adapted. Thence, the corollary, i.e. the in situ limiting factor of uptake rate and, hence, of growth, is determined by comparing K values and naturally occurring nutrient concentrations and/or by comparing actual U and U_{max} (Thomas 1970a, b; Paasche 1973; Smayda 1973; MacIsaac et al. 1974, 1979; Perry 1976). However, Carpenter and Guillard (1971) pointed out that consideration should be given to the history of the test strains to verify that kinetic values have not changed during maintenance in culture collection. That leads to the question: are the differences observed adaptive or selective? In other words, are the geographic strains a result of Darwinian selection or are the algae able to adapt their cell machinery to varied conditions? Because no physiological measurements were usually made immediately after isolation, no experimental data are available to ascertain that cultured cells have not changed at all. However, comparisons by Yoder (1979) between the cell division rate of natural populations of the diatom, *Skeletonema costatum*, grown in dialysis bags, and that predicted from a mathematical model based on laboratory data for cultured strains, supports the validity of the model and, therefore, indicates that algae remain physiologically unchanged in maintenance cultures. Moreover, Maestrini and Kossut (1981) demonstrated that the elemental composition, namely C/N, C/proteins, C/P, C/ATP, and C/chlorophyll a ratios, is restored promptly to a natural level when cells taken from culture collection are grown in situ in oligotrophic waters.

Comparison of theoretically predicted and observed behavior in phytoplankton communities — Whereas the preceding authors attempted to apply laboratory-obtained kinetic constant values to the algae of natural habitats, others endeavored to use the hyperbolic model to predict the steady-state outcome of competition between two or several species growing in controlled conditions. Generally such experiments were devised to test the validity of the models, and usually did, but frequently the methods represented an oversimplification, so their conclusions are not free of criticism.

Ross's (1973) attractive title is in fact a mathematical speculation free from considerations of the physiological patterns of the observed organisms, namely diatoms, that makes it useless for our application. Nevertheless, Ross's model predicts that the total biomass of two algae competing in the nutrient-balanced medium of a continuous culture is smaller than the sum of the individual biomasses at equilibrium in separated unialgal cultures. General considerations of Stewart and Levin (1973) and Taylor and Williams (1975) apply to all microorganisms, because they are based on the hyperbolic kinetics of growth, limited by one nutrient. Taylor and Williams' theoretical work led to several particularly interesting conclusions. They found that a mixed population growing in a continuous-flow system could remain in equilibrium if there were at least as many growth-limiting nutrients as there were different species. They predicted that aquatic biota, where a single or a few nutrients are limiting growth of microorganisms, will tend to produce populations of low species diversity. But they also stated that species that are unsuccessful competitors will be slowly eliminated. Because nitrogen is frequently considered to be the only limiting nutrient of algal growth in seawaters and phosphorus to have the same role in fresh waters, and given the usual complexity of the natural populations of phytoplankton, one is led to question the statements of Taylor and Williams, or the general agreement concerning the nature of the limiting nutrients, or both. Also, one should remark that the models cited do not separate the growth and uptake processes because they essentially refer to bacterial growth: bacteria metabolize nutrients so rapidly after uptake that separation is not essential. Likewise, this shortcut is the main criticism of Tilman's contribution, the first fully dedicated to algae with consideration to physiological features and the consequences for the species competition. Titman (1976) and Tilman (1977) predicted the outcome of the competition of the freshwater diatoms, *Asterionella formosa* and *Cyclotella meneghiniana*, competing for phosphate and silicium. The maximal growth rates (μ_{max}) of the two species are not significantly different, but *A. formosa* has a K for phosphorus lower than *C. meneghiniana* (0.04 μg–at·L^{-1} and 0.25 μg–at·L^{-1}, respectively) while the difference in K values for silicium is opposite (3.9 μg–at·L^{-1} for *A. formosa* and 1.4 μg–at·L^{-1} for *C. meneghiniana*). From these spe-

cific kinetic constant values, he established the range of nutrient conditions that allows one or other of the competitors to dominate in equilibrium; to do this, he used the hyperbolic model either with the Monod's (1942) equation (one-compartment model) or the Droop's (1974) model (two-compartment model). Both models predict that *C. meneghiniana* is the best competitor when the growth of both species is limited by silicium, whereas *A. formosa* is dominant when both species are phosphate limited. The two species stably coexist when each is limited by a different nutrient. A series of 76 long-term experiments in semicontinuous culture with high dilution rate enables the author (Titman = Tilman) to demonstrate that the predictions were valid, even those of the simple Monod's equation that also explain 75% of the variance in the relative abundance of the two species along a natural silicate-phosphate gradient in the lake from which experimental strains were isolated. Luxury uptake apparently did not influence the predicted outcome of the competition except at boundary ratios and slow flow rates. Hence, using a fast nutrient replacement was probably a bias that offset the role of the luxury uptake and Tilman's demonstration is partly negated where application to natural populations is concerned. Nevertheless, his great contribution is to have stressed the importance of the relative proportions, rather than concentrations, of nutrients in determining species interactions; this previous contributors did not do.

Moreover, slow algal growth and rapid uptake have been observed together, as well as actively dividing algal cells in nutrient-poor waters. This again raised the question of whether analyzed nutrients really act as limiting nutrients, and how closely uptake and growth processes are related. The former problem has been partly solved (Berland et al. 1980) and recent concepts will be discussed later. The latter has generated considerable literature since Caperon (1968) and Droop (1968) proved that uptake and growth are uncoupled and suggested that the intracellular nutrient quotas may rule primary algal growth.

Based on such a concept, the model of Grenney et al. (1973) considers an algal cell as a three-compartment unit: the reservoir of inorganic nutrients, organic intermediates, and proteins. Variations in the uptake rate with environmental concentrations of the limiting nutrient (nitrogen in Grenney et al.) and assimilation from cell nutrient reservoir into organic compounds follow the hyperbolic model. When comparing the abilities of several species with a slight advantage in either assimilation or uptake rates to compete for one limiting nutrient, the model predicts that species with a low K value for growth and high maximum uptake rate will dominate in high flux of nutrient input, while at low-nutrient concentrations species with a low K value for uptake are advantaged. This was predictable with a more simple model, but the model also points out that a short injection of limiting nutrient creates a transient high concentration that enables the species with high K for uptake to gain a competitive advantage. Grenney et al. pointed out that temporal variations in the limiting nutrient concentration may tender the environment suitable for coexistence of different species. Thus, rather than the magnitude of the characteristics themselves, variations may be the most important factors influencing species equilibrium. Indeed, the Grenney et al. model was a critical step; however, it did not involve light and temperature variations and assumed all species are limited by the same nutrient. These weaknesses were remedied later.

As a matter of fact, Lehman et al. (1975) proposed a theoretical framework that avoids the usual shortcoming of considering a natural population as a single unit, without any regard for physiological differences such as differences in nutrient uptake efficiencies. Their model integrates the nutrient constants of the hyperbolic model, assuming that uptake velocities are dependent on both internal and external concentrations, and includes luxury consumption, end-product inhibition of carbon fixation and nutrient uptake, and light and temperature response constants as well. It predicts that a species dominance ends and a succession occurs when cell-division rates of dominant species are slowed by nutrient shortage or physical limitations. This leads these algae to become less resistant to grazing and sinking, the primary processes of algal cell disappearance. The model can also predict the daily pulses related to light limitation of photosynthesis, and temporal changes in biomass and species composition. They did not use data to verify the ability of their model to apply to natural situations. However, they fitted the model to data for physiological constants and the exact values reported by Hutchinson for a pond he studied, i.e. nutrient contents of 0.1 μg-at-P·L^{-1} with a daily input of 0.0003 μg-at-P·L^{-1}, 8.6 μg-at-N·L^{-1} and 0.035 μg-at-N·L^{-1}·d^{-1}, and 142.8 μg-at-Si·L^{-1} and 0.125 μg-at-Si·L^{-1}·d^{-1}. Algal densities were 2000 cells·L^{-1} for diatoms, 1000 cells·L^{-1} for other taxa. Computation demonstrated that the diatoms are the first dominant algae. Nevertheless, they are the algae most susceptible to sinking due to their siliceous frustules and absence of motility. They need high turbulence and rapid division rate to produce heavy populations in pelagic biota. Because of their more efficient uptake of dissolved phosphorus and slower sinking rates, the chrysophytes continued to increase after diatom blooms collapsed. The other algae, namely chlorophytes and dinoflagellates, and cyanophytes never achieved substantial population densities

because of the low nutrient levels that follow diatom bloom. All Hutchinson's observations appeared to have been predictable, which enabled Lehman et al. (1975) to claim that detailed models, when correctly formulated, can predict general patterns precisely without costly simulation and that the simple model cannot. No model is perfect, in the sense that none can simultaneously satisfy all demands and prerequisites.

Mickelson et al. (1979) experimented on the competition of the diatoms *Chaetoceros septentrionalis*, *Skeletonema costatum*, and *Thalassiosira gravida* grown in nitrogen (NH$_1$)-limited continuous cultures, to estimate the relative change, if any, in the specific growth constants obtained from single-species chemostats, that may occur when two species are grown together. By inoculation of a small sample of an invader algal culture into a resident one (2–98%) they demonstrated that both *C. septentrionalis* and *S. costatum* rapidly dominated *T. gravida* which was displaced. Also, the latter strain was not able to grow in resident cultures of the two other diatoms. Behavior of mixed cultures of *C. septentrionalis* and *S. costatum* are related to initial proportions, i.e. the resident population (98%) displaced the invader, and the two species can coexist when relative initial biomasses are equal. Moreover, temperature stress (27°C) favored the growth of the less abundant species. Hence, two modes of dominance may occur; one based on the different physiological capabilities to compete for nutrient partition, and one related to species matching with equal success, in which take-over occurs only when an additional factor is detrimental to one species and favors the other. Finally, Mickelson et al. calculated the kinetic constants by Monod's (1942) equation (one-compartment model) and Droop's (1974) model (two-compartment model). Comparisons made with data in the literature and obtained by unialgal cultures demonstrated that no notable difference exists between the two sets of data. Hence, this contribution confirms the use of single-species growth kinetics as a basis for predicting the outcome of competition between two algae, by derivation of a theory described for bacteria by Veldkamp and Jannasch (1972) and Jannasch and Mateles (1974).

Validity of constant K-based predictions — From the main contributions cited, the kinetic constants of nutrient uptake and growth appear to reflect the capability of an alga to compete with others for nutrient partitioning, and to be valid for prediction of species succession as well. The half-saturation constants have been frequently used, probably because their dimensions are nutrient concentrations, which allow direct comparison with field data. Contrariwise, the maximal uptake or growth rates are pratically neglected. Healey (1980) criticized this misuse and recalled that the K values can be readily compared only when maximum rates are the same. To illustrate his argument he replotted the data of McCarthy (1972) that showed the diatoms *Thalassiosira fluviatilis* and *T. pseudonana* to have the same K value for urea uptake, but a quite different U_{max}. Hence, except at trace levels to which the algae will respond similarly, the species with the higher U_{max} will displace the other. Healey proposed to include both K and U_{max} values in one index, in order to get a more general application, namely the ratio $U_{max}:K$, which is the slope of Monod's model at lowest nutrient concentrations. If the ratio $U_{max}:K$ is found in uptake studies using cells with minimum cell quota (k_Q) it should provide an estimate of the $U_{max}:K$ ratio for growth which remains, the common result of all cellular processes. Healey's refinement is promising, indeed, and should certainly come into common use in the near future.

On the other hand, Crowley (1975), who discussed the role of natural selection on adjustment of half-saturation constants to relative ambient substrate concentrations, demonstrated that the relative fitnesses of the alternative evolutionary strategies determine these specific constants over evolutionary time. In other words, the algae can adapt towards the greater ability to take up the nutrient most bound (affinity strategy) or present at very low levels (efficiency strategy) or adapt to faster growth (velocity strategy). Doyle (1975) emphasized that adapting to a low nutrient concentration does not necessarily imply a decrease in the value of U_{max}. Slawyk (1980) confirmed this later by recording high K and U_{max} values with the phytoplankton of the Costa Rica dome. However, the half-saturation constant is still considered here as reflecting the specific capability of an alga to compete for nutrient partition. Gavis (1976) claimed the rate of diffusion transport of nutrients within the depleted area around any individual may govern nutrient-uptake rate and, hence, growth. By comparing the respective K and U_{max} and diffusion coefficients of the diatoms *Coscinodiscus lineatus* ($K = 2.8$ μg–at–N·L^{-1}) and *Ditylum brightwellii* ($K = 0.6$ μg–at–N·L^{-1}), he predicted the latter organism would absorb nutrients more rapidly than the former only at concentrations less than 0.75 μg–at–N·L^{-1}. This was not predictable by comparing only the K values. However, no experiment was done to verify whether the prediction pertains to reality. Altogether, there is often a significant discrepancy between predictions and the real behavior of natural populations, which has so far resisted elucidation so well that the term "paradox" was applied to it.

THE PARADOX OF THE PLANKTON

On the basis of general knowledge on species competition and algal physiology, one would expect that the one species best able to take up and use the limiting nutrient would displace all other species. If this rationale had been correct, the principle of "competitive exclusion" (as termed by Hardin (1960) but known earlier (see Udvardy 1959)) would have been obeyed; all aquatic habitats would contain few species and each ecological niche a single one. That is obviously not true; marine and fresh waters usually contain several tens of species in apparent competitive equilibrium. The violation of this principle by the phytoplankton was termed "the paradox of the plankton" by Hutchinson (1961). By using the word "paradox," Hutchinson symbolized the opinion of the whole community of planktonologists who were all deeply convinced that plankton must obey the principle of exclusion. When apparently it does not, the explanation must be that environmental perturbations have interupted and/or masked the normal behavior. Therefore, efforts were made to explain the paradox.

Hutchinson (1961) pointed out that the idealized conditions assumed in classical theories (i.e. space uniform, no temporal variations, and all species having the same mortality rate) are violated in a natural environment whose main characteristics include spatial and temporal complexities (resulting from light, temperature, and nutrient concentration variations), while grazing and sinking are species variable. Therefore, natural conditions are never stable long enough to allow the most efficient species at any time to eliminate the less successful species before the most efficient species loses dominance. Later, Richerson et al. (1970) insisted on the importance of patchiness, which results from insufficient rates of mixing compared with the reproductive rates of phytoplankton. The distinct patches or temporary niches separated in space represent different biota whose populations are then mixed by the net samplers commonly used. Grenney et al. (1974) discussed this suggestion and demonstrated that fluctuations in the supply of limiting nutrient would allow several species of algae to persist together. Combined with other factor variations, they provide an unlimited number of combinations of which one or several may correspond to the respective requirements of different algal species. If suitable combinations occur with sufficient frequency and duration, a species may be able to survive indefinitively. The dynamics of the system could be a major source of species diversity. Turpin and Harrison (1979) investigated this topic and demonstrated that, in marine waters, the diatoms *Chaetoceros socialis* and *C. constrictus* dominate in a homogeneous distribution of the limiting nutrient, while *Skeletonema costatum* was dominant in a patchy distribution, but at the same time that one nutrient is limiting for some species, other algae may be limited by other nutrients, and then numerous species can coexist in a complex environment.

Williams (1971) suggested that temporal separation of nutrient uptake activities of different algae of the same community could allow numerous species to coexist by increasing the number of the niches. Diel periodicity in nitrogen assimilation studied by Eppley et al. (1971) with *Skeletonema costatum* and *Coccolithus huxleyi* and diel-phased cell division of natural populations of *Ditylum brightwellii* observed by Smayda (1975), among others, support this statement. So pulses in nutrient supply have been associated with daily patterns of incorporation of carbon and nutrients to generate species coexistence by restricting the competitive advantage of each species to a part of the daily cycle. For instance, the introduction of a nitrogen pulse with a period greater than 10 d in the model of Grenney et al. (1973) led to prediction of species equilibrium. Doyle and Poore (1974), who observed that all dinoflagellate species present in the Gulf Stream divide simultaneously, suggested that diurnal oscillation of nutrient supply could be responsible for the synchrony, by eliminating from the plankton all those species not phased with it. However, this effect will be diminished when nutrient availability and grazing rates are both high; the timing of cell division and variations in nutrient concentrations will not be perfectly coupled. Stross and Pemrick (1974) reported conflicting results by observing a temporal stratification of nutrient niches in a lake that allows several functional groups of algae to take up nutrients at different times of the day. Weiler and Chisholm (1976) observed that three species of dinoflagellates, *Ceratium dens*, *C. furca*, and *Dinophysis fortii*, divide at different times of day in the waters of Santa Monica Bay and, hence, minimize respective nutrient privation. It appears, therefore, that temporal patchiness results not only from direct responses of cell machinery to fluctuations of environment, but also from species-specific physiological rhythms. The importance of biological clocks in algal physiology was demonstrated long ago (Sweeney and Hastings 1962) and has become part of the basic background, but their role in species competition has been recognized only recently. Otherwise, zooplankters that graze at night are supposed to liberate enough nutrient to allow phytoplankton to grow the following day (Wroblewski 1977). Computer simulation and experiments conducted with the fresh alga *Euglena gracilis* by Stross et al. (1973) and Chisholm and Nobbs (1976) and experiments by Chisholm et al. (1978) with a natural marine population dominated by diatoms are persuasive, but do not prove that properly phased daily rhythms in nutrient uptake and nutrient pulses can restrict the advantage of each species to a part of the cycle duration, and hence allow a multispecies co-occurrence.

O'Brien (1974), who simulated algal growth rate as a function of nutrient concentrations, and two-species competition, did not refer to the paradox. Notwithstanding, his speculations led to interesting remarks which may be relevant to this discussion. The cause of a population crash, he wrote, can be due to a large supply of nutrients in excess of that which allows a steady state, when mortality and growth are balanced. When that occurs, the daily rate of nutrient replacement is not fast enough to maintain the large algal biomass arising from the consumption of the whole nutrient pool; hence, a population crash follows the bloom. O'Brien's discussion demonstrated the importance of zooplankton and other selective causes of mortality in influencing species composition and succession of phytoplankton. He remarked that because K and μ_{max} are specific constants, if the death rate for all species was the same the one most able to take up nutrients would displace all others, whereas if the death rates vary within competitors several species can coexist at a given nutrient concentration. Subsequently, because grazing is the main mortality factor, it appears that the more different grazers present, the more variable the death rates of phytoplankton and, therefore, the more species able to coexist. This is an alternative explanation of the paradox, indeed.

Thus, all included, it seems to be quite clear that a natural population of algae could consist of an assemblage of species having a little overlap, although they share the same space. Most authors who discussed the "paradox" assumed that equilibrium is an asymptotic situation never fulfilled, because of successive and varied violations of normal behavior resulting from unstable environmental features. Recently, a few other authors have claimed that several species of phytoplankton can co-occur in a true competitive equilibrium, and others claim that competition for nutrients is a myth.

Theoretical speculations based on ability of species units to take up and assimilate nutrients led Stewart and Levin (1973) to state that coexistence of two species competing for a single resource can occur when one species grows faster at high concentration while the other grows faster at low concentrations of the limiting resource; at one intermediate concentration, the two relative capabilities equilibrate. Moreover, the total biomass of both species growing together is less than the biomass of either species in the same conditions; this was also independently predicted by Ross (1973). Petersen (1975) also simulated an algal competition. The model he ran involved the usual kinetic constants plus specific death rates and remineralization of dead cells as did O'Brien (1974), but it also permitted investigation of the consequences of different specific uptake capabilities. When a plurispecific equilibrium occurs, that implies (according to Petersen's statements), that (i) each species is more adapted than the others to acquire at least one of the nutrients that are present in limiting amounts, (ii) each species is less efficient in obtaining at low concentration the nonlimiting nutrient it requires in larger amounts to continue to grow, (iii) the set of respective algal capabilities are matched. Subsequently, the model predicted that the number of coexisting species cannot exceed the total number of limiting nutrients, a result also obtained spearately by Taylor and Williams (1975). It also predicts that oligotrophic waters should host communities richer in species than eutrophic waters, which, in fact, they do. Equilibrium is displaced either by depletion or by heavy enrichment of a single nutrient; both cases lead to single species dominance. Likewise, the invasion of one species most able to take up all nutrients at very low levels will displace all the resident competitors. Thus, Petersen's speculations have been really fruitful. Altogether the paradox, if not fully clarified, is no longer a frightening problem. But, on the other hand, the direct comparison of specific kinetic constants (common a decade ago) appears to be a simplification presently in extinction, whereas recent developments have complicated further this important scientific topic, by challenging the principle of nutrient limitation in natural condition.

ARE NATURAL PHYTOPLANKTON POPULATIONS NUTRIENT LIMITED?

That nutrient availability limits algal growth has been implicitly purported for as long as phytoplankton have been studied. But the word "growth" is inadequate here, in that it covers an array of processes that are sighted by two main consequences — the division rate of individuals and the crop of the population. O'Brien (1972, 1973) proposed to classify growth responses into type I, where growth continues longer and the final yield increases with increasing concentrations of the limiting nutrient, and type II, where growth rate increases and the yield remains constant. Holmes (1973) and Kelly and Hornberger (1973) severely criticized this concept and demonstrated the final yield will depend on the concentration of a limiting nutrient and not necessarily on how fast the algae grow, but a nutrient addition will usually increase both nutrient growth rate and final biomass of natural populations. O'Brien replied that these figures are unrealistic as populations do not have unlimited time to divide. They have to face severe causes of mortality that can be compensated only by rapid changes in growth rate, leading to the possibility of both unlimited growth rate and nutrient-limited yield, a concept also de-

fended by Fuhs et al. (1972). To clarify this contention, a didactic language is needed. If one accepts the concept that there is a specific minimum cell quota (Droop's k_Q) of each element to permit production of a cell, it becomes obvious that the magnitude of the biomass of a population is given by the reservoir of the nutrient least available with respect to the needs. Hence, nutrients limit growth. However, one can imagine that any individual may find sufficient nutrient supply to divide as fast as its cell machinery permits, so nutrients would be not limiting. That would lead to conflicting features — individuals not growth limited (growth = growth rate), the whole population growth limited (growth = yield). Is this speculation unrealistic? Certainly it is, if we refer to unialgal cultures, but not necessarily if daughter cells are eliminated as fast as they are produced, which can occur in natural conditions.

Hulburt (1970, 1976, 1977, 1979a, b) conceived a theory whose main feature was that planktonic algae are not competing for nutrients. This concept can be summarized as follows: (i) Most oceanic species do not vary in abundance over large areas of offshore waters, with the exception of a few like *Coccolithus huxleyi* in the western North Atlantic Ocean. These species show an appreciable decrease in shallow waters, while *C. huxleyi* is more abundant in coastal waters. (ii) This does not result either from competition for nutrients or from differential grazing pressure. (iii) Oceanic species grow too slowly to respond to increased nutrient contents of coastal waters, but their capability to take up nutrients at very low concentrations makes them successful in open ocean. (iv) In open ocean, cell densities of algal species do not vary very much because, when a mother cell produces two daughter cells, it decreases nutrients; when a daughter cell is grazed and remineralized it increases nutrients. Therefore, nutrients are never lacking, and the oceanic species are in a permanent equilibrium.

The basis of Hulburt's theory belongs to field observations, and refers essentially to the slight variations over wide areas of population densities, and nutrient concentrations, as well. The theory evidently applies also to the "paradox of the plankton" and provides an alternative explanation. Hulburt (personal communication) wrote: "If there is one nutrient concentration which is determined by every species, then every species determines its own different concentration of nutrient. One concentration of nutrient is maintained by mixing and extends over distances of a meter or more. Different concentrations of nutrient can be maintained theoretically about each cell for small distances only, $0.17–0.37 \times 10^{-3}$ cm^2 in the Sargasso Sea, for instance. This means that mixing always prevents any particular species from being in equilibrium with its own nutrient concentration as in a chemostat. So, all species but one are not competed out of existence by that one which can force the nutrient to the lowest concentration, i.e. its own equilibrium concentration." Yet this formulation is not quite clear, at least for us. The mechanism evoked is the same as that proposed by Petersen (1975), Taylor and Williams (1975), and Titman (1976) who stated that at equilibrium each species is limited by a different nutrient and, therefore, the number of coexisting species cannot exceed the total number of limiting nutrients. Their ideas diverge, however, because they assume the phytoplankton is nutrient limited, which Hulburt denies. By comparing specific K values to nutrient concentrations, several authors have also concluded that the populations they studied were nutrient unlimited (Thomas 1969, 1970a, b; MacIsaac and Dugdale 1969; Titman and Kilham 1976) and, hence, implicitly supported Hulburt's statement.

The contention will not be solved here; however, we are suspicious about how perfect and how permanent is the balance between absorption of nutrients for growth and production of nutrients through remineralization. Because the later process involved a series of mechanisms spread along the food chain, one can expect an algal cell to be able to grow faster than the nutrients are regenerated, thence to be nutrient limited, even though the K value would be very low. Moreover, some species are evidently nutrient limited as they grow faster as soon as they benefit from nutrient-rich waters. So does *Coccolithus huxleyi* in coastal waters as reported by Hulburt (1979a), for whom he implicitly does not deny that nutrients limit its growth in oceanic waters. To explain why oceanic species decrease in shallow waters, but *C. huxleyi* increases, Hulburt wrote: "One simple reason why oceanic species decrease in shallow water is that they get stuck on the bottom, stranded there. All cells of all species get stuck there, of course. But the slow growers grow too slowly to balance loss by stranding; and the fast growers, like *C. huxleyi*, grow faster, due to more nutrient, than they get stranded. More nutrient in shallow water is of no use to slow growers, since they are already growing at the maximum in low nutrient deep water." Hulburt's original insight implies that all species present in oceanic areas are physiologically adapted to take up nutrients at very low levels, a capability which had not been really explored until recently. But it still remains unclear how such an alga as *C. huxleyi* can live in equilibrium with species uniquely adapted to the oceanic conditions and can also bloom in nutrient-rich waters. Such a behavior implies that this alga has at one time, or can adapt rapidly to show, the following physiological capabilities: high specific growth rate, low K value, capability to take

up at very low nutrient levels, namely undetectable trace levels. Is that possible?

Steemann Nielsen (1978a, b) brought a new insight that could begin to answer the question. He investigated algal growth rate at very low nutrient levels, but he used a special batch technique that allowed him to record the growth of a population as rare as 10^3 cells $\cdot$ L^{-1}. With the fast-growing freshwater algal *Selenastrum capricornutum*, whose $\mu_{max} > 2$ divisions $\cdot$ d^{-1}, he demonstrated that 75% of μ_{max} occurs at concentrations as low as 0.02 μg–at–N (NH$_4$) $\cdot$ L^{-1}. The K value could not be determined because concentrations of NH$_4$ lower than 0.02 μg–at $\cdot$ L^{-1} could not be measured and, therefore, the 50% of μ_{max} never obtained. With NO$_3$, the nitrogen requirements are higher, and the K value could be determined to be 0.05 μg–at $\cdot$ L^{-1}, while 75% of μ_{max} is given by 0.2 μg–at $\cdot$ L^{-1}. Requirements for phosphorus are also very low: K was found at 7 ng–at $\cdot$ L^{-1}, which was the lowest concentration that could be produced. Although we can question why the uptake rates are so much different for N-NH$_4$ and N-NO$_3$, it remains quite clear that in nutrient-poor waters *S. capricornutum* is capable of growth as fast as its cell machinery permits, light and temperature permitting.

Similarly, Goldman et al. (1979) claimed that growth rates of natural phytoplankton populations in oceanic waters may be near maximal growth and, hence, not nutrient limited. They remarked that the cell contents of the algae *Dunaliella tertiolecta*, *Monochrysis lutheri* (now *Pavlova lutheri*), and *Thalassiosira pseudonana* 3H approach the Redfield ratio only at high growth rates. Hence, they discussed whether the chemical composition of natural marine phytoplankton is typically characterized by this ratio because growth rates in oceanic waters are quite high (Goldman 1980). Berland et al. (1972, p. 343) also remarked the natural populations have the same basic cellular composition as cultured cells growing in nutrient-unlimited conditions, namely the logarithmic phase of a batch culture in their experiments, and Slawyk et al. (1978) reported that the ratio POC:PON of marine phytoplankton of northwest African upwelling is similar to that found in steady-state chemostat cultures. Goldman et al. reconciled the steady state of chemostat and the euphotic zone of the open ocean by the following rationale: (i) In a chemostat, the growth rate equals dilution rate, but remains completely independent of the concentration of limiting nutrient. (ii) Residual limiting nutrient flowing into the "sump" are undetectable. (iii) Thus, it is possible to have simultaneously low or undetectable residual nutrient levels and high growth rates, as is shown in uptake measurements by McCarthy and Goldman (1979). McCarthy and Goldman demonstrated that the ratio of uptake rate of NH_4 versus growth rate of the diatom *T. pseudonana* increases from 1.1 to 33.9, when the dilution rate decreases. In other words, when the nutrient concentration decreases to very low levels, the uptake process is able to sustain a far higher division rate. Therefore, under conditions of severe starvation, a cell needs to be exposed to saturation NH_4 only for a very short period with regard to the doubling time to replenish its nutrient reservoir. It can do so by passing into microenvironments in which nutrient concentrations are elevated, for instance by excretion or by remineralization of dead organisms, whose existence is also defended by Wroblewski (1977).

This new concept on adaptation of algal physiology to conditions of nutrient depletion is surprising and leads to some questions. Is it, for instance, totally relevant to argue that an open ocean works as a steady state of a chemostat? In a chemostat, there are two privileged points generally separated by the largest distance flooded by the culture medium — the orifice of input and the orifice of output; between the two, nutrients disappear. The cells, which are randomly distributed by mixing, benefit, from time to time, from transient concentrations corresponding to those at which uptake machinery is efficient. McCarthy and Goldman assume that nutrient-rich microniches provide similar opportunities, and that phytoplankton might appear to be growing successfully at the expense of virtually undetectable small-scale nutrient pulses. Jackson (1980) denies the existence of such niches; his calculations prove the excreta of a protozoan are dispersed fast enough to make the concentration at the center of a 10-μm plume only 0.1% of the initial concentration within 0.1 s. Behind a swimming copepod a decrease to 1% of the concentration of the excreta will require only 100 s; yet the vicinity of a zooplankter is more often deadly, the phytoplankton will not encounter high-nutrient level there, except with macrozooplankters, which are very rare. Jackson also remarked that in the central North Pacific gyre the average division rate of the phytoplankton is 0.1 d^{-1}; the diatom *Thalassiosira pseudonana* would maintain such a growth rate with a NH_4 concentration of only 0.0008 μg-at$\cdot$$L^{-1}$. Thus, slow phytoplankton growth rates are consistent with low nutrient levels and slow zooplankton abundance and filtration rate. Williams and Muir (1981), on the basis of their own computations and those of Pasciak and Gavis (1974), established that molecular diffusion is sufficient to disperse microzones of excreted nutrients 50 times too rapidly to be taken up by phytoplankton. Enhanced uptake rates at very low substrate concentrations reported by McCarthy and Goldman (1979) can be suspected to have been overestimated. Because their short-term measurements (5 min) were made with relatively high concentrations of NH_4 (8

and 16 μg-at-N$\cdot$$L^{-1}$), a part of the NH_4 could have been absorbed and accounted for with that taken up, but killed-cell suspensions do not retain activity. Collos and Slawyk (1980), who replotted the data of Caperon and Meyer (1972), Eppley and Renger (1974), and McCarthy and Goldman (1979) obtained with the diatom *T. pseudonana*, remarked that from total nutrient depletion to trace concentrations (which allow a nitrogen cell content of about 0.5 μg-at$\cdot$ $cell^{-1}$), the specific uptake rate increases until a maximum, then decreases. Hence, the authors who worked with higher values (e.g. McCarthy and Goldman) have missed the left part of the peak and overestimated the algal capability to adapt the uptake at very low nutrient concentrations. In Collos and Slawyk's (1980) opinion, algae react to nitrogen limitation by reducing their cell quota (Dugdale 1977), thereby increasing their specific U_{max}; but there is a minimum cell quota (Droop 1974). Therefore, in case of extreme deficiency, a decrease in U_{max} cannot be compensated for by a parallel decrease in nitrogen cell quota; this leads to a decrease in specific U_{max}. Collos (1980) confirmed this proposed mechanism by investigating the response of the diatom *Phaeodactylum tricornutum* and demonstrating that it behaves similarly to *T. pseudonana*.

Otherwise, Stross (1980) suggested that an alternative arrangement may be conceived for diatoms living in oligotrophic fresh waters. For such organisms, when a small pool of phosphate becomes available it can be immediately used (*r* strategy) because the cell is equipped with efficient enzymes and excess of RNA, or can be deferred until the necessary RNA is made available (*K* strategy), and permits, in contrast, a larger biomass.

Beyond the problem of stating whether algal growth is nutrient limited or unlimited, the subsequent problem of estimating the importance of nutrient partition in species competition and succession arises. Obviously, if the concepts of Hulburt, Goldman, and McCarthy pertain to natural populations, the role of nutrients has been greatly overestimated; hence, most models will have to be reconsidered. However, prior to any hasty statement, one could remark that only a few species have been involved in experiments that demonstrate the algal capability to take up nutrient very rapidly. Goldman et al. (1979) and McCarthy and Goldman (1979) refer essentially to data obtained with *Thalassiosira pseudonana*, while similar capability reported by Conway et al. (1976), Conway and Harrison (1977), and Turpin and Harrison (1979) issued from experiments made with *Skeletonema costatum*. Both these diatoms are well known for their active metabolism, which makes them convenient experimental material; numerous others show less-efficient metabolism. Also, nitrogen was the only nutrient involved in the studies, while several workers demonstrated the importance of the silicium in seawater and phosphorus in fresh waters. Therefore, it is our opinion that there are so far no convincing reasons to generalize to all algal species. Hence, if the concept of nutrient-unlimited algal growth has to be restricted to some species having the ability to assimilate large quantities of nutrients in a short time duration and to shift their cell machinery to take advantage of any transient pulse of nutrients, others would have to face a drastic disadvantage. We should have just gone one step more in the discouraging complexity of the phytoplankton mechanisms of competition and coexistence; this is, unfortunately, what we have to expect.

Acknowledgments

We wish to thank greatly Dr Trevor Platt for revising the English manuscript.

References

AHLGREN, G. 1977. Growth of *Oscillatoria agardhii* in chemostat culture. I. Nitrogen and phosphorus requirements. Oikos 29: 209–224.

BERLAND, B. R., D. J. BONIN, P. L. LABORDE, AND S. Y. MAESTRINI. 1972. Variations de quelques facteurs estimatifs de la biomasse, et en particulier de l'ATP, chez plusieurs algues marines planctoniques. Mar. Biol. 13: 338–345.

BERLAND, B. R., D. J. BONIN, AND S. Y. MAESTRINI. 1980. Azote ou phosphore? Considérations sur le "paradoxe nutritionnel" de la mer Méditerranée. Oceanol. Acta 3: 135–142.

BREMER, H., AND P. P. DENNIS. 1975. Transition period following a nutritional shift-up in the bacterium *Escherichia coli* B/r: stable RNA and protein synthesis. J. Theor. Biol. 52: 365–382.

BROWN, E. J., AND R. F. HARRIS. 1978. Kinetics of algal transient phosphate, uptake and the cell quota concept. Limnol. Oceanogr. 23: 35–40.

BROWN, E. J., AND D. L. BUTTON. 1979. Phosphate-limited growth kinetics of *Selenastrum capricornutum* (Chlorophyceae). J. Phycol. 15: 305–311.

BUTTON, D. K. 1978. On the theory of control of microbial growth kinetics by limiting nutrient concentrations. Deep Sea Res. 25: 1163–1177.

CAPERON, J. 1967. Population growth in micro-organisms limited by food supply. Ecology 48: 715–721.

1968. Population growth response of *Isochrysis galbana* to nitrate variation at limiting concentrations. Ecology 49: 866–872.

CAPERON, J., AND J. MEYER. 1972. Nitrogen-limited growth of marine phytoplankton. II. Uptake kinetics and their role in nutrient-limited growth of phytoplankton. Deep Sea Res. 19: 619–632.

CARPENTER, E. J., AND R. R. L. GUILLARD. 1971. Intraspecific differences in nitrate half-saturation constants for three species of marine phytoplankton. Ecology 52: 183–185.

CHISHOLM, S. W., F. AZAM, AND R. W. EPPLEY. 1978. Silicic acid incorporation in marine diatoms on light: dark cycles: use as an assay for phased celle division. Limnol. Oceanogr. 23: 518–529.

CHISHOLM, S. M., AND P. A. NOBBS. 1976. Simulation of algal growth and competition in a phosphate-limited cyclostat, p. 337–355. *In* R. P. Canale [ed.] Modeling biochemical processes in aquatic ecosystems. Ann Arbor Sci. Publ., Ann Arbor, MI.

COLLOS, Y. 1980. Transient situations in nitrate assimilation by marine diatoms. 1. Changes in uptake parameters during nitrogen starvation. Limnol. Oceanogr. 25: 1075–1081.

COLLOS, Y., AND G. SLAWYK. 1980. Nitrogen uptake and assimilation by marine phytoplankton, p. 195–211. *In* P. Falkowsky [ed.] Primary productivity in the sea. Plenum Press, New York, NY.

CONWAY, H. L., AND P. J. HARRISON. 1977. Marine diatoms grown in chemostats under silicate or ammonium limitation. IV. Transient response of *Chaetoceros debilis*, *Skeletonema costatum* and *Thalassiosira gravida* to a single addition of the limiting nutrient. Mar. Biol. 43: 33–43.

CONWAY, H. L., P. J. HARRISON, AND C. O. DAVID. 1976. Marine diatoms grown in chemostats under silicate or ammonium limitation. II. Transient response of *Skeletonema costatum* to a single addition of the limiting nutrient. Mar. Biol. 35: 187–199.

CROWLEY, P. H. 1975. Natural selection and the Michaelis constant. J. Theor. Biol. 50: 461–475.

DOYLE, R. W. 1975. Upwelling, clone selection and the characteristic shape of nutrient uptake curves. Limnol. Oceanogr. 20: 487–489.

DOYLE, R. W., AND R. V. POORE. 1974. Nutrient competition and division synchrony in phytoplankton. J. Exp. Mar. Biol. Ecol. 14: 201–210.

DROOP, M. R. 1961. Vitamin B_{12} and marine ecology: the response of *Monochrysis lutheri*. J. Mar. Biol. Assoc. U.K. 41: 69–76.

1968. Vitamin B_{12} and marine ecology. IV. The kinetics of uptake, growth and inhibition in *Monochrysis lutheri*. J. Mar. Biol. Assoc. U.K. 48: 689–733.

1974. The nutrient status of algal cells in continuous culture. J. Mar. Biol. Assoc. U.K. 54: 825–855.

DUGDALE, R. C. 1967. Nutrient limitation in the sea: dynamics, identification and significance. Limnol. Oceanogr. 12: 685–695.

1977. Modeling, p. 789–806. *In* E. D. Goldberg [ed.] The sea: ideas and observations on progress in the study of the sea. J. Wiley and Sons, New York, NY.

DUGDALE, R. C., AND J. J. GOERING. 1967. Uptake of new and regenerated forms of nitrogen in primary productivity. Limnol. Oceanogr. 12: 196–206.

ELBRÄCHTER, M. 1977. On population dynamics in multi-species cultures of diatoms and dinoflagellates. Helgol. Wiss. Meeresunters. 30: 192–200.

EPPLEY, R. W., AND J. L. COATSWORTH. 1968. Uptake of nitrate and nitrite by *Ditylum brightwellii* – kinetics and mechanisms. J. Phycol. 4: 151–156.

EPPLEY, R. W., AND E. H. RENGER. 1974. Nitrogen assimilation of an oceanic diatom in nitrogen-limited continuous culture. J. Phycol. 10: 15–23.

EPPLEY, R. W., J. N. ROGERS, AND J. J. MCCARTHY. 1969. Half-saturation constants for uptake of nitrate and ammonium by marine phytoplankton. Limnol. Oceanogr. 14: 912–920.

EPPLEY, R. W., J. N. ROGERS, J. J. MCCARTHY, AND A. SOURNIA. 1971. Light/dark periodicity in nitrogen assimilation of the marine phytoplankters Skeletonema costatum and Coccolithus huxleyi in N-limited chemostat culture. J. Phycol. 7: 150–154.

EPPLEY, R. W., AND W. H. THOMAS. 1969. Comparison of half-saturation constants for growth and nitrate uptake of marine phytoplankton. J. Phycol. 5: 375–379.

ESTRADA, R. W., AND D. BLASCO. 1979. Two phases of the phytoplankton community in the Baja California upwelling. Limnol. Oceanogr. 24: 1065–1080.

FUHS, G. W., S. D. DEMMERLE, E. CANELLI, AND M. CHEN. 1972. Characterization of phosphorus-limited plankton algae (with reflexions on the limiting-nutrient concept), p. 113–132. In G. E. Likens [ed.] Nutrients and eutrophication. Vol. 1. Am. Soc. Limnol. Oceanogr. Spec. Symp.

GATES, W. E., AND J. T. MARLAR. 1968. Graphical analysis of batch culture data using the Monod expressions. J. Water Pollut. Control Fed. 40: R469–R476.

GAUSE, G. F. 1932a. Experimental studies on the struggle for existence. I. Mixed populations of two species of yeast. J. Exp. Biol. 9: 389–402.

1932b. Ecology of populations. Q. Rev. Biol. 7: 27–46.

GAVIS, J. 1976. Munk and Riley revisited: nutrient diffusion transport and rates of phytoplankton growth. J. Mar. Res. 34: 161–179.

GOLDMAN, J. C. 1980. Physiological processes, nutrient availability, and the concept of relative growth rate in marine phytoplankton ecology, p. 179–194. In P. Falkowsky [ed.] Primary productivity in the sea. Plenum Press, New York, NY.

GOLDMAN, J. C., W. J. OSWALD, AND D. JENKINS. 1974. The kinetics of inorganic carbon limited algal growth. J. Water Pollut. Control Fed. 46: 554–574.

GOLDMAN, J. C., J. J. MCCARTHY, AND D. G. PEAVEY. 1979. Growth rate influence on the chemical composition of phytoplankton in oceanic waters. Nature (London) 279: 210–215.

GRENNEY, W. J., D. A. BELLA, AND H. C. CURL JR. 1973. A theoretical approach to interspecific competition in phytoplankton communities. Am. Nat. 107: 405–425.

GRENNEY, W. J., D. A. BELLA, AND H. C. CURL JR. 1974. Effects of intracellular nutrient pools on growth dynamics of phytoplankton. J. Water Pollut. Control. Fed. 46: 1751–1760.

GUILLARD, R. R. L., P. KILHAM, AND T. A. JACKSON. 1973. Kinetics of silicon-limited growth in the marine diatom Thalassiosira pseudonana Hasle and Heimdal (= Cyclotella nana Hustedt). J. Phycol. 9: 233–237.

HARDIN, G. 1960. The competitive exclusion principle. Science (Washington, D.C.) 131: 1292–1297.

HARRISON, P. J., H. L. CONWAY, AND R. C. DUGDALE. 1976. Marine diatoms grown in chemostats under silicate or ammonium limitation. I. Cellular chemical composition and steady-state growth kinetics of Skeletonema costatum. Mar. Biol. 35: 177–186.

HEALEY, F. P. 1980. Slope of the Monod equation as an indicator of advantage in nutrient competition. Microbiol. Ecol. 5: 281–286.

HOLMES, P. 1973. Phytoplankton algae: nutrient concentrations and growth. Science (Washington, D.C.) 180: 1298–1299.

HOLMES, R. W., P. M. WILLIAMS, AND R. W. EPPLEY. 1967. Redwater in La Jolla Bay, 1964–1966. Limnol. Oceanogr. 12: 503–512.

HULBURT, E. M. 1970. Competition for nutrients by marine phytoplankton in oceanic, coastal, and estuarine regions. Ecology 51: 475–484.

1976. Limitation of phytoplankton species in the ocean off western Africa. Limnol. Oceanogr. 21: 193–211.

1977. Coexistence, equilibrium, and nutrient sharing among phytoplankton species of the gulf of Maine. Am. Nat. 111: 967–980.

1979a. An assymetric formulation of the distribution characteristics of phytoplankton species: an investigation in interpretation. Mar. Sci. Commun. 5: 245–268.

1979b. Russell's definite description analysis of production and limitation of phytoplankton species. Mar. Biol. 52: 321–329.

HUTCHINSON, G. E. 1961. The paradox of the plankton. Am. Nat. 95: 137–145.

JACKSON, G. A. 1980. Phytoplankton growth and zooplankton grazing in oligotrophic oceans. Nature (London) 284: 439–440.

JANNASCH, H. W., AND R. I. MATELES. 1974. Experimental bacterial ecology studied in continuous culture, p. 165–212. In A. H. Rose and D. W. Tempest [ed.] Advances in microbial physiology. Vol. 11. Academic Press, London.

KELLY, M. G., AND G. M. HORNBERGER. 1973. Phytoplankton algae: nutrient concentrations and growth. Science (Washington, D.C.) 180: 1298–1299.

KING, D. L., AND J. T. NOVAK. 1974. The kinetics of inorganic carbon-limited algal growth. J. Water Pollut. Control. Fed. 46 (7): 1812–1816.

LAW, A. T., AND D. K. BUTTON. 1977. Multiple-carbon-source-limited growth kinetics of a marine coryneform bacterium. J. Bacteriol. 129: 115–123.

LEHMAN, J. T., D. B. BOTKIN, AND G. E. LIKENS. 1975. The assumptions and rationales of a computer model of phytoplankton population dynamics. Limnol. Oceanogr. 20: 343–364.

LIEBIG, J. 1840. Die Chemie in ihrer Anwendung auf Agrikultur und Physiologie. (4th ed., 1847). Taylor & Walton, London.

LOTKA, A. J. 1920. Analytical note on certain rhythmic relations in organic systems. Proc. Natl. Acad. Sci. U.S.A. 6: 410–415.

1934. Théorie analytique des associations biologiques, p. 1–45. In G. Tessier [ed.] Exposés de biométrie et de statistique biologique. IV. Actual. Sci. Ind. 187.

McCARTHY, J. J. 1972. The uptake of urea by marine phytoplankton. J. Phycol. 8: 216–222.

McCARTHY, J. J., AND J. C. GOLDMAN. 1979. Nitrogenous nutrition of marine phytoplankton in nutrient-depleted waters. Science (Washington, D.C.) 203: 670–672.

MacISAAC, J. J., AND R. C. DUGDALE. 1969. The kinetics of nitrate and ammonia uptake by natural populations of marine phytoplankton. Deep Sea Res. 16: 45–57.

MacISAAC, J. J., R. C. DUGDALE, S. A. HUNTSMAN, AND H. L. CONWAY. 1979. The effect of sewage on uptake of inorganic nitrogen and carbon by natural populations of marine phytoplankton. J. Mar. Res. 37: 51–66.

MacISAAC, J. J., R. C. DUGDALE, AND G. SLAWYK. 1974. Nitrogen uptake in the northwest Africa upwelling area: results from the CINECA-Charcot II cruise. Tethys 6: 69–76.

MAESTRINI, S. Y., AND M. G. KOSSUT. 1981. In situ cell depletion of some marine algae enclosed in dialysis sacks and their use for the determination of nutrient limiting growth in Ligurian coastal waters (Mediterranean Sea). J. Exp. Mar. Biol. Ecol. 50: 1–19.

MICHAELIS, L., AND M. M. L. MENTEN. 1913. Die kinetik der Invertinwirkung. Biochem. Z. 49: 333–369.

MICKELSON, M. J., H. MASKE, AND R. C. DUGDALE. 1979. Nutrient-determined dominance in multispecies chemostat cultures of diatoms. Limnol. Oceanogr. 24: 298–315.

MONOD, J. 1942. Recherches sur la croissance des cultures bactériennes. 2nd ed. Hermann, Paris. 210 p.

O'BRIEN, W. J. 1972. Limiting factors in phytoplankton Algae: their meaning and measurement. Science (Washington, D.C.) 178: 616–617.

1973. Phytoplankton algae: nutrient concentrations and growth. (Reply to comments by Holmes and Kelly and Hornberger). Science (Washington, D.C.) 180: 1298–1300.

1974. The dynamics of nutrient limitation of phytoplankton algae: a model reconsidered. Ecology 55: 135–141.

PAASCHE, E. 1973. Silicon and the ecology of marine plankton diatoms. II. Silicate-uptake kinetics in five diatom species. Mar. Biol. 19: 262–269.

PARSONS, T. R., AND J. D. H. STRICKLAND. 1962. On the production of particulate organic carbon by heterotrophic processes in seawater. Deep Sea Res. 8: 211–222.

PASCIAK, W. J., AND J. GAVIS. 1974. Transport limitation of nutrient uptake in phytoplankton. Limnol. Oceanogr. 19: 881–888.

PERRY, M. J. 1976. Phosphate utilization by an oceanic diatom in phosphorus-limited chemostat culture and in the oligotrophic waters of the central North Pacific. Limnol. Oceanogr. 21: 88–107.

PETERSEN, R. 1975. The paradox of the plankton: an equilibrium hypothesis. Am. Nat. 109: 35–49.

PRICE, C. A., AND E. F. CARELL. 1964. Control by iron of chlorophyll formation and growth in *Euglena gracilis*. Plant Physiol. 39: 862–868.

PRICE, C. A., AND J. W. QUIGLEY. 1966. A method for determining quantitative zinc requirements for growth. Soil Sci. 101: 11–16.

PRUDER, G. D., AND E. T. BOLTON. 1979. The role of CO_2 enrichment of aerating gas in the growth of an estuarine diatom. Aquaculture 17: 1–15.

QASIM, S. Z., P. M. A. BHATTATHIRI, AND V. P. DEVASSY. 1973. Growth kinetics and nutrient requirements of two tropical marine phytoplankters. Mar. Biol. 21: 299–304.

RICHERSON, P., R. ARMSTRONG, AND C. R. GOLDMAN. 1970. Contemporaneous disequilibrium, a new hypothesis to explain the "paradox of the plankton." Proc. Natl. Acad. Sci. U.S.A. 67: 1710–1714.

RILEY, G. A. 1963. Theory of food chain relation in the ocean, p. 438–463. In M. N. Hill [ed.] The sea. Vol. 2. Interscience Publ., New York, NY.

ROSS, G. R. 1973. A model for the competitive growth of two diatoms. J. Theor. Biol. 42: 307–331.

SCHAECHTER, M. 1968. Growth: cells and populations, p. 136–162. In J. Mandelstam and K. McQuillen [ed.] Biochemistry of bacterial growth. J. Wiley and Sons, New York, NY.

SLAWYK, G. 1980. L'absorption de composés azotés par le phytoplancton marin: rôle dans la production primaire, relations avec la photosynthèse et les variables du milieu extra et intracellulaire. Thèse Doct. ès Sc., Univ. Aix-Marseille II. 213 p.

SLAWYK, G., Y. COLLOS, M. MINAS, AND J. R. GRALL. 1978. On the relationship between carbon-to-nitrogen composition ratios of the particulate matter and growth rate of marine phytoplankton from the northwest African upwelling area. J. Exp. Mar. Biol. Ecol. 33: 119–131.

SMAYDA, T. J. 1973. The growth of *Skeletonema costatum* during a winter–spring bloom in Narragansett Bay, Rhode Island. Norw. J. Bot. 20: 219–247.

1975. Phased cell division in natural populations of the marine diatom *Ditylum brightwellii* and the potential significance of diel phytoplankton behavior in the sea. Deep Sea Res. 22: 151–165.

STEELE, J. H. 1959. The quantitative ecology of marine phytoplankton. Biol. Rev. Cambridge Philos. Soc. 34: 129–158.

STEEMANN NIELSEN, E. 1978a. I. Productivity and modeling. Growth of the unicellular alga *Selenastrum capricornutum* as a function of P. With some information also on N. Verh. Int. Ver. Limnol. 20: 38–42.

1978b. Growth of plankton algae as a function of N-concentration, measured by means of a batch technique. Mar. Biol. 46: 185–189.

STEWART, F. M., AND B. R. LEVIN. 1973. Partioning of resources and the outcome of interspecific competition: a model and some general considerations. Am. Nat. 107: 171–198.

STROSS, R. G. 1980. Growth cycles and nutrient-limited photosynthesis in phytoplankton. Limnol. Oceanogr. 25: 538–544.

STROSS, R. G., S. W. CHISHOLM, AND T. A. DOWNING. 1973. Causes of daily rhythms in photosynthetic rates of phytoplankton. Biol. Bull. Woods Hole. 145: 200–209.

STROSS, R. G., AND S. M. PEMRICK. 1974. Nutrient uptake kinetics in phytoplankton: a basis for niche separation. J. Phycol. 10: 164–169.

SWEENEY, B. M., AND J. W. HASTINGS. 1962. Rhythms, p. 687–700. *In* R. A. Lewin [ed.] Physiology and biochemistry of algae. Academic Press, New York, NY.

TAYLOR, P. A., AND P. J. LE B. WILLIAMS. 1975. Theoretical studies on the coexistence of competing species under continuous-flow conditions. Can. J. Microbiol. 21: 90–98.

THOMAS, W. H. 1969. Phytoplankton nutrient enrichment experiments off Baja California and in the eastern tropical Pacific Ocean. J. Fish. Res. Board Can. 26: 1133–1145.

———. 1970a. On nitrogen deficiency in tropical pacific oceanic phytoplankton: photosynthetic parameters in poor and rich water. Limnol. Oceanogr. 15: 380–385.

———. 1970b. Effect of ammonium and nitrate concentration on chlorophyll increases in natural tropical pacific phytoplankton populations. Limnol. Oceanogr. 15: 386–394.

TILMAN, D. 1977. Resource competition between planctonic algae: an experimental and theoretical approach. Ecology 58: 338–348.

TITMAN, D. 1976. Ecological competition between algae: experimental confirmation of resource-based competition theory. Science (Washington, D.C.) 192: 463–465.

TITMAN, D., AND P. KILHAM. 1976. Sinking in freshwater phytoplankton: some ecological implications of cell nutrient status and physical mixing processes. Limnol. Oceanogr. 21: 409–417.

TURPIN, D. H., AND P. J. HARRISON. 1979. Limiting nutrient patchiness and its role in phytoplankton ecology. J. Exp. Mar. Biol. Ecol. 39: 151–166.

UDVARDY, M. F. D. 1959. Notes on the ecological concepts of habitat, biotope and niche. Ecology 40: 725–728.

VELDKAMP, H., AND H. W. JANNASCH. 1972. Mixed culture studies with the chemostat. J. Appl. Chem. Biotechnol. 22: 105–123.

VOLTERRA, V. 1926. Fluctuations in the abundance of a species considered mathematically. Nature (London) 118: 558–560.

VOLTERRA, V., AND U. D'ANCONA. 1935. Les associations biologiques au point de vue mathématique. *In* V. G. Tessier [ed.] Exposés de biométrie et de statistique biologique. Actual. Sci. Inc. 243.

WEILER, C. S., AND S. W. CHISHOLM. 1976. Phased cell division in natural populations of marine dinoflagellates from shipboard cultures. J. Exp. Mar. Biol. Ecol. 25: 239–247.

WILLIAMS, F. M. 1971. Dynamics of microbial populations, p. 197–267. *In* B. C. Patten [ed.] Systems analysis and simulation in ecology. Vol. 1. Academic Press, New York, NY.

WILLIAMS, P. J. LE B., AND L. R. MUIR. 1981. Diffusion as a constraint on the biological importance of microzones in the sea. Proc. 12th Colloq. Ocean Hydrodynam. Liège.

WROBLEWSKI, J. S. 1977. Vertically migrating herbivorous plankton. Their possible role in the creation of small scale phytoplankton patchiness in the ocean, p. 817–847. *In* N. R. Andersen and B. J. Zahuranec [ed.] Oceanic sound scattering prediction. Plenum Press, New York, NY.

YODER, J. A. 1979. A comparison between the cell division rate of natural populations of the marine diatom *Skeletonema costatum* (Greville) Cleve grown in dialysis culture and that predicted from a mathematical model. Limnol. Oceanogr. 24: 97–106.

Importance of Organic Nutrients for Phytoplankton Growth in Natural Environments: Implications for Algal Species Succession

DANIEL J. BONIN AND SERGE Y. MAESTRINI

Station Marine d'Endoume, Chemin de la Batterie des Lion, F-13007 Marseille

Introduction

One probable role of organic compounds in natural waters is to support the growth of phytoplankters when major inorganic nutrients are totally lacking or are present at a very low concentration, or when the light intensity is very low. The ecological importance of these phenomena has been strongly debated, in spite of the fact that heterotrophic assimilation capabilities have been observed in numerous freshwater and marine algae. As a matter of fact, the ability of many planktonic algae to use diverse organic nutrients in laboratory cultures is well documented. However, the kinetics of such uptake often appear to be quite inadequate for the low concentrations of organic compounds found in natural environments. The high half-saturation (K) values observed for organic nutrient assimilation by phytoplankters led to the conclusion that, typically, algae cannot compete with bacteria for the dilute organic substrates usually present in natural waters; and algal heterotrophy is then considered as a laboratory artifact arising from the axenic conditions in cultures and from the very high concentrations of substrates used in most experiments. The dependence of the phytoplankters on organic materials is not obligatory; it is facultative heterotrophy. The importance of this way of growth depends greatly on the general nutritional conditions, and differs according to the element given in organic form: carbon, nitrogen, or phosphorus.

Carbon

HISTORICAL AND PHYSIOLOGICAL FEATURES

From mud samples collected during the *Galathea* Expedition, in 1951, Wood (1956) found wellpreserved benthic diatoms, belonging to autochtonous populations and adapted to live at very great depths (7000–10 000 m). Bernard (1958) observed some Chrysomonads in the Mediterranean Sea in very deep layers (between 250 and 2000 m) where absolutely no light can penetrate. These organisms were in apparent good health. Obviously, in such conditions, if growth can occur, it should be dependent totally on organic material.

The significance of the utilization of organic compounds is very complex and varies with the algae (Droop 1974; Neilson and Lewin 1974; Hastings and Thomas 1977; Hellebust and Lewin 1977). Experimentally, it has been demonstrated that many algae can grow in the total dark if an organic compound is added in the medium. This has been observed for algae of all taxonomic groups. These compounds are used as energy source and sometimes also as carbon source. For example, it has been shown that when CO_2 is lacking in the medium, *Navicula pelliculosa* (Lewin 1953) can grow in presence of light if glycerol is added in the medium. Likewise, *Euglena gracilis* (Murray et al. 1970) can grow if glycolate, glycine, or serine is provided as single carbon source. On the other hand, it is mentioned that organic nutrients stimulate the growth of some obligatory photoautotrophs maintained in very dim light (Cheng and Antia 1970; Cooksey and Chansang 1976; Morrill and Loeblich 1979).

But no ecological significance can be attributed to these capabilities until more is known of the performance of the algae under natural conditions. Not only the concentrations and types of organic materials available in natural waters must be determined, but also the kinetics of uptake of organic compounds by the algae must be measured. Only then can the laboratory studies be extrapolated to natural environmental conditions to determine if the algae can successfully compete with bacteria for dissolved organic compounds. The first experiments made in this topic were not very encouraging. For example, Sloan and Strickland (1966) in their conclusions pointed out that, even if it is possible to find some heterotrophic capability in *Cyclotella cryptica* and *Thalassiosira rotula*, it takes a lag phase for the algae to adjust, and the uptake is too low, in the range of substrate concentrations in natural waters, to attach any ecological significance to the heterotrophy. Wright and Hobbie (1965) distinguished two different mechanisms in the uptake of organic materials by organisms. One responds to an enzymatic transport system which is probably unique to bacteria. The second one is linear: uptake by passive diffusion increases proportionally with increasing substrate concentration. It should be performed by organisms other than bacteria, such as phytoplankton. If so, obviously, the algae would be strongly disadvantaged relative to bacteria for the uptake of such compounds at low concentrations.

Somewhat later, Hellebust and Guillard (1967) demonstrated that the transport of organic compounds across the membrane of the cell is an active phenomenon depending on the external concentration of the metabolite and responding to a Michaelis-Menten type equation. Using this approach, it has been possible to characterize the affinities of the cells for different substrates. The algae show different characteristics in regard to this uptake. For instance, Lewin and Hellebust (1975, 1976, 1978) demonstrated that *Nitzschia angularis*, *Nitzschia laevis*, and *Navicula pavillardi* are able to utilize glutamate for heterotrophic growth but differ greatly in their heterotrophic capabilities with respect to glucose utilization: *Navicula pavillardi* is absolutely unable to utilize glucose; *Nitzschia angularis* takes up glucose as a substrate, in the presence of glumatate as energy source; *Nitzschia laevis* can grow when in presence of glucose as sole substrate. No lag phase is observed before growth takes place after transferring cells from autotrophic to heterotrophic conditions. This finding confirms the presence of a transport system in light-grown cells. The authors pointed out that it is not a rule and other algae behave differently. For instance, *Cyclotella cryptica* and *Cylindrotheca fusiformis* show a lag phase of about 2 d when transferred to the dark. There is a considerable variability in the characteristics of the responses of these diatoms to organic substrates. Furthermore, the affinity of the uptake system in *Nitzschia laevis* is rather high for glutamate ($K = 0.03$ mM), glucose ($K = 0.03$ mM), and alanine ($K = 0.02$ mM), but fairly low for lactate ($K = 0.4$ mM). The ability to take up organic carbon can vary also from dark to light exposure. For instance, Hellebust (1971) showed that glucose uptake by *Cyclotella cryptica* is induced in the dark and stopped during exposure to light. Various physical factors may react on this uptake capability, not only the light intensity and the temperature, but also the salinity. A shift in the salt balance may modify the characteristics of the uptake. Thus, Hellebust (1978) demonstrate that the transport system for glucose and amino acids is strongly related to the NaCl concentration. The relationship between uptake and NaCl concentration is hyperbolic.

ECOLOGICAL IMPLICATIONS

Acclimation to a shift in the energy source, light or organic carbon, can have considerable ecological significance because it is more or less easy for the facultative heterotrophs. For example, White (1974) pointed out that *Coscinodiscus* sp. and *Cyclotella cryptica*, grown in total darkness for 1 yr, keep their chlorophyll *a* and chlorophyll *c* contents.

Undoubtedly, facultative heterotrophy is of ecological benefit to these diatoms when they settle out of the photic layer into dimly lit or dark bottom waters, or in muds, rich in organic materials. They can remain viable there, even for long periods, until exposed to conditions suitable for photoautotrophic growth. And these algae are able to reoccupy the illuminated upper layers when the conditions become better. On the other hand, instead of total heterotrophy, a light-stimulated organic nutrient uptake (photoheterotrophy) may confer a biological advantage to species living preferentially in dim light. Bristol Roach (1928) already demonstrated that, for a soil alga exposed to a very attenuated light, autotrophic and heterotrophic uptakes are not exclusive processes, but, on the contrary, may be cumulative. Even if we have observed that some centric diatoms are capable of such an heterotrophic growth, most species showing these capabilities belong to the pennate group. Quantitative measurements for other algae are scarce and it is difficult to establish a good estimate of the real influence of this uptake by unstudied species of algae relative to the uptake by bacterial populations in the water column.

With differential filtration and autoradiographic methods, it has been possible to characterize the uptake of labeled organic compounds by various components of the pelagic ecosystem. The results obtained at sea and in lakes point out that the fraction that retains the most part of the radioactivity is of a very small size (under 1–2 μm) and likely mainly belongs to bacterial populations. Many works have been published on this topic (Williams 1970; Allen 1971; Berman 1975; Azam and Hodson 1977; Berman and Stiller 1977; Chrétiennot-Dinet and Vacelet 1978). These results are not surprising because, as stated before, the half-saturation constants of algae for uptake of the organic compounds are usually high. Bennett and Hobbie (1972) mentioned with glucose, $K = 5$ mg$\cdot$L^{-1} in *Chlamydomonas* sp.; this concentration is much higher than those observed in natural waters; consequently, such a transport system cannot in general be effective under natural conditions.

However, the concentrations of all the naturally occurring organic compounds increase significantly in peculiar situations: at the surface of organic aggregates (Riley 1963), in muddy sediments near the bottom, or in areas submitted to hypertrophication. The heterotrophic potential of the algae cannot be neglected in these conditions, since there is often a good correspondence between their heterotrophic capabilities and the organic trophic level of the ecosystem to which they belong. This has been observed more frequently in benthic diatoms (Admiraal and Peletier 1979) and less often in phytoplankton. For instance, Mahoney and McLaughlin

(1977) found that dinoflagellates, abundant during the blooms in the hypertrophicated New York Bay, are highly versatile and use more than half the 21 organic compounds tested, mainly sugars and derivatives. Obviously, the two dinoflagellates studied, *Massartia rotundata* and *Prorocentrum micans*, and the chrysophyte *Olithodiscus luteus* have a nutritional advantage in this environment. Because these organisms can reach densities over 200 million cells per litre, it is possible that the CO_2 becomes a limiting factor. In fact, one observes an increase of growth in these samples when bicarbonate is added. For these species, the use of organic carbon sources would likely help to mitigate the CO_2 deficiency. The role of organic compounds as alternative carbon sources has also been postulated in very soft water lakes, inadequatly buffered, where, at some period of the day, the intensive photosynthesis brings the pH abruptly to very high levels (Allen 1972). But, such improvements of growth by organic carbon compounds that act as a carbon source may be not very common and are mainly observed in very rich waters. As a matter of fact, it has been demonstrated that the availability of inorganic carbon from bicarbonate complex is sufficient in most natural waters to be much less limiting than other nutrients (Goldman et al. 1974; Caperon and Smith 1978).

The real demonstration and the final proof of heterotrophy in the natural environments, as stated Vincent and Goldman (1980), require the following: (i) analytical description of the ambient concentrations and rates of supply of usable substrates; (ii) in situ evidence that algae have a high affinity transport system which enables them to take up organic compounds at the in situ concentrations; (iii) demonstration that these algae are biochemically equipped to use these substrates for growth; (iv) estimation of the relative contribution of dissolved organic substances versus other nutrient or energetic factors. To get simultaneous information on these four points is very difficult indeed. But the same authors, Vincent and Goldman (1980), demonstrated that, in an oligotrophic lake (Lake Tahoe, USA), it is possible to find two species, *Monoraphidium contortum* and *Friedmannia* sp., that are able to take up organic compounds in the deeper layers of the lake but are usually not abundant in the surface euphotic zone. Furthermore, these species are capable of significant acetate transport, which varies with environmental conditions and ranges from 25 to 247% compared with the photosynthetic carbon uptake. But, at the bottom of the photic layer, the ratio of the organic carbon utilization by total phytoplankton is only 1.5–15.0% of the photosynthetic carbon uptake. On the other hand, in culture, these species have an extremely slow growth in the dark but are able to remain viable and to retain a fully operational

photosynthetic apparatus for very long periods. These observations lead the authors to assert that heterotrophic capability helps the cells to maintain good health in aphotic conditions, but does not contribute significantly to the total production of the water column.

In conclusion, when organic compounds are taken up by phytoplankters, they are used mainly as additional energy sources and less frequently as carbon source. Furthermore, it is doubtful that this kind of heterotrophy plays a major role in the trophic strategies of the greatest part of phytoplankters, in most natural environmental conditions. But, principally in locally enriched areas, heterotrophy and the photoheterotrophy might increase the survival potential of organisms during periods of low light intensity and might give them an advantage relative to their exclusive photoautotrophic competitors.

Nitrogen

INTRODUCTION AND GENERAL FEATURES

For many years, inorganic nitrogen was considered the sole potential source for the algae in natural waters. This tendency was so strong that even the role of ammonia was omitted completely in the computation of the available forms of nitrogen for the primary production. But, obviously, the metabolism of organic matter by animals, algae, and bacteria releases in the medium many organic forms of nitrogen and phosphorus, which are more or less rapidly oxidized to nitrates and phosphates. When the Redfield's (1958) ratio nitrogen: phosphorus is close to 15:1, the conclusion that organic forms do not interfere directly in plant growth could be accepted. But, often in neritic waters and at the end of the blooms in the open waters, and much more commonly in lakes, this ratio can vary considerably. Its variations are greater when only the amounts of nitrates and nitrites are taken into account and not the other forms of nitrogen (Harris and Riley 1956; Vaccaro 1963). Even if such organic compounds probably have only a slight influence on the total production of the waters, it is difficult to deny their role on phytoplankton populations, at least in peculiar conditions.

The concept of Dugdale and Goering (1967) has been very useful in this respect. These authors proposed the terms of "regenerated production" for the production due to rapidly recycled forms of nitrogen in the upper layers, and "new production" related to forms of nitrogen brought from the deep layers or from the atmosphere. When the hydrological conditions lead to an increase in the function of regenerated production relative to new production, the algae of natural assemblages that are able to take up and assimilate organic forms of nitrogen will be helped in their growth, and this capability could be an important factor in determining species succession. This role will be more important in oligotrophic waters where the concentrations of inorganic forms of nitrogen are low.

Indeed, algae are able to grow with organic nitrogen compounds as sole nitrogen source and this information is very old. Ternetz (1912) was probably the first to give such results, using *Euglena gracilis*. Since then, these potentialities have been observed in many algae (Syrett 1962; Van Baalen 1962; Guillard 1963; Lewin 1963; McCarthy 1972a; Wheeler et al. 1974; Antia et al. 1975, and many others). The aim of the earliest studies was often to characterize biochemically some strains or species, to differentiate them by their growth patterns which might be of some taxonomic utility. Each investigator chose his own set of experimental conditions, particularly the nitrogen source concentration. Unfortunately, it was frequently 100–1000 times higher than the values usually found in natural waters, and the results may not reflect the behavior of phytoplankters in their environment. Moreover, illumination conditions (intensity, quality, light–dark cycles) used in these experiments were also quite different. Because of that, these studies were not always directly useful for the ecologist, even if they offered a valuable insight into the metabolic potential of algae for utilization of various nitrogen sources. Anyhow, it is possible to retain some general features. (i) The responses greatly differ with the species and, even within one species, with the strains. All organic compounds tested (urea, uric acid, amino acids, amino sugars, purines) do not show the same capability of growth for each species. For instance, among 26 species belonging to all taxonomic groups present in the plankton, and grown on urea, glycine, glucosamine, and hypoxanthine, 88% showed a more or less good growth on urea, 69% on hypoxanthine, 50% on glycine, and 42% on glucosamine (Antia et al. 1975). Obviously, urea is a good potential nitrogen source for almost all the species studied and this is pointed out by many authors. Amino acids are used very differently by the different species and, in one species, by various clones (Cain 1965). Usually, glycine, glutamic acid, asparagine, and tryptophane are more frequently used than lysine, proline, phenylalanine and tyrosine (data from Turner 1979). Pyrimidic and puric bases are less frequently taken up. But hypoxanthine is proved as a good source of nitrogen (Antia et al. 1975). (ii) It is necessary to point out that the results may vary with the culture conditions, and conflicting results are not unusual. For example, the cyanophyta *Agmenellum quadruplicatum* strain PR6 shows different behaviors in different studies. Van Baalen

(1962) and Antia et al. (1975) did not observe any growth on glycine, the opposite results to that of Kapp et al. (1975). Liu and Hellebust (1974) observed successful growth of *Cyclotella cryptica* on urea but Antia et al. (1977) did not. Obviously, all experimental conditions (light, temperature, salinity strength) may react on the capacity for one strain to grow on a given organic compound. (iii) Another cause of discrepancies may lie in the fact that, for some species–organic compound associations, an adaptation phase may occur when the alga is transferred from a medium with inorganic source to a medium with an organic source. For instance, Antia et al. (1975) observed a very long period of adaptation (18–23 d) with *Prasinocladus marinus*, *Isochrysis galbana*, and *Hemiselmis virescens* cultivated on hypoxanthine before growth began; afterwards, these species appeared to utilize the purine as efficiently as they did ammonium or urea. On the other hand, it has been demonstrated that the capability of taking up such compounds may vary as a function of chemical conditions of the medium. North and Stephens (1967, 1969, 1971, 1972) mentioned uptake of amino acids by *Platymonas subcordiformis* and *Nitzschia ovalis*. They observed that a previous restriction of the nitrogen availability in the culture greatly accelerates the rate of amino acid uptake. As a matter of fact, it appears that the growth potentials of the nitrogen compounds depend on the nutritional history of the cells. (iv) Furthermore, the concentration of the nutrient plays a very important role in this capability of growth (Berland et al. 1976, 1979; Antia et al. 1977). An increase of the concentration enhances not only the frequency of appearance of the potentiality, but also the growth rate for several species which develop poorly at lower concentrations. Sometimes, it is necessary to reach very high levels (12.5 or 25 mM·L^{-1} of N compound) to observe any growth. But, such high values can be toxic for other strains and we have to be very cautious in extending such remarks to the ecological content, since these high concentrations are never found in natural waters.

In fact, some works demonstrate that many algae are able to effectively take up such compounds as urea and amino acids at concentrations rather close to the amounts existing in the waters.

AMINO ACIDS

Wheeler et al. (1974) studied 25 strains cultivated on nine amino acids, and observed that 75% of the strain–substrate combinations allowed a fairly good growth at a concentration of 1 µg-at·L^{-1} of N substrate. One conclusion was that, in most cases, species that could grow in culture on amino acids at high concentrations, could also take up amino acids at low concentrations. Therefore, these results showed that the high concentrations frequently used in culture often provide valuable and useful information on the real uptake potentialities of the algae in their natural environment. More generally, it must be concluded that many phytoplankters have transport systems that allow them to accumulate and assimilate amino acids at concentrations commonly found in natural waters. Such patterns appear preferentially in species that normally occur in inshore and littoral habitats where amino acid concentrations may be higher (Clark et al. 1972).

Another question which has to be resolved concerns the capability of these algae to take up and assimilate such compounds when different nitrogen sources are present simultaneously in the medium. Early research on the subject led to the conclusion that high concentrations of nitrate or ammonia did not interfere with amino acid uptake (North and Stephens 1971). But, further experiments gave opposite results. North and Stephens (1972) demonstrated with *Nitzschia ovalis* that the transport of all amino acids is repressed by high concentrations of nitrate in the medium. Likewise, Wheeler (1977) with *Platymonas subcordiformis* pointed out that ammonia is the most efficient N source in the repression of amino acid uptake. As the assimilation of nitrate is inhibited by ammonia in the medium, the uptake of amino acids seems directly related to the presence of inorganic nitrogen sources. Such results are scarce, but if they were generalized, they would lead us to believe that amino acid uptake could only occur with nitrogen-limiting conditions, contrary to what was earlier thought to be the case.

Stephens and North (1971) observed that the algae are able to retain the amino moiety of the molecule after taking it up and to extrude the carbon part. This negates the hypothesis of Algeus (1948) that amino acids are extracellularly deaminated. The mechanism of the amino acid uptake is really much more complex than initially expected. North and Stephens (1972) demonstrated by kinetic studies that *Nitzschia ovalis* possesses at least three amino acid uptake systems, specific for transporting acidic, polybasic, and neutral amino acids. The efficiencies of the three systems are not similar. Acidic and neutral amino acids are taken up only by nitrogen-depleted cells at the end of growth in batch cultures. On the contrary, the polybasic amino acid sites appear to be present throughout all phases of the growth. Likewise, Hellebust (1970) found at least three amino acid transport sites in the diatom *Melosira nummuloides*. Because several different compounds can compete for one site when analogues are present in the medium, they can prevent the uptake of amino acids as Pedersen and Knudsen (1974) demonstrated in *Chlorella fusca*. In the same way, Kirk and Kirk

(1978) showed the existence of amino acid specific carriers in various Chlorophyceae. These carriers can be loaded with several different amino acids or other compounds like urea, that would compete for the occupation of one site. In a given species, the carrier of one amino acid can be saturated by another and then can transport this latter, but with a lower efficiency. This discovery is very important because it implies that different organic compounds could act synergistically to modify the response observed with one compound alone; this synergistic action is not always positive. Likely, such systems exist in other groups of algae. Since the uptake systems may differ among species, the amino acid composition of the waters could preferentially enhance the growth of some species in comparison with the other components of natural phytoplankton assemblages.

Once taken up, all amino acids do not have the same evolution inside the cells. Wheeler and Stephens (1977) demonstrated that arginine, alanine, and lysine absorbed by *Platymonas* N-limited cells rapidly entered both anabolic and catabolic pathways. In N-nonlimited cells, all the soluble alanine, but only a part of the arginine and lysine were available for protein systhesis, suggesting two different metabolic pools of amino acids in the cells. In other words, all the amino acids seem not to be similarly used for protein synthesis, but we do not know enough about these metabolic pathways to assert that there is no difference, in qualitative needs for the amino acids, between algae belonging to different taxonomic groups.

This problem becomes much more complex if we consider all the organisms in the ecosystem able to take up amino acids. Bacteria from fresh and oceanic waters are the best equipped in this competition and develop very rapidly in culture, on almost all the amino acids. This is verified by size fractionation, microautoradiographic, and kinetics studies in natural communities (Hobbie et al. 1968; Williams 1970; Crawford et al. 1974; Paerl 1974; Hollibaugh 1976; and others). The main argument for this assessment is that bacterial uptake of organic substrates proceeds more rapidly and at a lower substrate concentrations than algal uptake. Furthermore, bacteria very rapidly adjust their uptake rates to high concentrations of amino acids by metabolic adaptations or activation involving the synthesis of inducible enzymes (Hollibaugh 1979). Very often, with the autoradiographic studies, it appears that the phytoplankton cells are not appreciably labeled. On the contrary, other studies do deny a total lack of influence of the amino acids on the growth of the phytoplankton in defined conditions. For example, Schell (1974) described situations in marine waters, southeast of Alaska, where the uptake of

N- and C-labeled glycine and glutamic acid showed utilization by natural assemblages at low but detectable rates compared with those of nitrate and ammonia. Consequently, the uptakes of the dissolved free amino acids may contribute to a small percentage of the nitrogen required by phytoplankton in surface waters severely depleted in inorganic nitrogen. The author even explains variations in turnover times of dissolved free amino acids by differences in the composition of the phytoplankton populations or by cell adaptations to more efficient use of organic compounds. At the entrance of Newport Bay (USA), Wheeler et al. (1977) observed the occurrence of activity in the nanoplankton size fraction, whereas only a slight uptake was coupled with the small particles of bacteria size. This fact could be explained by the activity of the bacteria attached to big particles which would be able to retain a great part of the amino acids; but, according to the authors, such an hypothesis is untenable in the water they studied and the role of uptake by nanoplankton cannot be neglected.

UREA

The influence of urea on the phytoplankton production has been easier to demonstrate. The attention has been more easily focused on this compound because it has been possible to observe very high concentrations of urea in several areas. Furthermore, the enzymes urease and ATP: urea amidolyase (UAL-ase) used in the initial step in urea metabolism are well known (Roon and Levenberg 1968), whereas the mechanism of uptake of amino acid is still almost unknown. It appeared that the two enzymes are not present together in the same alga (Leftley and Syrett 1973). Each organism has either one enzymatic activity or the other. According to the studies carried out so far, it seems that Chlorophyceae contain UAL-ase and the other algae, urease. The published data of K values with extracted urease are much higher than with UAL-ase (Syrett and Leftley 1976). But, in organisms, it appears that the activities of the two enzymes are very close and algae that possess UAL-ase are not at such an advantage to take up the urea at low concentrations as would be initially expected. For example, McCarthy (1972a) demonstrated that the marine diatoms *Cyclotella nana*, *Ditylum brightwelli*, *Lauderia* sp., *Skeletonema costatum*, and *Thalassiosira fluviatilis* have urea uptake K values ranging from 0.42 to 1.70 μg-at$\cdot$L^{-1} N. Furthermore, *Skeletonema costatum* and *Ditylum brightwelli* have urea uptake K values not really different from those observed with ammonia. The fact that half-saturation constants for urea uptake are equal or lower than the urea concentrations frequently measured in the oceans suggests that urea should be a valuable nitrogen source for many phytoplankters. Healey (1977) observed similar values for K constants in freshwater algae *Scenedesmus quadricauda* and *Pseudoanabaena catenata*. Since the urea concentrations in lakes and fresh waters are often higher than in the sea, it led the same author to assert that, in fresh waters, ammonia and urea are the main nitrogen sources and that, most often, nitrate and nitrite are not taken up by algae.

As observed with amino acids, bacteria can compete with algae for urea uptake, but it has been demonstrated that, in eutrophic areas where the urea concentrations are high, the phytoplankters are responsible for the major part of its decomposition. Remsem et al. (1972) showed this in estuaries of the Georgia coast (USA) where the urea concentration can reach 8.9 $\mu M \cdot L^{-1}$. In these brackish waters, the uptake by the cells is more efficient for marine algae than for freshwater ones, and higher for the large cells than small ones. In coastal waters off southern California, McCarthy (1972b) found that urea, particularly in the upper layers at stations where the amount of nitrates are very low, could constitute between 30 and 50% of the total nitrogen used by natural assemblages. In a polluted bay of the Hawaian Islands, Harvey and Caperon (1976) gave such findings with an urea uptake average that accounted for 53.5% of the total nitrogen uptake. For several stations, this percentage can reach 100%.

The real function of urea in the phytoplankton production is not easy to appreciate because it depends on the nature and concentrations of other nitrogen sources in the medium. McCarthy and Eppley's (1972) results on natural populations showed that urea and ammonia uptakes occurred simultaneously, but at different rates according to their relative concentrations. Urea inhibits nitrate uptake but at a lower level than ammonia. In Chesapeake Bay, over 13 mo, McCarthy et al. (1977) always observed a high phytoplankton preference for ammonia and urea over nitrate; urea was used after ammonia but before nitrate in order of preference. In another experiment, Eppley et al. (1971) did not observe a significant difference in the total crop of natural assemblages obtained after 3 d in outdoor cultures supplied with nitrate, ammonia, or urea at the same concentration. The average doubling rate of the cells is almost similar with the three substrates. But the behavior of the algae might differ from one species to the other when in presence of urea and other inorganic nitrogen sources. In fresh waters, Healey (1977) gave the results as follows: *Scenedesmus quadricauda* and *Pseudoanabaena catenata* do not respond in the same way when they have both urea and ammonia at their disposal. When the two substrates are present together, the rate of the urea uptake appears to dominate over ammonia uptake in *P. catenata*. On the contrary, *S. quadricauda* generally takes up ammonia two or three times faster than urea. The introduction of ammonia to a *S. quadricauda* culture severely depressed urea uptake whereas the introduction of urea caused a small depression of ammonia uptake. It is the opposite in *P. catenata*.

Even if all the uptake mechanisms are not yet completely elucidated in natural waters, the utilization of urea as a nitrogen source must be interpreted, in general, as a common and very important process in natural environments, the opposite of amino acid uptake. It might be possible that the presence of urea in the medium not only allows the crop to reach higher levels, but also may significantly help some species to outgrow their competitors. In other words, we agree totally with the statement of Butler et al. (1979): "There is now considerable evidence that some species of phytoplankton utilize at least part of the dissolved organic nitrogen directly. It therefore seems a reasonable hypothesis that as NO_3 is exhausted the phytoplankton population changes so that the species capable of utilizing other forms of N become dominant."

Phosphorus

PHOSPHORUS AS A LIMITING FACTOR FOR ALGAL GROWTH

The utilization of organic phosphorus compounds has been studied with less attention than nitrogen organic materials. Generally, phosphorus has been considered sufficient, relative to the nitrogen concentrations in seawater. On the contrary, in lakes, it frequently becomes the first limiting factor. Many works support this conclusion. For example, Healey and Hendzel (1980) measured physiological indicators of nitrogen and phosphorus deficiency of many lakes in the center of Canada, and concluded that the lakes severely or moderately deficient in phosphorus are much more numerous than nitrogen-deficient ones. Several other authors give similar conclusions.

Recently, the position of several scientists on the impossibility of phosphorus limiting the production in the sea has been reconsidered. Effectively, if ammonia and urea are included as available nitrogen in the Redfield's (1958) N:P ratio, it often becomes much more higher than 15:1 and the role of phosphorus in the limitation of the primary production would be emphasized. An example is given by Sander and Moore (1979) who observed a shift of the N:P atomic ratio from 9.8:1.0 to 28.8:1.0 in the first 100 m of the water column near Barbados, if ammonia is included. In some areas like the Mediterranean Sea, the ratio frequently reaches values over 20 (McGill 1965), and there, at many stations, it is possible to verify that phosphorus becomes more limiting than nitrogen (Berland et al.

1980). Steemann Nielsen (1978) observed good growth of *Selenastrum capricornutum* at very low concentrations of ammonia. He pointed out that such concentrations are very often observed in oligotrophic parts of the oceans and he asserted that, in these areas, it is wrong to conclude that nitrogen is the most limiting factor on the primary production only on the basis of the low concentrations of inorganic nitrogen.

Furthermore, algae have to compete with bacteria for phosphorus uptake. The role of bacteria in the consumption of inorganic phosphorus cannot be neglected. Harrison et al. (1977) pointed out that the fraction of inorganic phosphorus taken up by bacteria was always important in Saanich Inlet, British Columbia; at least 50% of the ^{32}P uptake is associated with particles under 1 μm. For the size fraction over 1 μm, the amount of phosphorus fixed by bacteria seems more important than for algae. Likewise, Paerl and Lean (1976), using the ^{32}P autoradiographic technique, found that, in lakes, bacteria are more strongly labeled by ^{32}P-labeled orthophosphates than are algae. Even if it seems that, in certain conditions, the affinity towards orthophosphates is lower for the bacteria than for the algae (Rhee 1972), there is a strong evidence that, in some natural waters, bacteria can successfully compete with algae for the utilization of inorganic phosphorus.

Otherwise, it is usually assumed that the deprivation of external phosphorus does not immediately damage the algal metabolism because of the internal pool of orthophosphates and polyphosphates stored inside the cell. Effectively, the algal capacity to store internal phosphorus is usually great. It is also observed that phosphorus starvation is followed by an increase of the phosphorus uptake after the replenishment of the medium. In cells newly enriched with phosphorus, the proportion of polyphosphates in the cell can reach very high values (Aitchison and Butt 1973) and this form of phosphorus can contribute as much as 50% of the total cell phosphorus (Perry 1976). Obviously, this reservoir dramatically enhances the capability of the algae to remain viable during phosphorus depletion and helps them to compete successfully with bacteria in which this property is less well developed. Such a demonstration has been made experimentally by Rhee (1972) in comparing the growth of the green alga *Scenedesmus* sp. with that of a strain of *Pseudomonas* in different environmental conditions. The algae also have the capability to take up polyphosphates in the medium. Such observations have often been made in cultures. Solorzano and Strickland (1968) mentioned it in *Skeletonema costatum* and *Amphidinium carteri*. Several authors also explain the high potential of the algae to keep their viability, even in phosphorus-deficient media, by a very rapid turnover of the ambient phosphate (Fitzgerald and Nelson 1966).

It is possible to believe that the total inorganic phosphorus may become limiting, at least in particular ecological conditions, and consequently, that organic compounds could be used as an alternative source of phosphorus.

DISSOLVED ORGANIC MATERIALS AS AN ALTERNATIVE SOURCE OF PHOSPHORUS

Steiner (1938) is the first to have foreseen the possible ecological importance of these compounds for phytoplankton growth. Later, Chu (1946) demonstrated experimentally that some sources of dissolved organic phosphorus, as phytin and glycerophosphate, support a fairly good growth of *Phaeodactylum tricornutum*. It was proved very quickly that many species of algae are capable of such growth in the absence of orthophosphates but in the presence of phosphoesters (Provasoli 1958). Therefore, it was assumed and verified later that algae, like bacteria, can produce a phosphatase that hydrolyzes the ester in, or on, the cell membrane, when the inorganic phosphorus becomes limiting. Kuenzler and Perras (1965) demonstrated that this enzyme exists in 27 strains of algae belonging to Chrysophyceae, Bacillariophyceae, Cryptophyceae, Cyanophyceae, Dinophyceae, and Chlorophyceae. They showed that the activity of the phosphatase could vary greatly according to the species. Furthermore, the optimum pH conditions for the highest enzymatic activity differs for each species. These results, with others dedicated to freshwater algae (Brandes and Elston 1956), were very provocative. As a matter of fact, since the activity of phosphatase, when present, could vary according to species and environmental conditions, this capability might ensure the algae which possess these enzymes a decisive advantage over other species, when inorganic phosphorus concentrations in the medium are low, compared with those of the esters.

Kuenzler (1970) verified the influence of these compounds on the species succession in an experimental ecosystem. He found that *Cyclotella cryptica*, *Phaeodactylum tricornutum*, *Dunaliella tertiolecta*, *Chlorella* sp., *Rhodomonas lens*, *Coccolithus huxleyi*, and *Synechococcus* sp. are capable of growing on filtrate from cultures of other strains but with various success. The diatoms were the most efficient in the uptake of organic phosphorus. On the contrary, *Dunaliella* and *Synechococcus*, which have an internal but no external phosphatase, and *Chlorella* and *Rhodomonas*, which have no efficient phosphatase in the experimental conditions, cannot take up most compounds released in the medium by the other algae. In these experiments, the fact that the amount of enzymes and the rate of uptake of dissolved

organic phosphorus are positively related demonstrates both the importance of the phosphatases in the uptake of DOP and the role of phosphomonoesters as a supplementary source of phosphorus. Such results showed the real potentiality of many algae to utilize DOP, but, because of the high concentrations used in the experiments, it was difficult to assert categorically that such utilization can really occur in natural environments.

As a matter of fact, the concentration of DOP is often very low in natural waters. In San Diego Harbor (USA) Solorzano and Strickland (1968) found concentrations ranging from 0.12 to 0.70 μg-at$\cdot$L^{-1}. In Chesapeake Bay, Taft et al. (1975, 1977) gave values between 0.12 and 0.53 μg-at$\cdot$L^{-1}. In the Seto Inland Sea (Japan), Matsuda et al. (1975) mentioned concentrations always lower than 0.75 μg-at$\cdot$L^{-1}. In the Dutch Wadden Sea, De Jonge and Postma (1974) indicated an average of 0.3 μg-at$\cdot$L^{-1}; in these waters, the DOP can be present at higher concentrations than the inorganic phosphorus, particularly in summer. Kobori and Taga (1979) gave similar conclusions for some bays in Japan. Moreover, all forms of inorganic phosphorus are not available at the same level. Data from fresh waters (Lean 1973) and seawaters (Strickland and Solórzano 1966) show that two general types of DOP exist. One contains the high molecular weight compounds, slowly degradable and supposed to be mainly constituted of nucleic acids. The second part, easily biodegradable and attacked by the phosphatases, includes all the phosphomonoesters. The latter is often found at relatively low concentrations regarding total DOP: 19% in Loch Creran, Scotland (Solórzano 1978); between 13 and 75% in Sagami Bay, Japan (Kobori and Taga 1979). But the fact that the easily degradable fraction of the DOP is usually at low concentration does not mean that this fraction has less influence on the phytoplankton production than the more stable one. The separation of the DOP in two fractions of inequal importance, one easily, the other slowly degradable, is probably an excessive simplification. As a matter of fact, using an artificial procedure (pH = 9; temperature = 37°C) Francko and Heath (1979), in two lakes in Ohio, found that 60–98% of the particulate phosphorus is hydrolyzed to orthophosphate by the alkaline phosphatase. Obviously, the easily hydrolyzable fraction effectively released by the organisms is much higher than that expected from concentrations usually found in the water.

The problem concerning the capability of algae to take up such phosphomonoesters is whether they are able to do it at very low concentrations. Taft et al. (1977) observed that in the Chesapeake Bay natural assemblages have uptake characteristics that permit utilization of phosphoesters at very low concentrations (K below 0.5 μg-at·L^{-1} with glucose-6-phosphate). In this uptake, the role of the bacteria seems to be less than 15% of the total absorption. This K value is close to those observed for the uptake of the inorganic phosphorus by various species: K (μg-at·L^{-1}) is 0.12 for *Asterionella japonica* (Thomas and Dodson 1968); 0.15 for *Ceratium furca* (Qasim et al. 1973); 0.6 for *Scenedesmus* sp. (Rhee 1973); 0.6 for *Thalassiosira pseudonana* (Perry 1976); values ranging from 0.11 to 1.72 for natural populations in the Chesapeake Bay (Taft et al. 1975). Such comparisons of K values allow us to assert without great risk that, in many algae, the organic compounds may be hydrolyzed by the phosphatase at concentrations not too different from the natural ones.

ALKALINE PHOSPHATASE ACTIVITY AS AN INDEX OF PHYTOPLANKTON GROWTH ON ORGANIC PHOSPHORUS

Another approach for investigating the limitation of inorganic phosphorus and the potential utilization by algae of DOP as monoesters is to measure the activity of the alkaline phosphatase in the plankton, since the activity of this enzyme has been reported to be directly related to inorganic phosphorus limitation. High phosphatase activities are induced or activated by low inorganic phosphorus concentrations. Conversely, phosphatases are repressed or inhibited by high inorganic phosphorus concentrations (Kuenzler and Perras 1965). Thus, it seems possible to associate the presence of the enzyme with (i) a lack of available phosphorus, (ii) consequently a limitation of the algal growth, and (iii) an eventual utilization of the organic phosphorus to compensate for the lack of inorganic phosphorus in the environment. In fact, it is absolutely impossible to assert that the presence of the enzyme is directly coupled with the utilization of phosphomonoesters by algae, and it now seems that the real significance of the phosphatase has not always been adequately evaluated in natural waters.

One difficulty in interpreting the significance of the presence of the enzyme is that bacteria are also able to use phosphomonoesters in natural waters. For example, the phosphatase-producing bacteria represent more than 40% of the total bacteria studied in some bays in Japan (Kobori and Taga 1979), and the profiles of the enzyme activity are well correlated with bacteria densities at various depths. Even more, because the phosphatase activity is significantly correlated with the number of bacteria, and the number of bacteria directly related to the quantity of organic materials in the water, several ecologists use the phosphatase activity as an index of the trophic level of the environment, both in seawaters (Taga and Kobori 1978) and in fresh waters (Jones 1972a,

b). In these conditions, if the inorganic phosphorus is not completely exhausted in the medium, the algae are not phosphorus-depleted and the phosphatase measurement has no real significance. On the contrary, when the amounts of inorganic phosphorus are very small, it is impossible to ignore the potential role of bacteria in the measurements. Using the phosphatase activity as an index of the nutrient depletion of phytoplankton becomes more difficult.

It is possible to find direct and good correlations between the chlorophyll *a* concentration and the activity of the alkaline phosphatase. Thus, in natural populations, Taft et al. (1977) demonstrated that the size fraction ranging from 0.8 to 5 μm, which corresponds to the major part (78%) of the plant biomass, is the most efficient (70%) in the uptake of the glucose-6-phosphate. Obviously, in this case, organic phosphorus is essentially taken up by algae and not by bacteria. But, generally there is no direct evidence for the simultaneous occurrence of phosphatase activity and esterphosphate uptake by algae. The presence of the phosphatase only indicates that the orthophosphate supply has dropped below a critical level, which corresponds to a very high internal N:P ratio and, therefore, that additional pathways for phosphorus uptake are in use. Usually, the critical value for the N:P ratio is about 30 (indications of Rhee 1973 on *Scenedesmus* sp. and Møller et al. 1975 on *Chaetoceros affinis*). As a matter of fact, the presence of the alkaline phosphatase in the plankton does not prove that the inorganic part of the dissolved phosphorus in the medium is utilized by algae. For example, Perry (1976) demonstrated that *Thalassiosira pseudonana* cultivated in a chemostat, on a medium made with inorganic, phosphorus-poor water sampled in the central North Pacific Ocean, did not use naturally occurring dissolved organic phosphorus in spite of the presence of phosphatase at the surface of the cells. In this experiment, all natural organic phosphorus compounds in the water were not hydrolyzable by the phosphatase. On the other hand, it has been demonstrated that phosphatase activity responds to diel rhythms. Rivkin and Swift (1979) showed it in the dinoflagellate *Pyrocystis noctiluca*, where the activity of the enzyme is directly coupled to the light–dark cycles, suggesting an endogenous control. Indeed, the meaning of the phosphatase occurrence in natural phytoplankton populations appears to be very complex.

Even if the metabolic action of the phosphatase is presently fairly well known in culture, "the actual role and importance of alkaline phosphatase in the mineral nutrition and ecology of marine phytoplankton is not yet known." This sentence written by Perry (1972) is still valid. It is still difficult to appreciate the real advantage in species competition held by those algae able to take up organically bound phosphorus.

Acknowledgments

We thank Dr Trevor Platt for revising the English manuscript and offering helpful suggestions.

References

ADMIRAAL, W., AND H. PELETIER. 1979. Influence of organic compounds and light limitation on the growth rate of estuarine benthic diatoms. Br. Phycol. J. 14: 197–206.

AITCHISON, P. A., AND V. S. BUTT. 1973. The relation between the synthesis of inorganic polyphosphate and phosphate uptake by Chlorella vulgaris. J. Exp. Bot. 24: 497–510.

ALGEUS, S. 1948. The deamination of glycocoll by green algae. Physiol. Plant. 1: 382–386.

ALLEN, H. L. 1971. Dissolved organic carbon utilization in size-fractionated algal and bacterial communities. Int. Rev. Gesamten Hydrobiol. 56: 731–749.

1972. Phytoplankton photosynthesis, micronutrient interactions, and inorganic carbon availability in á soft-water Vermont lake, p. 63–80. In Nutrients and eutrophication. Spec. Symp. Vol. I, Am. Soc. Limnol. Oceanogr.

ANTIA, N. J., B. R. BERLAND, D. J. BONIN, AND S. Y. MAESTRINI. 1975. Comparative evaluation of certain organic and inorganic sources of nitrogen for phototrophic growth of marine microalgae. J. Mar. Biol. Assoc. U.K. 55: 519–539.

1977. Effects of urea concentration in supporting growth of certain marine microplanktonic algae. Phycologia 16: 105–111.

AZAM, F., AND R. E. HODSON. 1977. Size distribution and activity of marine microheterotrophs. Limnol. Oceanogr. 22: 492–501.

BENNETT, M. E., AND J. E. HOBBIE. 1972. The uptake of glucose by Chlamydomonas sp. J. Phycol. 8: 392–398.

BERLAND, B. R., D. J. BONIN, O. GUERIN-ANCEY, AND N. J. ANTIA. 1979. Concentration requirement of glycine as nitrogen source for supporting effective growth of certain marine microplanktonic algae. Mar. Biol. 55: 83–92.

BERLAND, B. R., D. J. BONIN, AND S. Y. MAESTRINI. 1980. Azote ou phosphore? Considérations sur le "paradoxe nutritionnel" de la mer Méditerranée. Oceanol. Acta 3: 135–142.

BERLAND, B. R., D. J. BONIN, S. Y MAESTRINI, M. L. LIZÁRRAGA-PARTIDA, AND N. J. ANTIA. 1976. The nitrogen concentration requirement of D-glucosamine for supporting effective growth of marine microalgae. J. Mar. Biol. Assoc. U.K. 56: 629–637.

BERMAN, T. 1975. Size fractionation of natural aquatic populations associated with autotrophic and heterotrophic carbon uptake. Mar. Biol. 33: 215–220.

BERMAN, T., AND M. STILLER. 1977. Simultaneous measurement of phosphorus and carbon uptake in Lake Kinneret by multiple isotopic labelling and differential filtration. Microb. Ecol. 3: 279–288.

BERNARD, F. 1958. Données récentes sur la fertilité élémentaire en Méditerranée. Rapp. P.V. Cons. Cons. Int. Explor. Mer 144: 103–108.

BRANDES, D., AND R. N. ELSTON. 1956. An electron microscopical study of the histochemical localization of alkaline phosphatase in the cell wall of Chlorella vulgaris. Nature (London) 177: 274–275.

BRISTOL ROACH, B. M. 1928. On the influence of light and of glucose on the growth of a soil alga. Ann. Bot. London 42: 317–345.

BUTLER, E. I., S. KNOX, AND M. I. LIDDICOAT. 1979. The relationship between inorganic and organic nutrients in sea water. J. Mar. Biol. Assoc. U.K. 59: 239–250.

CAIN, J. 1965. Nitrogen utilization in 38 freshwater Chlamydomonas algae. Can. J. Bot. 43: 1367–1378.

CAPERON, J., AND D. F. SMITH. 1978. Photosynthetic rates of marine algae as a function of inorganic carbon concentration. Limnol. Oceanogr. 23: 704–708.

CHENG, J. Y., AND N. J. ANTIA. 1970. Enhancement by glycerol of phototrophic growth of marine planktonic algae and its significance to the ecology of glycerol pollution. J. Fish. Res. Board Can. 27: 335–346.

CHRETIENNOT-DINET, M. J., AND E. VACELET. 1978. Séparation fractionnée du phytoplancton et estimation de l'assimilation autotrophe et hétérotrophe de ^{14}C. Oceanol. Acta 1: 407–413.

CHU, S. P. 1946. The utilization of organic phosphorus by phytoplankton. J. Mar. Biol. Assoc. U.K. 26: 285–295.

CLARK, M. E., G. A. JACKSON, AND W. J. NORTH. 1972. Dissolved free amino acids in southern California coastal waters. Limnol. Oceanogr. 17: 749–758.

COOKSEY, K. E., AND H. CHANSANG. 1976. Isolation and physiological studies on three isolates of Amphora (Bacillariophyceae). J. Phycol. 12: 455–460.

CRAWFORD, C. C., J. E. HOBBIE, AND K. L. WEBB. 1974. The utilization of dissolved free amino acids by estuarine microorganisms. Ecology 55: 551–563.

DE JONGE, V. N., AND H. POSTMA. 1974. Phosphorus compounds in the Dutch Wadden Sea. Neth. J. Sea Res. 8: 139–153.

DROOP, M. R. 1974. Heterotrophy of carbon, p. 530–559. In W. D. P. Stewart [ed.] Algal physiology and biochemistry. Blackwell Scientific Publications, Oxford.

DUGDALE, R. C., AND J. J. GOERING. 1967. Uptake of new and regenerated forms of nitrogen in primary productivity. Limnol. Oceanogr. 12: 196–206.

EPPLEY, R. W. ET AL. 1971. Phytoplankton growth and composition in shipboard cultures supplied with nitrate, ammonium, or urea as the nitrogen source. Limnol. Oceanogr. 16: 741–751.

FITZGERALD, G. P., AND T. C. NELSON. 1966. Extractive and enzymatic analyses for limiting or surplus phosphorus in algae. J. Phycol. 2: 32–37.

FRANCKO, D. A., AND R. T. HEATH. 1979. Functionally distinct classes of complex phosphorus compounds in lake water. Limnol. Oceanogr. 24: 463–473.

GOLDMAN, J. C., W. J. OSWALD, AND D. JENKINS. 1974. The kinetics of inorganic carbon limited algal growth. J. Water Pollut. Control Fed. 46: 554–574.

GUILLARD, R. R. L. 1963. Organic sources of nitrogen for marine centric diatoms, p. 93–104. *In* C. H. Oppenheimer [ed.] Symposium on marine microbiology. C. C. Thomas, Springfield, IL.

HARRIS, E., AND G. A. RILEY. 1956. Oceanography of Long Island Sound, 1952–1954. VIII. Chemical composition of the plankton. Bull. Bingham. Oceanogr. Coll. 15: 315–323.

HARRISON, W. G., F. AZAM, E. H. RENGER, AND R. W. EPPLEY. 1977. Some experiments on phosphate assimilation by coastal marine plankton. Mar. Biol. 40: 9–18.

HARVEY, W. A., AND J. CAPERON. 1976. The rate of utilization of urea, ammonium, and nitrate by natural populations of marine phytoplankton in a eutrophic environment. Pac. Sci. 30: 329–340.

HASTINGS, J. L., AND W. H. THOMAS. 1977. Qualitative requirements and utilization of nutrients: algae, p. 87–163. *In* M. Rechcigl Jr. [ed.] Handbook series in nutrition and food, section D: Nutritional requirements. Vol. 1. CRC Press, Cleveland, Ohio.

HEALEY, F. P. 1977. Ammonium and urea uptake by some freshwater algae. Can. J. Bot. 55: 61–69.

HEALEY, F. P., AND L. L. HENDZEL. 1980. Physiological indicators of nutrient deficiency in lake phytoplankton. Can. J. Fish. Aquat. Sci. 37: 442–453.

HELLEBUST, J. A. 1970. The uptake and utilization of organic substances by marine phytoplankters, p. 223–256. *In* D. W. Hood [ed.] Symposium on organic matter in natural waters. Inst. Mar. Sci., Univ. Alaska, Occas. Publ. No. 1.

1971. Glucose uptake by *Cyclotella cryptica*: dark induction and light inactivation of transport system. J. Phycol. 7: 345–349.

1978. Uptake of organic substrates by *Cyclotella cryptica* (Bacillariophyceae): effects of ions, ionophores and metabolic and transport inhibitors. J. Phycol. 14: 79–83.

HELLEBUST, J. A., AND R. R. L. GUILLARD. 1967. Uptake specificity for organic substrates by the marine diatom *Melosira nummuloides*. J. Phycol. 3: 132–136.

HELLEBUST, J. A., AND J. LEWIN. 1972. Transport systems for organic acids induced in the marine pennate diatom *Cylindrotheca fusiformis*. Can. J. Microbiol. 18: 225–233.

1977. Heterotrophy, p. 169–197. *In* D. Werner [ed.] The biology of diatoms. Blackwell Scientific Publications, Oxford.

HOBBIE, J. E., C. C. CRAWFORD, AND K. L. WEBB. 1968. Amino acid flux in an estuary. Science (Washington, D.C.) 159: 1463–1464.

HOLLIBAUGH, J. T. 1976. The biological degradation of arginine and glutamic acid in seawater in relation to the growth of phytoplankton. Mar. Biol. 36: 303–312.

1979. Metabolic adaptation in natural bacterial populations supplemented with selected amino acids. Estuarine Coastal Mar. Sci. 9: 215–230.

JONES, J. G. 1972a. Studies on freshwater bacteria-association with algae and alkaline phosphatase activity. J. Ecol. 60: 59–75.

1972b. Studies on freshwater microorganisms-phosphatase activity in lakes of differing degrees of eutrophication. J. Ecol. 60: 777–791.

KAPP, R., S. E. STEVENS JR., AND J. L. FOX. 1975. A survey of available nitrogen sources for the growth of the blue-green alga, *Agmenellum quadruplicatum*. Arch. Microbiol. 104: 135–138.

KIRK, D. L., AND M. M. KIRK. 1978. Amino acid and urea uptake in ten species of Chlorophyta. J. Phycol. 14: 198–203.

KOBORI, H., AND N. TAGA. 1979. Phosphatase activity and its role in the mineralization of organic phosphorus in coastal sea water. J. Exp. Mar. Biol. Ecol. 36: 23–39.

KUENZLER, E. J. 1970. Dissolved organic phosphorus excretion by marine phytoplankton. J. Phycol. 6: 7–13.

KUENZLER, E. J., AND J. P. PERRAS. 1965. Phosphatases of marine algae. Biol. Bull. Woods Hole 128: 271–284.

LEAN, D. R. S. 1973. Movements of phosphorus between its biologically important forms in lake water. J. Fish. Res. Board Can. 30: 1525–1536.

LEFTLEY, J. W., AND P. J. SYRETT. 1973. Urease and ATP: urea amidolyase activity in unicellular algae. J. Gen. Microbiol. 77: 109–115.

LEWIN, J. C. 1953. Heterotrophy in diatoms. J. Gen. Microbiol. 9: 305–313.

1963. Heterotrophy in marine diatoms, p. 229–235. *In* C. H. Oppenheimer [ed.] Symposium on marine microbiology. C. C. Thomas, Springfield, IL.

LEWIN, J., AND J. A. HELLEBUST. 1975. Heterotrophic nutrition of the marine pennate diatom *Navicula pavillardi* Hustedt. Can. J. Microbiol. 21: 1335–1342.

1976. Heterotrophic nutrition of the marine pennate diatom *Nitzschia angularis* var. *affinis*. Mar. Biol. 36: 313–320.

1978. Utilization of glutamate and glucose for heterotrophic growth by the marine pennate diatom *Nitzschia laevis*. Mar. Biol. 47: 1–7.

LIU, M. S., AND J. A. HELLEBUST. 1974. Uptake of amino acids by the marine centric diatom *Cyclotella cryptica*. Can. J. Microbiol. 20: 1109–1118.

MAHONEY, J. B., AND J. J. A. MCLAUGHLIN. 1977. The association of phytoflagellate blooms in lower New York Bay with hypertrophication. J. Exp. Mar. Biol. Ecol. 28: 53–65.

MCCARTHY, J. J. 1972a. The uptake of urea by marine phytoplankton. J. Phycol. 8: 216–222.

1972b. The uptake of urea by natural populations of marine phytoplankton. Limnol. Oceanogr. 17: 738–748.

MCCARTHY, J. J., AND R. W. EPPLEY. 1972. A comparison of chemical, isotopic, and enzymatic methods for measuring nitrogen assimilation of marine phytoplankton. Limnol. Oceanogr. 17: 371–382.

MCCARTHY, J. J., W. R. TAYLOR, AND J. L. TAFT. 1977. Nitrogenous nutrition of the plankton in the Chesapeake Bay. I. Nutrient availability and phytoplankton preferences. Limnol. Oceanogr. 22: 996–1011.

MCGILL, D. A. 1965. The relative supplies of phosphate, nitrate and silicate in the Mediterranean Sea. Comm. Int. Explor. Sci. Mer. Medit., Rapp. P.V. Réun. 18: 737–744.

MØLLER, M., S. MYKLESTAD, AND A. HAUG. 1975. Alkaline and acid phosphatases of the marine diatoms *Chaetoceros affinis* var. *willei* (Gran) Hustedt and *Skeletonema costatum* (Grev.) Cleve. J. Exp. Mar. Biol. Ecol. 19: 217–226.

MORRILL, L. C., AND A. R. LOEBLICH III. 1979. An investigation of heterotrophic and photoheterotrophic capabilities in marine Pyrrhophyta. Phycologia 18: 394–404.

MURRAY, D. R., J. GIOVANELLI, AND R. M. SMILLIE. 1970. Photoassimilation of glycolate, glycine and serine by *Euglena gracilis*. J. Protozool. 17: 99–104.

NEILSON, A. H., AND R. A. LEWIN. 1974. The uptake and utilization of organic carbon by algae: an essay in comparative biochemistry. Phycologia 13: 227–264.

NORTH, B. B., AND G. C. STEPHENS. 1967. Uptake and assimilation of amino acids by *Platymonas*. Biol. Bull. Woods Hole 133: 391–400.

——— 1969. Dissolved amino acids and *Platymonas* nutrition. Proc. Int. Seaweed Symp. 6: 263–273.

——— 1971. Uptake and assimilation of amino acids by *Platymonas*. II. Increased uptake in nitrogen-deficient cells. Biol. Bull. Woods Hole 140: 242–254.

——— 1972. Amino acid transport in *Nitzschia ovalis* Arnott. J. Phycol. 8: 64–68.

PAERL, H. W. 1974. Bacterial uptake of dissolved organic matter in relation to detrital aggregation in marine and freshwater systems. Limnol. Oceanogr. 19: 966–972.

PAERL, H. W., AND D. R. S. LEAN. 1976. Visual observations of phosphorus movement between algae, bacteria, and abiotic particles in lake waters. J. Fish. Res. Board Can. 33: 2805–2813.

PEDERSEN, A. G., AND G. KNUTSEN. 1974. Uptake of L-phenylalanine in synchronous *Chlorella fusca*. Characterization of the uptake system. Physiol. Plant. 32: 294–300.

PERRY, M. J. 1972. Alkaline phosphatase activity in subtropical Central North Pacific waters using a sensitive fluorometric method. Mar. Biol. 15: 113–119.

——— 1976. Phosphate utilization by an oceanic diatom in phosphorus-limited chemostat culture and in the oligotrophic waters of the Central North Pacific. Limnol. Oceanogr. 21: 88–107.

PROVASOLI, L. 1958. Nutrition and ecology of protozoa and algae. Annu. Rev. Microbiol. 12: 279–308.

QASIM, S. Z., P. M. A. BHATTATHIRI, AND V. P. DEVASSY. 1973. Growth kinetics and nutrient requirements of two tropical marine phytoplankters. Mar. Biol. 21: 299–304.

REDFIELD, A. C. 1958. The biological control of chemical factors in the environment. Am. Sci. 46: 205–221.

REMSEN, C. C., E. J. CARPENTER, AND B. W. SCHROEDER. 1972. Competition for urea among estuarine microorganisms. Ecology 53: 921–926.

RHEE, G.-Y. 1972. Competition between an alga and an aquatic bacterium for phosphate. Limnol. Oceanogr. 17: 505–514.

——— 1973. A continuous culture study of phosphate uptake, growth rate and polyphosphate in *Scenedesmus* sp. J. Phycol. 9: 495–506.

RILEY, G. A. 1963. Organic aggregates in sea water and the dynamics of their formation and utilization. Limnol. Oceanogr. 8: 372–381.

RIVKIN, R. B., AND E. SWIFT. 1979. Diel and vertical patterns of alkaline phosphatase activity in the oceanic dinoflagellate *Pyrocystis noctiluca*. Limnol. Oceanogr. 24: 107–116.

ROON, R. J., AND B. LEVENBERG. 1968. An adenosine triphosphate-dependent, avidin-sensitive enzymatic cleavage of urea in yeast and green algae. J. Biol. Chem. 19: 5213–5215.

SANDER, F., AND E. MOORE. 1979. Significance of ammonia in determining the N:P ratio of the sea water off Barbados, West Indies. Mar. Biol. 55: 17–21.

SCHELL, D. M. 1974. Uptake and regeneration of free amino acids in marine waters of southeast Alaska. Limnol. Oceanogr. 19: 260–270.

SLOAN, P. R., AND J. D. H. STRICKLAND. 1966. Heterotrophy of four marine phytoplankters at low substrate concentrations. J. Phycol. 2: 29–32.

SOLÓRZANO, L. 1978. Soluble fractions of phosphorus compounds and alkaline phosphatase activity in Loch Creran and Loch Etive, Scotland. J. Exp. Mar. Biol. Ecol. 34: 227–232.

SOLÓRZANO, L., AND J. D. H. STRICKLAND. 1968. Polyphosphate in seawater. Limnol. Oceanogr. 13: 515–518.

STEEMANN NIELSEN, E. 1978. Growth of plankton algae as a function of N-concentration, measured by means of a batch technique. Mar. Biol. 46: 185–189.

STEINER, M. 1938. Zur Kenntnis des Phosphatkreislaufes in Seen. Naturwissenchaften 26: 723–724.

STEPHENS, G. C., AND B. B. NORTH. 1971. Extrusion of carbon accompanying uptake of amino acids by marine phytoplankters. Limnol. Oceanogr. 16: 752–757.

STRICKLAND, J. D. H., AND L. SOLÓRZANO. 1966. Determination of monoesterase hydrolysable phosphate and phosphomonoesterase activity in sea water, p. 665–674. *In* H. Barnes [ed.] Some contemporary studies in marine science. Allen and Unwin, London.

SYRETT, P. J. 1962. Nitrogen assimilation, p. 171–188. *In* R. A. Lewin [ed.] Physiology and biochemistry of algae. Academic Press, New York, NY.

SYRETT, P. J., AND J. W. LEFTLEY. 1976. Nitrate and urea assimilation by algae, p. 221–234. *In* N. Sunderland [ed.] Perspectives in experimental biology, Vol. 2: Botany. Pergamon Press, Oxford.

TAFT, J. L., M. E. LOFTUS, AND W. R. TAYLOR. 1977. Phosphate uptake from phosphomonoesters by phytoplankton in the Chesapeake Bay. Limnol. Oceanogr. 22: 1012–1021.

TAFT, J. L., W. R. TAYLOR, AND J. J. McCARTHY. 1975. Uptake and release of phosphorus by phytoplankton in the Chesapeake Bay estuary, USA. Mar. Biol. 33: 21–32.

TAGA, N., AND H. KOBORI. 1978. Phosphatase activity in eutrophic Tokyo Bay. Mar. Biol. 49: 223–229.

TERNETZ, C. 1912. Beiträge zur Morphologie und Physiologie der *Euglena gracilis* Klebs. Jahr. Wiss. Bot. 51: 435–514.

THOMAS, W. H., AND A. N. DODSON. 1968. Effects of phosphate concentration on cell division rates and yield of a tropical oceanic diatom. Biol. Bull. Woods Hole 134: 199–208.

TURNER, M. F. 1979. Nutrition of some marine microalgae with special reference to vitamin requirements and utilization of nitrogen and carbon sources. J. Mar. Biol. Assoc. U.K. 59: 535–552.

VACCARO, R. F. 1963. Available nitrogen and phosphorus and the biochemical cycle in the Atlantic off New England. J. Mar. Res. 21: 284–301.

VAN BAALEN, C. 1962. Studies on marine blue-green algae. Bot. Mar. 4: 129–139.

VINCENT, W. F., AND C. R. GOLDMAN. 1980. Evidence for algal heterotrophy in Lake Tahoe, California–Nevada. Limnol. Oceanogr. 25: 89–99.

WHEELER, P. A. 1977. Effect of nitrogen source on Platymonas (Chlorophyta) cell composition and amino acid uptake rates. J. Phycol. 13: 301–308.

WHEELER, P., B. NORTH, M. LITTLER, AND G. STEPHENS. 1977. Uptake of glycine by natural phytoplankton communities. Limnol. Oceanogr. 22: 900–910.

WHEELER, P. A., B. B. NORTH, AND G. C. STEPHENS. 1974. Amino acid uptake by marine phytoplankters. Limnol. Oceanogr. 19: 249–259.

WHEELER, P. A., AND G. C. STEPHENS. 1977. Metabolic segregation of intracellular free amino acids in Platymonas (Chlorophyta). J. Phycol. 13: 193–197.

WHITE, A. W. 1974. Growth of two facultatively heterotrophic marine centric diatoms. J. Phycol. 10: 292–300.

WILLIAMS, P. J. LE B. 1970. Heterotrophic utilization of dissolved organic compounds in the sea. I. Size distribution of population and relationship between respiration and incorporation of growth substrates. J. Mar. Biol. Assoc. U.K. 50: 859–870.

WOOD, E. J. 1956. Diatoms in the ocean deeps. Pac. Sci. 10: 377–381.

WRIGHT, R. T., AND J. E. HOBBIE. 1965. The uptake of organic solutes in lake water. Limnol. Oceanogr. 10: 22–28.

Some Processes and Physical Factors that Affect the Ability of Individual Species of Algae to Compete for Nutrient Partition

D. J. BONIN AND S. Y. MAESTRINI

Station marine d'Endoume, Chemin de la Batterie des Lions, F-13007 Marseille, France

AND J. W. LEFTLEY

Dunstaffnage Marine Research Laboratory, P.O. Box 3, Oban, Argyll PA34 4AD, Scotland

Introduction

Optimal algal anabolism requires nutrient sufficiency, optimal illumination, and temperature; on the other hand, there are extreme values at which growth stops. At intermediate levels, algae are assumed to grow according to parameters established on the basis of one-species and one-factor experiments (see reviews by Williams 1971; Soeder and Stengel 1974; Yentsch 1974; Finenko 1978). However, in an algal cell, all single-factor effects are combined to give an ultimate integrated result: the actual growth. These three parameters (nutrients, light, and temperature) vary both spatially and temporally and also govern simultaneously the species succession; therefore, it is impossible to discriminate completely between their respective effects. However, in spite of the fact that considering them separately has obvious weaknesses, there is practically no other way to discuss their roles.

Field observations indicate that temperature controls the horizontal distribution of many species of algae; convincing evidence has been gathered for freshwater phytoplankton (Hutchinson 1967) and marine phytoplankton (Raymont 1963; Gessner 1970; Guillard and Kilham 1977). Moreover, experimentally recorded ranges of temperatures suitable for species growth indicate that natural phytoplankton is usually well adapted to the local conditions and that death may occur when these conditions are experimentally modified (Hulburt and Guillard 1968). However, temporal fluctuations over a broad range of temperature, especially in temperate waters, may be such that the local species have to adapt and develop under rapidly changing conditions. As such populations show the most marked and characteristic species successions, one might suspect that temperature controls these successions. On the other hand, light is the energy source of photosynthesis and subsequently that of the whole food chain. Day length and light intensity are largely dependent on the latitude and climate. Moreover, light is progressively absorbed by the water with depth, so that the so-called euphotic zone may be spread over some tens

of metres, or a few metres, or less in areas where light-absorbing particles are especially dense. Furthermore, nutrients are also vertically distributed; usually nutrient concentrations decrease from the surface to the bottom of the oceans and deep lakes. Ultimately, both spatial and temporal distributions of energy source, nutrient supply, and temperature may vary so that they are differentially favorable. For instance, nutrient-rich waters are often cold and nutrient-poor waters well illuminated; but algae have to react to variations in all the physical and chemical parameters at the same time. The way by which an alga balances the different effects is species dependent and, therefore, helps us understand why some species dominate and regularly succeed others.

The importance of the interactions between the effects of light intensity, temperature, and nutrient concentrations on algal growth rate have been discussed (Eppley and Strickland 1968; Middlebrooks and Porcella 1971; Di Toro et al. 1971; MacIsaac and Dugdale 1972) and modeled (Kiefer and Enns 1976; Platt et al. 1977; Kremer and Nixon 1978; Nyholm 1978). But recent observations may render obsolete the early concepts as it has been shown that motile algae do not conform to the models established on the sole basis of fixed kinetic constants recorded with single species in laboratory cultures; such algae represent a fascinating adaptation to the competition for life.

Temperature

TEMPERATURE-GOVERNED SPECIES SUCCESSIONS

Whereas physiological adaptations for maintaining the cell machinery at its highest efficiency when nutrients and light are not optimum have been frequently studied and discussed (see below), the ways by which algae adapt to grow at different temperatures remain often unclear, although resistance to extreme and lethal temperatures has been the subject of much research. Frequently the role of temperature is expressed simply by ranges of values within which responses are maximal, or possible (e.g. Jitts et al. 1964). Nevertheless, an imperfect overlap of temperature ranges suitable for growth can govern the competition and/or the temporal succession of some species. Such an effect is, for instance, that of the tropical dinoflagellate *Gymnodinium breve* and the cyanophyte *Gomphosphaeria aponina*; the dinoflagellate, the growth of which is inhibited by external metabolites released by the cyanophyte, blooms at relatively low temperatures, i.e. 22–23°C, because the range of temperature suitable for its own growth (17–30°C) extends towards lower values than that (24–29°C) of its antagonistic companion species (Eng-Wilmot et al. 1977). Likewise, the dominance of the flagellate *Olisthodiscus luteus* during summer blooms in Narragansett Bay has been ascribed recently to temperature (Tomas 1980; for more details see Maestrini and Bonin 1981). Goldman and Ryther (1976) reported that the diatom *Skeletonema costatum* dominates outdoor continuous mass culture at temperatures below 10°C whereas *Phaeodactylum tricornutum* outgrows and replaces this species at higher temperatures. This displacement of naturally dominant species by high-temperature-adapted algae in power plant discharge plumes is also well established (Briand 1975). In this way, cyanophytes are often regarded as organisms favored by high temperature because they are the only oxygen-evolving photosynthetic organisms occurring in hot springs (Brock 1967) and because they are more abundant in tropical than in temperate waters (Fogg et al. 1973).

PHYSIOLOGICAL ADAPTATIONS TO SUBOPTIMAL TEMPERATURES

It is evident that temperature governs algal growth and species competition; but this statement does not establish whether algal response to temperature is direct.

Early work carried out with the diatom *Skeletonema costatum* prompted Jørgensen and Steemann Nielsen (see Jørgensen and Steemann Nielsen 1965; Jørgensen 1968; Steemann Nielsen and Jørgensen 1968a, b) to suggest that phytoplankton adapt to nonoptimal temperature by increasing their enzyme content to permit the rate of photosynthesis to remain constant. Due to the increase in the amount of all enzymes at low temperatures, the total amount of organic matter per cell also increases. This pioneer statement was first supported by Morris and Farrell (1971) who demonstrated that the green alga *Dunaliella tertiolecta* behaves like *S. costatum*; a real adaptation to resist unfavorable temperatures seemed to have been confirmed. But, a further study made on *Phaeodactylum tricornutum*, *Nitzschia closterium*, and *D. tertiolecta* led Morris and Glover (1974) to question the previous statement. Their experiments demonstrated that growth at low temperatures reduces

the algal photosynthetic ability at higher temperatures, but does not enhance the ability to photosynthesize at low temperatures. "The generally accepted hypothesis of temperature adaptation by algae is untenable" concluded Morris and Glover. Thus, a simple equation could be written by Eppley (1972) to describe the kinetics of maximum expected growth rate versus temperature lower than 40°C.

TEMPERATURE AND NUTRIENTS

Assuming the validity of the Eppley model for all species would mean that temperature would govern competition and species succession only through the different specific ranges of temperature suitable for growth, as predicted by many other models (e.g. Goldman and Carpenter 1974; Kiefer and Enns 1976; Kremer and Nixon 1978); this is denied by various observations. As a matter of fact, Goldman and associates (Goldman 1977, 1979; Goldman and McCarthy 1978; Goldman and Mann 1980) demonstrated that temperature strongly influences cellular chemical composition and that each species responds somewhat differently. At the lowest temperature at which growth occurs, *Dunaliella tertiolecta*, *Phaeodactylum tricornutum*, *Skeletonema costatum*, and *Pavlova lutheri* increase their cellular nitrogen content, while the particulate organic nitrogen (PON) per cell remains constant in *Thalassiosira pseudonana*. Yoder (1979) reported conflicting results in showing that temperature does not affect the cellular content of POC and PON in the diatom *Skeletonema costatum*, but influences the chlorophyll *a* content. Because cell division rates and nutrient uptake rates are uncoupled with respect to temperature, and because extreme and optimal temperatures are species related, there is evidence that nutrient uptake rates are not equally temperature-governed in all species.

As a matter of fact, in competition experiments by Goldman and co-workers, *S. costatum* was the most efficient species at assimilating inorganic nitrogen and was the dominant species at 10°C whereas *D. tertiolecta* dominated the other algae at 30°C. In another outdoor mass culture, the routine *S. costatum* dominance at winter low temperatures was prevented by an excess of nitrogen and phosphorus while silicon was lacking, and led to a permanent dominance of *P. tricornutum* through the whole range of temperatures. Finally, Goldman hypothesized that algae would be separated into a group of fast-growth species versus temperature, which includes *S. costatum* and *Thalassiosira pseudonana*, while other species, such as *Pavlova lutheri*, would comprise a group of algae with a low growth rate versus temperature. The first group would correspond to the curve of Eppley (1972) whereas the second one would not obey the model, especially at low temperatures. Other research, summarized by Li (1981), also indicated that the processes of cell division, production, and accumulation of some cell materials, for instance protein and POC, are affected differently according to the different species. Conversely, temperature alterations of chlorophyll *a* and PON contents might be similar in all species.

Whether and/or how temperature changes the nutrient uptake rate is poorly documented, probably because the growth kinetic parameters, such as K and μ_{max}, are implicitly considered to be species constants. The early work by McCombie (1960) showed that the temperature optimum for growth of the freshwater alga *Chlamydomonas reinhardii* decreases when the nutrient concentration increases, whereas Maddux and Jones (1964) reported that such an increase of nutrient supply widens the optimum temperature range of the marine algae *Nitzschia closterium* and *Tetraselmis* sp. Otherwise, it was reported that, at low temperatures, higher phosphate concentrations are required to produce the same biomass of freshwater algae (Borchardt and Azad 1968). Further research by Eppley et al. (1969) and Thomas and Dodson (1974) showed that the lower the temperature, the lower the K constant for nitrogen uptake in *Skeletonema costatum*, *Dunaliella* sp., and *Gymnodinium splendens*; Ahlgren's (1978) results with the cyanophyte *Oscillatoria agardhii* were similar. Hence, cells growing at higher temperatures show a higher requirement for the limiting nutrient. Nutrient-rich waters such as winter waters or newly upwelled marine waters are generally cold; these waters become warmer and nutrient-depleted while the algae grow. Therefore, the result is that algal nutrient requirements increase when available nutrients become scarce. The algae which profit in these conflicting situations are those able to migrate vertically and so take advantage of the beneficial effects of the two kinds of waters (see below).

COMBINED TEMPERATURE
AND LIGHT EFFECTS

The combination of light and temperature effects on algal photosynthesis leads to a secondary role for temperature in differentiating the specific capabilities of adapting to variable environmental conditions. For instance, it has been demonstrated that low temperature decreases the optimum light intensity for growth, and increases the inhibitory effect of high light intensities, in *Detonula confervacea* (Smayda 1969), *Cryptomonas ovata* (Cloern 1977), and *C. erosa* (Morgan and Kalff 1979). Otherwise, Li and Morris (1981) reported that *Phaeodactylum tricornutum* cells behave differently according to their history of adaptation: cells adapted to grow at high temperatures have a higher rate of photosynthesis than

unadapted cells. For instance, from 25 to 10°C, cells adapted to lower temperatures exhibit enhanced photosynthesis at that temperature, compared with cells adapted to high temperatures. At temperatures below 10°C, adapted cells do not exhibit enhanced photosynthesis but have a reduced optimal photosynthetic capability. On the other hand, Hitchcock (1980) found that the temperature dependence of growth rate is similar at light-limiting or light-saturated levels for the oceanic isolate *Thalassiosira pseudonana* 13-1, while for other neritic species, such as *Detonula confervacea*, *Skeletonema costatum*, and *Thalassiosira nordenskioldii*, the changes in division rates along with increasing temperatures differ when cells are adapted to high light intensities.

Indeed, all these insights lead to the opinion that the role of temperature in phytoplankton growth and succession is not as simple as previously assumed, and further complexity may be expected as research progresses.

Illumination

Reports that light is the major factor governing algal species competition have been hitherto rare. More often the authors' attention has been focused on specific metabolic adaptations, with special reference to pigment composition and the photosynthetic rate of the total crop. Species competition has been a secondary and subsequent topic of interest; hence the literature cited here on the subject is rather short.

LIGHT-SHADE AND LIGHT-SUN
PHYSIOLOGICAL ADAPTATIONS IN
PHYTOPLANKTON SPECIES:
MAIN BACKGROUND[3]

Early observations made with several species of the dinoflagellate *Ceratium* led Steemann Nielsen (1954, in Ryther and Menzel 1959) to remark that some species are characteristically found in surface waters whereas others are confined below the euphotic zone of the oceans (100 m in his example). On this basis, he termed "sun" species those growing in highly illuminated surface waters, and "shade" species those growing in the dim light prevailing in deep waters. Later on, the phytoplankton as a whole was sorted into sun and shade populations, both in fresh waters (Rhode et al. 1958) and in marine waters (Ryther and Menzel 1959). It has been demonstrated by the latter authors that temporal variations and mixing may modify significantly the conditions governing light adaptation. In winter,

---

[3] For further cytophysiological details, see Prézelin (1981).

when waters are isothermal and mixed below the euphotic zone, all phytoplankton forms are sun adapted. In summer, only surface phytoplankton is sun adapted; the deep components are shade adapted because of the strong stratification of the water. Steemann Nielsen and Hansen (1959) demonstrated that planktonic algae from the deeper waters are better able to utilize low-intensity light and , on the other hand, that a reduced light intensity for optimal photosynthesis does not mean an enhanced ability to utilize very low light. Data obtained by Ichimura (1960) and Aruga and Ichimura (1968) are consistent with this concept. Conversely, Yentsch and Lee (1966) questioned the reality of this adaptation and assumed that natural phytoplankton populations in suboptimal conditions do not adapt to maintain highest rates of growth, but simply respond to a physiologically inferior environment, i.e. light responses of algae at very low illumination are characterized by a low rate of carbon uptake, which is saturated at low light intensity. This rate remains low when light intensities increase because there are not enough enzyme molecules present to utilize the increased illumination.

However, on the basis of unialgal culture experiments, several other authors have claimed that algae adapt their physiology to different light intensities. Steemann Nielsen et al. (1962) and Jørgensen (1964) described two types of responses: the "Chlorella type" which adapts to a new light intensity by changing the pigment content, and the "Cyclotella type" which adapts only by changing the light saturating rate, suggesting a shift in the concentration of the enzymes involved in the dark reactions of photosynthesis. Later, Jørgensen (1969) focused attention on the fact that the two adaptation types are not sharply separated and that transition responses can occur between the two extreme types. Usually, marine phytoplankton respond to decreased light intensities by increasing photosynthetic pigment content, but the responses differ greatly among the species, which agrees well with Jørgensen's idea. Usually, chlorophytes have a more marked ability to modify their pigment concentrations than dinoflagellates and diatoms. For example, *Lauderia borealis* shows very slight variations in its pigment concentration when exposed to different light (Marra 1978). Brooks (1964 unpublished, in Prézelin and Matlick 1980) suggested that *Dunaliella tertiolecta* and *Skeletonema costatum* may also photoadapt (1) by a modification of the pigment concentration and (2) by a variation in the efficiency of the photosynthetic units (PSU) because the pigment concentration per cell varies much less than the shifts in optimal light intensities. Such results suggest that these algae photoadapt partly by increasing PSU size. The data concerning *Skeletonema costatum* have been con-

firmed and explained by Falkowski and Owens (1978). Likewise, Berseneva et al. (1978) demonstrated that *Ditylum brightwellii* and *Gyrodinium fissum* adapt to varying illumination by changing the rate of their enzymatic reactions while cellular chlorophyll content remains constant, whereas other species such as *Chaetoceros curvisetus*, *C. socialis*, *Gymnodinium kovalevskii*, *Peridinium trochoideum*, and *Scenedesmus quadricauda* photoadapt by modifying the chlorophyll concentration. Prézelin and Matlick (1980) also observed similar reactions with the dinoflagellate *Glenodinium* sp., which shows photosynthetic changes during light–dark cycles unrelated to variations in its pigmentation, and Prézelin and Sweeney (1979) demonstrated that the freshwater dinoflagellate *Peridinium cinetum* increases the total number of PSU per cell while pigmentation is unchanged.

Algal adaptation to new light conditions is usually swift. For example, a variation in cellular chlorophyll *a* corresponding to a change in light intensity can occur within 12 h at 18°C in *Skeletonema costatum* (Glooschenko et al. 1972) and a similar observation has been made with *Phaeodactylum tricornutum* at 20°C (Beardall and Morris 1976). Indeed, pigments, particularly chlorophyll *a*, very often have a short turnover time. Thus, Riper et al. (1979) reported such turnover times ranged from 3 to 10 h for chlorophyll *a* with *Skeletonema costatum*, depending on the growth conditions. Grumbach et al. (1978) mentioned a turnover time of only 1 h for chlorophyll *a* in the green alga *Chlorella pyrenoidosa*. The second photoadaptative strategy of phytoplankters, which belongs to, or is close to the "Cyclotella type," and consists of modifying the photosynthetic units without new chlorophyll synthesis, can be performed within an even shorter time period. That is, it can be achieved after only $\frac{1}{10}$ th the generation time according to Prézelin and Matlick (1980). Yet the ability to adjust the cell physiology to new light conditions, as reflected by the time required to show new photosynthetic patterns, differs greatly with the species. Such cell adaptability, usually high, is peculiar to algae; such fast light-governed adaptations are not observed in higher plants.

Otherwise, responses to illumination are not free from the influence of other physical and chemical factors. For instance, diatoms near their temperature optimum reach their maximum rates within only 24 h, when illumination increases to optimal intensities, but, conversely, when they grow at their temperature minimum, their division rates require more than 1 d to respond to variation in light intensity (Hitchcock 1981).

In natural waters, diel illumination variations and turbulence could also generate a light–shade

295

adaptation by modifying, on a short-term basis, the illumination received by an organism growing in the mixing layer. Waves, for instance, are able to change the illumination conditions sufficiently to control the photosynthetic patterns of the natural population: at high light intensity the waves depress the photosynthetic rate; conversely, they increase photosynthesis at low light intensities (Frechette and Legendre 1978). Furthermore, the cells do not remain at the same depth within a diel light–dark cycle. To summarize, a cell will be able to photoadapt only if its transport rate is slow enough compared with its adaptation time to adjust to the new light conditions. Subsequently, "if mixing-processes occur on a timescale shorter than it takes the cells to adapt to the variations in the light-regime, the vertical distribution of the light-dependent physiological characteristics would be expected to be more uniformly distributed" (Falkowski 1981). Hence, in a natural population, the fast-adapting algae are obviously at an advantage in the species competition. In any case, chlorophyll turnover times lower than one generation are of a great ecological significance for phytoplankters potentially exposed to considerable variations in light intensity during periods of a few hours (Riper et al. 1979). However, when the well-mixed layer extends beyond the 1% light penetration depth, as for instance in coastal upwelling, the phytoplankton populations stay within the euphotic zone for a shorter average time than they do in thermally well-stratified marine or fresh waters. Hence, not only the light regime but also the light-exposure history play a critical role in controlling the availability of nutrients (Nelson and Conway 1979).

LIGHT INTENSITY AND NUTRIENT CONTROLLED SPECIES SUCCESSIONS

The effects of illumination on species succession have been differentiated from the action of other factors only under experimental conditions, and reports on this subject are still rare. Recently, Mur et al. (1977, 1978) found that the maximal growth rate of the green alga Scenedesmus protuberans is far higher than that of the cyanophyte Oscillatoria agardhii, 1.58 and 0.86 divisions per day, respectively. Nevertheless, the cyanophyte periodically dominates the natural populations of many lakes. Light-effect studies demonstrated that the cyanophyte prefers low intensities and has the ability to select suitable conditions by modifying its buoyancy. Thus, a simple light-governed mechanism enables the cyanophyte to dominate. In nutrient-poor waters, high illumination prevents O. agardhii from blooming in surface waters; dense populations occur only in deeper layers. In eutrophic waters, this organism may multiply because, the growth potential being higher, the biomass becomes denser and leads to an intense light absorption; with such low illumination, the green alga cannot grow, although the cyanophyte does. Likewise, Foy et al. (1976) explained the dominance of Oscillatoria redekei over three other blue-green algae in an Irish lake during early spring by its ability to grow fastest under low light conditions. Competition between diatoms might also be governed by light intensity, in association with nutrient levels and temperature. For instance, Phaeodactylum tricornutum has been reported to dominate outdoor mass cultures when temperature ranges from 10 to 20°C, while the same species is poorly represented in all natural waters at the same temperature. Otherwise, many species such as the minute Thalassiosira pseudonana, which has high division rates, and which would grow well in natural waters in the same 10–20°C range, is usually outgrown by P. tricornutum in mass cultures. Further experiments performed by Nelson et al. (1979) demonstrated that P. tricornutum is able to sustain unusually high growth rates at low light intensities; this property contributes greatly to its success in nutrient-rich and highly turbid mass cultures, systems in which only this diatom dominates. Such examples show the importance of photoadaptation in species competition. But light intensity is not the only aspect of illumination; day length and light quality might also have an important role.

DAY LENGTH AND TEMPERATURE GOVERNED SPECIES SUCCESSIONS

Early studies made by Guillard and Ryther (1962) demonstrated that the diatom Detonula confervacea outgrows another diatom, Skeletonema costatum, when temperature is low (4°C) and the duration of illumination is long (12–16 h). Further research confirmed this finding and demonstrated that D. confervacea grows well at low light intensities (Holt and Smayda 1974). Comparison between its physiological characteristics and the field conditions suggests that the ambient light intensities during the winter bloom occurring in Narragansett Bay favor its growth, while the concomitant short day lengths are unfavorable and would become a limiting factor. At the beginning of the bloom, D. confervacea grows faster than Skeletonema costatum and Thalassiosira nordenskioldii; its rate of photosynthesis is higher and its compensation light levels for photosynthesis and growth are the lowest. Conversely, for some reason still unclear, D. confervacea dominance ends while the bloom is progressing. Durbin (1974) reported that a cultivated Thalassiosira nordenskioldii strain showed an optimal temperature which varied according to day length: at a longer day length, the optimum temperature and the optimum light intensities were lower than those required for a shorter day length, which is consistent with early results obtained with the same species (Jitts et al. 1964). Thus, though studies performed on this subject have been few, such algal responses related to variable day length and light intensities may be common.

LIGHT QUALITY AND LIGHT INTENSITY GOVERNED SPECIES COMPETITION AND SUCCESSION IN DOMINANCE

The selective attenuation of incident radiation by particulate and dissolved organic and inorganic compounds, and by the water itself, induces a change in the spectral composition of illumination with depth, while light intensity is also attenuated. Green and blue light penetrate to the greatest depths. Thus, the algae reaching the bottom of the euphotic layer will be illuminated mainly by blue light, particularly in oligotrophic waters. The dependence of algal photosynthetic response on wavelength of light has already been studied in detail since the early contributions by Emerson and Lewis (1943) and Haxo and Blinks (1950), while the "complementary chromatic adaptation," that is, the variation of pigment composition with light quality, is one of the oldest fields of algal research (Engelmann and Gaidukav 1902, in Halldal 1958); pertinent reviews on the topic can be found in Halldal (1970). Regarding this early attention, it is surprising that little has been done to investigate whether light quality might govern, in part, the species competition in phytoplankton populations, in spite of the fact that the vertical zonation of benthic seaweeds has been frequently related to the presence or the absence of pigments such as phycobilins which preferentially absorb short wavelengths and allow these plants to live in deeper waters (e.g. Levring 1966). Nevertheless, recent findings mitigate some of these early oversights (see for instance Ramus et al. 1976, 1977).

However, Wall and Briand (1979) investigated whether light intensity and color can play a major role in determining the vertical gradient observed in phytoplankton species composition in Heney Lake, Québec Natural populations were cultivated in situ in plexiglass cubes of different colors. Under red light, the proportions of cyanophytes, diatoms, and green algae increased, while those of dinoflagellates decreased. Chrysophytes and cryptophytes tended to be relatively enhanced by blue light. However, only four species were reported to react significantly to light at specific wavelengths; blue light enhanced the growth of the chrysophyte *Chrysocapsa* sp. and depressed that of the cyanophytes *Dactylococcopsis smithii* and *Rhabdoderma sigmoides*; under red light, the growth of the cyanophyte *Gloeotrichia echinulata* decreased. Responses to given light intensities are consistent with predictions, i.e. the diatoms and green algae dominate under high illumination whereas dino-

flagellates and other motile algae are favored by low intensities. Therefore, combining both light-intensity and light-color effects, Wall and Briand (1979) obtained responses consistent with distribution of different algae in the water column: cyanophytes, diatoms, and green algae were favored by high intensities and red light; these conditions occur in surface waters of many lakes where these algae dominate. In contrast, high intensities and red light induced the displacement of dinoflagellates from the top to the bottom of the euphotic layer during daytime. However, the most common and, hence, the most successful species belong to a group of minute and motile microflagellates in which no preference for a given wavelength of light has been recorded; the foremost light-induced cell adaptation could lie in this motility that allows them to maintain their vertical position in a layer corresponding to an optimal light regime.

Buoyancy and Motility

PHYTOPLANKTON STRATEGIES TO REMAIN IN NUTRIENT-RICH LAYERS

The success of a phytoplankter largely depends on its ability to remain suspended in the photic zone where sufficient light is available for the photosynthetic reactions. Unfortunately, the upper layers are not the richest in the water column. The nutrient richness often increases below the mixed layer at the bottom of the euphotic zone. In the upper nutrient-limited layers, the availability of light relative to the photochemical requirements of the alga exceeds that of inorganic nutrients relative to the requirements of the enzymatic processes. Conversely, in deeper layers, production is controlled primarily by availability of substrates for the photochemical system relative to its needs. Between these two extremes, represented by the upper and lower bounds of the photic zone, the relative availability of substrates varies systematically for a species according to the light and nutrient supply rate (Bienfang and Gundersen 1977) and differs in all species according to their biochemical characteristics. It explains why the chlorophyll maximum is not, generally, at the top of the water column but at depths where the availabilities of light and nutrients are still high enough to allow good production (Eppley et al. 1977).

In this respect, phytoplankters belong to two large families. Motile cells, such as dinoflagellates, are able to perform vertical migrations of a phototactic nature and to choose an optimum depth, at least between some limits (Seliger et al. 1970; Blasco 1978). On the other hand, nonmotile cells can counterbalance the natural movements of the water only by regulating their buoyancy, either by changing their own density as diatoms do, or by producing gas vacuoles, as cyanophytes do (Walsby 1972). It is obvious that the ability of all flagellates to migrate actively is an important advantage in obtaining sufficient nutrients and light (Gran 1929).

The species sinking rate is an important ecological factor in understanding succession, as stressed by Hutchinson (1967) who postulated that much of the seasonal species succession is due to the resulting effect of turbulence and sinking, and O'Brien (1974) who included the species specific loss rates as a major parameter in his nutrient-limitation models. An experimental demonstration of its importance was carried out by Knoechel and Kalff (1975), who concluded a study based on the track autoradiography technique by stating that the summer decline in a Canadian lake of the diatom population, dominated by *Tabellaria fenestra*, and the increase of the cyanophyte population, especially *Anabaena planctonica*, was mainly due to the lower sinking rate of the latter. In situ sinking rates are strongly affected by water mass stability. They depend on the size, shape, density of organisms, and also on the physiological characteristics of the cells (Smayda 1970; Sournia 1981). It is well known that buoyancy differs during light–dark cycles; for instance, Anderson and Sweeney (1978) showed that the diatom *Ditylum brightwellii* changes its ionic balance and is able to modify its density and, consequently, its buoyancy between day and night. The settling rate is lower in the dark. A very similar result is given by Schöne (1972); the specific gravity of *Thalassiosira rotula* is proportional to light intensity: with increasing light intensity, the sinking rate increases. Schöne gave no metabolic explanation for this mechanism. But, for the alga such a buoyancy control may be a direct response to an excessively bright light; *T. rotula* seems to be a shade cell and prefers low light intensities. Recently, Burns and Rosa (1980) studied the settling velocities of the main species of a lake phytoplankton population, and reported that velocities of nonliving particles were about equal for each size range and showed little diurnal variation whereas, in contrast, the algae showed considerable response to changing light intensity during the daytime. Some flagellates migrated downward at sunset; a species of diatom settled more slowly during daylight than at night; a blue-green alga showed maximum buoyancy at midnight; and some green algae changed from sinking on a bright day to upward movement on a dull day. These observations clearly indicate that settling rate is a result of various physiological processes and subsequent species-dependent changes in cell content, but such changes have been little studied. However, Jones and Galloway (1979) demonstrated experimentally that *Dunaliella tertiolecta* is able to modify its internal pool of organic compounds, and particularly its glycerol content, according to the intensity of different factors (particularly external molarity, light intensity, and quality). A positive correlation between the glycerol content and the age of the culture was found.

Usually, senescent cells sink faster than actively growing ones (Eppley et al. 1967). It has been verified that, in the sea, a positive buoyancy is often associated with cells in active growth, particularly at the beginning of blooms. But it is also possible to find high sinking rates during blooms (Lännergren 1979). Such high sinking rates may be interpreted as adaptations to a shift of the nutritional conditions. As a matter of fact, when the nutrients become less concentrated in the upper layers, an increase in the sinking rate leads the organisms to reach lower layers richer in nutrients and, thus, facilitates nutrient uptake. Such a phenomenon has been demonstrated by Kahn and Swift (1978), who showed that *Pyrocystis noctiluca* is neutrally buoyant when nutrient depleted, and positively buoyant after taking up nutrients at the bottom of the photic layer. Such explanations might be given to explain in part why the large diatoms usually appear during blooms, when nutrient concentrations are high. Under these conditions, without a variable buoyancy, it would be absolutely impossible for such large cells to remain in the photic layer because of an unfavorable surface/volume ratio at other times of the bloom. Later on, such algae are eliminated from the upper layers by sinking and are replaced by smaller cells, and particularly flagellates, with lower sinking rates or even a positive buoyancy. Usually, cells in deeper layers find better conditions in regard to nutrients, but worse conditions for growth if we consider also the physical factors, namely dim light and often lower temperature. There is, therefore, a very complex interrelationship between these physical factors and the physiological processes of nutrient uptake by algae, and it is difficult to study any individual element of the relationship in isolation from the others.

EFFICIENCY OF NUTRIENT CAPTURE
IN DEEP LAYERS

Various results, obtained both in the field and in the laboratory, support the hypothesis that the migration of dinoflagellates to nutrient-enriched deep waters is effective because the cells are able to take up nutrients at night. Such an uptake by natural populations or clones has often been observed and seems common even if rates are very low (Dugdale and Goering 1967; Holmes et al. 1967; Eppley and Harrison 1975). It has also been verified that the uptake in the dark is the response of algae to drastic N starvation (Syrett 1962). The more nutrient-depleted are the cells, the more important is uptake at night (Malone et al. 1975). But, besides slight dark uptake, it has been pointed out that, usually, maxima for nitrate and ammonia uptake by natural phytoplankton populations occur during daylight hours (Dugdale and Goering 1967; MacIsaac and Dugdale 1972; Packard and Blasco 1974). Because of the nocturnal migrations of the dinoflagellates, particularly during red tides, it had been suggested that only these organisms were able to take up nutrients in the dark, in contrast with the diatoms which could not do so. Harrison (1976) demonstrated that, in culture, Gonyaulax polyedra has the ability for both uptake and assimilation of nitrate in the dark and would be capable of meeting 50–100% of its daily nitrogen requirement for growth from dark assimilation only. In the same way, it has been verified that two dinoflagellates, Pyrocystis fusiformis and Dissodinium lunula, take up nitrate and ammonium at almost equal rates both day and night when preconditioned on 12:12 h night–day cycle at illuminations between 42 and 67 $\mu E \cdot m^{-2} \cdot s^{-1}$ (Bhovichitra and Swift 1977). However, the ability of algae to take up nitrogen sources in the dark varies greatly; for instance, Coccolithus huxleyi does so but the diatom Skeletonema costatum does not.

Unfortunately, field surveys are not often consistent with an ecological extension of these observations. For example, MacIsaac (1978), comparing her own data with those of MacIsaac and Dugdale (1972) on the waters off California and Peru, asserts that there is no evidence that dinoflagellates have a competitive advantage over diatoms under low light conditions. The dark uptake of nitrate is apparently characteristic of both starved dinoflagellates and diatoms. But the migratory capability of dinoflagellates may help them to occupy the most favorable levels of the water column where the concentration of nutrients is higher and may help them to persist in the blooms. This is the biggest advantage of the dinoflagellates over the diatoms, which cannot avoid sinking when turbulence is decreased. It explains why strong upwellings, with high nutrient conditions, are accompanied by diatom dominance, while a relaxation of the system leads rapidly to dinoflagellate dominance even at reduced nutrient levels (MacIsaac 1978). This has been verified experimentally by Eppley et al. (1978). More than dark uptake, the ability to take up nutrients at very low light levels is very important for phytoplankters. It is reported that light saturation of nitrate assimilation is much lower than that of photosynthesis (Hattori 1962). For instance, it has been observed that this light saturation for Pyrocystis sp. was about 10 times lower than that of photosynthesis (Swift and Meunier 1976; Bhovichitra and Swift 1977). In clear oceanic waters, such phytoplankters are able to take up nitrate at the maximum rate at a depth of 100 m.

Reaching such layers, if they are rich in nutrients, is undoubtedly an important advantage in the competition for growth. Reshkin and Knauer (1979) measured uptake of phosphate as a function of light intensity by natural phytoplankton populations and found a relationship which approximated to the Michaelis-Menten equation. Light "half-saturation constants" (K_L), corrected for dark uptake, were found to be 11.3–18.3% of the surface light intensity, which is comparable to K_L values for light-dependent uptake of nitrate and ammonium by phytoplankton found by MacIsaac and Dugdale (1972). The possible importance of dark uptake of phosphate by phytoplankton was also pointed out by Reshkin and Knauer (1979). They measured rates of dark uptake of phosphate that were 29.1–33.4% of the maximum uptake rate in the light. Although dark uptake of phosphate in natural waters has been attributed to bacteria, these workers suggest that, because Thalassiosira fluviatilis has been shown to accumulate phosphate in the dark, dark uptake by phytoplankton in general may also significantly affect calculations of K_L. The low K_L values calculated for phosphate, nitrate, and ammonia are in good agreement with the average incident light level in the photic zone of high-production areas. For example, Huntsman and Barber (1977) showed that, in the northwest Africa upwelling, phytoplankton had an effective exposure to a mean light intensity of 10% relative to the surface value.

NUTRIENT UPTAKE ENHANCEMENT BY CELL DISPLACEMENT

The migrations of small flagellates or the sinking of other algae have another very important effect on their ability to take up nutrients: the availability of dilute nutrients is enhanced by passive or active movements of the cells, or by movements of the medium (Munk and Riley 1952). In fact, the uptake rate of a nutrient by a cell can be limited by the inability of the nutrient to diffuse to the cell as rapidly as the cell can assimilate it at its ambient concentration. It has been demonstrated that the effect of transport limitation was decreased by mixing and that diffusion transport can influence uptake rates at low-nutrient concentrations (Pasciak and Gavis 1974, 1975). Hence, it is assumed that diffusion transport limitation may be so great that it can lead an alga to lose the competitive advantage that it might have had, given its uptake capabilities (Gavis 1976). This concept is very complex and depends on many factors (Hulburt 1970) — the effect of flow determined by cell size, shape, density, self movement, the "affinity" of the nutrient for the surface of the cell, the surface/volume ratio, and so on. The lower the nutrient concentration in the medium, the greater is the beneficial action of the sinking. As explained by Canelli and Fuhs (1976), an increase in sinking rate has two antagonistic actions: (1) the loss of organisms under a mixed and illuminated layer is linear; (2) the increase in nutrient uptake follows an hyperbolic curve versus the sinking velocity. Thus, there is an optimum value of sinking rate for each nutrient condition; for each species there is a sinking rate that allows an optimum of production for given nutrient concentrations. All species do not have the same characteristics and do not find the best conditions for maximum production at the same time.

ABILITY OF MOTILE CELLS TO CROSS OVER THE THERMOCLINE BARRIER

One other factor cannot be dissociated from buoyancy and the ability of phytoplankters to take up nutrients at lower depths in the water column: the strong density gradient of the thermocline which slows down the sinking of all particles; very often it is possible to observe an increase of cell numbers at this level. But some migrations of dinoflagellates traverse large temperature gradients and cross this hurdle. It has been shown that many freshwater dinoflagellates can cross this density hurdle, although there is considerable variation in their ability to do so. For instance, *Ceratium hirundinella* can cross a 2°C temperature gradient (Talling 1971), *Peridinium westii*, 4°C (Berman and Rhode 1971), *Cryptomonas marssonii*, 6°C (Soeder 1967), and *Pyrodinium bahamense*, 5°C (Seliger et al. 1970). The ability of marine phytoplankters to cross these gradients is somewhat less but they can often cross over a 2°C gradient and sometimes more (*Cachonina niei* migrates across 5°C). In very stratified waters such phytoplankters can cross the thermocline barrier and gain access to subthermocline nutrient pools. This ability may be of a great importance for these species because it has been pointed out that, below a temperature characteristic of each latitude, plant nutrients and temperature are inversely related (Kamykowski and Zentara 1977).

The problem in such situations is that, sometimes, the temperature below the thermocline is low enough to be under the temperature optimum and even below the temperature limit for the species growth. In these conditions, the benefit of higher nutrient concentrations is greatly diminished by the decrease in the rate of all the metabolic reactions. Furthermore, the ability for the cells to reach such deeper layers is strongly modified by the reduction of their motility.

Salinity

Algae living in an environment where salinities may change rapidly (such as estuaries, brackish water ponds, salt marshes, or rock pools) have to adapt their physiological processes rapidly to be able to maintain their growth as constant as possible. Likewise, freshwater algae reaching estuaries can survive only if they are somewhat euryhaline. Thus, in many coastal and usually nutrient-rich environments, salinity might be expected to shift the species dominance in a community reaching a variable salinity area, and to be responsible for the peculiar composition of resident populations (Lohmann 1908; Välinkangas 1926; Carter 1938; Droop 1953; Halim 1960; Hulburt 1963; Hulburt and Rodman 1963; Hobson 1966; Saugestad 1971; Podamo 1972; Chrétiennot 1974; Charpy-Roubaud and Charpy 1981). However, laboratory studies have shown that some species of algae are able to tolerate very large variations in salinity and this has stimulated studies on the physiological mechanisms allowing algae to resist osmotic stresses.

ALGAL RESISTANCE TO SALINITY VARIATIONS

Allen and Nelson (1910) and Allen (1914) first remarked that some marine algae, e.g. the diatoms *Biddulphia mobiliensis*, *Coscinodiscus excentricus*, *Skeletonema costatum*, and *Thalassiosira gravida*, were able to grow in different media, the salinity of which varied within a broad range, namely 17–50‰ for *T. gravida*. Braarud (1951) extended this concept to many phytoplankton species, especially dinoflagellates, which he studied in detail. By measuring the growth of cultured algae versus salinity, he demonstrated that the optimum salinity for growth is usually lower than that of the waters from which natural populations come, and that species are separated by the lowest salinity at which they can grow. From the available data (Braarud 1961; Williams 1964; Nakanishi and Monsi 1965; Smayda 1969; Ignatiades and Smayda 1970; Schöne 1974; Paasche 1975; Grant and Horner 1976; White 1978), it appears that such optimal values range from 15 to 20‰ for algae as different as coccolithophorids (e.g. *Coccolithus huxleyi* and *Syracosphaera carterae*), dinoflagellates (e.g. several *Ceratium* spp., *Exuviaella baltica*, *Peridinium trochoideum*), cryptomonads (e.g. *Hemiselmis virescens*), chrysomonads (e.g. *Pavlova lutheri*), and diatoms (e.g. *Asterionella japonica*, *Skeletonema costatum*). Furthermore, McLachlan (1960) reported that the green alga *Dunaliella tertiolecta* can grow in media having a salinity between 3.7 and 120‰ and Takano (1963) claimed that diatoms can also adapt to grow between broad-ranging values such as 6 and 45‰, e. g. *Cerataulina pelagica*, *Chaetoceros radians*, *Leptocylindrus danicus*, and *Thalassiosira decipiens*, while *Skeletonema costatum* can grow even at 3‰. This concept was supported by Bonin (1969), who reported that with *Chaetoceros affinis* growth can occur within a 5–50‰ range, and Tomas (1978), who demonstrated that the chrysophyte *Olisthodiscus luteus* tolerates a salinity range of 2–50‰.

EFFECTS OF SUBOPTIMAL SALINITIES

Thus, the ability of algae to grow at various salinities is a long-established concept and seems to be shared by many species belonging to different taxa. However, the effect of suboptimal salinities is poorly documented: often the only quantitative criterion used to record algal responses in such experiments is the cell density measurement, with sometimes the duration of lag phase, and few results are given on the physiological characteristics of the cells.

Yet, McLachlan (1961) demonstrated that the chlorophyll *a* content per cell of algae such as *Platymonas* sp. and *Porphyridium* sp. can be affected by suboptimal salinity, while growth itself is unaffected. For other species such as *Amphidinium carteri* and *Olisthodiscus* sp., growth and chlorophyll *a* content show a respective maximum rate for the same optimal salinity value. This author also reported that *Syracosphaera carterae*, *Pavlova lutheri*, and *Thalassiosira decipiens* show a very wide range of salinity values for optimal growth, which conflicts slightly with previous results given for these latter species. Otherwise, the chlorophyll content of the green alga *Platymonas subcordiformis* (Kirst 1975) and of the diatoms *Chaetoceros affinis* (Bonin 1969) and *Cyclotella cryptica* (Liu and Hellebust 1976a) has been reported not to vary very much in the range of optimal salinities, while it decreases sharply for values above and below this range. Other researchers using photosynthetic carbon uptake rate (Curl and McLeod 1961; Nakanishi and Monsi 1965) or oxygen production and respiration measurements (Ehrhardt and Dupont 1972) reported results similar to those obtained by recording cell-division rates or chlorophyll and production values. Otherwise, White (1978) demonstrated that maximum growth and toxin production in *Gonyaulax excavata* occur at different salinities, 30.5 and 37‰, respectively. But, more generally, little effort has hitherto been made to characterize the different responses of cell physiological processes to salinity variations. In particular nothing is known yet about inorganic nutrient uptake.

However, Liu and Hellebust (1976b) and Hellebust (1978) opened a new area of research when they demonstrated that the marine diatom *Cyclotella cryptica* increases its uptake rate of organic nutrients like glucose and amino acids, according to the increase of NaCl concentrations, from 0 mM (no uptake) to 100 mM (optimum uptake rate).

SALINITY-GOVERNED SPECIES DISTRIBUTION

On the basis of field observations and experimental data, many authors have stressed the importance of salinity in controlling phytoplankton distribution (Provasoli 1958; Braarud 1961; Carpelan 1964; Wood 1965; Riley 1967; Gessner and Schramm 1971; Rice and Ferguson 1975). But speculations based on both field evidence and laboratory studies are rather rare and open to criticism. For instance, Nakanishi and Monsi (1965) recorded the relationships between salinity and photosynthesis of phytoplankton sampled in Tokyo Bay and the brackish Lake Hinuma, and compared the data they obtained with the responses of three cultured algal strains, *Skeletonema costatum*, *Chaetoceros* sp., and *Chlorella ellipsoidea*, with the aim of explaining the dominance of some species in natural waters. They noted that the diatom *S. costatum* can grow down to 3‰, with optimum growth at 18‰, whereas *Chaetoceros* sp. shows its optimum at 34‰. This led them to remark that most species living in Tokyo Bay are euryhaline and have their optimum salinities markedly different from the salinities of their habitats. However, their discussion is quite unclear and failed to demonstrate that salinity governs the phytoplankton distribution in the studied areas. The main reason is that natural population responses were compared with responses of cultured strains not reported to be dominant, whereas the dominant species have not been put into culture.

Mahoney and McLaughlin (1979) observed that, in New York harbor, estuarine and oceanic waters are dominated primarily by several flagellates whose behavior seems to be closely related to salinity. As a matter of fact, in this area, algal blooms frequently develop in the harbor estuarine waters and then spread to both ocean and rivers; occasionally, the algae bloom in the river waters and then extend to estuarine and oceanic ones. However, in one such case, a dominant species in the tidal river waters (with salinity between 15 and 21‰), *Massartia rotundata*, lost its dominance in the marine waters in favor of *Prorocentrum micans* or *Olisthodiscus luteus*. Laboratory experiments demonstrated that *M. rotundata* shows the best growth in the range 24–30‰, *O. luteus* in the range 10–36‰, and *P. micans* within 27–36‰. Thus, the three optimum ranges for growth sufficiently match the salinities characteristic of the studied waters (17–32‰), eliminating salinity tolerance as a major factor in limiting the development of these species in these natural conditions. On the other hand, experiments carried out to study the influence of the change from brackish to ocean water salinities allow the authors to point out that these stress effects inhibit growth, especially in *M. rotundata* and *O. luteus*, but that the latter species is able to recover its growth rate faster. Indeed, Mahoney and McLaughlin's interpretation of their experimental data fit well with the observed natural distribution of these phytoflagellates. But the authors did not give any physiological explanation of the three different species responses.

In fact, all early reports left unclear the physiological mechanisms by which the cells adapt to osmotic stress, although some speculations on the subject had been formulated (see review by Guillard 1962). However, more recently, promising research has been initiated in this field.

PHYSIOLOGICAL AND BIOCHEMICAL ADAPTATIONS TO OSMOTIC STRESS

It has been shown that many algae respond to increasing concentrations of external solute by increasing the intracellular concentration of certain osmotic solutes, particularly polyols such as glycerol, mannitol, and sorbitol, and the amino acid proline (Hellebust 1976a, b; Liu and Hellebust 1976a, b; Brown and Hellebust 1978b; Kauss 1974, 1977, 1978, 1979; Kirst 1979; Schobert 1979). The change in concentration of these solutes has been interpreted as being a simple osmotic mechanism causing water reflux and balancing the difference in water potential between the inside and the outside of the cell. However, although any intracellular solute (other than the dominant extracellular solute) which responded appropriately to changes in extracellular water activity could function as an osmoregulator, it is remarkable that the major solutes accumulated under water stress by a wide range of algae and higher plants are usually of only two types, polyols and proline. Schobert (1977, 1979, 1980a) and Brown and Borowitzka (1979) have argued that polyols and proline are "compatible solutes" which, because of their unique properties, have a special role in water regulation other than simply acting as osmoregulators.

"Compatible solute" was a term originally coined by Brown and Simpson (1972), and may be defined as a solute that is compatible with cellular metabolism because, even when present at very high concentrations, there is minimal inhibition of enzymes and, hence, biochemical reactions. The reasons why the physico-chemical properties of polyols and proline make them eminently suitable as compatible solutes have been examined in detail by Schobert (1977, 1979, 1980a). It is not possible to reiterate this work fully here without a lengthy discussion of the physico-chemical properties of water and the compatible solutes. Suffice it to say that, under conditions of water stress, the reduction in cellular water activity is assumed to impair the hydration sphere of cellular constituents, particularly macromolecules. It is proposed that the compatible solutes function primarily by improving the solubility of macromolecules by interacting with them to preserve the surrounding water structure, thus preventing precipitation of these molecules and irreversible damage to the algal cell.

Only a few algae have been studied with regard to the biochemical changes that occur in response to osmotic stress. Kauss (1974, 1979) has shown that, in *Ochromonas*, increasing the concentration of external solutes causes an increase in the internal concentration of isofloridoside (α-1,1,-galactosylglycerol) and, to a lesser extent, potassium and free amino acids. Decreasing the external osmotic value stimulates the rapid transformation of isofloridoside to a reserve glucan.

The pathway of isofloridoside synthesis has also been studied: initiation of biosynthesis appears to involve the proteolytic activation of an inactive precursor of the enzyme isofloridoside–phosphate synthase in response to changes in external water potential. Kreuzer and Kauss (1980) have also shown that there is de novo synthesis of the enzyme α-galactosidase in response to hyperosmotic conditions. The regulatory signal and regulatory sites of the isofloridoside pathway have yet to be elucidated.

The osmoregulatory mechanism in *Cylindrotheca closterium* seems to parallel that in *Ochromonas*. Intracellular concentrations of free mannose and polymannose in this diatom appear to be in dynamic equilibrium and change in response to changing external water potential (Paul 1979). Increasing salinity shifted the equilibrium towards production of free mannose, and the rate of CO_2 fixation also increased. Decreasing salinity stimulated the polymerization of mannose. It was also found that the enzymes involved in the mannose/polymannose conversion appeared to respond to changes in water potential rather than to changes in any particular ion, as varying the water potential with sorbitol was equally as effective as using inorganic salts.

Phaeodactylum tricornutum responds to increasing osmolarity of the external medium by accumulating proline: this accumulation appears to be due to inhibition of proline catabolism (Schobert 1980b).

The osmotically stimulated production of glycerol in *Dunaliella* has been intensively studied. The relevant literature has been reviewed by Brown and Borowitzka (1979). *Dunaliella* is remarkably adaptable to a wide range of salt concentrations. For example, *D. tertiolecta* is able to grow within a range of NaCl concentrations from 0.06 to > 3.6 M (Borowitzka et al. 1977). If transferred to concentrated salt solutions, *Dunaliella* responds immediately by initiating synthesis of glycerol, which continues for about 90 min, after which the normal cell volume is regained (Kessly unpublished results, quoted in Brown and Borowitzka 1979). Therefore, there must be some other mechanism that allows certain metabolic functions to continue during this period while the osmotic equilibrium is being restored. The energy for glycerol synthesis seems to come primarily from respiration. *Dunaliella* is able to control closely its glycerol content in response to salinity and it is thought that a probable regulatory site is an NADP-specific glycerol dehydrogenase, but the exact nature of the regulatory signal that initiates changes in glycerol metabolism is not yet understood (Brown and Borowitzka 1979).

The discussion so far has centered on adaptation to decreasing water potential, but phytoplankters must also be able to adapt quickly to increasing water potential (osmotic downshock). Algae which are downshocked are faced with the problem of increasing their internal water potential and various types of response have been observed. For example, *Ochromonas malhamensis* (Kauss 1974) and *Cylindrotheca fusiformis* (Paul 1979) respond to mild osmotic downshock by repolymerizing the compatible solute. In *Dunaliella* the effect of dilution shock is to cause a metabolic dissimilation of intracellular glycerol, a process that begins within minutes of downshock and is complete within about an hour (Kessly unpublished, in Brown and Borowitzka 1979). The metabolic dissimilation of glycerol is not fully understood, but must obviously involve conversion to nonosmotically active compounds, most likely starch and/or CO_2. Even with a relatively large downshock, very little glycerol is lost by leakage from *Dunaliella* spp. (Brown and Borowitzka 1979). In contrast, some algae respond to downshock by rapid ejection of low molecular weight compounds from the cell, followed by a period of metabolic adjustment of various processes — respiration, photosynthesis, and membrane permeability. Algae that show this type of adaptation are *Pavlova* (= *Monochrysis*) *lutheri* (Craigie 1969), *Platymonas suecica* (Hellebust 1976b), *Platymonas subcordiformis* (Kirst 1979), and *Phaeodactylum tricornutum* (Schobert 1980b). This mechanism allows the algae to reduce very quickly the internal concentration of osmotically active solutes, thereby obviating possible lysis of the cell due to greatly increased turgor pressure.

Moreover, Brown and Hellebust (1978a) demonstrated the very important role of the concentration of particular ionic species in deplasmolysis. They focused attention on KCl, the only electrolyte capable of allowing deplasmolysis of *Cyclotella cryptica* cells when supplied alone in the medium. On the other hand, Ca^{2+}, Mg^{2+}, and Na^+, which are involved in the energy-dependent uptake of K^+, strongly enhance the ability of the alga to adapt at various salinities. Furthermore, it has been observed that the energy used in this regulation has not always the same origin. Some algae, like *Cyclotella cryptica*, are able to deplasmolyze in the dark, whereas others, like *Scenedesmus obliquus* (Wetherell 1963) need light to do so.

SALINITY-GOVERNED SPECIES COMPETITION: PROSPECTS

Although there are many publications describing one species based ecophysiological experiments that stress the importance of salinity as an ecological factor in estuarine and coastal waters, it is surprising to find a lack of experimental studies and in situ observations of the potential role of salinity in nutrient partition between species and, subsequently, in phytoplankton succession. Nevertheless, the shift in species dominance from tidal river to brackish and marine waters, reported by Mahoney and McLaughlin (1979), and the failure of oceanic strains to dominate in coastal waters as a result of their inability to increase their growth rate at higher nutrient concentrations (Hulburt 1979), indicate that the relationships between dominant species and osmotic strength in salinity-variable environments are not yet at all clear, at least as far as ecophysiological processes are concerned.

As a matter of fact, in such studies it is absolutely necessary to consider separately in the natural environment the action (1) of the total dissolved salts, (2) of the minimum requirements for predominant anions and cations, and (3) the influence of the different ionic ratios in the water. In many estuaries, where the salt concentration is low enough and the ionic ratios may vary considerably depending on the origin of the water, such parameters, among many others, may explain the composition of species assemblages that cannot otherwise be understood only in terms of the direct influence of the total osmotic strength. Since it has been demonstrated that the concentration of particular ions directly governs the ability to take up some organic molecules by algae, it is possible to believe that, more generally, the concentrations of certain conservative ions might affect the uptake rate of inorganic nutrients. Hence, research into salinity and ion balance paralleling that already carried out with combined variations of nutrients and illumination and/or temperature might give exciting results and bring a new insight in estuarine phytoplankton ecology.

Acknowledgment

We wish to thank Dr Trevor Platt for a critical review of the manuscript.

References

AHLGREN, G. 1978. Growth of *Oscillatoria agardhii* in chemostat culture. 2. Dependence of growth constants on temperature. Mitt. Int. Ver. Limnol. 21: 88–102.

ALLEN, E. J. 1914. On the culture of the plankton diatom *Thalassiosira gravida* Cleve, in artificial sea-water. J. Mar. Biol. Assoc. U.K. 10: 417–439.

ALLEN, E. J., AND E. W. NELSON. 1910. On the artificial culture of marine plankton organisms. J. Mar. Biol. Assoc. U.K. 8: 421–474.

ANDERSON, L. W. J., AND B. M. SWEENEY. 1978. Role of inorganic ions in controlling sedimentation rate of a marine centric diatom *Ditylum brightwelli*. J. Phycol. 14: 204–214.

ARUGA, Y., AND S. E. ICHIMURA. 1968. Characteristics of photosynthesis of phytoplankton and primary production in the Kuroshio. Bull. Misaki Mar. Biol. Inst. Kyoto Univ. 12: 3–20.

BEARDALL, J., AND I. MORRIS. 1976. The concept of light intensity adaptation in marine phytoplankton: some experiments with *Phaeodactylum tricornutum*. Mar. Biol. 37: 377–387.

BERMAN, T., AND W. RHODE. 1971. Distribution and migration of *Peridinium* in Lake Kinneret. Verh. Int. Ver. Limnol. 19: 266–276.

BERSENEVA, G. P., L. M. SERGEYEVA, AND Z. Z. FINENKO. 1978. Adaptation of marine planktonic algae to light. Oceanology 18: 197–201.

BHOVICHITRA, M., AND E. SWIFT. 1977. Light and dark uptake of nitrate and ammonium by large oceanic dinoflagellates: *Pyrocystis noctiluca*, *Pyrocystis fusiformis*, and *Dissodinium lunula*. Limnol. Oceanogr. 22: 73–83.

BIENFANG, P., AND K. GUNDERSEN. 1977. Light effects on nutrient-limited, oceanic primary production. Mar. Biol. 43: 187–199.

BLASCO, D. 1978. Observations on the diel migration of marine dinoflagellates off the Baja California coast. Mar. Biol. 46: 41–47.

BONIN, D. J. 1969. Influence de différents facteurs écologiques sur la croissance de la diatomée marine *Chaetoceros affinis* Lauder en culture. Téthys 1: 173–238.

BORCHARDT, J. A., AND H. S. AZAD. 1968. Biological extraction of nutrients. J. Water Pollut. Control Fed. 40: 1739–1754.

BOROWITZKA, L. J., D. S. KESSLY, AND A. D. BROWN. 1977. The salt relations of *Dunaliella*. Further observations on glycerol production and its regulation. Arch. Microbiol. 113: 131–138.

BRAARUD, T. 1951. Salinity as an ecological factor in marine phytoplankton. Physiol. Plant. 4: 28–34.

———— 1961. Cultivation of marine organisms as a means of understanding environmental influences on populations, p. 271–298. *In* M. Sears [ed.] Oceanography. Am. Assoc. Adv. Sci. Publ. 67.

BRIAND, F. J. P. 1975. Effects of power-plant cooling systems on marine phytoplankton. Mar. Biol. 33: 135–146.

BROCK, T. D. 1967. Micro-organisms adapted to high temperatures. Nature (London) 214: 882–885.

BROWN, A. D., AND L. J. BOROWITZKA. 1979. Halotolerance of *Dunaliella*, p. 139–190. *In* M. Levandowsky and S. H. Hutner [ed.] Biochemistry and physiology of protozoa. 2nd ed. Vol. 1. Academic Press, New York, NY.

BROWN, A. D., AND J. R. SIMPSON. 1972. Water-relations of sugar-tolerant yeasts: the role of intracellular polyols. J. Gen. Microbiol. 72: 589–591.

BROWN, L. M., AND J. A. HELLEBUST. 1978a. Ionic dependence of deplasmolysis in the euryhaline diatom *Cyclotella cryptica*. Can. J. Bot. 56: 408–412.

———— 1978b. Sorbitol and proline as intracellular osmotic solutes in the green alga *Stichococcus bacillaris*. Can. J. Bot. 56: 676–679.

BURNS, N. M., AND F. ROSA. 1980. In situ measurement of the settling vlocity of organic carbon particles and 10 species of phytoplankton. Limnol. Oceanogr. 25: 855–864.

CANELLI, E., AND G. W. FUHS. 1976. Effect of the sinking rate of two diatoms (*Thalassiosira* spp.) on uptake from low concentrations of phosphate. J. Phycol. 12: 93–99.

CARPELAN, L. H. 1964. Effects of salinity on algal distribution. Ecology 45: 70–77.

CARTER, N. 1938. New or interesting algae from brackish water. Arch. Protistenk. 90: 1–68.

CHARPY-ROUBAUD, C. J., AND L. J. CHARPY. 1981. A biomassa fitoplanctonica do Saco Justino (32°S, Lagoa dos Patos, Rio Grande do Sul). Bolm Inst. Oceanogr. São Paulo. (In press)

CHRETIENNOT, M.-J. 1974. Nanoplancton de flaques supralittorales de la région de Marseille. I. Étude qualitative et écologie. Protistologica 10: 469–476.

CLOERN, J. E. 1977. Effects of light intensity and temperature on *Cryptomonas ovata* (Cryptophyceae) growth and nutrient uptake rates. J. Phycol. 13: 389–395.

CRAIGIE, J. S. 1969. Some salinity-induced changes in growth, pigments, and cyclohexanetetrol content of *Monochrysis lutheri*. J. Fish Res. Board Can. 26: 2959–2967.

CURL, H., AND G. C. MCLEOD. 1961. The physiological ecology of a marine diatom *Skeletonema costatum* (Grev.) Cleve. J. Mar. Res. 19: 70–88.

DI TORO, D. M., D. J. O'CONNER, AND R. V. THOMANN. 1971. A dynamic model of the phytoplankton population in the Sacramento–San Joaquim Delta, p. 131–180. *In* J. D. Hem [ed.] Nonequilibrium systems in natural water chemistry. Adv. Chem. Ser. 106.

DROOP, M. R. 1953. On the ecology of flagellates from some brackish and fresh water rockpools of Finland. Acta Bot. Fenn. 51: 1–52.

DUGDALE, R. C., AND J. J. GOERING. 1967. Uptake of new and regenerated forms of nitrogen in primary productivity. Limnol. Oceanogr. 12: 196–206.

DURBIN, E. G. 1974. Studies on the autecology of the marine diatom *Thalassiosira nordenskiöldii* Cleve. I. The influence of daylength, light intensity and temperature on growth. J. Phycol. 10: 220–225.

EHRHARDT, J. P., AND J. DUPONT. 1972. Effets de la salinité du milieu de culture sur les activités photosynthétiques et respiratoires de *Dunaliella salina* (Dunal) Theodoresco. C. R. Soc. Biol. 166: 516–519.

EMERSON, R., AND C. M. LEWIS. 1943. The dependence of the quantum yield of *Chlorella* photosynthesis on wave length of light. Am. J. Bot. 30: 165–178.

ENG-WILMOT, D. L., W. S. HITCHCOCK, AND D. F. MARTIN. 1977. Effect of temperature on the prolif-

304

eration of *Gymnodinium breve* and *Gomphosphaeria aponina*. Mar. Biol. 41: 71–77.

EPPLEY, R. W. 1972. Temperature and phytoplankton growth in the sea. Fish. Bull. 70: 1063–1085.

EPPLEY, R. W., AND W. G. HARRISON. 1975. Physiological ecology of *Gonyaulax polyedra*, a red water dinoflagellate of Southern California, p. 11–22. *In* V. R. LoCicero [ed.] Proc. 1st Int. Conf. Toxic Dino-Flagellate Blooms, Nov. 1974. Massachusetts Science and Technology Foundation, Wakefield, MA.

EPPLEY, R. W., R. W. HOLMES, AND J. D. H. STRICKLAND. 1967. Sinking rates of marine phytoplankton measured with a fluorometer. J. Exp. Mar. Biol. Ecol. 1: 191–208.

EPPLEY, R. W., P. KOELLER, AND G. T. WALLACE JR. 1978. Stirring influences the phytoplankton species composition within enclosed columns of coastal sea water. J. Exp. Mar. Biol. Ecol. 32: 219–239.

EPPLEY, R. W., J. N. ROGERS, AND J. J. MCCARTHY. 1969. Half-saturation constants for uptake of nitrate and ammonium by marine phytoplankton. Limnol. Oceanogr. 14: 912–920.

EPPLEY, R. W., J. N. ROGERS, J. J. MCCARTHY, AND A. SOURNIA. 1971. Light/dark periodicity in nitrogen assimilation of the marine phytoplankters *Skeletonema costatum* and *Coccolithus huxleyi* in N-limited chemostat culture. J. Phycol. 7: 150–154.

EPPLEY, R. W., J. H. SHARP, E. H. RENGER, M. J. PERRY, AND W. G. HARRISON. 1977. Nitrogen assimilation by phytoplankton and other microorganisms in the surface waters of the Central North Pacific Ocean. Mar. Biol. 39: 111–120.

EPPLEY, R. W., AND J. D. H. STRICKLAND. 1968. Kinetics of marine phytoplankton growth, p. 23–62. *In* M. R. Droop and E. J. Ferguson-Wood [ed.] Advances in microbiology of the sea. Vol. 1. Academic Press, New York, NY.

FALKOWSKI, P. G. 1981. Light-shade adaptation in marine phytoplankton, p. 99–119. *In* P. G. Falkowski [ed.] Primary productivity in the sea. Environmental Science Research Series. Vol. 19 Plenum Press, New York, NY.

FALKOWSKI, P. G., AND T. G. OWENS. 1978. Effects of light intensity on photosynthesis and dark respiration in six species of marine phytoplankton. Mar. Biol. 45: 289–295.

FINENKO, Z. Z. 1978. Production in plant populations, p. 13–87. *In* O. Kinne [ed.] Marine ecology. Vol. 4: Dynamics. Wiley Interscience, London.

FOGG, G. E., W. D. P. STEWART, P. FAY, AND A. E. WALSBY. 1973. The blue-green algae. Academic Press, London. 459 p.

FOY, R. H., C. E. GIBSON, AND R. V. SMITH. 1976. The influence of daylength, light intensity and temperature on the growth rates of planktonic blue-green algae. Br. Phycol. J. 11: 151–163.

FRECHETTE, M., AND L. LEGENDRE. 1978. Photosynthèse phytoplanctonique : réponse à un stimulus simple, imitant les variations rapides de la lumière engendrées par les vagues. J. Exp. Mar. Biol. Ecol. 32: 15–25.

GAVIS, J. 1976. Munk and Riley revisited: nutrient diffusion transport and rates of phytoplankton growth. J. Mar. Res. 34: 161–179.

GESSNER, F. 1970. Temperature. Plants, p. 362–406. *In* O. Kinne [ed.] Marine ecology. Vol. 1: Environmental factors, part 1. Wiley Interscience, London.

GESSNER, F., AND W. SCHRAMM. 1971. Salinity. Plants, p. 705–820. *In* O. Kinne [ed.] Marine ecology. Vol. 1: Environmental factors, part 2. Wiley Interscience, London.

GLOOSCHENKO, W. A., H. CURL, AND L. F. SMALL JR. 1972. Diel periodicity of chlorophyll-*a* concentration in Oregon coastal waters. J. Fish. Res. Board Can. 29: 1253–1259.

GOLDMAN, J. C. 1977. Temperature effects on phytoplankton growth in continuous culture. Limnol. Oceanogr. 22: 932–936.

1979. Temperature effects on steady-state growth, phosphorus uptake, and the chemical composition of a marine phytoplankton. Microb. Ecol. 5: 153–166.

GOLDMAN, J. C., AND E. J. CARPENTER. 1974. A kinetic approach to the effect of temperature on algal growth. Limnol. Oceanogr. 19: 756–766.

GOLDMAN, J. C., AND R. MANN. 1980. Temperature-influenced variations in speciation and chemical composition of marine phytoplankton in outdoor mass cultures. J. Exp. Mar. Biol. Ecol. 46: 29–39.

GOLDMAN, J. C., AND J. J. MCCARTHY. 1978. Steady state growth and ammonium uptake of a fast-growing marine diatom. Limnol. Oceanogr. 23: 695–703.

GOLDMAN, J. C., AND J. H. RYTHER. 1976. Temperature-influenced species competition in mass cultures of marine phytoplankton. Biotechnol. Bioeng. 18: 1125–1144.

GRAN, H. H. 1929. Investigation of the production of plankton outside the Romsdalsfjord 1926–1927. Rapp. P.V. Réun. Cons. Int. Explor. Mer 56: 1–112.

GRANT, W. S., AND R. A. HORNER. 1976. Growth responses to salinity variation in four arctic ice diatoms. J. Phycol. 12: 180–185.

GRUMBACH, K. H., H. K. LICHTENTHALER, AND K. H. ERISMANN. 1978. Incorporation of $^{14}CO_2$ in photosynthetic pigments of *Chlorella pyrenoidosa*. Planta 140: 37–43.

GUILLARD, R. R. L. 1962. Salt and osmotic balance, p. 529–540. *In* R. A. Lewin [ed.] Physiology and biochemistry of algae. Academic Press, New York, NY.

GUILLARD, R. R. L., AND P. KILHAM. 1977. The ecology of marine phytoplanktonic diatoms, p. 372–469. *In* D. Werner [ed.] The biology of diatoms. Blackwell, Oxford.

GUILLARD, R. R. L., AND J. H. RYTHER. 1962. Studies of marine planktonic diatoms. I. *Cyclotella nana* Hustedt and *Detonula confervacea* (Cleve) Gran. Can. J. Microbiol. 8: 229–239.

HALIM, Y. 1960. Observations on the Nile bloom of phytoplankton in the Mediterranean. J. Cons. Int. Explor. Mer 26: 57–67.

HALLDAL, P. 1958. Pigment formation and growth in blue-green algae in crossed gradients of light intensity and temperature. Physiol. Plant. 11: 401–420.

HALLDAL, P. [ed.] 1970. Photobiology of microorganisms. Wiley Interscience, London. 479 p.

HARRISON, W. G. 1976. Nitrate metabolism of the red tide dinoflagellate *Gonyaulax polyedra* Stein. J. Exp. Mar. Biol. Ecol. 21: 199–209.

HATTORI, A. 1962. Light induced reduction of nitrate, nitrite and hydroxylamine in a blue-green alga *Anabaena cylindrica*. Plant Cell Physiol. 3: 355–369.

HAXO, F. T., AND L. R. BLINKS. 1950. Photosynthetic action spectra of marine algae. J. Gen. Physiol. 33: 389–422.

HELLEBUST, J. A. 1976a. Osmoregulation. Annu. Rev. Plant Physiol. 27: 485–505.

_____ 1976b. Effect of salinity on photosynthesis and mannitol synthesis in the green flagellate *Platymonas suecica*. Can. J. Bot. 54: 1735–1741.

_____ 1978. Uptake of organic substrates by *Cyclotella cryptica* (Bacillariophyceae): effects of ions, ionophores and metabolic and transport inhibitors. J. Phycol. 14: 79–83.

HITCHCOCK, G. L. 1980. Influence of temperature on the growth rate of *Skeletonema costatum* in response to variations in daily light intensity. Mar. Biol. 57: 261–269.

HOBSON, L. A. 1966. Some influences of the Columbia river effluent on marine phytoplankton during January 1961. Limnol. Oceanogr. 11: 223–234.

HOLMES, R. W., P. M. WILLIAMS, AND R. W. EPPLEY. 1967. Red water in La Jolla Bay, 1964–1966. Limnol. Oceanogr. 12: 503–512.

HOLT, M. G., AND T. J. SMAYDA. 1974. The effect of daylength and light intensity on the growth rate of the marine diatom *Detonula confervacea* (Cleve) Gran. J. Phycol. 10: 231–237.

HULBURT, E. M. 1963. The diversity of phytoplanktonic populations in oceanic, coastal, and estuarine regions. J. Mar. Res. 21: 81–93.

_____ 1970. Competition for nutrients by marine phytoplankton in oceanic, coastal, and estuarine regions. Ecology 51: 475–484.

_____ 1979. An asymmetric formulation of the distribution characteristics of phytoplankton species: an investigation in interpretation. Mar. Sci. Commun. 5: 245–268.

HULBURT, E. M., AND R. R. L. GUILLARD. 1968. The relationship of the distribution of the diatom *Skeletonema tropicum* to temperature. Ecology 49: 337–339.

HULBURT, E. M., AND J. RODMAN. 1963. Distributions of phytoplankton species with respect to salinity between the coast of southern New England and Bermuda. Limnol. Oceanogr. 8: 263–269.

HUNTSMAN, S. H., AND R. T. BARBER. 1977. Primary production off Northwest Africa: the relationship to wind and nutrient conditions. Deep-Sea Res. 24: 7–23.

HUTCHINSON, G. E. 1967. A treatise on limnology. Vol. 2: Introduction to lake biology and the limnoplankton. Wiley, New York, NY. 1115 p.

ICHIMURA, S. E. 1960. Photosynthesis pattern of natural phytoplankton relating to light intensity. Bot. Mag. Tokyo 73: 458–467.

IGNATIADES, L., AND T. J. SMAYDA. 1970. Autoecological studies on the marine diatom *Rhizosolenia fragilissima* Bergon. I. The influence of light, temperature, and salinity. J. Phycol. 6: 332–339.

JITTS, H. R., C. D. MCALLISTER, K. STEPHENS, AND J. D. H. STRICKLAND. 1964. The cell division rates of some marine phytoplankters as a function of light and temperature. J. Fish. Res. Board Can. 21: 139–157.

JONES, T. W., AND R. A. GALLOWAY. 1979. Effect of light quality and intensity on glycerol content in *Dunaliella tertiolecta* (Chorophyceae) and the relationship to cell growth/osmoregulation. J. Phycol. 15: 101–106.

JØRGENSEN, E. G. 1964. Adaptation to different light intensities in the diatom *Cyclotella meneghiniana* Kütz. Physiol. Plant. 17: 136–145.

_____ 1968. The adaptation of plankton algae. II. Aspects of the temperature adaptation of *Skeletonema costatum*. Physiol. Plant. 21: 423–427.

_____ 1969. The adaptation of plankton algae. IV. Light adaptation in different algal species. Physiol. Plant. 22: 1307–1315.

JØRGENSEN, E. G., AND E. STEEMANN NIELSEN. 1965. The adaptation in plankton algae. Mem. Ist. Ital. Idrobiol. 18 (suppl.): 37–46.

KAHN, N., AND E. SWIFT. 1978. Positive buoyancy through ionic control in the nonmotile marine dinoflagellate *Pyrocystis noctiluca* Murray ex Schuett. Limnol. Oceanogr. 23: 649–658.

KAMYKOWSKI, D., AND S. J. ZENTARA. 1977. The diurnal vertical migration of motile phytoplankton through temperature gradients. Limnol. Oceanogr. 22: 148–151.

KAUSS, H. 1974. Osmoregulation in *Ochromonas*, p. 90–94. *In* U. Zimmermann and J. Dainty [ed.] Membrane transport in plants. Springer Verlag, Berlin.

_____ 1977. Biochemistry of osmotic regulation. Int. Rev. Biochem. (Plant Biochem. II) 13: 119–140.

_____ 1978. Osmotic regulation in algae. Prog. Phytochem. 5: 1–27.

_____ 1979. Biochemistry of osmotic regulation in *Poterioochromonas malhamensis*. Ber. Dtsch. Bot. Ges. 92: 11–22.

KIEFER, D. A., AND T. ENNS. 1976. A steady-state model of light-, temperature-, and carbon-limited growth of phytoplankton, p. 319–336. *In* R. P. Canale [ed.] Modeling biochemical processes in aquatic ecosystems. Ann Arbor Sci. Publ., Ann Harbor, MI.

KIRST, G. O. 1975. Wirkung unterschiedlicher Konzentrationen von NaCl und anderen osmotisch wirksamen Substanzen auf die CO_2^- Fixierung der einzelligen Alge *Platymonas subcordiformis*. Oecologia 20: 237–254.

_____ 1979. Osmotic adaptations of the marine plankton alga *Platymonas subcordiformis* (Hazen). Ber. Dtsch. Bot. Ges. 92: 31–42.

KNOECHEL, R., AND J. KALFF. 1975. Algal sedimentation: the cause of a diatom-blue-green succession. Verh. Int. Ver. Limnol. 19: 745–754.

KREMER, J. N., AND S. W. NIXON. 1978. A coastal marine ecosystem. Simulation and analysis. Ecological Studies No. 24. Springer-Verlag, Berlin. 217 p.

KREUZER, H. P., AND H. KAUSS. 1980. Role of α galactosidase in the osmotic regulation of *Poterioochromonas malhamensis*. Planta 147: 435–438.

LÄNNERGREN, C. 1979. Buoyancy of natural populations of marine phytoplankton. Mar. Biol. 54: 1–10.

LEVRING, T. 1966. Submarine light and algal shore zonation, p. 305–318. *In* R. E. Bainbridge and E. G. C. Rackham [ed.] Light as an ecological factor. Wiley, New York, NY.

LI, W. K. W. 1981. Temperature adaptation in phytoplankton: cellular and photosynthetic characteristics, p. 259–279. *In* P. G. Falkowski [ed.] Primary productivity in the sea. Environmental Science Research Series. Vol. 19. Plenum Press, New York, NY.

LI, W. K. W., AND I. MORRIS. 1981. Photosynthetic adaptation and adjustment to temperature in *Phaeodactylum tricornutum*. J. Exp. Mar. Biol. Ecol. (In press)

LIU, M. S., AND J. A. HELLEBUST. 1976a. Effects of salinity changes on growth and metabolism of the marine centric diatom *Cyclotella cryptica*. Can. J. Bot. 54: 930–937.

1976b. Effects of salinity and osmolarity of the medium on amino acid metabolism in *Cyclotella cryptica*. Can. J. Bot. 54: 938–948.

LOHMANN, H. 1908. Untersuchungen zur Feststellung des vollständigen Gehaltes des Meeres an Plankton. Wiss. Meeresunters. Abt. Kiel. 10: 131–370.

MACISAAC, J. J. 1978. Diel cycles of inorganic nitrogen uptake in a natural phytoplankton population dominated by *Gonyaulax polyedra*. Limnol. Oceanogr. 23: 1–9.

MACISAAC, J. J., AND R. C. DUGDALE. 1972. Interactions of light and inorganic nitrogen in controlling nitrogen uptake in the sea. Deep-Sea Res. 19: 209–232.

MADDUX, W. S., AND R. F. JONES. 1964. Some interactions of temperature, light intensity, and nutrient concentration during the continuous culture of *Nitzschia closterium* and *Tetraselmis* sp. Limnol. Oceanogr. 9: 79–86.

MAESTRINI, S. Y., AND D. J. BONIN. 1981. Allelopathic relationships between phytoplankton species. Can. Bull. Fish. Aquat. Sci. 210: 323–338.

MAHONEY, J. B., AND J. J. A. MCLAUGHLIN. 1979. Salinity influence on the ecology of phytoflagellate blooms in lower New York Bay and adjacent waters. J. Exp. Mar. Biol. Ecol. 37: 213–223.

MALONE, T. C., C. GARSIDE, K. C. HAINES, AND O. A. ROELS. 1975. Nitrate uptake and growth of *Chaetoceros* sp. in large outdoor continuous cultures. Limnol. Oceanogr. 20: 9–19.

MARRA, J. 1978. Effect of short-term variations in light intensity on photosynthesis of a marine phytoplankter: a laboratory simulation study. Mar. Biol. 46: 191–202.

MCCOMBIE, A. M. 1960. Actions and interactions of temperature, light intensity and nutrient concentration on the green alga, *Chlamydomonas reinhardi*. J. Fish. Res. Board Can. 17: 871–894.

MCLACHLAN, J. 1960. The culture of *Dunaliella tertiolecta* Butcher — a euryhaline organism. Can. J. Microbiol. 6: 367–379.

1961. The effect of salinity on growth and chlorophyll content in representative classes of unicellular marine algae. Can. J. Microbiol. 7: 399–406.

MIDDLEBROOKS, E. J., AND D. B. PORCELLA. 1971. Rational multivariate algal growth kinetics. J. Sanit. Eng. Div. Proc. Am. Soc. Civ. Eng. 97 (SAI): 135–140.

MORGAN, K. C., AND J. KALFF. 1979. Effect of light and temperature interactions on growth of *Cryptomonas erosa* (Cryptophyceae). J. Phycol. 15: 127–134.

MORRIS, I., AND K. FARRELL. 1971. Photosynthetic rates, gross patterns of carbon dioxide assimilation and activities of ribulose diphosphate carboxylase in marine algae grown at different temperatures. Physiol. Plant. 25: 372–377.

MORRIS, I., AND H. E. GLOVER. 1974. Questions on the mechanism of temperature adaptation in marine phytoplankton. Mar. Biol. 24: 147–154.

MUNK, W. H., AND G. A. RILEY. 1952. Absorption of nutrients by aquatic plants. J. Mar. Res. 11: 215–240.

MUR, L. R., H. J. GONS, AND L. VAN LIERE. 1977. Some experiments on the competition between algae and blue-green bacteria in light-limited environments. FEMS Microb. Lett. 1: 335–338.

1978. Competition of the green algae *Scenedesmus* and the blue-green alga *Oscillatoria*. Mitt. Int. Ver. Limnol. 21: 473–479.

NAKANISHI, M., AND M. MONSI. 1965. Effect of variation in salinity on photosynthesis of phytoplankton growing in estuaries. J. Fac. Sci. Univ. Tokyo Sect. III Bot. 9: 19–42.

NELSON, D. M., AND H. L. CONWAY. 1979. Effects of the light regime on nutrient assimilation by phytoplankton in the Baja California and northwest Africa upwelling systems. J. Mar. Res. 37: 301–318.

NELSON, D. M., C. F. D'ELIA, AND R. R. L. GUILLARD. 1979. Growth and competition of the marine diatoms *Phaeodactylum tricornutum* and *Thalassiosira pseudonana*. II. Light limitation. Mar. Biol. 50: 313–318.

NYHOLM, N. 1978. A mathematical model for growth of phytoplankton. Mitt. Int. Ver. Limnol. 21: 193–206.

O'BRIEN, W. J. 1974. The dynamics of nutrient limitation of phytoplankton algae: a model reconsidered. Ecology 55: 135–141.

PAASCHE, E. 1975. The influence of salinity on the growth of some plankton diatoms from brackish water. Norw. J. Bot. 22: 209–215.

PACKARD, T. T., AND D. BLASCO. 1974. Nitrate reductase activity in upwelling regions. 2. Ammonia and light dependence. Téthys 6: 269–280.

PASCIAK, W. J., AND J. GAVIS. 1974. Transport limitation of nutrient uptake in phytoplankton. Limnol. Oceanogr. 19: 881–888.

1975. Transport limited nutrient uptake rates in *Ditylum brightwellii*. Limnol. Oceanogr. 20: 604–617.

PAUL, J. S. 1979. Osmoregulation in the marine diatom *Cylindrotheca fusiformis*. J. Phycol. 15: 280–284.

PLATT, T., K. L. DENMAN, AND A. D. JASSBY. 1977. Modeling the productivity of phytoplankton, p. 807–856. *In* E. D. Goldberg et al. [ed.] The sea: ideas and observations on progress in the study of the seas. Vol. 6. Wiley, New York, NY.

PODAMO, J. 1972. Contribution à l'étude biologique et chimique du port d'Ostende. Ann. Soc. R. Zool. Belg. 102: 105–127.

PRÉZELIN, B. 1981. The light reaction of photosynthesis. Can. Bull. Fish. Aquat. Sci. 210: 1–43.

PRÉZELIN, B. B., AND H. A. MATLICK. 1980. Time-course of photoadaptation in the photosynthetic-irradiance relationship of a dinoflagellate exhibiting photosynthetic periodicity. Mar. Biol. 58: 85–96.

Prézelin, B. B., and B. M. Sweeney. 1979. Photo-adaptation of photosynthesis in two bloom-forming dinoflagellates, p. 101–106. *In* D. L. Taylor and A. N. Seliger [ed.] Toxic dinoflagellate blooms. Proc. 2nd Int. Conf. Toxic Dinoflagellate Blooms. Elsevier, Amsterdam.

Provasoli, L. 1958. Nutrition and ecology of protozoa and algae. Annu. Rev. Microbiol. 12: 279–308.

Ramus, J., S. I. Beale, D. Mauzerall, and K. L. Howard. 1976. Changes in photosynthetic pigment concentration in seaweeds as a function of water depth. Mar. Biol. 37: 223–229.

Ramus, J., F. Lemons, and C. Zimmerman. 1977. Adaptation of light-harvesting pigments to downwelling light and the consequent photosynthetic performance of the eulittoral rockweeds *Ascophyllum nodosum* and *Fucus vesiculosus*. Mar. Biol. 42: 293–303.

Raymont, J. E. 1963. Plankton and productivity in the oceans. Pergamon Press, Oxford. 660 p.

Reshkin, S. J., and G. A. Knauer. 1979. Light stimulation of phosphate uptake in natural assemblages of phytoplankton. Limnol. Oceanogr. 24: 1121–1124.

Rhode, W., R. A. Vollenweider, and A. Nauwerck. 1958. The primary production and standing crop of phytoplankton, p. 299–322. *In* A. A. Buzzati-Traverso [ed.] Perspectives in marine biology. Univ. Calif. Press, Berkeley.

Rice, T. R., and R. L. Ferguson. 1975. Response of estuarine phytoplankton to environmental conditions, p. 1–43. *In* F. J. Vernberg [ed.] Physiological ecology of estuarine organisms. Univ. S. Carolina Press.

Riley, G. A. 1967. The plankton of estuaries, p. 316–326. *In* G. H. Lauff [ed.] Estuaries. Am. Assoc. Adv. Sci. Publ. 83.

Riper, D. M., T. G. Owens, and P. G. Falkowski. 1979. Chlorophyll turnover in *Skeletonema costatum*, a marine plankton diatom. Plant Physiol. 64: 49–54.

Ryther, J. H., and D. W. Menzel. 1959. Light adaptation by marine phytoplankton. Limnol. Oceanogr. 4: 492–497.

Saugestad, T. 1971. Microflora in supralittoral rockpools in a costal area south of Bergen, Norway. Sarsia 46: 79–95.

Schobert, B. 1977. Is there an osmotic regulatory mechanism in algae and higher plants? J. Theor. Biol. 68: 17–26.

1979. Proline accumulation in *Phaeodactylum tricornutum* and the function of the compatible solutes in plant cells under water stress. Ber. Dtsch. Bot. Ges. 92: 23–30.

1980a. The importance of water activity and water structure during hyperosmotic stress in algae and higher plants. Biochem. Physiol. Pflanz. 175: 91–103.

1980b. Proline metabolism, relaxation of osmotic strain and membrane permeability in the diatom *Phaeodactylum tricornutum*. Physiol. Plant. 50: 37–42.

Schöne, H. K. 1972. Experimentelle Untersuchungen zur Ökologie der marinen Kieselalge *Thalassiosira rotula*. I. Temperatur und Licht. Mar. Biol. 13: 284–291.

1974. Experimentelle Untersuchungen zur Ökologie der marinen Kieselalge *Thalassiosira rotula*.

II. Der Einfluss des Salzgehaltes. Mar. Biol. 27: 287–298.

Seliger, H. H., J. H. Carpenter, M. Loftus, and W. D. McElroy. 1970. Mechanisms for the accumulation of high concentrations of dinoflagellates in a bioluminescent bay. Limnol. Oceanogr. 15: 234–245.

Smayda, T. J. 1969. Experimental observations on the influence of temperature, light, and salinity on cell division of the marine diatom *Detonula confervacea* (Cleve) Gran. J. Phycol. 5: 150–157.

1970. The suspension and sinking of phytoplankton in the sea. Oceanogr. Mar. Biol. Annu. Rev. 8: 353–414.

Soeder, C. J. 1967. Tagesperiodische Vertikalwanderung bei begeisselten Planktonalgen. Umsch. Wiss. Tech. 67: 388.

Soeder, C., and E. Stengel. 1974. Physico-chemical factors affecting metabolism and growth rate, p. 714–740. *In* W. D. P. Stewart [ed.] Algal physiology and biochemistry. Blackwell, Oxford.

Sournia, A. 1981. Morphological basis of competition and succession. Can. Bull. Fish. Aquat. Sci. 210: 339–346.

Steemann Nielsen, E., and V. K. Hansen. 1959. Light adaptation in marine phytoplankton populations and its interrelation with temperature. Physiol. Plant. 12: 353–370.

Steemann Nielsen, E., V. K. Hansen, and E. G. Jørgensen. 1962. The adaptation to different light intensities in *Chlorella vulgaris* and the time dependence on transfer to a new light intensity. Physiol. Plant. 15: 505–517.

Steemann Nielsen, E., and E. G. Jørgensen. 1968a. The adaptation of plankton algae. I. General part. Physiol. Plant. 21: 401–433.

1968b. The adaptation of plankton algae. III. With special consideration on the importance in nature. Physiol. Plant. 21: 647–654.

Swift, E., and V. Meunier. 1976. ffects of light intensity on division rate, stimulable bioluminescence and cell size of the oceanic dinoflagellates *Dissodinium lunula*, *Pyrocystis fusiformis* and *P. noctiluca*. J. Phycol. 12: 14–22.

Syrett, P. J. 1962. Nitrogen assimilation, p. 171–188. *In* R. A. Lewin [ed.] Physiology and biochemistry of algae. Academic Press, New York, NY.

Takano, H. 1963. Diatom culture in artificial sea water. I. Experiments on five pelagic species. Bull. Tokai Reg. Fish. Res. Lab. 37: 17–25.

Talling, J. F. 1971. The underwater light climate as a controlling factor in the production ecology of freshwater phytoplankton. Verh. Int. Ver. Limnol. 19: 214–243.

Thomas, W. H., and A. N. Dodson. 1974. Effect of interactions between temperature and nitrate supply on the cell-division rates of two marine phytoflagellates. Mar. Biol. 24: 213–217.

Tomas, C. R. 1978. *Olisthodiscus luteus* (Chrysophyceae). I. Effects of salinity and temperature on growth, motility and survival. J. Phycol. 14: 309–313.

1980. *Olisthodiscus luteus* (Chrysophyceae). V. Its occurrence, abundance and dynamics in Narragansett Bay, Rhode Island. J. Phycol. 16: 157–166.

VÄLIKANGAS, I. 1926. Planktologische Untersuchungen im Hafengebiet von Helsingfors. I. Über das Plankton insbesondere das Netz-Zooplankton des Sommer-halbjahres. Acta Zool. Fenn. 1: 1–298.

WALL, D., AND F. BRIAND. 1979. Response of lake phytoplankton communities to in situ manipulations of light intensity and colour. J. Plankton Res. 1: 103–112.

WALSBY, A. E. 1972. Structure and function of gas vacu-oles. Bacteriol. Rev. 36: 1–32.

WETHERELL, D. F. 1963. Osmotic equilibration and growth of *Scenedesmus obliquus* in saline media. Physiol. Plant. 16: 82–91.

WHITE, A. W. 1978. Salinity effects on growth and toxin content of *Gonyaulax excavata*, a marine dinoflagellate causing paralytic shellfish poisoning. J. Phycol. 14: 475–479.

WILLIAMS, F. M. 1971. Dynamics of microbial popu-lations, p. 197–267. *In* B. C. Patten [ed.] Systems analysis and simulation in ecology. Vol. 1. Academic Press, New York, NY.

WILLIAMS, R. B. 1964. Division rates of salt marsh diatoms in relation to salinity and cell size. Ecology 45: 877–880.

WOOD, E. J. F. 1965. Marine microbial ecology. Chapman & Hall Ltd., London. 243 p.

YENTSCH, C. S. 1974. Some aspects of the environmental physiology of marine phytoplankton: a second look. Oceanogr. Mar. Biol. Annu. Rev. 12: 41–75.

YENTSCH, C. S., AND R. W. LEE. 1966. A study of photosynthetic light relations, and a new interpretation of sun and shade phytoplankton. J. Mar. Res. 24: 319–337.

YODER, J. A. 1979. Effect of temperature on light-limited growth and chemical composition of *Skeletonema costatum* (Bacillariophyceae). J. Phycol. 15: 362–370.

The Role of Phytohormones and Vitamins in Species Succession of Phytoplankton

D. J. Bonin and S. Y. Maestrini

Station Marine d'Endoume, Chemin de la Batterie des Lions, F 13007 Marseille, France

and J. W. Leftley

Dunstaffnage Marine Research Laboratory, P.O. Box 3, Oban, Argyll PA34 4AD, Scotland

Introduction

It is very difficult to give a good definition of growth-promoting substances. All the metabolites produced by one organism that may enhance the growth of others, whatever the nature of their action might be, are included in this family. Nevertheless, it is possible to separate these organic compounds into three large groups: (1) organic compounds that can be used directly by organisms as sources of energy, carbon, or other elements when they are lacking in inorganic form in the environment; (2) compounds that are solubilizers or chelators and make inorganic nutrients more available; (3) organic compounds that participate in metabolic reactions and are usually essential for algal growth: they are of vitamin or plant hormone nature. In this review, we shall discuss the role of metabolites belonging only to the third group. Because the relative need for each nutrient is different for each phytoplankter present at any one time, all these substances lead to a modification of the nutritional characteristics of the medium and, therefore, contribute to the modification of the growth of several phytoplankton species. Consequently, they may interact with other nutritional and physical factors in the species succession.

Growth-promoting substances such as hormones and vitamins are compounds of various origins and are very different in structure and function. Some algae (auxotrophs) are absolutely unable to synthesize some of their own growth factors and depend wholly on the medium for these requirements. Auxotrophy does not relate to the sources of energy used by the algae and some obligate photoautotrophic algae, as well as heterotrophic algae, may need vitamins. On the other hand, exogenous plant hormones are never absolutely necessary. However, in some cases, mainly in seaweeds but sometimes also in unicellular planktonic algae, it appears that they can modify several aspects of growth.

Hormones

In higher plants, hormones are characterized by effecting improvements in growth and cell divi-sion, blossoming of flowers, development of fruit, increase of roots and shoots, and control of dormancy in seeds. These substances can be separated into three groups: (1) auxins, activating cell growth, for example, indole acetic acid (IAA) and its numerous analogues and derivatives; (2) gibberellins, for example, gibberellic acid (GA) and some analogues acting principally on cell growth but also on division rate and maturation of organs; (3) kinetins, acting particularly on cell division.

As soon as auxins were characterized by Thimann (1934) and their action as growth factors became established in plants, it was tempting to ascribe various positive interactions, observed between different algae in culture, to a common factor of auxinic nature. As a matter of fact, this hypothesis remained unproven until the 1960s when liberation of several auxinlike substances by cultured algae was verified, for example, the work of Bentley (1958, 1959) on *Chlorella pyrenoidosa*, *Oscillatoria* sp., and *Anabaena cylindrica* and that of Tauts and Semenenko (1971) on *Chlorella* sp. Simultaneously, a large number of substances of hormonal origin have been characterized in unicellular and, more frequently, multicellular marine and freshwater algae. It was evident that if these substances exist in the cytoplasm, they could also exist in that fraction of organic matter, sometimes very large, which is excreted by algae during growth. The size of this fraction differs according to various authors and the experimental conditions used. For example, it can vary from 7 to 50% of the biomass in fresh-water (Fogg 1966) and from 35 to 40% of the carbon assimilated in seawater (Antia et al. 1963).

In this respect, the first significant work was that of Van Overbeek (1940a, b) on some 15 algae, and particularly on a mixture of diatoms (*Melosira* sp. and *Biddulphia* sp.). Van Overbeek demon-strated that all the algae studied contained more or less high quantities of substances producing an auxinlike response with the coleoptile test. Later on, it was verified that some of the substances really are auxins having biochemical characteristics similar to those of IAA and that they are more abundant in growing algae than in senescent algae (Schiewer 1967, on *Enteromorpha*; Augier 1965, on *Botryo-*

cladia botryoides). Also, the existence of gibberellin-like substances has been demonstrated in *Tetraselmis*, *Fucus spiralis*, and numerous diatoms from natural plankton samples (Mowat 1963). Likewise, substances closely related to cytokinins have been found by Bentley-Mowat and Reid (1967) in *Gymnodinium splendens* and *Phaeodactylum tricornutum*. These three chemical families do not appear as frequently in algae. Indeed, analyzing the data presented by Augier (1977) in his review of the subject, and taking into account the difficulty of interpreting the indefinite results given by different authors, we can state that, among 416 assays for determination of growth substances in algae, one finds 127 indoliclike substances (IAA, analogues, derivatives, and precursors), 18 gibberellinlike compounds, and 12 cytokininlike ones. Are these numbers valid? Surely not, and for several reasons. These substances are extremely photo- and thermo-labile; their extraction can lead to a significant diminution or even to the total disappearance of activity in the extract. The difficulty of extraction is increased by the fact that hormones are distributed diffusely throughout the whole algal cell and are not concentrated in glands, as in animals. Therefore, it is necessary to use a complete thallus to obtain a small amount of active substance in the final extract; the same applies to unicellular algae. In these conditions, chemical analysis leads to a precise determination of the nature of the molecule but gives unreliable information about the real quantity in the algae. On the other hand, biological tests are very sensitive for quantitative evaluation but give no information on the chemical nature of the product. It is not surprising to find IAA and its derivatives in diverse groups of algae as these substances are known to be produced during metabolism of the important aromatic amino acid, tryptophan. If investigation and extraction methods could be improved, indoliclike compounds probably could be found in many plant cells.

More important for the ecologist is the aim to define whether an exogenous source of phytohormone can effect improvements in growth processes. There are numerous reports of the action of various concentrations of auxins and other phytohormones on algae in culture, but their interpretation is very difficult. The early studies were too imprecise, both in the description of the experiments themselves and in the presentation of the results; many of them must be disregarded. Most were realized with nonaxenic cultures. The extracts were used directly such that the measured growth could have resulted from action of the solvent (ethanol) itself (Bach and Fellig 1958). The experimental conditions (nutrition of the algae, light, and temperature) are often imprecisely specified. Results are also given in an ambiguous form; for instance, improvement of growth can be expressed either as an increase of cell division rate or as a doubling rate of the total biomass of the culture, as these hormones act on cell size as demonstrated in several experiments (Bentley-Mowat 1967; Bonin 1969). It is not surprising to find in the literature contradictory and even directly opposite conclusions. Thus, working at the same time, but separately, Brannon and Sell (1945) and Manos (1945) found exactly conflicting results in their studies on the influence of IAA at a 10 mg·L^{-1} concentration on *Chlorella*. When an effect is observed after addition of auxin, it is often an inhibitory action for the highest concentrations and no action at all with the lowest ones. Augier (1976) gathered results on the influence of exogenous phytohormones on the growth of different algae. The same statement can be made about these data as that made by Brian (1963), i.e. that responses to phytohormones are less characteristic in unicellular algae than in coenocytic algae and in seaweeds. Among 72 IAA positive-reacting strains, 21 are unicellular and 51 multicellular, and among 24 IAA nonreactive strains, 17 are unicellular and 7 are multicellular. On the other hand, the different families of products do not act with the same relative frequency on all the groups of algae: on diatoms, IAA is less often stimulatory than GA, and on Chlorophyceae, IAA is beneficial as frequently as GA; but on these two groups kinetins do not usually have a pronounced action.

Are these results understandable, given that they are obtained in nutrient media that are so varied, but at the same time always excessively rich? Algeus (1946) had already noted that the results could be very different according to the medium used and the culture conditions. On the other hand, are these unialgal experiments significant for the ecologist? On this subject, Johnston's (1963) interesting work has to be mentioned. He compared growth of the different components of a natural planktonic sample exposed to various concentrations of gibberellins. He concluded that there is very often "no significant effect" but in some cases beneficial effects can be discerned on several of the algae studied. After 8 d of culture a change appears in the dominance of algae; for example, GA$_7$ at 0.1 mg·L^{-1} promotes growth of *Ditylum brightwelli* more than that of *Nitzschia delicatissima*.

Another subject of interest in Johnston's work was a simultaneous experiment on 10 replicate samples for the same GA concentration, which produced very scattered results. Are such conclusions valid? What can we think of other studies carried out without any statistical basis? Virtually no results are presented in kinetic terms for growth measurements, so no real conclusion can be given on the exact influence of addition of exogenous phytohormones. On the contrary, there are no studies showing that a total lack of hormones in the medium stops growth. In other words, it means that all the algae studied are able to synthesize their own phytohormones or that their metabolic reactions do not require the presence of hormones.

One more problem has to be discussed; it concerns the concentration of hormone for which an increase in growth is observed. Most workers have used high concentrations based on those active in higher plants. Therefore, data obtained with algae may not reflect the real potential of the hormones as might be revealed at lower concentrations. For any one given substance, the beneficial action appears at different concentrations according to various authors and the algae they have studied. The sensitivity of a clone to a certain substance can be large. For example, Kim and Greulach (1961) showed that IAA at 1 mg·L^{-1} had no effect on *Chlorella pyrenoidosa*, at 5 mg·L^{-1} it favored growth, but at 20 mg·L^{-1} it was quite toxic. Also, when the same species has been studied by other authors, the results have been quite different. On the basis of the data collected by Augier (1976), it is possible to find differences ranging from 10 μg·L^{-1} (Gray 1962) to 100 mg·L^{-1} (Bendana and Fried 1967) for concentrations of GA improving growth of *Chlorella pyrenoidosa*.

It would be interesting to find whether differences exist between freshwater and marine algae concerning their requirement for hormones. Is this requirement dependent on the original biotope? An answer cannot be given to this question because most authors do not specify the ecological characteristics of the strain they study. Bentley (1958) and Johnston (1959, 1963) admitted that unicellular marine algae are generally very sensitive to auxins and antimetabolites. As a matter of fact, concentrations of 100 and even 10 μg·L^{-1} of GA lead to inhibition of the growth in several unicellular marine algae although higher concentrations of the same compound favor growth of *Chlorella pyrenoidosa*; that is what Johnston's (1963) work demonstrated. With *Skeletonema costatum*, Bentley (1958) found beneficial concentrations of IAA-like substances ranging from 10 to 100 ng·L^{-1}. Bonin (1969) mentioned that concentrations of 100 ng·L^{-1} of IAA and 1 μg·L^{-1} of GA favored growth of *Chaetoceros lauderi*. Thus, it seems that planktonic marine algae are sensitive to concentrations ranging from 10 ng·L^{-1} to 1 μg·L^{-1}. At lower values, hormones, principally indolic ones, have no apparent effect.

It is interesting to know the concentrations of these substances in natural waters. Bentley (1960) found some compounds in offshore waters with characteristics close to those of IAA. They were biologically tested with the coleoptile test and they appeared to be present at a very low concentration, around 3 ng·L^{-1}, i.e. about 10 times less than the lowest values known to give a positive effect on growth of *Skeletonema costatum*. In such a case,

auxinlike substances found in seawater are unlikely to have any action on the growth of this alga. In littoral zones, where plant biomass is composed predominantly of seaweeds, growth-promoting substances have been detected. Augier (1972) found IAA and GA in the midlittoral zone of the Mediterranean shore. Likewise, Pedersen and Fridborg (1972) noted an improvement in growth of seaweeds cultivated in a medium containing seawater from the *Fucus–Ascophyllum* zone and Pedersen (1973) isolated a cytokinin from these waters. The culture improvement could really be due to this cytokinin. Consequently, one may think that regulation by such substances can occur in areas where plant materials are important. But, according to the few results we collected, this action is less in unicellular algae than in seaweeds.

Is it possible to make useful conclusions if the various extracts have shown positive effects on growth, but have not been chemically characterized? Provasoli and Carlucci (1974) noted that there is no proof that algae normally employ exogenous higher plant hormones to regulate their biochemical processes. As a matter of fact, land plants respond differently to various forms of auxins, gibberellins, and cytokinins. It must be the same for algae. The only means to answer these questions would be a biochemical analysis of those algal extracts that show a positive effect on growth. It seems that physiologists have focussed too much on a systematic search for previously known substances associated with the phanerogams.

Vitamins

GENERAL FEATURES

It has been known for many years that vitamins play a positive role in the growth of microorganisms in culture. This idea was first proposed by Lwoff and Lederer (1935) and it was verified by Lwoff and Dusi (1937) who demonstrated the pyrimidine and thiazole requirements of the flagellate *Polytomella caeca*.

Progress in purification and synthesis allowed the demonstration that some form of vitamin requirement is widespread among algal taxa (see reviews by Droop 1962; Provasoli 1963, 1971; Provasoli and Carlucci 1974; Berland et al. 1978; Swift 1981). Hence, we shall not give too many details here concerning the frequency of this requirement, but only some examples: Droop (1962), reviewing 179 species mentioned in the literature, noted that 95 are auxotrophic, 80% of which depend on B$_{12}$, 53% on thiamine, and 10% on biotin. Subsequently, Provasoli and Carlucci (1974) reviewed a larger group of species (388) and found 203 auxotrophs, 85% of which required B$_{12}$, 40% thiamine, and 7% biotin. These results are similar to those of Droop, and all the authors cited note that other water-soluble vitamin requirements are much rarer. If requirements are classified according to taxonomy, one also finds significant differences between the algal groups. Numerous centric diatoms, half of the pennate diatoms, most of Haptophyceae, 90% of Dinophyceae, only 20% of Cyanophyceae, and just a few Chlorophyceae require vitamin B_{12}. Exogenous thiamine is less frequently required in these groups, and biotin very rarely, except in some Dinophyceae and Chrysophyceae. Hitherto, no diatoms or Haptophyceae have seemed to be dependent on biotin (see Swift 1981).

These data have to be considered as approximate and relative indices. As a matter of fact, in nature the percentages of these requirements may be modified for several reasons. In the earliest experimental studies, the workers often made a selection of species before undertaking the experiments. Also, very rich media were used that could modify strongly the exact nutritional status of the species as found in nature. Swift (1981) points out that green algae are very often isolated in media without organic matter such that their vitamin requirements tend to be statistically underestimated. On the other hand, Droop (1962) thought that vitamin requirements were overestimated because, when authors gathered data, they did not pay enough attention to the possible negative effects of vitamins, which were not, therefore, always very clearly expressed in the literature. Some data are difficult to interpret because they come from experiments carried out with a mixture of vitamins, some of which are well characterized whereas others are not. Moreover, some strains can require simultaneously two, three, or possibly more vitamins, a phenomenon that complicates the survey of the requirements of the algae; for example, *Prorocentrum micans* needs B_{12} and biotin, and *Amphidinium carteri* and *Gymnodinium breve* require B_{12}, thiamine, and biotin.

A pertinent question which may be posed is: Are vitamin requirements, demonstrated in a given species, always constant or do they depend on the experimental conditions? For example, Herdman and Carr (1972) had greater success than previous workers in isolating auxotrophic strains of *Anacystis nidulans* because they used different mutagenic and culture techniques. Ideally, research on vitamin requirements should be done on newly isolated strains in which natural characteristics still exist. In fact this is rarely done because, most frequently, scientists try to improve their knowledge of nutritional requirements of strains about which information already exists.

Vitamin requirements also vary according to other nutritional factors, as demonstrated by Hutner et al. (1953). They showed that B_{12} is necessary for growth of *Ochromonas* but is no longer necessary,

or is required at lower concentrations, if methionine is added to the culture medium. The explanation of this phenomenon is that B_{12} is an essential cofactor in transmethylation reactions in the biosynthesis of certain amino acids, but the B_{12} requirement disappears if such amino acids are supplied directly to the alga. Rahat and Reich (1963) demonstrated a related phenomenon in *Prymnesium parvum*; methionine could not replace B_{12} or reduce the requirement for the vitamin. However, in the presence of vitamin B_{12}, methionine counteracted the inhibition of growth caused by some B_{12} analogues substituted at the benzimidazole part of the molecule, but no such effect was observed against inhibition by other analogues. α-(5-hydroxybenzimidazolyl)-cobamide cyanide (factor III) replaced B_{12} in the presence of methionine and, to a lesser extent, in the presence of other methyl donors such as betaine. These workers concluded that factor III was capable of replacing B_{12} in most B_{12}-requiring biochemical pathways in *Prymnesium* except for methyl-group synthesis. Although these two examples may not be exceptional, they allow us to suppose the existence of such phenomena in many other algae. But it is not universal as Van Baalen (1961) demonstrated that, in *Synechocystis* sp., methionine could not substitute for B_{12}. This could simply mean that the alga is impermeable to this amino acid. Hutner et al. (1957) also mentioned that B_{12} requirements in *Ochromonas* vary strongly according to temperature, but they could not give any explanation for this phenomenon.

SPECIES-SPECIFIC REQUIREMENTS

Algae do not have the same requirements with respect to the molecular structure of the vitamin offered to them. For instance, it has been demonstrated that, with thiamine, several microorganisms require only the thiazole moiety of the molecule whereas others require only the pyrimidine. Some algae need both parts of the molecule even if given separately whereas others require the complete compound. Lewin (1961) showed that among 41 algal strains he studied, only one required the complete molecule. The exact form of this requirement may be very important ecologically because the quantities needed depend on the kind of requirement. Droop (1958) noted that algae which require thiazole only need a greater quantity of the vitamin than those which need only the pyrimidine moiety.

The growth response towards vitamin B_{12} (cyanocobalamin) is even more complex. The cobalamins consist of a cobalt-containing corrin ring nucleus to which a nucleotide is attached. Specificity of organisms towards naturally occurring and artificial variants of the vitamin is determined by the nature of the nucleotide. Thus B_{12}-requiring organisms fall generally into three groups: (1) those like mammals which need a benzimidazole type of base in the nucleotide; (2) those like *Lactobacillus leichmannii* which can also use an adeninelike base; and (3) those like *Escherichia coli* which require no more than the nucleotide-free nucleus. B_{12}-requiring unicellular algae fall into one of these three categories of specificity, but the "mammalian" response is the most frequent (Droop et al. 1959; Provasoli 1971). However, Guillard (1968) claimed that, at least for diatoms, these response categories are somewhat arbitrary. He tested the growth response of 23 isolates (21 species) of marine diatoms to B_{12} analogues compared with B_{12} when supplied at the "ecologically significant" concentration of 4 ng·L^{-1}. The growth response was not "all or none" but varied continuously depending on the percentage response (B_{12} = 100%) chosen by the experimenter. At the 10% level of response, 11 clones had coliform, 4 lactobacillus, and 8 mammalian specificity patterns, whereas at the 1% response level 14 appeared to have coliform, 5 lactobacillus, and 4 mammalian specificities. To the writers this seems to be a somewhat subjective approach.

At a given concentration of a given analogue of B_{12}, algae respond differently according to the presence or the absence of other B_{12} analogues or of substances acting as antimetabolites (work of Ford 1958 on *Ochromonas malhamensis*). A very complete study carried out on *Euglena gracilis* with 300 different compounds (Epstein and Timmis 1963) (purines, pteridines, and nicotinamides) showed that, for similar or even lower concentrations than that of the vitamin, these compounds are inhibitory because they interfere with cofactors closely concerned with the utilization of B_{12}. The analogues show a great variation in their toxicity and in some cases they can even give a positive response of the lactobacillus type (Jacobsen et al. 1975).

Taking into account these findings, it is evident that vitamin requirements can vary for each species and even within the same species, depending on culture conditions; this has caused many difficulties in experimental studies. It is nevertheless important to quantify this vitamin requirement for each alga as it tells us whether the growth factor may play a direct role in the species succession, depending on the concentrations found in situ. The subject has been approached indirectly through vitamin bioassay. Indeed, such measurements are based on the fact that experimentally, at least in given limits, one can find a good linear relationship between the concentration of the growth factor tested and the number of cells observed at the end of the experiment. In this way, it has been possible to establish the relation between the number of molecules of vitamin used by a single cell of a given species. Guillard

and Cassie (1963) in such a study indicated values ranging from 6.5 to 15 molecules of B_{12} for a cubic micrometre of cell volume. It seems that these values vary between experiments, but the variations could be due to experimental artefacts; Droop (1961) had already raised this point. These results indicate that the growth limit (in terms of cytoplasmic yield) allowed by a certain concentration of a given vitamin is nearly constant regardless of species. Nevertheless, Guillard and Cassie thought that this conclusion does not deny the role of vitamins in the succession of populations. As a matter of fact, the same concentration of vitamin may lead to various rates of metabolic synthesis, according to the species, and may also be important in certain stages of the reproductive cycle, such as auxospore formation in diatoms.

The first studies carried out to evaluate the action of vitamin concentrations on growth rate using kinetic methods gave encouraging results. Droop (1961) noticed that division rate in *Monochrysis lutheri* does not change when B_{12} concentrations vary from 0.1 to 100 ng·L^{-1} under constant experimental conditions. If concentrations of B_{12} are to be limiting, according to Monod's law the B_{12} concentration must be lower than 0.1 ng·L^{-1}. Lewin (1954), Droop (1954), and Cowey (1956), in different neritic and oceanic areas, measured B_{12} concentrations ranging from 0.2 to 20 ng·L^{-1}. Therefore, in natural waters (the vitamin-poorest ones excepted) B_{12} has no regulating effect on the growth rate of *Monochrysis lutheri*, as its concentration is always sufficient for maximum growth. Droop (1961) compared the B_{12}-dependent growth of *Monochrysis* with that of *Ochromonas malhamensis*, using data obtained for the latter alga by Ford (1958). *Ochromonas* shows a decrease of cell division rate as soon as the 13 ng·L^{-1} concentration is reached. Although it is difficult to compare the growth characteristics of the two algae, it seems clear that, for B_{12} concentrations ranging from 0.1 to 13 ng·L^{-1}, *Monochrysis* would have a much higher growth rate than *Ochromonas*. Swift and Taylor (1974) also compared growth kinetics in three marine species according to B_{12} concentration and observed different characteristics for these species. The half-saturation constant is 0.39 (ng·L^{-1}) for *Thalassiosira pseudonana*, 1.69 for *Isochrysis galbana*, and 2.77 for *Monochrysis lutheri*, i.e. for the last one, slightly higher values than those mentioned by Droop. With respect to B_{12} (concentrations of about 1 ng·L^{-1} found in marine waters) Swift and Taylor thought that, at a certain phase of the life cycle, the development of these three species could be limited by availability of B_{12}.

VITAMIN B_{12} BINDING PROTEIN

Many unicellular algae, and other microorganisms, produce an extracellular "binding factor" which strongly sequesters vitamin B_{12}. The historical background to the discovery and characterization of this factor has been dealt with in detail by Provasoli and Carlucci (1974) and Pintner and Altmeyer (1979).

Droop (1968) and Pintner and Altmeyer (1979) have shown that extracellular B_{12}-binder is produced by a wide range of algae (diatoms, cryptophytes, chrysophytes, dinoflagellates, and green algae) including organisms that are not auxotrophic for the vitamin. Culture filtrates containing the factor will inhibit the growth of B_{12}-requirers when added to fresh culture medium. The binder produced by each class of algae seems to have the same general properties: it is heat labile, inhibition of the growth of B_{12}-requirers is nonspecific, and the inhibition can be abolished by adding excess B_{12}.

To date, only the B_{12} binding protein from *Euglena gracilis* has been biochemically characterized in any detail (Daisley 1970). Binder from cell extracts, and that excreted into the medium, was purified and found to be of a similar nature, a glycoprotein of molecular weight of about 200 000. The extracellular binder had a greater binding capacity than that from cell extracts, but both preparations of binder were heterogeneous, tending to disaggregate during purification, which suggested an oligomeric molecule.

The metabolic role of B_{12} binding protein is not clear; the function of the analogous mammalian "intrinsic factor," also a glycoprotein, is to facilitate transport of B_{12} across the intestinal membrane (Glass 1963). Provasoli and Carlucci (1974) suggested that the protein is involved in active uptake of B_{12} by algae and that any excess is excreted into the medium. Certainly, non-B_{12}-requirers which produce B_{12}-binder can actively take up the vitamin (Droop 1968). However, there is presently no data as to whether, or how, algal B_{12}-binder functions in the uptake of the vitamin.

Ford (1958) proposed that B_{12} was bound at the surface of *Ochromonas* cells, and Droop (1968) assumed that this was also the case for *Monochrysis*. However, Daisley (1970) prepared antiserum against partially purified binder from *Euglena* but this failed to agglutinate *Euglena* cells, indicating that binding does not take place at the surface of this alga. Sarhan et al. (1980) concluded from their data that the majority of binding sites in *Euglena* are associated with the chloroplasts. Modern affinity cytochemistry techniques may help to solve this problem.

The physiology of uptake of B_{12} has been studied in only a few algae: *Ochromonas malhamensis* (Reeves and Fay 1966; Bradbeer 1971), *Euglena gracilis* (Varma et al. 1961; Sarhan et al. 1980), and *Monochrysis* (= *Pavlova*) *lutheri* (Droop 1968). In all these algae, uptake of the vitamin

follows the same pattern, which is similar to that shown in bacteria. A primary uptake phase, characterized by very rapid uptake, is unaffected by metabolic inhibitors and is somewhat insensitive to temperature. Bradbeer (1971) found that, in *Ochromonas*, this primary phase showed saturation kinetics, with a K_m (B_{12}) of 4 nM and a V_{max} of $5 \times 10^1 B_{12}$ molecules$\cdot s^{-1} \cdot$cell^{-1}. In contrast, Sarhan et al. (1980) found that although the initial uptake of B_{12} by *Euglena* showed saturation kinetics, these did not conform to the Michaelis-Menten equation. The primary phase is followed by a secondary phase where the uptake rate is somewhat slower, and the process is sensitive to both metabolic inhibitors and to temperature. The primary phase has been interpreted as corresponding to the binding of B_{12} to specific receptors, and the secondary phase as corresponding to active transport of B_{12}, and possibly de novo synthesis of new binding sites, both processes requiring metabolic energy.

The ability to accumulate B_{12} very rapidly from the medium, even when it is present at very low concentrations, is obviously advantageous to an alga. For example, Bradbeer (1971) pointed out that, even at concentrations of B_{12} only 0.01 of the measured K_m for initial uptake (4 nM), the minimal amount of vitamin necessary for a new generation of cells could be taken up in only 3 s by *Ochromonas*; he also noted that this alga, per cell, stores B_{12} in bound form about 10^3 times the minimal requirement, which would permit growth for a subsequent 10 generations in absence of vitamin. Also, Sarhan et al. (1980) found that *Euglena* could accumulate 600 times the minimal cell requirement of B_{12}, which was sufficient to support 10 subsequent generations of algae. These workers suggested that this "luxury consumption" might have an ecological significance in that it would enable the population to survive during periods of vitamin depletion and also to compete with other auxotrophs that did not have such a high affinity for the vitamin.

The importance of B_{12} binding factor in natural populations is open to debate. Droop (1968) pointed out that inhibitory effect of binding factor was apparent in chemostat experiments with cell concentrations of *Monochrysis* as low as 0.4 million$\cdot$mL^{-1} and, because this alga can reach a density of 40 million cells$\cdot$mL^{-1} in supralittoral rock pools, the effect of the binder would probably be significant. He went on to suggest that B_{12}-binder could also be important in the open ocean. Once the producer of the binder became dominant, the dominance would be effectively maintained by the inhibitor because other B_{12} auxotrophs would be unable to take up the sequestered vitamin whereas the dominant species would have already accumulated sufficient B_{12} to be almost immune from the effect of the binder.

A similar hypothesis was proposed by Provasoli (1971) to explain the continuing abundance of diatoms for more or less long periods at the end of their blooms. But, of course, algae prototrophic for B_{12} would also be unaffected by presence of the binder. Also, if B_{12} was present in sufficient quantities to saturate the binder, its effect would be neutralized. An additional complication is that we have no data concerning the specificity and affinity of algal B_{12}-binder for B_{12} derivatives that are probably present in seawater; those algae able to utilize B_{12} derivatives not bound, or only loosely bound, would be at an advantage.

ALGAE AS VITAMIN PRODUCERS

Another discovery made by using experimental culture methods was the excretion of vitamins by algal cells themselves. This challenged early concepts because, for a very long time, bacteria were assumed to be the only vitamin producers in natural media. Indeed, many bacteria do excrete vitamins (Ericson and Lewis 1953; Starr et al. 1957; Burkholder 1959). It appears, furthermore, that in several biotopes, strains that can provide one of the three essential vitamins are more numerous than those which need them (Berland et al. 1976). In mixed cultures, it had been already demonstrated that the vitamin B_{12} requirement of several marine diatoms could be satisfied totally by heterotrophic marine bacteria isolated from the same biotope (Haines and Guillard 1974). Although the available data did not give any information about the vitamin flux between organisms in natural environments, it was tempting to suppose that bacteria were the main producers of those vitamins which became available for auxotrophic microorganisms and especially for algae. But it was known already that vitamins were excreted by various algae: biotin by *Chlorella pyrenoidosa* (Bednar and Holm-Hansen 1964), nicotinic acid by *Chlamydomonas* (Nakamura and Gowans 1964), and numerous growth factors by *Ochromonas danica* (Aaronson et al. 1971). However, demonstrating that algae are able to produce vitamins is one thing, but proving that the excretion is sufficient to allow growth of other plytoplankters from the same biotope is quite another, and needs various experiments using mixed cultures of vitamin-producing and vitamin-requiring organisms. Carlucci and Bowes (1970b) demonstrated that such successions can be obtained in experimental studies. Thus, *Dunaliella tertiolecta* and *Skeletonema costatum* produced thiamine that *Coccolithus huxleyi* could use, *Phaeodactylum tricornutum* and *Skeletonema costatum* produced biotin which was used by *Amphidinium carterae*, and *Coccolithus huxleyi* excreted B_{12} that *Cyclotella nana* could use. In these three cases, the biomass reached by the vitamin-requiring algae was very significant and sometimes superior to those of the producing species. But such an experimental demonstration might hardly be extrapolated to natural conditions. Indeed, nutrient concentrations used in the culture media, about 500 μg–at $N \cdot L^{-1}$ and 50 μg–at $P \cdot L^{-1}$, were considerably higher than in natural waters. According to Carlucci and Bowes (1970a), if we consider nutrient concentrations 10 times lower than those in their experiment, it is possible to calculate that *Coccolithus huxleyi* releases vitamin B_{12} at a concentration of 2.5 ng $\cdot L^{-1}$ at the end of growth, or about the same order of magnitude as found in seawater. Therefore, it is permissible to suppose that such a model would be applicable to natural waters.

Another important aspect of these experiments is that liberation of vitamin has been shown to be a phenomenon which takes place during exponential growth and not only when the culture reaches the stationary phase, although, at that stage, the dissolved vitamin concentrations are considerably increased. The rate of vitamin excretion is also a function of the culture conditions. Thus, in the preceding experiments it was demonstrated that the quantity of vitamin released by a unit of producing cells depends on the concentration of another vitamin required by the producer. All biological, biochemical, and physical factors of the environment interfere with the capability of the alga to excrete vitamin, and that problem is that much more complicated.

ALGAE AS COMPETITORS FOR
VITAMIN PARTITION

The fact that prototrophic algae are known to take up vitamins may have some ecological significance. Droop (1968) observed that *Phaeodactylum*, which does not require B_{12}, took up the vitamin in a similar fashion to B_{12} auxotrophs; Carlucci and Bowes (1970b) observed a stimulation of growth of this alga, which was probably due to B_{12}. Subsequently, Swift and Guillard (1978) demonstrated that the addition of vitamin B_{12} to the culture medium of 12 clones belonging to the genera *Thalassiosira*, *Porosira*, and *Chaetoceros*, which are not absolutely B_{12}-requiring, improved growth by increasing the growth rate and decreasing the lag period. These algae are able to use the growth factor when it is present in the medium, but also excrete the vitamin when they are grown in B_{12}-free medium. Swift and Guillard described this characteristic as "facultative autotrophy" and suggested that it might help such diatoms to compete well with auxotrophs at the beginning of a bloom. However, further work needs to be done before we can understand fully the phenomenon of facultative autotrophy and whether it has any ecological significance.

ROLE OF VITAMINS IN ALGAL SPECIES SUCCESSION

Is it possible from the experimental data already discussed to postulate the possible influence of vitamins on primary production processes and on species succession in natural waters? It has been observed that vitamins follow annual cycles in many natural biotopes, but it is much more difficult to elucidate their exact role in succession. Very often, authors' conclusions are more hypotheses than assertions. Interpretation of vitamin bioassays is indeed difficult; even if they do permit an appreciation of the real effect of vitamins, analogues, and derivatives on a given species, they only specify the concentrations of the active substances as a whole for the organism used in the test. But, typically, this organism is not the most representative of the community in the natural environment. Bioassays carried out with only one species allow comparison between different waters, but it is usually prohibitive to increase by very much the number of assay specimens. Consequently, it becomes impossible to characterize every area with the organisms of greatest ecological significance.

Menzel and Spaeth (1962) were the first to try to establish the role of vitamin B_{12} in species succession. They found that, in the upper layers of the Sargasso Sea during the spring bloom, B_{12} concentrations increased with abundance of centric diatoms, some of which were found to be B_{12} dependent (Guillard 1968). Later on in the year when B_{12} concentration decreases, *Coccolithus huxleyi*, which is only thiamine dependent, becomes dominant in the phytoplankton population. At the same time, in Long Island Sound, Vishniac and Riley (1961) ascertained that the maximum B_{12} concentration appears in the middle of the winter and remains at a high level until a bloom of *Skeletonema costatum* and other centric diatoms occurs.

Negative correlations between vitamin concentrations and algal abundance are often encountered. Thus, Cattell (1973) found one between B_{12} and a dinoflagellate population at different stations surveyed in the Strait of Georgia, British Columbia, showing that B_{12} might be used by the phytoplankters. Carlucci (1970) observed a similar situation with *Gonyaulax polyedra* off La Jolla, California. Parker (1977) noticed it during the development of Cyanophyceae belonging to the genus *Oscillatoria* in Lake Washington. Likewise, Kurata et al. (1976) found these inverse relationships between B_{12} and thiamine concentrations and growth of small planktonic forms, essentially represented by *Tabellaria flocculosa* and *Mougeotia* sp. in Lake Mergozzo, Italy. Many more examples could be given. Such observations allow us to assert that the algae use the vitamin only if we have parallel evidence from experimental studies that these organisms are really auxotrophic for it.

In other cases, such negative correlations are not evident and the simultaneous evolution of vitamins and species densities is not resolved. Several algae are able to produce vitamins and, in this case, we may observe a positive correlation between the vitamin concentration and the abundance of cells producing them. Ohwada and Taga (1972b) observed such production in Lake Sagami, Japan, where biotin and thiamine concentrations increased when *Cyclotella* sp., *Fragilaria crotonensis*, and *Synedra acus* became dominant in the plankton; simultaneously B_{12} values fell. The study of such patterns is not easy because the capacity of algae to release vitamins in the medium is much less understood than their auxotrophic requirements.

Interpreting the simultaneous evolution of vitamins and growth of phytoplankton populations is a difficult task, and does not always yield clear-cut results and, hence, reliable conclusions. There are many reasons for this; the correlation could be regarded as significant only if there is prior evidence from test organisms for which the vitamin response is very close to that of the algae well represented in the natural sample. For instance, Bruno and Staker (1978) could not entirely explain the succession of populations in Block Island Sound, New York, according to variations in vitamin B_{12} concentrations. They measured the B_{12} concentrations in these waters with *Thalassiosira pseudonana* 3H, which has a totally "mammalian" type of response, although in these samples one of the most abundant species was *Skeletonema costatum*, which has a "coliform" type response. Other vitamin B_{12} derivatives that could be utilized by *Skeletonema* would not be measured by the *Thalassiosira* bioassay. In the Gulf of Maine, Swift and Guillard (1977) found that, in a 150-m water column, the ratio of total cobamides versus true B_{12} can vary between 3.3 and 1.4. In freshwater, Kurata et al. (1976) found even higher ratios at some stations in Lake Mergozzo, Italy. More recently, Sharma et al. (1979) compared radioisotope dilution techniques with bioassays for vitamin B_{12} in seawater. The radioisotope techniques gave results from 4 to 6 times higher than results obtained by standard microbiological assays (two strains of *Thalassiosira pseudonana* were used). Radioisotope dilution assays can be carried out very much quicker than bioassays, but tend to be less specific as they may determine the sum of B_{12} and its derivatives whether the latter are biologically active or not. Sharma et al. suggested that only 25–40% of cobalamin molecules measured by the radioassays were vitamin B_{12}, pseudovitamin B_{12}, and their analogues, and that the remaining 60–75% were transformation products formed by the action of

317

light and seawater on cobalamins. However, they could not exclude the possibility that this large fraction might include cobalamins that were not utilized by the bioassay organisms. This work highlights the difficulty of using highly specific bioassays to measure a wide spectrum of potentially biologically active molecules. These molecules could be measured chemically (Beck 1978; Kolhouse and Allen 1978) but there would still be the problem of assessing which of the B_{12} derivatives could be used by each organism in a natural assemblage.

Thus, in any attempt to correlate dissolved vitamin concentrations with species composition and succession, ideally it is necessary to know the vitamin requirements of each phytoplankter present in the sample. But this is not always practicable. Under such conditions, it is tempting to use relationships between the vitamin concentration and the phytoplankton biomass as a whole, by particulate carbon or chlorophyll a measurements. The results obtained in this way are not always similar. For example, Benoit (1957) noted that, in lakes, the proportion of total cobalt tied up in vitamin B_{12} is about 10% in the epilimnion where production is maximum and only 4% or less in the hypolimnion. In an oligotrophic lake (Lake Tahoe), Carlucci and Bowes (1972) found that, usually, concentrations of all three vitamins are low or undetectable in deeper waters. The highest concentrations of vitamins were observed in the waters from 60 m, and especially in summer at a time when phytoplankton usually reaches the highest densities. Similar results are given by Natarajan and Dugdale (1966) for surface seawater in the Gulf of Alaska where, throughout the year, thiamine concentrations are found to range from undetectable levels up to 490 ng$\cdot$L^{-1}. The amounts of dissolved vitamin are usually high in coastal regions and low in the open sea; below the euphotic zone, these values are generally very low or even undetectable. Ohwada and Taga (1972a) observed in the North Pacific Ocean and in the China Sea that the concentrations of dissolved vitamin B_{12}, thiamine, and biotin generally showed patterns similar to those of chlorophyll a, with a maximum in July and a strong decrease with depth. Usually, vitamin B_{12} is less correlated with chlorophyll a than are the other vitamins. But, on the other hand, Daisley and Fisher (1958), in the Bay of Biscay, found low B_{12} concentrations in the upper illuminated zone and at the greatest depths, with a maximum at intermediate depth. Likewise, Carlucci and Silbernagel (1966) measured higher concentrations from 200 m and below in the Northeast Pacific Ocean, with maximum at intermediate depth (average of 500 m), and an inverse chlorophyll a–vitamin B_{12} relationship in the upper waters. However, these latter results are of little interest to the ecologist as they cannot give a

reliable explanation for the role of vitamins in the growth of each component of the crop. Furthermore, it is always necessary in these observations to make a distinction between vitamin B_{12}, thiamine, and biotin. The experimental method proves that thiamine is not as significant ecologically as B_{12} as relatively fewer organisms require it, and this statement is even more applicable to biotin.

On the other hand, it is difficult to understand the relationships between the different parameters when sampling is not frequent enough; the usual time interval between two samplings at sea is about a month or 2 wk. An example is given by the experiment of Antia et al. (1963) using a large-volume plastic sphere. They found a slight decrease of vitamin B_{12} when *Skeletonema costatum* dominated the phytoplankton. Afterwards, other pelagic species followed the *S. costatum* bloom and, at the end of the experiment, the B_{12} concentration reached values higher than those at the beginning (8 ng$\cdot$L^{-1} vs. 3 ng$\cdot$L^{-1}). The chlorophyll a concentrations also showed the same trend. Comparing parameters at the beginning and at the end of the experiment would have led to a totally mistaken interpretation of the relationship between the phytoplankton standing crop and the B_{12} concentration. Only high frequency of sampling allows the authors to give a reliable account of the biological sequence.

One more difficulty in interpreting the exact influence of vitamins on algal growth and, therefore, on species succession is the interaction between requirements for vitamins and other nutrients. Obviously, the limiting action of the vitamin is easier to demonstrate when other nutrients are not limiting. Often there is an intimate relation between the content of nutrient salts and that of vitamins: that is what Kashiwada and Kakimoto (1962) showed when comparing Japanese lakes and marshes belonging to the eutrophic, merotrophic, and oligotrophic types. Daisley (1969) observed similar results in the English Lake District. The primitive rocky lakes with low productivity are poor in vitamin B_{12}. The evolved silted lakes, richer in sediments and, therefore, in nutrients and organisms, have higher concentrations of vitamin. Such results are common in the study of well-defined ecosystems. But in the open sea the observations are less clear. One way to elucidate the role of vitamins on production is to measure both the soluble and the particulate fractions of the vitamins. If the soluble fraction is always significant and if the particulate one is small, it is possible to assert that the vitamin is not a limiting factor. For example, Ohwada and Taga (1972b) showed that particulate thiamine and biotin correspond to only 1% of that of the dissolved form in the surface waters of the North Pacific Ocean. In coastal waters, on the contrary, they were 144 and 54%, respectively.

Obviously, factors other than these two vitamins were limiting algal growth in the open sea. In the same way, Natarajan (1970) mentioned that high concentrations of vitamins were usually found in low-nutrient areas. Thiamine particularly showed a negative correlation with PO_4-P and NO_3-N whereas vitamin B_{12} had a less significant correlation with all the other parameters measured. In this case, such results indicate that the thiamine content of the sea is sufficient to support a level of production which is then limited by other factors, such as availability of other nutrients. In such areas, where vitamins are quantitatively sufficient with respect to other nutrients, they have no effect on production and only a slight effect on species succession. But vitamins, especially B_{12}, show low values in waters where some macronutrients could be limiting and where physical factors, such as temperature and light, are not optimal for growth. An example is the antarctic and subantarctic waters where it has not yet been possible to find reliable correlations between the chemical and physical parameters and primary production (Carlucci and Cuhel 1977; Holm-Hansen et al. 1977; Fiala 1980).

COMMENTS AND PROSPECTS

The only approach to understanding the precise role of vitamins among the other limiting factors on each component of the ecosystem would be to know exactly the physiological responses to vitamins of *all* the species present in the waters, and not just the most abundant species in the crop. It would also help to know (1) the importance of upwelling from deep waters and the exact nature of all the analogues carried up with them, (2) the ability of the growth factors to remain in active form in spite of the potentially destructive action of physical, chemical, and biological agents which vary greatly with climate and origin of the waters, (3) the turnover time of the vitamin molecules in the upper layers, and (4) the composition and the physiological characteristics of bacterial populations that obviously interfere with the response of the phytoplankton. Generally, as long as we do not know much about these processes, it will be very difficult to understand the exact function of the main growth factors and regulators in the equilibrium of ecosystems.

Nevertheless, as Swift (1981) says, auxotrophs are usually important in natural waters. This implies that vitamin concentrations are frequently sufficient to allow maximum growth rates for many of them. Another argument in support of this statement is that, if it is not so, the autotrophs that do not require vitamins would always dominate when competition occurs. When an organism requires a growth factor in vitro this metabolite, or its physiological equivalent, should be found in significant amounts in its

natural environment, and that is what has been verified by the measurements of vitamin concentrations in natural waters and by experimental studies. But, because vitamin concentrations sometimes vary greatly in natural waters, a lack or an excess of these natural compounds can enable some species (obviously not the same ones) to grow faster and then can act directly on the succession. Indeed, in peculiar situations it is possible to observe such a direct interaction between species belonging to bacterio- and phyto-plankton, and so to explain local succession. But, more usually, when vitamins and other nutritional elements interact as limiting factors, such explanations are more difficult to give. The action of vitamins remains very complex and its quantitative evaluation difficult.

Acknowledgments

We are grateful to Dr Trevor Platt for an initial critical review of the manuscript. We also wish to express our appreciation to Drs Henry Augier, Michel Fiala, and Dorothy Swift for helpful discussion.

References

AARONSON, S., B. DE ANGELIS, O. FRANK, AND H. BAKER. 1971. Secretion of vitamins and amino acids into the environment by *Ochromonas danica*. J. Phycol. 7: 215–218.

ALGEUS, S. 1946. Untersuchungen über die Ernährungsphysiologie der Chlorophyceen. Mit besonderer Berücksichtigung von Indolylessigsäure, Ascorbinsäure und Aneurin. Bot. Not. 2: 129–278.

ANTIA, N. J., C. D. MCALLISTER, T. R. PARSONS, K. STEPHENS, AND J. D. H. STRICKLAND. 1963. Further measurements of primary production using a large volume plastic sphere. Limnol. Oceanogr. 8: 166–183.

AUGIER, H. 1965. Les substances de croissance chez la Rhodophycée *Botryocladia botryoides*. C.R. Acad. Sci. Paris 260: 2304–2306.

———— 1972. Contribution à l'étude biochimique et physiologique des substances de croissance chez les algues. Thèse Doct. ès Sci. Univ. Aix-Marseille II. 323 p.

———— 1976. Les hormones des algues. État actuel des connaissances. III. Rôle des hormones dans la croissance et le développement des algues. Bot. Mar. 19: 351–377.

———— 1977. Les hormones des algues. État actuel des connaissances. V. Index alphabétique par espèce des travaux de caractérisation des hormones endogènes. Bot. Mar. 20: 187–203.

BACH, M. K., AND J. FELLIG. 1958. Auxins and their effect on the growth of unicellular algae. Nature (London) 182: 1359–1360.

BECK, R. A. 1978. Competitive intrinsic factor binding assay technique for cobalamins in natural waters. Anal. Chem. 50: 200–202.

BEDNAR, T. W., AND O. HOLM-HANSEN. 1964. Biotin liberation by the lichen alga *Coccomyxa* sp. and by *Chlorella pyrenoidosa*. Plant Cell Physiol. 5: 297–303.

BENDANA, F. E., AND M. FRIED. 1967. Stimulatory effects of gibberellins on the growth of *Chlorella pyrenoidosa*. Life Sci. 6: 1023–1033.

BENOIT, R. J. 1957. Preliminary observations on cobalt and vitamin B_{12} in fresh water. Limnol. Oceanogr. 2: 233–240.

BENTLEY, J. A. 1958. Role of plant hormones in algal metabolism and ecology. Nature (London) 181: 1499–1502.

———— 1959. Auxin like substances in algae. Annu. Rep. Challenger Soc. 3: 20.

———— 1960. Plant hormones in marine phytoplankton, zooplankton and sea water. J. Mar. Biol. Assoc. U.K. 39: 433–444.

BENTLEY-MOWAT, J. A. 1967. Do plant growth-substances affect the development and ecology of unicellular algae? Wiss. Z. Univ. Rostock Math. Naturwiss. Reihe 16: 445–449.

BENTLEY-MOWAT, J. A., AND S. M. REID. 1967. Effect of gibberellins, kinetin and other factors on the growth of unicellular marine algae in culture. Bot. Mar. 12: 185–199.

BERLAND, B. R., D. J. BONIN, J. P. DURBEC, AND S. Y. MAESTRINI. 1976. Bactéries hétérotrophes aérobies prélevées devant le delta du Rhône. IV. Besoins en vitamines et libération de ces substances. Hydrobiologia 50: 167–172.

BERLAND, B. R., D. J. BONIN, M. FIALA, AND S. Y. MAESTRINI. 1978. Importance des vitamines en mer. Consommation et production par les algues et les bactéries, p. 121–146. *In* Les substances organiques naturelles dissoutes dans l'eau de mer. Colloque GABIM-CNRS, 1976. CNRS, Paris.

BONIN, D. 1969. Influence de différents facteurs écologiques sur la croissance de la diatomée marine *Chaetoceros affinis* Lauder en culture. Tethys 1: 173–238.

BRADBEER, C. 1971. Transport of vitamin B_{12} in *Ochromonas malhamensis*. Arch. Biochem. Biophys. 144: 184–192.

BRANNON, M. A., AND H. M. SELL. 1945. The effect of IAA on dry weight of *Chlorella pyrenoidosa*. Am. J. Bot. 32: 257–258.

BRIAN, P. W. 1963. Growth regulating hormones in lower plants. Sci. Prog. 51: 226–238.

BRUNO, S. F., AND R. D. STAKER. 1978. Seasonal vitamin B_{12} and phytoplankton distribution near Napeague Bay, New York (Block Island Sound). Limnol. Oceanogr. 23: 1045–1051.

BURKHOLDER, P. R. 1959. Vitamin producing bacteria in the sea, p. 912–913. *In* M. Sears [ed.] International oceanographic congress, preprints. Am. Assoc. Adv. Sci.

CARLUCCI, A. F. 1970. The ecology of the plankton off La Jolla, California, in the period April through September, 1967. II. Vitamin B_{12}, thiamine and biotin. Bull. Scripps Inst. Oceanogr. 17: 23–31.

CARLUCCI, A. F., AND P. M. BOWES. 1970a. Production of vitamin B_{12}, thiamine and biotin by phytoplankton. J. Phycol. 6: 351–357.

———— 1970b. Vitamin production and utilization by phytoplankton in mixed culture. J. Phycol. 6: 393–400.

———— 1972. Determination of vitamin B_{12}, thiamine, and biotin in Lake Tahoe waters using modified marine bioassay techniques. Limnol. Oceanogr. 17: 774–777.

CARLUCCI, A. F., AND R. L. CUHEL. 1977. Vitamins in the South Polar Seas: distribution and significance of dissolved and particulate vitamin B_{12}, thiamine, and biotin in the Southern Indian Ocean, p. 115–128. *In* G. A. Llano [ed.] Adaptations within antarctic ecosystems. Third SCAR Symposium on antarctic biology. Smithsonian Institution, Washington, DC.

CARLUCCI, A. F., AND S. B. SILBERNAGEL. 1966. Bioassay of seawater. III. Distribution of vitamin B_{12} in the northeast Pacific Ocean. Limnol. Oceanogr. 11: 642–646.

CATTELL, S. A. 1973. The seasonal cycle of vitamin B_{12} in the Strait of Georgia, British Columbia. J. Fish. Res. Board Can. 30: 215–222.

COWEY, C. B. 1956. A preliminary investigation of the variation of vitamin B_{12} in oceanic and coastal waters. J. Mar. Biol. Assoc. U.K. 35: 609–620.

DAISLEY, K. W. 1969. Monthly survey of vitamin B_{12} concentrations in some waters of the English Lake District. Limnol. Oceanogr. 14: 224–228.

———— 1970. The occurrence and nature of *Euglena gracilis* proteins that bind vitamin B_{12}. Int. J. Biochem. 1: 561–574.

DAISLEY, K. W., AND L. R. FISHER. 1958. Vertical distribution of vitamin B_{12} in the sea. J. Mar. Biol. Assoc. U.K. 37: 683–686.

DROOP, M. R. 1954. Cobalamin requirement in Chrysophyceae. Nature (London) 174: 520.

———— 1958. Requirement for thiamine among some marine and supralittoral protista. J. Mar. Biol. Assoc. U.K. 37: 323–329.

———— 1961. Vitamin B_{12} and marine ecology: the response of *Monochrysis lutheri*. J. Mar. Biol. Assoc. U.K. 41: 69–76.

———— 1962. Organic micronutrients, p. 141–159. *In* R. A. Lewin [ed.] Physiology and biochemistry of algae. Academic Press, New York, NY.

———— 1968. Vitamin B_{12} and marine ecology. IV. The kinetics of uptake, growth and inhibition in *Monochrysis lutheri*. J. Mar. Biol. Assoc. U.K. 48: 689–733.

DROOP, M. R., J. J. A. MCLAUGHLIN, I. J. PINTNER, AND L. PROVASOLI. 1959. Specificity of some protophytes toward some vitamin B_{12}-like compounds, p. 916–918. *In* M. Sears [ed.] International oceanographic congress, preprints. Am. Assoc. Adv. Sci.

EPSTEIN, S. S., AND G. M. TIMMIS. 1963. Simple antimetabolites of vitamin B_{12}. J. Protozool. 10: 63–73.

ERICSON, L. E., AND L. LEWIS. 1953. On the occurrence of vitamin B_{12}-factors in marine algae. Ark. Kemi 6: 427–442.

FIALA, M. 1980. Vitamine B_{12} et phytoplancton dans

diverses régions marines. Thèse Doct. ès Sci. Univ. Pierre et Marie Curie, Paris. 128 p.

FOGG, G. E. 1966. The extracellular products of algae. Oceanogr. Mar. Biol. Annu. Rev. 4: 195–212.

FORD, J. E. 1958. B_{12}-vitamins and growth of the flagellate *Ochromonas malhamensis*. J. Gen. Microbiol. 19: 161–172.

GLASS, G. B. J. 1963. Gastric intrinsic factor and its function in the metabolism of vitamin B_{12}. Physiol. Rev. 43: 529–849.

GRAY, N. J. P. 1962. The effects of gibberellins on *Chlorella*. Phycol. Soc. Am. News Bull. 15: 34.

GUILLARD, R. R. L. 1968. B_{12} specificity of marine centric diatoms. J. Phycol. 4: 59–64.

GUILLARD, R. R. L., AND V. CASSIE. 1963. Minimum cyanocobalamin requirements of some marine centric diatoms. Limnol. Oceanogr. 8: 161–165.

HAINES, K. C., AND R. R. L. GUILLARD. 1974. Growth of vitamin B_{12}-requiring marine diatoms in mixed laboratory cultures with vitamin B_{12}-producing marine bacteria. J. Phycol. 10: 245–252.

HERDMAN, M., AND N. G. CARR. 1972. The isolation and characterization of mutant strains of the blue-green alga, *Anacystis nidulans*. J. Gen. Microbiol. 70: 213–220.

HOLM-HANSEN, O., S. Z. EL-SAYED, G. A. FRANCESCHINI, AND R. L. CUHEL. 1977. Primary production and the factors controlling phytoplankton growth in the southern ocean, p. 11–50. *In* G. A. Llano [ed.] Adaptations within antarctic ecosystems. Third SCAR Symposium on antarctic biology. Academic Press, New York, NY.

HUTNER, S. H., H. BAKER, S. AARONSON, H. A. NATHAN, E. RODRIGUEZ, S. LOCKWOOD, M. SANDERS, AND R. A. PETERSON. 1957. Growing *Ochromonas malhamensis* above 35°C. J. Protozool. 4: 259–269.

HUTNER, S. H., L. PROVASOLI, AND J. FILFUS. 1953. Nutrition of some phagotrophic freshwater chrysomonads. Ann. N.Y. Acad. Sci. 56: 852–862.

JACOBSEN, D. W., P. M. DiGirolamo, AND F. M. HUENNEKENS. 1975. Adenosylcobalamin analogues as inhibitors of ribonucleotide reductase and vitamin B_{12} transport. Mol. Pharmacol. 11: 174–184.

JOHNSTON, R. 1959. Antimetabolites and marine algae, p. 918–920. *In* M. Sears [ed.] International oceanographic congress, preprints. Am. Assoc. Adv. Sci.

——— 1963. Effects of gibberellins on marine algae in mixed cultures. Limnol. Oceanogr. 8: 270–275.

KASHIWADA, K., AND D. KAKIMOTO. 1962. Studies on vitamin B_{12} in natural water. VII. Relation between the fertility and the vitamin B_{12} content of lakes. Bull. Jpn. Soc. Sci. Fish. 28: 352–360.

KIM, W. K., AND V. A. GREULACH. 1961. Promotion of algal growth by IAA, GA and kinetin. Plant. Physiol. 36 (suppl.): 14.

KOLHOUSE, F. J., AND R. H. ALLEN. 1978. Isolation of cobalamin and cobalamin analogues by reverse affinity chromatography. Anal. Biochem. 84: 486–490.

KURATA, A., C. SARACENI, D. RUGGIU, M. NAKANISHI, U. MELCHIORRI-SANTOLINI, AND H. KADOTA. 1976. Relationship between B group vitamins and

primary production and phytoplankton population in lake Mergozzo (Northern Italy). Mem. Ist. Ital. Idrobiol. 33: 257–284.

LEWIN, R. A. 1954. A marine *Stichococcus* sp. which requires vitamin B_{12} (cobalamin). J. Gen. Microbiol. 10: 93–96.

——— 1961. Phytoflagellates and algae, p. 401–417. *In* W. Ruhland [ed.] Handbuch der Pflanzenphysiologie, Vol. 14. Springer Verlag, Berlin.

LWOFF, A., AND H. DUSI. 1937. La pyrimidine et le thiazol, facteurs de croissance pour le flagellé *Polytomella coeca*. C. R. Acad. Sci. Paris 205: 630.

LWOFF, A., AND E. LEDERER. 1935. Remarques sur l'"extrait de terre" envisagé comme facteur de croissance pour les flagellés. C.R. Soc. Biol. 119: 971–973.

MANOS, E. 1945. The effect of heteroauxin on the growth of *Chlorella*. Biol. Bull. 7: 11.

MENZEL, D. W., AND J. P. SPAETH. 1962. Occurrence of vitamin B_{12} in the Sargasso Sea. Limnol. Oceanogr. 7: 151–154.

MOWAT, J. A. 1963. Gibberellin-like substances in algae. Nature (London) 200: 453–455.

NAKAMURA, K., AND C. S. GOWANS. 1964. Nicotinic acid-excreting mutants of *Chlamydomonas*. Nature (London) 202: 826–827.

NATARAJAN, K. V. 1970. Distribution and significance of vitamin B_{12} and thiamine in the subarctic Pacific Ocean. Limnol. Oceanogr. 15: 655–659.

NATARAJAN, K. V., AND R. C. DUGDALE. 1966. Bioassay and distribution of thiamine in the sea. Limnol. Oceanogr. 11: 621–629.

OHWADA, K., AND N. TAGA. 1972a. Vitamin B_{12}, thiamine and biotin in Lake Sagami. Limnol. Oceanogr. 27: 315–320.

——— 1972b. Distribution and seasonal variation of vitamin B_{12}, thiamine and biotin in the sea. Mar. Chem. 1: 61–73.

PARKER, M. 1977. Vitamin B_{12} in Lake Washington, USA: concentration and rate of uptake. Limnol. Oceanogr. 22: 527–538.

PEDERSEN, M. 1973. Identification of a cytokinin, 6-(3-methyl-2-butenylamino) purine, in sea water and the effect of cytokinins on brown algae. Physiol. Plant. 28: 101–105.

PEDERSEN, M., AND G. FRIDBORG. 1972. Cytokinin-like activity in sea water from the *Fucus-Ascophyllum* zone. Experientia 28: 111–112.

PINTNER, I. J., AND V. L. ALTMEYER. 1979. Vitamin B_{12}-binder and other algal inhibitors. J. Phycol. 15: 391–398.

PROVASOLI, L. 1963. Organic regulation of phytoplankton fertility, p. 165–219. *In* M. H. Hill [ed.] The sea, Vol. 2. Interscience Publications, New York, NY.

——— 1971. Nutritional relationships in marine organisms, p. 369–382. *In* J. D. Costlow [ed.] Fertility of the sea, Vol. 2. Gordon and Breach, New York, NY.

PROVASOLI, L., AND A. F. CARLUCCI. 1974. Vitamins and growth regulators, p. 741–787. *In* W. D. P. Stewart [ed.] Algal physiology and biochemistry. Blackwell Scientific Publications, Oxford, U.K.

RAHAT, M., AND K. REICH. 1963. The B_{12} vitamins and

growth of the flagellate *Prymnesium parvum*. J. Gen. Microbiol. 31: 195–202.

REEVES, B. R., AND S. F. FAY. 1966. Cyanocobalamin (vitamin B$_{12}$) uptake by *Ochromonas malhamensis*. Am. J. Physiol. 210: 1273–1278.

SARHAN, F., M. HOUDE, AND J. P. CHENEVAL. 1980. The role of vitamin B$_{12}$ binding in the uptake of the vitamin by *Euglena gracilis*. J. Protozool. 27: 235–238.

SHARMA, G. M., H. R. DuBOIS, A. T. PASTORE, AND S. F. BRUNO. 1979. Comparison of the determination of cobalamins in ocean waters by radioisotope dilution and bioassay techniques. Anal. Chem. 51: 196–199.

SCHIEWER, U. 1967. Auxinvorkommen und Auxinstoffwechsel bei mehrzelligen Ostseealgen. I. Zum Vorkommen von Indol-3-Essigsaüre. Planta 74: 313–323.

STARR, T. J., M. E. JONES, AND D. MARTINEZ. 1957. The production of vitamin B$_{12}$-active substances by marine bacteria. Limnol. Oceanogr. 2: 114–119.

SWIFT, D. G. 1981. Vitamins and phytoplankton growth, p. 329–368. *In* I. Morris [ed.] Primary productivity of natural waters. Blackwell Scientific Publications, Oxford, UK.

SWIFT, D. G., AND R. R. L. GUILLARD. 1977. Diatoms as tools for assay of total B$_{12}$ activity and cyanocobalamin activity in sea water. J. Mar. Res. 35: 309–320.

1978. Unexpected response to vitamin B$_{12}$ of dominant centric diatoms from the spring bloom in the Gulf of Maine (Northeast Atlantic Ocean). J. Phycol. 14: 377–386.

SWIFT, D. G., AND W. R. TAYLOR. 1974. Growth of vitamin B$_{12}$-limited cultures: *Thalassiosira pseudonana, Monochrysis lutheri*, and *Isochrysis galbana*. J. Phycol. 10: 385–391.

TAUTS, M. I., AND V. E. SEMENENKO. 1971. Isolation and identification of physiologically active agents of indol nature in extracellular *Chlorella* metabolites. Dokl. Akad. Nauk. SSSR. 198: 970–973. (In Russian)

THIMANN, K. V. 1934. Studies on the growth hormone of plants. IV. The distribution of the growth substances in plants. J. Gen. Physiol. 18: 23–34.

VAN BAALEN, C. 1961. Vitamin B$_{12}$ requirement of a marine blue-green alga. Science (Washington, D.C.) 133: 1922–1923.

VAN OVERBEEK, F. 1940a. Auxin in marine algae. Plant Physiol. 15: 291–299.

1940b. Auxin in marine plants. II. Bot. Gaz. 101: 940–947.

VARMA, T. N. S., A. ABRAHAM, AND I. A. HANSEN. 1961. Accumulation of Co^{58}–vitamin B$_{12}$ by *Euglena gracilis*. J. Protozool. 8: 212–216.

VISHNIAC, H. S., AND G. A. RILEY. 1961. Cobalamin and thiamine in Long Island Sound: patterns of distribution and ecological significance. Limnol. Oceanogr. 6: 36–41.

Allelopathic Relationships Between Phytoplankton Species

SERGE Y. MAESTRINI AND DANIEL J. BONIN

Station Marine d'Endoume
Chemin de la Batterie des Lions
F-13007 Marseille

Introduction

The first mention of the importance of dissolved organic matter for aquatic life (i.e. nutrition) goes back to Thomson (1874); the analysis and experiment phase began with Pütter (1907a, b). However, Akehurst (1931) was probably the first to suggest the existence between phytoplankton species of non-nutritional relationships mediated by organic substances. From his findings on fluctuations of algal populations in inland ponds, he supposed that most algae secrete extracellular organic compounds into the surrounding water that can inhibit the growth of some algae and favor the growth of others. Lucas (1938) extended these ideas to marine life and, later (Lucas 1947) developed a broad concept and named substances produced and released by various living organisms, which can affect other individuals or species at a distance, "external metabolites" or "ectocrines." These external metabolites can be growth-promoting or growth-inhibiting compounds or micronutrients, and are specially important for microorganisms. Lucas believed that during the course of evolution many organisms have adapted themselves to tolerate or take advantage of these substances released by their neighbors, and organisms that failed to do so must have become extinct or have evolved some avoiding mechanisms. This concept is vitally concerned with community integration, competition, and succession of algal species.

Among all problems pointed out by Lucas (1947), it was contention about the importance of the antibacterial substances released by algae that drew the attention of the scientific community and stimulated most research. The numerous papers on this field have been frequently reviewed (Lucas 1947, 1955, 1961; Nigrelli 1958; Sieburth 1964, 1968; Aubert 1971, 1978; Berland et al. 1974) and sometimes overreviewed. On the other hand, it has been demonstrated that substances released by bacteria can inhibit bacterial growth (Rosenfeld and Zobell 1947; Krasil'Nikova 1964; Burkholder et al. 1966) or algal growth (Fitzgerald 1969; Berland et al. 1972a, b), but little attention has been paid to growth-limiting bacterial ectocrines, and their importance has rarely been discussed. Such a discussion will not be attempted in this paper, as bacteria are beyond the scope of the review.

Substances released by algae that are toxic to other algae have been studied for a long time, but not all contributions have been critical. Thus, only few experimental data are really pertinent and the question of the importance of these substances is still open. Reproducing an exhaustive list of published articles would be useless. The reader can find all references needed in the reviews of Lefevre (1964) and Tassigny and Lefevre (1971), who were specially dedicated to antialgal–algal ectocrines; the reviews of Lucas (1947, 1955, 1961) and Pourriot (1966), who discussed the biochemical interactions between aquatic organisms as a whole; and Saunders (1957), Hartman (1960), Fogg (1962), Provasoli (1963), Whittaker and Feeny (1971), Hellebust (1974), and Rice and Ferguson (1975), who included this topic in their discussions of algal physiology and ecology. Only a brief summary of the conceptual progress before these reviews will be given here. Subsequent papers will be dealt with in more detail.

ANTIALGAL ECTOCRINES RELEASED BY ALGAE: HISTORICAL BACKGROUND

It is obvious that marine biologists are indebted to inland aquatic microbiologists for making the basic discoveries (see summary in Table 1).

Step one — Pütter's (1907a, b) pioneering ideas opened a new field in biology (Ranson 1935, 1936; Johnston 1972), but he obviously overemphasized by one order of magnitude the quantitative importance of both algal secretion and seawater content of dissolved organic substances. With Krogh (1931), who was a critical chemist, the dissolved organic matter content of seawater became accurately known. From the data tabled in the review of Williams (1975) and Whittle (1977) it appears that the approximate mean concentration of dissolved organic carbon (DOC) in surface seawaters ranges from 1 mg $C \cdot L^{-1}$ to 1.5 mg $C \cdot L^{-1}$. These values will be useful for later discussion. Recent developments of the analytical technology by Lindroth and Mopper (1979) made available a new method, i.e. the high perfor-

323

TABLE 1. Allelopathic interactions between phytoplankton species: progress of concepts from early contributions to last comprehensive reviews (Hellebust 1974; Rice and Ferguson 1975).

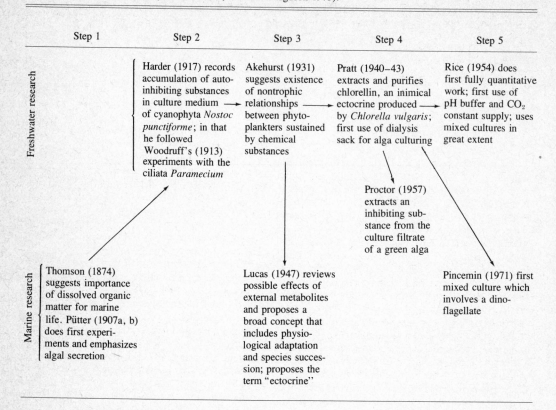

	Step 1	Step 2	Step 3	Step 4	Step 5
Freshwater research		Harder (1917) records accumulation of auto-inhibiting substances in culture medium of cyanophyta *Nostoc punctiforme*; in that he followed Woodruff's (1913) experiments with the ciliata *Paramecium*	Akehurst (1931) suggests existence of nontrophic relationships between phyto-plankters sustained by chemical substances	Pratt (1940–43) extracts and purifies chlorellin, an inimical ectocrine produced by *Chlorella vulgaris*; first use of dialysis sack for alga culturing	Rice (1954) does first fully quantitative work; first use of pH buffer and CO_2 constant supply; uses mixed cultures in great extent
				Proctor (1957) extracts an inhibiting substance from the culture filtrate of a green alga	
Marine research	Thomson (1874) suggests importance of dissolved organic matter for marine life. Pütter (1907a, b) does first experiments and emphasizes algal secretion		Lucas (1947) reviews possible effects of external metabolites and proposes a broad concept that includes physiological adaptation and species succession; proposes the term "ectocrine"		Pincemin (1971) first mixed culture which involves a dino-flagellate

mance liquid chromatography with fluorescence derivatization that decreases by 10 times the duration of analysis, 100 times the volume of sample required, and increases the sensitivity by 1000 times.

Step 2 — Harder (1917) recorded accumulation, in the culture medium of the cyanophyte *Nostoc punctiforme*, of organic substances that are auto-inhibiting for the organism that produced them. In this he emulated Woodruff's (1913) work and results with the ciliate *Paramecium*. Hence, it appears that the dissolved organic matter (DOM) can be poisonous and may have a role other than trophic. Since then, similar observations have been made either with marine or freshwater species, but no critical progress was made as most data published were obtained in such a way they are vulnerable to several of the following criticisms: (1) Algal cultures are not bacteria-free; that is another potential source of production or destruction of growth-inhibiting algal substances. (2) Filtrates are prepared with ordinary paper filters that might contain particles and bacteria. (3) Most experiments are made by filtering an algal culture and subculturing another algae in the filtrate; no

mixed cultures are done with a view to separating the effects of nutrient competition and "chemical war" between the test species (Fig. 1). (4) In sub-culturing experiments, pH varies; no buffer is used; no attention is paid to the decreased CO_2 content of the subculture. (5) Some experiments are made by extracting the inimical substances from packed cells or dried cells; no attempt has been made to extract the active substance from the filtrate. (6) Inhibiting effects are often observed only on morphological basis. (7) Test algae are cultured in nutrient-rich medium; thus, algal biomass may produce external metabolites at very high levels. Because their activity is growth-promoting at low concentrations and growth-inhibiting at high concentration, in vitro data are irrelevant to statements on their role at ecological level. (8) Active algae might have been isolated from different locations and may never belong to the same natural community.

Step 3 — In the 1930s, the aquatic scientific community was already preoccupied with changes in nutrition resulting from the accumulation of excretory products in the culture medium of a growing

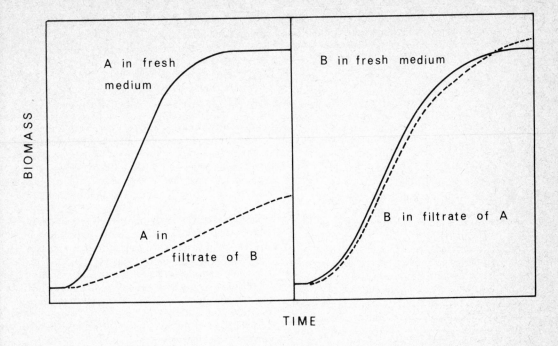

FIG. 1. Scheme of classic method used to demonstrate allelopathic interactions between two algal species. The following operations are usually done with unialgal or axenic strains: (i) species A and B are separately grown in batch cultures; (ii) species A is subcultured in nutrient-reinriched, cell-free culture medium of species B, species B is similarly subcultured in filtrate medium of species A; (iii) biomass increases are recorded and plotted versus time duration; (iv) growths of species A and B in preconditioned media are compared with respective controls; (v) conclusions are: species B inhibits species A, species A does not inhibit species B.

population. However, this "group effect" was hitherto studied mainly in vitro with various organisms, mostly animals (see Allee 1934). But at that time the scientific community represented "a few small groups of near-amateurs with enthusiasm and interest in a wide range of disciplines" (French 1979), prior to becoming a "very large number of groups all intent on a small segment of science and seemingly with little interest in followers of other subjects." Thus, Akehurst (1931) certainly was aware of studies done in other fields when he tried to extend to field conditions some principles elucidated by laboratory research. In an inland pond, he observed a roughly rhythmical rise and decline in numbers of different species of phytoplankton that he related partly to the physical and nutrient conditions, and partly to other factors that he called "toxines." These substances were defined by Akehurst as "an excretory product or products of indefined chemical constitution which may also serve as an accessory food and may inhibit or stimulate growth." The phytoplankton was considered to consist of two main groups, when classified according to cell reserves: the oil group and the starch group. Akehurst wrote

that the autotoxins of the oil group become an accessory food for the starch group and vice versa, and he thought this process explains why the growth of almost the entire oil group ceases at the same time and why no recovery is shown until the starch period has passed through its phase of abundance.

Later work refined the critical observations of the 1930s, either in freshwater blooms or marine species succession (see Lefevre et al. 1952; Pratt 1965, 1966), but no new concept was proposed. At most, autoantagonistic substances were demonstrated to be also inimical for other algae. Thus, in the ecological perspective, the broad concept of Lucas (1947) appears to be an extension of Akehurst's statement, but Lucas expressed clearly the theory of the nonpredatory relationships linking marine organisms and showed its peculiar importance for marine microorganisms. His discussion was documented by results which showed that algae excrete various nutrients, that vitamins are present in waters and produced by bacteria and algae, and by the isolation of a purified algal antibiotic, the "chlorellin," by Pratt and Fong (1940, 1944). The rapid development of antibiotic use, and the recognition of their

325

production by various microorganisms, certainly helped Lucas (1947) to extend to aquatic life some principles well established for land or soil fungi and bacteria (Waksman 1941).

Step 4 — By measuring the variations of yield as a function of nutrient concentration of the medium, Pratt (1940) and Pratt and Fong (1940) demonstrated that the green alga *Chlorella vulgaris* produces and liberates a substance that tends to retard its own growth, adding a new species to the list of algae producing autoinhibiting substances. But later, Pratt (1942) cultured the alga in a collodion dialysis membrane and demonstrated the production of the inhibiting substance by healthy growing cells. Then, he extracted the substance from dried cells using organic solvents and eliminated the chlorophyll and much of the extraneous organic matter. Thus, he could attempt a tentative chemical determination of the active substance he named "chlorellin," and study its properties. Logically, he continued by using the purified substance to run an experiment that allowed him to express the results versus the number of cells needed to produce enough substance to reach the threshold concentration for inhibiting effect (Pratt 1943). From his data, it appeared that 1.8×10^6 cells $\cdot$ mL^{-1} are needed for a visible inhibition. He also demonstrated that chlorellin is active against other algae (Pratt 1943) and bacteria (Pratt and Fong 1944). Thus, Pratt and co-workers took a critical step by producing the first reliable data for the significance of in vitro results in natural conditions; but, curiously, Pratt did not make this extension.

The production of hetero-inimical ectocrines being well established, and Proctor (1957) having extracted purified substances from cultures filtrates, one wonders that few have followed Pratt's example. It is also surprising that little attention has been paid so far to the discrepancy between the density of cells involved in laboratory experiments versus those in natural populations with regard to the real ecological role of the antimetabolites. Apparently the aquatic biologists preferred to avoid time-consuming biochemical methods in favor of experiments on mixed cultures.

Step 5 — Many aquatic biologists have experimented with simple systems of two or a few species of microorganisms since Gause (1932) first tried to set up a theoretical model from experimental data obtained with mixed cultures of two species of yeast. However, most experiments with two or more algae were made on a morphological basis (see Lefevre 1964) and the first fully quantitative study appears to be that of Rice (1954). Rice cultured bacteria-free strains of the green alga *Chlorella vulgaris* and the diatom *Nitzschia frustulum* in mixed liquid or agar plate batch cultures, with various combinations

of nutrient supply, pH buffer, and air bubbling to eliminate lack of CO_2. He found that biological production of poisonous ectocrines is responsible for antagonistic growth inhibition whether or not there is nutrient competition, but densities obtained in experimental pure cultures were much higher than those ordinarily found in nature. As a matter of fact, the greatest inhibition in the growth of *N. frustulum* occurred when 5×10^9 *C. vulgaris* cells per litre were present; only 70% inhibition occurred in the division rate of the diatom then. Application to natural populations was uncertain, indeed. The same remark can be made about the work of McVeigh and Brown (1954) who, nevertheless, introduced a new refinement. They separated the two algae they used by enclosing the cells in two dialysis sacks, but allowed the external metabolites to act by immersion of the two coupled sacks in the same medium flask. Unfortunately, their strains were not bacteria-free and contained a strain whose ectocrines inhibited or enhanced the growth of algae tested. They also did not pay any attention to the pH and CO_2 effects in crossed subculturing experiments and, thus, 17 yr passed before results based on a satisfactory technical approach were published.

Contributions Published and Progress Made During the Past Decade

The main feature of recent research seems to be that research programs have become more comprehensive, involving observations of natural processes and experiments in the laboratory on strains of the same origin. Further, the different cell functions such as nutrition, excretion, mobility, or production of inimical ectocrine are now not separated. It also appears that production of inimical ectocrines is no longer considered a permanent avantage, but a potential cell weapon, acting in defined situations. Apparently this marks a welcome shift from the concept of "chemical warfare" among microorganisms of the 1960s (Sieburth 1962).

Most researchers at present pay attention to the fact that all physiological mechanisms can interact and that "weapons" used in species competition may vary greatly when environmental conditions change. Understanding when and why they are acting or useful seems to be the aim of the foremost works. There is also an impressive development of research done with dinoflagellates (which have been too long ignored); improvement of culture media for growing these peculiar algae certainly stimulated the growing interest in them. Since the foremost research involves different methods of study at one time, or in successive steps, papers relevant to a particular study may appear over an extended period. Thus, chronological priority is sometimes misleading.

TABLE 2. Allelopathic interactions between phytoplankton species. Critical progress made during the past decade (for steps 1 to 5, see Table 1).

Step 6	Step 7	Step 8
		Fully integrated field observations and experiments done with locally isolated strains
Kroes (1971, 1972) avoids all previous technical shortcomings, devises a filter bialgal culture method, and extends the inimical ectocrines from cell-free filtrates	Bialgal cultures of two dino-flagellates demonstrate that respective behaviors greatly depend on relative cell proportions (Elbrächter 1976)	Keating (1977, 1978) made observations over 5 yr and indicated that diatom blooms vary inversely with density of preceding cyanophyta populations; crude lake water contains heat-labile substances which inhibit diatoms; dominant species produce only inhibiting or neutral effects on immediate predecessors, and only beneficial or neutral effects on immediate successors; strains of same species but from other locations are less susceptible; bacteria act by destroying active substances
Ranges of concentrations for some allelopathic effects are determined: 10–50 mg·L^{-1} (Jüttner 1976–79); 25 mg·L^{-1} (Mc Cracken et al. 1980)	Gauthier et al. (1975) integrate field observations and laboratory experiments	
	Similar approach demonstrates a naturally occurring cyanophyte may govern growth of a toxigenic dinoflagellate (Martin and co-workers 1974–79)	
Substances excreted by an alga might have different effects with different phases of growth (Federov and Kustenko 1972)		From Pratt (1965) to Tomas (1978–80). Blooms of Skeletonema costatum and Olithodiscus luteus alternate; subculture in 10^8 cells·L^{-1} filtrate of O. luteus suppresses growth of S. costatum, whereas low densities stimulate; O. luteus ability to take up nutrients is regular, notwithstanding it blooms in nutrient-depleted waters; S. costatum grows well in dialysis sacks incubated when O. luteus blooms; O. luteus escape grazing possibly by production of an ectocrine repellent
The cyanophyta Anaboena inhibits growth of its companion species by producing a strong iron chelator found both in culture and natural lake waters (Murphy et al. 1976)	Experiments made with natural waters where actual dominant species are blooming and preceding dominant species are becoming scarce (Honjo et al. 1978)	

(Lake research applies to the upper grouping; Marine research applies to the lower grouping in Step 8.)

ALLELOPATHIC INTERACTION BY CROSSED SUBCULTURING

Harris (1970, 1971) surveyed the auto- and hetero-inhibition of 11 freshwater algae by crossed subculturing cell-free culture filtrates (however, not reenriched), and found that all species produced inhibiting substances, specially Pandorina morum, Volvulina pringsheimii, Eudorina cylindrica, and E. illinoisensis. By comparing the growths of the cyanophyte Microcystis aeruginosa and the green algae Monoraphidium minutum and Scenedesmus abundans in monocultures and bicultures, Krzywicka and Krupa (1975) found that the cyanophyte reproduces more slowly than the green algae in bicultures. They suspected that the green algae excrete into the environment some toxic substances that inhibit development, but they did not try either to isolate the active substance or to question if nutrient competition might be responsible for the reduced growth. On the contrary, Lange (1974) showed that in a mixed experimental cyanophyte system of Microcystis aeruginosa, Nostoc muscorum, and Phormidium foveolarum one species may exclude the other two

with an exhaustion of selected nutrient elements. Crossed subculturing of the pool of three species in culture filtrates with or without associated bacteria demonstrated that no toxic or allelopathic matter acts between the cells. However, it should be noted the three strains used were obtained from different culture collections and thus were isolated from different origins, so the data are not entirely free from criticism. Schenk and Jüttner (1974), Jüttner (1976), Herrmann and Jüttner (1977), and Jüttner (1979) studied the excretion products of freshwater algae both from pelleted cells of naturally occurring bloom cyanophyte and from cultured cells. By using laboratory bioassays, they demonstrated that norcarotenoid excreted by Cyanidium caldarium inhibits the growths of Anabaena variabilis, Nannochloris coccoides, and synechococcus sp. within a range of 10–50 mg·L^{-1}. Although these contributions provide some rare quantitative data on inhibiting substances, they help but little the present discussion because their aim is different and their experimental protocols are questionable. The data of Chan et al. (1980) are equally questionable. These authors reported the inhibition of the diatom Cylindrotheca

327

fusiformis by a dozen other algae belonging to several taxa, including diatoms and dinoflagellates, but they used the plating bioassay technique with methanol extracts of packed algal cells or algal–culture filtrates. Hence, they did not get any evidence that the zones of inhibition observed around the impregnated disks really reflect an in situ occurring process. Chan et al. did not claim such implications and did not ignore the shortcomings of their experiments. They just wanted to survey many species in order to get a convenient material for further experiments. However, for such an aim, in our opinion, the method used by Berland et al. (1973) for surveying alga–bacterium allelopathic interactions could be a better approach, because it allows both the antagonistic species on the same agar medium to grow, and this procedure avoids many artefacts and saves time (Fig. 2).

Sze and Kingsbury (1974) studied fresh waters heavily polluted by copper but with enough nutrients to support the resident phytoplankton growth without limitation. This pollution has not resulted in a phytoplankton flora of only a few well-adapted species as might be expected; a large number of species and a regular succession are still found. Among them, a *Chlamydomonas* species appears every year in several brief but dense peaks; in contrast, another alga, *Staurastrum paradoxum*, is present permanently but in low abundance. Sze and Kingsburry hypothesized that an allelopathic interaction controlled the observed fluctuations in populations. They did several experiments with mixed cultures and crossed subcultures in culture filtrates and found that neither the presence of an inhibitor nor nutrient competition could explain the reduced growth of the planktonic alga, *S. paradoxum*, when cultured with the *Chlamydomonas* strain. They concluded that the interactions reported are similar to the dynamics observed in natural waters and may describe some population fluctuations, even though the experimental conditions differed significantly from the natural conditions. This is by no means clear, but nevertheless, it is almost certain that several *Chlamydomonas* species are able to produce and release one or several substances inimical to other algae. McCracken et al. (1980) studied the same strain of *C. reinhardtii* used by Proctor (1957), who demonstrated that a substance produced by this alga is toxic to another species. The latter is inhibited when grown in cell-free filtrate that McCracken et al. demonstrated to be a mixture of three fatty acids active against six of seven test algae, including two strains (*Haematococcus lacustris* and *Oocystis* sp.) which are killed by 25 mg·L^{-1} of crude extract. Unfortunately, McCracken et al. did not completely follow Proctor; they extracted the active substance from the total culture (i.e. including the cells). This does not help

attempts to extend the conclusions to natural conditions. Because, in addition, they do not say how many cells are required to produce 25 mg of active extract, their data contribute little to our discussion. Lam and Silvester (1979) studied the growth interactions among the cyanophyte *Anabaena oscillarioides* and *Microcystis aeruginosa* and the green alga *Chlorella* sp., by using both standard mixed cultures and cultures separated by a membrane filter. They demonstrated that *A. oscillarioides* and *M. aeruginosa* both inhibit the growth of the *Chlorella* strain. *Microcystis aeruginosa* probably acts by releasing an inhibiting substance, while the inhibiting effect of *A. oscillarioides* on *Chlorella* sp. is mostly the consequence of a competition for uptake of phosphorus. This mechanism can explain why in nature *M. aeruginosa* is one of the most common bloom-forming species, even if its nutritional characteristics leave it vulnerable to domination by other species. The demonstration of Lam and Silvester is not, however, totally convincing, because they used isolates from different origins and grew the algae in a very rich nutrient medium, which gave artificially high cell densities (i.e. up to 16×10^9 cells·L^{-1}).

IMPROVED TECHNOLOGIES LEAD TO MORE CONVINCING DEMONSTRATIONS

Kroes (1971, 1972a, b) developed a filter culture method in which two separate cultures of different species are connected via a filtering system, through which medium is exchanged while the cells themselves are kept separate. The culture medium was Tris-buffered and air-bubbled. Algal strains were axenic. With such equipment, Kroes demonstrated that *Chlorococcum ellipsoideum* inhibits the growth of *Chlamydomonas globosa*, but not vice versa. The most important finding was that there are many different extracellular compounds released by *C. ellipsoideum* and that each fraction isolated from the culture filtrate had its own specific, but small, effect on the growth of other alga. He also pointed out that the role of pH is more important in interactions than extracellular substances. In that, Kroes' statement differs from those of previous authors who assumed that in the algal ecosystem strongly inhibitory substances were responsible for the observed phenomena, and paid little, if any, attention to the pH (except Proctor 1957). Then, in a further technical improvement, Kroes (1973) designed a new apparatus that, for practical purposes, excludes pH as an element of the interspecies interaction, and thus let the algae compete only by competitive nutrient uptake and by production of inimical extocrine. Scott and Ball (1975) built improved equipment derived from Kroes' remarks, but no experiment has been reported yet.

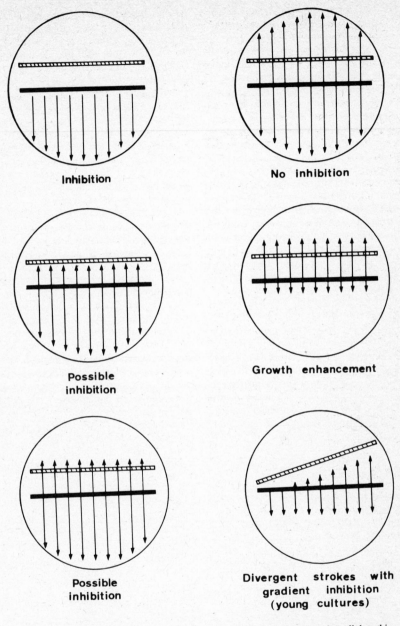

Inhibition

No inhibition

Possible
inhibition

Growth enhancement

Possible
inhibition

Divergent strokes with
gradient inhibition
(young cultures)

Fig. 2. Scheme of method used by Berland et al. (1973) for screening allelopathic interactions between a gliding alga and a nonmotile microorganism. Experiments are done in Petri dishes and agar medium. The gliding alga is inoculated with a wire loop; a stroke (solid bar) is made at the center of the plate. A stroke (hatched bar) of the potentially antagonistic strain parallels the first. When the nonmotile microorganism releases an extremely inhibitory substance, the alga moves (black arrows) exclusively in the opposite direction (inhibition); the antagonistic strain stroke may appear like a fence. When inhibition is not so strong, the gliding alga may touch the other strain (possible inhibition). If no inhibiting substance is involved, the gliding alga grows as usual and covers the whole agar medium (no inhibition). Growth-promoting substances may be released by the nonmotile cells; this leads the gliding companion species to grow towards it faster (growth enhancement).

Fedorov and Kustenko (1972) studied the competition between the diatoms *Thalassiosira nitzschioides* and *Skeletonema costatum* for uptake of nitrogen and demonstrated that neither of the two algae can gain the upper hand over the other in mixed culture with the same initial cell density. However, the shape of the growth curves points to the existence of a reciprocal inhibition that was ascribed to the production of external metabolites. By adding the filtrates from actively dividing, non-growing, or autolysing cultures, they demonstrated that actively growing cells of *T. nitzschioides* do not substantially affect the growth of *S. costatum*. On the contrary, the latter species releases substances capable of inhibiting active division of *T. nitzschioides*, even in the early stage of its own growth, that allows it to become dominant in mixed cultures. Filtrate from stationary phase or autolysing cells of both species have no inhibiting effect; on the contrary, cell-free filtrates of aged *S. costatum* are beneficial to *T. nitzschioides*, explaining why the latter alga cannot be displaced by the former in mixed cultures, when cultured over a long period. These results are interesting in that they demonstrate that the substances excreted by an alga might have different effects according to the phase of growth and subsequent algal physiological status. However, because the experiments were done at high cell densities (up to 10^9 cells $\cdot$ L^{-1}) extension of conclusions to the relations between partners in a natural association is hazardous (as Fedorov and Kustenko admit). Kustenko (1979) improved the method used, but does not report any new pertinent data.

Another interaction between the marine diatoms *Thalassiosira pseudonana* and *Phaeodactylum tricornutum* has been studied by Sharp et al. (1979), with the goal of designing a protocol to favor the growth of the first and eliminate the second from mass cultures used to feed commercial shellfishes. *Phaeodactylum tricornutum*, which is considered to be a poor food and, therefore, undesirable, dominates continuous mass cultures and eliminates other species. Experiments done with both crossed subculturing in filtered reenriched culture media and batch or continuous bialgal cultures allowed the observation in laboratory conditions of the inhibition of *S. costatum* growth by a heat labile substance released in the medium by *P. tricornutum*. Because, in addition, none of the relative growth constants of the two species can explain the dominance of *P. tricornutum*, it was concluded by Sharp et al. that an allelopathic effect was responsible for this process. However, the inimical effects arise from populations that are three orders of magnitude denser than natural phytoplankton cell densities. *Phaeodactylum tricornutum* is always rare in natural population and the authors do not try to extend their results to natural waters, but

notice that allelopathy (inimical effect) may play an important role in large enriched, outdoor cultures. The dominant production of the undesired *P. tricornutum* on Woods Hole mass cultures (Ryther et al. 1975) may support this opinion. The similar results of Pintner and Altmeyer (1979) pertain to a similar technological approach, but their study, which involved 21 algal species belonging to different taxa, led them to conclude that heat-stable substances excreted by several species are lethal to other species. Their effects are species-specific and each species has different patterns and degrees of inhibition depending also on the test organism. The most active algae are diatoms, among which *P. tricornutum* appeared to be the most efficient.

Altogether, the above-cited contributions left unclear whether or not the excreted antialgal substances act at naturally occurring concentrations. Such a lack greatly diminishes most published statements or generalizations. However, Honjo et al. (1978) attempted to use natural water samples and, subsequently, their results could contribute to ascertaining the reality of the allelopathic relationships among phytoplankters. Daily sampling and counting allowed these authors to observe that, in Hakata Bay (Japan), the phytoplankton species association and dominance changed, at the end of spring, from several diatoms and nanoflagellates to dinoflagellates and an intensive bloom of *Heterosigma* sp. These observations led the authors to assume that species associated in dominance did not compete with each other for growth. On the contrary, the species of the first group were inhibited by those of the second group; namely, the blooming of the large diatom *Heterosigma* sp. temporarily inhibited the growth of the nanoflagellates and completely prevented the growth of most diatoms. Experiments made with culture filtrates and nutrient-enriched seawater collected during *Heterosigma* sp. bloom, conducted with locally isolated strains, demonstrated that *Heterosigma* sp. releases an inhibiting ectocrine acting against most diatoms, especially *Skeletonema costatum*, but has no effect against others, i.e. *Nitzschia closterium* and *Phaeodactylum tricornutum*, which are able to remain present during the in situ *Heterosigma* sp. bloom. Unfortunately, the authors seem not to have investigated and separated the respective effects of the nutrient competition and the production of inimical extocrines on the observed species succession.

DINOFLAGELLATES AS GROWTH-INHIBITING SUBSTANCE PRODUCERS

The association of dense populations of marine dinoflagellates and toxic effects for a large variety of organisms has been known for many years (Kofoid

330

1911; Liebert and Deerns 1920). Accumulation of information on the toxic substances released by these peculiar algae is impressive, indeed. In spite of the disappearance of other taxa of algae during the so-called red-tide blooms of toxic dinoflagellates, relatively little attention has been paid to the advantage given to them by their external metabolites in competition for nutrients and population dominance.

Pincemin (1969) observed the inhibition of growth of a small *Chaetoceros* in Mediterranean waters on development of a red tide of *Cochlodinium* sp. and claimed the presence of a strong inhibiting substance. In further research Pincemin (1971) experimented with another diatom, *Asterionella japonica* and another dinoflagellate, *Glenodinium monotis*. With cross-subculturings and reenrichments of the cultures he demonstrated the production of autoinhibiting substances by both species and the toxic effect for the diatom of the substances released by the dinoflagellate. Unfortunately, he did not pay attention to the pH increase and CO_2 concentration decrease subsequent to the first culture, and used cultured strains from different origins. Altogether, this work (the first to involve a dinoflagellate in a mixed culture) did not avoid the shortcomings of the older research and, hence, brings little new information. In a related work Pincemin and other workers of the same laboratory (Aubert et al. 1970; Gauthier et al. 1978) reported that the dinoflagellate *Prorocentrum micans* releases some substances which inhibit the production of an antibacterial compound by the diatoms *Asterionella japonica* and *Chaetoceros lauderi*, which remain otherwise capable of growth. This might be an interesting secondary effect of the heteroantagonism between algal species. Further research is needed to confirm this effect and assess its importance in situ, because the strain used to test the antibacterial effect was a *Staphylococcus aureus*, obviously not an aquatic bacterium. Also, the substances were extracted from heavy bulks of packed cells and were active at concentrations which represent several thousands times the cell densities of the two diatoms in the marine phytoplankton. Production of diatom-inhibitory substance by *P. micans* in nutrient-rich medium was also described by Uchida (1977, 1981). In bialgal cultures, the dinoflagellate overcomes *Skeletonema costatum* and *Chaetoceros didymus* and, when subcultured in cell-free culture filtrate of *P. micans* reenriched with fresh nutrients, the two diatoms are also inhibited. In Uchida's opinion, the production of diatom-inhibiting substance might explain the bloom of *P. micans*, which succeeds the diatom flowering in natural waters of the Japanese coast. However, Uchida reports that, in mixed cultures, inhibition of diatom growth begins only after 3 d incubation; hence, the initial dinoflagellate population ($10^6 - 2 \times 10^6$ cells·L^{-1}) might well have overtaken the maximum natural population (3×10^6 cells·L^{-1}) he observed.

Gauthier et al. (1975) reported another study in which field observations and laboratory experiments are investigated. They surveyed the evolution of bacterial and algal populations, nutrient concentrations, and temperature in shallow coastal Mediterranean waters. They observed that from winter to summer the densities of diatom and flagellate populations decrease continuously; the dominant diatoms were such species as *Skeletonema costatum*, *Asterionella japonica*, *Phaeodactylum tricornutum*, and some *Navicula* species. In warm summer waters, blooms of green flagellates may occur, but they end when oxygen content is reduced by bacterial activity. The green flagellates are then replaced by some dinoflagellates, namely *Prorocentrum micans*, *Gymnodinium* sp., and *Glenodinium* sp. Diatoms and green algae reappear only when the dinoflagellates have disappeared and the oxygen content has been restored. To explain this succession, the authors do not invoke nutrient concentration and do not give any information about their seasonal evolution, but from one of their figures one can read that in surface water the nutrient content is very high (P–PO_4 = 240 μg–at·L^{-1}; N–NO_3 = 67 μg–at·L^{-1}), reflecting a eutrophicated situation. Gauthier et al. suggested a chemical interaction between the above species. To prove their hypothesis, they isolated some of the main species, i.e. *P. micans*, *S. costatum*, *A. japonica*, and *Tetraselmis maculata*, and carried out several bicultures and crossed unicultures in culture filtrates. Having observed some inhibition of growth of *T. maculata* when cultured in these conditions, they concluded that the observed algal competition is a result of the effect of external metabolites released by the algae. Their statement seems to be convincing, but the time has come to be cautious with such extension of conclusions from laboratory experiments to natural conditions. Gauthier et al. grew their strains in a nutrient-rich medium (Provasoli's medium). Their apparently most convincing experiment consists of injecting a small inoculum of the second alga into a well-established culture of the first alga. For instance, 1840 cells of *T. maculata* are mixed with 5490 cells of *P. micans* (resident species); because *T. maculata* divides only 7.6 times (whereas in a fresh medium control such an inoculum divides 9.9 times), it is concluded that *T. maculata* is inhibited by substances released by *P. micans*, which divides as much as in unialgal culture. Such a slight difference is not fully convincing because the experimental device does not offset the role of competition for nutrient partition that is related more to the respective specific kinetic constants of uptake than to the cell densities.

Elbrächter (1976) cultivated two dinoflagellates in bialgal cultures: *Prorocentrum micans* and *Gymnodinium splendens* and also did several crossed cultures with reenriched culture filtrates. The two species do not show the same growth capacity. It is presumed that *G. splendens* can excrete an inhibiting factor affecting the growth of *P. micans*, whereas the effect on *G. splendens* production by *P. micans* is limited to nutrient competition. Thus the behavior of a mixed culture depends greatly on the relative cell proportions; the toxigenic species can dominate the other one only when enough cells are present to produce the ectocrine above the acting concentration. Elbrächter points out that because the cell densities normally involved do not occur in nature and because the toxic inhibition was not lethal but extended the lag phase, the results do not constitute a direct proof. However he is convinced that the results he obtained in vitro also apply to natural habitats. In a further development of this research, Elbrächter (1977) ran several combinations of mixed cultures of two diatoms — *Biddulphia regia* and *Coscinodiscus concinnus* — and two dinoflagellates — *Ceratium horridum* and *Prorocentrum micans*. Cultures were initiated with cell densities and nutrient levels corresponding to those prevailing in the natural environment from which they were all isolated. From data obtained, he could state that changes in growth rates, which resulted for each species from association with other species, were not due to inhibition caused by excreted substances, but rather by nutrient competition. Unfortunately, this conclusion concerned all the nutrients as a whole and was not investigated in more detail. In other words, not enough was done to describe how these species adapt to the nutrient competition. Kayser (1979) used batch cultures, crossed subculturing in cell-free culture filtrates, and continuous cultures of combinations of three dinoflagellates — *Gymnodinium splendens*, *prorocentrum micans*, and *Scrippsiella faeroense* — also isolated from Heligoland waters, with a view to separating the phenomena of nutrient competition and interactions of external metabolites. From the data obtained, he could state that in multispecies populations the exponential growth is mainly regulated by nutrient competition, while inhibiting metabolic products act secondarily at maximum cell densities. Whether this inhibiting effect is caused by toxic algal excretions or bacterial decomposition products of dead cells could not be determined.

During the course of investigations of a red tide, Kutt and Martin (1974) isolated from the same sample a toxigenic dinoflagellate (*Gymnodinium breve*) and a cyanobacterium (*Gomphosphaeria aponina*) which they cultivated in mixed culture. They observed that the presence of the cyanobac-

terium inhibits the growth of the dinoflagellate. Further research (Kutt and Martin 1975; Martin and Martin 1976; McCoy and Martin 1977; McCoy et al. 1979; Moon and Martin 1979) demonstrated that the inhibition did not result from nutrient competition but from the production of an antialgal substance by the cyanobacterium. This substance, named "aponin," was first extracted from packed cells and later from cell-free culture medium, indicating that it is primarily an exotoxin. The crude aponin is heat stable to 110°C, and acid stable. In nutrient-rich medium the lethal effect is obtained with 6×10^6 cells $\cdot$ L^{-1} of *G. aponina*, whereas the minimum detectable effect on *G. breve* after 24 h of incubation is achieved by only 60 μg $\cdot$ L^{-1} of crude aponin. This substance was purified by a broad array of biochemical treatments, including HPLC, and proved to be a chemically defined sterol. Aponin can reduce the production of ichthyotoxic substances by *G. breve* and, hence, may mitigate the effects of the dinoflagellate products on marine life, but it has no direct effect on fishes, crustaceans, and bacteria. Aponin is a substance specifically antialgal and antifungal. Likewise, the toxin produced by *G. breve* has no effect on *G. aponina*. On the other hand, considering the responses to temperature and comparing with naturally occurring temperatures in surface waters of coastal Florida waters, Martin and associates postulated that *G. breve* should have optimal proliferation during midspring and late autumn, and *G. aponina* may proliferate during late spring and early summer and autumn. As a matter of fact, several red tides have occurred during late autumn and one during midspring, exactly during the postulated periods, namely when *G. aponina* cannot grow, supporting the opinion that the mechanisms postulated from in vitro experiments really occur in situ. Ultimately, these scientists suggest using the aponin or *G. aponina* freezed-dried cells as a biological tool in red-tide management.

FIELD OBSERVATIONS, LABORATORY-STUDIED PROCESSES, AND LOCALLY ISOLATED STRAINS INVOLVED IN THE SAME INVESTIGATION

Keating (1977, 1978) reported that observations made over a 5-yr period in a eutrophicated lake indicate that diatom blooms vary inversely with the density of the preceding cyanophyta populations. A successsion of dominant cyanophyte species was also recorded. Then, she tried to explain these processes by ecophysiological mechanisms. By using seven crude (only filtered) lake waters collected over an 18-mo period for bioassays, she demonstrated that lake waters contain a heat-labile substance that inhibits diatom growth. Then, subculturing in cell-free culture filtrates confirmed that the producers of these substances were cyanophyta rather than other organisms. Succession of dominant cyanophyta is also explained by allelopathic effects among species. By bioassays with predecessors and successors of a dominant species, she demonstrated that dominant species produce only inhibiting or neutral effects on their immediate predecessors, and, in contrast, only beneficial or neutral effect on their immediate successors. Hence, both patterns of interaction enhance the competitive position of the organism that will dominate an impending bloom. As a matter of fact, in vitro allelopathic effects are well correlated with annual in situ succession patterns. Keating's experiments were done with eight cyanophytes isolated from the same waters. Diatoms tested for their susceptibility to crude lake water or to cyanophyta external products have also the same origin. There were from 7 to 9 species or, exceptionally, 3, 13, 18, and 29 species. Each cyanophyte appears to produce a substance inhibiting most and even all diatoms, but effects against diatoms were notably decreased when strains isolated from other lakes were used for comparison. The role of bacteria was also investigated by using axenic or bacterized algal strains. They have no qualitative effect but decrease the inhibition of diatom growth, probably by degrading the active substances. This bacterial role might turn out to be critical, because Keating also demonstrated that reducing filtrates to 33% of normal strength by dilution eliminates the inhibition, proving that the substances act like antibacterial antibiotics, i.e. they are inhibiting above a threshold concentration and have no action or are enhancing (hormesis) below this concentration. In addition, the substances released by the cyanophyta are not all toxic for diatoms. Physically extracted (ultrafiltration) substances from culture filtrate of *Anaboena holsaticum* are shown by chemical separation to contain a diatom growth promoting compound associated with an inhibiting one. The effect of the former compound is masked in full-strength filtrates but appears when filtrates are diluted. Keating's contribution is impressive, indeed. By selecting a broad array of naturally cooccuring strains and using algal biomass and nutrient concentrations at ecological levels (e.g. she adds 12.3 μg–at–N$\cdot$L^{-1}, 0.57 μg–at–P$\cdot$L^{-1}, and other nutrients at balanced levels), she overcame the main shortcomings that led to questionable results in the past. Prior to inoculation of test cells, she allowed CO_2 content and pH to come to their original values after autoclaving, if any, and she duplicated experiments with axenic or bacterized cultures, something never done before, at least in experiments designed with all refinements at one time. Unfortunately, the growth characteristics (K_s, V_{max}, etc.) of the cyanophyta were not established, so one cannot separate clearly nutrient competition from the role of the external metabolites in the species succession, but, the results demonstrate that ectocrines are certainly part of the fine control in determination of bloom sequence (Keating 1977). Hence, their role is not negligible, even if the coarse controls, such as light and macronutrients, determine the growth potential of the system and the major categories of dominant algae.

The physiological mechanism of the algal inhibition has also been little studied, but Murphy et al. (1976) remarked that in a eutrophic lake the sudden dominance of cyanophytes of genus *Anaboena* coincided with the production of strong iron chelators and an active uptake of iron. Several experiments, ascertained by further research of Bailey and Taub (1980), led them to propose a hypothesis: cyanophyta have a strong iron uptake system and excrete hydroxamate siderochromes that act as strong iron binders. Thus, the cyanophytes remain capable of taking up iron while they suppress the availability of iron to other species, which are inhibited, therefore, by a secondary nutrient starvation effect. As hydroxamates were found in supernatant of ultrafiltered natural lake waters, this process might be of ecological interest and a promising research direction, but, of course, it does not exclude the direct poisonous effect of inimical ectocrines on one or several biochemical pathways.

Another example of antagonism between organisms belonging to different taxonomic groups was described in marine waters. Weekly observations by Pratt (1965), over a 7-yr period, showed that the phytoplankton of the Narragansett Bay is dominated during spring and summer by alternate brief blooms of the diatom *Skeletonema costatum* and the chrysophycean flagellate *Olithodiscus luteus*. "Environmental factors measured did not provide any clue to the sequence and did not appear to favor either species over the other, but there were some indications that each actor awaits the other's exit before coming on stage," said Pratt, who suggested that the succession is mediated by an interaction between the two algae whose mechanism was not indicated by the field data. Then, he continued his investigation with in vitro experiments (Pratt 1966). By the use of bialgal cultures and crossed subculturing in nutrient reenriched filtrates, he demonstrated that a concentration of more than 100 $\times$ 10^6 cells$\cdot$L^{-1} of *O. luteus* inhibits the growth of *S. costatum* by secreting a tanninlike substance. A concentration of less than this value stimulates the growth of the diatom, with a maximal effect at 20 $\times$ 10^5 cells$\cdot$L^{-1}, but effective up to 4 $\times$ 10^6 cells$\cdot$L^{-1}. Pratt's demonstration provided a fascinating theory to explain the natural processes he observed: when circumstances combine to give *O. luteus* a sufficient relative abundance, it suppresses the growth of *S. costatum* by release of large quantities of an ectocrine. When

S. costatum outstrips *O. luteus* in competition, it does so primarily by virtue of its much greater rate of multiplication, thus monopolizing the available nutrients. But, further, in small competing populations, the slight amount of the presumed tannin produced by the *O. luteus* cells favors *S. costatum* growth, perhaps by metal chelation. Unfortunately, cell concentrations required to produce the inimical ectocrine were two orders of magnitude higher than the highest cell density of *O. luteus* in Narragansett Bay. Pratt stated this criticism himself and called for further work. The challenge was taken up by Stuart (1972), who first demonstrated that prevention of *S. costatum* growth in *O. luteus* conditioned and nutrient-restored medium was only temporary; with time, rapid growth occurred. Hence, final cell population, maximal biomass, and growth rate were unaffected. Because autoclaving removed inhibition and doubling trace metals caused mortality, he could suggest that chelation and trace metal availability might be involved in the inhibition. Then chemical separations indicated that substances having a molar mass below 2000 cause the lag effect in the growth of *S. costatum*. However, conversely, in bialgal culture, *S. costatum* takes the upper hand over *O. luteus* which grows poorly, having a longer lag phase and a lower growth rate than those of the diatom; thus, there is a discrepancy with Pratt's (1966) findings. This probably originates in the different cell densities involved, wrote Stuart (1972), who used $27–190 \times 10^6$ cells $\cdot$ L^{-1} instead of the $400–452 \times 10^6$ cells $\cdot$ L^{-1} used by Pratt. But the latter also pointed out that the inhibition begins with 190×10^6 cells $\cdot$ L^{-1} of *O. luteus*. In addition, both Pratt and Stuart used nonaxenic strains whose bacteria might have enhanced or suppressed any effect of extracellular substances. Thus, altogether their results do not unequivocably confirm the inhibition of *S. costatum* by these substances liberated by *O. luteus*. Further research was still needed. Tomas's (1978, 1979, 1980) continuing studies of the autoecology of *O. luteus* provided physiological information for this species that allowed him to compare the two competitors on the basis of a broad array of physiological patterns. But it appears that this chrysophyte has not any exceptional abilities for the uptake and utilization of nutrients, notwithstanding that it is reported to occur in spring blooms in nutrient-depleted waters. Likewise, cells divide actively in a broad range of temperature and light intensities, but so do those of *S. costatum*. Hence, most mechanisms that act in species competition seem to be little involved. Tomas (1980) reexamined the Pratt hypothesis of biochemical interaction between the two species and stated that *S. costatum* grows well in dialysis sacs incubated in situ during periods when *O. luteus* is naturally abundant. Because

the dialysis walls allow the passage of the substance released by *O. luteus* (M < 2000) (Tomas 1980) the inhibition should have been observed, if it was there. Thus, if the ectocrine inhibition might occur for short periods of time in restricted areas where maximum densities are high, no clear explanation of the apparent reciprocal codominance of *S. costatum* and *O. luteus* in Narragansett Bay is yet available. In addition, Tomas observed there is no apparent predator on *O. luteus*, whereas *S. costatum* is actively grazed on by small zooplankton. During the bimodal periods of increasing abundance of *O. luteus* (May and October), large populations of zooplankton are present and *S. costatum* is scarce. During the midsummer decline of the chrysophytes, copepods are reduced to low levels by ctenophore predation and the diatom blooms. Hence, the decrease of *O. luteus* and concomitant increase of *S. costatum* and vice versa may be events mediated more by grazing pressure than through direct physiological interactions. This raises a new question: why is *O. luteus* avoided by zooplankters? Observations reported by Tomas (1980) of noxious effects on zooplankton and even fishes again call attention to the inimical ectocrines released by this species and the need for more research.

IMPORTANCE OF GROWTH-INHIBITING ECTOCRINES IN ALGAL COMPETITION AND SPECIES SUCCESSION

That some algae in their growth stages are able to produce and release substances that are inhibiting to other algae is well confirmed. However, three important questions remain: (i) How many species are capable of it? (ii) Do these substances really act in situ? (iii) When do they confer a stronger advantage, if at all, to the producing alga than other physiological processes? The answers to these questions will state the real importance of this physiological adaptation.

Except for a few recent contributions, the strains used in experiments were choosen mainly for their availability in culture collections. Thus, the total number of species known to produce antialgal ectocrines does not represent more than a couple of dozen for freshwater algae and even less for marine phytoplankton. This small array might be readily increased if all or most species could be tested. On the other hand, the number of species producing ectocrines relative to the total number of species would be of greater ecological importance, by allowing an estimate of the average numbers of ectocrine-producing cells in a natural population under study; this has not been done yet. Collecting strains from different origins may build artificial communities that never occur in situ, but modern researchers usually avoid this problem and study naturally occurring competitors. Nevertheless, only two or a few species are involved in experiments and, unfortunately, this is not sufficient. Keating (1978) demonstrated that different isolates belonging to the same species, but from different origins, may have different responses, which called in question most published data. In addition, the few species involved in experiments are mostly competing dominant species, which can explain the reciprocal codominance of these species through production of inimical ectocrines, but leaves the outcome over other species unstudied. Only Keating tested most naturally companion species of several dominant algae-producing ectocrines. With such an approach, she could demonstrate that most cyanophytes of the lake she studied produce substances that inhibit most, if not all, the diatoms living in the same waters. By choosing the susceptible strains, other authors might have overestimated dramatically the inhibiting effects of ectocrines, when considered in the natural population as a whole. In addition, for marine algae, almost all the strains used in experiments were isolated from coastal waters. Because of the great differences between neritic and oceanic waters in nutrient content and phytoplankton composition, extension of published results to the world ocean could be misleading. Thus, all told, the relative number of algae-producing antialgal external metabolites is still unknown, even tentatively, either for fresh waters or marine species.

That antialgal ectocrines are released by several algae does not necessarily mean the substances are active in situ or provide an obvious advantage to the producers in species competition. Based on laboratory experiments, some previous statements like those of Hartman (1960) and Lefevre (1964), to cite only the main reviewers, have certainly overestimated this case by ignoring the criticisms and/or generalizing to the global scale a few results belonging to discrete communities. During the past decade, most experimental shortcomings have been overcome. Hence, several contributions have ascertained the potentiality of the nontrophic relationships among algal populations, but pertinent demonstrations of inimical ectocrines acting in situ are scarce and related to particular conditions. As a matter of fact, most laboratory experiments are biased in that they involve nutrient-rich culture media and subsequent dense algal populations that far exceed those occurring in situ. Hence, the substances excreted may reach very high concentrations that pass the threshold concentration for inhibiting activity. Computations to transfer results to in situ conditions by dividing the inhibiting effect by the ratio of in vitro/in situ algal densities or ectocrines concentrations are certainly wrong, as the external metabolite is ineffective or even enhancing below the activity threshold.

From the few quantitative data reported, these threshold concentrations seem to be high; $10-50$ mg $\cdot$ L^{-1} (Jüttner 1979) and 25 mg $\cdot$ L^{-1} (McCracken et al. 1980). Obviously, these are far above the average concentration of dissolved organic matter in aquatic habitats, and it is unreasonable to postulate that all dissolved organic matter could be composed of one substance, namely the inhibiting one. However, some algae may produce external metabolites acting at very low levels, as low as 60 μg $\cdot$ L^{-1} as reported by Martin and associates. Because of the growing prevalence of eutrophication in fresh waters and coastal marine waters, subsequent algal blooming may produce cell densities as high as those that cause inhibiting effects in laboratory conditions. The use of batch culturing is probably the main cause of artifacts, in that it allows the substances excreted by algae to accumulate, while in nature they are immediately diluted. This dispersal is more critical for oceans because the volume/surface ratio is far greater and, therefore, algae are concentrated in upper layer. The remark of Tomas (1980), who points out that *Skeletonema costatum* is strongly inhibited in vitro by *Olisthodiscus luteus* but grows well in situ when enclosed in dialysis sacks and immersed in *O. luteus* conditioned waters, is of primary importance and should prevent premature extrapolation and imprudent generalization. A continuous culturing with an apparatus as developed by Kroes (1973) is certainly a more pertinent approach, but one must remark that data obtained by Elbrächter (1976) and Kayser (1979) diminish the role of external metabolites, when nutrients are added at natural levels. The presence of bacteria is a source of confusion; to prove that the inhibitions observed are really caused by algae, axenic strains are needed, but, on the other hand, absence of bacteria is misleading because they naturally destroy the dissolved organic matter and thus prevent accumulation, if any. This suggests we use axenic strains only for preliminary survey of potential ectocrine-producing algae, and naturally bacterized strains for critical experiments. Because demonstration of direct inhibition by crude natural waters (only filtered) of several isolated algae has been done only once (Keating 1978), a clear answer cannot be given to the second question. Nevertheless, we think that recent contributions supply growing evidence that aquatic habitats should be classified according to a nutrient criterion. Those where naturally occurring conditions make nutrient-rich waters, and those which are eutrophicated may support a heavy algal biomass that can produce great quantities of external metabolites; hence, these substances may really act in situ. Such conditions are certainly more frequent in inland waters, because land drainage of natural substances and farm fertilizers enrich stagnant waters (lake or pond waters where these "water blooms" of a few species occur impressed Lefevre (1964)). Shallow coastal waters may be similar; for instance, those studied by Gauthier et al. (1975, 1978) were far richer in nutrients than the natural Mediterranean waters and almost free from mixing. All things considered, within the red-tide plumes, ectocrine inhibition is probably a means of competition for the dominant species. On the other hand, in oligotrophic waters (e.g. all oceanic waters and mountain lakes) all published data are consistent with the view that external metabolites have no role in algal competition or in species succession, but no direct proof is available.

Acknowledgments

We wish to gratefully thank Dr Trevor Platt for revising the English manuscript.

References

AKEHURST, S. C. 1931. Observations on pond life, with special reference to the possible causation of swarming of phytoplankton. J. R. Microsc. Soc. 51: 237–265.

ALLEE, W. C. 1934. Recent studies in mass physiology. Biol. Rev. Camb. Philos. Soc. 9: 1–48.

AUBERT, M. 1971. Télémédiateurs chimiques et équilibre biologique océanique. Première partie. Théorie générale. Rev. Int. Oceanogr. Med. 21: 3–16.

1978. Télémédiateurs et rapports inter-espèces dans le domaine des micro-organismes marins, p. 179–200. In Actualités de biochimie marine. Colloq. GABIM-CNRS.

AUBERT, M., D. PESANDO, AND J. M. PINCEMIN. 1970. Médiateur chimique et relations inter-espèces. Mise en évidence d'un inhibiteur de synthèse métabolique d'une diatomée produit par un péridinien (étude "in vitro"). Rev. Int. Oceanogr. Med. 17: 5–21.

BAILEY, K. M., AND F. B. TAUB. 1980. Effects of hydroxamate siderophores (strong Fe (III) chelators) on the growth of algae. J. Phycol. 16: 334–339.

BERLAND, B. R., D. J. BONIN, AND S. Y. MAESTRINI. 1972a. Are some bacteria toxic for marine algae? Mar. Biol. 12: 189–192.

1972b. Étude des relations algues-bactéries du milieu marin : possibilités d'inhibition des algues par les bactéries. Tethys 4: 339–348.

1973. Study of bacteria inhibiting marine algae: a method of screening which uses gliding algae. Mem. Biol. Mar. Oceanogr. 3: 1–10.

1974. Importance des substances inhibitrices dans le contrôle des populations d'algues et de bactéries du plancton marin. Mem. Biol. Mar. Oceanogr. 4: 63–97.

BURKHOLDER, P. R., R. M. PFISTER, AND F. M. LEITZ. 1966. Production of a pyrrole antibiotic by a marine bacterium. Appl. Microbiol. 14: 649–653.

CHAN, A. T., R. J. ANDERSEN, M. J. LE BLANC, AND P. J. HARRISON. 1980. Algae plating as a tool for investigating allelopathy among marine microalgae. Mar. Biol. 59: 7–13.

ELBRÄCHTER, M. 1976. Population dynamic studies on phytoplankton cultures. Mar. Biol. 35: 201–209.

1977. On population dynamics in multi-species cultures of diatoms and dinoflagellates. Helgol. Wiss. Meeresunters. 30: 192–200.

FEDOROV, V. D., AND N. G. KUSTENKO. 1972. Competition between marine planktonic diatoms in monoculture and mixed culture. Oceanology 12: 91–100.

FITZGERALD, G. P. 1969. Some factors in the competition or antagonism among bacteria, algae, and aquatic weeds. J. Phycol. 5: 351–359.

FOGG, G. E. 1962. Extracellular products, p. 475–489. In R. A. Lewin [ed.] Physiology and biochemistry of algae. Academic Press, New York, NY.

FRENCH, C. S. 1979. Fifty years of photosynthesis. Annu. Rev. Plant Physiol. 30: 1–26.

GAUSE, G. F. 1932. Experimental studies on the struggle for existence. I. Mixed populations of two species of yeast. J. Exp. Biol. 9: 389–402.

GAUTHIER, M. J., P. BERNARD, AND M. AUBERT. 1978. Modification de la fonction antibiotique de deux diatomées marines, Asterionella japonica (Cleve) et Chaetoceros lauderi (Ralfs) par le dinoflagellé Prorocentrum micans (Ehrenberg). J. Exp. Mar. Biol. Ecol. 33: 37–50.

GAUTHIER, M. J., J. P. BREITTMAYER, AND M. AUBERT. 1975. Étude des facteurs responsables de dérives écologiques en milieu marin méditerranéen côtier. 10th Eur. Symp. Mar. Biol., Ostend, Belgium, Sept. 17–23. Vol. 2: 271–283.

HARDER, R. 1917. Ernährungsphysiologische Untersuchungen an Cyanophyceen, hauptsächlich dem endophytischen Nostoc punctiforme. Z. Bot. 9: 145–242.

HARRIS, D. O. 1970. An autoinhibitory substance produced by Platydorina caudata Kofoid. Plant Physiol. 45: 210–214.

1971. Growth inhibitors produced by the green algae (Volvocaceae). Arch. Mikrobiol. 76: 47–50.

HARTMAN, R. T. 1960. Algae and metabolites of natural waters, p. 38–55. In C. A. Tryon Jr. and R. T. Hartman [ed.] The ecology of algae. Univ. Pittsburgh Press.

HELLEBUST, J. A. 1974. Extracellular products, p. 838–863. In W. D. P. Stewart [ed.] Algal physiology and Biochemistry. Blackwell Scientific Publications, Oxford.

HERRMANN, V., AND F. JÜTTNER. 1977. Excretion products of algae. Identification of biogenic amines by gas-liquid chromatography and mass spectrometry of their trifluoroacetamides. Anal. Biochem. 78: 365–373.

HONJO, T., T. SHIMOUSE, N. UEDA, AND T. HANAOKA. 1978. Changes of phytoplankton composition and its characteristics during red tide season. Bull. Plankton Soc. Jpn. 25: 13–19.

JOHNSTON, R. 1972. The theories of August Pütter. Proc. R. Soc. Edinb. Sect. B 72: 401–409.

JÜTTNER, F. 1976. β-cyclocitral and alkanes in Microcystis (Cyanophyceae). Z. Naturforsch. Teil C 31: 491–495.

1979. Nor-carotenoids as the major volatile excretion products of *Cyanidium*. Z. Naturforsch. Teil C 34: 186–191.

KAYSER, H. 1979. Growth interactions between marine dinoflagellates in multispecies culture experiments. Mar. Biol. 52: 357–369.

KEATING, K. I. 1977. Allelopathic influence on blue-green bloom sequence in a eutrophic lake. Science (Washington, D.C.) 196: 885–887.

——— 1978. Blue-green algal inhibition of diatom growth: transition from mesotrophic to eutrophic community structure. Science (Washington, D.C.) 199: 971–973.

KOFOID, C. A. 1911. Dinoflagellata of the San Diego region. IV. The genus *Gonyaulax*. Univ. Calif. Publ. Zool. 8: 187–286.

KRASIL'NIKOVA, E. N. 1964. Antagonism in marine microorganisms, p. 208–229. *In* A. E. Kriss, I. E. Mishustina, N. Mitskevich, and E. V. Zemtsova [ed.] Microbial population of oceans and seas. Nauka Zhizn. (Transl. from Russian by G. E. Fogg)

KROES, H. W. 1971. Growth interactions between *Chlamydomonas globosa* Snow and *Chlorococcum ellipsoideum* Deason and Bold under different experimental conditions, with special attention to the role of pH. Limnol. Oceanogr. 16: 869–879.

——— 1972a. Growth interactions between *Chlamydomonas globosa* Snow and *Chlorococcum ellipsoideum* Deason and Bold: the role of extracellular products. Limnol. Oceanogr. 17: 423–432.

——— 1972b. Extracellular products from *Chlorococcum ellipsoideum* and *Chlamydomonas globosa*. Arch. Mikrobiol. 84: 270–274.

——— 1973. A spin filter system for the study of algal interactions. Oecologia Berl. 11: 93–98.

KROGH, A. 1931. Dissolved substances as food of aquatic organisms. Rapp. P. V. Reun. Cons. Int. Explor. Mer. 75: 7–36.

KRZYWICKA, A., AND D. KRUPA. 1975. Preliminary investigations on mutual growth relations of the populations of the blue-green alga *Microcystis aeruginosa* and green algae *Monoraphidium minutum* and *Scenedesmus abundans* in bicultures. Acta Hydrobiol. 17: 81–88.

KUSTENKO, N. G. 1979. Application of factor experiment plans in studies of algae relationship in culture. Gidrobiol. Zh. 15: 79–80. (In Russian)

KUTT, E. C., AND D. F. MARTIN. 1974. Effect of selected surfactants on the growth characteristics of *Gymdinium breve*. Mar. Biol. 28: 253–259.

——— 1975. Report on a biochemical red tide repressive agent. Environ. Lett. 9: 195–208.

LAM, C. W. Y., AND W. B. SILVESTER. 1979. Growth interactions among blue-green (*Anabaena oscillarioides, Microcystis aeruginosa*) and green (*Chlorella* sp.) algae. Hydrobiologia 63: 135–143.

LANGE, W. 1974. Competitive exclusion among three planktonic blue-green algal species. J. Phycol. 10: 411–414.

LEFEVRE, M. 1964. Extracellular products of algae, p. 337–367. *In* D. F. Jackson [ed.] Algae and man. Plenum Press, New York, NY.

LEFEVRE, M., H. JAKOB, AND M. NISBET. 1952. Auto et hétéroantagonisme chez les algues d'eau in vitro et dans les collections d'eau naturelles. Ann. Stn. Cent. Hydrobiol. Appl. 4: 5–199.

LIEBERT, F., AND W. M. DEERNS. 1920. Onderzoek naar de Oozaak van een Vischsterfte in den polder Wookumer-Nieuwland, Nabij Workum. Verh. Rijksinst. Visschonderz. 1: 81.

LINDROTH, P., AND K. MOPPER. 1979. High performance liquid chromatographic determination of subpicomole amounts of amino acids by precolumn fluorescence derivatization with O-phthaldialdehyde. Anal. Chem. 51: 1667–1674.

LUCAS, C. E. 1938. Some aspects of integration in plankton communities. J. Cons. Cons. Int. Explor. Mer. 8: 309–322.

——— 1947. The ecological effects of external metabolites. Biol. Rev. 22: 270–295.

——— 1955. External metabolites in the sea. Papers in marine biology and oceanography. Deep Sea Res. 3 (suppl.): 139–148.

——— 1961. On the significance of external metabolites in ecology. Symp. Soc. Exp. Biol. 15: 190–206.

MARTIN, D. F., AND B. B. MARTIN. 1976. Aponin, a cytolytic factor toward the red tide organism, *Gymnodinium breve*. Biological assay and preliminary characterization. J. Environ. Sci. Health Part A 11: 613–622.

McCOY, L. F. JR., AND D. F. MARTIN. 1977. The influence of *Gomphosphaeria aponina* on the growth of *Gymnodinium breve* and the effect of aponin on the ichthyotoxicity of *Gymnodinium breve*. Chem. Biol. Interact. 17: 17–24.

McCOY, L. F. JR., D. L. ENG-WILMOT, AND D. T. MARTIN. 1979. Isolation and partial purification of a red tide (*Gymnodinium breve*) cytolytic factor (s) from cultures of *Gomphosphaeria aponina*. Agric. Food Chem. 27: 69–74.

McCRACKEN, M. D., R. E. MIDDAUGH, AND R. S. MIDDAUGH. 1980. A chemical characterization of an algal inhibitor obtained from *Chlamydomonas*. Hydrobiologia 70 (3): 271–276.

McVEIGH, I., AND W. H. BROWN. 1954. In vitro growth of *Chlamydomonas chlamydogama* Bold and *Haematococcus pluvialis* Flotow Em. Wille in mixed cultures. Bull. Torrey Bot. Club. 81: 218–233.

MOON, R. E., AND D. F. MARTIN. 1979. Potential management of red tide blooms. Treatment with concentrated frozen *Gomphosphaeria aponina* cultures. J. Environ. Sci. Health Part A 14: 195–199.

MURPHY, T. P., D. R. S. LEAN, AND C. NALEWAJKO. 1976. Blue-green algae: their excretion of iron-selective chelators enables them to dominate other algae. Science (Washington, D.C.) 192: 900–902.

NIGRELLI, R. F. 1958. Dutchman's baccy juice of growth-promoting and growth-inhibiting substances of marine origin. Trans. N.Y. Acad. Sci. Ser. II(20): 248–262.

PINCEMIN, J. M. 1969. Apparition d'une eau rouge a *Cochlodinium* sp. devant Juan-les-Pins. Rev. Int. Oceanogr. Med. 13/14: 205–216.

——— 1971. Télémédiateurs chimiques et équilibre biologique océanique. Troisième partie. Étude in vitro de relations entre populations phytoplanctoniques. Rev. Int. Oceanogr. Med. 22/23: 165–196.

PINTNER, I. J., AND V. ALTMEYER. 1979. Vitamin B$_{12}$-binder and other algal inhibitors. J. Phycol. 15: 391–398.

POURRIOT, R. 1966. Métabolites externes et interactions biochimiques chez les organismes aquatiques. Ann. Biol. 5: 337–374.

PRATT, D. M. 1965. The winter–spring diatom flowering in Narragansett Bay. Limnol. Oceanogr. 10: 173–184.

——— 1966. Competition between *Skeletonema costatum* and *Olithodiscus luteus* in Narragansett Bay and in culture. Limnol. Oceanogr. 11: 447–455.

PRATT, R. 1940. Studies on *Chlorella vulgaris*. I. Influence of the size of the inoculum on the growth of *Chlorella vulgaris* in freshly prepared culture medium. Am. J. Bot. 27: 52–56.

——— 1942. Studies on *Chlorella vulgaris*. V. Some properties of the growth-inhibitor formed by *Chlorella* cells. Am. J. Bot. 29: 142–148.

——— 1943. Studies on *Chlorella vulgaris*. VI. Retardation of photosynthesis by growth-inhibiting substance from *Chlorella vulgaris*. Am. J. Bot. 30: 32–33.

PRATT, R., AND J. FONG. 1940. Studies on *Chlorella vulgaris*. II. Further evidence that *Chlorella* cells form a growth-inhibiting substance. Am. J. Bot. 27: 431–436.

——— 1944. Chlorellin, an antibacterial substance from *Chlorella*. Science (Washington, D.C.) 99: 351–352.

PROCTOR, V. W. 1957. Studies on algal antibiosis using *Haematococcus* and *Chlamydomonas*. Limnol. Oceanogr. 2: 125–139.

PROVASOLI, L. 1963. Organic regulation of phytoplankton fertility, p. 165–219. *In* M. N. Hill [ed.] The sea. Vol. 2. J. Wiley & Sons, New York, NY.

PÜTTER, A. 1907a. Die Ernährung der Wassertiere. Z. Allg. Physiol. 7: 283–320.

——— 1907b. Der Stoffhaushalt des Meeres. Z. Allg. Physiol. 7: 321–368.

RANSON, G. 1935. Le rôle de la matière organique dissoute dans l'eau et les théories de Pütter. Bull. Mus. Natl. Hist. Nat. 2 (7): 359–366.

——— 1936. Le rôle de la matière organique dissoute dans l'eau et les théories de Pütter (suite). Bull. Mus. Natl. Hist. Nat. (2)8: 160–172.

RICE, T. R. 1954. Biotic influences affecting population growth of planktonic algae. Fish. Bull. 54: 227–245.

RICE, T. R., AND R. L. FERGUSON. 1975. Response of estuarine phytoplankton to environmental conditions, p. 1–43. *In* F. J. Vernberg [ed.] Physiological ecology of estuarine organisms. Univ. South Carolina Press, Columbia, SC.

ROSENFELD, D. W., AND C. E. ZOBELL. 1947. Antibiotic production by marine micro-organisms. J. Bacteriol. 54: 393–398.

RYTHER, J. H. 1975. Physical models of integrated waste recycling marine polyculture systems. Aquaculture 5: 163–177.

SAUNDERS, G. W. 1957. Interrelations of dissolved organic matter and phytoplankton. Bot. Rev. 23: 389–409.

SCHENK, H. E. A., AND F. JÜTTNER. 1974. Nachweis extracellulärer Murein-Hydrolase-Aktivität beim Zusammenbruch einer Blüte von *Anabaena solitaria* Kleb. Arch. Hydrobiol. 74: 1–7.

SCOTT, T. G., AND A. J. S. BALL. 1975. An apparatus for studying syntrophic interaction between micro-organisms. Limnol. Oceanogr. 20: 291–295.

SHARP, J. H., P. A. UNDERHILL, AND D. J. HUGHES. 1979. Interaction (allelopathy) between marine diatoms: *Thalassiosira pseudonana* and *Phaeodactylum tricornutum*. J. Phycol. 15: 353–362.

SIEBURTH, J. M. 1962. Biochemical warfare among the microbes of the sea. Honors lecture, Univ. Rhode Island, Kingston. 13 p.

——— 1964. Antibacterial substances produced by marine algae. Dev. Ind. Microbiol. 5: 124–134.

——— 1968. The influence of algal antibiosis on the ecology of marine micro-organisms, p. 63–94. *In* M. R. Droop and E. J. Ferguson Wood [ed.] Advances in microbiology of the sea. Vol. 1. Academic Press, London.

STUART, M. 1972. The effects of *Olisthodiscus luteus* Carter upon the growth of *Skeletonema costatum* (Grev.) Cleve. M. S. Thesis, Univ. Rhode Island, Kingston. 82 p.

SZE, P., AND J. M. KINGSBURY. 1974. Interactions of phytoplankters cultured from a polluted saline lake, Onondaga Lake, New York. J. Phycol. 10: 5–8.

TASSIGNY, M., AND M. LEFEVRE. 1971. Auto., hétéroantagonisme et autres conséquences des excrétions d'algues d'eau douce ou thermale. Verh. Int. Ver. Limnol. 19: 26–38.

THOMSON, W. 1874. Les abîmes de la mer. Traduction de 1875.

TOMAS, C. 1978. *Olisthodiscus luteus* (Chrysophyceae). I. Effects of salinity and temperature on growth, motility and survival. J. Phycol. 14: 309–313.

——— 1979. *Olisthodiscus luteus* (Chrysophyceae). III. Uptake and utilization of nitrogen and phosphorus. J. Phycol. 15: 5–12.

——— 1980. *Olisthodiscus luteus* (Chrysophyceae). V. Its occurrence, abundance and dynamics in Narragansett Bay, Rhode Island. J. Phycol. 16: 157–166.

UCHIDA, T. 1977. Excretion of a diatom-inhibitory substance by *Prorocentrum micans* Ehrenberg. Jpn. J. Ecol. 27: 1–4.

——— 1981. The relationships between *Prorocentrum micans*-growth and its ecological environment. Sci. Pap. Inst. Algol. Res. Fac. Sci. Hokkaido Univ. (In press)

WAKSMAN, S. A. 1941. Antagonistic relations of micro-organisms. Bacteriol. Rev. 5: 231–291.

WHITTAKER, R. H., AND P. P. FEENY. 1971. Allelochemics: chemical interactions between species. Science (Washington, D.C.) 171: 757–770.

WHITTLE, K. J. 1977. Marine organisms and their contribution to organic matter in the ocean. Mar. Chem. 5: 381–411.

WILLIAMS, P. J. LE B. 1975. Biological and chemical aspects of dissolved organic material in sea water, p. 301–363. *In* J. P. Riley and G. Skirrow [ed.] Chemical oceanography, 2 nd Ed. Academic Press, London.

WOODRUFF, L. L. 1913. Effect of excretion products of Infusoria. J. Exp. Zool. 14: 575–582.

Morphological Bases of Competition and Succession

ALAIN SOURNIA

*Laboratoire d'Ichtyologie, Muséum National d'Histoire Naturelle,
43, rue Cuvier, 75231 Paris 05, France*

My idea about this school is that
it should try to bring everyone to
a common level of ignorance.
TREVOR PLATT

The above quotation is taken from a letter that the Chairman sent to the lecturers during the preparation of this seminar. It reminds me of the philosophy of cardinal Nicholas of Cusa (1401–64). Looking for truth is tantamount to appraising ignorance, says a major theme of his *Docta ignorantia*. In the following pages, I will strictly obey the principles of Nicholas and Trevor. The data under examination will be used, hopefully, to fill the gaps in our knowledge. I would like also to regain the ingenuousness of the child who asks about whatever he may come across: "What is this used for?" since the usefulness (in biological terms: the ecological, physiological, or evolutionary significance) of the morphological features of phytoplankton cells, frankly speaking, remains practically unknown.

At present, phytoplanktologists are divided into several races, or at least they behave as if they were. Although excellent works are produced in one field or another, it would seem that microscopists work on morpho-cells, ecologists on eco-cells, physiologists on physio-cells, and so on. However, in so far as our common aim is to understand the nature of phytoplankton better, the different races of workers should not only treat each other with indulgence in a spirit of peaceful coexistence, but they desperately need to cooperate. Don't we, all of us, work on the same cells?

Morphological and Cytological Features

According to the current classifications (there are several of them), algae are separated into 12–16 groups, usually classes. It may then be said that virtually all of them are present in marine plankton, providing that the following restrictions are made:
— Charophycean algae (either as a class or a subclass) are totally absent of the marine plankton;
— Phaeophyceae can be encountered there only as spores, since the vegetative forms are benthic macrophytes. Thus, they will be omitted here;
— Cyanophyceae are present, but many authors would rather consider them as bacteria. They are included here for practical reasons.

Any review on phytoplankton should include the phototrophic bacteria. In spite of an increasing interest in this category (see e.g. Fujita and Zenitani 1975; Sieburth 1979), bacteria will be omitted here on "practical grounds." These two words emphasize that we consider all the phototrophic species that are amenable to routine planktological methods. (In this perspective, one flaw is that the smaller Cyanophyceae may escape such methods; but we need a perspective nevertheless.)

Some algal classes in marine plankton are merely incidenal, whereas others predominate in numbers or biomass. However, all of them will be taken into account with equal interest. Thirteen algal classes are of concern here. Their main morphological and cytological characteristics are summarized in Table 1. Because the taxonomical literature is extremely profuse and scattered, only a few recent books and reviews are referred to: Dodge (1973, 1979), Stewart (1974), Werner (1977), and Sieburth (1979).

SHAPES AND SIZES

The sizes of marine phytoplankters range from a few micrometres (or even 1 μm) to a few millimetres; hence, there is a range of three orders of magnitude for the average linear dimension on a worldwide basis. If cell volumes are compared, the extreme cases known may differ by a factor of one million or more. Practically, in a given area or study, cell volumes will commonly encompass a span of 4–5 orders of magnitude.

As a consequence, a number of classifications into size groups have been proposed. They are too numerous and too divergent to be reviewed here. The more commonly accepted separation is made between "microplankton" and "nannoplankton" (or nanoplankton) but the criterion for this varies largely according to authors (the 20-μm size is recommended as the limit between the two groups).

Algologically speaking, marine plankters may be one of the following: (1) unicells, either flagellated or not; (2) colonies, usually nonmotile as far as marine forms are concerned; (3) seldom, filaments; (4) exceptionally, coenocytic or thallic.

Morphodynamically, the same organisms may be ascribed to various geometrical types. The ones proposed by Schütt (1892) and Gran (1912) are classical but should not be thought of as obsolete, as they represent truly unique features, not to be found in any environment other than planktonic. These are (1) the bladder type, large, thin-walled cells, possibly including a large vacuole; (2) the ribbon type, flattened, thin-walled cells; (3) the hair type, cells elongated and/or grouped into elongated chains; (4) the branching type, with spiny or lamellar extensions. A fifth, mucous type, was implicitly added (with mucilage sheaths or filaments), which is rather rare in the sea compared with fresh waters. Although such types are obviously arbitrary and somewhat restrictive, their respective values, on adaptative or competitive grounds, have never been assessed experimentally.

Morphodynamically again, one may recognize several levels of organization in the occupation of space. The following scheme was derived by Lewis (1976) from the study of a tropical lake; it would merit examination by oceanographers as well. Four levels are distinguished: "(i) primary structure, determined by the shape and size of cells comprising the biomass unit; (ii) secondary structure, determined by the arrangement of cells with respect to each other as a result of physical connections between them; (iii) tertiary structure, resulting from the coiling, twisting, or bending of multicellular units; and (iv) quaternary structure, arising from the combination of similar multicellular subunits. Less than half of the phytoplankton species show only primary structure, half or more show secondary structure, and only a few show structure at all levels."

It may not be of much use to dwell on the diversity of shapes among phytoplankters. On one hand, every marine biologist is more or less familiar with it. On the other hand, no one has ever attempted to evaluate its significance. On the contrary, most planktologists in their everyday labor tend to cancel out the morphological variability, cell counts being expressed as numbers of individuals or converted into biochemical units; even taxonomical diversity (when this painful task is carried out) does not tell us anything about morphological diversity because the species recognized may be quite different (as two species of different genera often are) as well as closely similar (as congeneric species usually are).

Some aspects of the geometry of the cells will be discussed later.

FLAGELLA

Most algal classes of marine plankton are flagellated, the exceptions being Bacillariophyceae (diatoms), Cyanophyceae, Eustigmatophyceae, Rhodophyceae, and Xanthophyceae. The three or four last groups, however, are quantitatively unimportant. Note that flagellated classes may include nonflagellated genera, whereas nonflagellated classes may exhibit flagellated spores and gametes.

There may be up to eight flagella on a cell. They are equal or subequal or quite different in structure and function. They may be anchored in a depression or gullet of the cell, or not; be partly or entirely lodged in a groove, or completely free; be inserted apically or laterally; beat forward (thus pulling the cell) or backward (pushing it).

Usually, flagella bear secondary branchings called mastigonemes (or simply, hairs) of various kinds. These are inserted in one or two rows or in a spiral manner, and an apical tuft may be present. The flagella of some classes or genera bear tiny scales, either organic or mineralized. In some cases, the main axis of the flagellum, or axonema, is lined by a sheath, a rod, or a striated strand.

Although the internal structure of all flagella presents some universal features, such as the organization of the axonema into 9 doublets plus 2 fibrils, the other components of the flagellar apparatus, such as the "roots," seem to be highly variable, but they have not been studied extensively yet.

The haptonema is a very special kind of flagellum, only present in the Prymnesiophyceae, inserted between the two normal flagella. It is contractile or of varying length, has no roots, and its ultrastructure departs from the "9 + 2" model.

As far as marine plankton is concerned, the behavioral and ecological significance of none of the above features has ever been investigated (except the observation that haptonema may serve for attachment).

The swimming speed of a relatively minute number of species has been measured. This can be done directly under the microscope or indirectly from cell counts along a vertical profile at sea, units being $\mu m \cdot s^{-1}$ or $m \cdot d^{-1}$, respectively (see, for instance, Throndsen (1973) and Eppley et al. (1968) for each respective case). The data are much too scarce to answer questions such as which class is the fastest? or which flagellar type is best?, but an order of magnitude can be set forth. This would be about 150 $\mu m \cdot s^{-1}$ or 15 $m \cdot d^{-1}$.

CELL WALLS

Only a very few species of marine phytoplankton may properly be called "naked," in the sense that their cell is not limited by anything other than the cellular membrane (or plasmalemma). This happens in the chlorophycean *Dunaliella*, in two minor classes, and in various spores and gametes. In all other cases, the term "naked" is just erroneous.

Thus, the great majority of organisms are included in some kind of wall, or covering, or skeleton

TABLE 1. Morphological and cytological characteristics of the various taxonomical classes of marine planktonic algae. (Note: Whe▮

	Bacillariophyceae	Chloromonadophyceae = Rhaphidophyceae	Chlorophyceae	Chrysop▮
Cell shape	Boxlike ± prominences, fairly geometrical	Rounded or flattened	Highly variable; marine plankters often rounded	Highly v▮ rounded
Grouping of cells	Colonies frequent in plankton	Solitary	All algal types; marine plankters solitary	Mostly s▮ colony, ▮ marine p▮
Size	From a few μm to 2 mm	Rather small (nannoplankton)	All algal sizes; marine plankters small (nannoplankton)	Usually s▮ (nannopl▮
Flagella	None (gametes may be flagellated)	Two flagella (one forward and hair-bearing, the other backward and smooth), or no flagella	0, 2, 4 or 8; all apparently smooth	Usually 2▮ hair-bear▮ and smoo▮ sheath; o▮
Cell wall and skeleton	"Frustule," a siliceous external skeleton made of two "valves" and a "girdle"	None	None; or a cellulosic wall	None; or "lorica," exception▮ spines, in▮ skeleton
Chloroplasts	Highly variable in shape and arrangement; usually two or more	Numerous, in an outer region of the cytoplasm	Usually one, cup-shaped	One (bilo▮ to 6
Eyespot	None	None	Common at some stages of the life cycle	Common
Ejectile bodies	None	Trichocysts; mucocysts	None	Discobolo▮ (exception▮
Reproduction (where relevant to marine plankton)	Division of the frustule into its 2 halves; auxospores; statospores; diatoms are diploid			Siliceous ▮ sexuality ▮
Additional characters	Several Golgi bodies	Peculiar ring of Golgi bodies around the nucleus; contractile vacuoles		Mucous bo▮ vacuoles; (pseudopo▮ heterotroph▮
World abundance	All habitats, often abundant	A small class	Mostly fresh water	Mostly fre▮
Abundance in marine plankton	Very common, frequently dominant	Minor although locally dominant in some cases	Minor; higher in brackish waters	Not very c▮ ever domin▮

dinium. Then, whereas routine counts usually include several nonphotosynthetic taxa (mainly dinoflagellates), the same counts omit various protozoan species which are ascribed to microzooplankton but, because they harbor algal symbionts, should be regarded functionally as phytoplankters.

A granular, carotenoid-containing organelle, called the stigma or eyespot, is common in the Chrysophyceae, Prasinophyceae, and Xanthophyceae, while rare or absent elsewhere. It is either included in the chloroplast or not, and associated with the flagella or not. Its function has presumably . . . something to do with light. Ejectile bodies of various kinds (trichocysts, mucocysts, and others) are known in about one-half of the marine algal groups. Their function is also hypothetical. It is surprising that both series of organelles are generally considered as animal characters, although so many algae possess them. (One may add motility as another alleged "animality" of many phytoplankters.)

A large vacuole often fills much of the cell in the centric diatoms. Coccolithophorids seem to contain a large vacuole too. Nothing general can be said about the other groups. Contractile vacuoles with an obvious osmoregulatory function are probably common among the Chrysophyceae and rare in two other classes. A peculiar, permanent osmoregulatory vacuole, termed the pusule, is specific to the Dinophyceae where it encompasses a large range of structures. Digestive vacuoles are reported in the Dinophyceae and the Prasinophyceae. Gas vacuoles, better to be called pseudovacuoles, are restricted to a few cyanophycean genera, e.g. *Oscillatoria* (= *Trichodesmium*) which they may render positively buoyant.

Endosymbiotic bacteria may be common in dinoflagellate cells and should be looked for in the other groups. Viruses are but seldom mentioned.

Morphological Auto-Correlations

The functional significance of the above features, if we may repeat it, remains largely unknown.

A possible way to understanding their significance would be to investigate the internal correlations that may exist between such features. To this end, intraspecific as well as interspecific and intergeneric variability would be equally relevant. Here are a few examples of the questions to be answered:
— Why does the valve of the centric diatoms, in a given species, seem to flatten with increasing valve diameter (personal and subjective observations on *Rhizosolenia* and *Corethron* spp.)?
— Do spiny or horny cells tend to be also the larger or the smaller cells, and to be thin- or thick-walled cells?

— Are colonies formed preferentially among small cells or small species, as suggested by Beklemishev (1959)?
— Are all the combinations of characters (e.g. motility, elongation, gigantism, presence of trichocysts, and so on) equally met with in nature? If not (as it seems), which are the preferred combinations, which others are avoided, and why?

Cell Size as an Eco-Physiological Factor

Cell Volume

It seems to be a biological law that smaller organisms are metabolically more active than larger ones. In other words, metabolic rates per unit volume or unit weight decrease with increasing sizes of the organisms. In the field of unicellular algae, this is substantiated in the following ways:

	With increasing size
Growth rate	Decreases
Respiration per unit weight	Decreases
Photosynthesis per unit weight, assimilation number	Decrease
Half-saturation constants of nutrient assimilation	Increase
(Sinking velocity)	(Increases)

These are general trends that may suffer a few exceptions; sinking rate is added here for convenience.

Then, considering that the first three rates all decrease with increasing size, one may wonder: how do they decrease with respect to each other? For instance, how does the ratio "net production:gross production" behave? This remains controversial. Laws (1975) reviewed the available data and concluded that respiration drops in such a way that large cells gain advantage over the smaller, but Banse (1976), on the account of the same data, reached the opposite conclusion that "growth efficiency" is not size dependent.

As regards physical factors, a large amount of work in the past has been done to correlate cell size with temperature, either on specific, interspecific, or intergeneric bases. The data are so conflicting that the hope of finding any simple, universal relationship has been more or less abandoned, the same being true for salinity. This just means that things are more intricate.

Therefore, recent approaches aim to correlate the size of phytoplankton cells at sea with a number of parameters simultaneously. What may be called the "soviet school" (e.g. Semina 1972; Semina et al.

(none of these expressions has been clearly defined and no attempt will be made here). The different types of "cell walls" (in the broad sense) can be briefly described, recalling that the position of the wall with respect to the plasmalemma is controversial in some classes; thus it cannot be said firmly whether these classes have an external or an internal skeleton.

Periplast, cuticle, and pellicle — The first two terms are generally synonymous and apply mostly to the Cryptophyceae. Within this class, the periplast consists of very small plates, probably proteinaceous, with a larger system of grooves and ridges. Above it is the plasmalemma, then an external "fuzz" of granular or fibrillar material.

The pellicle, proper to the Euglenophyceae, is made of proteinaceous bands that encircle the cell (inside of the plasmalemma too) and give it a striated appearance.

Amphiesma — To avoid the ambiguity of the term "theca," the cell wall of the Dinophyceae is better referred to as an amphiesma, from an old name revived by Loeblich (1970). Even when apparently "naked," dinoflagellates bear a multilayered and vesicular wall made, from inside to outside, of (1) a continuous, fibrous, noncellulosic layer, (2) a system of vesicles and membranes, enclosing or not cellulosic plates that are easily visible in the "armored" species, (3) an external membrane or the plasmalemma, depending on the author. The plates, when present, are highly variable with respect to thickness, shape, size, number, and arrangement; they may or may not possess pores, spines, crests, ridges, and lamellae.

Frustule — The skeleton of the Bacillariophyceae is truly external, in the sense that all authors agree that the plasmalemma lies under it. It is also true that the new frustule of the dividing cell is formed in vesicles (that soon merge into a continuous "silicalemma") situated beneath the cell membrane. Thus, some questions remain about what is lost and what is newly formed when the new frustule resumes an external position.

The overall organization of the frustule consists of the well-known boxlike structure (the familiar lid and bottom called the "valves" and joined together by a "girdle"). No detail can be added here, due to the complexity of the subject and the amount of data available. Three remarks will be made, however.

The "glass box" or "Petri dish" commonplaces are best forgotten, as a significant part of the frustule is organic and its mineralized fraction is made of amorphous, hydrated silica.

The ultrastructure of the frustule, recently revealed by the scanning electron microscope, does *not* lead to a discouraging multiplicity of trifling details, but rather to a reasonable array of unitary elements whose disposition and number, but not nature, differ widely among genera and species.

In the few cases that have been studied, the frustule has been shown to be covered by a two- or multi-layered coating, part of which may serve silica deposition and part of which may control cellular exchanges (Hecky et al. 1973). On the other hand, a few, but taxonomically unrelated species can secrete polysaccharidic microfibrils, hardly visible by electron microscopy, and this has not been investigated extensively. Should these features prove to be of general occurrence, the skeleton of diatoms could no longer be reasonably called "external."

Organic and mineralized scales — Organic scales are common in the Prasinophyceae and the Prymnesiophyceae, rare among the Chrysophyceae, and exceptional in some Dinophyceae. They are made of microfibrils arranged in regular and/or irregular layers. They originate in the Golgi bodies and then migrate outside the plasmalemma. Two or more different types are commonly present on the same species.

In addition, a number of the Prymnesiophyceae, forming the Coccolithophorids, bear calcareous scales or coccoliths. A coccolith is made of several elements in an organic matrix and is (always?) surrounded by an organic skin.

Siliceous scales are found in some members of the Chrysophyceae.

Lorica — Some Prasinophyceae and Chrysophyceae are included in an armor of agglomerated grains or fibrils called the lorica. This skeleton is usually cellulosic and truly external.

CELL ORGANELLES

The number, shape, size, and arrangement of chloroplasts in the cells of planktonic algae are highly variable. Some classes may show a more or less typical pattern, such as the Prasinophyceae with their single, cup-shaped plastid, but most classes, including diatoms and dinoflagellates, display a large range of types under the light microscope. As to the ultrastructure, most phytoplanktologists ignore it. Yet, why do most algae have three thylakoids per lamella, Cryptophyceae only two, and Chlorophyceae and Prasinophyceae from one to six? Why do the chloroplastic envelopes (they are made of 2 to 4 membranes) and their connection with the endoplasmic reticulum differ so widely among the classes? Similarly, why are some pyrenoids embedded within the plastid and others stalked on it, and why do some genera apparently lack them?

Marine phytoplankton offers a diversified choice of cases where the chloroplasts do not belong to the cell itself, but to an algal symbiont. The best-known examples are found in the dinoflagellates *Ornithocercus* or *Noctiluca* and the ciliate *Meso-*

1976) faces the problem of cell size as a global, average, and adaptative response of phytoplankton to its environment. In this way, cell size in the Pacific Ocean was shown to be (a) negatively correlated with the velocity of vertical water transport, (b) positively correlated with the density gradient in the main pycnocline, and (c) more or less dependent on nutrient concentrations. Following a different philosophy, Parsons and Takahashi (1973, 1974) focus attention on the competition of phytoplankters which inhabit the same ecological "niche." They developed an equation in which the growth rate of a given cell or species is a function of the six following factors: (1) incident light, (2) extinction coefficient, (3) depth of the mixed layer, (4) upwelling velocity, (5) rate of nutrient input to the cell, and (6) sinking rate of the cell. Then, comparing the growth rates of a small coccolithophorid and a large diatom whose characteristics were already available, they conclude that "only in a region of high light intensity and high nutrient concentration it is possible for the larger phytoplankter to grow faster than the small phytoplankter." As the authors note, this would beautifully explain why nannoplankton quantitatively overwhelm microplankton in most seas of the world. A shrewd and fruitful criticism of this model was given by Hecky and Kilham (1974).

THE SURFACE:VOLUME RATIO

The surface area of a cell is of obvious interest as it permits and limits the exchange of energy (light absorption, thermic balance) and matter (osmotic equilibration, nutrient assimilation). This is why cell surface is a useful index, or the best one in several cases, of phytoplankton activity (Paasche 1960; Smayda 1965). It is worth remembering here that Rubner's "surface rule" (as cited in Bertalanffy 1951), according to which "the metabolic rate per unit weight decreases with increasing size, but is constant per unit surface," has not been evaluated in the case of unicellular algae.

Then, a ratio such as "surface area of the cell: cell volume" (hereafter S/V) is of obvious interest too, as it relates the exchange potential to the biomass present. Two geometrical considerations are essential in this connection.

1) For any given shape of cell, S/V will decrease with increasing size.

2) At any given size, a spherical shape provides the smallest S/V.

Because S/V and size are inversely correlated, one would expect the growth rate and S/V to be positively correlated. In effect, this is known from laboratory cultures (e.g. Eppley and Sloan 1966) and has been observed at sea (Margalef 1957). The

same is true for photosynthetic rates, in the lab (Taguchi 1976) as well as in the sea (Smayda 1965). As for nutrients, one laboratory work at least showed that S/V is increased in deficient media (Harrison et al. 1977), substantiating the opinion that oligotrophic seas favor large S/V (which improve nutrient assimilation), that is to say, smaller cells.

According to a study (already mentioned) by Lewis (1976) on a tropical lake, natural populations of phytoplankton keep the range of S/V values within limits that are much narrower than they would be if random combinations of sizes and shapes were all "permitted." Although this kind of paradox has not been identified rigorously in marine plankton, we already have some indications: suffice it to examine a taxonomical list where both sizes and S/V are reported, for example that of Smayda (1965) for the diatoms of the Gulf of Panama, then it becomes evident, although intuitively, that S/V values vary considerably less than random values of the linear dimensions would allow them to do.

Cell Morphology and the Planktonic Way of Life

FLOTATION AND SINKING

According to a myth which originates in the early times of planktology (V. Hensen, F. Schütt, W. Ostwald, and others) and that still persists in many of the recent textbooks, the morphological peculiarities of phytoplankton are efficient "flotation mechanisms." Because phytoplankton is observed to live in the upper layer of the ocean, it was and still is blindly assumed that its curious shapes cannot aim at anything else than ensuring the best flotation as possible! Breaking off with this obsession, Munk and Riley (1952) pointed out that phytoplankton has not only to keep itself in the top of the ocean, but also to absorb nutrients and avoid grazing. They made bold to say, and were able to demonstrate, that sinking aids the absorption of nutrients. Some years later, a freshwater planktologist wrote: "So far we have had as a background the view that perfect flotation or a density equal to that of the surrounding medium is a desirable property. Yet it is quite likely that it is not the case under most conditions" (Lund 1959). These new views were then extended by Smayda (1970) in a thorough review, the title of which duly associated the two words "suspension" and "sinking."

Before examining the various components involved in flotation and sinking, let us remind ourselves that a phytoplankter may behave in three different ways with respect to depth. It may be either neutrally buoyant (this would be rather common according to Eppley et al. 1968), or swimming (if motile), or sinking down. In the latter case, how fast does it sink? A rough average of the available data would be $1 \ m \cdot d^{-1}$, which is rather slow (and slower by one order of magnitude than the swimming velocity, as mentioned in the first section).

Let v stand for the sinking velocity.

All things being equal (which never holds true in nature), small cells sink slower. As to the overall shape (disc, ribbon, and so on), things are not simple as each shape has its own size/v function. The incidence of cellular appendages (horns, setae, and so on) is still more complicated as any departure from the spherical or spheroidal shapes will simultaneously:
— increase the drag resistance, then lower v;
— increase the specific weight, then increase v;
— make cells more subjected to passive entrainment;
— modify the orientation of the sinking cell in an unknown way; in this connection, two sorts of effects have to be distinguished: (1) the geometrical shape of the cell and the resulting projections, (2) the distribution of weight within the volume of the cell.

The role of mucous threads or sheaths remains unclear or controversial because mucus simultaneously lessens the total weight and increases the size.

In spite of the common preconception, colonies sink faster than unicells, and long colonies sink faster than short ones. The most obvious reason is that the total area of a colony is smaller than the sum of the areas of the isolated cells.

As to cellular content, it has long been suggested that lipidic inclusions (the so-called oil droplets) may compensate for the excess gravity, but precise calculations as well as experimental measurements make this possibility more and more doubtful (see e.g. Anderson and Sweeney 1977). On the other hand, the ancient theory of a regulation by ionic exchange, after being severely criticized, has been revived recently (see for instance the last reference).

It is well known that the viscosity of seawater is inversely correlated with temperature. As a consequence, v is accelerated by about 4% with a rise of 1°C and is approximately doubled when temperature rises from 0 to 27°C. However, the viscosity of the medium differs from that in the immediate environment of the cells, as suggested by Margalef (1957) and demonstrated by Chase (1979). This should stimulate experimental measurements on some selected species.

A common observation in the laboratory is that planktonic algae sink faster when either light or nutrients are deficient, and when cells are aging. Reasons for this are not clear. As regards light, the clue may be that active transport of ions, which is involved in flotation to some extent, is an energy-requiring process.

One of the merits of Smayda's review (1970) has been to emphasize the effects of the physical movements of water on the suspension of phytoplankters. Such movements include turbulence, wind-induced patterns, thermic convection, and various water transports. According to Smayda, their velocity exceeds v by 2 or 3 orders of magnitude. Thanks to this physical aid, plankters would be allowed to explore the vertical dimension and benefit temporarily from the deeper and more nutritive layers. Morphological features, instead of assisting flotation, would thus ensure passive entrainment and even sinking. Thus the etymology of "plankton" ($\pi\lambda\alpha\gamma\kappa\tau\acute{o}\varsigma$ = unstable, wandering) is better understood. In this modern approach as well as in the older one, our ignorance remains complete as to the exact function of the morphological features and the functional differences, if any, among taxonomical classes, genera, and species.

More details on the problem of suspension can be found in the reviews by Hutchinson (1967), Smayda (1970), and Walsby and Reynolds (1981). Suffice it here to conclude that floating is not always a requirement for phytoplankters and that, in all cases, an interaction of counteracting factors is involved.

Nutrient and Light Requirements

The dependence of the absorption of nutrients on cell morphology has been established on theoretical (or, sometimes, subjective) grounds only.

If there are good theoretical reasons to believe that small and motile cells are best adapted to absorption (Munk and Riley 1952), the other relations are rather hypothetical. For instance, the formation of colonies is thought by Beklemishev (1959) to be unfavorable, due to the reduction of the absorbing surfaces, whereas Margalef (1978) points out that colonies are more efficiently tossed about and washed by turbulence, hence an improved absorption. The same author estimates that mucilages hinder absorption and serve as a restraint upon excessive growth. In all respects, experimental data are desperately needed, particularly with regard to the incidence of the various kinds of cell walls and skeletons.

Concerning light, the main cytological differences among phytoplankters may lie in their respective pigmentary equipment, a matter which is beyond the present subject. Truly morphological adaptations to light have not been studied, except for the "shade flora" question. The shade flora consist principally of several genera or species of dinoflagellates which occur preferentially at the bottom of the euphotic layer, or even somewhat below. Unfortunately, it has not been possible so far to identify any morphological character that would be common to such species. For instance, if one considers the single genus *Ceratium*, its half-dozen "shade species" are either flattenned, or delicately elongated, or strongly constructed!

GRAZING PRESSURE

Because the grazing of phytoplankton by herbivorous zooplankton (and sometimes nekton directly) is largely an active and selective process, grazing pressure can be expected to modify the size distribution and the taxonomical spectrum of planktonic algae in the sea. Munk and Riley (1952) again may be consulted for a theoretical approach, and experimental evidence may be found in Parsons et al. (1967).

It has been frequently reported that the smaller forms are less actively preyed upon than larger ones; the same for long-horned organisms as compared with smooth ones, colonies as compared with unicells, and so on. Any generalization would be quite hazardous, however, and no algal category of any kind can be guaranteed against grazing in any case. Obviously, grazing involves reciprocal conditions of suitability between the morphology of the prey and the anatomy of the grazer, the details of which depend on the specific food chain under consideration.

Again, the suitability of the different groups of phytoplankton with respect to grazing remains to be evaluated. For instance, there are indications that trichocysts may be an efficient protection and that bioluminescent species of dinoflagellates discourage copepods.

THE ECOLOGICAL SUCCESSION

According to the synthetic views of R. Margalef on the ecology of phytoplankton, the morphological, cytological, and physiological properties of the planktonic algae become integral components of the ecological succession (Margalef 1958, 1978).

Thus, cells at the early stage of the succession are typically small and often rounded, have a high surface:volume ratio, assimilate nutrients intensively, and multiply rapidly. As one proceeds in the space–time continuum towards conditions of thermal stratification and nutrient impoverishment, phytoplankters tend to exhibit a larger size, a lower S/V ratio, and a reduced rate of cellular exchanges, together with motility, long generation time, and morphological specialization. At the same time, the taxonomical diversity of the community is considerably increased.

Some Concluding Remarks

In the present state of the communication of information between microscopists and taxonomists

on one hand, ecologists and physiologists on the other hand, the great amount of morphological data may well be considered as luxurious and superfluous knowledge. It will remain so until a bridge connects both sides of planktology, a bridge that may be called eco-physio-morphology, or simply, functional morphology.

Two series of questions may be asked. The function of the various geometrical and cytological features is to be defined, and the functional differences between the taxa are to be investigated. In both ways, the simpler the question will be, the best it will be (for instance, what is an eyespot used for? and which flagellates swim faster?).

Hopefully, this will enlighten the classical "plankton paradox" of G. E. Hutchinson. Are those categories that we call species functionally redundant, or does each of them occupy a distinct micro-niche in the ecosystem? All that can be said today about morphological diversity is, plagiarizing E. F. Schumacher's views in economics, that diverse is beautiful. This is not a scientific statement, however.

Acknowledgments

The comments of Prof. P. Bourrelly and Dr M.-J. Chrétiennot-Dinet on Table 1 are gratefully acknowledged. Dr A. E. Walsby helped to improve both the style and the substance of the manuscript.

References[1]

ANDERSON, L. W. J., AND B. M. SWEENEY. 1977. Diel changes in sedimentation characteristics of *Ditylum brightwellii*: changes in cellular lipid and effects of respiratory inhibitors and ion-transport modifiers. Limnol. Oceanogr. 22: 539–552.

BANSE, K. 1976. Rates of growth, respiration and photosynthesis of unicellular algae as related to cell size — a review. J. Phycol. 12: 135–140.

BEKLEMISHEV, C. W. 1959. Sur la colonialité des diatomées planctoniques. Int. Rev. Gesamten Hydrobiol. 44: 11–26.

BERTALANFFY, L. VON. 1951. Metabolic types and growth types. Am. Nat. 85: 111–117.

CHASE, R. R. P. 1979. Settling behavior of natural aquatic particulates. Limnol. Oceanogr. 24: 417–426.

DODGE, J. D. 1973. The fine structure of algal cells. Academic Press, London and New York. 261 p.

1979. The phytoflagellates: fine structure and phylogeny, p. 7–57. *In* M. Levandowsky and S. H. Hutner [ed.] Biochemistry and physiology of protozoa.

---

[1] In this paper, the references have been deliberately kept to a minimum. A more extensive bibliography will be given in a later review.

2nd ed. Vol. I. Academic Press, New York, London, Toronto, Sydney, and San Francisco.

EPPLEY, R. W., O. HOLM-HANSEN, AND J. D. H. STRICKLAND. 1968. Some observations on the vertical migration of dinoflagellates. J. Phycol. 4: 333–340.

EPPLEY, R. W., AND P. R. SLOAN. 1966. Growth rates of marine phytoplankton: correlation with light absorption by cell chlorophyll *a*. Physiol. Plant. 19: 47–59.

FUJITA, Y., AND B. ZENITANI. 1975. Distribution of phototrophic bacteria in Omura Bay during the summer with special reference to brown *Chlorobium*. J. Oceanogr. Soc. Jpn. 31: 124–130.

GRAN, H. 1912. Pelagic plant life, p. 307–386. *In* J. Murray and J. Hjort [ed.] The depths of the ocean. MacMillan, London.

HARRISON, P. J., H. L. CONWAY, R. W. HOLMES, AND C. O. DAVIS. 1977. Marine diatoms grown in chemostats under silicate or ammonium limitation. III. Cellular chemical composition and morphology of *Chaetoceros debilis*, *Skeletonema costatum*, and *Thalassiosira gravida*. Mar. Biol. 43: 19–31.

HECKY, R. E., AND P. KILHAM. 1974. Environmental control of phytoplankton cell size. Limnol. Oceanogr. 19: 361–366.

HECKY, R. E., K. MOPPER, P. KILHAM, AND E. T. DEGENS. 1973. The aminoacid and sugar composition of diatom cell-walls. Mar. Biol. 19: 323–331.

HUTCHINSON, G. E. 1967. A treatise on limnology. Vol. II — Introduction to lake biology and the limnoplankton. John Wiley and Sons, New York, London, Sydney. 1115 p. [Chap. 20. The hydromechanics of the plankton, p. 245–305.]

LAWS, E. A. 1975. The importance of respiration losses in controlling the size distribution of marine phytoplankton. Ecology 56: 419–426.

LEWIS, W. M. JR. 1976. Surface/volume ratio: implications for phytoplankton morphology. Science (Washington, D.C.) 192 (4242): 885–887.

LOEBLICH, A. R. III. 1970. The amphiesma or dinoflagellate cell covering. Proc. N. Am. Paleontol. Convention, Chicago 1969. Part G: 867–929.

LUND, J. W. G. 1959. Buoyancy in relation to the ecology of the freshwater phytoplankton, Br. Phycol. Bull. 7: 1–17.

MARGALEF, R. 1957. Nuevos aspectos del problema de la suspensión en los organismos planctónicos. Invest. Pesq. 7: 105–116.

1958. Temporal succession and spatial heterogeneity in phytoplankton, p. 323–349. *In* A. A. Buzzati-Traverso [ed.] Perspectives in marine biology. Univ. California Press, Berkeley and Los Angeles; Union internationale des sciences biologiques, Paris.

1978. Life-forms of phytoplankton as survival alternatives in an unstable environment. Oceanol. Acta 1: 493–509.

MUNK, W. H., AND G. A. RILEY. 1952. Absorption of nutrients by aquatic plants. J. Mar. Res. 11: 215–240.

PAASCHE, E. 1960. On the relationship between primary production and standing crop of phytoplankton. J. Cons. Perm. Int. Explor. Mer 26: 33–48.

PARSONS, T. R., R. J. LEBRASSEUR, AND J. D. FULTON. 1967. Some observations on the dependence of zooplankton grazing on the cell size and concentration of phytoplankton blooms. J. Oceanogr. Soc. Jpn. 23: 10–17.

PARSONS, T. R., AND M. TAKAHASHI. 1973. Environmental control of phytoplankton cell size. Limnol. Oceanogr. 18: 511–515.

1974. A rebuttal to the comment by Hecky and Kilham. Limnol. Oceanogr. 19: 366–368.

SCHÜTT, F. 1892, 1893. Das Pflanzenleben der Hochsee. Kiel & Leipzig, 76 p. (1892); Ergebn. Plankton Exped. Humbold Stift. 1A: 243–314 (1893).

SEMINA, H. J. 1972. The size of phytoplankton cells in the Pacific ocean. Int. Rev. Gesamten Hydrobiol. 57: 177–205.

SEMINA, H. J., I. A. TARKHOVA, AND TRUONG NGOC AN. 1976. Patterns of phytoplankton distribution, cell size, species composition and abundance. Mar. Biol. 37: 389–395.

SIEBURTH, J. McN. 1979. Sea microbes. Oxford Univ. Press, New York, NY. 491 p.

SMAYDA, T. J. 1965. A quantitative analysis of the phytoplankton of the Gulf of Panama. II. On the relationship between C14 assimilation and the diatom standing crop. Inter-Am. Trop. Tuna Comm. Bull. 9: 465–531.

1970. The suspension and sinking of phytoplankton in the sea. Oceanogr. Mar. Biol. A. Rev. 8: 353–414, 1 pl., 1 table.

STEWART, W. D. P. [ed.]. 1974. Algal physiology and biochemistry. Blackwell Scient. Publ. Oxford, London, Edinburgh, and Melbourne (Bot. Monogr. 10). 989 p.

TAGUCHI, S. 1976. Relationship between photosynthesis and cell size of marine diatoms. J. Phycol. 12: 185–189.

THRONDSEN, J. 1973. Motility in some marine nanoplankton flagellates. Norw. J. Zool. 21: 193–200.

WALSBY, A. E., AND C. S. REYNOLDS. 1981. Sinking and floating. *In* I. Morris [ed.] Physiological ecology of phytoplankton. Blackwell Scient. Publ., Oxford. (In press)

WERNER, D. [ed.]. 1977. The biology of diatoms. Blackwell Scient. Publ., Oxford, London, Edinburgh, and Melbourne (Bot. Monogr. 13). 498 p.